D0896581

The Dance of Anger

The Dance of Intimacy

The Dance of Deception

The Dance of Anger

❖

The Dance of Intimacy

❖

The Dance of Deception

HARRIET LERNER, PH.D.

L.C.C.C. LIBRARY
DISCARD

ONE SPIRIT

New York

The Dance of Anger
Copyright © 1985, 1997 by Harriet G. Lerner

The Dance of Anger accurately conveys the themes that are most central in women's lives, but all names and all identifying characteristics of the individuals mentioned in the book have been changed in order to protect their privacy.

The Dance of Intimacy
Copyright © 1989 by Harriet Goldhor Lerner

The Dance of Deception
Copyright © 1993 by Harriet G. Lerner

This edition was especially created in 2003 for One Spirit by arrangement with HarperCollins Publishers Inc. This edition copyright © 2003 by Bookspan. All rights reserved.

Printed in the United States of America

The Dance of Anger

*A Woman's Guide to Changing
the Patterns of Intimate Relationships*

For my first family:

My mother, *Rose Rubin Goldhor*
My father, *Archie Goldhor*
My sister, *Susan Henne Goldhor*

And in memory
of my grandparents:

Henne Salkind Rubin and *Morris Rubin*
Teibel Goldhor and *Benny Hazel Goldhor*

CONTENTS

PREFACE

I recently read *The Dance of Anger* again with an eye toward updating its contents for this new edition. Although the book was first published more than a decade ago, I found that I still agreed with everything I said back then.

This was both good news and bad news. The good news is that I had nothing more to do.

The bad news is that anger is still with us, and for obvious reasons. Intimate relationships are still a source of suffering, disappointment, and just plain hard times. Families continue to be dysfunctional (I like Mary Karr's definition of a dysfunctional family as "any family with more than one person in it"). And the world of work is neither fair nor hospitable to women. Anyone who claims to have nothing to be angry about these days is sleepwalking.

Anger is one of the most painful emotions we experience, and the most difficult to use wisely and well. Yet our anger is an important signal that always deserves our attention and respect. The difficulty is that feeling angry doesn't tell us what is wrong, or what specifically we can do that will make things better rather than worse. That's why I wrote *The Dance of Anger*—to help readers not only to identify the true sources of their anger, but also to learn how to change the patterns from which anger springs.

The challenge of anger is at the heart of our struggle to achieve intimacy, self-esteem, and joy. Learning how to deal with it is worth the journey, even though there are no six-easy-steps to personal fulfillment and relational bliss. *The Dance of Anger* teaches readers to understand how relationships operate and how to change our part in them. It encourages readers to go the hard route.

My own attitude toward the self-help world has changed since *The Dance of Anger* was first published in 1985. During the early stages of my writing, colleagues often asked, "Do you really think a *book* (as opposed to *therapy*, they meant) can help people?" It was a fair question. Real change occurs slowly, sometimes at glacial speed even with professional help. My honest response was, "I don't know." But I hoped that it could make a difference in people's lives.

I also worried that I would never find out. For a very long time, it appeared as if *The Dance of Anger* would never see the light of day. My first publisher hired, fired, rehired, and then fired me again. This was the beginning of an endless series of rejections from just about every publisher on the planet over a period of years. I often quip that I could wallpaper the largest room of my home with rejection slips—hardly an exaggeration. No one wanted to publish a book on the subject of women's anger. When *The Dance of Anger* finally did hit the stores, I was convinced that no one other than my mother and my five best friends would buy it.

Today, with twenty-five foreign editions and sales of over two million copies in English, I have only my readers to thank. Word of mouth keeps *The Dance of Anger* circulating, and I am continually moved by the "you changed my life" stories that come my way. Once, after a lecture, a seventy-three-year-old woman came up and introduced me to her ninety-five-year-old mother. They were holding hands. The daughter told me that they hadn't spoken to each other for over two decades until they read my book. This story, along with many others, stays with me, reminding me during the inevitable down periods of authorhood that it is all worthwhile.

Finally, I want to mention the availability of a booklet called *A Reader's Guide to the Work of Harriet Lerner*, which your local bookstore can order for you free of charge. You can also call toll-free 1-800-242-7737 and order by ISBN (0-06-099359-6) or visit the HarperCollins home page (http://www.harpercollins.com). All around the country, women have gathered together in book groups to discuss ideas that interest them. Some of these groups are salon-style arrangements where participants share ideas only, while other groups encourage self-examination and more personal sharing. The reader's guide includes information about me as an author, tips for forming a book (or "Dance") group, and questions for your own group to discuss. Reading groups like these are wonderful and anyone can start one—on my books or on those of other favorite authors.

What my readers have taught me is that, yes, a book really can change lives. Or, as the saying goes, "When the student is ready the teacher arrives"—and sometimes in the form of the written word. I'm continually amazed that so many women and men have been able to grab a bit of wisdom and advice from *The Dance of Anger* and run with it. Appreciative letters from my readers now far outnumber my old rejections slips. I am very grateful, indeed.

Harriet Lerner, January 1997

ACKNOWLEDGMENTS

I have many people to thank.

Sandra Elkin, my literary agent, steered me from professional to popular writing in 1979, and planted the seeds for this book. She saw me through an unanticipated series of literary ups and downs and demonstrated a remarkable capacity to maintain her sense of humor and clarity of direction, no matter what. Eleanor Rawson also helped me to develop as a popular writer by challenging my distant, scholarly style and encouraging me to connect more directly and personally with my readers.

In the early stages of this project, many friends and colleagues at the Menninger Foundation read manuscripts and offered valuable criticism and conversation. My thanks to Shirley Bonney, Nancy Gordon, Arthur Herman, Maria Luisa Leichtman, Arthur Mandelbaum, Sharon Nathan, Gavin Newsom, Dale Roskos, and especially to Meredith Titus. From outside of Topeka, Nancy Chodorow, Sally McNall, and Robert Seidenberg read chapters and offered feedback. While the bulk of my early writing did not find its way into the final version of this book, the feedback that I received from these people helped shape the course and direction of the final product.

Marianne Ault-Riché developed and named the "Talking Straight and Fighting Fair" workshops that we took on the road together as I gathered additional data about women and anger. Observing Marianne in action was inspirational to me; what I learned from her—of content, spirit, and courage—is reflected in this book.

I owe much to Sherry Levy-Reiner who carefully read and re-read chapters at the shortest notice, giving generously of time that she did not have. In addition to her vital suggestions, she offered me emotional support and feminist companionship at the Menninger Foundation, until her departure in 1982. I am similarly indebted to Emily Kofron whose loving friendship, camaraderie, and belief in my work nourished me through the good and bad times.

Katherine Glenn Kent has been, as always, an unfailing source of new ideas, which she translates with stunning lucidity and imagination into clinical work. She introduced me to Bowen Family Systems Theory and helped me to put it into practice in my own life. What I have learned from her over our many years of friendship is incalculable, although I suspect that she would credit Murray Bowen with as much vigor and enthusiasm as that with which I now credit her.

Betty Hoppes typed the bulk of this book and worked second hardest next to myself. In addition to her outstanding secretarial skills, her support, wisdom, and generosity of spirit helped see me through. Thanks also to Mary McLin, who helped with the typing of early final drafts and to Aleta Pennington, Debi Smith, and Jeannine Riddle, who worked magic with the word processor.

I could not have written this book had I not been relieved of other professional responsibilities. I am grateful to the Menninger Foundation for supporting part-time employment and for making it possible for me to pursue my own work. My particular thanks to Donald Colson, Leonard Horwitz, and Irwin Rosen. Thanks also to Roy Menninger, president of the Menninger Foundation, for his generous encouragement and support of my activities.

Under the superb direction of Alice Brand, the professional library at the Menninger Foundation is nothing short of a scholar's dream. The library staff has retrieved all my requests with accuracy and expedience, and, in addition, has sent me numerous references that I did not request, but should have. The Menninger Library staff may be guilty of making it impossible for me to ever leave Topeka.

Janet Goldstein, my editor at Harper & Row, joined this project in its latter stages and proved to be everything that a writer could wish for. Her suggestions and criticisms were so clear, helpful, and wise, that the final rewriting of this book was ... well, almost fun. It is a blessing that my manuscript ended up in her gifted and enthusiastic hands. Susan Philipson did an excellent job copyediting the final manuscript.

There is no way that I can adequately acknowledge or name the influence of my parents in shaping my life and writing. I thank my mother for her warmth, her intelligence, her quiet dignity and courage, her love of life and remarkable spirit of survival, and her capacity to give generously to others in even the most difficult of personal circumstances. I thank my father for his wonderful humor and wit, for his appreciation of words and language, which he taught both his daughters, and for his loving, albeit unsuccessful attempts to steer me away from comic books and rock-and-roll during my formative years in Brooklyn. Finally, I thank my sister, Susan, for her correspondence and companionship, for her help with this project, and for being the very best of big sisters.

I wish also to thank the following people: My women's group for hand-holding and sympathy; Susi Kaplow for her pioneering article "Getting Angry"; Teresa Bernardez for inspiring the subject of this book and for being the most loving and demanding of critics; Judie Koontz for being such a good friend; Carol Tavris for providing long-distance, big-sisterly reassurance that this book would come out in my lifetime; Anthony Kowalski for having sensitively provided conditions for emotional and intellectual openness; Peter Novotny for encouraging my work all along; Susan Kraus for her special way of cheering me on; Ann Carver for reminding me through her gentle and graceful teaching of yoga that I cannot work and create as a disembodied spirit. I also want to thank the larger community of women, including many I have not met, who have reached out over long distances, even oceans, to encourage my ideas and to share their own. For this network, and for feminism itself, I will always stand in debt.

Last and most significantly, my love and gratitude goes to Stephen Lerner. He has been, along with everything else, the finest of editors, the best of friends, and the most nurturant of husbands. I thank him for his patience, his proddings, his all-around helpfulness and expert advice, for his seriousness as well as his irrepressible silliness. All this, combined with the bright faces and wonderful personalities of our two sons Matthew and Benjamin, have made me feel very lucky indeed.

This book, like others of its kind, is the product of many people's work. While I have tried in my Notes to acknowledge the specific contributions of others, those credited do not necessarily share my views. For example, I have used ideas and language from Bowen Family Systems Theory; however, my interpretation and application of Bowen's work has been heavily influenced by my psychoanalytic and feminist background. In sum, others have influenced this book, but the final responsibility throughout is mine.

1
THE CHALLENGE
OF ANGER

Anger is a signal, and one worth listening to. Our anger may be a message that we are being hurt, that our rights are being violated, that our needs or wants are not being adequately met, or simply that something is not right. Our anger may tell us that we are not addressing an important emotional issue in our lives, or that too much of our self—our beliefs, values, desires, or ambitions—is being compromised in a relationship. Our anger may be a signal that we are doing more and giving more than we can comfortably do or give. Or our anger may warn us that others are doing too much for us, at the expense of our own competence and growth. Just as physical pain tells us to take our hand off the hot stove, the pain of our anger preserves the very integrity of our self. Our anger can motivate us to say "no" to the ways in which we are defined by others and "yes" to the dictates of our inner self.

Women, however, have long been discouraged from the awareness and forthright expression of anger. Sugar and spice are the ingredients from which we are made. We are the nurturers, the soothers, the peacemakers, and the steadiers of rocked boats. It is our job to please, protect, and placate the world. We may hold relationships in place as if our lives depended on it.

Women who openly express anger at men are especially suspect. Even when society is sympathetic to our goals of equality, we all know that "those angry women" turn everybody off. Unlike our male heroes, who fight and even die for what they believe in, women may be condemned for waging a bloodless and humane revolution for their own rights. The direct expression of anger, especially at men, makes us unladylike, unfeminine, unmaternal, sexually unattractive, or, more recently, "strident." Even our language condemns such women as "shrews," "witches," "bitches," "hags," "nags," "man-haters," and "castrators." They are unloving and unlovable. They are devoid of femininity. Certainly, you do not wish to become one of *them*. It is an interesting sidelight that our language—created and codified by men—does not have *one* unflattering term to describe men who vent their anger at women. Even such epithets as "bastard" and "son of a bitch" do not condemn the man but place the blame on a woman—his mother!

The taboos against our feeling and expressing anger are so powerful that even *knowing* when we are angry is not a simple matter. When a woman shows her anger, she is likely to be dismissed as irrational or worse. At a professional conference I attended recently, a young doctor presented a paper about battered women. She shared many new and exciting ideas and conveyed a deep and personal involvement in her subject. In the middle of her presentation, a well-known psychiatrist who was seated behind me got up to leave. As he stood, he turned to the man next to him and made his diagnostic pronouncement: "Now, *that* is a *very* angry woman." That was that! The fact that he detected—or thought he detected—an angry tone to her voice disqualified not only what she had to say but also who she was. Because the very possibility that we are angry often meets with rejection and disapproval from others, it is no wonder that it is hard for us to know, let alone admit, that we are angry.

Why are angry women so threatening to others? If we are guilty, depressed, or self-doubting, we stay in place. We do not take action except against our own selves and we are unlikely to be agents of personal and social change. In contrast, angry women may change and challenge the lives of us all, as witnessed by the past decade of feminism. And change is an anxiety-arousing and difficult business for everyone, including those of us who are actively pushing for it.

Thus, we too learn to fear our own anger, not only because it brings about the disapproval of others, but also because it signals the necessity for change. We may begin to ask ourselves questions that serve to block or invalidate our own experience of anger: "Is my anger legitimate?" "Do I have a right to be angry?" "What's the use of my getting angry?" "What good will it do?" These questions can be excellent ways of silencing ourselves and shutting off our anger.

Let us question these questions. Anger is neither legitimate nor illegitimate, meaningful nor pointless. Anger simply is. To ask, "Is my anger legitimate?" is similar to asking, "Do I have a right to be thirsty? After all, I just had a glass of water fifteen minutes ago. Surely my thirst is not legitimate. And besides, what's the point of getting thirsty when I can't get anything to drink now, anyway?"

Anger is something we feel. It exists for a reason and always deserves our respect and attention. We all have a right to *everything* we feel—and certainly our anger is no exception.

There *are* questions about anger, however, that may be helpful to ask ourselves: "What am I really angry about?" "What is the problem, and whose problem is it?" "How can I sort out who is responsible for what?" "How can I learn to express my anger in a way that will not leave me feeling helpless and powerless?" "When I'm angry, how can I clearly communicate my position without becoming defensive or attacking?" "What risks and losses might I face if I become clearer and more assertive?" "If getting angry is not working for me, what can I do differently?" These are questions that we will be addressing in subsequent chapters, with the goal, not of getting rid of our anger or doubting its validity, but of gaining greater clarity about its sources and then learning to take a new and different action on our own behalf.

There is, however, another side of the coin: If *feeling* angry signals a problem, *venting* anger does not solve it. *Venting anger may serve to maintain, and even rigidify, the old rules and patterns in a relationship, thus ensuring that change does not occur.* When emotional intensity is high, many of us engage in nonproductive efforts to change the other person, and in so doing, fail to exercise our power to clarify and change our own selves. The old anger-in/anger-out theory, which states that letting it all hang out offers protection from the psychological hazards of keeping it all pent up, is simply not true. Feelings of depression, low self-esteem, self-betrayal, and even self-hatred are inevitable when we fight but continue to submit to unfair circumstances, when we complain but live in a way that betrays our hopes, values and potentials, or when we find ourselves fulfilling society's stereotype of the bitchy, nagging, bitter, or destructive woman.

Those of us who are locked into ineffective expressions of anger suffer as deeply as those of us who dare not get angry at all.

ANGER GONE WRONG

If our old familiar ways of managing anger are not working for us, chances are that we fall into one or both of the following categories: In the "nice-lady" category, we attempt to avoid anger and conflict at all costs. In the "bitch" category, we get angry with ease, but we participate in ineffective fighting, complaining, and blaming that leads to no constructive resolution.

These two styles of managing anger may appear to be as different as night and day. In reality, they both serve equally well to protect others, to blur our clarity of self, and to ensure that change does not occur. Let's see how this works.

The "Nice Lady" Syndrome

If we are "nice ladies," how do we behave? In situations that might realistically evoke anger or protest, we stay silent—or become tearful, self-critical, or "hurt." If we do feel angry, we keep it to ourselves in order to avoid the possibility of open conflict. But it is not just our anger that we keep to ourselves; in addition, we may avoid making clear statements about what we think and feel, when we suspect that such clarity would make another person uncomfortable and expose differences between us.

When we behave in this way, our primary energy is directed toward protecting another person and preserving the harmony of our relationships at the expense of defining a clear self. Over time we may lose our clarity of self, because we are putting so much effort into "reading" other people's reactions and ensuring that we don't rock the boat, we may become less and less of an expert about our own thoughts, feelings, and wants.

The more we are "nice" in these ways, the more we accumulate a storehouse of unconscious anger and rage. Anger is inevitable when our lives consist of giving in and going along; when we assume responsibility for other people's feelings and reactions; when we relinquish our primary responsibility to proceed with our own growth and ensure the quality of our own lives; when we behave as if having a relationship is more important than having a self. Of course, we are forbidden from experiencing this anger directly, since "nice ladies," by definition, are not "angry women."

Thus begins a self-defeating and self-perpetuating cycle. The more we give in and go along, the more our anger builds. The more we intensify our repressive efforts, the more we unconsciously fear a volcanic eruption should we begin to let our anger out. So, the more desperately we repress . . . and so it goes. When we finally do "blow," we may then confirm our worst fears that our anger is indeed "irrational" and "destructive." And other people may write us off as neurotic, while the real issues go unaddressed, and the cycle begins again.

Although "nice ladies" are not very good at feeling angry, we may be great at feeling guilty. As with depression or feeling hurt, we may cultivate guilt in order to blot out the awareness of our own anger. Anger and guilt are just about incompatible. If we feel guilty about not *giving* enough or not *doing* enough for others, it is unlikely we will be angry about not *getting* enough. If we feel guilty that we are not properly fulfilling our prescribed feminine role, we will have neither the energy nor the insight to question the prescription itself—or who has done the prescribing. Nothing, but nothing, will block the awareness of anger so effectively as guilt and self-doubt. Our society cultivates guilt feelings in women such that many of us still feel guilty if we are anything less than an emotional service station to others.

Nor is it easy to gain the courage to stop feeling guilty and begin to use our anger to question and define what is right and appropriate for our own lives. Just at that point when we are serious about change, others may redouble their guilt-inducing tactics. We may be called "selfish," "immature," "egocentric," "rebellious," "unfeminine," "neurotic," "irresponsible," "ungiving," "cold," or "castrating." Such slurs on our character and femininity are perhaps more than many of us can bear. When we are taught that our worth and identity are to be found in loving and being loved, it is indeed devastating to have our attractiveness and womanliness questioned. How tempting it may be to shuffle apologetically back to our "proper place" in order to regain the approval of others.

Unlike the "bitches" among us, who are doomed to lose popularity contests—if not our jobs—"nice ladies" are rewarded by society. The personal costs, however, are very high and affect every aspect of our emotional and intellectual life. "See no evil, hear no evil, speak no evil" becomes the unconscious rule for those of us who must deny the awareness and expression of our anger. The "evil" that we must avoid includes any number of thoughts, feelings, and actions that might bring us into open conflict, or even disagreement, with important others. To obey this rule, we must become sleep-walkers. We must not see clearly, think precisely, or remember freely. The amount of creative, intellectual, and sexual energy that is trapped by this need to repress anger and remain unaware of its sources is simply incalculable.

The "Bitchy" Woman

Those of us who are "bitches" are not shy about getting angry and stating our differences. However, in a society that does not particularly value angry women, this puts us in danger of earning one or another of those labels that serve as a warning to silence us when we threaten others, especially men. Like the word "unfeminine" but even more so, these labels may have the power either to shock us into silence, or to further inflame us by intensifying our feelings of injustice and powerlessness. In the latter case, a label like "castrating bitch" can become a self-fulfilling prophecy.

But this is only part of the story. The negative words and images that depict women who do speak out are more than just cruel sexist stereotypes; they also hint at a painful reality. Words like "nagging," "complaining," and "bitching" are words of helplessness and powerlessness, which do not imply even the possibility of change. They are words that reflect the "stuck" position that characterizes our lives when a great deal of emotion is flying around and nothing is really changing.

When we vent our anger ineffectively, we can easily get locked into a self-perpetuating, downward cycle of behavior. We *do* have something to be angry about, but our complaints are not clearly voiced and we may elicit other people's disapproval instead of their sympathy. This only increases our sense of bitterness and injustice; yet, all the while, the actual issues go unidentified. On top of that, we may become a prime scapegoat for men who dread female anger and for women who wish to avoid their own.

Obviously it requires courage to know when we are angry and to let others hear about it. The problem occurs when we get stuck in a pattern of ineffective fighting, complaining, and blaming that only preserves the status quo. When this happens, we unwittingly protect others at our own expense. On the one hand, an angry woman is threatening. When we voice our anger ineffectively, however— without clarity, direction, and control—it may, in the end, be reassuring to others. We allow ourselves to be written off and we provide others with an excuse not to take us seriously and hear what we are saying. In fact, we even help others to stay calm. Have you ever watched another person get cooler, calmer, and more intellectual as you became more infuriated and "hysterical"? Here the nature of our fighting or angry accusations may actually allow the other person to get off the hook.

Those of us who fight ineffectively are usually caught up in unsuccessful efforts to change a person who does not want to change. When our attempts to change the other person's beliefs, feelings, reactions, or behaviors do not work, we may then continue to do more of the same, reacting in predictable, patterned ways that only escalate the very problems we complain about. We may be so driven by emotionality that we do not reflect on our options for behaving differently or even believe that new options are possible. Thus, our fighting protects the old familiar patterns in our relationships as surely as does the silence of "nice ladies."

We have all had firsthand experience with both of these self-defeating and self-perpetuating behavior patterns. Indeed, "nice ladies" and "bitches" are simply two sides of the same coin, despite their radically different appearance. After all is said and done—or *not* said and done—the outcome is the same: We are left feeling helpless and powerless. We do not feel in control of the quality and direction of our lives. Our sense of dignity and self-esteem suffers because we have not effectively clarified and addressed the real issues at hand. And nothing changes.

Most of us have received little help in learning to use our anger to clarify and strengthen ourselves and our relationships. Instead, our lessons have encouraged us to fear anger excessively, to deny it entirely, to displace it onto inappropriate targets, or to turn it against ourselves. We learn to deny that there is any cause for anger, to close our eyes to its true sources, or to vent anger ineffectively, in a manner that only maintains rather than challenges, the status quo. Let us begin to unlearn these things so that we can use our "anger energy" in the service of our own dignity and growth.

THE ROAD AHEAD

This book is designed to help women move away from styles of managing anger that do not work for us in the long run. These include *silent submission, ineffective fighting and blaming,* and *emotional distancing.* My task is to provide the reader with the insight and practical skills to stop behaving in our old predictable ways and begin to use anger to clarify a new position in significant relationships.

What Is the Focus of This Book? Because the subject of anger touches on every aspect of our lives, I have made some choices. In order to avoid writing an unmanageably fat volume, I have decided to focus largely, although not exclusively, on the family. We know our greatest anger, as well as our deepest love, in our roles as daughters, sisters, lovers, wives, and mothers. Family relationships are the most influential in our lives, and the most difficult. It is here that closeness often leads to "stuckness," and our efforts to change things only lead to more of the same. When we can learn to use our anger energy to get unstuck in our closest and stickiest relationships, we will begin to move with greater clarity, control, and calm in every relationship we are in, be it with a friend, a co-worker, or the corner grocer. Issues that go unaddressed with members of our first family only fuel our fires in other relationships.

What Is the Scope of This Book? I have written this book specifically with the goal that it be useful. I have sacrificed theory, no matter how interesting, if I did not think that it had a clear, practical application to the real lives of real women. Yet, in the process of writing about anger, I found that I not only had to narrow my subject; I also had to broaden it. The reader should be forewarned that this book does not lay out rules on "how to do it" in ten easy steps. This is because the ability to use anger as a tool for change requires that we gain a deeper understanding and knowledge of how relationships operate.

Thus, we will be looking at the ways in which we betray and sacrifice the self in order to preserve harmony with others ("de-selfing"); we will be exploring the delicate balance between individuality (the "I") and togetherness (the "we") in relationships; we will be examining some of the roles and rules that define our lives and serve to elicit our deepest anger while forbidding its expression; we will be analyzing how relationships get stuck and how they can get unstuck. We will see how close relationships are akin to circular dances, in which the behavior of each partner provokes and maintains the behavior of the other. In a nutshell, we can learn how to use our anger as a starting point to *change patterns* rather than *blame people*.

How Does One Make Use of This Book? Very slowly. No matter how crazy or self-defeating our current behavior appears to be, it exists for a reason and may serve a positive and protective function for ourselves or others. If we want to change, it is important to do so slowly so that we have the opportunity to observe and test out the impact of one small but significant change on a relationship system. If we get ambitious and try to change too much too fast, we may not change at all. Instead, we may stir up so much anxiety and emotional intensity within ourselves and others as to eventually reinstate old patterns and behaviors. Or we may end up hastily cutting off from an important relationship, which is not necessarily a good solution.

This book will be most useful if you read it all. Don't skip the discussions about children because you don't have kids, or the chapter on husbands because you are single or divorced. What is important is the relationship patterns that I will describe. The specific partners are less the issue than the form of the dance and how it works. Remember that each chapter contains information that has relevance for any relationship that you are in. As you read, you can generalize to other settings and relationships, and the exercise of doing so is a useful one.

In order to use our anger as a tool for change in relationships, we will be learning to develop and sharpen our skills in four areas:

1. We Can Learn to Tune In to the True Sources of Our Anger and Clarify Where We Stand. "What about the situation makes me angry?" "What is the real issue here?" "What do I think and feel?" "What do I want to accomplish?" "Who is responsible for what?" "What, specifically, do I want to change?" "What are the things I will and will not do?" These may seem like simple questions, but we will see later just how complex they can be. It is amazing how frequently we march off to battle without knowing what the war is all about. We may be putting our anger energy into trying to change or control a person who does not want to change, rather than putting that same energy into getting clear about our own position and choices. This is especially true in our closest relationships, where, if we do not learn to use our anger first to clarify our own thoughts, feelings, priorities, and choices, we can easily get trapped in endless cycles of fighting and blaming that go nowhere. Managing anger effectively goes hand in hand with developing a clearer "I" and becoming a better expert on the self.

2. We Can Learn Communication Skills. This will maximize the chances that we will be heard and that conflicts and differences will be negotiated. On the one hand, there may be nothing wrong with venting our anger spontaneously, as we feel it, and without intervening thought and deliberation. There are circumstances in which this is helpful and those in which it is simply necessary—that is, if we are not abusive in doing so. Many times, however, blowing up or fighting may offer temporary relief, but when the storm passes, we find that nothing has really changed. Further, there are certain relationships in which maintaining a calm, nonblaming position is essential in order for lasting change to occur.

3. We Can Learn to Observe and Interrupt Nonproductive Patterns of Interaction. Communicating clearly and effectively is difficult even in the best of circumstances. When we are angry, it is more difficult still. It is hardly possible to be self-observant or flexible in the midst of a tornado. When emotions are high, we can learn to calm down and stand back a bit in order to sort out the part we play in the interactions that we complain about.

Learning to observe and change our part in relationship patterns goes hand in hand with an increased sense of personal responsibility in every relationship that we are in. By "responsibility," I do not mean self-blame or the labeling of ourselves as the "cause" of the problem. Rather, I speak here of "response-ability"—that is, the ability to observe ourselves and others in interaction and to respond to a familiar situation in a new and different way. We cannot make another person change his or her steps to an old dance, but if we change our own steps, the dance no longer can continue in the same predictable pattern.

4. We Can Learn to Anticipate and Deal with Counter-moves or "Change back!" Reactions from Others. Each of us belongs to larger groups or systems that have some investment in our staying exactly the same as we are now. If we begin to change our old patterns of silence or vagueness or ineffective fighting and blaming, we will inevitably meet with a strong resistance or countermove. This "Change back!" reaction will come both from inside our own selves and from significant others around us. We will see how it is those closest to us who often have the greatest investment in our staying the same, despite whatever criticisms and complaints they may openly voice. We also resist the very changes that we seek. This resistance to change, like the will to change, is a natural and universal aspect of all human systems.

In the chapters that follow, we will be taking a close look at the strong anxiety that inevitably is aroused when we begin to use our anger to define our own selves and the terms of our own lives more clearly. Some of us are able to *start out* being clear in our communications and firm in our resolve to change, only to back down in the face of another person's defensiveness or attempts to disqualify what we are saying. If we are serious about change, we can learn to anticipate and manage the anxiety and guilt evoked in us in response to the countermoves or "Change back!" reactions of others. More difficult still is acknowledging that part of our inner selves that fears and resists change.

For now, let me say that it is never easy to move away from silent submission or ineffective fighting toward a calm but firm assertion of who we are, where we stand, what we want, and what is and is not acceptable to us. Our anxiety about clarifying what we think and how we feel may be greatest in our most important relationships. As we become truly clear and direct, other people may become just as clear and direct about their own thoughts and feelings or about the fact that they are not going to change. When we accept these realities, we may have some painful choices to make: Do we choose to stay in a particular relationship or situation? Do we choose to leave? Do we stay and try to do something different ourselves? If so, what? These are not easy questions to answer or even to think about.

In the short run, it is sometimes simpler to continue with our old familiar ways, even when personal experience has shown them to be less than effective. In the long run, however, there is much to be gained by putting the lessons of this book into practice. Not only can we acquire new ways of managing old angers; we can also gain a clearer and stronger "I" and, with it, the capacity for a more intimate and gratifying "we." Many of our problems with anger occur when we choose between having a relationship and having a self. This book is about having both.

OLD MOVES, NEW MOVES, AND COUNTERMOVES

The evening before my workshop on anger was scheduled to take place, a woman named Barbara telephoned me at home to cancel her registration. In a voice that conveyed both resentment and distress, she told me the following:

"I so much wanted to come to your workshop, but my husband put his foot down. I fought with him until I was blue in the face, but he won't let me come."

"What was his objection?" I inquired.

"You!" she said. "He said that you were a radical women's libber and that the workshop was not worth the money. I told him that you were a well-known psychologist and that the workshop would certainly be very good. I'm *sure* the workshop is worth the money, but I couldn't convince him of that. 'No' was his final word."

"I'm sorry," I said.

"Yes, so am I," she continued. "And I've had a terrible headache since then and a good cry. But I did put up quite a fight. In fact, my husband even agreed that I could use some kind of help with my anger because I behaved so badly."

I hung up the telephone and thought about the brief conversation that had just taken place. Clearly, this woman did not *have* to cancel her registration to the workshop. She could have chosen to do otherwise. She could not, however, have chosen to do otherwise without consequences. Perhaps the consequence that she feared was the loss of her most important relationship.

What is *your* reaction to the telephone conversation?

Do you think . . .
"Her husband is a real chauvinist!"
    Or . . .
"What an insecure and frightened man."

Do you think . . .
"I feel sorry for this poor woman."
    Or . . .
"This masochistic woman could sure use psychotherapy."
    Or . . .
"Why didn't she pick herself up and go to the workshop!"

Do you think . . .
"He is to blame. How can he do this to her!"
    Or . . .
"She is to blame. How can she allow him to make decisions about *her* life!"
    Or . . .
"Society is to blame. How sad it is that we teach men to do this and teach women to take it."

Do you think . . .

"She is upset because her husband won't let her go to the workshop."

Or . . .

"She is upset because she is giving in."

Do you think . . .

"I can see myself in her."

Or . . .

"I can't relate to this at all."

We may each have our own personal reaction to what Barbara says. Many of us will not *want* to identify with her story. Yet, what she does, and how she feels, is far from outdated or unique:

She submits to unfair circumstances.

She does not feel in control of her life.

She has not effectively addressed the real issues at hand.

She is unclear about her own contribution to her dilemma.

She sacrifices her own growth to bolster and protect her husband.

She preserves the status quo in her marriage at the expense of her own self.

She avoids testing how much flexibility her marriage has to tolerate change on her part.

She feels helpless and powerless.

She turns anger into tears.

She gets a headache.

She does not like herself.

She believes that she behaves badly.

Are any of the above unfamiliar to you? Probably not. One or all of these things happen to us when we engage in ineffective fighting and blaming or when we are afraid to fight at all.

Unlike some women who dare not differ with their husbands, or lovers, Barbara has no problem getting angry. Her problem is that she fights in a manner that ensures that change will not occur and she *protects* her husband and the status quo of their relationship at the expense of her own growth. Carry on as she may, Barbara does not challenge the basic rule in the relationship—that her husband makes the rules. She "de-selfs" herself for her man.

What is "de-selfing?" Obviously, we do not always get our way in a relationship or do everything that we would like to do. When two people live under the same roof, differences inevitably arise which require compromise, negotiation, and give and take. If Barbara's husband was upset about the workshop, and if the workshop was not really that important to her, she might have decided to forget it. This in itself would not necessarily be a problem for her.

The problem occurs when one person—often a wife—does more giving in and going along than is her share and does not have a sense of clarity about her decisions and control over her choices. De-selfing means that too much of one's self (including one's thoughts, wants, beliefs, and ambitions) is "negotiable" under pressures from the relationship. Even when the person doing the most compromising of self is not aware of it, de-selfing takes its inevitable toll. The partner who is doing the most sacrificing of self stores up the most repressed anger and is especially vulnerable to becoming depressed and developing other emotional problems. She (and in some cases he) may end up in a therapist's office, or even in a medical or psychiatric hospital, saying, "What is wrong with *me?*" rather than asking, "What is wrong with this relationship?" Or she may express her anger, but at inappropriate times, over petty issues, in a manner that may invite others simply to ignore her or to view her as irrational or sick.

A form of de-selfing, common to women, is called "underfunctioning." The "underfunctioning-overfunctioning" pattern is a familiar one in couples. How does it work? Research in marital systems has demonstrated that when women and men pair up, and stay paired up, they are usually at the *same* level of "independence," or emotional maturity. *Like a seesaw, it is the underfunctioning of one individual that allows for the overfunctioning of the other.*

A wife, for example, may become increasingly entrenched in the role of the weak, vulnerable, dependent, or otherwise dysfunctional partner. Her husband, to the same degree, may disown and deny these qualities in himself. He may begin to direct the bulk of his emotional energy toward reacting to his spouse's problems, rather than identifying and sharing his own. Underfunctioners and overfunctioners provoke and reinforce each other's behavior, so that the seesaw becomes increasingly hard to balance over time. The more the man avoids sharing his own weaknesses, neediness, and vulnerability, the more his woman may experience and express more than her share. The more the woman avoids showing her competence and strength, the more her man will have an inflated sense of his own. And if the underfunctioning partner starts looking better, the overfunctioning partner will start looking worse.

My brief telephone conversation with Barbara suggests

that she is the underfunctioner in her marriage. Of course, not all women sit on the bottom of the seesaw in their relationships. In real life, there are any number of happy and unhappy arrangements. A man may sit on the bottom of the seesaw, or a couple may keep the seesaw moving over time, or each partner may compete with the other for the more helpless, one-down position.

What is important is that being at the bottom of the seesaw relationship is *culturally prescribed* for women. While individual women may defy or even reverse the prescription, it in fact underlies our very definitions of "femininity" and the whole ethos of male dominance. Women are actively taught to cultivate and express all those qualities that men fear in themselves and do not wish to be "weakened" by. And, of course, cultural teachings that discourage us from competing with men or expressing anger at them are paradoxical warnings of how hurtful and destructive the "weaker sex" might be to men if we were simply to be ourselves!

Sure enough, those old dictates to "play dumb," "let the man win," or "pretend he's boss"—are out of vogue. But their message still remains a guiding rule that lurks in the unconscious of countless women: *The weaker sex must protect the stronger sex from recognizing the strength of the weaker sex lest the stronger sex feel weakened by the strength of the weaker sex.* We learn to act weaker to help men feel stronger and to strengthen men by relinquishing our own strength.

Underfunctioning can take any number of forms. It may be as subtle as a wife's turning down a job opportunity or avoiding a new challenge when her husband gives a covert communication that he would prefer things to remain as they are or when she fears he would feel threatened by such a change. A woman may protect her man by confining herself to work that he prefers not to do and by failing to recognize and develop interests and skills in "his" areas. She may, in the process, acquire emotional or physical problems. Underlying her various complaints lurks the unconscious conviction that she must remain in a position of relative weakness for her most important relationship to survive. If the woman is further convinced that she herself cannot survive without the relationship, she will—like Barbara—vent her anger in a manner that only reinforces the old familiar patterns from which her anger stems.

INEFFECTIVE BLAMING VERSUS ASSERTIVE CLAIMING

How does fighting and blaming actually serve to *block* rather than *facilitate* change? Let's analyze Barbara's situation more closely. To begin with, Barbara participated in a dead-end battle about going to the workshop and used her anger energy to try to make her husband see things her way. There are two problems with her efforts to change her husband's mind: First, he has as much right to his opinions and speculations about the workshop as she has to hers. Second, it is hardly likely that she is going to succeed in this venture. She may know from past experience that this particular workshop is just the thing that her husband would say no to. As she said in her phone call, "I'm *sure* the workshop is worth the money, but I couldn't convince him of that. 'No' was his final word."

By engaging in a battle that she could only lose, she failed to exercise the power that she really did have—the power to take charge of her own self. Barbara would have taken a significant step out of her de-selfed position had she clarified her own priorities and taken action on her own behalf. She might have refused to fight entirely and instead said to her husband, "Good or bad, radical or not, the workshop is important to me. If I cancel my registration because you want me to, I will end up feeling angry and resentful. I look forward to the workshop and I plan to go."

What prevented Barbara from moving from ineffective fighting and complaining to clear and assertive claiming? Perhaps she feared paying a very high price for this move. Many of us who fight ineffectively, like those of us who don't fight at all, have an unconscious belief that the other person would have a very hard time if we were clear and strong. *Our anxiety and guilt about the potential loss of a relationship may make it difficult for us to change in the first place—and then to stay on course when our partner reacts strongly to our new and different behavior.*

Making Changes—Taking Chances

What if Barbara did something different and clarified a new position with her husband? What if she approached him at a time when he would be most receptive to hearing her and stated her position firmly and calmly without anger or tears? For instance: "I know that you don't think the workshop is worth the money and I appreciate that this is your opinion. However, I'm a grown woman and I need to make my own decisions. I don't expect you to approve of the workshop or to be happy about my going, but I *do* need to make this decision for myself."

Let us imagine that Barbara could stand firm on the *real* issue here ("I will make my own decisions") and avoid getting sidetracked into arguing other points, such as the value of the workshop or my character and credentials. Let us suppose that without fighting, blaming, accusing, or trying to change her husband's mind, she simply held to her statement of what she wanted to do: "Right or wrong, good or bad, I need to make this choice for myself."

What next? What would happen to this couple if Barbara challenged the status quo by calmly asserting her decision to attend the workshop? What would her husband's next move be? Would he draw the line and say, "If you go, I'll leave you?" Would he say nothing but then hit the bottle, have an affair, or become abusive in some way? Would he respond more mildly and become grouchy or depressed for several days?

Of course, we don't have the slightest idea. We know little about this couple. One thing, however, is certain: Whenever one person makes a move to rebalance the seesaw, there is a countermove by the other party. If Barbara behaved in this new way, her husband would make some "Change back!" maneuver as an attempt to reduce his own anxiety and reinstate the old familiar patterns of fighting. Such a maneuver would occur not because he no longer loved his wife or because he was intimidated by this particular workshop, but because he felt threatened by the new level of assertiveness, separateness, and maturity that Barbara was demonstrating.

Barbara's new position would have implications far beyond the question of her attendance at an anger workshop. It would be a statement that it is her responsibility, not his, to make decisions about what she will and will not do. In calmly and firmly clarifying this important issue in the relationship, she would no longer be the same woman whom he married and with whom he feels comfortable and secure. She, too, would be feeling very anxious and uncertain if she behaved in this new and different way. *There are few things more anxiety-arousing than shifting to a higher level of self-assertion and separateness in an important relationship and maintaining this position despite the countermoves of the other person.*

If Barbara gives up her fantasy that she can change her husband and starts using that same anger energy to clarify her choices and take new actions on her own behalf, she will be less troubled by the "anger problems" that spring from her de-selfed or underfunctioning position: headaches, low self-esteem, and chronic bitterness and dissatisfaction, to name just a few. The price she will pay is that her marriage, at least for a while, will likely be rougher than ever. Underlying issues and conflicts will begin to surface. She may start asking herself some serious questions: "Who is responsible for making decisions about my life?" "How are power and decision-making shared in this relationship?" "What will happen in my marriage if I become stronger and more assertive?" "If my choice is either to sacrifice myself to keep the marriage calm, or to grow and risk losing the relationship, which do I want?"

Perhaps Barbara is not ready to be struggling with such threatening issues at this time. Perhaps she would get very little support in such a venture. Perhaps she believes that any relationship is better than no relationship at all. For all we know, she herself is scared to attend the workshop and is unconsciously inviting her husband to express all the negative feelings for both of them.

It is important to appreciate that there are real dangers here. If Barbara was to stand firm about the workshop, she would inevitably feel an internal pressure to take a stand on other issues as well. Whereas in the past she and her husband may have fit together like two pieces of a puzzle, she would now be in the process of changing her shape. Would he change along with her so that they could continue to fit together, or would he eventually leave her? Would she, while making her own changes, decide that she needed to leave him? At least for now, Barbara has made her choice to protect her husband and continue in the old ways. It is not simply an act of "passive submission"; rather, it may well be an active choice to safeguard the predictable familiarity and security of her most important relationship—her marriage.

PEACE AT ANY PRICE

In a certain way, Barbara is not so "unliberated" as she may seem. She is able to express ideas and opinions that are different from her husband's. She can recognize that what she wants for herself is not the same as what her husband wants for her. She also knows her priorities. She would prefer, at least in this instance, to accommodate to her husband's wishes rather than risk rocking the marital boat.

Many of us make such choices without being consciously aware of what we are doing and why we are doing it. We do not allow our own selves to know that we would like to attend a workshop on anger. We avoid entertaining new ideas and ways of thinking that would lead to overt conflict and disagreement in our relationships with important others. We may not allow ourselves to identify the unfair arrangements in which we participate. We may also cancel our registration to things new and different, but we may be unaware of the sacrifices we make to keep things on an even keel and ensure that peace reigns.

How might such a peace-keeper have handled the

workshop situation? Most likely, she would not have struggled with her partner, because there would have been nothing to fight about. She would not have considered attending an anger workshop in the first place. She would not allow herself to become seriously interested in anything that would threaten another person or disrupt the status quo in an important relationship. If she did allow herself some initial interest in the workshop, she might test out her partner's reaction before she signed up. She might approach him and say, "Listen, I'm thinking about attending this workshop. . . ." And then she would sensitively evaluate his spoken and unspoken response. If she picked up any signals that he felt threatened or was disapproving, she would move in quickly to protect him. She might say to herself, "Well, the workshop probably wouldn't be that good," or, "We don't have the money now," or, "I'm not really in the mood to go, anyway."

In this way, a woman avoids conflict by defining her own wishes and preferences as being the same as what her partner wishes and prefers her to be. She defines her own self as he defines her. She sacrifices her awareness of who she is in her efforts to conform to his wants and expectations. The entire de-selfing process goes on unconsciously so that she may experience herself in perfect harmony with her husband. If she develops emotional or physical problems, she may not associate her dysfunction with the self-sacrifices that she has made in order to protect another person or keep a relationship calm.

In a somewhat less extreme position is the woman who would be able to maintain her interest in the workshop despite the risk of recognizing that she and her partner were not of one mind. She would allow herself to be aware that she is a separate and different person from him, with ideas and preferences no less deserving of respect than his. Nonetheless, she might still find a way to avoid bringing differences between her and her partner into bold relief and incurring his disapproval. She might say to herself, "Well, I do want to go to the workshop, but I can tell there's going to be a big hassle if I push it and it's not worth the fight." _"It's not worth the fight"_ is a familiar phrase that protects many of us from confronting the challenge of changing our behavior. As Barbara's situation illustrates, fighting per se is not the issue. What matters is the degree to which we are able to take a clear position in a relationship and behave in ways that are congruent with our stated beliefs.

Women who fall into the peace-maker or "nice lady" category are by no means passive, wishy-washy losers. Quite to the contrary, we have developed an important and complex interpersonal skill that requires a great deal of inner activity and sensitivity. We are good at anticipating other people's reactions, and we are experts at protecting others from uncomfortable feelings. This is a highly developed social skill that is all too frequently absent in men. If only we could take this very same skill and redirect it inward in order to become experts on our own selves.

SEPARATION AND TOGETHERNESS

Making a long-term relationship work is a difficult business because it requires the capacity to strike a balance between individualism (the "I") and togetherness (the "we"). The tugs in both directions are very strong. On the one hand, we want to be separate, independent individuals—self-contained persons in our own right; on the other, we seek a sense of connectedness and intimacy with another person, as well as a sense of belongingness to a family or a group. When a couple gets out of balance in either direction, there is a problem.

What happens if there is not enough "we" in our relationship? The result may be a case of "emotional divorce." Two people can end up isolated and alone in an empty-shell marriage where they do not share personal feelings and experiences. When the "separateness force" is overriding, an "I-don't-need-you" attitude may be expressed by one or both partners—a stance that is a far cry from a truly autonomous position. There may be little fighting in the relationship, but little closeness as well.

What happens if there is not enough "I" in our relationship? Here, we sacrifice our clear and separate identity and our sense of responsibility for, and control over, our own life. When the "togetherness force" is overriding, a lot of energy goes into trying to "be for" the other person, and trying to make the other person think or behave differently. Instead of taking responsibility for our own selves, we tend to feel responsible for the emotional well-being of the other person and hold the other person responsible for ours. When this reversal of individual responsibility is set in motion, each partner may become very emotionally reactive to what the other says and does, and there may be a lot of fighting and blaming, as in Barbara's case.

Another outcome of excessive togetherness is a pseudo-harmonious "we," where there is little overt conflict because a submissive spouse accepts the "reality" of the dominant spouse, or both may behave as if they share a common brain and bloodline. The "urge to merge" may be universal, but when acted out in extreme forms, these "fusion relationships" place us in a terribly vulnerable position. If two people become one, a separation can feel like a psychological or a physical death. We may have nothing—not even a self to fall back on—when an important relationship ends.

We all need to have both an "I" and a "we" that nourish and give meaning to each other. There is no formula for the "right" amount of separateness and togetherness for all couples or even for the same couple over time. Each member of a couple is constantly monitoring the balance of these two forces, automatically and unconsciously making moves to restore more separateness (when anxiety about fusion sets in) or more togetherness (when anxiety about unrelatedness sets in). The balance of these two forces is constantly in motion in every couple. One common "solution" or "division of labor" that couples unconsciously arrange is that the woman will express the wish for "togetherness"; the man, the wish for "separateness." We will be taking a closer look at this dance between the "pursuing female" and the "distancing male" in Chapter 3.

If we are chronically angry or bitter in a particular relationship, that may be a message to clarify and strengthen the "I" a bit more. We must re-examine our own selves with a view toward discovering what we think, feel, and want and what we need to do differently in our lives. The more we carve out a clear and separate "I," the more we can experience and enjoy both intimacy and aloneness. Our intimacy need not be "sameness" or "oneness" or loss of self; our aloneness and separateness need not be distance and isolation.

Why is strengthening the "I" such a difficult task? There are many factors, but if we keep a narrow focus on the here and now, Barbara's situation illustrates how scary it can be to move to a higher level of clarity and assertiveness. Barbara could not give up her old ways and try out some new ones without experiencing an anxiety-arousing feeling of separateness and without making waves in her marriage. Since this is true in all relationships, let's take a closer look.

Clarity and the Fear of Loss

If Barbara had a clearer "I" to begin with, she would not define her problem as: "My husband won't let me go to the workshop." Instead, she might say something like the following to herself: "My problem is this: If I cancel the workshop, I will feel bitter and resentful. If I go to the workshop, my husband will feel bitter and resentful. Which do I choose?" After some thought, she might decide that the workshop was not that important or that the timing just wasn't right for her to make waves in the marriage. Or, she might conclude that the workshop was a non-negotiable issue on which she would not compromise. In this case, she might think about how to present her decision to her husband in a way that would minimize the power struggle. Or, she might simply inform him that she was going. Later, when things were calm, she might initiate a discussion about decision-making in the marriage and explain that while she was interested in his opinions, she was ultimately in charge of making her own decisions.

What stopped Barbara from achieving this kind of clarity? Why would any of us end up as chronic fighters and complainers, rather than identify our problems and choices and clarify our position? No, women do not gain a secret masochistic gratification from being in the victimized, one-down position. Quite to the contrary, the woman who sits at the bottom of a seesaw marriage accumulates a great amount of rage, which is in direct proportion to the degree of her submission and sacrifice.

The dilemma is that we may unconsciously be convinced that our important relationships can survive only if we continue to remain one down. To do better—to become clearer, to act stronger, to be more separate, to take action on our own behalf—may be unconsciously equated with a destructive act that will diminish and threaten our partner, who might then retaliate or leave. Sometimes, to develop a stronger "I" is to come to terms with our deep-seated wish to leave an unsatisfactory marriage, and this possibility may be no less frightening than the fear of being left.

Perhaps Barbara is not ready to face the risk of putting her husband and herself to the test of whether change is possible. She may already be convinced that the relationship cannot tolerate much change. She may be caught between a rock and a hard place: Neither is she ready to say to herself, "I am choosing to stay in this unhappy marriage with a man who is not going to change," nor can she clarify a bottom line and say, "If these things do not change, I will leave." Or perhaps Barbara is not yet ready to face anxiety or the "funny depression" that often hits us when we take a clearer and more separate stance in a meaningful relationship. *Fighting and blaming is sometimes a way both to protest and to protect the status quo when we are not quite ready to make a move in one direction or another.*

COUNTERMOVES AND "CHANGE BACK!" REACTIONS

I do not wish to convey the bleak impression that we must stay put on the bottom of the seesaw lest our partner, as well as our relationship, come tumbling down. In some cases, this may happen as a consequence of our change and growth. But more frequently, and depending on how we proceed, the other person will grow along with us, and our emotional ties will ultimately be strengthened. We can learn to strengthen our own selves in a way that will maximize the chances that we will enhance rather than threaten our relationships. Making a change, however, never occurs easily and smoothly.

We meet with a countermove or "Change back!" reaction from the other person whenever we begin to give up the old ways of silence, vagueness, or ineffective fighting and begin to make clear statements about the needs, wants, beliefs, and priorities of the self. In fact, Murray Bowen, the originator of Bowen Family Systems Theory, emphasizes the fact that in *all* families there is a powerful opposition to one member defining a more independent self. According to Bowen, the opposition invariably goes in successive steps:

1. "You are wrong," with volumes of reasons to support this.
2. "Change back and we will accept you again."
3. "If you don't change back, these are the consequences," which are then listed.

What are some common countermoves? We may be accused of coldness, disloyalty, selfishness, or disregard for others. ("How could you upset your mother by saying that to her!") We may receive verbal or nonverbal threats that the other person will withdraw or terminate the relationship. ("We can't be close if you feel that way." "How can we have a relationship if you really mean that?") Countermoves take any number of forms. For example, a person may have an asthma attack or even a stroke.

Countermoves are the other person's unconscious attempt to restore a relationship to its prior balance or equilibrium, when anxiety about separateness and change gets too high. Other people do not make countermoves simply because they are dominating, controlling, or chauvinistic. They may or may not be these things, but that is almost beside the point. Countermoves are an expression of anxiety, as well as of closeness and attachment.

Our job is to keep clear about our own position in the face of a countermove—not to prevent it from happening or to tell the other person that he or she should not be reacting that way. Most of us want the impossible. We want to control not only our own decisions and choices but also the other person's *reactions* to them. We not only want to make a change; we want the other person to *like* the change that we make. We want to move ahead to a higher level of assertiveness and clarity and then receive praise and reinforcement from those very people who have chosen us for our old familiar ways.

Countermoves aside, our *own* resistance to change is just as formidable a force. Barbara's position in her marriage, for example, may have roots in patterns that go back for many generations. Barbara's mother and other women relatives who came before her may have assumed a de-selfed position in marriage, or may have paired up with de-selfed husbands. There may not be a tradition in Barbara's family for marriages in which *both* partners can be clear and competent in making decisions about their own lives and negotiating differences. All of us are deeply affected by the patterns and traditions of past generations even if—and especially if—we are not consciously aware of them. Like many women, Barbara may feel guilty if she strives to have for herself what her own mother could not. Deep in her unconscious mind, Barbara may view her attempt at self-assertion as an act of disloyalty—a betrayal not only of her husband but also of generations of women in her family. If this is the case, she will unconsciously resist the changes that she seeks.

To complicate matters further, unresolved issues from our past inevitably surface in our current relationships. If Barbara is stuck in a pattern of chronic marital fighting and blaming, that may be a sign that she has not negotiated her separateness and independence within her first family and that she needs to do some work here (see Chapter 4). How well is Barbara able to take a firm position on important issues with members of her first family? Is she able to make clear and direct statements of her own thoughts and feelings? Is she able to be who she is and not what other family members want or expect her to be—and allow others to do the same? If Barbara is having difficulty staying in emotional contact with living members of her first family and defining a clear and separate "I" within this context, she may have difficulty doing so in her marriage. As a psychotherapist I often help women to clarify and to change their relationships with siblings, parents, and grandparents so that underground family conflicts and patterns will not be replayed—nor buried anger and anxieties pop up—in another close relationship, making for a painful degree of reactivity to others.

WHERE ARE WE?

Barbara's telephone call provided us with an excellent example of ineffective fighting that ensures non-change, because she did two things that we all do when we are stuck and spinning our wheels: First, she fought about a false issue.

Second, she put her energy into trying to change the other person.

Pseudo Issues

Barbara and her husband probably put a great deal of energy into fighting about the value of my workshop, which is, like most things in life, a matter of personal opinion. More to the point, it's a pseudo issue. It has nothing to do with Barbara's real problem, which concerns her struggle between her wish to make responsible decisions for her own life and her wish to preserve togetherness in her marriage and protect the status quo.

All couples fight over pseudo issues some of the time, and often with great intensity. I will never forget the very first couple I saw in marital therapy. There in my office they sat, quarreling bitterly over whether they would eat their dinner that evening at McDonald's or Long John Silver's. Each of these intelligent people put forth the most compelling arguments regarding the relative merits of hamburger or fish, and neither would give an inch. Being new at marital therapy, I was not quite certain how to be helpful to this couple, but I did know one thing for sure: The impassioned argument I was witnessing between two people who were obviously in a great deal of pain had nothing to do with the respective value of burgers and fish.

Identifying the *real* issues is no easy matter. It is particularly difficult among family members, because when two adults have a conflict, they often bring in a third party (perhaps a child or an in-law) to form a triangle, which then makes it even harder for the two people involved to identify and work out their problems. For example:

A wife says to her husband, "I am terribly angry about the way you ignore our son. I feel like he's growing up without a father." The real issue not addressed is: "I feel ignored and I am angry that you do not spend more time with me."

A husband says to his wife, who is considering a new job, "The children need you at home. I support your working, but I do not like to see the kids and the household neglected." The real issue not addressed is: "I am scared and worried about your making this change. I am not sure how your career will affect our relationship, and your enthusiasm about this new work is putting me in touch with my dissatisfaction with my own job."

A wife says to her husband, "Your mother is driving me crazy. She's intrusive and controlling and she treats you like you're her husband and little boy all wrapped up in one." The real issue not addressed is: "I wish you could be more assertive with your mother and set some limits. Sometimes I wonder whether your primary commitment is to me or to her."

When we learn about triangles (Chapter 8), we will see that it is difficult to sort out not only *what* we are angry about but also *whom* we are angry at.

Trying to Change Him

Barbara, like most of us, was putting her "anger energy" into trying to change the other person. She was trying to change her husband's thoughts and feelings about the workshop and his reactions to her going. She wanted him to approve of the workshop and she wanted him to *want* her to go. In short, she wanted him to think and feel about the workshop as she did. Of course, most of us secretly believe that we have the corner on the "truth" and that this would be a much better world if everyone else believed and reacted exactly as we do. But one of the hallmarks of emotional maturity is to recognize the validity of multiple realities and to understand that people think, feel, and react differently. Often we behave as if "closeness" means "sameness." Married couples and family members are especially prone to behave as if there is one "reality" that should be agreed upon by all.

It is extremely difficult to learn, with our hearts as well as our heads, that we have a right to everything we think and feel—and so does everyone else. It *is* our job to state our thoughts and feelings clearly and to make responsible decisions that are congruent with our values and beliefs. It is *not* our job to make another person think and feel the way we do or the way we want them to. If we try, we can end up in a relationship in which a lot of personal pain and emotional intensity are being expended and nothing is changing.

There is nothing wrong with *wanting* to change someone else. The problem is that it usually doesn't work. No matter how skilled we become in dealing with our anger, we cannot ensure that another person will do what we want him or her to or see things our way, nor are we guaranteed that justice will prevail. We are able to move away from ineffective fighting only when we give up the fantasy that we can change or control another person. It is only then that we can reclaim the power that is truly ours—the power to change our own selves and take a new and different action on our own behalf.

In the chapters that follow, we will learn how to put the lessons from Barbara's phone call into practice. What are these seemingly simple lessons?

First, "letting it all hang out" may not be helpful, because venting anger may protect rather than challenge the old rules and patterns in a relationship. Second, the only person we can change and control is our own self. Third, changing our own self can feel so threatening and difficult that it is often easier to continue an old pattern of silent withdrawal or ineffective fighting and blaming. And, finally, de-selfing is at the heart of our most serious anger problems.

3

CIRCULAR DANCES
IN COUPLES

*When Getting Angry
Is Getting Nowhere*

Six months after the birth of my first son, I was vacationing with my family in Berkeley, California. Browsing through a secondhand bookstore, I came upon a volume by a foremost expert in child development. My heart sank slightly as I noted that my baby was not doing the things that the book said were appropriate for his age. "My God," I thought to myself, "my child is slow!" I flashed back on the complications that had characterized my pregnancy, and I froze. Was something wrong with my baby?

When I saw my husband, Steve, later in the day, I anxiously told him my fears. He responded with uncharacteristic insensitivity. "Forget it," he said matter-of-factly. "Babies develop at different rates. He's fine." His response (which I heard as an attempt to silence me) only upset me further. I reacted by trying to prove my point. I told him in detail what the book said, and I reminded him of the problems I had experienced throughout the pregnancy. He accused me of exaggerating the problem and of worrying excessively. *Nothing* was wrong. I accused him of denying and minimizing the problem. Something *might* be wrong. He reminded me coldly that my mother was a "worrier" and that, clearly, I was following in her footsteps. I reminded him angrily that worrying was not permitted in *his* family, since problems were not to be noticed. And then followed more of the same.

We repeated this *same* fight, in its *same* form, countless times over the next six months as our son continued even more conspicuously *not* to do what the book said he should be doing. The psychologist who tested him at nine months (at my initiation) said that he was, in fact, quite slow in certain areas but that it was too early to know what this meant. She suggested that we wait a while and then consult with a pediatric neurologist if we were still concerned.

Steve and I became even more rigidly polarized in our fights, and we fought with increasing frequency. Like robots, we took the same repetitive positions, and the sequence unfolded as neatly as clockwork: The more I expressed worry and concern, the more Steve distanced and minimized; the more he distanced and minimized, the more I exaggerated my position. This sequence would escalate until it finally became intolerable, at which point each of us would angrily point the finger at the other for "starting it."

We were stuck. Our years of psychological training and intellectual sophistication went down the drain. It was clear enough that what each of us was doing only provoked a more vehement stance in the other. Yet, somehow, neither Steve nor I was able to do something different ourselves.

"Your baby is fine," a top pediatric neurologist in Kansas City reported blandly. Our son was almost a year old. "He has an atypical developmental pattern. There are certain babies who don't do much of anything until they walk." Sure enough, our son began to walk (right on schedule, no less) without having crawled, scooted, or in any way moved about preceding this. And so ended our chronic repetitive fights.

Later, we were able to recognize the unconscious benefits we got by maintaining these fights. Fighting with each other helped both of us to worry a little less about our son, and deflected our attention from other concerns we had about becoming new parents. But what was most impressive at the time was how irrevocably stuck we were. We both behaved as if there was only one "right" way to respond to a stressful situation in the family, and we engaged in a dance in which we were trying to get the *other* person to change steps while we would not change our own. The outcome was that nothing changed at all.

GETTING STUCK—GETTING UNSTUCK

How do couples get stuck? The inability to express anger is not always at the heart of the problem. Many women, like myself, get angry with ease and have no difficulty showing it. Instead, the problem is that getting angry is getting nowhere, or even making things worse.

If what we are doing with our anger is not achieving the desired result, it would seem logical to try something different. In my case, I could have changed my behavior with Steve in a number of ways. Surely, it was clear to me that my anxious expressions of worry only provoked his denial, which then provoked more worry on my part. For example, I might have taken my worry to a good friend for several weeks and stopped expressing it to Steve. Perhaps then Steve would have had the opportunity to experience his own worry. Or, I might have approached Steve at a time when we were close, and shared with him that I was worrying a lot about our baby and that I hoped for his help and support as I struggled with this. Such an approach would have been quite different from my usual behavior, which involved speaking out at the very height of my anxiety and then implying that Steve was at fault for not reacting the same way as I. Steve, too, might easily have broken the pattern of our fights by doing something different himself. For example, *he* might have initiated a talk in which he expressed concern for our son.

We all recognize intellectually that repeating our ineffective efforts achieves nothing and can even make things worse. Yet, oddly enough, most of us continue to do *more of the same,* especially under stress. For example, a wife who lectures her husband about his failure to stay on his diet increases the intensity or frequency of her lectures when he overeats. A woman whose lover becomes cooler when she angrily presses him to express feelings presses on even harder, her problem being not that she is unable to get angry but that she's doing something with her anger that isn't working and yet keeps doing it.

Even rats in a maze learn to vary their behavior if they keep hitting a dead end. Why in the world, then, do we behave less intelligently than laboratory animals? The answer, by now, may be obvious. Repeating the same old fights protects us from the anxieties we are bound to experience when we make a change. Ineffective fighting allows us to stop the clock when our efforts to achieve greater clarity become too threatening. Sometimes staying stuck is what we need to do until the time comes when we are confident that it is safe to get unstuck.

Sometimes, however, even when we *are* ready to risk

change, we still keep participating in the same old familiar fights that go nowhere. Human nature is such that when we are angry, we tend to become so emotionally reactive to what the other person is doing to us that we lose our ability to observe our own part in the interaction. Self-observation is not at all the same as self-blame, at which some women are experts. Rather, self-observation is the process of seeing the interaction of ourselves and others, and recognizing that the ways other people behave with us has something to do with the way we behave with them. We cannot *make* another person be different, but when we do something different ourselves, the old dance can no longer continue as usual.

The story of Sandra and Larry, a couple who sought my help, is a story about getting unstuck. While the *content* of their struggles may or may not hit home, the *form* of the dance they do together is almost universal. For this couple, like many, was caught in a circular dance in which the behavior of each served to maintain and provoke that of the other. Once we are part of an established twosome—married or unmarried, lesbian or straight—we may easily become caught in such a dance. When this happens, the more each person tries to change things, the more things stay the same.

SANDRA AND LARRY

"Well, how do each of you see the problem in your marriage?" I inquired. It was my first meeting with Sandra and Larry, who had requested marital therapy at Sandra's initiative. My eyes fell first on Larry and then on Sandra, who quickly picked up the invitation to speak. She turned her body in my direction and cupped her hands against her face. Like blinders, they blocked Larry from her view.

With unveiled anger in her voice, Sandra listed her complaints. It was evident that she had told her story before. It was also evident that she thought the "problem" was her husband.

"First of all, he's a workaholic," she began. "He neglects the kids and me. I don't even think he knows how to relate to us anymore. He's a stranger in his own family." Sandra paused for a moment, drew a deep breath, and continued: "He acts like he expects me to run the house and deal with the kids all by myself, and then when something goes wrong, he tells me I'm crazy to be reacting so emotionally. He's not available and he never expresses his feelings about things that should worry him."

"When Larry comes home, and you're upset about something at home, how do you ask for his support and help?" I asked.

"I tell him that I'm really upset, that I'm worried about our money situation, and that Jeff is sick, and that I had to miss my class, and that I'm going nuts with the baby today. But he just looks at me and criticizes me that the dinner isn't ready, or tells me that I'm overreacting. He always says, 'Why do you get so damn emotional about everything?' He makes me want to scream!"

Sandra fell silent and Larry said nothing. After several minutes, Sandra continued, her anger now laced with tears: "I'm tired of being at the bottom of his list of priorities. He hardly ever takes the initiative to relate to me and he neglects the kids, too. And then, when he *does* decide that he wants to be a father, he just takes over like he's the only one in charge."

"For example?" I asked.

"For example, he goes out and buys Lori, our oldest

daughter, this expensive dressing table that she's had her eye on, and he doesn't even consult me! He just tells me after the fact!" Sandra is now glaring at Larry, who refuses to meet her eye.

"When Larry does something that you disapprove of, like the dressing-table incident, how do you let him know?"

"It's impossible!" Sandra said emphatically. "It's simply impossible!"

"*What* is impossible?" I persisted.

"Talking to him! Confronting him! He doesn't talk about feelings. He doesn't know how to discuss things. He just doesn't respond. He clams up and wants to be left alone. He doesn't even know how to fight. Either he talks in this superlogical manner, or he refuses to talk at all. He'd rather read a book or turn on the television."

"Okay," I said, "I think I understand how you see the problem." It was Larry's turn now: "How do you define the problem in your marriage, Larry?"

Larry proceeded to speak in a controlled and deliberate voice that almost masked the fact that he was as angry as his wife: "Sandra isn't supportive enough, she doesn't give enough, and she's always on my back. I think that's the main problem." Larry fell silent, as if he was finished for the day.

"In what ways does Sandra fail to support you or give to you? Can you share a specific example?"

"Well, it's hard to say. She cuts me down a lot, for one thing. Or, I walk in the door at six o'clock, and I'm tired and wanting some peace and quiet, and she just rattles on about the kids' problems or her problems, or she just complains about one thing or another. Or, if I sit down to relax for five minutes, she's on my back to discuss some earthshaking matter—like the garbage disposal is broken." Larry was angry, but he managed to sound as if he was discussing the Dow-Jones average.

"Are you saying that you need some space?" I asked.

"Not exactly," replied Larry. "I'm saying that Sandra is very overreactive. She's very overemotional. She creates problems where they don't even exist. Everything is a major case. And, yes, I suppose I am saying that I need more space."

"What about the kids? Do you—" I had not finished my question when Larry interrupted:

"Sandra is a very overinvolved mother," he explained carefully, as if he were describing a patient at a clinical conference. "She worries excessively about the children. She inherited it from her mother. And, if you could meet her mother, you would understand."

"Do you worry about the kids?" I inquired.

"Only when there's something to worry about. For Sandra, it seems to be a full-time job."

Although one would not have guessed it from this first session, Sandra and Larry were deeply committed to each other. At our initial meeting, however, they appeared to share only one thing in common—blaming. Like many couples, each spouse saw the locus of his or her marital difficulties as existing entirely within the other person, and each had the same unstated goal for marital therapy—that the *other* would be "fixed up" and "straightened out."

Let's take a closer look at the details of Sandra and Larry's story, for there is much to be learned. Though couples differ markedly in how they present themselves, the ways in which they get stuck are very much the same.

"He Just Doesn't Respond!"
"She's Very Overemotional!"

Sound familiar? Sandra and Larry's central complaints about each other will ring a bell for many couples. His unfeelingness, unavailability, and distance is a major source of her anger: "My husband withdraws from confrontation and cannot share his real feelings." "My husband is like a machine." "My husband refuses to talk about things." "My husband is more invested in his work than in his family." And it is no coincidence that men have a reciprocal complaint: "My wife is much too reactive." "She gets irrational much too easily." "I wish that she would back off and stop nagging and bitching." "My wife wants to talk everything to death."

As typically happens, the very qualities that each partner complains of in the other are those that attracted them to each other to begin with. Sandra, for example, had been drawn to Larry's orderly, even-keel temperament, just as he had admired her capacity to be emotional and spontaneous. Her reactive, feeling-oriented approach to the world balanced his distant, logical reserve—and vice versa. Opposites attract—right?

Opposites do attract, but they do not always live happily ever after. On the one hand, it is reassuring to live with someone who will express parts of one's own self that one is afraid to acknowledge; yet, the arrangement has its inevitable costs: The woman who is expressing feelings not only for herself but also for her husband will indeed end up behaving "hysterically" and "irrationally." The man who relies on his wife to do the "feeling work" for him will increasingly lose touch with this important part of himself, and when the time comes that he needs to draw upon his emotional resources, he may find that nobody's at home.

In the majority of couples, men sit on the bottom of the seesaw when it comes to emotional competence. We all know about the man who can tie good knots on packages and fix things that break, yet fails to notice that his wife is depressed. He may have little emotional relatedness to his own family and lack even one close friend with whom honest self-disclosure takes place. This is the "masculinity" that our society breeds—the male who feels at home in the world of things and abstract ideas but who has little empathic connection to others, little attunement to his own internal world, and little willingness or capacity to "hang in" when a relationship becomes conflicted and stressful. In the traditional division of labor, men are encouraged to develop one kind of intelligence, but they fall short of another that is equally important. The majority *underfunction* in the realm of emotional competence, and their underfunctioning is closely related to women's *overfunctioning* in this area. It is not by accident that the "hysterical," overemotional female ends up under the same roof as the unemotional, distant male.

The marital seesaw is hard to balance. When couples do try to balance it, especially under stress, their solutions often exacerbate the problem. The emotional, feeling-oriented wife who gets on her husband's back to open up and express feelings will find that he becomes cooler and even less available. The cool, intellectual husband who tries calmly to use logic to quiet his overemotional wife will find that she becomes even more agitated. True to stereotype, each partner continues to do the *same old thing* while trying to change the other. The solution for righting the balance *becomes* the problem.

DOING THE "FEELING WORK" FOR LARRY

Sandra had long been furious at Larry's lack of reactivity without realizing her own part in the circular dance. She failed to recognize that she was so skilled and comfortable in expressing feelings that she was doing the job for the two of them, thus protecting her husband from feeling what he would otherwise feel. Doing the "feeling work," like cleaning up, has long been defined as "woman's work," and lots of women are good at it. As with cleaning up, men will not begin to do their share until women no longer do it for them.

Although it was not her conscious intent, Sandra helped Larry to maintain his underemotional stance by expressing more than her share of emotionality. The unconscious contract for this couple was that Sandra would be the emotional reactor and Larry the rational planner. And so, Sandra reacted *for* Larry. She did so in response not only to family stresses that concerned them both but also to problems that were really Larry's to struggle with. Here are two examples of how Sandra protected Larry by doing the feeling work for him:

An Injustice on the Job

One evening when Larry returned from work, he told Sandra that a co-worker had gotten credit for an idea that was originally his. As he began to outline the details of the incident, Sandra became upset and expressed her strong anger at the injustice. As her emotional involvement in the incident increased, she noticed that Larry was becoming cooler and more removed. "Aren't you upset about this?" she demanded. "It's your life, you know! Don't you have any feelings about it?"

Of course Larry had feelings about it. It was his career and the injustice had been done him. However, his style of reacting, as well as his tempo and timing, was very different from his wife's. Also, Larry was using Sandra to react *for* him. Her quick outburst actually took him off the hook. He did not have to feel upset about the incident because she was doing all the work. The more emotion Sandra displayed, the less Larry felt within himself.

Sandra was consciously angry and frustrated at Larry's apparent lack of feelings about the incident, yet she was unconsciously helping him to maintain his strong, cool, masculine position. By criticizing him for not showing feelings and demonstrating the appropriate degree of distress, she was applying a solution that only reinforced the very problem she complained of. Sandra could not *make* Larry react differently. However, she could do something different herself. When Sandra stopped doing the feeling work for Larry, the circular dance was broken.

It was not easy for Sandra to change her behavior, but eventually she did make an important shift: Sometime later, when Larry shared a crisis at work, Sandra listened calmly and quietly. She did not express feelings that appropriately belonged to Larry, nor did she offer solutions to a problem that was not hers. Given sufficient time and space around him, Larry did, indeed, begin to react to his own problem and struggle with his own dilemma. In fact, he became depressed. But, while this was the very reaction Sandra had overtly sought and wished for ("That cool bastard doesn't react to anything!"), she was uncomfortable seeing her husband vulnerable and struggling. She realized, to her surprise, that part of her wanted Larry to maintain the role of the cool, strong, unruffled partner.

A Problem with Larry's Parents

Sandra also protected Larry from recognizing his anger at his own parents. She did this by criticizing them and fuming at them *for* him. Larry, then, was left with the simpler job of coming to their defense.

This pattern began at the time of the birth of their first child. Larry's parents, who were quite wealthy, were spending the year in Paris and did not acknowledge their new granddaughter with enthusiasm or show interest in seeing her. Sandra reacted with outrage, declaring to Larry that they were cold and selfish people who thought only of themselves. Years later she still spoke heatedly about their neglectful attitude, although always to Larry and never to his parents.

What did Larry do? He made excuses for his parents and found logical reasons for their behavior, which only made Sandra angrier. It was another circular dance in which the behavior of each provoked the other into doing more of the same. The more Sandra criticized her in-laws to Larry, the more Larry came to their defense; the more Larry came to their defense, the more openly critical Sandra became.

Deep down, of course, Larry was considerably more affected than Sandra by his parents' behavior. They were, after all, his parents, and he was their son. But because of Sandra's readiness to do the feeling work for him, Larry was in touch only with his loyalty to his parents who were under his wife's attack.

Sandra's focus on Larry's behavior with *his* parents, as opposed to her own relationship with *her* in-laws, complicated the problem and the solution. In fact, Sandra's focus on her husband obscured her own need to change matters.

Larry's parents, who traveled a great deal, visited once a year. These visits were initiated by Larry's father, who would write a letter informing the couple when they would arrive and for how long they would stay. Being told rather than asked annoyed Sandra no end. She then put pressure on Larry to confront his parents regarding this matter and he would refuse. In the face of Sandra's anger and criticisms, Larry predictably sided with them, putting forth logical arguments as to why his parents needed to schedule visits as they did.

Sandra felt helpless, and for good reason: First, she was trying to make Larry do something and it wasn't working. Second, she was doing the feeling work for him. Down the road a bit, Sandra changed both of these patterns.

At some point Sandra recognized that if the behavior of Larry's parents upset her, it was her job to deal with this herself. So she did. In a letter that was neither attacking nor blaming, Sandra explained to her in-laws that it was important to her to be consulted in arranging a mutually agreeable time for their visits. She stated her position warmly but with clarity and directness, and she did not back down in the face of their initial defensiveness. Much to her surprise, her long-pent-up anger at her in-laws began to dissipate as she became more confident that she could speak effectively to issues that were not to her liking. Also to her surprise, Larry's parents, in the end, responded warmly and affirmatively, thanking Sandra for her straightforwardness. This was the first step in Sandra's taking care of her own business with her in-laws, and, in the process, opening up a more direct person-to-person relationship with each of them.

Larry, threatened by the new assertiveness that his wife was expressing, initially protested the very idea that she would write such a letter. In his typical style, he presented her with a dozen intellectual arguments to back his disapproval. Sandra, however, was clear in her resolve to change things and resisted fighting back, since her experience had taught her that such arguments led nowhere. Instead, she explained to Larry that although she appreciated his point of view, she needed to make her own decisions about how, when, and if she would deal with issues that were important to her.

When Larry observed that Sandra was continuing to address issues directly with his parents without criticizing or attacking them, a predictable next step occurred: His own unresolved issues with his mother and father surfaced full force. Sandra was no longer complaining to Larry about his parents but managing her own business with them. In response to this, Larry began to feel an internal pressure to take care of his own.

When a woman vents her anger ineffectively (like Sandra complaining to Larry about his parents, which surely wasn't going to change anything), or expresses it in an overemotional style, she does *not* threaten her man. If anything, she helps him to maintain his masculine cool, while she herself is perceived as infantile or irrational. When a woman clarifies the issues and uses her anger to move toward something new and different, then change occurs. If she stops *overfunctioning* for others and starts acting for herself, her *underfunctioning* man is likely to acknowledge and deal with his own anxieties.

THE BLAMING GAME

Sandra and Larry had expended enormous amounts of energy blaming each other for their endless fights. Like many of us, their method of attributing blame was to look for the one who started it. The search for a beginning of a sequence is a common blaming game in couples.

Consider, for example, the interaction between a nagging wife and a distant, withdrawing husband. The more he withdraws, the more she nags, and the more she nags, the more he withdraws, and so on. . . . So, who is to blame?

"I know!" says one observer of this sequence. "She is to blame. *First* she nags him and gets on his case for all kinds of things, and *then* the poor guy withdraws."

"No," says a second observer, "you have it all wrong. He is! *First* he buries himself in his work and ignores his family, and *then* his wife goes after him."

This is the who-started-it game—the search for a beginning of a sequence, where the aim is to proclaim which person is to blame for the behavior of both. But we know that this interaction is really a circular dance in which the behavior of one partner maintains and provokes the behavior of the other. The circular dance has no beginning and no end. In the final analysis, it matters little who started it. The question of greater significance is: "How do we break out of it?"

A good way to make this break is to recognize the part we play in maintaining and provoking the other person's behavior. Even if we are convinced that the other person is ninety-seven percent to blame, we are still in control of changing our own three percent. So the central question becomes: "How can I change *my* steps in the circular dance?" This is not to say that we don't have good reason to be furious with the other person. Nor is it to say that our current sex roles and gender arrangements, which breed these sorts of dances, are not at fault—they are. Rather, it is simply to say that we don't have the power to change another person who does not want to change, and our attempts to do so may actually *protect* him or her from change. This is the paradox of the circular dances in which we all participate.

EMOTIONAL PURSUER—EMOTIONAL DISTANCER
A VERY OLD DANCE

Emotional pursuers are persons who reduce their anxiety by sharing feelings and seeking close emotional contact. Emotional distancers are persons who reduce their anxiety by intellectualizing and withdrawing. As with Sandra and Larry, it is most often the woman who is the emotional pursuer and the man who is the emotional distancer.

When the waters are calm, the pursuer and the distancer may seem like the perfect complementary couple. She is spontaneous, lively, and emotionally responsive. He is reserved, calm, and logical. When the waters are rough, however, each exaggerates his or her own style, and that's where the trouble begins.

What happens when the inevitable stresses of life hit this couple? It may be an illness, a child in difficulty, a financial worry, or a possible career move. No matter what the content of the problem, these two styles of responding suddenly seem at odds. She reacts quickly, seeking direct contact and refuge in togetherness. She shares her feelings and wants him to do the same. He reacts very logically and rationally in a manner that is not acceptable to her. So, she pursues harder, wanting to know more of what he is thinking and feeling, and he distances further. The more he distances, the more she pursues, and the more she pursues, the more he distances. She accuses him of being cold, unresponsive, and inhuman. He accuses her of being pushy, hysterical, and controlling.

What is the common outcome of this classic scenario? After this escalating dance of pursuit and withdrawal proceeds for some time, the woman goes into what therapists call "reactive distance." Feeling rejected and fed up, she at last proceeds to go about her own business. The man now has even more space than he is comfortable with, and in time he moves closer to her in the hope of making contact. But it's too late. "Where were you when I needed you!" she says angrily. At this point, distancer and pursuer might even reverse their roles for a while.

Emotional pursuers protect emotional distancers. By doing the work of expressing the neediness, clingingness, and wish for closeness for both partners, pursuers make it possible for distancers to avoid confronting their own dependency wishes and insecurities. As long as one person is pursuing, the other has the luxury of experiencing a cool independence and a need for space. It is hardly surprising, considering her upbringing, that the woman is usually, though by no means always, the pursuer. It is another example of doing the feeling work for men. When a pursuer learns to back off and put her energies into her own life— especially if she can do this with dignity and *without hostility*— the distancer is more likely to recognize his own needs for contact and closeness . . . and begin to pursue. But beware, this is no easy task. Most women who are emotional pursuers go off into a cold or angry "reactive distance," which only temporarily reverses the pursuit cycle or has little effect at all.

BREAKING THE PURSUIT CYCLE

Sandra and Larry were caught in an escalating cycle of pursuit and distance for many years prior to their seeking help. Since the birth of their first child, Larry was decreasing his emotional involvement with Sandra as he increased the energy he put into work and hobbies. Sandra alternated between active pursuit, angry criticism, and a cold, bitter withdrawal. Sadly, but predictably, their relationship had gone from bad to worse.

On one particular Friday night, almost a year following our first meeting, Sandra broke the pursuit cycle. It was her increased sense of personal responsibility to provide for her own needs, as well as her growing awareness that she could not change her husband, that allowed her to do something new and different. And something new and different is exactly what Sandra did.

This Friday evening began like all others. The children were in bed, and Larry was shuffling through his briefcase about to pull out a couple hours' work. Sandra came and sat down next to him on the couch. Larry bristled, expecting the usual attack, but it did not come. Instead, Sandra began to speak warmly and with assurance:

"Larry, I feel like I owe you an apology. I've been on your back for a long time. I realize that I have been wanting you to provide me with something that really *I* need to provide for myself. Perhaps part of the problem is that you have family and work and I have only you and the kids. It's my problem and I recognize that I need to do something about it."

"Oh," muttered Larry, with a somewhat unsettled look on his face. He seemed at an uncharacteristic loss for words. "Well, that's nice. . . ."

The very next night, Sandra asked Larry if he would mind putting the children to bed himself on Tuesday and Friday because she was planning to go out. Larry protested that he had too much work. Instead of arguing, Sandra called the sitter to come in and help on those evenings. On Tuesday night Sandra joined a yoga class that met weekly. On Friday night she went to the movies with a friend and then out for a glass of wine. She did not pursue Larry in any way, nor did she distance from him or withdraw coldly. If anything, she was warmer to him than usual, although clearly directing much of her energy toward her own interests and scheduling.

After three weeks of this, Larry, who had wanted nothing more than to be left alone, began to get nervous. Much to his surprise, he became quite uncomfortable when his wife's bleep was off his radar screen. At first, he tried to provoke her into fighting by attempting to control what she could or could not do with her evenings. Without retaliating, Sandra explained to Larry that she was a social person with social needs and that she was no longer able to neglect this important part of her life. Her warm firmness on this issue communicated clearly to Larry that she was acting *for herself* and not *against him*.

Next, Larry started to pursue her. Instead of bringing his work home, he suggested they use the sitter to go out together—something they almost never did on a week night. As Larry increasingly began to experience and express his own dependency and insecurity, a funny thing happened: Sandra, for the first time, got in touch with her own wish to be left alone. For a while, they simply reversed their roles as pursuer and distancer until, finally, they got things in balance. And when that occurred, Sandra and Larry were able to recognize that each of them harbored strong dependency wishes, as well as a wish to flee when things became "too close."

Why was it Sandra who finally took the initiative in breaking the circular dance? Sandra was in greater emotional pain than Larry, and her role as the pursuer in the relationship placed her in a more emotionally vulnerable position. When she became convinced that her old ways simply were not working for her, she found the motivation to move differently. Why did *she* have to take the responsibility to make the change? Simply because no one else was going to do it for her.

Breaking the pursuit cycle did not in itself lead to emotional closeness for Sandra and Larry; there were important barriers to intimacy that the two of them were left to struggle with. However, Sandra and Larry could work more successfully on their relationship once they recognized that they shared a common problem: Both of them wished for closeness and also feared it. Before Sandra broke the pursuit cycle, Larry had the false but comforting fantasy that all of the neediness and wish for closeness was in Sandra. Likewise, Sandra imagined that all of the avoidance of and flight from intimacy was in Larry.

When a pursuer stops pursuing and begins to put her energy back into her own life—without distancing or expressing anger at the other person—the circular dance has been broken. Because this may smack of the old "hard-to-get" tactics that women have been taught to play, it may sound inauthentic or manipulative. But continuing the old dance of pursuit or cold withdrawal is *not* more honest. In fact, it only leaves the woman feeling the neediness and dependency for two people, while her partner can disown these same qualities within himself. Our experience of a relationship becomes more "true" and balanced as the pursuer can allow herself to acknowledge and express more of her own wish for independence and space, and, in turn, the distancer can begin to acknowledge more of his dependency and wish for closeness.

OVERINVOLVED MOTHER—UNDERINVOLVED FATHER: THE LAST DANCE

"Sandra is a very overinvolved mother. She inherited it from her mother." These were Larry's words about Sandra's mothering during our first meeting. And it was true. Sandra did worry excessively about the children, as her own mother had worried about her. She became upset when her children were upset, and she had difficulty allowing them to handle their own disappointments and deal with their own sadness and anger. She was quick to spot potential "problems" in her children in a way that actually invited them to give her something to worry about. Larry was correct that Sandra was an overinvolved mother. However, he was unaware of his part in provoking and maintaining that circular dance.

Larry's singular pursuit of career goals had left him estranged from his wife and children and lacking in parenting skills. As Sandra moved in even closer to fill the empty space left by Larry, Larry felt more shut out and withdrew further. Whenever his anger about being on the periphery caught up with him, he moved in with a bang! As Sandra described in our initial meeting, he then took over in a unilateral way, as if he was the only one in charge. Underlying his sporadic displays of paternal dominance was his sadness and anger about his actual position as "odd man out" in the family. And so, Sandra and Larry were caught in another dance in which the behavior of each spouse provokes and reinforces the behavior of the other. Larry's underinvolvement provoked Sandra's overinvolvement, which provoked Larry's underinvolvement . . . Thus, the vicious cycle continued, punctuated by Larry's occasional displays of dominance, following which their life returned to its usual pattern.

This dance was very difficult to disrupt, because the entire family was working overtime to keep it going: On the one hand, Sandra and Larry each demanded that the other change. Larry criticized Sandra's overinvolvement with the children as harshly as she criticized his token fathering. Yet, each of them also wanted to keep the old dance going. "Please change!" and "Change back!" was the double message they gave each other. Like most couples, each partner wished for the other's change and growth, yet feared and resisted it.

Sandra, for example, complained incessantly about Larry's underinvolvement with the children. Yet, when he did make a tentative move closer to the family, she would correct some detail of his parenting, criticize some aspect of his behavior, or advise him on how to better interact with the children. It was extremely difficult for her to simply stay out and allow him to relate to the children in his own way. Sandra wanted Larry to become more involved, but she also wanted to maintain her special role as the more dominant and influential parent. If she relinquished that special status, her feelings of uselessness threatened to become intolerably strong, and her discontent with her marriage would be experienced with even greater intensity. She thus gave Larry mixed messages. She encouraged him to be more available to the kids but then, without being aware of it, undermined his tentative attempts to do so. Larry, in a similar fashion, gave Sandra the same "Please change!" and "Change back!" messages.

Toward the end of marital therapy, Sandra was able to do different steps in *this* dance, too. As she became increasingly invested in fostering her own growth and development, she became less tightly enmeshed with her children and no longer looked to them to fill up the emptiness she had been experiencing. Sandra's earlier focus on her husband and children had protected her from confronting some difficult questions: "What are my priorities right now?" "Are there interests and skills that I would like to develop?" "What are my personal goals over the next several years?" As Sandra began to put her energy into struggling with these difficult issues, she was better able to allow Larry to relate to the children in his own way without correcting him or getting in the middle. As Sandra backed off, Larry moved in. The children, too, sensed that their mother was putting her energy into her own life and no longer needed them to be "loyal" to her as the "number-one" parent. Thus, they became freer to be close with their dad without anxiety and guilt. This was a difficult shift for Larry, because he was faced head on with his own worries about being a father and his concerns about his competence in this area.

TRYING TO CHANGE HIM

Sandra had spent many years trying to change Larry. "If only he would change!" "If only he would be different!" She truly believed that a change in Larry would secure her happiness. But the more Sandra put her energies into trying to change and control Larry, the more things stayed the same. For trying to change or control another person is a solution that never, never works. And while Sandra poured all that effort into trying to change someone she could not change, she failed to exercise the power that *was* hers—*the power to change her own self.*

Sandra's realization that she could not change Larry did not mean that she silently swallowed her anger and dissatisfaction. If anything, she learned to articulate her reactions to Larry with clarity and assurance. She was aware, however, that in response to these statements of her own wishes and preferences, Larry would change or not change. And if he did *not* change, it was Sandra's job to decide what *she* would or would not do from there. This is something more difficult than participating in further fighting that only maintains the status quo.

For example, Larry's pattern of leaving household jobs half finished was a real irritant to Sandra. The typical old pattern was that Sandra would push Larry to finish a task, in response to which he would procrastinate further, which provoked Sandra into pushing harder. The circular dance was procrastinate-push-procrastinate-push . . . Sandra would continue to try to *make* Larry finish the job despite the likelihood that it would not get done.

As is often the case, Sandra's pushing actually helped Larry to be more comfortable with his irresponsible behavior. He would become angry and defensive in the face of her criticisms, which protected him from feeling guilty and concerned about his difficulty completing tasks. Sandra's attempts to change Larry only made it easier for him to avoid confronting his own problem.

Now, Sandra is clear in telling Larry that she becomes upset when the bathroom ceiling remains half painted and buckets of paint are lying around the house. If Larry shows no positive response to her complaint, Sandra then puts her energy into determining what she will do or will not do in order to take care of her own needs. She is able to do this when she *begins* to feel resentful, so that her anger does not build up. Thus, she can talk to Larry without hostility and let him know that she is needing to do something *for* herself and not *to* him.

After considering the options open to her, she may choose to say any number of things to Larry. It may be: "Okay, I don't like it, but I can live with it." Or: "Larry, I would rather you finish what you began, but if you are unable to do so this week, it is bothersome enough to me that I will do it myself. I can paint it without becoming angry, so that's okay with me." Or: "I can only tolerate looking at this unfinished job for one week, and I can't complete it myself without becoming angry about it. So, what might we do that you don't feel pushed and I don't become furious? One idea I have is to call the painter if it's not done by Saturday." Obviously, there is *something* Sandra can do about the ceiling, for if Larry were to disappear from the earth, it is highly unlikely that she would live out the rest of her life with a half-painted ceiling. In the old pattern, however, Sandra put so much effort into trying to change Larry that she obscured from herself her own power to act and make choices. And this, in the end, is the only real power we have.

4

ANGER AT OUR IMPOSSIBLE MOTHERS

The Story of Maggie

Turning theory and good intentions into practice is especially challenging with members of our first family. Our relationships with our parents and siblings are the most influential in our lives and they are never simple. Families tend to establish rigid rules and roles that govern how each member is to think, feel, and behave, and these are not easily challenged or changed. When one individual in a family begins to behave in a new way that does not conform to the old family scripts, anxiety skyrockets and before long everyone is trying to reinstate the old familiar patterns.

Rather than face the strong feelings of anxiety and discomfort that are inevitably evoked when we clarify a new position in an old relationship, we may instead do the very two things with our anger that only serve to block the possibility that change will occur.

First, we may "confront" members of our family by telling them what's wrong with them and how they should think, feel, or behave differently. That is, we try to change the *other* person. This other person typically (and understandably) becomes upset and defensive. We then become frustrated or guilty and allow things to return to the usual pattern. "My mother (father, sister, brother) can't change!" is our subsequent conclusion.

Second, we may cut ourselves off from our parents or siblings emotionally and/or geographically. Surely, the fastest cure for chronic anger or frustration is simply to leave home, to move across the country (better yet, to a different country), or to find a sympathetic therapist who will "re-parent" us. We can keep family visits few and far between or we can keep them polite and superficial. True enough, such distancing does bring short-term relief by lowering the anxiety and emotional intensity in these relationships and freeing us of the uncomfortable feelings that may be evoked upon closer emotional contact. The problem is that there is a long-term cost. All the unresolved emotional intensity is likely to get played out in another important relationship, such as that with a spouse, a lover, or, if we ourselves are parents, a child. No less important is the fact that emotional distancing from our first family prevents us from proceeding calmly and clearly in new relationships. When we learn to move differently in our family and get "unstuck" in these important relationships, we will function with greater satisfaction in every relationship we are in. And, as Maggie's story illustrates, we *can* go home again. We can learn to do something different with our anger.

THE WAY IT WAS

Maggie, a twenty-eight-year-old graduate student at a local university, came to see me because of her recurrent migraine headaches and her lack of sexual interest in her husband, Bob. Beginning with our first therapy session, however, she maintained an almost single-minded focus on her mother. Although Maggie lived in Kansas and her mother in California, time and space had healed no wounds.

Maggie had no problem getting in touch with her anger at her mother, and if left to herself, she spoke of little else. From Maggie's description, she and her mother had never gotten along well, nor had their relationship improved when Maggie left home and started a family of her own. Maggie's mother and father were divorced five years prior to her starting therapy, shortly after she married Bob and moved away from the west coast. Since that time, Maggie and her father had become increasingly distant, while her relationship with her mother had become more intense, even though they were physically apart.

Maggie dutifully invited her mother for annual visits, but by the third day Maggie would feel frustration and rage. During her therapy sessions, she would describe the horrors of the particular visit to which she was being subjected. With despair and anger in her voice, she would recite her mother's crime sheet, which was endless. In vivid detail, she would document her mother's unrelenting negativism and intrusiveness. During one visit, for example, Maggie reported the following events: Maggie and Bob had redecorated their living room; mother hadn't noticed. Bob had just learned of his forthcoming promotion; mother didn't comment. Maggie and Bob effortfully prepared fancy dinners; mother complained that the food was too rich. To top it all off, mother lectured Maggie about her messy kitchen and criticized her management of money. And when Maggie announced that she was three months pregnant, mother replied, "How will you deal with a child when you can hardly make time to clean your house?"

About all this, Maggie had said nothing, except for a few sarcastic comments and one enormous blowup to mark the day of her mother's departure. Maggie was furious and she saw therapy as a place where she could safely vent her anger. But that's about all she did. She did not, for example, say to her mother, "Mom, this pregnancy means a great deal to Bob and me. We're excited about it, and although I worry sometimes, I'm confident that we'll do just fine." Nor did she say, "Mother, I know that I manage money in a way that's very different from your way. But what I do is working okay for me, just as your way works for you." Instead, Maggie tended to keep quiet when she felt unappreciated or put down. She alternated between seething silently, emotionally distancing herself, and finally blowing up. None of these reactions was helpful to her.

Obviously, it is not necessary, or even desirable, to personally address every injustice and irritation that comes our way. It can be an act of maturity to let something go. But for Maggie, not speaking up—and then blowing up—had become the painful rule in her relationship with mother. Maggie was de-selfing herself by failing to address issues that mattered to her, and as a result, she felt angry, frustrated, victimized, and depressed.

When I asked Maggie about her silences, she provided countless justifications for her failure to speak up. Among them were: "I could never say that!" "My mother can't hear." "It would only make things worse." "I've tried it a hundred times and it doesn't work." "The situation is hopeless." "It would kill my mother if I said that." "It's just not important enough to me anymore." "You just don't know my mother!"

Sound familiar? When emotional intensity is high in a family, most of us put the entire responsibility for poor communication on the other person. It is one's mother/father/sister/brother who is deaf, defensive, crazy, hopeless, helpless, fragile, or set in their ways. Always, we perceive that it is the *other* who prevents us from speaking and keeps the relationship from changing. We disown our own part in the interactions we complain of and, with it, our power to bring about a change.

Maggie acted as if her only options were either to keep quiet or to argue and fight, although she knew from experience that neither worked. Indeed, when she did vent her anger, the result left her feeling so frustrated that she would begin yet another cycle of silence and emotional withdrawal.

ONE YEAR LATER: GOING TO BATTLE

Amy—Maggie and Bob's new baby—was two months old when Maggie's mother made her next visit. Tensions between the two women were already sky high by the time mother's suitcase was unpacked, and only seemed to escalate as the visit progressed. Having a new baby brought out the fighter in Maggie, and she and her mother were constantly locking horns, especially on the subject of Amy's care.

When Maggie decided to let Amy cry herself to sleep, her mother suggested that she be picked up, insisting that such neglect might have potentially damaging effects. When Maggie nursed her baby on demand, her mother advised her to nurse on a fixed schedule and warned that Maggie was spoiling Amy by overly long feedings. And so it went.

On this particular visit, Maggie did not sit still through her mother's lectures and criticisms. Armed with supporting evidence from physicians, psychologists, and child-care experts, Maggie set out to prove her wrong on every count. She debated her mother constantly. The more thoroughly Maggie martialed her evidence, the more tenaciously her mother clung to her own opinions. When finally this sequence reached an intolerable point, Maggie would angrily accuse her mother of being rigid, controlling, and unable to listen. Her mother would then become sullen and withdrawn, in response to which Maggie retreated into silence. Things would settle down for a while and then the fighting would begin again.

Four days into the visit, Maggie reported that her nerves were on edge and she was at the tail end of a migraine headache. She once again diagnosed her mother as "a hopeless case" and stated bitterly that she had no option but to retreat to her earlier style of silent suffering and to see her mother as little as possible in the future.

What Went Wrong?

One problem with Maggie's style of fighting with her mother may already be obvious: Maggie was trying to change her mother rather than clearly state her own beliefs and convictions and stand behind them. To attempt to change another person, particularly a parent, is a self-defeating move. Predictably, Maggie's mother would only cling with greater determination to her own beliefs in the face of her daughter's pressuring her to admit error. Maggie had yet to learn that she cannot control or change another person's thoughts and feelings. Her attempts to do so in fact provoked the very rigidity in her mother that she found so disturbing.

Perhaps the reader can identify a second problematic aspect of Maggie's fights with her mother. Maggie had not yet identified the true source of her anger. As is often the case, mother and daughter were fighting about a pseudo issue. Arguing about such child-rearing practices as feeding Amy on schedule or demand, or rocking her to sleep rather than letting her cry it out, only masks the *real* issue here: Maggie's independence from her mother.

Maggie's intense reactivity to her mother also prevented her from being able to think about her situation in a clear, focused way. Until she can calm down enough to become more reflective, she is unlikely to identify her main problem and decide how she wants to deal with it. Simply giving vent to stored-up anger has no particular therapeutic value. Such catharsis may indeed offer feelings of relief—especially for the person doing the venting—and the accused party usually survives the verbal onslaught. But this solution can only be temporary.

Taking Stock of the Situation

During one particular psychotherapy hour when Maggie was describing yet another frustrating battle with mother on some question of Amy's care, I decided to interrupt her:

"You know, I'm struck by your protectiveness of your mother," I remarked.

"Protectiveness?" exclaimed Maggie, looking at me as if I had surely gone mad. "She's driving me crazy. I'm not protecting her! I'm fighting with her constantly."

"And what's the outcome of these fights?" It was a rhetorical question.

"Nothing! Nothing ever changes!" Maggie declared.

"Exactly," I said. "And that is how you protect her. By

participating in fights that lead nowhere and never speaking directly to the real issue. You fight with your mother rather than let her know where you stand."

"Where I stand on what?" asked Maggie.

"Where you stand on the question of who is in charge of your baby and who has the authority to make decisions about her care."

Maggie was silent for a long moment. The anger on her face changed slowly to a look of mild depression and concern. "Maybe I'm not sure where I stand."

"Perhaps, then," I responded, "we had better take a look at that issue first."

After this exchange, Maggie began to move in a new direction. She began to *think* carefully about her situation, as opposed to expressing feelings about it, and to clarify where *she* stood, rather than continuing to criticize her mother. In this process, Maggie gained a new perspective on her pattern of relating to her mother. To her surprise, she discovered that she felt guilty about excluding her mother from her new family; part of her wanted to "share" her children so that her mother would not feel left out or depressed. Maggie thought about her parents' divorce, which followed on the heels of her own marriage to Bob, and she wondered out loud whether her leaving home and getting married were somehow linked to the ending of her parents' marriage. She then revealed a critical piece of information that she had failed to mention in all of our time working together: her mother had received electroshock therapy for a post-partum depression following Maggie's birth. Although Maggie was not at first aware of it, she was worried that following the event of Amy's birth, her mother would again become depressed.

In the months that followed, Maggie explored many facets of the deep bond between herself and her mother. She began to feel less angry and more empathic toward her mother as she understood better how every member of the family, including herself, had unconsciously tried to protect her mother from loneliness and depression whether, in reality, she wanted this protection or not. More important, Maggie was able to recognize her own wish to maintain the status quo—to hold on to her mother and be close in the old ways. And as long as Maggie chose to fight, or to remain silent on issues that mattered to her, she would never really leave home. Even if she moved to the moon, she would still be her mother's little girl.

As Maggie became less scared and guilty about showing her mother her own strong and separate self, she became more ready to make a change in this relationship. She was no longer going to participate in the same old fights. Nor would she sit silently seething when she felt that her authority as both a mother and an adult woman was being questioned. Maggie was going to demonstrate her independence.

BREAKING A PATTERN—MOTHER'S NEXT VISIT

Amy was almost a year and half now. It was a hot Sunday afternoon, the second day of Maggie's mother's visit, and Bob was out playing tennis with his friends. Maggie had just put Amy down for a nap and she was crying in her crib. Only five minutes had passed when her mother suddenly jumped up from her chair, scooped Amy out of the crib, and said to Maggie, "I just can't stand to hear her cry! I'm going to rock her to sleep!"

Anger welled up inside Maggie and for a moment she

felt like yelling at her mother. But she was now aware that fighting was a way of protecting both her mother and herself. And silence was the same. For both fighting and silence would insure that Maggie would never declare her independence from her mother. Suddenly, she simmered down.

With as much poise as Maggie could muster, she stood up, lifted Amy from her mother's arms, and placed her gently back in the crib. Then she turned to her mother and said, without anger or criticism in her voice, "Mom, let's go out on the porch. I really want to talk with you about something important to me."

Maggie's heart was beating so fast, it occurred to her that she might faint. She realized in a split second that it would be easier to fight than to do what she needed to do. She was about to show her mother her separateness and independence. And she was going to proceed to do so in a mature and responsible fashion. Her mother was clearly nervous, too; it was unlike her daughter to speak to her in a calm but firm manner.

The two women were seated on the porch swing. Maggie's mother spoke first, with anger that barely masked the anxiety in her voice: "Margaret" (it was the name her mother had always used when she was upset with Maggie), "I cannot stand to hear that child cry. When a child needs to be picked up, I just can't sit there pretending I don't hear her screaming."

Maggie's voice was level and sure. She looked at her mother directly and spoke without anger. "Mom," she said, "I appreciate how concerned you are about Amy. I know it's important to you that your grandchildren are well-cared-for. But there's something I feel I must tell you. . . ."

Maggie paused for a moment. She felt an icy fear in her

chest without knowing why. She guessed that her mother felt it, too. But she kept her composure.

"You see, Mom, Amy is *my* child. And I'm struggling hard to learn to be a good mother and to establish a good relationship with her. It's very important to me that with *my* child, I do what *I* think is right. I know that sometimes I'll make mistakes, sometimes I'll do the wrong thing. But right now I need to take care of Amy in a way that *I* see fit. I need to do that for her and I need to do that for me. And I very much want to have your support in that." Maggie heard the strength and maturity in her own voice and it surprised her. She continued with a warmth that was beginning to feel genuine: "Mom, when you tell me what to do with Amy, or correct me, or take things into your own hands, it's not helpful to me. It would mean a whole lot to me if you would not do that anymore."

There was a moment of dead silence. Maggie felt as if she had stabbed her mother with a knife. Then her mother's voice came back, familiar and angry. It was as if she had not heard:

"Maggie, I cannot stand to see that child suffer. A child of Amy's age must not be left to sob uncontrollably in her crib." Mother continued to speak at length about the adverse psychological effects of Maggie's practice.

Maggie was tempted to bolster her own position, but she refrained from doing so. Arguing, she realized, deflected attention from the issue Maggie was at last beginning to speak to—that of her being a separate and different person from her mother, with her own unique way of being in the world.

Maggie listened patiently and respectfully until her mother was through. She did not contradict her, nor did she fight back. Maggie was doing something very different, and both she and her mother knew it.

"Mom," Maggie said softly, "I don't think you're hearing me. Perhaps I'm wrong about the question of Amy's crying in her crib, or perhaps I'm right. I can't know for sure. But what's most important to me right now is that, as Amy's mother, I do what *I* feel is best. I'm not saying that I'll never make mistakes or that I have the final word on things. What I am saying is that I'm working hard to be independent and to gain confidence in myself as Amy's mother. It's very important to me that with *my* child, I do what *I* think is right."

Her mother became more anxious and upped the ante: "I've raised four children. Are you telling me that you don't want any advice at all? That I have nothing worthwhile to say? Are you saying that I should have stayed home? I can leave, you know, if I'm just in the way. It sounds like I've been making things worse rather than better!"

Maggie felt a new wave of anger rising up, but this time it disappeared quickly. Maggie had her feet on the ground. She knew she was not going to accept the invitation to fight, and thus reinstate old patterns. Instead, she said, "Mother, I very much appreciate your being here. I'm aware how much you know about raising children. And maybe at some point when I am more secure in my own independence and my own mothering skills, I'll be asking you for some advice."

"But you don't want my advice now?" It was more an accusation than a question.

"That's right, Mother," Maggie answered. "Unless I specifically ask for advice, I don't want it."

"I can't stand by and watch you ruin that child." Maggie's mother was becoming more irrational and provocative, unconsciously trying to draw Maggie back into fighting in order to reinstate their earlier, predictable relationship.

"You know, Mother," Maggie said, "Bob and I have our struggles as parents. But I think that we're pretty good at it and that we'll get better. I'm confident that we won't ruin Amy."

"And you're just criticizing me!" Mother continued, as if Maggie had not just spoken. "I've been trying to help you and you just throw it back in my face!"

"Mom"—Maggie's voice was still calm—"I'm not criticizing you. I'm not saying that you're doing the wrong thing. I'm sharing *my* reaction. When you do something like pick up Amy when I put her down, I get upset because I'm trying to develop my confidence as a mother on my own. I'm not criticizing you. I am sharing with you how I feel and what I want."

Maggie's mother rose abruptly and went back into the house, slamming the screen door behind her. Maggie had the terrifying fantasy that her mother was going to kill herself and that she would never see her again. Suddenly, Maggie noticed that her own knees were shaking and she felt dizzy. Both Maggie and her mother were experiencing "separation anxiety." Maggie was beginning to leave home.

UNDERSTANDING MOTHER'S REACTION

When Maggie stepped out of her characteristic position in her relationship with her mother, she experienced a panicky feeling about herself and her mother's well-being. Her mother responded to Maggie's changed style of communication by intensifying her own position, almost to absurd proportions, in a powerful effort to protect both herself and her daughter from the strong anxiety that standing on one's own can evoke in parties who are close to each other.

What might at first glance appear to be an obnoxious, unfeeling response on her mother's part reflects her deep wish to stay close to her daughter and to spare them both the painful solitude of greater separateness and independence. Indeed, if her mother had been able to respond calmly and rationally, Maggie herself would have been left to experience even more of the separation anxiety that welled up in her from time to time during their talk. Adding to each woman's deep-seated fear of losing the other was the fact that their old pattern of interaction was so long standing, neither Maggie nor her mother knew a different way of relating. Precisely what kind of relationship could replace this one was a scary unknown to both of them. Thus, when Maggie broke the old repetitive pattern of communicating, her mother, unconsciously sensing a threat to their relationship, rallied to keep it intact.

Although Maggie was intellectually prepared for the sequence of events that occurred, she still found herself feeling shaken and depressed. "Have I made a mistake?" she asked herself. "Is my mother acting crazy?" "Will I lose my mother forever just because I finally had the courage to state my own point of view?"

The answer is no. Countermoves are par for the course when we begin to define a stronger self in a family relationship. Maggie's mother's "Change back!" reaction was her way of communicating that Maggie's act of independence— her statement of self—was a cruel rejection of her. The threats—some overt, some disguised—were that her mother would become depressed, that she would withdraw, that she would fall apart, and that the relationship between her and Maggie would be severed. As we have seen, this powerful emotional counterforce ("You're wrong"; "Change back!"; "Or else . . .") is predictable, understandable, and, to some extent, universal. What happens next is up to Maggie.

A New Dance—One Step at a Time

Maggie's work had just begun. As her mother angrily retreated to her room, Maggie felt scared and guilty. More than anything, she wanted to get away from her mother—to "leave the field." She had said what she needed to say and now her only wish was that she or her mother would disappear.

It doesn't work. "Hit-and-run" confrontation in an important relationship does not lead to lasting change. If Maggie is really serious about change, she still has a challenging road to walk.

First, Maggie needs to show (for her own sake as well as her mother's) that at last she is declaring her separateness and independence from mother, but that she is *not* declaring a lack of caring or closeness. *Independence means that we clearly define our own selves on emotionally important issues, but it does not mean emotional distance.* Thus, Maggie needs to show, through her behavior, that although she will stand behind her own wants and convictions, she is still her mother's daughter and loves her mother very much.

The work of negotiating greater independence—especially between a mother and a daughter—may be so fraught with mutual anxieties about rejection and loss that the person making the move (in this case, Maggie) must be responsible for maintaining emotional contact with the other (her mother). If Maggie fails in this regard, her mother will feel rejected and upset; Maggie will feel anxious and guilty; and both mother and daughter will unconsciously agree to return their relationship to the old predictable pattern.

How can Maggie best maintain emotional closeness with her mother at this time? She might ask her mother questions about her interests and activities. She can express interest in learning more about her mother's own past and personal history. This is one of the best ways to stay emotionally connected to members of our family and, at the same time, learn more about our selves (see Chapter 6). When things cool off a bit and the relationship is calm, Maggie might initiate a dialogue with her mother on the subject of raising children—an area in which mother has valuable expertise. For example, Maggie might say, "You know, Mother, sometimes I try to comfort Amy and she keeps crying and crying. Did you go through that when we were little? How did you handle it?" Or, "What was it like for you to raise four children, especially when two of us were only a year apart?" If her mother were to reply in a huff, "Well, I thought *you* had enough of *my* advice!" Maggie might respond, "Actually, I don't find advice helpful—even good advice—because I need to struggle with the problem myself and find my own solution. But I do find it very useful to learn more about your own experience and how you handled things." Blocking advice-giving—if that is one of the problems—is not the same as cutting off the lines of communication. As we become more independent we learn *more* about our family members, not less, and we are able to share more about our selves.

In addition to the task of being the caretaker in maintaining emotional contact, Maggie will now face a series of "tests," for her mother will need to determine whether Maggie really "means it," or whether she is willing to return to the previous pattern of interaction. Again, this is not because Maggie's mother is a rigid, crazy woman, but because this is the predictable reaction in all family systems. It is as basic as a law of physics. Maggie must be prepared to have her mother attack, withdraw, threaten, and "do her old thing" with Maggie's baby, Amy. And she must be equally prepared to restate her convictions like a broken record if necessary, yet retain emotional contact with her mother as best she can. The point cannot be emphasized enough: No successful move toward greater independence occurs in one "hit-and-run" confrontation.

And so, Maggie's work was far from over at the point when her mother rose and retreated to her room. On this particular day, Maggie had only begun the process of attaining a higher level of separateness from her first family. If she can stay on course, over time she will achieve greater independence and clarity of self that will manifest itself in all her important relationships. Her mother, too, is likely to shift to a more separate mode of interacting and to proceed in her own life with greater emotional maturity.

Will Maggie be able to tolerate the anxiety and guilt associated with clarifying a more independent self, or will she become so emotionally caught up in her mother's reactions as to lapse back into the reassuringly familiar fights that kept her and her mother close in the old way? The ball is in Maggie's court. And the difficult choice is hers.

Together, Differently

As it happened, Maggie chose to work on changing the old pattern. She fell on her face many times and temporarily slipped back into fighting, instructing, criticizing her mother, or distancing herself from the relationship. But most important, she was able to pick herself up each time and get back on course. She continued to make her declaration of independence with increasingly less blaming and distancing as time progressed. In doing so, she established a new, more adult relationship with her mother and began to talk with her about topics that had previously been eclipsed by their endless years of fighting. Maggie began to ask her mother more about her past life, about her own mother and father and her childhood and memorable events. She even initiated discussions about subjects that had formerly been "taboo" ("Mom, how do you understand that you got so depressed after I was born?"). Maggie talked with her mother in a way that neither of them had previously done, since their interactions were so heavily based on silence, sarcasm, outright fighting, and emotional distancing. As they talked more and more often in this new way, Maggie was able to see her mother's old "obnoxious" behaviors in a different light. She came to appreciate that her mother's apparent intrusiveness and criticism were in fact expressions of her own wish to be helpful to her daughter, as well as her fear that were she not, she would lose Maggie. Besides advising and criticizing, her mother had been as bewildered as Maggie about how to be helpful and close. She, too, sensed Maggie's need not to let go—to hold on in the old ways. Maggie also learned that her mother had had much the same kind of relationship with *her* mother, maintaining closeness through constant squabbling.

And what about Maggie's father? Like many fathers, he was most conspicuous by his absence. Maggie's distant relationship with her father had become even more pronounced following her parents' divorce, in part because of an unspoken family rule that Maggie was to be her mother's "ally" as her parents negotiated the divorce. When Maggie herself no longer needed to maintain her special bond with mother in the old way, she began working on having an adult, one-to-one relationship with her father as well.

This was not an easy task, because both Maggie and her father had a good share of anxiety and discomfort about establishing an emotionally close relationship. When Maggie first began to write to her dad, he reacted by distancing himself further, which was one of a number of countermoves, in response to her initiating a change. Indeed, her father's "Change back!" reactions were as dramatic as her mother's, although they took a different form. Much to Maggie's credit, she was able to maintain a calm, nonreactive position and she persisted, in a low-keyed way, to write to him and share the important events and issues going on in her life. Although mother and father were still fighting it out, Maggie's new level of independence helped her to stay out of the conflicts between them—a feat that required considerable assertiveness on her part. Over time, her relationship with her father developed and deepened.

As a result of the changes that Maggie made with her mother and father, she became free of the symptoms that first brought her to see me. Her headaches did not return and she became more sexually responsive with her husband, Bob. She also felt clearer and more assertive in all of her other relationships.

The work that Maggie did will have reverberations in the next generation. When her children are older, she will be better able to allow them the appropriate degree of independence and separateness, for the degree of independence that we achieve from our own family of origin is always played out in the following generation. Had Maggie not done this work, she would in time have found herself overinvolved and intensely reactive to one or more of her children. Or, alternatively, she might have been overly distant and emotionally cut off when her children were grown, which is simply the other side of the same coin. Although Maggie is not yet aware of it, the work that she did is the best "parent-effectiveness training" that money can buy.

BECOMING OUR OWN PERSON

Autonomy, separateness, independence, selfhood—these are all concepts that psychotherapists embrace as primary values and goals. And so do the women who seek help: "I want to find myself." "I want to discover who I really am and what I want." "I don't want to be so concerned with other people's approval." "I want to have a close relationship and still be my own person."

The task of defining (and maintaining) a separate self within our closest relationships is one that begins in our first family but does not end there. Like Maggie, we can proceed to work on achieving greater independence (and with it, an increased capacity for intimacy and togetherness) at any stage of our lives. Renegotiating relationships with persons on our own family tree yields especially rich rewards, because the degree of self that we carve out in this arena will greatly influence the nature of our current relationships.

In this lifelong task of forging a clear self, our anger is a double-edged sword. On the one hand, it helps to preserve our integrity and self-regard. Maggie's anger at her mother was the signal that let her know she was not comfortable in the old pattern of relating to her mother and that she needed to make a change. However, as we have seen, venting anger does not solve the problem that anger signals. To the contrary, Maggie's success at becoming her own separate person rested on her ability to share something about herself with her mother and father in a straightforward, nonblaming way while maintaining emotional contact with them throughout the process. It required, also, that Maggie uphold her position with persistence and calm, without getting emotionally buffeted about by the inevitable countermoves and "Change back!" reactions we meet whenever we assume a more autonomous position in an important relationship. This is what achieving selfhood and independence is all about. And it requires, among other things, a particular way of talking and a degree of clarity that are especially difficult to achieve when we are angry.

5

USING ANGER AS A GUIDE
The Road to a Clearer Self

I was first introduced to the notion of turning anger into "I messages" some years back when I read Thomas Gordon's best-selling book, *Parent Effectiveness Training*. I still recall the first time I put his theory into practice. I was standing in the kitchen washing dishes when I noticed my son, Matthew, who was then three, sitting at the kitchen table about to cut an apple with a sharp knife. The conversation that followed went something like this:

> ME: "Matthew, put that knife down. You're going to cut yourself."
>
> MATTHEW: "No, I'm not."
>
> ME (getting angry): "Yes, you are!"
>
> MATTHEW (getting angrier): "No, I'm not!"
>
> ME (even louder): "Yes, you are! Put it down!"
>
> MATTHEW: "No!"

At this point in the escalating power struggle, I remembered what I had read about "I" messages. Every "you" message (for example, "You're going to cut yourself") could be turned into an "I" message—that is, a nonblaming state-ment about one's own self. So, in a split second's time, I made the conversion:

"Matthew," I said again (this time without anger), "when I see you with that sharp knife, I feel scared. I am worried that you will cut yourself." At this point Matthew paused, looked me straight in the eye, and said calmly, "That's *your* problem." To which I replied, "You're absolutely right. It *is* my problem that I'm scared and I'm going to take care of my problem right now by taking that knife away from you." And so I did.

What was interesting to me was that Matthew relin-quished the knife easily, without the usual anger and struggle and with no loss of pride. I was taking the knife away from him because I was worried, and exercised my parental authority in that light. I owned the problem ("I feel scared") and I took responsibility for my feelings. Later, I was to learn that Matthew had been cutting apples with a sharp knife for over a month in his Montessori preschool, but that is beside the point. What is important is that I was able to shift from "You're going to cut yourself" (did I have a crystal ball?) to "It *is* my problem. . . ."

Of course, no one talks in calm "I messages" all the time. When my husband broke my favorite ceramic mug that had been with me since college, I did not turn to him with perfect serenity and say, "You know, dear, when you knock my cup off the table, my reaction is to feel angry and upset. It would mean a great deal to me if you would be more careful next time." Instead, I cursed him and created a small scene. He apologized, and a few minutes later we were the best of friends again.

There is nothing inherently virtuous in using "I messages" in all circumstances. If our goal is simply to let someone know we're angry, we can do it in our own personal style, and our style may do the job, or at least makes us feel better.

If, however, our goal is to break a pattern in an important relationship and/or to develop a stronger sense of self that we can bring to all our relationships, it is essential that we learn to translate our anger into clear, nonblaming statements about our own self.

There are any number of self-help books and assertiveness-training courses that teach men and women how to change "You are ..." communications into "I feel ..." communications. Certainly we maximize the opportunity for constructive dialogue if we say "I feel like I'm not being heard" rather than "You don't know how to listen." The story of how Maggie changed her relationship with her mother is a vivid illustration of this point. Shaping up our communication, however, is only a small part of the picture.

The more significant issue for women is that we may not have a clear "I" to communicate about, and we are not prepared to handle the intense negative reactions that come our way when we do begin to define and assert the self.

As we have seen, women often fear that having a clear "I" means *threatening* a relationship or *losing* an important person. Thus, rather than using our anger as a challenge to think more clearly about the "I" in our relationships, we may, when angry, actually blur what personal clarity we *do* have. And we may do this not only under our own roof with intimate others but on the job as well with office mates. Karen's difficulty maintaining a clear "I" will ring a bell for those of us who have occasion to fall into the "nice lady" category at work.

FROM ANGER TO TEARS

Karen was one of two young women who sold life insurance in an otherwise all-male firm. After her first year on the job, she received a written evaluation from her boss that placed her in the "Very Satisfactory" performance range. From Karen's perspective, her work was in the "Superior" range. By objective criteria, her sales record was right at the top.

This evaluation meant much to Karen, since only employees rated "Superior" received a special salary bonus along with the opportunity to attend out-of-state seminars. Karen was raising two children with little financial support from her ex-husband. She needed the money and wanted the educational opportunities that would allow her to advance.

When Karen brought her story to group psychotherapy, she had tears in her eyes. "I'm hurt," said Karen. "It's just not fair!" When asked what she planned to do, Karen said flatly, "Nothing." As she put it, "It's just not worth the hassle."

"Aren't you angry?" a group member inquired. "Why should I be angry?" responded Karen. "Where will it get me? It only makes things worse." These were the things that Karen would predictably say to avoid taking her anger seriously.

With help from the other group members, Karen was finally able to acknowledge her anger and mobilize the courage to meet with her boss to discuss the evaluation. She got off to a good start with him by lucidly stating why she believed she deserved the higher rating. At first, her boss seemed to listen attentively, but it soon became evident that he was feeling defensive and wasn't really considering her view of the matter. When she finished talking, he brushed aside the valid points that she had made and began instead to focus on certain problems that he had noticed in *her* work. These problems, although real, were trivial and unrelated to the question of whether or not Karen deserved a "Superior" rating. Then he added that "other people" in the office thought she was "a little rough around the edges."

"What do you mean?" asked Karen.

"Perhaps it's a personality issue," he continued, "but you give the impression to some people that you are less committed to your work than you might be."

At this point, Karen's eyes filled with tears and she felt totally inarticulate. "I don't understand that," she said softly, doing her best not to burst out crying. She then proceeded to tell her boss how unappreciated she felt because she was struggling so hard to raise two children and to succeed in a full-time job as well. Now that tears and "hurt" had replaced Karen's calm assertiveness, her boss shifted from defensiveness to paternalistic concern. He reassured Karen that she showed a great deal of potential in her work, and he empathized with the difficult task of being a single parent. The meeting ended with Karen's sharing some of the emotional struggles she was having since her divorce, while her boss lent a sympathetic ear. She did not mention anything further about the evaluation, nor did he. Karen left the office feeling relieved that she had not alienated her boss and that their meeting had ended on a warm note.

When Karen told us her story at the next group-therapy session, she concluded with the following words: "You see— it doesn't do any good to confront him. He doesn't listen. Anyway, the evaluation is really no big deal. To tell the truth, it really doesn't matter that much to me."

But the other group members did not drop the subject

so easily. They had a number of questions for Karen that forced her to confront her own uncertainty.

Who were these "other people" in the office who questioned Karen's commitment and who told the boss that she was "a little rough around the edges?"

Karen had no idea who her critics were.

What did "a little rough around the edges" mean?

Karen wasn't sure: "Something to do with my personality or character . . ."

What, specifically, would she have to do differently to get a "Superior" rating?

Karen didn't know.

It was not only that Karen failed to restate her position following her boss's initial defensiveness; she did not even allow herself to clarify the issues with him. She did not ask, "Who in the office is criticizing me?" Or, "Could you be more specific about my personality problems?" Or, "What, specifically, must I change in order to get a 'Superior' rating?" Karen's emotional reaction to her boss's criticism obscured her thinking about what she wanted to ask and what she wanted to say.

Feeling fuzzy-headed, inarticulate, and not so smart are common reactions experienced by women as we struggle to take a stand on our own behalf. _It is not just anger and fighting that we learn to fear; we avoid asking precise questions and making clear statements when we unconsciously suspect that doing so would expose our differences, make the other person feel uncomfortable, and leave us standing alone._

"But my boss _intimidates_ me!" said Karen.

That's a cover story. Karen was really afraid of rocking the boat in an important relationship by persisting in her efforts to take up her own cause in a mature and articulate manner. Her tears and her willingness to let her boss play the role of advisor and confidant were, in part, her unconscious way of reinstating the status quo and apologizing for the "separateness" inherent in her initial position of disagreement. Karen's tears may also have been an unconscious attempt to make her boss feel guilty ("See how you've hurt me?")—a frequent practice for women who are blocked from making a direct statement of where we stand.

"But I'm not angry about it anymore," protested Karen. "It just doesn't matter."

Of *course* Karen is still angry. She just doesn't recognize it. Anger is inevitable when we submit to unfair circumstances and when we protect another person at our own expense.

Karen's denial of her anger and her failure to stand behind her position had inevitable costs. She felt tired and less enthusiastic at work. Two weeks after her evaluation, Karen misplaced a folder of important forms and she was seriously reprimanded. This self-sabotaging act was perhaps an unconscious attempt to put herself in the role of the "bad guy" who did not really deserve the "Superior" evaluation, rather than stand firm in her opinion that her boss had failed to give her the evaluation that she believed she deserved.

DENYING ANGER: THE UNCONSCIOUS IN ACTION

Have you ever initiated a confrontation at work, only to transform your anger into tears, apologies, guilt, confusion, or self-criticism? Karen's behavior may well strike a familiar, if not universal, chord among women. How can we better understand some of the deeper, unconscious reasons why any of us would attempt to deny our anger and sacrifice one of our most precious possessions—our personal clarity?

The Fear of Destructiveness

Karen's failure to defend her position in an articulate and persistent fashion with her boss was a pattern in her personal relationships as well. The explanations that she gave herself were just the tip of the iceberg: "I get intimidated." "I just can't think straight when I'm dealing with an authority figure." "I guess I don't have faith in my own convictions." Karen *did* lose her confidence when her ideas were not given the stamp of other people's approval, but this lack of confidence masked a more serious problem: Karen was *afraid* to be clear about the correctness of her position, because she would then experience pressure to *continue* to take up her own cause. And to do this might make her the *target* of her boss's anger and disapproval. As Karen put it, a "real fight" might ensue.

This idea frightened Karen, partly for realistic reasons, such as the possibility that her work situation would become difficult and uncomfortable or that she might even be fired. Surely, fighting would escalate the tensions between Karen and her boss, making it even less likely that she would be heard. Reality aside, however, Karen had a deep unconscious fear that fighting might unleash her fantasied destructive potential, although it had never seen the light of day. If she lost control of her anger, would she destroy everything? It was as if Karen feared that the full venting of her outrage might cause the entire office building to go up in flames. Also, like most women, Karen had little practice expressing her anger in a controlled, direct, and effective fashion.

It is not surprising that Karen had deep-seated fears of her own omnipotent destructiveness and the vulnerability of men. Our very definitions of "masculinity" and "femininity" are based on the notion that women must function as nonthreatening helpmates and ego builders to men lest men feel castrated and weakened. The problem for Karen was that this irrational fear had a high cost. Not only did she avoid fighting; she also avoided asserting her viewpoint, requesting explanations from others, and stating her wants. All of the above fell into the category of potentially destructive acts that might hurt or diminish others.

The Fear of Separateness

As much as Karen feared a volcanic eruption, she had an even greater fear, also safely tucked away in her subconscious. Karen was afraid of transforming her anger into concise statements of her thoughts and feelings lest she evoke that disturbing sense of separateness and aloneness that we experience when we make our differences known and encourage others to do the same. Maggie, for example, felt this "separation anxiety" when she talked with her mother about her baby in a new, more adult way. Sandra felt it when she apologized to Larry for being so critical and assumed more responsibility to provide for her own happiness. Barbara *would* have felt it had she stopped fighting and calmly told her husband that she planned to go to the "anger" workshop.

Separation anxiety may creep up on us whenever we shift to a more autonomous, nonblaming position in a relationship, or even when we simply consider the possibility. Sometimes such anxiety is based on a realistic fear that if we assume a bottom-line stance ("I am sorry, but I will not do what you are asking of me"), we risk losing a relationship or a job. More often, and more crucially, separation anxiety is based on an underlying discomfort with separateness and individuality that has its roots in our early family experience, where the unspoken expectation may have been that we keep a lid on our expressions of self. Daughters are especially sensitive to such demands and may become far more skilled at protecting the relational "we" than asserting the autonomous "I."

Karen was not aware of her separation anxiety, but it led her to transform her initially clear and strong position into tears and hurt. Expressing hurt allowed her boss to be helpful and restored her sense of connectedness to him— which made her feel safe despite the self-betrayal involved in this transformation. Karen had a long-standing pattern of attempting to restore the togetherness of her relationships by crying, criticizing herself, becoming confused, or prematurely making peace. At the heart of the problem was the fact that Karen (like Maggie, in Chapter 4) needed to work harder at the task of clarifying her separateness and independence within her first family. If Karen can stay in contact with family members and make progress in this arena, she will find that she will proceed more effectively when she is angry at work and with less fear of standing separate and alone, on her own two feet.

Moving Differently

If Karen were to do it all over again, how might she transform her anger into productive action? First, she can better prepare herself to deal with her boss's countermoves, which in this case consisted of his indirectly criticizing her work and deflecting her from the issue. Karen shouldn't try to change or control his reactions (which is not possible, anyway). Nor should she allow herself to be controlled by them. She can simply stay on course by listening to what he has to say and then restating her initial position. There is nothing wrong with sounding like a broken record now and then.

What if Karen starts to feel tearful or emotionally intense during the interaction? If this happens, she can take time out to regain her composure: She can say, "I need a little time to sort my thoughts out. Let's set up another time to talk more about it."

What if her supervisor refuses to consider changing the evaluation? Karen can then begin to give some thought to her next move. She may request a third party to review her evaluation. She may simply say to her boss, "I don't like it, but I can live with it." She may ask for specific instructions on how she might secure a "Superior" evaluation the next time around. No matter how skilled Karen becomes in handling her anger, she cannot *make* her boss change his mind or ensure that justice will prevail. She *can* state her position, recognize her choices, and make responsible decisions on her own behalf. The calmer and clearer that Karen can be with her boss, the clearer *he* will become about his own perspective on the evaluation and what *he* will and will not do. Could it be that Karen unconsciously preferred to avoid this kind of clarity so as to maintain the image of her boss as a "good guy?"

Karen's story illustrates how our unconscious fears of destructiveness and of separateness may block us from maintaining our clarity and using our anger as a challenge to take a new position or action on our own behalf. In some instances, however, our problem is not the *fear* of clarity but the *absence* of it. That we are angry is obvious. But we may have little perspective on the "I," as a result of focusing exclusively on what the *other* person is doing to us. Here is a personal example:

THE FRYING-PAN STORY

During a visit some years ago from my older sister, Susan, the two of us set off to Macy's, where I planned to buy a non-stick frying pan. Without much forethought, I picked up a pan that looked fine to me and began to head over to the cashier. Before I could take two steps, my sister informed me that I was buying the wrong pan. Not only did the tone of Susan's voice express supreme confidence in her own judgment, but her advice was accompanied by a rather detailed and technical account regarding the problems with the particular finish I had selected—a subject about which I knew nothing and cared even less. My initial reaction was to be once again impressed by my big sister's encyclopedic mind, but, as she continued on, I felt a growing anger. Who asked for her opinion? Why did she always think she was right? Why did she behave like the world's expert on all subjects? I briefly toyed with the idea of bopping her on the head with the pan I had in hand, but resisted the impulse. Instead, I marched over to the cashier like a sullen and rebellious little sister and paid for the pan I had chosen myself. It proved to be of poor quality and short-lived—just as Susan had predicted.

An old saying tells us: "We teach what we most need to learn." When I was recounting the incident to my friend Marianne Ault-Riché, who conducts anger workshops with me, I was as far from personal clarity as any person could be. Why was I angry? The answer was simple: because my sister was so difficult! She had caused my anger by her opinionated style and by her need to be an expert on all matters. Everything I said to Marianne about my anger was a statement about my sister—not one word about my own self.

Marianne listened and then responded lightly, "I'd love to take your sister shopping along with me! I would have been fascinated to learn about different types of non-stick cookware. Susan is so knowledgeable!"

Marianne was speaking honestly. If she had been in my shoes, her reaction to Susan's knowledge and personality would have been entirely positive. Indeed, the very qualities that I was criticizing were those that endeared Susan to certain others, my parents included. At that moment, I recognized what is so obvious to me in other people—that my blaming stance was preventing me from gaining an understanding of my heated reaction.

What was it about Susan's advice-giving and expertise that annoyed me? Why was it a problem for me? What was the pattern in our relationship, and what was my participation in it? Only after I was able to reflect on these questions was I able to tell Susan what was bothering me, without implying that her personality or way of being in the world was at fault.

First, I used my anger as an incentive to sort out what I wanted and then to set a limit with my sister. As Maggie did with her mother, I clarified with Susan that I wanted her advice only when I asked for it. It was understandably difficult for Susan to accept that I would choose to avoid helpful and sound advice, since she herself would welcome it, solicited or not. To help explain the problem that I had receiving her advice, I told her a bit about my experience of being a younger sister:

"You know, Susan, all my life I've seen you as a brilliant star. I've always looked up to you as the person who had all the answers. I felt you knew everything and could do anything. And I felt I was in a one-down position, like I didn't have much to teach or to offer you in return. In fact, when I feel intimidated by your brilliance, I react by becoming even less competent.

"Our relationship is very important to me and I'm trying to work on getting things more in balance for myself. What I think will help me is to steer clear of my big sister's help and advice for a while. I know that may sound silly and ungrateful, because you are so good at being helpful, but that's what would be most useful to me at this time."

I was, in fact, asking my sister to make a change in her behavior. However, I was asking her to make a change not because her advice-giving was bad or wrong or excessive but rather because that would be helpful to me, in light of my reactions to big-sisterly advice—reactions for which I took full responsibility.

Sharing my dilemma with Susan (including my envy about her being the brilliant star in the family) was an important step in breaking out of an old overfunctioning-underfunctioning pattern in which Susan was in the role of the competent helper and I in that of the less competent helpee. In the past, the more Susan expressed enough wisdom and competence for the two of us, the more I would react by de-selfing myself into a state of conspicuous fuzzy-headedness. As I verbalized my wish to be able to provide something for my sister (rather than always being on the receiving end of her big-sisterly wisdom), Susan responded by sharing some of *her* problems with me, and it became evident to me, for the first time, that she valued my perspective. Over time, our relationship became more balanced and

I no longer felt myself to be at the bottom of the seesaw. Today, I do value her advice—solicited or not—on any number of subjects, non-stick cookware included.

Using our anger as a starting point to become more knowledgeable about the self does not require that we analyze ourselves and provide lengthy psychological explanations of our reactions, as I did with Susan. If I had not identified some long-standing relationship issues, I might simply have told my sister that I didn't want advice and really wasn't clear about why. The essential ingredient of this story is that I used my anger to clarify a request based on my own personal wants, and not because I sought to become an uninvited authority on how Susan should best conduct herself.

Anger is a tool for change when it challenges us to become more of an expert on the self and less of an expert on others.

TAKING A FIRM STAND

Learning to use our anger effectively requires some letting go—letting go of blaming that other person whom we see as causing our problems and failing to provide for our happiness; letting go of the notion that it is our job to change other people or tell them how they should think, feel, behave. Yet, this does not mean that we passively accept or go along with any behavior. In fact, a "live-and-let-live" attitude can signal a de-selfed position, if we fail to clarify what is and is not acceptable or desirable to us in a relationship. The main issue is *how* we clarify our position.

Recently I worked with a woman named Ruth who was furious over her husband's neglect of his health. He had received poor medical treatment for a serious leg problem that was worsening, and he had no plans to seek further help. Ruth expressed her anger by lecturing him on what he should do for himself and interpreting his feelings and behavior. ("You're being self-destructive." "You're neglecting yourself the way your father did." "You're denying your own fears," etc.) Her husband, in response, adopted an increasingly bland attitude toward his problem (which was understandable, since his wife was voicing enough worry for both of them) and became more dogmatic in his refusal to consider further treatment. It was an escalating circular dance in which Ruth's "I-know-what's-best-for-you" attitude only intensified her husband's willful assertion of his independence on this issue, which led to longer and more frequent lectures on Ruth's part about what he should do and what he was *really* feeling. Like many women, Ruth was becoming the emotional reactor *for* her man, while he played out the role of the emotional dumbbell.

It was a big step for Ruth to recognize that it was up to her husband to determine his own feelings, to choose his own risks, and to assume the primary responsibility for his own health. This was his job, not hers. But it was equally important for Ruth to take her anger seriously—to use it to clarify, first to herself and then to her husband, that she was unable to live with the status quo and go about business as usual.

Ruth made an important change when she talked to her husband about her own feelings instead of criticizing and instructing him. Ruth's father had died from a degenerative illness when she was twelve and she now found herself scared of losing her husband as well. Instead of focusing on her husband's "self-destructiveness" or "neglect," Ruth was able to request that her husband seek medical help because of her own needs and feelings. She explained that her fears and anxieties were so great that she could not go about her day-to-day activities as if nothing was happening. She did not blame her husband for her reaction, nor did she say that she knew what was best for him. Rather, Ruth was now sharing *her* problem with the situation and asking her husband to respect the intensity of her discomfort. He did agree to go to the doctor, although he made it perfectly clear that he was going for *her* sake, not his own.

When we use our anger to make statements about the self, we assume a position of strength, because no one can argue with our own thoughts and feelings. They may try, but in response, we need not provide logical arguments in our defense. Instead, we can simply say, "Well, it may seem crazy or irrational to you, but this is the way I see it." Of course, there is never a guarantee that other people will alter their behavior in the way that we want them to. Joan's story is illustrative.

A Bottom-Line Position

Joan and Carl had been living together for a year and had maintained their separate friendships with both sexes. They were in agreement that they were committed to monogamy, but did not want to sacrifice the opportunity to have close friends. This informal contract proved to be workable, until Carl began spending time with his young research assistant who was in the process of going through a divorce. In response, Joan found herself feeling jealous, threatened, and angry.

For almost a year the relationship between Carl and his assistant remained the focus of nonproductive fighting. Joan would question whether Carl's feelings were truly platonic and Carl, in turn, would accuse her of being paranoid and possessive. They had countless intellectual debates regarding boundary issues: Was it appropriate for Carl's assistant to call him at home in the evening to talk about her divorce? Was it okay for Carl to have dinner with her or just lunch? Joan shifted back and forth between blaming Carl and blaming herself, while nothing was resolved. Her recurrent anger, however, was a strong signal that despite the passage of time, she was not at peace with this relationship.

The turning point came when Joan stopped complaining about Carl's behavior and stated openly that the situation was not acceptable to her. She did not criticize him for doing something bad or wrong, and she even acknowledged that another woman in her shoes might not complain or might even welcome the opportunity to do the same herself. Joan's point was simply that she was experiencing more jealousy and anger than she could live with.

When Carl interpreted her reaction as "pathological" and "middle-class," Joan did not fight or become defensive. Instead she said, "Well, my feelings are my feelings. And I am having such a painful reaction to your relationship with this woman that I want you to end it. It may be ninety-nine percent my problem, but I'm unable to live with it and still feel okay about us. I'm just finding it too difficult." Joan upheld this position with dignity and firmness.

Joan's clarity about her emotional anguish forced Carl to clarify his own priorities—and his first priority was not Joan. Carl refused to end his relationship with his research assistant. Joan, after considerable personal turmoil, finally took a bottom-line position and said, "I can't continue to live with you if you continue in this relationship." She said this not as a threat or as an attempt at emotional blackmail but rather to share what she was experiencing and declare what was possible for her. Carl didn't respond and continued on as usual, and Joan requested that he move out. Soon afterward, Carl left Joan entirely and moved in with his research assistant.

Joan suffered a great deal; however, she felt good about the position she had taken. She had lost Carl, but she had saved her dignity and self-respect. Did she do the right thing? Joan did the right thing for Joan, but some of us in her place might have chosen to do something different—or not have known what to do at all.

In using our anger as a guide to determining our innermost needs, values, and priorities, we should not be distressed if we discover just how unclear we are. If we feel chronically angry or bitter in an important relationship, this is a signal that too much of the self has been compromised and we are uncertain about what new position to take or what options we have available to us. To recognize our lack of clarity is not a weakness but an opportunity, a challenge, and a strength.

There is no reason why women *should* be clear about the "I." "Who am I?" "What do I want?" "What do I deserve?" These are questions that we all struggle with—and for good reason. For too long, we have been encouraged *not* to question but to accept other-defined notions of our "true nature," our "appropriate place," our "maternal responsibilities," our "feminine role," and so forth. Or we have been taught to substitute other questions: "How can I please others?" "How can I win love and approval?" "How can I keep the peace?" We suffer most when we fail to grapple with the "Who am I?" questions and when we deny feeling the anger that signals that such questions are there for us to consider.

It is an act of courage to acknowledge our own uncertainty and sit with it for a while. Too often, anger propels us to take positions that we have not thought through carefully enough or that we are not really ready to take. Nor does it help that those around us may be full of advice and encouragement to act: "Leave that man, already!" "Tell your boss that you won't do the assignment." "You just can't let him treat you that way." "Tell her you won't be friends with her anymore if she does that again." "Just tell him no."

Slow down! Our anger can be a powerful vehicle for personal growth and change if it does nothing more than help us recognize that we are not yet clear about something and that it is our job to keep struggling with it. Let us look at one woman's journey from an angry, blaming position to a productive confronting of her own confusion.

6

UP AND DOWN THE GENERATIONS

Katy and Her Aging Father

Katy is a fifty-year-old homemaker whose youngest child has just left home for college. Her father is a seventy-two-year-old retired teacher who has been widowed for ten years and who is in moderately poor health. Katy called me at the Menninger Foundation because she had heard that I was an "anger expert." During our initial telephone conversation, she described a pattern that has been the source of her anger for almost a decade.

"My father has a big problem," she explained, with unveiled desperation in her voice. "He makes excessive demands on me, especially since he can't drive anymore because he lost some vision following a stroke. I'm supposed to take him shopping when he calls and drive him to his appointments. He asks me to do things for him in his apartment and then criticizes me for not doing them right. There are many things he could do for himself, but he acts like a big baby. Sometimes he calls me two or three times in one day. When I tell him no, he withdraws and makes me feel guilty. I'm really at the end of my rope."

When I met with Katy for the first time and requested clarification, I heard more of the same:

"What is your problem as you see it?"
KATY: "My problem is that my father doesn't realize I have my own life. He thinks my world should revolve around him. Since my mother's death, he uses me to fill in the empty space and take over."

"What, specifically, have you said to your father about the problem?"
KATY: " 'Father, you have to realize that I have my own life and that you are asking too much. I wish you would stop making me feel guilty when I don't come around. I think you need to get out and meet people and not just isolate yourself and rely on me.' "

"How does your father respond to this?"
KATY: "He gets upset and won't speak to me for a while. Or sometimes he starts talking about his poor health and he makes me feel so guilty that it's not worth it."

"What do you do then?"
KATY: "Nothing. Nothing works—that is why I'm here."

What was striking, and also quite typical, about Katy's brief synopsis was that everything she said was about her father:

"My father doesn't realize I have my own life."
"My father thinks my world should revolve around him."
"My father uses me."
"My father asks too much."
"My father makes me feel guilty."

"My father needs to get out and meet people."

Katy is doing what most of us do when we are angry. She is judging, blaming, criticizing, moralizing, preaching, instructing, interpreting, and psychoanalyzing. There is not one statement from Katy that is truly about her own self.

As you read ahead, keep in mind the lessons you have learned from the previous chapters. Katy's problem with her father has certain similarities to Maggie's problem with her mother. Struggle a bit with your own thoughts and reactions to the questions that follow before reading mine.

Is Katy's Father Wrong to Make Such Demands? I don't know. Who among us can say with certainty how many demands this particular seventy-two-year-old widowed father should rightfully make on his grown daughter? If we were to ask ten different people for their opinion, we might get ten different answers, depending on the respondent's age, religion, nationality, socioeconomic class, sibling position, and family background. If I were in Katy's shoes, I would probably also complain that my father was "too demanding." But that's because I'm me. Another person in the same spot might feel happy to be so needed.

If we are searching for the ultimate "truth" of the matter (How much should a parent ask? How much should a daughter give?), we may be failing to appreciate that there are multiple ways of perceiving the same situation and that people think, feel, and react differently. If I persist in repeating this point, it is because it is an extremely difficult concept to grasp, and hold on to, when we are angry. Conflicting wants and different perceptions of the world do not mean that one party is "right" and the other is "wrong."

Does Katy Have a Right to be Angry? Is Her Anger at Her Father Legitimate? Of course. As I stated earlier, feeling angry is neither right nor wrong, legitimate nor illegitimate. We have a right to everything we feel, and Katy's anger deserves her attention and respect. But Katy's right to be angry does not mean that her father is to blame. Rather, Katy's chronic anger and resentment is a signal that she needs to re-evaluate her participation in her interactions with her father and consider how she might move differently in this important relationship.

What's Wrong with Katy's Communications to Her Dad? For starters, Katy is not being particularly tactful or strategic. Few people are able to listen well when they are being criticized or told what's wrong with them. Unless Katy has a remarkably flexible father, her statements are likely to elicit further defensiveness on his part and make it less likely that she will be heard.

Second, Katy's communications convey that she is an expert on her father's experience. Katy diagnoses her father as a selfish, neurotic, and demanding man who is using his daughter to fill up the empty space left by his deceased wife. This psychological interpretation may or may not fit. There are countless other possible explanations for father's behavior, as well.

Diagnosing the other person is a favorite pastime for most of us when stress is high. Although it can reflect a wish to provide a truly helpful insight, more often it is a subtle form of blaming and one-upmanship. When we diagnose, we assume that we can know what another person *really* thinks, feels, or wants, or how the other person *should* think, feel, or behave. But we can't know these things for sure. It is difficult enough to know these things about our own selves.

Who Has the Problem? "My father has a big problem. He makes excessive demands on me." These statements—Katy's opening words to me on the phone—reflect her conviction that it is her *father* who has the problem. And yet, from Katy's description, her father is able to identify his wishes, state them clearly, and even get what he wants.

Katy has the problem. She has yet to find a way to identify and clarify her own limits with her father so that she is not left feeling bitter and resentful. It is Katy who is struggling and in pain. This is *her* problem.

To say that Katy has a problem, however, is not to imply that she is wrong or to blame or at fault. "Who has the problem?" is a question that has nothing to do with guilt or culpability. The one who has the problem is simply the party who is dissatisfied with or troubled by a particular situation.

What Is Katy's Problem? Katy's problem is that she has not sorted out some major questions in her own mind: "What is my responsibility for my own life, and what is my responsibility toward my father?" "What is being selfish, and what is being true to my own wants and priorities?" "What amount of help *can* I give to my father without feeling angry or resentful?" Not until she comes up with clear-cut answers to these difficult questions can she meet her father on a different plane.

Katy's problem is not that her father "makes" her feel guilty. Another person cannot "make" us feel guilty; they can only try. Katy's father will predictably give her a hard time if she shifts the old pattern, but she alone is responsible for her own feelings—guilt included.

Surely, there are no simple answers. What would *your* reaction be if Katy were to clarify new limits with her father? Would you view her as selfish or would you cheer her new claim to selfhood? Who knows? How many of us can distinguish with confidence where our responsibilities to others begin and end? How can women—trained from birth to define ourselves through our loving care of others—know with confidence when it is time to finally say "Enough!"?

"A woman's work is never done" was the credo that Katy had lived out with her children, and now that the youngest was leaving home, she was continuing the drama with her elderly father. Katy, I learned, had been "giving" for most of her life, as her mother and grandmother had before her. Deep down, she felt too scared and guilty to reveal that long-buried part of herself that wanted to put forth her own needs and begin to take. Katy had devoted herself so exclusively to the needs of others that she had betrayed, if not lost, her own self. She felt the rage of her buried self but hadn't yet been able to use it in order to make changes.

No matter how much we sympathize or identify with Katy's situation, it is her problem, nonetheless. This is not to imply that Katy is neurotic, misguided, or wrong. Nor is it to say that she is the "cause" of her dilemma. The rules and roles of our families and society make it especially difficult for women to define ourselves apart from the wishes and expectations of others—and negative reactions from others, when we begin to pay primary attention to the quality and direction of our own lives, may certainly invite us to become anxious and guilty.

If, however, we do not use our anger to define ourselves clearly in every important relationship we are in—and manage our feelings as they arise—no one else will assume this responsibility for us.

Harnessing Unclarity

Katy sought my help because she wanted to "do something" with her father and she wanted me to tell her what that something was. The fact of the matter was that Katy—like most women—had more than enough people telling her what to do. Her mother, by example, had taught her that selflessness, self-sacrifice, and service were a woman's calling, and now Katy's friends were telling her that self-assertion was the key to her liberation. "Don't say yes when you really mean no" was the most oft-repeated statement that Katy heard from her advisers, until she herself began to believe that her problem might be solved if she could only find the courage to mutter this unspeakable two-letter word.

What Katy really needed to do was to calm down and do nothing, at least for a while. It is not wise to make decisions or to attempt to change a relationship at a time when we are feeling angry and intense. Also, Katy has really not thought very much about her situation, because she is too busy reacting to it.

Katy would get off to a good start if she stopped blaming and diagnosing her father. She could begin to recognize that it is *her* job to separate herself a bit from his wishes and expectations in order to clarify her own values, to evaluate her own choices and priorities and to make decisions regarding what she will and will not do. Katy could also recognize that she is not yet clear about these things and does not know how to solve her problem. Acknowledging our unclarity is, in itself, a significant step.

What could Katy do next? What can any of us do when we feel angry in reaction to demands being placed upon us but see no new options for changing our behavior? Our anger signals a problem, but it provides us with no answers—not even a clue—as to how to solve it. Anger is simply something we feel—or allow ourselves to feel. At the same time it tells us that we need to slow down and think more clearly about the self, our anger can make clear thinking difficult indeed!

At this point, Katy's task is not to "do something" with her anger, although criticizing her father and inviting others to do the same may bring her short-term relief or at least a sense of moral superiority. In terms of lasting change, Katy's job is to strive to achieve a lower degree of emotional reactivity and a higher degree of self-clarity. How? Katy will become clearer about her convictions and options if she does the following: First, she can *share her problem* with other family members, including her father; second, she can *gather data* about how other relatives—especially the women in her family—have dealt with similar problems over the generations.

"Dad, I Have a Problem"

When Katy told her father a little about her problem, it was a high-anxiety moment and no less significant than Maggie's talk with her mother. By calmly sharing something about where she stood on an emotional issue in the family, Katy shifted the old rigid pattern in the relationship. The conversation went something like this:

"You know, Dad, I have a problem. I haven't figured

out how to balance the responsibility I feel toward you and the responsibility I feel toward myself. Last week when I took you shopping two times and also drove you to your doctor's appointment, I found myself feeling tense and uncomfortable, because I really wanted some of that time just for me. But when I say no and go about my own personal business, I end up feeling guilty—like I'm looking over my shoulder to see how you're doing."

"Well, if I'm that much of a burden, I can just stay away," father said coldly. He looked as if he had been physically struck.

Katy had prepared herself for her father's countermoves so that she could stand her ground when they came, without getting sucked into that intense field of emotional reactivity that characterized their relationship. "No, Dad," she replied, "I wouldn't want that. I'm not saying that *you* are burdening me. In fact, I would like to get a little better myself at asking people for help. What I'm talking about is *my* problem getting clear about what feels comfortable for me. I need to figure out how much I can do for you and when I need to say no and put myself first."

"Katy, you surprise me," said her father. "Your mother took care of both her parents when they were old and she never complained about it. Your mother would certainly not be very proud of you."

"I know what you mean, Dad." Katy refused to bite the bait and she continued to calmly address her own issue. "I was always impressed by Mom's willingness to take care of both her parents. It seemed to me that she had an amazing capacity to be giving, without feeling short-changed or resentful. But I'm not Mom. I'm different, and I really don't think I could do that. I guess I *am* more selfish than Mother was."

There was an awkward silence, which her father broke: "Well, Katy, is there something I'm supposed to do about this problem of yours?" The mixture of sarcasm and hurt in his voice couldn't be missed.

For a moment, Katy felt that old pressure to give her father advice and suggest ways that he could meet people and make use of the resources available to him. She knew from experience, however, that it didn't work. Instead, she stayed on course and continued to discuss her own problem:

"I wish someone else could solve my problem and make my decisions for me, but I know that's really my job." Katy became thoughtful. "Actually, Dad, it would be helpful to me, in my attempts to get clear about all this, if you could share some of your own experience with me. Have you ever struggled with anything like this? What was it like for you when your mother became ill and couldn't take care of herself anymore? Who in the family made the decision to put her in the nursing home, and what was your perspective on that?"

By directly addressing a family issue (in this case, "Who takes care of an elderly parent?") rather than angrily *reacting* to it, Katy detoxified the subject by getting it out on the table. As a result, the underground anxiety that surrounds unaddressed emotional issues will diminish and Katy will find that she is able to think more objectively about her situation. In addition, Katy is beginning to question her dad about his own experience with elderly parents. Learning how other family members have handled problems similar to our own, down through the generations, is one of the most effective routes to lowering reactivity and heightening self-clarity. In fact, *before* Katy could initiate this talk with her dad in so solid a fashion, she had to learn more about the legacy of caretaking in her family background.

LEARNING ABOUT OUR LEGACY

Which women in Katy's extended family have struggled with a similar problem and how have they attempted to solve it? How have other women in Katy's family—her sister, aunts, and grandmothers—balanced their responsibility to others with their responsibility to their selves? How successful have they been?

How did it happen that Katy's mother took on the sole responsibility of caring for her aging parents? What is the perspective of her mother's sister and brothers about how well this arrangement worked out?

How did decisions get made, down through the generations, about who took care of family members who were not able to care for themselves?

We are never the first in our family to wrestle with a problem, although it may feel that way. All of us inherit the unsolved problems of our past; and whatever we are struggling with has its legacy in the struggles of prior generations. *If we do not know about our own family history, we are more likely to repeat past patterns or mindlessly rebel against them, without much clarity about who we really are, how we are similar to and different from other family members, and how we might best proceed in our own life.*

Using our anger effectively requires first and foremost a clear "I," and women have been blocked from selfhood at every turn. We cannot hope to realize the self, however, in isolation from individuals on our family tree. No book—or psychotherapist, for that matter—can help us with this task if we stay cut off from our roots. Most of us react strongly to family members—especially our mothers—but we do not talk to them in depth and gather data about their experience. We may know virtually nothing about the forces that shaped our parents' lives as they shaped ours, or how our mothers and grandmothers dealt with problems similar to ours. When we do not know these things, we do not know the self. And without a clear self, rooted in our history, we will be prone to intense angry reactions in all sorts of situations, in response to which we will blame others, distance ourselves, passively comply, or otherwise spin our wheels.

And so, Katy had some "family work" to do. She contacted a wide representation of family members—especially the women—and learned firsthand about their experience and perspective as they grappled with issues not unlike her own. From living family members, she learned more about those who had died, including her mother. In so doing, Katy was able to see her problem with her father in its broader context.

Katy discovered that women in her family tended to fall into two opposite camps: those who, like her mother, made large personal sacrifices to care for aging parents and grandparents; and those who, like her mother's sister, Aunt Peggy, stuck their heads in the sand as aging family members became unable to care for themselves. Within these camps were several warring factions. Katy's mother, for example, did not speak to her sister for several years following their mother's death, because she felt that Peggy had not pitched in her share of the caretaking. From Peggy's perspective

Katy's mother had made unilateral and unwise decisions about their mother's care. Caring for elderly parents had been such a loaded issue in the previous generations that it was predictable that Katy would have a hard time finding a middle ground, and striking a comfortable balance between her responsibility for herself and her responsibility to her father.

As Katy connected to her family and gathered information, she felt calmer about her situation and was able to think about new options for herself with her father, where before she had been convinced that none were possible. There were no easy answers or painless solutions. Katy once summarized her dilemma this way: "No matter how long I'm in therapy, I'm still going to feel guilty if I say no to my father. But if I keep saying yes, I'm going to feel angry. So, if I'm going to change, I guess I will just have to learn to live with some guilt for a while." This is exactly what Katy did: She lived with some guilt, which did not prove fatal and which eventually subsided.

The specific changes that Katy made with her father may seem small and unimpressive to an outsider. She decided to have dinner with him twice rather than three times a week, and told him that she would shop for him on Saturday rather than on an "on-call" basis during the week. These were the only changes that she initiated, but she held to them and they made a big difference in her life. Soon thereafter, her father initiated a change of his own: He became good friends with an older woman in his neighborhood and they would talk for several hours each day. Katy felt reassured but also disquieted by this event. She began to realize how much her preoccupation with her father had organized her life and helped her to avoid confronting her isolation from her own peers. She also learned that she was far more skilled at giving help than asking for it.

The specifics of what Katy decided to do and not do for her father is the least important part of her story. Katy's solution would not necessarily be the right one for you or me. What is more significant is the work that she did in her own family which gave her a greater sense of connectedness to her roots and of her separateness and clarity as an individual. Now she could better use her anger as a spring-board for *thinking* about her situation rather than remaining a victim of it. And as we will see, thinking clearly about the questions "What am I responsible for?" and "What am I *not* responsible for?" is a difficult challenge for all of us.

7

WHO'S RESPONSIBLE FOR WHAT

The Trickiest
Anger Question

While attending a conference in New York one spring, I rode by bus to the Metropolitan Museum with two colleagues. I had lost my old familiarity with the city, and my companions, Celia and Janet, felt like foreigners in a strange land. Perhaps as a result of our "big-city" anxiety, we reminded the bus driver—once too often—to announce our stop. In a sudden and unexpected fury, he launched into a vitriolic attack that turned heads throughout the crowded bus. The three of us stood in stunned silence.

Later, over coffee, we shared our personal reactions to this incident. Celia felt mildly depressed. She was reminded of her abusive ex-husband and this particular week was the anniversary of their divorce. Janet reacted with anger, which seemed to dissipate as she drummed up clever retorts to the driver's outburst and hilarious revenge fantasies. My own reaction was nostalgia. I had been feeling homesick for New York and almost welcomed the contrast to the midwestern politeness to which I had become accustomed. It was a New

York City "happening" that I could take back to Topeka, Kansas.

Suppose we reflect briefly on this incident. We might all agree that the bus driver behaved badly. But is he also responsible for the reactions of three women? Did he *cause* Celia's depression and Janet's anger? Did he *make* me feel nostalgic for my past? And if one of us had reacted to this man's surliness by jumping off the Brooklyn Bridge that night, should he be held accountable for a death? Or, viewed from another perspective, were *we* responsible for his outburst to begin with?

It is tempting to view human transactions in simple cause-and-effect terms. If we are angry, someone else *caused* it. Or, if we are the target of someone else's anger, we must be to *blame;* or, alternately—if we are convinced of our innocence—we may conclude that the other person has no *right* to feel angry. The more our relationships in our first family are fused (meaning the togetherness force is so powerful that there is a loss of the separate "I's" within the "we"), the more we learn to take responsibility for other people's feelings and reactions and blame them for our own. ("You always make Mom feel guilty." "You give Dad headaches." "She caused her husband to drink.") Likewise, family members assume responsibility for *causing* other people's thoughts, feelings, and behavior.

Human relationships, however, don't work that way— or at least not very well. We begin to use our anger as a vehicle for change when we are able to share our reactions without holding the other person responsible for causing our feelings, and without blaming ourselves for the reactions that other people have in response to our choices and actions.

We *are* responsible for our own behavior. But we are *not* responsible for other people's reactions; nor are they responsible for ours. Women often learn to reverse this order of things: *We put our energy into taking responsibility for other people's feelings, thoughts, and behavior and hand over to others responsibility for our own.* When this happens, it becomes difficult, if not impossible, for the old rules of a relationship to change.

To illustrate the point, let's return to Katy's problem with her widowed father, whom she initially described as excessively demanding and guilt-inducing. If Katy perceives her father as unilaterally causing her anger and/or guilt, she is at a dead end. She will feel helpless and powerless because she cannot change him. Similarly, if Katy takes responsibility for causing her father's feelings and reactions, she is also stuck. Why? Because if Katy does make a change in the status quo, her father will become emotionally reactive to her new behavior. If Katy then feels responsible for causing his reactions, she may reinstate the old pattern in order to protect her father (and herself) from uncomfortable feelings and to safeguard the predictable sameness of the relationship. ("My father got so angry and crazy when I said no that there was just nothing I could do.") The situation is then defined as hopeless.

Why is the question "Who is responsible for what?" such a puzzle for women? Women in particular have been discouraged from taking responsibility for solving our own problems, determining our own choices, and taking control of the quality and direction of our own lives. As we learn to relinquish responsibility for the self, we are prone to blame others for failing to fill up our emptiness or provide for our happiness—which is not their job. At the same time, however, we may feel responsible for just about everything that goes on around us. We are quick to be blamed for other people's problems and pain and quick to accept the verdict of guilty. We also, in the process, develop the belief that we *can* avert problems if only we try hard enough. Indeed, guilt and self-blame are a "woman's problem" of epidemic proportion. A colleague tells the story of pausing on a ski slope to admire the view, only to be knocked down by a careless skier who apparently did not notice her. "I'm s-o-r-r-y," she reflexively yelled after him from her prone position as he whizzed on by.

In this chapter we will see how confusion about "Who is responsible for what?" is one source of nonproductive self-blaming and other-blaming, as well as a roadblock to changing our situation. How can we learn to take *more* responsibility for the self and *less* for the thoughts, feelings, and behavior of others? At this point, you should be clearer on the subject than when you started out, but let's continue to try our hand at sorting out the elements of this perplexing question. Remember—assuming responsibility for the self means not only clarifying the "I" but also observing and changing our part in the patterns that keep us stuck. In this chapter we will be looking carefully at the *overfunctioning-underfunctioning patterns* in which we all participate.

A CRISIS AT MIDNIGHT

Jane and Stephanie have lived together for eight years and have raised a German shepherd who is a much-loved member of their household. One evening the dog woke them in the middle of the night and was obviously quite ill. Stephanie thought that the situation was serious enough to warrant an immediate call to the vet. Jane insisted that it could wait till morning. She accused Stephanie of being excessively worried and overreactive.

When they awoke the next morning, their dog's condition had worsened. When the veterinarian examined him, she said, "You should have called me immediately. Your dog could have died." Stephanie was furious at Jane. "If anything had happened," she said, "*you* would have been to blame!"

What is your perspective on this situation?

How would you react if you were in Stephanie's shoes at this point?

How do you view the responsibility of each party in contributing to Stephanie's anger?

We may empathize with Stephanie's anger, but she is nonetheless confused about who is responsible for what. Let's analyze the situation in more detail.

It is Jane's responsibility to clarify her beliefs and take action in accord with them. She did this. It was her opinion that the dog did not need immediate medical attention and so she did not call the doctor. Stephanie, too, is responsible for clarifying *her* beliefs and acting upon them. She did *not* do this. She was worried that the dog might need immediate attention and still she did not call the vet.

I am not suggesting that Stephanie should not feel angry with Jane. If she is angry, she is angry. She may be angry that Jane put down her fears, minimized her concerns, disqualified her perception of reality, or acted like a know-it-all. Nonetheless, it is Stephanie, not Jane, who has the ultimate responsibility for what Stephanie decides to do or not to do.

"But You Don't Know Jane!"

"The reason I didn't call," Stephanie explained later, "is that Jane would never have let me hear the end of it if I was wrong. If I had woken the vet up in the middle of the night for nothing, Jane would have been on my case for weeks and she'd have one more reason to label me a neurotic worrier. I love Jane, but you don't know how difficult she can be! She is so sure of herself that it makes me question my own opinions." In this formulation, Stephanie continues to blame Jane for her (Stephanie's) behavior.

Of course, if Stephanie does begin to assert her own self, Jane may have an intense reaction—especially if Jane has operated as the dominant partner whenever decisions had to be made. But if Stephanie can stick to her position without emotionally distancing or escalating tensions further, chances are that over time Jane will manage her own feelings and reactions just fine.

What are the steps we can take to translate our anger into a clear sense of personal responsibility that will result in more functional relationships with others? Some steps for Stephanie are: observation, clarifying the pattern, and gathering data.

OBSERVATION

Imagine that you are in Stephanie's shoes and feeling angry—not just about the dog incident but also about the relationship pattern that this incident brought to light. What might be your next step?

The first step in the direction of gaining greater clarity about who is responsible for what is to begin to *carefully observe* the sequences of interaction that lead up to our feeling angry or emotionally intense. For example, Stephanie might observe that the pattern around decision-making often goes like this:

A situation occurs (in this case, a sick dog) that requires a decision. Stephanie tends to respond first by voicing a rather tentative opinion. Jane then states her own opinion, which may be different, in a supremely confident manner. Stephanie then begins to doubt her initial opinion, or simply concludes that "it's not worth the fight." In either case, she defers to Jane. Often this pattern works fine for both of them and things remain calm. But when anxiety and stress are high (as in the present example), Stephanie becomes angry with Jane if the outcome of Jane's decision-making is not to her liking. Stephanie then either withdraws from Jane or criticizes her decision. If she does the latter, a fight ensues, and by the next day things are usually calm again.

CLARIFYING THE PATTERN

Although she might define it differently, Stephanie is beginning to identify an overfunctioning-underfunctioning pattern around decision-making. The more Jane *overfunctions* (jumps in to make decisions for the two of them; fails to express any doubt or insecurity about her own judgment; behaves as if she does not benefit from Stephanie's help and advice), the more Stephanie *underfunctions* (spaces out or does nothing when a decision is to be made; relies on Jane to take over; feels lazy or less competent to make important decisions). And the more Stephanie *underfunctions*, the more Jane will *overfunction*. Overfunctioners and underfunctioners reinforce each other's behavior in a circular fashion.

Approaching a relationship pattern in this way—gathering the objective data about who does what, when, and in what order—is difficult enough when things are calm. It is next to impossible if we are locked into emotionally intense and blaming behavior. We have seen how women learn to be the emotional reactors in our relationships, especially when stress hits, so we may need to make a conscious effort to become less reactive in order to focus our attention on the task of getting the facts.

GATHERING DATA

Stephanie will also benefit from gathering some data about how this pattern of relating to Jane fits with her own family tradition over the generations. For example, how did Stephanie's parents, and their parents before them, negotiate issues of decision-making? In Stephanie's extended family, which relationships were characterized by a balance of power and which marriages had one dominant (overfunctioning) partner who was viewed as having the corner on competence? How is Stephanie's relationship with Jane similar to and different from her parents' relationship with regard to the sharing of decision-making power? What other women in Stephanie's family have struggled to shift away from the underfunctioning position and how successful were they? As we saw with Katy, our current relationship struggles are part of a legacy that began long before our birth. A familiarity with this legacy helps us gain objectivity when evaluating our behavior in relationships.

Birth order is another factor that strongly influences our way of negotiating relationships. In Stephanie and Jane's case, for example, their pattern around decision-making fits their sibling positions. Jane is the older of two sisters. It is characteristic of one in this sibling position to be a natural leader and to believe, in one's heart of hearts, that one truly knows best, not only for oneself, but for the other person as well. Stephanie is the younger of the two sisters in her family, and, in the manner of one in that position, is often comfortable letting other people do things for her. Although she may compete fiercely with the "leader," she may also shun leadership should it be offered her. Simply being aware that one's sibling position within the family affects one's approach to life can be extremely helpful. If Stephanie finds herself having a hard time taking charge of things, and Jane an equally hard time *not* taking charge, they will both be able to deal with their situation with more humor and less self-criticism if they can appreciate the fact that they are behaving much the way people in their sibling positions behave under stress.

SO WHO HAS THE PROBLEM?

Let us suppose that Stephanie has taken the following steps since the dog incident: First, she has let go of her blaming position ("If anything had happened, *you* would have been to blame!") and has begun to *think* about, rather than simply react to, the problem. Second, she has pretty clearly figured out who does what, when, and in what order; when stress hits, Stephanie underfunctions and Jane overfunctions. Third, Stephanie has thought about how this pattern fits with the traditions in her own family. Finally, she has concluded that she is in a de-selfed position and that her anger is a signal that she would like to achieve more balance in her relationship with Jane when it comes to decision-making.

The following dialogues reflect two modes of using our anger: The first assumes that Jane has the problem and it is her responsibility to take care of it. The second assumes that

Stephanie has the problem and it is her responsibility to take care of it.

"Jane, you are so damned sure of yourself. You're impossible to argue with because you're always right and you don't really listen to my opinions in any open way. You come on so strong that no one can argue with you. I'm really fed up with your know-it-all attitude. When I give my opinion, you pronounce it true or not true, like you're God or something. You make me feel totally insecure about my own thinking. And you always take over and manipulate things to get your way."

"You know, Jane, I've been thinking about the problem that I have in our relationship. I think it has to do with how difficult it is for me to make decisions and take charge of things. I didn't call the vet the other night because when you expressed such confidence in your opinion, I began to doubt my own. And when you were critical of my opinion and put me down for being so worried—which I don't like—I reacted by being even more ready to back down. I'm aware that I do this a lot. And I'm planning to work harder to make my own decisions and stand behind them. I'm sure I'll make mistakes and our relationship might be more tense for a while—but I'm just not satisfied with things as they are. However, I'm also aware that the women in my family haven't done too well making their own decisions—so it may not be easy for me to be a pioneer in this way."

What about dialogue 1? Some relationships thrive on

tough confrontation, and feedback of this sort and fighting it out may be viewed by both partners as a valuable and spicy aspect of the relationship. For all we know, Jane might respond to dialogue 1 by becoming thoughtful and saying, "You know, I've been told that before by other people in my life. I think you have something there. I'm sorry for coming on so strong and I'll try to watch it."

This dialogue does, however, reflect Stephanie's confusion about the matter of individual responsibility. Can you spot the problem? She holds Jane responsible for Jane's behavior (putting Stephanie down), which is fair enough; but she also holds Jane responsible for Stephanie's behavior (feeling insecure and manipulated and failing to stand firmly behind her own opinion), which is not fair at all. Blaming of this sort blurs the boundaries between self and other in a close relationship.

What about dialogue 2? Here, Stephanie shares something about herself and does not assume to be an expert on Jane. She talks about her own dilemma in the relationship and takes responsibility for her own participation in the pattern. While dialogue 1 might lead to a further escalation of an already stressful situation, dialogue 2 would probably calm things down a bit and foster greater objectivity on both women's parts.

Which dialogue better suits your personal style? For me, it depends on the relationship. With my husband, Steve, I sometimes dissipate tension by fighting dialogue-1 style, although with less frequency and intensity as I get older. At work, however, and during visits from long-distance friends and family, I end up feeling much better if I communicate in dialogue-2 style, and I find that these relationships do better, too. It all depends on what the circumstances are, what your goals are, and what in the past has left you feeling better or worse in the long run.

Of course, what is most important is not what Stephanie says to Jane but what she does. Next time around, perhaps Stephanie will listen to Jane and consider her perspective but then take responsibility to make her own reasoned decision about what she will and won't do. Stephanie's communication style will make little difference if she does not modify her own underfunctioning position.

As we learn to identify relationship patterns, we are faced with a peculiar paradox: On the one hand, our job is to learn to take responsibility for our thoughts, feelings, and behavior and to recognize that other people are responsible for their own. Yet, at the same time, how we react with others has a great deal to do with how they react with us. We cannot *not* influence a relationship pattern. Once a relationship is locked into a circular pattern, the whole cycle will change when one person takes the responsibility for changing her or his own part in the sequence.

Assuming this responsibility does not mean we take a self-blaming or self-deprecating position. Learning to observe and change our behavior is a self-loving process that can't take place in an atmosphere of self-criticism or self-blame. Such attitudes frequently undermine, rather than enhance, our ability to observe relationship patterns. They may even be part of the game we learn to play in which the unconscious goal is to safeguard relationships by being one down in order to help the other person feel one up.

In contrast, it is a position of dignity and strength that allows us to say to ourselves or others, "You know, I observe that this is what I am doing in this relationship and I am now going to work to change it." Such owning of responsibility does not let the other person off the hook. To the contrary, we have seen how it brings our "separateness" into bold relief and confronts others with the fact that we alone bear the ultimate responsibility for defining our selves and the terms of our own lives. It respectfully allows others to do the same.

WHO'S DOING THE HOUSEWORK?

After countless housework battles with her husband, Lisa decided to cease and desist from the old fights and begin to clarify her own problem. She chose a moment when things were relatively calm and close between them and said, "Rich, I'm having a problem with the amount of housework I do. When I take on more than half the responsibility for cooking and cleaning, I end up feeling resentful, because the way I see it, I'm pulling more than my fair share of the load. I'm exhausted as well. I guess my biggest problem is that I am tired too much of the time and I need to find a way to conserve my energy and have more time for myself." Then Lisa told Rich specifically what she would like him to do in order to help out.

Lisa did not criticize her husband or instruct him on how a good man behaves; rather, she was sharing her feelings about a situation that had become increasingly problematic for her. When Rich said, "Well, other women I know seem to manage just fine," Lisa said lightly, "Well, I'm not other women. I'm me."

Several months later, Rich was doing nothing more than taking the garbage out and tending to yard work and Lisa was still angry. As she and I talked, however, I became aware that she had made no change in her own behavior. As usual, she was entertaining Rich's colleagues, doing his laundry, cooking dinner, washing the dishes, even vacuuming his study. Lisa's words were saying, "I'm tired and resentful and I need to do something about it." Her actions, however, were maintaining the status quo. She was not taking responsibility for doing something about her problem.

But why should she? Isn't Rich the one who should change his behavior? Is it not his responsibility to behave fairly and considerately toward his wife? Lisa is forever trying to initiate change in this relationship—so, isn't it Rich's turn?

You and I may think so, but that's beside the point. Rich does not have a problem with the current situation. He is satisfied with things as they are and he is not interested in making a change. If Lisa does not proceed to take care of what is *her* problem, no one else will do it for her, her husband included.

When the day came that Lisa could no longer stand her predicament, she began to make her actions congruent with her words. First, Lisa figured out a plan. She made a list of tasks that she would continue to do (for example, a clean living room and kitchen were extremely important to her, so she would not let things pile up here) and a list of those that she would no longer do. For these, she hoped that Rich would fill in, but if not, they would just live without their being done. Then she shared the plan with Rich and put it into force.

Lisa stood behind her position as Rich tested her out for two months by becoming even more of a slob than usual. Lisa continued to do more of the housework because a clean house was more important to her than it was to Rich. She found other ways, however, to save her time and energy.

For three nights a week she made sandwiches for her and the kids for dinner and let Rich prepare his own meals when he came home from work. If Rich invited his friends or colleagues to dinner, she did not shop or cook for the event, although she was glad to help out. Lisa carefully sorted out where she wanted to put her time and energy and where she could conserve it.

Lisa made these changes out of a sense of responsibility for herself—not as a move against Rich. If she had gone "on strike," or this was no more than a plot to shape Rich up or to get back at him, the probable outcome for this couple might well have been an escalation of their difficulties.

As a postscript, I might add that as Rich made some changes of his own, Lisa, in reaction, made some counter-moves. If you recall, "Please change!" and "Change back!" are the mixed messages that we often give each other. When Rich took the initiative to do housework, Lisa was right there to offer unsolicited advice or to criticize him for not being thorough enough. To ask a person to do more housework (or parenting) and then say "Do it the way I would do it" or "Do it the way I want you to" is a *move that blocks change.* If Lisa is truly ready to have Rich more involved with the housework (which means that she is willing to give up some control in this area), she must also be ready to *let Rich do it his own way.* If she wants him to stop underfunctioning in this area, she must be willing to stop overfunctioning. Obviously, Rich may never clean house up to her standards, which are likely to be different from his. However, if Lisa can credit his attempts and truly stay out (unless he asks for her advice or feedback), his housekeeping skills will get better in time.

Lisa had an additional problem as Rich began to change:

She not only wanted him to do more of the housework; she wanted him to *want* to. "He did the dishes last night," she moaned, "but he sulked and pouted for the rest of the evening. It's just not worth it." Again, we see Lisa's discomfort with change. Sulking and pouting is *Rich's* problem, and it is not Lisa's business or responsibility to fix or take away his feelings. Although no one has died from sulking yet, women, the emotional rescuers of the world, can have a terribly difficult time allowing others just to sit with their feelings and learn to handle them. If Lisa can avoid becoming distant and critical, and if she can allow Rich the space to sulk as he pleases without reacting to it, his sulking will eventually subside. But when she says "It's just not worth it," this *is* Lisa's problem and reflects her own mixed feelings about changing a long-standing relationship pattern.

Why should it be easy for Lisa to relinquish control in an area where female authority and competence have gone unquestioned generation after generation? When Lisa does housework, she is linked to her mother, to her grandmothers, and to all the women who have come before. It is part of her heritage and tradition, to say nothing of the fact that homemaking is important and valuable work—no matter how little recognition it gets. Sure, housework can be tedious and daily living easier when it is shared, but it is understandable that Lisa may have some complicated feelings about it all. And perhaps Lisa has few other areas where she, rather than Rich, can assume the role of the competent expert.

One last question: If Lisa is serious about change, why not a good let-it-all-hang-out fight? Can't Lisa let Rich know by the volume of her voice that she really means business? *Nothing is wrong with fighting if it leaves Lisa feeling better and if it is part of a process by which Lisa gains a greater*

clarity that she will not proceed with things as usual. In
ongoing battles of this sort, the single most important factor
is not whether we fight or not, or whether our voice is raised
or calm; it is the growing inner conviction that we can no
longer continue to overfunction (in Lisa's case, on the domestic
scene), for our own sake.

Emotional Overfunctioning—
More "Women's Work"

Earlier we noted the ways in which de-selfing and *underfunctioning* are prescribed for women—and so they are.
Thus, when we have our own area of *overfunctioning,* we
may do it with a vengeance while complaining all the way,
as Lisa did with housework. In addition to picking up
someone else's socks, how else are we likely to overfunction?

Often in relationships, women overfunction by assuming
a "rescuing" or "fix-it" position. We behave as if it is our
responsibility to shape up other people or solve their problems, and further, that it is in our power to do so. We may
become reactive to every move that a person makes or fails
to make, our emotions ranging from annoyance to intense
anger or despair. And when we realize that our attempts to
be helpful are not working, do we stop and do something
different? Of course not! As we saw with Sandra and Larry
(Chapter 3), we may redouble our unsuccessful efforts, only
to become angrier and angrier at that underfunctioning
individual who is not shaping up.

What a difficult time we may have maintaining the
degree of separateness that allows others the space to manage
their own pain and solve their own problems! Men also have
this difficulty balancing the forces of separateness and togetherness; however, they tend to handle anxiety by emotional

distancing and disengaging (thus, sacrificing the "we" for the "I"), whereas women more frequently handle anxiety by fusion and emotional overfunctioning (thus, sacrificing the "I" for the "we"). The sex-role division for these two unhappy and out-of-balance alternatives is hardly surprising. Our society undervalues the importance of close relationships for men and fosters their emotional isolation and disconnectedness. Women, on the other hand, receive an opposite message that encourages us to be excessively focused on, and fused with, the problems of others, rather than putting our primary "worry energy" into our own problems. _When we do not put our primary emotional energy into solving our own problems, we take on other people's problems as our own._

But what is wrong with taking responsibility for others? In some respects, nothing. For generations, women have gained both identity and esteem from our deep investment in protecting, helping, nurturing, and comforting others. Surely, connectedness to others, empathy and loving regard for our fellow human beings, and investment in facilitating the growth of the young are virtues of the highest order for both women and men. The problem arises when we are excessively reactive to other people's problems, when we assume responsibility for things that we are not responsible for, and when we attempt to control things that are not in our control. When we overfunction for another individual, we end up very angry, and in the process, we facilitate the growth of no one.

The saga of overfunctioning will come more clearly to light as we unravel the story of Lois and her brother. As you read, keep in mind that it could as easily be Lois and her son, her grandfather, her mother-in-law, her employee, or her friend.

"MY BROTHER IS A MESS!"

"I don't mean to sound unsympathetic or callous," explained Lois, who sounded as if she was about to disown her younger brother, Brian. "Obviously, I'm very concerned about Brian because he's so screwed up. But I also find myself angry with him. Two things that he does irritate the hell out of me: First, he always calls in the middle of some kind of crisis and wants to borrow some money and ask for advice. Then he spends the money—which he never pays back—and ignores the advice. I've referred him to two therapists, but he didn't stick with it. I've suggested books for him to read to get his life together. I've talked on the phone with him when he calls me—collect, of course—and I tell him what he can do to get his act together. Brian listens and then he doesn't do it. I've tried some tough confrontation and that doesn't work, either. I'm feeling drained and I'm feeling angry. Yet, he's my brother and I can't turn him away. He's alienated my parents and he has nowhere else to go."

What is the pattern of interaction between Lois and her brother? Brian calls, saying "Help!" Lois jumps in to help. Brian then continues his old ways, and sooner or later he calls again with a new crisis. Lois takes either a tough or a sympathetic approach, but in either case she continues to tell her little brother (who is twenty-four years old) how to shape up. Brian does not shape up. Lois gets angry and the cycle continues.

So, who is to blame for this merry-go-round? Hopefully, by now you are no longer thinking in these terms. Relationships are circular (A and B are mutually reinforcing) rather than linear (A causes B or B causes A). *Once a pattern is established in a relationship, it is perpetuated by both parties.*

What is Lois's part in keeping the circular dance going? The more she overfunctions, the more Brian will underfunction—which means that the more Lois is helpful, the more Brian will need her help. The more Lois fails to express her own doubts, vulnerability, or incompetence to Brian, the more Brian will express enough for both of them. The more emotional Lois gets about Brian's problems, the more he won't care enough about himself. Lois's big-sisterly sense of responsibility may have many positive aspects. Nonetheless, she is functioning at the expense of her brother's competence.

Does this mean that Lois is responsible for her brother's problems? Not at all. She does not *make* Brian incompetent to manage his life any more than Brian *makes* Lois rescue him. Lois's role as rescuer and Brian's as rescuee have their roots in family patterns that can be traced back for generations. They are each responsible for their own behavior, and Lois's behavior is fifty percent of the problem she complains of. What are your thoughts about the specific steps Lois might take to change it?

What about sharing her problem with Brian in a non-blaming way? Lois could approach him when things are calm in their relationship and say, "When you call me to ask for money and advice, my initial reaction is to give it. But after I give it and I see that it hasn't really helped, I start to feel resentful. Maybe it's partly from my own wish to be helpful that I end up feeling frustrated. But I don't want things to continue this way. Please don't ask me to lend you money unless you can pay it back. And please don't ask me for advice if you're just going to do your own thing anyway."

It won't work—or at least it won't change the pattern.

Communication of this sort is preferable to blaming Brian ("Brian, you're an exploitative, irresponsible, manipulative psychopath") or interpreting his motives ("I think you are using me"). Nonetheless, if Lois wishes to change this over-functioning-underfunctioning pattern, she cannot do so simply by expressing her feelings or asking Brian to change. *She will have to stop overfunctioning.* What specifically does this mean?

Learning How Not to Be Helpful

If Lois wants to change the old pattern with Brian, she can put the brakes on being helpful. Sound simple? For those of us who believe it is our sacred calling to save other people and shape them up, the hardest thing in the world is to *stop* trying to be helpful.

How does one go about not trying to be helpful? How does one stop rescuing another family member? Here's an example:

The next time Brian calls Lois in distress, Lois can listen sympathetically and ask him questions about his situation. And she can say in a low-keyed way, "It sounds like you're really having a hard time, Brian. I'm sorry to hear that."

If Brian asks her for money, she can say, "I've decided not to lend you any more money, Brian. There are a bunch of things that I'm saving for and I've decided that's my first priority—you're on your own, kid." If Lois can do this with warmth and humor, all the better. For example, if Brian says accusingly, "That's selfish," Lois might say, "You're probably right. I think I am getting more selfish in my old age."

If Brian courts her advice, Lois can bite her tongue and say, "Well, I really just don't know," or, "I wish I could be helpful, but you know, Brian, I just don't know what to say."

Then Lois might proceed to share a little bit about what she is currently struggling with and perhaps ask Brian if he has any thoughts about *her* dilemma. Another thing Lois can do is to express confidence in Brian's ability to find his own solutions: "I know you've been struggling for a long time to get on top of things, but I have faith that you'll eventually work it out. I think you're a really bright guy."

Learning how not to be helpful requires a certain attitude toward relationships and an ability to strike the right balance between the forces of separateness and togetherness. If Lois's tone is, "Don't try to involve *me*, it's not *my* problem," the old pattern won't change. This is a reactive and distancing position. Similarly, if Lois says, "Well, I'm not going to give you any advice or money from now on because it's not good for *you*, Brian," she is simply doing another variation of her therapeutic "I-really-know-what's-best-for-you" attitude. Learning how *not* to be helpful requires that we begin to acknowledge that we do not have the answers or solutions to other people's problems. In fact, we don't even have the answers to all of our own.

What's Wrong with Advice-Giving?

Does this mean that Lois should never, ever offer Brian advice for as long as they both shall live? Down the road a bit, as the pattern starts to shift, Lois might give Brian advice *if* he asks for it and *if* she observes that it's useful. But there is advice-giving—and then there is advice-giving!

There is nothing wrong with giving another person advice ("This is what I think . . ." or, "In my experience, this has worked for me") as long as we recognize that we are stating an opinion that may or may not fit for the other person. We start to overfunction, however, when we assume that we know what's best for the other person and we want them to do it our way. If Lois feels angry when Brian does not follow her advice, that's a good indication that she should not be giving it.

It is also the case that those closest to us may have the greatest difficulty considering our advice if we come across as though we have the final word on their lives. Lois's typical style, for example, is to lecture Brian about the importance of his getting professional help and then to get angry at him for not following through. Brian would have a better opportunity to evaluate this option if Lois were to say (and only if asked), "Well, therapy has been pretty helpful to me in my own life, so I'm all for it. But not everyone is alike and you may be more of a do-it-yourselfer. What do you think?" Giving advice in this way is not just a strategic move; it is a mature approach that takes into account the separateness and "otherness" of her brother. Further, it acknowledges that people are different and that we all have the ability to become the best experts on our own selves.

Hanging In

As we saw with Maggie and her mother, there is hardly anything more important than emotionally hanging in— especially when we are shifting a pattern. Lois's task is to show her concern for Brian at the same time that she stops trying to help him solve his problems. How can she do this?

Lois can call Brian while he's having a hard time simply to touch base with him. She might say, "I know I'm not much help to you at this time, but I just wanted to hear how you're doing and let you know that I care about you." She might increase her contact with Brian and invite him to have dinner with her family. *Stepping back and allowing the other person to struggle with his or her own problems is not the same as emotional withdrawal.* Lois can stop trying to bail Brian out, yet still express her support and interest as he goes through a difficult time.

Maintaining emotional contact is never easy at this point in a changing relationship. Our natural tendency may be either to fight or to emotionally distance ourselves because we are uncertain about our position and how to maintain it in the face of pressures to do otherwise, a big part of which is our own anxiety about really changing. Hanging in requires us to move against enormous internal resistance, which is most often experienced as anger ("Why should I get in touch with him when he's acting this way?") or inertia ("I just don't feel like taking the initiative").

Sharing Our Underfunctioning Side

In therapy sessions, Lois discussed her problems and pain with me, but within her own family, and especially with Brian, she was always fine and didn't need anything from anybody. Like all good overfunctioners, Lois was convinced that sharing her struggles and vulnerability with Brian was absolutely out of the question. ("I would never tell Brian that I was depressed; I have absolutely no desire to do so and he has more than enough problems of his own." "Brian can't deal with my feelings." "Why burden him; there is no way he can be helpful to me.") The relationship between Lois and Brian was extremely polarized, with Brian expressing only his weakness and Lois only her competence.

If Lois wants to shift the old pattern, she can present a more balanced picture of herself and begin to share a bit about her own travails with Brian. For example, when Brian calls to talk about his recent crises, Lois can say, "Brian, I wish I could be more useful, but I'm no good for much of anything right now. In fact, I've been feeling lousy all day. I'm sorry you're feeling bad, but I just don't have much energy to give to anyone else. Part of the problem is that I've been feeling dissatisfied with my job for a long time, but today it really came to a head and I got real down in the dumps." If we are dealing with depressed or underfunctioning individuals, the least helpful thing we can do is to keep focusing on *their* problems and trying to be helpful. *The most helpful thing we can do is begin to share part of our own underfunctioning side.*

Ah, Yes, Countermoves!

Finally, Lois must be prepared to deal with Brian's countermoves. As sure as the sun rises in the morning, Brian will up the ante and attempt to reinstate the old pattern. If he has been requesting money to help pay his electric bills, his next request is bound to find him starving to death or about to be thrown in jail. This is the point at which we are truly put to the test. We either give ourselves an excuse to go back to our old ways and blame the other party ("Well, I couldn't let my own brother die in the streets, could I?"), or we sit with some anxiety and guilt and maintain our new position. If Lois can calmly continue not to rescue Brian or attempt to solve his problems—while offering him emotional support and contact—his countermoves are likely to decrease rather dramatically. They will pop up only periodically as he tests out the waters of their relationship over time.

What light does Lois's story shed on the question we started out with: "Who is responsible for what?" It provides us with a good example of how we may be too responsible for another person and, at the same time, not responsible enough for our own behavior. Lois is feeling angry because she assumes too much responsibility for her brother's problems; she advises, rescues, and bails Brian out. She has difficulty simply being there and letting him struggle on his own. At the same time, however, Lois does not assume enough responsibility for examining how her own behavior contributes to the pattern she's so eager to change. She is stuck in a position that blocks her from reflecting upon her situation and figuring out how she can take a new stance that will free her from the old rules and roles.

While it is hard to change in the short run, there are long-term costs of maintaining the status quo. Most obvious are the costs for Brian. Lois is a devoted big sister, but, by persisting in her unsuccessful attempts to advise and rescue her brother and failing to show him her own vulnerable side, she is doing the least helpful things that one can do with an underfunctioning individual. Less obvious but no less important is the price that Lois pays personally for the position she holds in this relationship, as evidenced by her chronic anger and high level of stress. When we overfunction, we may have a difficult time allowing others to take over and care for us, so that we can just relax or have the luxury of falling apart for a little while. Lois, the caretaker and helper for others, has lost sight of her own needs and challenges of continued growth, which she can sweep under the rug because she "needs to care for her brother." By continuing to feel responsible for the other party, Lois ends up underfunctioning for her own self.

ANGER AT KIDS

Self-blaming and child-blaming remain an occupational hazard for many mothers today. "What's wrong with me?" and/or "What's wrong with this child?" are the two questions mothers learn to ask themselves as they are handed over the primary responsibility for all family problems. We have fostered in mothers the omnipotent fantasy that their child's behavior—their very "being"—is mother's doing: If the child performs well, she is considered a "good mother"; if poorly, a "bad mother," who caused the problem. It is as if the mother *is* the child's environment. Until recently, father, the family, the society in which the family is embedded—all these did not *really* count.

As mothers, we are led to believe that we *can*, and *should*, control things that are not realistically within our control. Many of us do feel an excessive need to control our children's behavior, to prove to ourselves, to our own mothers, and to the world that we are good mothers. However, the mother who is dominated by anger because she feels helpless to control her child is often caught in that paradox that underlies our difficulties with this emotion. We may view it as our responsibility to control something that is not in fact within our control and yet fail to exercise the power and authority that we *do* have over our own behavior. Mothers cannot *make* children think, feel, or be a certain way, but we can be firm, consistent, and clear about what *behavior* we will and will not tolerate, and what the consequences are for misbehavior. We can also change our part in patterns that keep family members stuck. At the same time we are doomed to failure with any self-help venture if we view the problem as existing within ourselves—or within the child or the child's father, for that matter. There is never one villain in family life, although it may appear that way on the surface.

Angry power struggles with kids often boil down to this: We may *overfunction*, or move in too much, when it comes to their thoughts and feelings. At the same time, we may *underfunction* when it comes to clarifying our own position and setting rules about behavior. Here is a typical example:

CLAUDIA: A FOUR-YEAR-OLD DICTATOR

Alicia, who had been divorced for several months, was starting to date a man named Carlos. "I like him, but my daughter doesn't," Alicia explained. "Whenever Carlos and I are about to leave the house together, Claudia, who's four, begins to sob mournfully as if her little heart is breaking. Perhaps it has to do with her loyalty to her father, but she just doesn't like Carlos and she doesn't like me to be alone with him. She treats him rudely and refuses to speak to him. Sometimes she has a full-blown temper tantrum when the two of us are about to walk out the door. I feel such rage at her that I can't even be sympathetic."

"And what do you do when Claudia does these things?" I inquired.

"When I'm feeling calm, I try to *reason* with her," explained Alicia. "I let her know that I need to go out and that there is no reason for her to be upset about it. I tell her that soon she will get used to my going out and then it won't bother her. I explain to her that Carlos is a very nice man and that if only she would make the effort, she would like him."

"And how does your daughter react?" I asked.

"She just doesn't listen to reason. She'll climb under the covers or put her hands over her ears. Or she'll get even louder and more upset. Last week it was so bad that I canceled my plans with Carlos and sent him and the baby-sitter home. Usually I go out, but then I feel so guilty that I don't enjoy myself. I know that Claudia is having a hard time with the divorce, but I end up *furious* with her for being so controlling. That kid is a little dictator."

What is going wrong here? Can you identify Alicia's problem?

Reasoning with Kids?

Reasoning with kids sounds like a good thing for any enlightened parent to do. In practice, however, it usually boils down to trying to convince them to see things our way. Alicia communicates to Claudia that Claudia's anger and distress are "wrong," excessive, or uncalled-for. Alicia not only wants to date Carlos; she also wants her daughter to *want* her to date Carlos. She not only wants her daughter to cut out the rude behavior (which is certainly a reasonable request); she also wants Claudia to *like* Carlos and to think that he is a nice man. It makes perfect sense that Alicia wishes that this were the case. But it is not possible to change our children's thoughts and feelings. More importantly, it is not our job. Trying will only leave us feeling angry and frustrated. It will also hinder our child's efforts to carve out a clear and separate "I" within the family.

Why is Alicia having such a difficult time simply accepting her daughter's feelings of anger and sadness? Perhaps Alicia herself is anxious about going out, although she may not be aware of it. Perhaps she overfunctions or "rescues" when it comes to other people's feelings—especially those of her child. So many of us do this. As soon as our son or daughter expresses sadness, anger, hurt, or jealousy, our first reaction may be to rush in and "do something" to take it away or to make things better. The "something" may be to give advice, interpretations, or reassurance. We may try to change the subject or cheer the child up. We may try to convince our child that she or he doesn't, or shouldn't, feel that way.

Emotional overfunctioning reflects the fusion in family relationships. Family roles and rules are structured in a way that fosters overly distant fathering and overly intense mothering. If our child itches, we scratch. This togetherness force between mother and child may be so strong that many of us have difficulty achieving the degree of separateness that would allow us to listen to our children in an empathic, low-keyed way, inviting them to talk more and elaborate as they wish. When we learn to stay in our own skin and avoid assuming an overfunctioning or "fix-it" position, children— whether they are four or forty—demonstrate a remarkable capacity to manage their own feelings, find solutions to their problems, and ask for help when they want it.

What would you do in Alicia's place? Claudia calmed down considerably when Alicia was able to take the following three steps:

First, Alicia listened to Claudia's thoughts and feelings without trying to change them or take them away. She did not offer her daughter advice, reassurance, criticism, interpretation, or instruction. Instead, she made empathic, non-fix-it statements, such as: "It sounds like you are pretty angry that I'm going out tonight"; "You really don't like Carlos very much, do you?" Claudia felt reassured by her mother's calm, nonreactive listening, and she began to more openly express her anger, fears, and unhappiness about her parents' divorce. Alicia felt as though a burden had been lifted from her shoulders when she learned to listen to her daughter's problems without having to "do something."

Second, Alicia realized that it was her responsibility to make her own decisions about dating Carlos—or about anything else, for that matter—and that these decisions were not based on her daughter's emotionality. Alicia communicated that she respected her daughter's feelings and took them into account but that she would not make her decisions in reaction to her daughter's emotional outbursts. For example, Alicia would say, "I know you are having a hard time tonight, but Carlos and I are still going to the movies and then out to dinner. I will be home at about eleven-thirty, after you are asleep." And when Claudia said tearfully, "I hate him," Alicia simply replied, "I understand that." Claudia, like all children, was ultimately reassured to know that she could express the full range of her thoughts and feelings but that her mother was separate and mature enough to take responsibility for making her own independent, thought-through decisions, for herself and for Claudia as well. In the old pattern, Alicia would give in to Claudia and then angrily blame her for being manipulative ("That kid always gets her way!").

Third, Alicia took responsibility for setting clear rules about behavior and enforcing them. For example, throwing a tantrum was unacceptable behavior. If Claudia did this, Alicia would pick her up and take her to her room, where she would have to stay until she calmed down. Alicia also clarified that it was not acceptable for Claudia to continue to ignore Carlos whenever he spoke to her. "You do not have to talk to Carlos if you don't want to," Alicia said to her daughter. "But if he asks you a question, *tell* him if you don't want to talk about it instead of just ignoring him." For several weeks Claudia proceeded to say "I don't want to talk about it" every time Carlos initiated a conversation. Alicia decided that she could live with this behavior. Alicia also observed that the more she pursued her daughter to relate to Carlos, and the more Carlos attempted to move closer to Claudia, the more Claudia distanced. She and Carlos were both able to back off a bit and provide Claudia with the space she wanted. When Claudia no longer felt pressured to like Carlos or to feel close to him, she felt more comfortable and relaxed in his presence and in time she began to warm up to him.

With children, as with adults, change comes about when we stop trying to shape up the other person and begin to observe patterns and find new options for our own behavior. As we sharpen our observational skills, some patterns may be easy to identify ("I notice that the more I ask Claudia to discuss her feelings about the divorce, the more she closes up. But when I leave her alone and calmly share some of my own reactions to the divorce, she will sometimes begin to talk about herself.") Other patterns that involve *three* key people are more difficult to observe, as we shall see in the next chapter.

8

THINKING IN THREES

Stepping Out of Family Triangles

Recently I visited my parents in Phoenix. I made this particular trip because my father—who prides himself on having made it to age seventy-five without even a sniffle—suddenly had a heart attack. It was a wonderful visit, but after I returned, I found myself feeling intense surges of anger toward my children. During the next few days, Matthew began waking up with headaches, Ben became increasingly rambunctious, and the boys fought constantly with each other. My two children became the prime target for my free-floating anger.

As I talked my situation over with my friend Kay Kent, a sensitive expert on families, I began to make the connection between my anger toward my children and my visit home to my parents. The good time that I had had with my parents was a reminder, not only of the geographical distance between us, but also of how much I would miss them when they were no longer around. On this particular visit, I could no longer deny their age. My father was tired, considerably slowed down, and easily out of breath. My mother, a spirited survivor of two cancers and a recent surgery, seemed her usual self; however, I was all too aware of her mortality.

Kay suggested that I address this new awareness directly with my children and parents, and so I did. At the dinner table the following night, I apologized to my whole family for being such a grouch and grump and I explained to Matt and Ben that I was really feeling sad following my Phoenix trip because Grandma and Grandpa were getting old and Grandpa's heart attack was a reminder to me that they would not be around forever and that one of them might die soon. "That," I explained, "is why I've been so angry." I also wrote a letter to my folks telling them how much I had enjoyed my visit and how, after my return home, I had come in touch with my concerns about their aging and my sadness about my eventual future without them.

What followed was quite dramatic: Both boys relaxed considerably and the fighting diminished. Each asked questions about death and dying and inquired for the first time about the specifics of their grandfather's heart attack and grandmother's cancer. I stopped feeling angry and things returned to normal.

The following week I received a letter from my father, who gave only a perfunctory reply to my self-disclosure by suggesting I not dwell on the morbid side of life. In the same envelope, however, he enclosed a separate lengthy letter to each of the boys explaining how the heart works and exactly what had happened in his own case. He concluded his letter to Matthew by directly addressing the subject of death. These letters, which were factual and warm, began the first correspondence between the two generations.

Underground issues from one relationship or context invariably fuel our fires in another. When we are aware of this process, we can pay our apologies to the misplaced target of our anger and get back on course: "I'm sorry I snapped at you, but I had a terrible day with my supervisor at work." "I'm scared about my health and I guess that's why I blew up at you." "I've been angry at everybody all day and then I remembered today is the anniversary of my brother's death." Sometimes, however, we are not aware that we are detouring strong feelings of anger from one person to another—or that underground anxiety from one situation is popping up as anger somewhere else.

It is not simply that we displace a *feeling* from one person to another; rather, *we reduce anxiety in one relationship by focusing on a third party, who we unconsciously pull into the situation to lower the emotional intensity in the original pair.* For example, if I had continued to direct my anger toward my misbehaving boys (who, in response, would have misbehaved more), I would have felt less directly anxious about the life-cycle issue with my aging parents. In all likelihood, I would not have identified and spoken to the real emotional issue at all.

This pattern is called a "triangle," and triangles can take many forms. On a transient basis triangles operate automatically and unconsciously in all human contexts including our family, our work setting, and our friendship networks. But triangles can also become rigidly entrenched, blocking the growth of the individuals in them and keeping us from identifying the actual sources of conflict in our relationships. The example below illustrates first a transient, benign triangle and then a problematic, entrenched one.

A Triangle on the Home Front

Judy is a real estate agent and Victor, her husband, is a salesman for the telephone company. On this particular day

Victor has a meeting after work and phones Judy to tell her that he will not be home until seven o'clock. Judy has been with the children all afternoon and finds herself tense and tired by the time the evening meal rolls around. She cooks dinner for the children, who, sensing her mood, act out more than usual, which only puts a greater strain on her. She cleans up, and watches the clock for Victor to come home. At seven-thirty Victor walks through the front door.

"I'm sorry I'm late," he says. "There was an accident on the road and I got stuck."

It is an entirely reasonable excuse, but Judy is furious. Not, however—as she experiences it—because of her *own* needs. She is not able to acknowledge that.

"I'm really upset!" she says, with intense anger in her voice. "Johnny and Mary [the children] have been waiting all day for you to come home. Now it's almost their bedtime. And I'm especially worried about Johnny. You've hardly been with him this week. He has been missing you terribly. He is a son without a father!"

What is happening here? The question of Victor's parenting may be a worthwhile subject for discussion, but it is not to the point. At this moment Judy is using the children as a deflection from an important issue between her and Victor. Victor, too, may have his own motives for colluding with this deflection.

Perhaps Judy feels that she has no right to be angry about Victor's late return. After all, the meeting was an important part of his job and the traffic jam was not his doing. Her belief that her anger is not rational, legitimate, or mature may prevent her from being able to articulate it, even to herself. Or it may be that the issue is a loaded one. Victor's lateness may touch on Judy's long-buried anger regarding the extent to which Victor is pulling his weight in the marriage.

If Judy and Victor have a flexible relationship, free from unmanageable levels of anxiety, the triangle will be temporary and of little consequence. When Judy cools off a bit, she will be able to share her feelings with Victor, including what a hard day she had and how angry and frustrated she felt when he did not return at five to offer her company and relief. But what if Judy does not feel safe speaking to Victor in her own voice? What if this couple is rigidly guarded against identifying the underground conflicts in their marriage?

Over time, a triangle consisting of Judy, Victor, and one of the children may become rigidly entrenched. Judy may find herself constantly blowing up at one of the kids instead of at Victor or she may intensify her relationship with Mary or Johnny in a manner that will help keep things calm on the marital front. This can happen in any number of ways: Mother and Johnny may form an overly close relationship that will compensate for a distant marriage and help keep father in an outside position in the family. Mother may complain to her daughter about her husband, rather than confining these issues to the marriage, where they belong. Or one of the children may become a major focus for concern, perhaps through the development of an emotional or behavior problem, thus drawing Judy's attention away from her own dissatisfaction in the marriage and perhaps enabling Victor and Judy to experience a pseudo-closeness as parents attempting to care for their troubled child.

The third leg of the triangle need not be a child. It could be Judy's mother, an in-law, or a person with whom Judy or Victor is having an affair. Triangles take on an endless variety of forms; but in each case, the intensity between Judy and a third party will be fueled by unaddressed issues in her marriage, and marital issues will become increasingly difficult to work on as the triangle becomes more entrenched. Of course, Judy's anger at her husband may be gaining steam from unaddressed issues with others, such as her own mother or father.

People of both sexes and all ages participate in multiple, interlocking triangles that may span several generations. But, as we have seen, women often have a greater, exaggerated fear about rocking the boat in an important relationship with a man. Thus, we are likely to avoid a direct confrontation and instead detour our anger through a relationship with a less powerful person, such as a child or another woman. How might such a triangle operate at work?

A Triangle on the Job

Melissa was a bright young woman who was appointed Director of Nursing in a small private hospital run almost exclusively by men. As it turned out, she was occupying a token position that afforded her little real authority. Month after month, Melissa sat in meetings where her contributions were ignored and where she felt increasingly powerless to influence institutional policy affecting the nursing discipline.

Melissa's sense of gratitude for being among the "chosen few," her dread of her own anger at male authorities, and her unconscious fear that greater personal clarity might lead to a confrontation that would lose her the approval of those in power—all combined to keep her from feeling angry and addressing issues directly where they belonged. Melissa's customary style was to behave deferentially to high-status males and to protect men in authority from the criticisms of other women. Perhaps this style played some part in her landing the director's position to begin with.

Melissa began to deal with her underground anxiety and anger in a triangular fashion. First she began to supervise her nursing staff very closely, moving in quickly at the slightest hint of a problem. Over time she became increasingly reactive to one particular nurse, Suzanne, who became the third leg of the triangle. Suzanne was an outspoken, highly competent young woman who was not particularly mindful of rules and paperwork deadlines and who easily voiced the anger at male leadership that Melissa could not. Melissa overreacted to any careless error that Suzanne made or paperwork deadline that she failed to meet, and began to treat her as a "special problem" who needed to be watched. For example, Melissa wrote long memos to another of Suzanne's supervisors about Suzanne's late paperwork rather than express her concerns directly to Suzanne. As Suzanne's anxiety skyrocketed, she unwittingly escalated things further by running around and trying to form allies among her fellow nurses to join her in criticizing Melissa. Tensions between the two women continued to mount. Suzanne's late paperwork became a more serious problem and six months down the road Melissa fired her, with the seal of approval from her male superiors.

Melissa and Suzanne were involved in a triangle that began at the highest levels of the organization. The relationship between Melissa and her male superiors could stay calm and nonconflictual because the underground anger was played out lower down the hierarchy, in this case at Suzanne's expense. Melissa made no moves to empower the nursing staff within the organization, and this remained the unspoken and unacknowledged hot issue between her and the male authorities.

Was Melissa, then, the *cause* of the problem? Did it start with her? Of course not. If Melissa had been in an institution where women were truly empowered and where she, as a female, was not a numerically scarce commodity at the top, her behavior would have been quite different. In fact, research indicates that women who hold positions of authority in male-dominated settings are not able to clearly define their own selves or successfully identify issues common to women until the relative numbers of men and women become more balanced. No one person was to blame for the scapegoating of Suzanne, nor was she a helpless victim of circumstances who had no participation in her fate.

In the best of all possible worlds, we might envision separate, person-to-person relationships with our friends, co-workers, and family members that were *not* excessively influenced by other relationships. For example, our relation-ship with our mother and that with our father would not be largely defined by the fact that they were battling something out together. We would stay out of conflicts between other parties and keep other people from getting in the middle of our own fights. If we were angry at Sue, we would go to Sue about it and not complain to Sally about Sue. We would not detour anger and intensity from one relationship to another. That's the ideal. However, we achieve it only more or less. Triangles are present in all human systems. When anxiety mounts between two people or conflicts begin to surface, a third party will automatically and unconsciously be drawn in. All of us participate in numerous interlocking triangles we are not even aware of. Many of these are not particularly problematic, but one or more may well be. How do we get out of something that we may not even realize we're in?

Understanding triangles requires that we keep an eye on two things: First, what unresolved and unaddressed issues with an important other (not infrequently someone from an earlier generation) are getting played out in our current relationships? Intense anger at someone close to us can signal that we are carrying around strong, unacknowledged emotions from another important relationship. Second, what is our part in maintaining triangular patterns that keep us stuck? To find out, we must begin the complex task of observing our three-person patterns. Let's consider a key triangle in a family that was plagued by anger and anxiety on all fronts.

A MULTIGENERATIONAL TRIANGLE IN ACTION: THE KESLER FAMILY

"I'm here because I'm very worried about my son Billy," explained Ms. Kesler, who had called the Menninger Foundation to request help with her oldest son and to get some relief from her own feelings of chronic anger and stress. "He's always been a pretty good kid, but since third grade this year, he's been having school problems. Billy and his father are at each other's throats about it and their relationship is deteriorating. I've done everything I can to change the situation between Billy and his dad and to help Billy be more responsible at school. Nothing helps. I'm feeling angry at Billy and I'm also angry at my husband, John, who is taking a punitive approach with the boy. I tried to get John to come with me today, but he's not interested. He thinks that therapist are quacks and that this is a lot of bunk."

In the first few minutes of our first appointment, Ms. Kesler's view of the problem became clear. The "problem" in the family was Billy and Billy's father. If we could ask Mr. Kesler, he might see the "problem" as Billy and Billy's mother. It is expectable, predictable, and quite normal for family members to define a problem in this way. When we feel angry, we tend to see *people* rather than *patterns* as the problem.

Below is a diagram of the Keslers' nuclear family. Squares stand for males and circles for females. The horizontal line connecting a square and a circle indicates a marriage. Children are drawn on vertical lines coming down from the marriage line, in chronological order, beginning with the oldest on the left. We can see that eight-year-old Billy is the first-born child, who has a six-year-old brother, Joe, and a four-year-old sister, Ann.

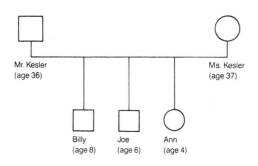

Who Does What . . . in Response to Whom . . . and Then What?

What is the interactional pattern in the Kesler family that gets set in motion around Billy's school problem? All of us—

individuals and families—react to stress in predictable patterned ways. If Ms. Kesler is to use her anger as a guide for
changing her position in the family, her first task is to learn
to observe the current "stuck" patterns. When I questioned
Ms. Kesler about specific details, she described a sequence of
events that had occurred the previous evening:

Billy watched television after dinner instead of doing
some math problems that he had agreed to finish at this
time. Father noticed first and sternly reprimanded Billy for
behaving "irresponsibly" and "failing to meet his agreement."
Billy hedged ("I'll do it after this program is over") and his
father became angrier. Mother, who was doing the dishes
and listening from the next room, yelled from the kitchen,
"John, there is no need to be so hard on the boy. The
program will be over in fifteen minutes." Father yelled back,
"You stay out of this! If you didn't spoil Billy to begin with,
the situation in school would never have gotten this far!"
Mother and father continued to argue while Billy retreated
to his room and lay down on the bed. Father then distanced
from mother, who pursued him unsuccessfully and then
withdrew herself.

Before Ms. Kesler spoke up, the triangle consisted of
two calm sides and one conflictual side between father and
son:

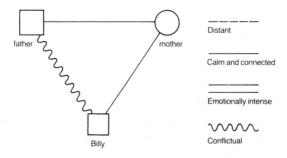

When Ms. Kesler entered the interaction in a rescuing position toward Billy, she became the focus of Mr. Kesler's criticisms and the triangle shifted:

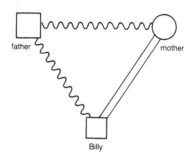

SCENARIO 1

This triangle would not necessarily be problematic if the pattern was transient and flexible. Let us suppose, for example, that the following events occurred later that evening: After Billy went to sleep, Mr. and Ms. Kesler talked together about their different perspectives on Billy's problem. They recognized that they had different opinions about the meanings of their son's behavior but were nonetheless able to reach a consensus on how to handle Billy that they both could support. Mr. Kesler then shared with his wife that he was upset about an incident at work and perhaps that was part of the reason why he had reacted so strongly to Billy. Ms. Kesler speculated that perhaps she was especially sensitive to his criticizing Billy because her own dad was always fighting with her older brother (also a first-born son, like Billy) and this had been very stressful for her. Mr. and Ms. Kesler would leave the subject of Billy behind as they moved on to talk about other issues in their personal or work lives or in their relationship together.

SCENARIO 2

But such flexibility did not characterize the Kesler family. Instead, Ms. Kesler was describing a repetitive pattern that was moving in increasingly rapid and intense cycles. When this family was under stress, the following occurred:

Father was stuck in a *blaming* position toward Billy. He became intense at the first sign of misbehavior or irresponsibility on the part of his son. ("You're going to get into deep trouble if you don't shape up!")

Mother was stuck in a *rescuing* position toward Billy and a *blaming* position toward father. ("John, that boy needs a little love and understanding from you, not an iron hand!") Sometimes she would adopt the role of the *mediating,* or *fix-it,* person. She would offer both her husband and her son advice on how they might better handle each other and themselves.

Billy was stuck in the *underfunctioning* position in the family. He had already acquired the label "problem child" at home and in school and he was the overriding focus of parental worry and concern.

Last but not least, Mr. and Ms. Kesler were stuck in repetitive cycles of fighting over how to parent, in which Mr. Kesler stood for "law and order" and Ms. Kesler for "love and understanding." The emotional intensity of these fights deflected and obscured other important issues in their marriage and their personal lives.

WHAT NOW, MS. KESLER?

During the following weeks, Ms. Kesler learned to observe her own anger as well as the family's pattern of interaction around Billy's problematic behavior. Now she could more clearly identify her characteristic style of handling stress. She saw that she assumed a rescuing position toward Billy, a blaming position toward her husband, and occasionally a peacemaking or mediating position between Billy and his father.

Ms. Kesler also noted that her participation in the old pattern was not effective: Whenever she tried to come to Billy's defense, her husband perceived her as siding with Billy and turned his criticisms against her. Ms. Kesler was now ready to think about her options for moving differently.

Getting Out of the Middle

When we continue unsuccessful efforts to intervene in another relationship, we are part of a triangle. *The most difficult job that Ms. Kesler had before her was to let her husband and son fend for themselves and manage their own relationship without her.* Here's what she did:

First, she went to her husband and apologized to him for interfering in his relationship with Billy. She admitted that she might have made things worse by thinking that she had any answers or advice for either of them about their relationship. She empathized with her husband's worry about Billy and praised his involvement as a father and his efforts to help his son grow up to be a responsible person. She expressed confidence that he and Billy could work out whatever problems they had.

To her son, she said, "Billy, I realize that I've been getting exhausted by rushing in and playing the role of the American Red Cross when you and your dad argue. You're a smart kid and you know what gets your dad's goat. I am sure that you and your dad will be able to work things out together, and from now on you're on your own."

Next, Ms. Kesler did her best to *stay calm* and *stay out* when the countermoves came rolling in. Predictably, the other family members made some attempt to up the ante and reinstate the old triangle. Father took off his belt to Billy, whereas previously he had gone after his son only with harsh words. Billy ran to his mother, tearfully complaining about his father's cruelty. Even Billy's younger siblings got into the act. ("Mom, Dad's going after Billy again!") A typical "test" from Billy would go something like this:

> BILLY: "Daddy says I can't go to the baseball game tomorrow night, and I'm the catcher! Can't you make him change his mind?"
>
> MOTHER: "That's between you and Dad, Billy. Talk to him about it if it's bothering you."
>
> BILLY (*crying*): "But he doesn't listen!"
>
> MOTHER: "Well, Billy, this is between you and Dad to work out. You're both smart people. Try to work it out the best you can."
>
> BILLY: "Daddy isn't fair! *You* wouldn't make me miss the game!"
>
> MOTHER: "Daddy and I may set different rules sometimes. This is Daddy's rule, and whether you go to the game or don't go to the game is up to Dad. This is between you and Dad."

Although Billy tried to draw his mother back in the middle, he was enormously reassured by her new position. In a way, Billy was unconsciously testing out whether he truly had his mother's "permission" to have a separate relationship with his dad, or whether his mother needed him to be loyal to her, with the two of them subtly in alliance against a father labeled "unfair" or "incompetent." Through her new behavior, Ms. Kesler was letting Billy know that she did not need to keep up the old triangle, in which father would be on the outside. Billy could work things out with his dad without having to worry so much about his mom.

Maintaining her new position was anything but easy. "I get terribly tense when John and Billy go at it," Ms. Kesler explained to me. "When I hear John go on and on, I start feeling upset and ready to blow. Sometimes I go to the bathroom just to get away or leave the house to take a walk." Ms. Kesler was able to take this distance when she needed it, without criticizing her husband. In a calm, nonblaming manner she explained to him, "When you and Billy start getting riled up, I sometimes react by getting uncomfortable and upset. I'm not sure what my reaction is about, but when I start to feel this way, I may leave the room or take a walk because that helps." She made it clear to her husband that she took responsibility for her own feelings and reactions and she was not blaming him for "causing" her discomfort. Throughout the process, Ms. Kesler conveyed confidence that her husband and son could take care of their own relationship without her help.

But what if Ms. Kesler believes that her husband might physically abuse their son? Obviously, she will need to take a firm position against violence and protect Billy as best she can, even if this means calling the police. However, violence will be least likely to occur if she can do this without reinstating the old triangle, because *triangles greatly increase the probability of escalating aggression.* For example, she might say to her husband (ideally, at a relatively calm moment): "I need to tell you that I have a real fear that things between you and Billy will heat up to the point where he gets injured. I know that I can't solve anything between the two of you, but I can't live with violence. If that happens, I will do whatever is necessary to separate the two of you." To Billy, she might say pretty much the same thing: "I know that in the long run you and your dad have to work out your own problems. But, as I told Dad yesterday, I will step in if I get worried that things are getting so heated up that someone might get hurt." Taking a responsible position with each party need *not* mean falling back into the old pattern.

What happened in the Kesler family as a consequence of Ms. Kesler's getting out of the triangle? Mr. Kesler became less reactive to Billy's problems and provocations. He moved in less quickly and intensely. Billy, in turn, began to take more responsibility for his own behavior and his school problems all but disappeared. The relationship between father and son was greatly improved. Does this sound like the Kesler family lived happily ever after?

Not exactly. First mother and Billy started to have open conflict in *their* relationship. Further, marital issues concerning closeness and distance surfaced between husband and wife. Mr. Kesler became depressed and called me for an appointment despite his disapproval of psychotherapy.

Why did this happen? Triangles serve to keep anxiety-arousing issues underground, and that is why we all participate in them. When a triangle is disrupted and we begin to have a person-to-person relationship with each family member, without a third party interfering, hidden issues surface. This is emotionally difficult, but it also provides us with an opportunity to stop focusing on others and look more closely at our selves.

LOOKING BACKWARD: OUR FIRST FAMILY

When things settled down with Billy, the next step for Mr. and Ms. Kesler was to turn attention to their families of origin and begin to gather some data about the past. When a child or spouse is underfunctioning and has become the primary focus of our anger, worry, or concern, it is helpful to take a look at the larger family picture.

A broad approach to the problem will help to shed light on a number of questions: Why was Billy targeted to become a "problem child" in this family, rather than his younger brother or sister? Why did family interactions suddenly heat up when Billy entered third grade? Why was Mr. Kesler so reactive to the issue of "responsibility" in his son? Why was Ms. Kesler so reactive to her husband and son's fighting? Why did Mr. Kesler become depressed after he and Billy resolved their former conflicts? Most important, what work can Mr. and Ms. Kesler do to best ensure that no one family member will seriously underfunction or become the "problem," as Billy did?

Let's take a look at an expanded family diagram of the Kesler family and gather a few more facts. If you are feeling ambitious, you may want to draw a diagram of your own family, including, if you can, at least three generations. The diagram of the Kesler family, on the following page, is incomplete, in order to keep it uncluttered and to highlight certain key points. A complete family diagram would include the dates of births, deaths, serious illnesses, marriages, and divorces and the highest level of formal education for every member of the extended family, for as far back as we can go. An X in a circle or square indicates that the person is dead. Two diagonal lines across a marriage line indicate a divorce.

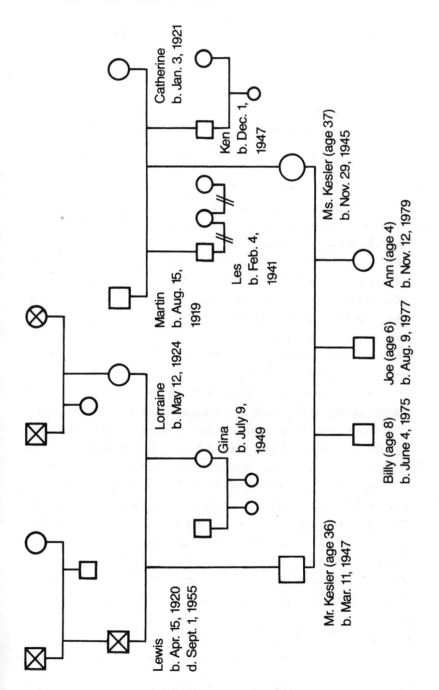

What does this family diagram tell us? Looking at father's side of the family, we see that he has a younger sister, Gina, who is married and has two daughters. If we do some simple arithmetic, we learn that Mr. Kesler's father, Lewis, was a first-born son who died at age thirty-five, when Mr. Kesler was eight years old. Mr. Kesler's mother, Lorraine, is the younger sister of a sister and did not remarry following her husband's death.

Looking at mother's family of origin, we see that she is a middle child. Her older brother, Les, is twice-divorced and her younger brother, Ken, is married and has one daughter. I learned from Ms. Kesler that Les is the "black sheep" in the family. In her words, "Les is an alcoholic who can always be counted on to screw up in business and marriage." Ms. Kesler's parents, Martin and Catherine, alternate between distancing emotionally from Les and bailing him out financially. Ms. Kesler is cut off from her brother and sees him only every few years at family gatherings.

Let us first examine father's side of the family diagram, with an eye toward linking the patterns of the past with those of the present.

Mourning a Father

When I gathered the above data during my initial appointment with Ms. Kesler, I understood why the relationship between Billy and his father had become intense and conflictual when Billy turned eight and entered third grade: Billy is now the age that Mr. Kesler was when he lost his father. In addition, Mr. Kesler is thirty-six years old, just past the age that his father was when he died. It is predictable that Mr. Kesler would have an "anniversary reaction" at this time and experience a reactivation of buried emotions that surrounded the loss of his dad.

Mr. Kesler did not directly mourn his dad or consciously experience the associated feelings of anger, anxiety, and loss as this anniversary date arrived. Instead, as is typical, he focused his emotional energy on a third party—his son—and became very reactive to any sign of trouble in Billy. *It is the intensity of our reactions toward another person's problem that ensures not only the escalation but also the continuation of the problem itself.* Billy's lack of cooperativeness increased in direct proportion to father's emotional reactivity (and mother's reactivity to father), setting a circular dance in motion.

Why did Mr. Kesler handle his anxiety by becoming focused on a child? This is a common way for mothers to manage emotional intensity and stress—as our social education actually fosters this child focus—but men are not immune from this triangle. Other triangular patterns might also have arisen. Mr. Kesler, for example, might have had an affair or left his wife at the time of this anniversary reaction. He might have distanced from her by becoming increasingly work-focused, which is a typical male pattern of managing anxiety. He himself might have underfunctioned and developed a new physical or emotional problem. He might have constantly found fault with his wife, leaving his children free from his emotional focus. We all handle stress in one or more of the above ways and, ideally, in more than one way. If the *only* way a family handles stress is to focus on a "problem child," the outcome will be a severely troubled child. If the *only* way a family handles stress is through marital fighting, the outcome will be a severely troubled marriage.

Why Billy?

Father and Billy share the same sibling position as first-born males. Father is thus more likely to identify with Billy than with his other children, to confuse Billy with himself, and to have more intense reactions to the strengths and weaknesses he perceives in his first-born son. Predictably, this might be the most problematic or intense relationship for Mr. Kesler, and the intensity would increase at a time of high stress. The fact that Mr. Kesler's own father was also a first-born further magnifies the emotional charge of Mr. Kesler's relationship with Billy. Birth order is an enormously important factor in determining how our parents perceive and label us and how we do likewise with our own children.

"Be Responsible, Son!"

Nothing pushed Mr. Kesler's buttons more than seeing Billy behave in a way that was not competent and responsible. Why?

The family diagram alone provides some good clues. At age eight Mr. Kesler lost his father and was left with his mother, Lorraine, who was the younger sister of a sister. What is known about the typical characteristics of a younger sister of a sister? As parents, often they are not comfortable taking charge, assuming a position of authority, and taking the initiative to do what has to be done. As a first-born child (and *son*), Mr. Kesler might have exercised *his* typical characteristics of "responsibility" and "leadership" at a very early age, perhaps trying to fill his father's shoes and help his widowed mother out.

When I met with Mr. Kesler, my speculations were confirmed. He had been a "little man" at an early age, and his own need to be a kid who could goof up and let others care for him was buried under a lifetime of overfunctioning and worrying about other family members. He was quick to react to the first sign of irresponsibility in Billy because Mr.

Kesler was *so* responsible as a child that he never really had much of a childhood. As he was later able to say to me, "I think I get so hot under the collar when I see Billy goofing off to have fun, because I'm a little jealous. After my father died, I stopped being a kid and became a worrier, long before I was really ready. My problem is that I feel *too* responsible for things."

"I Have a Problem"

Sometime later, during a week when Mr. Kesler found himself particularly reactive and angry in response to his son's casual attitude toward school, he took Billy on his lap and told him the following:

"Billy, this week I've been getting very upset and grouchy when I see you goofing up at school. I sure have been getting on your case. I think I figured out what my problem is. You know, Billy, when I was eight years old, my dad died and I was left without a dad. I felt angry and sad and frightened. And now that you are eight years old, like I was at that time, a lot of those old feelings are coming back. And sometimes the way that I deal with those feelings is to get on your back and fight with you so that I don't have to feel so sad about my own dad."

Billy looked at him wide-eyed. Then he said, "That's not fair! It doesn't make sense."

Mr. Kesler replied, "You're right, Billy, sometimes dads do things that don't make too much sense. I sure owe you an apology. It's my job to work on these old feelings I have about my dad dying. It's your job to decide what sort of student you're going to be in school. I'm going to do my best to try to work on *my* job and try to stay out of *your* job. I won't be successful all the time, but I'll be working on it."

"Does this mean that I can play with my friends and not have to do my homework?" asked Billy, with some mixture of anxiety and glee.

"Not a chance!" said Mr. Kesler, giving Billy a playful punch on the arm. "You know what the rules are, kid, and it's up to you to follow them. But you're going to have to decide what sort of student you'll be in school and I can't decide that for you, even though I may try sometimes." Billy said nothing, but several weeks later he began to ask all kinds of questions about Grandfather Lewis.

Taking the emotional focus off Billy did not mean adopting a "do-whatever-you-please-and-I-don't-care" attitude. Mr. Kesler's own style was to set pretty strict rules about the consequences of misbehavior. The degree of strictness or permissiveness will vary from family to family and is not, of itself, a problem. What is important is that Mr. Kesler enforced his rules without getting emotionally intense and blaming, and he made it clear to Billy that he (father) was dealing with his own issues and problems. It is also crucial that each parent support, rather than undermine, the rule-setting of the other, even if they don't always see eye to eye.

Most of us would not think of sharing something personal about our struggles with our children, as Mr. Kesler did—or as I did following my visit to my parents in Phoenix. Yet, there is hardly a more effective way to break a circular pattern. We maximize the opportunity for growth for all family members when we stop focusing our primary worry energy and anger energy on the underfunctioning individual and begin to share a bit about our own problem with the situation. This involves a shift from "You have a problem" to "I have a problem." In time—after working on the task of mourning his dad and modifying his overfunctioning position with his mother and sister—Mr. Kesler was able to do more of this.

What about Ms. Kesler? As we look at her side of the family diagram, what predictions might we make about her relationship with Billy?

A "Black-Sheep" Brother

Billy is in the same sibling position as Les—Ms. Kesler's "black-sheep" brother, who has made countless "bad moves" with jobs and women. In this key family triangle, Les is in the outside, underfunctioning role. Both his parents are in a blaming position toward him, while his sister, Ms. Kesler, takes a distancing position from him and a "fix-it" role with her parents. At times of low stress, she gossips with other family members about Les and his problems, and at times of high stress, she advises her parents on how to handle him and then gets angry when they ignore her advice.

While the emotional cutoff between Ms. Kesler and her brother keeps the anxiety down in *that* relationship, it is re-energized in her relationship with her son Billy, partly because he is in the same sibling position as Les and also because he happens to possess some actual physical and personality characteristics that remind mother of her big brother. Often, the underground intensity from a cutoff is not re-energized until an anniversary date comes up—for example, when Billy turns twelve, which is the age at which Les began getting into trouble, or twenty-three, Les's age when Ms. Kesler cut off from him. In the Kesler family, the intensity between mother and Billy began to surface when Ms. Kesler got out of the middle of the relationship between her husband and son and things calmed down on that front.

To some extent, we are all prone to confuse our children

with ourselves and with other family members. We project onto our children who we are and what we unconsciously wish, fear, and need. This process of projection gains steam from our unfinished business with siblings and parents. If mother makes no changes in her own family of origin, her projections onto current family members may be especially intense. She may, for example, encourage Billy to be a star in the family—an especially good child who will show none of the black-sheep qualities that she sees in her brother or fears in herself. Or, she may anxiously worry that Billy will turn out to be an irresponsible and troubled child like Les and unwittingly encourage this behavior by the intensity of her watchful focus on it. Billy may sense that his mother needs him to be a certain way for her own sake, and proceed to accommodate to or rebel against her needs. In either case, both Ms. Kesler and Billy become less able to directly manage the challenge of their own personal growth.

Like her husband, Ms. Kesler had "homework" to do with her family of origin.

Over time, Ms. Kesler gathered more data about her mother's and father's families, which provided her with a more sympathetic and objective understanding of why Les (rather than she) was more likely to underfunction and live out the black-sheep role. She learned to observe the patterns and triangles in her family of origin, as she had in her current nuclear family, and she took steps to get out of the middle of the relationship between Les and her parents. She did this by maintaining one-to-one emotional contact with all parties, without advising, taking sides, or talking with her parents about Les's problems. To do this required her to initiate closer contact with her brother, and she began to gradually share with him more about her life, including her own underfunctioning side. Eventually, she became much less focused on and reactive to the behavior of her husband and son, and she no longer felt dominated by anger and worry in these important relationships.

What Mr. and Ms. Kesler both learned is that children have a remarkable capacity to handle their problems when we begin to take care of our own. The work they each did with their own families was like money in the bank for Billy and his two siblings, because children are the carriers of whatever has been left unresolved from the generations that went before. Talking about the fact that Mr. Kesler lost his father and Ms. Kesler was cut off from her older brother may seem a bit removed from the subject of women and anger. *Yet all of us are vulnerable to intense, nonproductive angry reactions in our current relationships if we do not deal openly and directly with emotional issues from our first family—in particular, losses and cutoffs.* If we do not observe and understand how our triangles operate, our anger can keep us stuck in the past, rather than serving as an incentive and guide to form more productive relationship patterns for the future.

Let's take a look at a simpler family triangle in order to review the major points we have learned about observing and changing three-person relationship patterns.

WHY CAN'T HE MARRY A NICE JEWISH GIRL?

Sarah's son, Jerry, turned thirty-four the very day that Sarah showed up at my office. "My son, Jerry, is dating a non-Jewish woman for over three years," Sarah explained. "This girl—Julie is her name—is not even good for him and she has terrible problems herself. My husband and I know that he will be unhappy if he marries her, but my son won't listen to reason." Sarah told me that she was very *worried* about Jerry, but even a casual observer could see that she was also very *angry*. In fact, an atmosphere of chronic anger and tension permeated their relationship.

Jerry, I learned, was the younger of two brothers and still living at home. Although he graduated with honors from college, he had since been shifting from job to job, and his lack of direction was a source of family concern. Jerry, then, was in an underfunctioning position in the family.

Sarah's story is more than familiar to us by now. She is engaging in increasingly intense efforts to change her son despite the fact that such efforts only help keep the old pattern going.

What is the pattern? According to Sarah's description of her interactions, she blames and then distances under stress. Sometimes she blames Julie ("She just doesn't consider other people very much, does she?") and sometimes she blames Jerry ("I think you are rebelling against your family rather than making a mature choice"). When Jerry comes to Julie's defense or to his own, Sarah fights and then distances. While this is going on, Jerry's father distances from both his wife and his son, and then later unites with his wife in their shared concern over Jerry.

Sarah describes herself as occupying the outside position in the key triangle between herself, Jerry, and Julie.

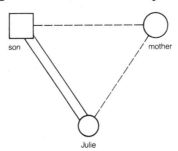

When Sarah criticizes Julie to her son, she implicitly invites him to side with her against his girlfriend. Should Jerry go along with this, he and his mother would have a closer relationship at Julie's expense and Julie would temporarily occupy the outside position in the triangle.

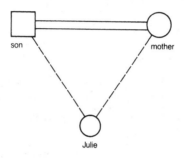

What more typically happens, however, is that Jerry comes to Julie's defense, which Sarah experiences as siding against her. At this point, conflict is likely to break out between mother and son.

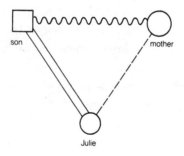

Why Shouldn't Sarah Let Her Son Know That She Does Not Approve of His Dating a Non-Jewish Woman? She should. Sarah ought to feel free to share her thoughts and feelings about important issues like this one with Jerry. She might, for example, let her son know what her problem is with the situation. Instead, she criticizes, advises, and blames. Now, nothing would be wrong with this if Sarah were satisfied with the situation. But she's not. As Sarah describes it, her interactions with Jerry frequently end in conflict and/or distance. The pattern has been going on for a long time, and Sarah is feeling angry and dissatisfied.

What Might the Payoffs Be for This Family in Maintaining the Status Quo? The old pattern will keep Sarah and her son stuck together in a close way (albeit negative closeness)—just like Maggie and her mother (Chapter 4), who fought about the baby in order to avoid negotiating their ultimate separateness and independence. The triangle between mother, son, and girlfriend here serves to reduce anxiety in the family by keeping other important issues between family members underground. It also protects Jerry and Julie from squarely identifying issues and conflicts in their own relationship.

What Can Sarah Do to Get Out of the Triangle? The three essential ingredients of extricating oneself from a triangle are: staying calm, staying out, and hanging in.

Staying calm means that Sarah can underreact and take a low-keyed approach when stress hits. Anxiety and intensity are the driving force behind triangles.

Staying out means that Sarah leaves Jerry and Julie on their own to manage their relationship. Therefore, no advising, no helping, no criticizing, no blaming, no fixing, no lecturing, no analyzing, and no taking sides in their problems.

Hanging in means that Sarah maintains emotional closeness with her son and makes some emotional contact with

Julie, as well. Sarah may temporarily seek distance when things get hot; but when "staying out" means cutting off, patterns tend not to change.

New Steps to an Old Dance

When Sarah was ready to get out of the old triangle, the following dialogue ensued:

"You know, Jerry, I owe you an apology for giving you such a hard time about Julie. What a terrible time I've had thinking about my son marrying a woman who's not Jewish—and it still is not easy for me. Sometimes I react with a lot of anger and hurt, and I guess you've been the target for that. But I'm beginning to realize that my feelings are my own responsibility and that it's not your job to ensure your mother's happiness. *Your* job is to find the very best relationship that you can for yourself—and only you can decide if that's going to be with Julie. Certainly, I'm in no position to make that decision for you or even to know what's best. I haven't even given Julie half a chance!"

Jerry stared at his mother as if she had just come down from another planet.

"Even though I've been on your back," Sarah continued, "I know that you're perfectly capable of making the best choice for yourself without my help. You know, I was just remembering something the other day. Before I met your dad, I was dating someone my parents didn't approve of. I never really stood up to them even though I was grown up and earning my own money. Do you know what I did? I would sneak out of the house and see him in secret! Later, when my parents disapproved so strongly of your father, we ran off and eloped!"

Sarah let out a big laugh and Jerry closed his mouth, which had been hanging open. He looked at his mother with curiosity. *This was the first time that his mother had shared something about her own experience as it related to their angry struggle.*

"Did *you* ever date a man who wasn't Jewish?" he asked, not knowing what to expect next.

"You know, I simply never considered it. I really don't think that it would have been possible for me. It just wasn't an option." Sarah became thoughtful and then continued: "But that was me, at another time. You and I are two different people."

Sarah felt wonderful after this talk, but that night as she got into bed, she was mildly depressed. She felt irritated with her husband, Paul, and provoked a fight with him, which eased her tension a bit about the change she was making with her son. What Sarah felt is simply the discomfort that occurs as we begin to move differently in an old pattern and navigate a more separate and mature relationship with another family member. As we have seen, pressures to reinstate the old pattern come from both within and without.

Two weeks later, Sarah encountered some tough tests of her resolve to move differently. Jerry dropped hints that he and Julie were talking about getting married. Sarah was able to stay calm and underreact. She did not hide the fact that she had always hoped for a Jewish daughter-in-law; however, her attitude conveyed respect for Jerry's judgment and recognition that choosing a wife was his job and not hers.

Jerry then began a new series of countermoves, as he started to criticize Julie to his mother. "Do you know, Mother, Julie's father had a birthday today and I couldn't even get Julie to call him or stop by." With increasing frequency and ingenuity, Jerry invited his mother to join him in criticizing Julie. Sarah bit her tongue so as not to bite the bait. Instead

she said, "Well, you know Julie much better than I do. If
that bothers you, perhaps you can talk with her about it and
let her know your feelings." Or, "Whatever the problem is,
I'm sure the two of you can work it out." Sarah herself
was initiating more contact with Julie and was discovering
things about her she genuinely liked and respected.

*Had Sarah joined with her son in criticizing Julie, she
would have reinstated the old triangle.* The only difference
would be that Julie, not Sarah, would occupy the outside
position. People would change their positions in the triangle,
but the triangle itself would remain unchanged. Anxiety
would be reduced, but at the expense of each participant's
ability to identify and negotiate issues with other parties.

If triangles keep underlying issues in each two-person
relationship from surfacing, what happens when a triangle
breaks up? Here is a brief look at some of the changes that
had occurred in this family eight months later as a result of
Sarah's extricating herself from a key triangle:

Jerry and Julie

Jerry and Julie were aware of some significant difficulties in
their relationship and Jerry was expressing genuine uncertainty about whether Julie was the woman he wanted to
marry. His critical feelings about Julie and his *own* ambivalence about marrying outside his religion had previously
been held in check by the old pattern in which mother
criticized Julie and he was free to come to her defense.

It was predictable that when Sarah got out of the middle
of this relationship and gave Jerry her blessings to do the
very best for himself, the real issues between Jerry and Julie
would surface. If their relationship had been on firmer
ground, it might well have been strengthened at this point.
Apparently this was not the case.

Sarah and Jerry

The relationship between Sarah and her son became calmer and more open as Sarah became genuinely less reactive to her son's relationship with Julie. With the intense focus off this third party, the important issue of negotiating separateness and independence surfaced between her and Jerry. During one of our sessions together, Sarah said to me for the first time, "Julie or no Julie, I'm beginning to think that Jerry is having a hard time leaving home. What is a grown man doing still living with his parents? I find myself wondering if there's some connection between *his* problem leaving home and *my* problem letting him go. You know, I was never really very independent from my own mother. When she protested my marriage to Paul, we ran off and eloped and I didn't write to her for several months. I didn't have the courage to say to her, 'I love you, Mom, but I love Paul, too, and it's my life.' I just cut off from her and didn't face the issue."

Sarah and Paul

Paul was a quiet, withdrawn man who was not very comfortable with closeness. The mother-son-girlfriend triangle served him well because it basically left him out of this intense family dynamic and kept him and his wife focused on *parental* rather than *marital* issues. When Sarah stopped focusing her major "worry energy" on her son, she and Paul came face to face with the distance and dissatisfaction that each of them experienced in their marriage, and they were forced to pay closer attention to their own relationship. As a consequence, Sarah and Paul informed Jerry that he was to move out because they were getting older and wanted to enjoy some time and space for themselves. Jerry did find his own apartment, but he still attempted to hang on harder to test out whether his parents really meant business. When Jerry learned that they had no plans to take him back in and that they were managing just fine without him, he began to put his energy into coming to grips with his own pattern of multiple failures at work and in relationships.

Focusing on a "problem child" can work like magic to deflect awareness away from a potentially troubled marriage or a difficult emotional issue we may have with a parent or grandparent. Children have a radarlike sensitivity to the quality of their parents' lives and they may unconsciously try to help the family out through their own underfunctioning behavior. The "difficult child" is often doing his or her very best to solve a problem for the family and keep anxiety-arousing issues from coming out in the open.

Sarah and Sarah

Sarah's focus on Jerry and Julie also protected her from thinking about her own life goals. When she removed herself from the old triangle, she was suddenly confronted by some serious questions: What were her current priorities? What goals did she want to pursue at this point in her life? Sarah came face to face with her own self. How easy it is to avoid this challenge of self-confrontation by keeping our emotional energy narrowly focused on men and children, just as society encourages us to do.

If you are directing your primary emotional energy toward an underfunctioning family member, have you ever wondered where all that worry energy or anger energy would go if that individual was off the map? When Sarah stopped busying herself with her son's life, she began to worry about her own. Jerry, in turn, began to worry about his.

9

TASKS FOR THE DARING
AND COURAGEOUS

Jog, meditate, ventilate, bite your tongue, silently count to ten . . .

There is no shortage of advice about what you can do with anger in the short run. Some experts will tell you to get it out of your system as quickly as possible and others offer different advice. In the long run, however, it is not what you do or don't do with your anger at a particular moment that counts. The important issue is whether, over time, you can use your anger as an incentive to achieve greater self-clarity and discover new ways to navigate old relationships. *We have seen how getting angry gets us nowhere if we unwittingly perpetuate the old patterns from which our anger springs.*

If you are serious about making a change in a relationship, you may want to read this book more than once. The important how-to-do-it lessons are contained in each woman's story. It is up to you to connect these with your own life. The patterns I have described are universal among women and you have undoubtedly recognized yourself many times. Nonetheless, you may initially feel discouraged when you try to move differently in *your* relationships. When you are *in* the dance, it is especially difficult to observe the broader pattern and change your own part. In this chapter I will suggest a few tasks to help you review some of what you have learned, add to your understanding of triangles and circular dances, and test out your ability to move differently in relationships. You may want to get together with a friend or form a group with other women who have read this book and who share your new vocabulary and insights.

PRACTICING OBSERVATION

Begin to observe your characteristic style of managing anger. Do you turn anger into tears, hurt, and self-doubt, as Karen did with her boss? Do you alternate between silent submission and nonproductive blaming, as Maggie did with her mother? We all have predictable patterned ways of managing anger and conflict, though they may vary in different relationships. For example, when conflict is about to surface, you may *fight* with your mother, *distance* from your father, *underfunction* with your boss, and *pursue* your boyfriend.

Give some thought to your usual style of negotiating relationships when anxiety and stress are high. My own pattern goes something like this: When stress mounts, I tend to *underfunction* with my family of origin (I forget birthdays, become incompetent, and end up with a headache, diarrhea, a cold, or all of the above); I *overfunction* at work (I have advice for everyone and I am convinced that my way is best); I *distance* from my husband (both emotionally and physically); and I assume an angry, *blaming* position with my kids.

If you are having difficulty labeling your own style, use the following as a guide:

PURSUERS

- react to anxiety by seeking greater togetherness in a relationship.

- place a high value on talking things out and expressing feelings, and believe others should do the same.

- feel rejected and take it personally when someone close to them wants more time and space alone or away from the relationship.

- tend to pursue harder and then coldly withdraw when an important person seeks distance.

- may negatively label themselves as "too dependent" or "too demanding" in a relationship.

- tend to criticize their partner as someone who can't handle feelings or tolerate closeness.

DISTANCERS

- seek emotional distance or physical space when stress is high.

- consider themselves to be self-reliant and private persons—more "do-it-yourselfers" than help-seekers.

- have difficulty showing their needy, vulnerable, and dependent sides.

- receive such labels as "emotionally unavailable," "withholding," "unable to deal with feelings" from significant others.

- manage anxiety in personal relationships by intensifying work-related projects.

- may cut off a relationship entirely when things get intense, rather than hanging in and working it out.

- open up most freely when they are not pushed or pursued.

UNDERFUNCTIONERS

- tend to have several areas where they just can't get organized.
- become less competent under stress, thus inviting others to take over.
- tend to develop physical or emotional symptoms when stress is high in either the family or the work situation.
- may become the focus of family gossip, worry, or concern.
- earn such labels as the "patient," the "fragile one," the "sick one," the "problem," the "irresponsible one."
- have difficulty showing their strong, competent side to intimate others.

OVERFUNCTIONERS

- know what's best not only for themselves but for others as well.
- move in quickly to advise, rescue, and take over when stress hits.
- have difficulty staying out and allowing others to struggle with their own problems.
- avoid worrying about their own personal goals and problems by focusing on others.
- have difficulty sharing their own vulnerable, under-functioning side, especially with those people who are viewed as having problems.
- may be labeled the person who is "always reliable" or "always together."

BLAMERS

- respond to anxiety with emotional intensity and fighting.
- have a short fuse.

- expend high levels of energy trying to change someone who does not want to change.
- engage in repetitive cycles of fighting that relieve tension but perpetuate the old pattern.
- hold another person responsible for one's own feelings and actions.
- see others as the sole obstacle to making changes.

As we have seen, women are trained to be pursuers and underfunctioners with men except in the areas of housework, child work, and feeling work, where we may overfunction with a vengeance. Men characteristically distance under relationship stress and are excused, if not rewarded, for this style. Both sexes blame, but women may do it more conspicuously than men, and for very good reasons indeed. These reasons include our deep-seated anger about our culturally prescribed de-selfed and one-down position, combined with the taboos against recognizing and directly protesting our subordinate status, as well as our fear and guilt about the potential loss of a relationship. Barbara's blaming, underfunctioning position with her husband, who refused to "allow" her to attend the anger workshop (Chapter 2), was the first of many examples illustrating how blaming both protests and protects the status quo and how it differs from effectively taking a stand.

In thinking about your own patterns of response, remember that none of the above categories are good or bad, right or wrong. They are simply *different* ways of managing anxiety. You will have a problem, however, if you are in an *extreme* position in any one of these categories or if you are unable to observe and change your pattern when it is keeping you *angry* and *stuck*.

Begin to observe other people's characteristic style of managing anger and negotiating relationships under stress. How does their style interact with your own? For example, if you are an overfunctioner who lives or works in close quarters with another overfunctioner, you may admire each other's competence when anxiety is low. When anxiety is high, however, there may be some head-banging and locking of horns regarding the question of who's in charge, who's in control, and who has the right answers. ("Why did you go ahead and make a decision without consulting me!") The most likely candidates for this pattern might be two first-borns, especially if each has a same-sex younger sibling. If you are an underfunctioner in a love or work relationship with another underfunctioner, each party may be angrily accusing the other of not assuming enough responsibility or simply not doing enough. Perhaps the bills aren't getting paid or no one wants to get out of bed when the baby cries. When overfunctioners and underfunctioners—or distancers and pursuers—pair up, we have seen the kind of escalating pattern that gets set in motion under stress.

Get as much practice as you can observing the interactional sequences in which your anger is embedded. That is, when things get hot, step back a bit in order to keep track of who does what, when . . . and then what. Observing is a skill that is definitely worth developing before you attempt to perform a daring and courageous act!

CHOOSING A COURAGEOUS ACT

Make a plan to do something different with your anger in a relationship—something that is *not* in keeping with your usual pattern. Using the earlier chapters as a guide, *choose one small, specific task that you can calmly carry out and maintain when the countermoves begin and your own anxiety mounts.* Anticipate the other person's reaction and what you will do then. Even if you don't hold your ground, moving differently in a relationship is the best way to learn about your own self and the relationship. *Only after you begin to change a relationship can you really see it.* Here are some examples:

BREAKING OUT OF A CIRCULAR DANCE

If you are *pursuing* a distancer in a romantic relationship or marriage, carefully reread Chapter 3, which describes how Sandra broke out of the pursuit cycle with Larry. If you are *overfunctioning* for a child, reread Chapter 8, focusing on the changes that Mr. and Ms. Kesler made in their relationships with their children. If you are in an *underfunctioning* position with your partner, go back to Stephanie's relationship with Jane (Chapter 7) or Barbara's dilemma with her husband (Chapter 2). Decide in advance on a length of time (for example, three weeks) that you will hold to a new position and see what happens.

DEFINING A SELF

Think of one or two ways in which you can more clearly define who you are with family members, without criticizing or trying to change them and without becoming defensive when anxiety mounts. For some of us, sharing our competence and strength is a move toward defining a whole, more balanced self. For others, a more courageous move may be to let others know that we have been depressed lately and that we are struggling with work or with a relationship. Stating a clear difference of opinion and standing behind it in a relationship where we have been the accommodating partner is another significant move toward defining a self. The more we work on this task, the clearer our thinking about our anger and how best to make it work for us.

MOVING AGAINST CUTOFFS

If you have been emotionally cut off from a family member, it can be an act of courage simply to send a birthday card or holiday greeting. Keep in mind that people—like other growing things—do not hold up well in the long run when severed from their roots. If you are emotionally disconnected from family members, you will be more intense and reactive in other relationships. An emotional cutoff with an important family member generates an underground anxiety that can pop up as anger somewhere else. Be brave and stay in touch.

MOVING SLOWLY AND THINKING SMALL

If you are feeling angry, think very carefully about what new position you want to take before doing anything. By its very nature anger propels us into quick action, so guard against this. You will only fall on your face if you attempt to take a new position that you are not yet ready to take or that you have only casually thought through.

Alice was furious with an ex-roommate who had moved to Denver a year ago but was still storing her belongings in Alice's basement. There was plenty of storage space, but for personal reasons Alice wanted the belongings out and was becoming increasingly angry with the excuses coming from

Denver. ("I can't afford to do it right now." "The weather is too cold for me to move my stuff.") Alice had a long history of overfunctioning for her ex-roommate and rescuing her from stressful situations, so this scenario was nothing new.

After attending an anger workshop that I conducted, Alice enthusiastically rushed home and wrote the following letter to her ex-roommate:

> Dear Leslie,
>
> I am having a terrible problem with your belongings in my basement. It may be selfish or irrational of me, but for whatever reason, I just can't live with it any longer. If you do not get your stuff out within three weeks, I am giving everything to the Salvation Army.
>
> Regretfully,
> Alice

Leslie did not get her stuff out and Alice gave it to the Salvation Army. Leslie acted furious and despairing, and Alice, in response, became guilty, remorseful, and depressed. It is not that Alice did the *wrong* thing. The problem was that she too quickly defined and acted on a position that was not comfortable for *her.* Katy's struggle to set new limits with her elderly father (Chapter 6) illustrates that it often takes time and effort to define a position that is congruent with our beliefs and values—a position that we can stick to without suffering undue anxiety and guilt when the countermoves start rolling in.

Remember that women have a long legacy of assuming responsibility for other people's feelings and for caring for others at the expense of the self. Some of us may care for others by picking up their dirty socks or doing their "feeling work"; some by being less strong, self-directed, and competent than we can be so as to avoid threatening those important to us. Changing our legacy is possible but not easy. Think small to begin with, but *think*.

PREPARING FOR RESISTANCE

As you attempt to shift a pattern, prepare yourself not only for intense reactions from others but also for the *inner* resistance that you will meet. Elizabeth was a twenty-nine-year-old lawyer who had been chronically angry with her parents, who she felt kept her in a childlike role by refusing to be guests in her home. Whenever they visited her apartment, they would insist on taking her to dinner at a restaurant—and picking up the check, as well. When Elizabeth *herself* was ready for a change, she found a way to let her parents know that it was important to her to be a hostess to them on her own turf. She cooked them an elegant gourmet dinner that was an undeniable statement of her competence and adulthood, and to her surprise, both her mother and father praised her profusely.

The next morning Elizabeth woke up depressed and with a headache. She was beginning to mourn the loss of the old stuck-together bond with her parents that protected her from that funny feeling of separateness and aloneness that accompanies our moving from a fused to a more mature relationship. That same week her father fell on the golf course and ended up with his leg in a cast. You can't be *too* prepared for the power of countermoves, as well as your own resistance to change. If *you* are planning to initiate a more adult, person-to-person relationship with a family member, read the chapter about Maggie and her mother (Chapter 4) several times.

As you think about this book or discuss it with a friend, you will come up with your own ideas for a bold and courageous act. If anxiety about change is very high in your family or other intimate relationships, you may want to begin working on a relationship that is more flexible and less intense for you, perhaps with a co-worker, neighbor, or friend. Wherever you begin and whatever task you choose for yourself, here is a review of some basic do's and don'ts to keep in mind when you are feeling angry:

1. *Do speak up when an issue is important to you.* Obviously, we do not have to address personally every injustice and irritation that comes along. To simply let something go can be an act of maturity. But it is a mistake to stay silent if the cost is to feel bitter, resentful, or unhappy. We de-self ourselves when we fail to take a stand on issues that matter to us.

2. *Don't strike while the iron is hot.* A good fight will clear the air in some relationships, but if your goal is to change an entrenched pattern, the worst time to speak up may be when you are feeling angry or intense. If your fires start rising in the middle of a conversation, you can always say, "I need a little time to sort my thoughts out. Let's set up another time to talk about it more." Seeking *temporary* distance is not the same as a cold withdrawal or an emotional cutoff.

3. *Do take time out to think about the problem and to clarify your position.* Before you speak out, ask yourself the following questions: "What is it about the situation that makes me angry?" "What is the real issue here?" "Where do I stand?" "What do I want to accomplish?" "Who is responsible for what?" "What, specifically, do I want to change?" "What

are the things I will and will not do?"

4. *Don't use "below-the-belt" tactics.* These include: blaming, interpreting, diagnosing, labeling, analyzing, preaching, moralizing, ordering, warning, interrogating, ridiculing, and lecturing. Don't put the other person down.

5. *Do speak in "I" language.* Learn to say, "I think . . ." "I feel . . ." "I fear . . ." "I want . . ." A true "I" statement says something about the self without criticizing or blaming the other person and without holding the other person responsible for our feelings or reactions. Watch out for disguised "you" statements or pseudo-"I" statements. ("*I* think *you* are controlling and self-centered.")

6. *Don't make vague requests.* ("I want you to be more sensitive to my needs.") Let the other person know specifically what you want. ("The best way that you can help me now is simply to listen. I really don't want advice at this time.") Don't expect people to anticipate your needs or do things that you have not requested. Even those who love you can't read your mind.

7. *Do try to appreciate the fact that people are different.* We move away from fused relationships when we recognize that there are as many ways of seeing the world as there are people in it. If you're fighting about who has the "truth," you may be missing the point. Different perspectives and ways of reacting do not necessarily mean that one person is "right" and the other "wrong."

8. *Don't participate in intellectual arguments that go nowhere.* Don't spin your wheels trying to convince others of the "rightness" of your position. If the other person is not hearing you, simply say, "Well, it may sound crazy to you, but this is how I feel." Or, "I understand that you disagree, but I guess we see it differently."

9. _Do recognize that each person is responsible for his or her own behavior._ Don't blame your dad's new wife because she "won't let him" be close to you. If you are angry about the distance between you and your dad, it is _your_ responsibility to find a new way to approach the situation. Your dad's behavior is _his_ responsibility, not his wife's.

10. _Don't tell another person what she or he thinks or feels or "should" think or feel._ If another person gets angry in reaction to a change you make, don't criticize their feelings or tell them they have no right to be angry. Better to say, "I understand that you're angry, and if I were in your shoes, perhaps I'd be angry, too. But I've thought it over and this is my decision." Remember that one person's right to be angry does not mean that the other person is to blame.

11. _Do try to avoid speaking through a third party._ If you are angry with your brother's behavior, don't say, "I think my daughter felt terrible when you didn't find the time to come to her school play." Instead, try, "I was upset when you didn't come. You're important to me and I really wanted you to be there."

12. _Don't expect change to come about from hit-and-run confrontations._ Change occurs slowly in close relationships. If you make even a small change, you will be tested many times to see if you "really mean it." Don't get discouraged if you fall on your face several times as you try to put theory into practice. You may find that you start out fine but then blow it when things heat up. Getting derailed is just part of the process, so be patient with yourself. You will have many opportunities to get back on track . . . and try again.

Of course, most important of all is our ability to take responsibility for our own part in maintaining the very patterns that evoke our anger. Triangles are the most complex relationship patterns to get a handle on, so let's move on to review this subject.

NO MORE GOSSIPING

If you are angry at Sue, is she the first or the last person to know about it? If you are irritated by your father's behavior, do you deal with him directly or do you go tell your mother? Do you pick up your phone to call your daughter if you are angry with your ex-husband or your son? If you are angry that your co-worker is not doing her job, do you tell her directly or do you talk to her supervisor behind her back in order to express your "concern" about her work?

When two people gossip, they are having a relationship *at the expense of a third party*. That's a variation of the triangle. Because triangles lower anxiety, they are not necessarily problematic when they are transient and flexible. When a triangle becomes *rigidly entrenched* in a family, friendship, or work situation such that it interferes with healthy person-to-person relationships, then the connecting legs must be broken.

Triangles at Work

Suppose, for example, that you are angry at Sue at the office because she takes extra-long coffee breaks, and as a result, additional work falls into your lap. You try to talk to Sue about it, but her first response is to get angry and defensive. You then stop Sally in the hallway and invite Sally to agree with you that Sue is selfish and unfair. If Sally listens sympathetically, your anxiety diminishes. Perhaps this helps you to calm down and think more clearly about how to go back to Sue and manage your relationship with her. This would be an example of a transient triangle with no particular cost to anybody.

On the other hand, suppose that you and Sally continue to talk about Sue behind her back. This *deflects* you from dealing directly with Sue to work out the problem. You will feel closer to Sally because of Sue's outside position, and in this way you *detour* your anger rather than deal with it. If the triangle continues to persist over time, any one of the following is likely to occur:

- Sally's relationship with Sue will be influenced by the unresolved issues between you and Sue. For example, Sally may become more distant from Sue or more reactive to her. If Sally begins to like Sue, she (Sally) may feel disloyal to you.

- Sue's anxiety will rise and she may begin to under-function more at work. The more that two people talk about an underfunctioning individual (rather than each working directly on that relationship), the more that party will have to work even harder to gain competence.

- You will have increasing difficulty calmly and clearly negotiating your differences with Sue and maximizing the chances that the two of you will have the most comfortable work relationship possible.

Can't it be helpful to talk with Sally if you're angry with Sue? If your intention is to get Sally's perspective on your problem, and if Sally is able to provide it without taking sides, diagnosing, or criticizing either one of you, then a triangle will be avoided. More typically, however, we may begin with the virtuous intentions of clarifying the problem and trying to understand why someone is performing poorly, only to have our efforts turn into mutual criticizing sessions and the start of an entrenched triangle. It never helps anybody's performance to talk *about* them rather than *to* them. The more other people get involved in a conflict between you and another person, the less likely you'll be to resolve it with minimal anxiety and maximum clarity.

Here are a few do's and don'ts to help you avoid setting up triangles at work. The following advice holds for a friendship or a family situation as well:

1. *If you are angry with someone, that's the person you should tell.* Even if Sue is resistant, rebellious, or rude, she is still the person to deal with. And dealing with her doesn't necessarily mean venting your anger at her. It means making use of everything that you have learned in this book—not with a third party but directly with Sue.

2. *If you want to go up the hierarchy with your anger, make sure to go through the appropriate channels and be open about it.* For example, suppose that Karen (Chapter 5) asked her boss to change her job rating from "Very Satisfactory" to "Superior" and he refused. If Karen wants a third party to review her evaluation, she can find out what the acceptable procedure is and tell her boss that she plans to go over his head and why. If you are open about bringing in another party and you make sure to use the appropriate hierarchy, you may avoid forming a triangle that will escalate anger and stress in the long run.

3. *When you are angry, speak in your own voice.* Whether you are addressing a subordinate or a superior, don't bring in an anonymous third party by saying, "Other people think you're difficult to work with," or, "There have

been some complaints about your attitude." Nameless, faceless criticism increases anxiety and is neither fair nor helpful. If you have an issue with someone, use the word "I." ("I think . . ." "I feel . . ." "I want . . ." "I am concerned . . .") Let other people speak for themselves.

4. *Avoid secrets.* If you believe that it is your job to let someone (Esther) know that she is being criticized or gossiped about—"Esther, I want you to know that Tom is telling people that you are alienating customers"—understand that Esther may want to go directly to the gossiping party to clarify the problem. If you plan to swear someone to secrecy— "Esther, please don't mention anything to Tom or he'll know I said something to you"—better to say nothing at all.

5. *Don't become the third party in someone else's triangle.* If someone complains to you, you can listen sympathetically, but without blaming or taking sides. Often this doesn't occur to us, but with practice it's not hard to do. Remember that the best reason to avoid quickly becoming someone's emotional ally is that others have the best chance of working out their own anger and negotiating their differences if you stay calm, stay out, and stay emotionally connected.

This concerned but neutral position is, in the long run, the most supportive one to take, for it helps facilitate creative problem solving in others. Suppose, for example, that *you* are supervising Esther, and Tom is complaining to you that she is rude to her customers. You can first encourage Tom to deal with her directly. If Tom says, "But I told her twice and she doesn't listen," you might tease him a bit and encourage him to grab Esther by the collar and try a third time. Or when you see Esther, you might say lightly, "Hey, I think Tom has a gripe about you. Why don't you meet with him and straighten it out." If you can maintain a low-keyed, nonreactive, noncritical position and express confidence that both parties can work out their difficulties, chances are that Esther and Tom will do surprisingly well.

Triangles Begin at Home

You have just finished cleaning up your kitchen when the phone rings. It is your mother calling and she sounds quite worked up. "Let me tell you what your brother, Joe, is doing now! He's drinking again and he is about to lose another job. I wonder if he'll ever grow up and find himself." Or, "I'm so upset that your father will not pay any of your sister's college tuition. He's always been cheap, and since he married Debbie, the situation is even worse."

What do you do?

POSITION 1

You join your mother in her anger and criticalness. Or perhaps you listen sympathetically and then spend the next ten minutes talking with her about Joe's emotional problems or your father's penny-pinching.

POSITION 2

You come to the other person's defense: "Well, Mother, if you didn't keep bailing Joe out, he wouldn't be in such a mess." Or, "I really don't think you appreciate Dad's financial situation right now."

POSITION 3

You give advice, doing your best to stay neutral. You may attempt to explain the behavior of each party to the other or try to help your mother be more "objective" or "reasonable."

POSITION 4

You clutch inside and feel very angry at your mother for putting you in this position. You silently decide that you will avoid her as much as possible because she is so difficult to deal with. Perhaps you make plans to move to Alaska.

Can you find yourself in one or more of the above responses? Let's look at each position more carefully:

Position 1. Here, you have a closer relationship with your mother at the expense of either your dad or your brother, who is in the outside position in the triangle. You are allied with your mother in a blaming position toward another family member.

Position 2. Here, your mother will feel like the outsider in the triangle and she may redirect her anger toward you for not supporting her or not seeing the "truth" about your father or your brother. You are in a blaming position toward your mother and a rescuing position toward the other party.

Position 3. Here, you try to help both parties and be a therapist in your own family, which is not possible. Your mother will either ignore your advice or tell you why it won't work. You are in a "fix-it" or "peacemaking" position in the triangle.

Position 4. Here, you try to lower your stress level by avoiding your mother, resolving nothing in the long run and ensuring that the underground anger and intensity will emerge elsewhere. You are in a blaming and distancing position toward your mother in the triangle.

None of the above positions is inherently troublesome if

it is flexible and temporary. As the Kesler family illustrates, however, positions in a family triangle can become rigid and fixed. As *daughters,* we are frequently participating in a triangle with our mother and one other family member— our father (if our parents are legally but not emotionally divorced, this triangle may be especially intense), our mother's mother, or a sibling. As long as we take part in this triangle, our relationship with our mother is heavily influenced by *her* relationship with the other party. And our relationship with the other party is heavily influenced by that person's relationship with our mother. In fact, every relationship on all three sides of the triangle is influenced by issues from another relationship. When triangles heat up, a lot of anger and stress may fly around, but salient issues do not get clarified or resolved. Remember also, a triangle is not something that another person *does* to you. Triangles require the participation of all three parties, and any one party can get out of a triangle—that is, if you can tolerate the anxiety involved in the process.

If you can do some work on an important triangle in your first family, it will not only help you with your anger; it will influence every relationship that you are in. Do you want to give it a try? The first step, as always, is observation!

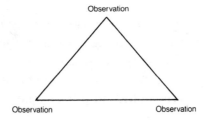

Observation

Observation   Observation

Sharpening Your Observational Skills

As you learn to observe your own position in a family triangle, you may want to diagram it. For example, when your mother calls and says, "Let me tell you what your brother, Joe, is doing now," you might participate in a triangle involving you, your mother, and your brother.

When things are calm in the family, you and your mother discuss Joe's problems (Position A). The relationship between your mother and Joe remains calm and distant because your mother is lowering her anxiety by talking with you, rather than dealing directly with her son. The relationship between you and your mother stays calm and close as you focus attention on your brother's problems instead of identifying and addressing issues in the relationship between the two of you. Here, the triangle looks like this:

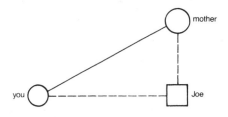

When stress increases, open conflict may break out between your mother and brother. You may then take a mediating position in the triangle, trying to be helpful to each party (Position C). You may say to your brother, "Mother really loves you." To your mother you may advise, "I think what Joe needs from you is a firm hand. It's not that he's bad; he's just testing the limits." Your relationship with both your mother and your brother intensifies, while the conflictual side of the triangle is between your mother and brother. Here, the triangle looks like this:

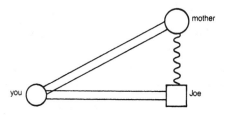

If tension escalates further, the triangle may shift again. Your mother may get angry at you for not seeing the "truth" about your brother, Joe may get angry at you for not taking his side against mother, and you may get angry at one or both of them for the way they are behaving with you or each other. All three of you are in a blaming position and there is conflict on all sides of the triangle:

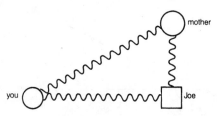

Can you now begin to identify your own position in a key family triangle? "Joe" may be your father, your grand-mother, your cousin, or your aunt. If you're saying, "This doesn't apply to *my* family," keep thinking about it.

How would you respond to your mother's telephone call if your task was to move out of the triangle rather than participate in it? Close this book and get clear on what you would say, before reading further. If you feel stuck and unclear, reread Chapter 8.

Detriangulating Moves

When your mother calls to talk about Joe (or he talks about her), you can casually show disinterest. Remember that triangles are driven by emotionality and anxiety (our own included), so that the more low-keyed you can be, the better. You might say, "Well, I'm not sure what Joe is up to. Beats me what it's all about. I just don't know what to say. To change the subject, Mother, what are you up to lately?" When one party pressures you to give advice or take sides, you can do neither, and instead express your confidence in both parties: "Well, I don't have the slightest idea about what's going on, but I love you both a lot and I trust that the two of you can work it out." If your mother's focus on your brother remains persistent and intense, you might address the issue more directly in a nonblaming way. "You know, Mother, I feel kind of selfish about our time together and I'd like to use it talking about us and what's happening in our lives without bringing my brother in. I know you're struggling with him, but I don't have the slightest idea how to be helpful, and it takes time away from you and me. When I'm with you, I like to talk about you, and when I'm with him, I like to talk about him. Right now I'm much more interested in hearing about ..." In extremely rigid triangles, even greater directness may be required: "Mom, I just can't listen to you talk about Joe [Dad, etc.] anymore. I love you both and I need to work on my own relationship with each of you. I've no way to be helpful, and for some reason I just start feeling tense when you talk about him."

The exact words you choose are far less important than your ability to maintain a warm, nonjudgmental, nonreactive position. That is, you can calmly communicate that your relationship to both parties is important to you and that you have nothing to offer in the way of help, advice, blame, or criticism as far as their struggle with each other is concerned. Keep in mind that changing a pattern is never a one-shot deal but something we do over time—getting derailed when intensity mounts and then getting back on track again.

Do's and Don'ts

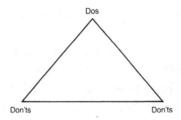

Dos

Don'ts   Don'ts

Here are some do's and don'ts to keep in mind if you are in the blaming position in a family triangle, as mother is in the above example. It's not only hard work to stay out of other people's conflicts, it requires just as much courage to keep other people out of our own. These suggestions can apply to any relationship network that you are in:

1. *If you are angry with one family member, put your emotional energy into dealing directly with that person.* If your reaction is, "But I've tried everything and nothing works," reread this book and think about new ways to move differently. If you feel stuck in an unsatisfying relationship and you want to talk about what is wrong with the other person, talk to someone outside the immediate family who does not have a relationship with the person at whom you are angry. It can be enormously helpful to share your struggle with a close female relative who may have been through a similar

experience, *if* you can steer clear of a blaming position as you learn more about how she handled her own problem.

2. *Avoid using a child (even a grown-up one) as a marital therapist or a confidant.* Don't try to protect your children by telling them what's wrong with their father even if you are convinced that it will help them to know the "truth." Children need to discover their own truths about family members by navigating their own relationships.

3. *Distinguish between privacy and secrecy.* Each generation needs its privacy. Siblings need privacy from parents, and parents need privacy of their own. Secrecy, however, is a cardinal sign of a triangle when it crosses the generations. ("Don't tell your father that you had an abortion, because it will upset him too much." "Don't tell your sister that Dad lost his job, because she'll tell the neighbors." "Dad, I'm living with Alex now, but you can't tell Mom about it.") We may have the loftiest motives ("So-and-so just couldn't handle the information"), but the bottom line is that we are asking one person to be closer to us at the expense of another. If you are at the listening end of the secret-keeping business, you can let people know that there are certain secrets that you're just not comfortable keeping.

4. *Keep the lines of communication open in the family without inviting others to blame or take sides in your battles.* It's fine to tell your mother or your kids, "Yes, Frank and I are really having a hard time in our marriage now. We have many differences and we are struggling to work them out." This is quite different from inviting a family member to be your ally or take your side. Do your best to block other family members from getting involved in your battles. If little Susie says, "Daddy is just terrible to divorce you," you can say, "Susie, I am feeling angry with your father now, but it's

my job to work on that, and not yours. Your job is to work on having the best relationship with me and with your dad that *you* can."

All of the above are different reminders that every family member needs to have his or her own person-to-person relationship with every other family member—that is separate from your anger and your relationship issues with a particular party. You may be enraged at your ex-husband or black-sheep sister, but try not to discourage other family members from having the best relationship with that person that they can. Not only will others be *more* sympathetic with your situation in the long run, but you will be less likely to get entrenched in a bitter position in which your anger only serves to hold the clock still.

LEARNING ABOUT YOUR FAMILY

Katy's story (Chapter 6) is one illustration of how useful it can be, not only to share our problems with other family members, but also to solicit from them information about how they dealt with similar issues.

If you didn't do so when you read about the Kesler family (Chapter 7), *put together your own family diagram.* You'll be surprised at how many things—birth order of aunts and uncles, marriage dates, causes and dates of grandparents' deaths—you don't know. You may also be surprised at the connections you can make if you study this diagram. For example, you may notice that the year that you and your brother were constantly at each other's throats was the same year that your grandmother's health began deteriorating. Perhaps the fighting between you and your brother reflected the chronically high level of anxiety in the family at that time. The more you can enlarge your focus to the broader multigenerational picture, the less likely you will be to blame or diagnose yourself or others.

Many of us *think* we know our family background. Certainly we all have stories we tell about our family to other people. Such stories may elicit their admiration ("Your mother sounds like an incredible person!") or their anger ("How horrible that your father treated you that way!") or their pity ("What a terrible childhood you've had!"). We may tell these stories over and over during our lifetime, constructing explanations for things that we seek to understand. ("My mother always put me down; that is why I have such a bad self-concept.") However, these stories, including the psychological interpretations that we learn to apply to ourselves and others, are not substitutes for knowing our family in the sense of asking questions of our parents, grandparents, and other relatives and inviting them to share their experience. Most of us *react* to other family members, but we do not *know* them.

Give it a try. Use the diagram of the Kesler family on page 172 as a model for your own. The typical amount of information on a family diagram includes the dates of births, deaths, marriages, divorces, and illnesses, as well as the highest level of formal education and occupation for all family members, going back as many generations as you can. This may sound like a boring and tedious job, but you may be amazed at what you will learn about your family and yourself if you go about the task, perhaps reconnecting with family members along the way to get the information. Don't write off your "crazy Aunt Pearl" or "black-sheep cousin Joe" as sources of information just because they are the family underfunctioners. *Every* family member has a unique and valuable perspective and may be surprisingly eager to share it, if approached with genuine interest and respect.

Is learning more about our family truly a daring and courageous act? Yes, it is. It is not easy to give up the fixed notions that we have about our family. Whether we rage against one family member or place another on a pedestal (two sides of the same coin), we don't want the "stuck-togetherness" of our family to be befuddled by the facts about *real people*. In addition, we may not want to openly ask questions about taboo subjects in our family, such as our aunt's suicide or our grandfather's alcoholism. The problem is that when we are low on facts, and when important issues stay underground, we are high on fantasy and emotionality—anger included. We are more vulnerable to having intense reactions to any of the inevitable stresses that life brings—and to get stuck in them.

Remember that we all contain within us—and act out with others—family patterns and unresolved issues that are passed down from many generations. The *less* we know about our family history, and the *less* we are in emotional contact with people on our family diagram, the *more* likely we are to repeat those patterns and behaviors that we most want to avoid. Remember the old adage "What you don't know won't hurt you?" Well, research on families just doesn't support that one! Rather, it is the very process of sharing our experiences with others in the family and learning about theirs that lowers anxiety and helps us to consolidate our identity in the long run, allowing us to proceed more calmly and clearly in *all* of our relationships. "But my parents won't talk!" Well, gathering family data is a skill that can be practiced and learned; how you do it determines what you get.

The Courageous Act of Questioning

Pick an emotionally loaded subject in your family. The "hot issue" may be sex, marriage, cancer, success, fat, alcohol, or Uncle Charley. If it is a "hot issue" with your mother, for example, chances are you feel angry and "clutch" inside whenever the subject comes up. Perhaps the subject rarely comes up these days because you have taken a strong "I-don't-want-to-talk-about-it" stance.

Your courageous act is to stop reacting with anger long enough to open up a real dialogue on the subject by *sharing something about yourself* and *asking questions of others*. Your task in questioning is to gain some perspective on what has occurred in the previous generations that has loaded a particular issue to make it "hot." Only by gathering the broader family picture can you replace your angry responses toward family members with empathic and thoughtful ones. Let us take a couple of specific examples:

Suppose that one hot issue is your single status; every time you go home, your mother gets around to taking a jab at your unmarried state. What is your task?

First, calmly share something about where you stand on the subject. For instance: "Mom, I can see that you are concerned about my not being married. To tell you the truth, there are times when I feel concerned about it, too. At this point, I don't know if I'm scared of commitment, if Mr. Right just hasn't come along yet, or if I don't *want* to get married. I'm not clear about it yet, but I'm working on sorting it out." If you are an underfunctioner, guard against presenting your problem as if you are just a bundle of weakness and vulnerability; if you are an overfunctioner, try not to make it appear as if you have it all together and don't need anything from anyone.

Second, open a dialogue with your mother about how the issue of female singleness versus marriage has been experienced in her family. *Block advice-giving and other "fix-it" moves by clarifying that you are not interested in solutions right now but in your mother's own perspective and experience instead.* You might then ask your mother any number of questions, such as:

> "I've been wondering, have *you* ever struggled with the question of whether marriage was right for you? And if so, how did you reach a conclusion?"
>
> "What worries do you have about me if I don't get married?"
>
> "If you yourself hadn't married, how do you think your life would have gone differently? What sort of work would you picture yourself doing?"
>
> "What was your mother's attitude about marriage and how would she have reacted if you had stayed single? How would your father have reacted?"
>
> "How did each of your parents react when Aunt Ruth didn't marry and worked on her career instead?"
>
> "Who in our extended family has not married, and how have they fared in your eyes?"

Questions like these will allow you to break the old communication pattern, reconnect with your mother in a more mature and separate way, detoxify the marriage issue by getting it out from under the table, and learn more about yourself and your family history. You may also learn about alternatives the family has found acceptable in the past, and prepare your mother for a greater range of outcomes in the future.

Now suppose that the "hot issue" for you in your family is your mother's ignoring your intellect and achievements and focusing on the successes of your brother. Again, your task would be to share some difficulty you're having in this area and then to ask your mother to help you out by sharing more about her own experience and perspective. What is most useful is to formulate questions that will allow you to get a picture of how the same emotionally loaded issue was played out a generation back with your mother and her family. For example, write your mother a letter explaining that it is difficult for you to work at succeeding and that the reactions of others are often *too* important to you. Then ask:

"How did *your* mother and father react to your talents and achievements?"

"Were you seen as smart in your family?"

"Which of your brothers and sisters were viewed as smart or not smart?"

"Did you ever think about going to college? What were your parents' attitudes about that?"

"If you had started a profession early in life, what career would have been your first choice?"

"Do you think you would have been successful at it? What might have stood in your way?"

"How was it decided that your brother was able to go to college and you weren't? What were your feelings about that?"

"What was it like for you to have so much responsibility in your family when you were growing up?"

"Did both your mother and father view themselves as smart and competent? Did they view each other that way?"

If you develop your skills in questioning, you will find that family members usually *do* want to share their experience if we first share something we are currently struggling with and assure them of our sincere interest in learning how they dealt with similar problems. *Parents and grandparents do not think to tell us their own experience. Instead, they tell us what they think we should hear or what they believe will be helpful to us.* Unless you are a good questioner, members of the previous generations are unlikely to tell you what it was really like for them.

A final postscript about fathers and mothers: If you take the initiative to move closer to your more distant parent (usually, but not always, your father)—by sharing more about yourself and asking more about him—you may find yourself feeling a bit disloyal to the other parent. For example, the distance that so often exists between us and our fathers may be the source of our angry complaints ("My father has no concern about me whatsoever"); yet we may actively (although unconsciously) go along with our father's "odd-man-out" position in a family triangle.

Be courageous! Defining a self rests on your ability to establish a person-to-person relationship with *each* family member that is not at the expense of another family member who is in an "outside" position. Also, keep in mind that if a parent reacts with increased distance to your initial efforts to be more in contact, this countermove is an expression of anxiety, not lack of love. Hang in, in a low-keyed way, and stay in touch. Remember, what is important in the long run is not the reactions you get from others but what *you* do—and how you define your own self and your personal ground in relationships.

EPILOGUE
Beyond Self-Help

"Defining a self" or "becoming one's own person" is a task that one ultimately does alone. No one else can or will do it for you, although others may try and we may invite them to do so. In the end, *I* define what I think, feel, and believe. *We* do not define what I think, feel, and believe. Yet, this lonely and challenging task cannot be accomplished in isolation. We can only accomplish it through our connectedness with others and the new learning about ourselves our relationships provide.

Self-help advice can be bad for our emotional well-being if it ends up conveying the message that major changes can be made easily or quickly—that, for example, if only you are motivated enough and follow this book carefully enough, you will achieve the happily-ever-after life. It is my hope that I have provided my readers with new perspectives on old angers; applying even one or two lessons from this book can make a significant difference in your life. But we both know that lasting change does not come about in a smooth, stepwise fashion and many of the women described in these chapters had the benefit of long-term psychotherapy to help them along.

Self-help advice can also be hazardous to our health if a "do-it-yourself" approach isolates us from other women. Throughout this book I have stressed the importance of learning about the experience of family members and sharing our own. Now I want to add that I believe it to be equally crucial for us to connect with the family of womankind, to share what it is really like for us, and to learn about the experience of others. It is through this process of reconnecting and sharing—of learning firsthand how we are similar to and different from other women—that allows us to go beyond the myths that are generated by the dominant group culture, transmitted through the family, and internalized by the self. Before the second wave of feminism, many of us suffered privately with our anger and dissatisfaction, maintaining a single-minded focus on the question "What's wrong with me?" Together with other women, however, we could stop blaming ourselves and begin to bring the old roles and rules into question.

Finally, self-help advice always runs the risk of fostering a narrow focus on our personal problems, to the exclusion of the social conditions that create and perpetuate them. This book has been about personal anger and personal change, but as feminism has taught us, "The personal is political." This means that there is a circular connection between the patterns of our intimate relationships and the degree to which women are represented, valued, and empowered in every aspect of society and culture. The patterns that keep us stuck in our close relationships derive their shape and form from the patterns of a stuck society. For this reason it is not sufficient for individual women to learn to move differently in personal relationships. If we do not also challenge and change the societal institutions that keep women in a subordinate and de-selfed position *outside* the home, what goes on *inside* the home will continue to be problematic for us all.

I believe that women today are nothing short of pioneers in the process of personal and social change. And pioneers we must be. For as we use our anger to create new, more functional relationship patterns, we may find that we have no models to follow. Whether the problem we face is a marital battle, or the escalating nuclear arms race, women and men both have a long legacy of blaming people rather than understanding patterns. Our challenge is to listen carefully to our own anger and use it in the service of change—while we hold tight to all that is valuable in our female heritage and tradition. If we can do this, we will surely make the best of pioneers.

NOTES

Chapter 1   **The Challenge of Anger**

1-2   Psychiatrist Teresa Bernardez was the first person to explore the powerful forces that prohibit female anger, rebellion, and protest, and to describe the psychological consequences of such prohibitions. See Teresa Bernardez-Bonesatti's "Women and Anger: Conflicts with Aggression in Contemporary Women," in the *Journal of the American Medical Women's Association* 33 (1978): 215-19. See also Harriet Lerner's "Taboos Against Female Anger," in *Menninger Perspective* 8 (1977): 4-11, which also appeared in *Cosmopolitan* (November 1979, pp. 331-33).

4   A well-known advocate of the let-it-all-hang-out theory is Theodore Isaac Rubin, author of *The Angry Book* (New York: Collier, 1970).

For a critique of Rubin's theory, as well as a comprehensive and enjoyable book on anger, see Carol Tavris's *Anger: The Misunderstood Emotion* (New York: Simon & Schuster, 1982).

Chapter 2   Old Moves, New Moves, and Countermoves

21   The concepts of "underfunctioning" and "overfunctioning" are from Bowen Family Systems Theory. However, Murray Bowen discounts the far-reaching implications of gender and sex-role stereotypes. For a comprehensive review of Bowen's theory, see Michael Kerr's "Family Systems Theory and Therapy," in Alan S. Gurman and David P. Kniskern,

PAGE   eds., *Handbook of Family Therapy* (New York: Brunner/ Mazel, 1981), pp. 226–64.

22   In her book *Toward a New Psychology of Women* (Boston: Beacon Press, 1976), Jean Baker Miller discusses the subject of women as carriers of those aspects of the human experience that men fear and wish to deny in themselves.

23   On de-selfing and dependency in women, see Harriet Lerner's "Female Dependency in Context: Some Theoretical and Technical Considerations," in the *American Journal of Orthopsychiatry* 53 (1983): 697–705, which also appeared in P. Reiker and E. Carmen, eds., *The Gender Gap in Psychotherapy* (New York: Plenum Press, 1984).

23   While women have been labeled "the dependent sex," I have argued (ibid.) that women are not dependent enough. Most women are far more expert at attending to the needs of others than identifying and assertively claiming the needs of the self. Luise Eichenbaum and Susie Orbach have illustrated how women learn to be depended *upon* and not to feel entitled to have their own emotional needs met. See *What Do Women Want* (New York: Coward McCann, 1983).

29   For a more technical discussion of the forces of separateness and togetherness in relationships, see Mark Karpel's "From Fusion to Dialogue," in *Family Process* 15 (1976): 65–82.

32   Jean Baker Miller (op. cit., 1976) describes women's fears of hurting or losing a relationship as they move toward greater authenticity and personal growth.

34   On countermoves and "change back!" reactions, see Murray Bowen, *Family Therapy in Clinical Practice* (New York: Jason Aronson, 1978), p. 495.

Chapter 3   **Circular Dances in Couples**

43   Paul Watzlawick, John Weakland, and Richard Fisch have written about the "more of the same" (or "when the

PAGE   solution becomes the problem") phenomenon of human nature. See Chapter 3 of *Change* (New York: Norton, 1974).

57   The marital pattern of distance and pursuit has been so widely described in the family literature that it is difficult to trace its origins. See especially Philip Guerin and Katherine Buckley Guerin's article, "Theoretical Aspects and Clinical Relevance of the Multigenerational Model of Family Therapy," in Philip Guerin, ed., *Family Therapy* (New York: Gardner Press, 1976), pp. 91–110. Also see Marianne Ault-Riché's article "Drowning in the Communication Gap," *Menninger Perspective* (Summer 1977, pp. 10–14).

Chapter 4   Anger at Our Impossible Mothers

68   On the subject of emotional distance and emotional cutoffs in families, see Michael Kerr's article on Bowen Family Systems Theory (op. cit., 1981).

69   On mothers and daughters, see *Mothers and Daughters*, by E. Carter, P. Papp, and O. Silverstein (Washington: The Women's Project in Family Therapy, Monograph Series, vol. 1, no. 1). See also (by same authors) *Mothers and Sons, Fathers and Daughters* (Monograph Series, vol. 2, no. 1, The Women's Project, 2153 Newport Place, N.W., Washington, DC 20037).

80   At the societal level, the same emotional counterforce ("You're wrong"; "Change Back!"; "Or else . . .") will occur when a de-selfed or subordinate group moves to a higher level of autonomy and self-definition. Feminists, for example, have been labeled selfish, misguided, and neurotic and warned that if they persisted in their efforts toward self-definition and self-determination, they would diminish men, ruin children, and threaten the very fabric of American life. In both family and societal systems, it is a difficult challenge indeed to stay connected and remain on course in the face of countermoves that invite nonproductive fighting and/or emotional cutoffs.

81   For a brief and highly readable summary on moving differently in one's own family system, see "Family Therapy with One Person and the Family Therapist's own Family," by Elizabeth Carter and Monica McGoldrick Orfanidis, in Philip Guerin's book *Family Therapy* (op. cit., 1976).

86   Maggie's story illustrates how we may resist change and sacrifice autonomy out of an unconscious belief that our further growth and self-definition will hurt other family members. It also illustrates that our resistance to change must be understood in the context of the powerful pressures against change exerted by the family system. For a more in-depth discussion of these concepts, see S. Lerner and H. Lerner's "A Systemic Approach to Resistance: Theoretical and Technical Considerations," in the *American Journal of Psychotherapy* 37 (1983): 387–99.

Chapter 5 Using Anger as a Guide

88   My thanks to Thomas Gordon for his pioneering work on "I-messages." I recommend *Parent Effectiveness Training* highly as a model of communication and relatedness that is applicable not only to parents and children but to adult relationships as well.

91   This vignette about Karen first appeared in "Good and Mad: How to Handle Anger on the Job," in *Working Mother* (March 1983, pp. 43–49).

95   For a more technical discussion of women's unconscious fears of their omnipotent destructiveness as well as the separation anxiety that leads women to transform anger into fears and "hurt," see Harriet Lerner's "Internal Prohibitions Against Female Anger," in the *American Journal of Psychoanalysis* 40 (1980): 137–47. Also see Teresa Bernardez (op. cit., 1978).

Many psychoanalytic and feminist thinkers have discussed the irrational dread of female anger and power

PAGE   that both sexes share, dating back to our earliest years of helpless dependency on woman (i.e., mother), and have suggested that until parenting is shared in a more balanced way by men and women, such irrational fears may persist.

102   Hopefully my statement that we let go "of angrily blaming that other person whom we see as causing our problems and failing to provide for our happiness" will not be misinterpreted. Here and throughout this book, I am referring to nonproductive blaming that perpetuates the status quo; this must be distinguished from other-directed anger that challenges it. Obviously, the ability to voice anger at discrimination and injustice is necessary not only for the maintenance of self-esteem but for the very process of personal and social change as well. Teresa Bernardez (op. cit., 1978) has summarized the crucial importance of women gaining the freedom to voice anger and protest on their own behalf.

Chapter 6   **Up and Down the Generations**

112   The assumption that "Katy has the problem" is not meant to obscure the fact that personal struggles are rooted in social conditions. Ultimately, the question "Who takes care of elderly parents?" cannot be solved by individual women in their individual psychotherapies. A crucial arena for change is the creation of a cooperative and caring society that provides for human needs, including those of elderly persons. While social and political change is not the subject of this book, the sociopolitical context gives shape and form to our most intimate struggles.

113   For an excellent discussion of the problems as well as the special strengths that derive from women's assigned role as caretaker to others, see Jean Baker Miller (op. cit., 1976).

118   Gathering information about one's emotional legacy, including facts about the extended family, is an essential part of Bowen Family Systems Theory. In clinical work derived from this theory, one would not be encouraged

PAGE to open up a toxic issue in the family or to move differently with a parent until one had obtained a calm, objective view of the multigenerational family process and one's own part in it. It is important to keep in mind that Katy spent quite a long time in psychotherapy, gathering facts and examining patterns in her extended family, prior to initiating the talk ("Dad, I have a problem . . .") with her father. For more about this process, see Carter and Orfanidis (op. cit.).

Chapter 7 Who's Responsible for What

125 Thanks to Meredith Titus for her ski-slope story.

129 How sibling position affects our world view depends on many factors, which include the number of years between siblings, and the sibling position of each parent. Walter Toman in his book *Family Constellation* (New York: Springer, 1976) presents profiles of different sibling positions, which are informative and fun to read despite the author's unexamined biases toward women, which color his presentation.

134 This vignette "Who's Doing the Housework?" first appeared in *Working Mother* ("I Don't Need Anything from Anybody," November 1984, pp. 144–48).

134–38 Lisa's problem with housework is another example of the inseparable nature of our personal dilemmas and the societal context. Were it not for the feminist movement and the collective anger and protest of many women, Lisa would probably not be struggling with the housework issue to begin with. If she felt exhausted and dissatisfied with her situation, she might have believed that she was at fault for feeling this way, and might simply have deepened her resolve to "adjust." As we do our best to define a position in a relationship, we are always influenced by predominant cultural definitions of what is right, "natural," and appropriate for our sex.

PAGE

142–47   My thanks to Katherine Glenn Kent for her excellent teaching on the fine points of the underfunctioning–overfunctioning polarity.

151   I recommend Thomas Gordon's *Parent Effectiveness Training* to help parents learn to listen to children without assuming a rescuing or "fix it" position. See especially his chapter on "active listening."

Chapter 8 **Thinking in Threes**

156   Much of what I know about triangles (a central concept in Bowen Family Systems Theory) I have learned from Katherine Glenn Kent.

161   See Rosabeth Moss Kanter's book *Men and Women of the Corporation* (New York: Basic Books, 1977) for an excellent analysis of tokenism and the special problems of women who are numerically scarce individuals in a dominant male work culture. For shorter reading, see Kanter's article "Some Effects on Group Life," in the *American Journal of Sociology* 82 (1977): 965–90.

162   My work with Mr. and Ms. Kesler illustrates an important epistemological shift toward systems thinking in the mental health field. This shift rejects the old linear model, which looks for a person to label as the "cause" of a problem (usually mother) and instead examines the reciprocal, repetitive, circular patterns maintained by all family members. Thinking in terms of family systems is a way of understanding people; it has nothing to do with whether a therapist sees one person individually or meets with a couple or family together.

171   For an informative videotape on how to construct a family diagram and its usefulness in understanding human behavior, see *Constructing the Multigenerational Family Genogram: Exploring a Problem in Context* (Educational Video

Productions, The Menninger Foundation, Box 829, Topeka, KS 66601).

180   The psychotherapy described for the Kesler family is based largely on the theoretical concepts of Murray Bowen. While I have done my best to highlight key aspects of the process of change, it is important to note that this work is often a lengthy process requiring the help of a professional therapist who has worked systematically on his or her own family of origin.

180   For a videotape describing aspects of the clinical work derived from Bowen Family Systems Theory, see *Love and Work: One Woman's Study of Her Family of Origin* (Educational Video Productions, The Menninger Foundation, Box 829, Topeka, KS 66601).

Chapter 9 Tasks for the Daring and Courageous

205   Obviously, we may wish to support a coworker or join forces with other women to form an open alliance for a worthwhile purpose. Mara Selvini Palazzoli has written a brief piece on organizational systems that touches upon the difference between a functional alliance, on the one hand, and a covert coalition or triangle, on the other. This is a difficult distinction because in both family and work systems a triangle is invariably presented as an alliance with someone for a good cause and not as a coalition at the expense of another person. See "Behind the Scenes of the Organization: Some Guidelines for the Expert in Human Relations," in the *Journal of Family Therapy* 6 (1984): 299–307.

Epilogue

223   To keep informed about issues and events affecting women, I recommend subscribing to *New Directions for Women* (published since 1972), 108 West Palisade Avenue, Englewood, NJ 07631.

INDEX

The Dance of Intimacy

*A Woman's Guide to Courageous
Acts of Change in Key Relationships*

For Steve Lerner

Contents

Contents

Acknowledgments

Although *The Dance of Anger* was a five-year undertaking, this book was finished in less than a year and a half. Happily, I have fewer people to thank.

My friends Emily Kofron and Jeffrey Ann Goudie read drafts on short notice, never failing to offer encouragement and good advice. Mary Ann Clifft generously put her editorial skills to use, going through chapters with a detective's eye. Other friends and colleagues responded to my call for help along the way; my thanks to Susan Kraus, Tom Averill, Monica McGoldrick, Jo-Ann Krestan, Claudia Bepko, Meredith Titus, and Nolan Brohaugh.

I am especially grateful to Katherine Glenn Kent for all she has taught me about Bowen theory and systems thinking during our many years of friendship. Her influence is reflected in all my work, and this book would not be the same, nor as good, without her. I am also indebted to the Menninger Clinic for providing an atmosphere that has challenged me to clarify my own ideas and to write. From the time of my arrival in 1972 as a postdoctoral fellow in clinical psychology, I have been blessed with dedicated teachers and colleagues, a superb secretarial and support staff, an unparalleled professional library, flexible work hours, and remarkably diverse opportunities for learning. All this, combined with my growing love for Kansas skies and the simple life, has led me to forgo Big-City living to settle down in the Midwest.

For the second time around I have been fortunate to be under the wing of Janet Goldstein, my editor at Harper & Row, who has influenced this book from start to finish, suggesting changes with clarity, delicacy, and tact, while respecting my need to proceed in my own way. I appreciate the careful work of the book's production editor at Harper & Row, Debra Elfenbein, and the fastidious copyediting by Andree Pages. My agent, Sandra Elkin, played a major role in making all this happen, and I thank her as well.

Many others have helped out in important ways. My friends in Topeka have closely shared my frustrations and successes as a writer, offering sympathy or champagne at the appropriate stages. Aleta Pennington and Chuck Baird have been generous-hearted and patient in the face of my computer anxiety. Jeannine Riddle worked beyond the call of duty when it came down to the final push. Betty Hoppes has facilitated my career from the start. Judie Koontz, Marianne Ault-Riché, and Ellen Safier have provided emotional support at home base. My long-distance community of feminist friends and colleagues has energized and sustained me through the best and worst of times. Countless readers of my first book have sent messages of overwhelming gratitude and affection, reminding me at the inevitable low points of authorhood that it is all worthwhile.

This book does not create a new epistemological framework for the understanding of relationships. Rather, I have worked to translate and bring to life what I have found to be empowering, theoretically sound, and useful in my personal life and professional work. In this regard I owe the greatest intellectual debt to Murray Bowen, founder of Bowen family systems theory, for the ideas and concepts that make up the very fabric of this book. At the same time, my interpretation and application of Bowen's work has been influenced by my feminist and psychoanalytic background, and by a worldview that differs significantly from Bowen and his colleagues at the Georgetown Family Center. For this reason, *The Dance of Intimacy* is by no means a pure translation of Bowen theory and as always, the ultimate responsibility for this work is my own.

It is understandably difficult to find words to thank those with whom one shares the most complex ties. I am grateful to my parents for all that they have given me throughout my lifetime and for being people I have come to so deeply admire and love. My sister, Susan, is an enthusiastic supporter of my work, and our friendship has flourished in our adult years despite geographical distance. My husband, Steve, has been my intimate partner in love and work for two decades; I thank him for his help with all my projects, including this one, and for our good life together. Finally, our two sons, Matthew and Benjamin, are a source of great joy. I thank all these people for what they have taught me firsthand about intimacy and for reminding me that being in relationships is a rich challenge indeed.

Except for the friends and family who have given permission to appear in this book, all names and all identifying characteristics of individuals mentioned have been changed in order to protect their privacy.

1

The Pursuit of Intimacy: Is It Women's Work?

I was cleaning my attic when I came across a poem I wrote during my sophomore year of college in Madison, Wisconsin. I vaguely recalled the brief attachment that inspired these lines—a steamy start which turned into an unbridgeable distance before either of us knew what was happening:

> Once you held me so hard
> and we were so close
> that belly to belly we fused
> passed through each other
> and back to back
> stood strangers again.

Neither the poem nor the romance was memorable, and my words certainly did not capture the anguish I felt when an initially blissful relationship failed. But I was reminded of what intimacy is not. And also what it is.

"All beginnings are lovely," a French proverb reminds us, but intimacy is not about that initial "Velcro stage" of relationships. It is when we stay in a relationship *over time*—whether by necessity or choice—that our capacity for intimacy is truly put to the test. It is only in long-term relationships that we are called upon to navigate that delicate balance between separateness and connectedness and that we confront the challenge of sustaining both—without losing either when the going gets rough.

Nor is intimacy the same as intensity, although we are a culture that confuses these two words. Intense feelings—no matter how positive—are hardly a measure of true and enduring closeness. In fact, intense feelings may block us from taking a careful and objective look at the dance we are doing with significant people in our lives. And as my poem illustrates, intense togetherness can easily flip into intense distance—or intense conflict, for that matter.

Finally, the challenge of intimacy is by no means limited to the subject of men, marriage, or romantic encounters, although some of us may equate "intimacy" with images of blissful heterosexual pairings. A primary commitment to a man reflects only one opportunity for intimacy in a world that is rich with possibilities for connectedness and attachment.

Whatever your own definition of intimacy, this book is designed to challenge and enlarge it. It will not teach you things to do to make him (or her) admire you. It does not provide guidelines for a love-in. It is not even about *feeling* close in the usual and immediate sense of the word. And certainly it is not about changing the other person, which is not possible. Instead, it is a book about making responsible and lasting changes that enhance our capacity for genuine closeness *over the long haul.*

Toward Defining Our Terms

Let's attempt a working definition of an *intimate relationship*. What does it require of us?

For starters, intimacy means that we can be who we are in a relationship, and allow the other person to do the same. "Being who we are" requires that we can talk openly about things that are important to us, that we take a clear position on where we stand on important emotional issues, and that we clarify the limits of what is acceptable and tolerable to us in a relationship. "Allowing the other person to do the same" means that we can stay emotionally connected to that other party who thinks, feels, and believes differently, without needing to change, convince, or fix the other.

An intimate relationship is one in which neither party silences, sacrifices, or betrays the self and each party expresses strength and vulnerability, weakness and competence in a balanced way.

Of course, there is much more to this business of navigating separateness (the "I") and connectedness (the "we"), but I will avoid spelling it out in dry theory. The subject, in all of its complexity, will come to life in later chapters as we examine turning points in the lives of women who courageously changed their steps in relationship dances that were painful and going badly. In each case, these changes were made in the direction of defining a more whole and separate "I." In each case, this work provided the foundation for a more intimate and gratifying "we." In no case was change easy or comfortable

In the chapters that follow, we will continue to evolve a new and more complex definition of intimacy, as well as guidelines for change that are based on a solid theory of how relationship patterns operate and why they get into trouble. The courageous acts of change that we will explore in detail are "the differences that make a difference"—the specific moves we can make with key persons in our lives that will most profoundly affect our sense of self and how we navigate closeness with others. *Our goal will be to have relationships with both men and women that do not operate at the expense of the self, and to have a self that does not operate at the expense of the other.* This is a tall order, or, more accurately, a lifelong challenge. But it is the heart and soul of intimacy.

Caveat Emptor (Buyer Beware!)

I believe that women should approach all self-help books, including this one, with a healthy degree of skepticism. We are forever exhorted to change ourselves—to become better wives, lovers, or mothers—to attract men more or to need them less, to do better at balancing work and family, or to lose those ten extra pounds. There are already more than enough books in print for women who love too much, or not enough, or in the wrong way, or with a foolishly chosen partner. Surely, we do not need more of the same. Yet just as surely, on our own behalf, we may need to become more effective agents of change in our primary relationships.

Perhaps we should first take time to contemplate why tending to relationships, like changing diapers, is predominantly women's work. Caring about relationships, working on them, and upgrading our how-to skills have traditionally been women's domain. When something goes wrong, we are usually the first to react, to feel pain, to seek help, and to try to initiate change. This is not to say that women *need* relationships more than men do. Contrary to popular mythology, research has shown that women do far better alone than do their male counterparts and do not benefit as much from marriage. Yet men often seem oddly unconcerned about improving or changing a relationship once they have one. Men are rarely ambitious about improving their people skills, unless doing so will help them move up—or measure up—on the job.

This being the case, we might ask ourselves some hard questions. Why are women so concerned about upgrading their relationship skills, especially with men? Why are men relatively unconcerned? To understand the origins of this difference, let's look at traditional love and marriage, for it is here that the imbalance in "relationship work" is most conspicuous.

Women Are the Experts

I grew up at a time when relationship skills for girls and women were nothing short of tools for survival. The rules of the game were clear and simple: Men were to seek their fortune, and women were to seek men. A man's job was to make something of himself in the world; a woman's job was to find herself a successful man. Despite my own career plans, I felt it to be the most basic and immutable difference between the sexes. Men must *be* somebody; women must *find* somebody. Nor was "finding somebody" (to say nothing of "keeping" that somebody) a task to be taken lightly. The brilliance that my college friends and I put into our discussions of men far outshone what we put into our academic studies.

Today, women are no longer exclusively defined by our connection to men and children, yet we still remain dedicated experts on the subject of relationships. Although females may have some biological edge in our interest in and attunement to the nuances of interactions, the bulk of our wisdom does not come to us through the magical gift of "feminine intuition" which is carried on the X chromosome. *Rather, in relationships between dominant and subordinate groups, the subordinate group members always possess a far greater understanding of dominant group members and their culture than vice versa.* Blacks, for example, know a great deal about the rules and roles of white culture and relationships. Whites do not possess a similar sensitivity to and knowledge about blacks.

While women once acquired relationship skills to "hook," "snare," or "catch" a husband who would provide access to economic security and social status, the position of contemporary women has not changed that radically. Much of our success still depends on our attunement to "male culture," our ability to please men, and our readiness to conform to the masculine values of our institutions. In my own career, for example, these skills, and my willingness to use them, influence whether my papers will be accepted in professional journals, whether I will move up in my work-place, and whether my projects will be perceived as trivial or significant. Before the recent feminist movement, women depended entirely on men for the validation and dissemination of our ideas and for our definition of what was important. Whether we work in the home, in the "pink-collar ghetto," or at the top of the executive ladder, women cannot easily afford to alienate men or to be ignorant about their psychology. Even today, a woman who loses her husband will also probably lose her social status and her (and her children's) standard of living along with him.

Finally, our society still does not accord equal value to women without a male partner, despite the fact that a good man is indeed hard to find—even more so as we become older and more mature. Having absorbed the lesson that "half a loaf is better than none" (i.e., *any* man is better than *no* man), we may compromise our standards more than we are later comfortable with. We may then put our energies into trying to change him, which can be as energy-consuming as it is impossible. Pushing a partner to change is about as effective as trying to make friends with a squirrel by chasing it.

To say that our orientation toward relationships evolves, in part, from women's subordinate status does not imply that our feelings are misguided, excessive, or wrong. To the contrary, the valuing of intimacy and attachment is an asset, not a liability. Surely, women's commitment to relationships is part of our proud legacy and strength. The problem arises, however, when we confuse intimacy with winning approval, when we look to intimate relationships as our sole source of self-esteem, and when we enter relationships at the expense of the self. Historically speaking, women have learned to sacrifice the "I" for the "we," just as men have been encouraged to do the opposite and bolster the "I" at the expense of responsible connectedness to others.

Men's Lack of Concern

Men seldom become scholars on the subject of changing their intimate relationships, because they do not yet need to. Women often demand surprisingly little in relationships with men, whether the issue at hand is emotional nurturance or who cleans up the kitchen. We may settle for small change with a lover or husband and tolerate behaviors and living arrangements that we would not find acceptable or deem fair in a close female friendship. Parents, too, may expect less from their sons ("Boys will be boys") than from their daughters in the realm of communication and responsible connectedness, while children learn to expect less from their fathers. Until we are able to expect more from men in order to stay with them or continue business as usual, it is unlikely that men will feel called upon to change or even to pay attention.

In marriage, the gap between men and women in their attunement to relationships often widens dramatically over time. Dad need not notice that little Sam has holes in his sneakers, or even that his mother's birthday is coming up, if his wife moves in to take up the slack and handle the problem. Nor need he put much emotional energy into his parents' arrival for an extended visit if his spouse will plan their entertainment or make sure that there is toilet paper in the house. As long as women function *for* men, men will have no need to change.

Men often feel at a loss about how to become experts on close relationships, although their anxiety may be masked by apathy or disinterest. Many men have been raised by fathers who were most conspicuous by their emotional or physical absence, and by omnipresent mothers whose very "feminine" qualities and traits they, as males, were taught to repudiate in themselves. The old definition of "family" hardly provided a good training ground for developing a clear male self in the context of emotional connectedness to others. Men tend to distance from a partner (or get a new one) when the going gets rough, rather than to hang in and struggle for change.

Finally—and perhaps most significantly—males are not rewarded for investing in the emotional component of human relationships. In our production-oriented society, no accolades are given to men who value personal ties at the expense of making one more sale, seeing one more client, or publishing one more paper. There is a popular joke in my profession about the psychoanalyst's son who reports that he wants to be "a patient" when he grows up. "That way," the small boy explains, "I'll get to see my father five times a week!" Such jokes are told with barely disguised pride, not with apology, by men who are truly dedicated to their work. Let's face it, fame and glory do not come to men who strive to keep their lives in balance and who refuse to neglect their important relationships. The rewards in doing so can only be private ones.

I believe that for both women and men the most significant area of learning is that of understanding and enhancing our intimate relationships with our friends, lovers, and kin. Although I have chosen to speak directly to women, the subject is no less relevant to men, whom I also invite to read this book. All of us develop through our emotional connectedness to others, and we continue to need close relationships throughout our lives. Only through our connectedness to others can we really know and enhance the self. And only through working on the self can we begin to enhance our connectedness to others.

When we distance from significant others or pretend we don't need people, we get in trouble. Similarly, we get in trouble when a relationship begins to go badly and we ignore it or put no energy into generating new options for change. Fortunately it is never too late to learn to move differently in our key relationships. While in the short run the changes we make—and the initial reactions we evoke—may leave us feeling scared, frustrated, angry, and very separate, like many things in life it's a matter of sitting with short-term anxiety for long-term gain.

2

The Challenge of Change

At the heart of it all, this is a book about change. My hope is not that you will acquire a list of how-to-do-it techniques for "getting close," but rather that you will become more knowledgeable on the dynamics of change than you ever imagined possible.

Why change? Only by working to develop and redefine the self in our key relationships can we really increase our capacity for intimacy. There is, quite simply, no other way.

To Change or Not to Change

In our rapidly changing society we can count on only two things that will never change. What will never change is the will to change and the fear of change. It is the will to change that motivates us to seek help. It is the fear of change that motivates us to resist the very help we seek.

A story is told of a New England farmer asked to attend a forthcoming meeting at the county seat. The farmer asked, "Why should I attend the meeting? What benefit will I get from attendance?" "Well, the meeting will teach you how to

10

be a better farmer," came the enthusiastic reply. The farmer was thoughtful for a few moments and then commented, "Why should I learn how to be a better farmer when I'm not being as good a farmer as I know how to be now?"

All of us have deeply ambivalent feelings about change. We seek the wisdom of others when we are not making full use of our own and then we resist applying the wisdom that we *do* seek even when we're paying for it. We do this not because we are neurotic or cowardly, but because both the will to change and the desire to maintain sameness coexist for good reason. Both are essential to our emotional well-being and equally deserve our attention and respect.

A Conservative Policy

While my own associations to the word "conservative" are not great ones, this word best describes my attitude toward personal change. Just as we strive for change, we also strive to conserve what is most valuable and familiar in our selves. And in a society where we are constantly being pressured to improve, actualize, and perfect our selves, it is probably wise to question why we should change at all and who is prescribing the changes.

Often we wish to get rid of some part of our selves—as we would an inflamed appendix—without recognizing the positive aspects of a particular "negative" trait or behavior. Few things are "all good" or "all bad." I recall a meeting of my women's group many years back when we had a little too much to drink and went around the circle sharing what we liked the *very best* and the *very least* about each other. Interestingly, what was labeled "the best" and "the worst" for each person turned out to be one and the same, or more accurately, different variations on the same theme. If *least liked* was one woman's tendency to hog the group spotlight, what was *most liked* was her energetic and entertaining personality. If *least liked* was another woman's failure to be straightforward, direct, and spontaneous, what was *most liked* was her kindness, tact, and respect for the feelings of others. If another's sense of entitlement and "Me first!" attitude pushed the group's buttons, it was her ability to identify her own goals and "go for it" that was most admired. And so it went. That evening I began to have a renewed appreciation for the inseparable nature of our strengths and weaknesses. Far from being opposites, they are woven from the same strands.

This experience also reinforced a direction I was moving in professionally. Early on in my career as a therapist, I deemed it my job to help my patients rid themselves of certain qualities—stubbornness, silence, demandingness, oppositionalism, or any other trait or behavior that seemed to make their life (or my work) especially difficult. Or perhaps I wanted them to be closer to their fathers, more independent from their mothers, or more (or less) ambitious, self-seeking, self-disclosing, or assertive. I discovered, however, that I could be far more helpful when I was able to identify and appreciate the *positive* aspects of what was seemingly most negative. Paradoxically, this appreciation was what left my clients freer to get on with the business of change.

Problems Serve a Purpose

Later in my career I began studying families, and came to further appreciate how negative behaviors often serve important and positive functions—even when these behaviors push others away or antagonize them. Let's consider the following example.

Seven-year-old Judy is brought into therapy by her concerned parents because she has temper tantrums and stomachaches and is demonstrating a whole variety of obnoxious misbehaviors. She is labeled "the problem" in the family—the patient, the sick one, the one to be fixed. Judy's parents hope that I *can change Judy* and rid her of her disruptive and self-defeating behaviors.

Upon careful questioning I learn that Judy's problems began soon after the death of her paternal grandfather to whom she was quite attached. The family is not processing or even talking much about this loss. In addition Judy's father has become increasingly withdrawn and depressed since losing his dad. His growing distance from both his wife and his daughter—as well as his obvious depression, *which no one mentions*—has everyone quite anxious. Judy's mother, however, does not openly address her concern about her husband or her distant marriage. Instead, she has increased her focus on her daughter.

When specifically does Judy act up and act out? From what I can piece together, this occurs when her father's distance and her mother's anxious focus on Judy reach intolerable proportions. And what is the *outcome* of Judy's troublemaking and tantrums? Distant Dad is roped back into the family (and is helped to become more angry than depressed), and the parents are able to pull together, temporarily united by their shared concern for their child.

Judy's behavior is, in part, an attempt to solve a problem in the family. It also reflects the high level of anxiety in this family at a particularly stressful point in their lives. More frequently than not, what we label "the problem" to be changed or fixed is not the problem at all. As Judy's story illustrates, it may even be a misguided attempt at the solution. And the "solution" we or others apply (which for Judy's parents involved increasing their focus on Judy and decreasing their focus on their own issues) just evokes and maintains the very problem we are trying to repair.

Small Changes

A conservative approach to personal change also means that we proceed slowly—and with the understanding that our moves forward will be accompanied by inevitable frustrations and derailments. Thinking small provides us with the opportunity to observe and check out the impact of each new behavior on a relationship system, and to sit with the benefits and costs of change. It also militates against our natural tendency to move in with a big bang and then drop out entirely when initial responses are not to our liking.

When an acquaintance of mine announced she was going to approach her father during the holiday vacation to try to "get close" to him by "breaking through his brick wall," I suspected she was doomed to failure. While I didn't know exactly what "breaking through his brick wall" might entail, I was not surprised when she returned home feeling grumpy and defeated.

The outcome might have been different if she had been less ambitious—if she had planned one specific move toward her goal. For example, she might have requested some one-to-one time with her dad, perhaps for coffee or a short walk. Because she and her father never had "alone time" in the midst of family visits, this in itself would have been a significant change, even if they had talked about nothing more than the weather. And had he resisted her efforts, she would then know she needed to begin with a smaller move still.

From a more conservative standpoint, it may have been premature for my acquaintance to make *any* new move until after she had taken time to get a calmer, less blaming perspective on the distance between herself and her dad. Perhaps she set up a confrontation that she unconsciously knew was doomed to fail, because *she herself* needed to reinforce her own distant position from her father, as well as her perception of herself as the one who could be close. In any case, breaking down someone's brick wall is hardly an example of moving slow and thinking small.

Substantive change in important relationships rarely comes about through intense confrontation. Rather, it more frequently results from careful thinking and from planning for small, manageable moves based on a solid understanding of the problem, including our own part in it. We are unlikely to be agents of change when we hold our nose, close our eyes, and jump!

Reassuring Sameness

Of course, it would be nice if we could make major changes quickly—*or would it?* Babies and small children have such an extraordinary capacity for change and growth, we may well wonder why grown-ups can't hold on to it. When my younger son, Ben, was six years old and my first book finally made its appearance, I overheard him exclaim to a small friend, "Do you know that my mother worked on her book for *my whole life!*" It was true enough. And while I had accomplished a great deal during that time, what had Ben done in the same number of years? From a scrawling, barely formed self with the most limited repertoire of language, movement, and understanding, he had transformed himself into a distinct six-year-old personality who was knowledgeable about some of the innermost workings of the New York publishing world. Now *that's* change!

Later that afternoon a friend and I were musing about how incredible it would be if adults could retain that extraordinary capacity for learning and change. Actually, it would be a total nightmare, if you really stop to think about it. Our very identity, our sense of continuity and stability in this world, and all our key relationships depend on our maintaining a high degree of sameness, predictability, and non-change. If we visit our father after a three-year absence, we count on him being pretty much the same person he's always been, no matter how loudly we may complain about the sort of person he is. In fact, we may count on this so much that we fail to validate and credit some real changes he has, in fact, made.

At the same time, change is inevitable and constant. No matter how effortfully we resist, no matter how hard we try to hold the clock still or attempt to view our world in static terms ("Someday I'll have my house/job/body/personality *exactly* as I want it and then I'll relax!"), we are always evolving and forever monitoring our steps in that complex dance of change. It is indeed a slow dance that we do with ourselves and others: moving back and forth between our will to change and our will not to change, between other people's desire for us to change and their anxiety and protest about our doing so, between our own wish for closeness when anxiety about isolation sets in and our need for distance when "togetherness" gets too sticky or suffocating.

When Relationships Are Stuck

The challenge of change is greatest when a relationship becomes a source of negative energy and frustration and our attempts to fix things only lead to more of the same. It is these times that we will pay special attention to in the examples to come. These stuck relationships are often *"too intense,"* and/or *"too distant,"* precluding real intimacy.

Too much intensity means that one party is overfocused on the other in a blaming or worried way or in an attempt to fix or shape up the other person. Or each party may be overfocused on the other and underfocused on the self. *Too much distance* means that there is little togetherness and real sharing of one's true self in the relationship. Important issues are pushed underground rather than being aired and worked on. Many distant relationships are also intense because distance is one way we manage intensity. If you haven't seen your ex-husband in five years and can't talk with him about the kids without clutching inside, then you have a *very* intense relationship.

Once a relationship is stuck, the motivation to change things is not sufficient to make it happen. For one thing, we may be so buffeted about by strong feelings that we can't think clearly and objectively about the problem, including our own part in it. When intensity is high, we *react* (rather than observe and think), we overfocus on the *other* (rather than on the self), and we find ourselves in polarized positions where we are unable to see more than one side of an issue (our own) and find new ways to move differently. We may navigate relationships in ways that lower our anxiety in the short run, but that diminish our capacity for intimacy over the long haul.

In addition, we may have a strong wish for change but be unaware of the actual sources of anxiety that are fueling a relationship problem and blocking intimacy. We are banging heads in *one* relationship, but the source of the problem is something we are not paying attention to, or do not want to pay attention to. We become much like the proverbial man who had too much to drink and lost his keys in the alley, but looked for them under the lamp post because the light was better. In Judy's case, for example, her behavior was defined as "the problem," but the anxiety in the family was actually evoked by an important loss. All family relationships had become distant because the grandfather's death could not be talked about and processed.

If we are going through a particularly painful time in a relationship, *that* is what we want to talk about and change. Our desire to focus where it hurts makes sense and sometimes we need to go no further. Frequently, however, a problem in one relationship is fueled by unaddressed issues —past and present—in another arena. Sometimes you can't become more intimate with your husband or boyfriend until *after* you have addressed something with your father, taken a new position with your mother, changed your part in an old family pattern, or learned more about the death of Uncle Charlie.

In this book we will be exploring stuck relationships in depth, as we follow the specific steps some women took toward a more solid self and a more intimate connectedness with others. We will see that changing *any* relationship problem rests directly on our ability to work on bringing *more of a self* to that relationship. Without a clear, whole, and separate "I," relationships *do* become overly intense, overly distant, or alternate between the two. We want closeness, but we become ineffective and fuzzy agents of change, moving in this week with angry complaints and distancing next week with cold withdrawal—none of which leads to anything new. Without a clear "I" we become overly reactive to what the other person is doing *to* us, or not doing *for* us—and we end up feeling helpless and powerless to define a new position in the relationship.

Our society places a great emphasis on developing the "I." Words like "autonomy," "independence," "separateness," "authenticity," and "selfhood" are popular if not universal goals. Yet there is much misunderstanding about what these words actually mean, who defines them, and how we can evaluate and improve where we stand on the "selfhood scale." Because mature intimacy rests so heavily on this business of *self*, let's take a careful look.

3

Selfhood:
At What Cost?

Messages everywhere exhort us to achieve selfhood—to find and express our true selves. Perhaps a more candid response to this glorification of self in our culture is captured in the following incident. An aspiring young writer had spent long hours polishing up a composition for her sophomore English class, only to receive the grade of C-plus. "Be your *self!*" her professor wrote in bold red letters, underlining the word *self* several times. Underneath, perhaps as an afterthought, this same professor penned in, "If this is your self, be someone else."

Perhaps existence would be simpler if all the important figures in our lives could be that open and upfront about the contradictory messages they communicate. Most mixed messages are so subtle and covert that we are not aware of sending or receiving them. "Be independent!" is the spoken message we hear from a parent or spouse—but then "Be like me!" or even "Be for me!" may be the disqualifying communication. "Don't be so clingy," a boyfriend may tell us, as he unconsciously encourages us to express the neediness and dependency that he fears to acknowledge within himself. "Why don't you get your life together?" a husband complains, but when we finally make the move to apply to graduate school, he becomes depressed and resentful.

From the time we are first wrapped in a pink blanket, family members encourage us to be our authentic selves, while they also unconsciously encourage us to express certain traits, qualities, or behaviors and to deny or inhibit others. People need us to be a certain way *for their own sake,* and for the most complex variety of unconscious reasons. Throughout our lives, we learn that the survival of our relationships, and the very integrity of our family, depend on our being this way or that. We, too, unwittingly communicate such messages to others. Of course, learning what others want and expect from us is a necessary part of becoming a civilized human being. There is no "true self" that unfolds in a vacuum, free from the influence of family and culture. However, it is the *unconscious* or covert communications—those outside the awareness of sender and receiver —that often carry the most negative power.

The dilemma of defining a self is a particularly complex one for women. Because we are a subordinate group, our "true nature" and "appropriate place" have forever been defined by the wishes and fears of men. How, then, do we approach the task of carving out a clear and authentic self from the myriad of mixed messages and injunctions that surround us from the cradle to the grave?

At the simplest level, "being a self" means we can be pretty much who we are in relationships rather than what others wish, need, and expect us to be. It also means that we can allow others to do the same. It means we do not participate in relationships at the expense of the "I" (as women are encouraged to do) and we do not bolster the "I" at the expense of the other (as men are encouraged to do). As simple as this may sound, its translation into action is enormously complex. In fact, any sustained move in the direction of "more self" is a difficult challenge and not without risk.

For women, the emphasis on *selfhood* is a recent historical development. Selflessness, self-sacrifice, and service were time-honored virtues for our mothers and grandmothers. In contrast, we are now bombarded with messages that we should be strong, assertive, separate, independent selves, at least in the abstract. (In any specific relationship, such qualities may be less than welcome.) If we now fail to make use of the how-to skills or inspirational messages available to us, we may feel terrible about ourselves. Little attention is paid to the enormity of the task at hand, or even to respecting the good reasons why we may be unable to change. The story below illustrates one such reason.

"Dear Editor . . ."

Some years back, this letter to the editor appeared in *Ms.* magazine:

> It is with much regret that I must ask you to cancel my subscription. . . . Over the years I have enjoyed *Ms.* immensely, but for the last two months I've had to *hide* the magazine in my dresser drawer. My supposedly "liberal and understanding" husband believes the magazine is changing my personality, making me less flexible to his demands. In an effort to "save" my marriage, I am canceling the subscription. I feel like crying. . . .

"Here," I thought to myself, "is a woman with the will *not* to change." I clipped the letter and shared it with a small group of psychology students over lunch, inviting their reactions. The first student studied the letter and concluded that the husband was the cause of the wife's problem. The second student felt angry at the wife for giving her husband the power to make decisions for her—and then blaming him for it. The third saw the culprit as our patriarchal culture—the deep-rooted ethos of male dominance that affects us all. The fourth student chomped on her chicken salad sandwich and remarked glibly, "Well, there's a couple who deserve each other."

These students—two women and two men—differed in where they placed their sympathy and their blame. But as the discussion continued, it was clear that they all agreed on one essential point. We all can change and make choices. This woman does not *have* to hide the magazine in her dresser drawer, nor does she *have* to cancel her subscription to *Ms.* She could choose to do otherwise. That is, as one student added emphatically, "if she *really* wants to change."

Let's examine this assumption carefully, with an eye toward determining what might block this woman from altering her key relationship by changing and strengthening her own self. This understanding will help us to more fully appreciate the dilemma of change.

Now is a good time to pause and give some thought to the anonymous author (let's call her Jo-Anne) of the letter to the editor. How do *you* understand Jo-Anne's willingness to compromise so much of her self under pressure? What in her past history might have led her to this place and what in her present context might keep her there? What is the worst-case scenario—both in the short run *and* the long run—that Jo-Anne might envision should she do something different and clarify a position of "more self" with her husband ("I don't expect you to like *Ms.* or to approve of it, but I do insist on making my own decisions about what I read")? If the cost of change is high, what is the cost for Jo-Anne of *not* changing—of continuing in this same pattern over the next ten years? What adjectives might you use to describe Jo-Anne's personality or character?

A Problem in Context

Perhaps your reaction to Jo-Anne's dilemma is decidedly unsympathetic. You may see her as an infantile woman who enjoys being her husband's child and who refuses to grow up and take responsibility for herself. Maybe she even *likes* suffering and emotional pain—you know, one of those "masochistic" types who derive a secret unconscious pleasure from their victimized position. Or Jo-Anne may be downright immature, lazy, and unmotivated—unwilling to put forth the effort that change requires. If we keep a narrow spotlight on Jo-Anne and view the problem as existing entirely under her skin, these are the kinds of interpretations we are likely to come up with.

Suppose instead, we are able to view Jo-Anne's problem in a broader context and examine her situation through a wide-angle lens. *Would any of the following facts make a difference in how you understand her decision to hide* Ms. *from her husband and ultimately cancel her subscription?*

Would it make a difference if Jo-Anne was a middle-aged woman with three dependent children, little formal education, and no support systems or marketable skills? Would it make a difference to know that changes in the direction of "more self" would be intolerable enough to her husband that he would ultimately leave her? Does Jo-Anne's resistance to change make more sense if we know that she is quite literally one husband away from a welfare check?

Would it make a difference if this husband's apparent good functioning rests on Jo-Anne's poor functioning—that whenever *she* begins to look better, he begins to look worse? Does it make a difference to know that her husband has a history of violent behavior, as well as severe depression —but that he has been functioning well since Jo-Anne has moved into a more accommodating, submissive role in their marriage?

Would it make a difference if in Jo-Anne's first family there was a powerful taboo against expressing differences, and that early in life Jo-Anne learned that asserting the "I" would threaten the most important family relationships on which she depended totally?

Would it make a difference to know that in canceling her subscription to *Ms.* magazine, Jo-Anne is doing exactly what women in her family have done for at least three hundred years? That accommodating to one's husband is a deep-rooted family tradition that links Jo-Anne to the important women in her past? That for Jo-Anne to do otherwise, or differently, would be to challenge the very "reality" of generations of women in her family and would constitute, at least unconsciously, a betrayal—a loss of identity and meaning?

Does any of this information, these small additional pieces of a much larger picture, change or inform your per-

sonal reaction to Jo-Anne's decision to cancel her subscription to *Ms.?* Or do you think, like the psychology students,
that Jo-Anne could certainly make a change within her marriage "if she *really* wanted to change"?

How Much We Don't Know

All of us are psychologists of sorts, even if this is not our
trade. When we are not able to make a desired change, we
will construct an explanation to make sense of our painful
experience. We may diagnose ourselves ("I'm scared of my
sexuality, that's why I can't lose weight") or the other person
("He just can't deal with intimacy"). We may blame our
mothers, our genes, our hormones, or the stars, but in each
case our understanding of the problem is just a small piece
of the elephant.

*We actually know very little about the strong human will not
to change.* If Jo-Anne were to go to ten therapists—and then
resist their efforts to help her become a more assertive person—she would probably be on the receiving end of ten
different interpretations. Each interpretation would be
based on the therapist's own particular theory or belief system about Jo-Anne's resistance to change. All these theories
and interpretations might be wrong. Or all might be correct,
with each representing a small part of a much larger and
more complicated picture. We are encouraged to accept
"expert advice" as truth, when in reality a great deal about
human behavior is unknown.

Perhaps the best truth we have is that no expert can
know with 100 percent certainty what is best for Jo-Anne at a
particular point in time or what changes she can tolerate. On
the one hand, the costs of *non*change are often clearly apparent. For Jo-Anne, these costs may include chronic anger and

bitterness, feelings of depression, anxiety, low self-esteem, or even self-hatred. They may include sexual or work inhibitions, physical complaints, or any other symptom in the book. We *do* know there is a price we pay when we betray and sacrifice the self, when too much of the self becomes negotiable under relationship pressures.

What is far more difficult to determine—what we cannot know completely or with certainty—is the price Jo-Anne would have to pay for change at this time. In fact, Jo-Anne herself can only begin to know this *after* she makes a change ("I will choose what I read in this marriage, whether you approve of it or not") and as she *holds to her decision* through the inevitable turmoil and anxiety that such a change inevitably evokes. As Margaret Mead so aptly pointed out, the disruption caused by change can only be solved by *more change,* and so one thing leads to another. If Jo-Anne decides she will *not* cancel her subscription to *Ms.,* she will begin to feel an internal pressure to take a position on other issues that are important to her. As the old marital equilibrium is disrupted, her husband will also be called upon to change. How much change can these two, as individuals and as a couple, manage over time? The answer is that we do not know.

Change requires courage, but the failure to change does not signify the lack of it. Women are quick to blame themselves— and to be blamed by others—when we are not able to make the changes that we ourselves seek or that others prescribe for us. We fail to respect the wisdom of the unconscious, which may tell us "No!" as our conscious mind says "Go!"

Keep in mind how little even the experts know about the process of change. And remember also that even the most self-defeating and problematic behavior patterns may exist for a good reason. We saw this in the brief example of seven-year-old Judy (Chapter 1). Here is a firsthand account.

The Will Not to Change: A Personal Story

When I was twelve years old, my mother was diagnosed with advanced endometrial cancer. Earlier symptoms of the disease had been misdiagnosed as menopause, and when the correct diagnosis was finally made, she was given a very poor prognosis. This was in the fifties, a time when children were typically "protected" from such painful information through secrecy and silence. No facts were provided about my mother's health problem, although it seemed obvious that she was dying. The level of anxiety in my family was chronically high, but the source of the anxiety was not mentioned. The word "cancer" was never spoken.

My older sister, Susan (a typical firstborn), managed her anxiety by *overfunctioning,* and I (a typical youngest) managed my anxiety by *underfunctioning.* Over time our positions became polarized and rigidly entrenched. The more my sister overfunctioned the more I underfunctioned, and vice versa. Here's how it went.

Susan, then a freshman at Barnard College, traveled three hours each day on the subway between Brooklyn and Manhattan, returning home to organize and take care of the entire household. She cooked, cleaned, ironed, and did everything that needed to be done with perfect competence and without complaint. If she felt scared, vulnerable, angry, or unhappy, she hid these feelings, even from herself. I, on the other hand, expressed enough of these feelings for the entire family. I became as bad as she was good—creating various scenes, making impossible demands for clothes that my family could not afford, and messing things up as quickly as my sister was able to clean and straighten them. I acted up in school and my parents were informed that I would never be "college material."

My father distanced (a typical male pattern of managing stress) and my mother handled her anxiety by *focusing on me.* Indeed, about 98 percent of her worry energy went in my direction. She became concerned, if not preoccupied, with the thought that I would not make it if she died. (Susan, she concluded, would do just fine.) My mother, who has always prided herself on being a "fighter" and a "survivor," decided that *for my sake,* she could not die. And die she did not. Even today (as I write this, she is pushing eighty), my mother does not hesitate for a moment when she is asked how she stayed alive against all medical odds. "You see," she explains, as if the answer is perfectly logical and merits no further explanation, "I could not die at that time. Harriet needed me. She was such a mess!"

A mess I was—and an incorrigible one at that. I was sent to a psychotherapist who did his best to straighten me out, but my unconscious will *not* to change was stronger than his best efforts to offer help. I remained a mess until I felt more confident that my mother was out of the woods.

Did my being a mess keep my mother alive? Recently, I called her in Phoenix and put this question to her directly. Now that our family is able to talk much more openly about difficult emotional issues, I continue to process this painful period of my life in a way that was not possible at the time. I asked my mother whether she *truly* believed that it was my being a mess that allowed her to live. Would she *actually* have died—as she now sees it—had I given her the impression that I was doing just fine?

My mother's most honest and thoughtful reaction was to say that looking back, she really was not sure. When the cancer was diagnosed, she had "no self"; although she could give and do for her children, she could not give and do on her own behalf. At first, she explained, she was fighting the cancer 80 percent for me, and 20 percent for herself. Over time, the balance began to shift as my mother learned to value her own life and make it a priority.

Did my being a mess *really* allow my mother to survive? We cannot know for sure. I am confident, however, of one thing. At some unconscious level, this twelve-year-old child believed it was my job in the family to keep my mother alive by being a mess. I believed this as deeply as my sister, Susan, believed that the integrity of the family depended on her being the all-good, all-responsible daughter who would hide any sign of vulnerability and pain. I was steadfast in my unconscious determination to resist all efforts to help me shape up. And sadly, we did not have the kind of help that our family actually needed, help that would have made it possible for all four of us to process my mother's cancer in a more open and direct way.

I have shared this story with you, and asked you to reflect on one woman's letter to the editor, in the hope that you will approach your own attempts at change with patience. The ideas and suggestions that lie ahead will be most useful to you if you can greet them with an open, courageous, and experimental attitude. But also keep in mind that no one else can tell you what changes you *should* make, at what speed, and at what cost. No expert, not even your therapist, can know for certain when it is the right time for you to change, how much change is tolerable and in what doses, and how various moves forward and backward will affect your emotional well-being, your relationships, your sense of self, your moorings in this world, and your (or someone else's) immune system.

Fortunately, the unconscious is very wise. What you read in this book will always be there for you—long after you think you have forgotten it—until the time is right for you to make use of it. Respect the fact that all you do and are now, has evolved for a good reason and serves an important purpose. Trust your own way more than the experts who promote change, myself included, because ultimately you are the best expert on your own self.

Selfhood or De-Selfing: Defining Our Terms

If our capacity for intimacy rests first and foremost on our continued efforts to be *more of a self,* how can we judge where we are on the "selfhood scale"? How can we measure the degree to which we are able to carve out a separate, whole, independent self within our closest relationships? Whether we call it "selfhood" or prefer a different word, such as "autonomy" or "independence," what are the criteria for having a lot of it—or not very much? Before reading on, you might want to jot down your own standards of measurement. How do *you* define it? Exactly what do you mean when you say, "She (or he) is a *very* independent person!"

Let me begin by sharing what I do *not* mean when I use these words. I do *not* mean, "She sits on the board of General Motors." I do *not* mean, "He really doesn't seem to need other people very much." I do *not* mean, "She doesn't care what other people think of her." I do *not* mean, "He has it all together—no problems." These statements refer more to *pseudo-independence* than to real self. We *all* need people, we are *all* deeply affected by how other people treat us. No one is without vulnerability, anxieties, and problems. And despite its rewards, there is nothing particularly "independent" about moving up the ladder of success. In fact, success in the public domain may require a high degree of conformity and sacrifice of personal values.

If, however, we have come to believe that such is the *real stuff* of which independence or selfhood is made, then men may appear to have far more of it than women. That's not the case. What *is* the case is that many men have more *pseudo-self* or *pseudo-independence,* often acquired at the expense of others: women, children, and less powerful men.

How, then, can we think in a more objective way about this business of "self"? How do we begin to define our term

What's "Low" on the Selfhood Scale?

Jo-Anne's letter to the editor provides us with an obvious example of a couple that is operating at the low end of the selfhood scale. Her husband, we can assume, is threatened by the emergence of *differences* in their relationship and by his wife's own growth. His position of dominance (being the one who makes the rules in the relationship) may give him a sense of pseudo-self (or pseudo-independence), but this rests on his wife's one-down, accommodating stance. Jo-Anne, for her part, sacrifices a great deal of self in her marriage. Surely, subscribing to *Ms.* is not the only issue in their relationship on which she fails to take a stand and thus behaves in ways that are not congruent with her own beliefs and values. This is not to say that this couple's behavior is without sense or reason. In fact, this marital dance is an exaggeration of one that is encouraged and prescribed in our culture and held in place by social and economic arrangements. But it is probably clear to even the casual reader that neither husband nor wife would rate at the top of the selfhood scale.

There are other ways in which we sacrifice or lose self that are less obvious to observe or label. When anxiety is high, and particularly if it remains high over a long period of time, *we are likely to get into extreme positions in relationships where the self is out of balance, and our relationships become polarized.* Consider how my own family operated during the period of high stress following the diagnosis of my mother's cancer.

For starters, my own role as "the mess" in the family, or "the problem child," was a de-selfed position. I was not able to free myself from the anxious, emotional family field in order to make use of my competence and show my strong, positive side to others. Like Jo-Anne, I believed that the integrity of my relationships, perhaps my very survival, depended on my giving up self. Unlike Jo-Anne, I could not have articulated my dilemma. I did not *consciously* give up self, as she did.

What about my sister? She behaved so competently, maturely, and responsibly—and so clearly seemed to have it all together—that surely *she* would be high on the selfhood scale. That's how others saw it, including my parents, who viewed Susan as sailing through the crisis. And yet Susan's overfunctioning behavior was as de-selfed as my own under-functioning behavior. She was no higher on the selfhood scale, she was only sitting on the opposite end of the seesaw. All of us have a vulnerable side, just as all of us have strength and competence. When we cannot express *both* sides with some balance, then we are not operating with a whole and authentic self.

What about my father? Like many men, he distanced. This may have been his attempt at helping the family, and certainly at lowering his own anxiety. Distant people are often labeled as "having no feelings," but *distancing is actually a way of managing very intense feelings*. It is also a de-selfed position. We are not high on the selfhood scale when we cannot stay emotionally connected to family members and speak directly to the important and difficult issues in our lives.

And my mother? By her own report she did not have enough self to choose life on her own behalf. My mother can now speak eloquently about how the cancer (and a trip to the Grand Canyon) challenged her to be her self and to be *for* her self. But this came later. Also, focusing on a child (or on any other family member) is another way that we manage anxiety, but at cost to both the self and the focused-on individual.

Toward More Self

It is not my intention to portray my family as a neurotic group of nonselves. Quite the contrary. My mother, father, sister, and I were simply behaving as individuals and families behave under stress. *Overfunctioning, underfunctioning, fighting, pursuing, distancing,* and *child-focus* (or *other-focus*) are normal, patterned ways to manage anxiety. One way is not better or more virtuous than another.

But when anxiety is high enough or lasts long enough, we get locked into rigid and extreme positions on these dimensions. Then our relationships become polarized and stuck, and we may have difficulty finding creative new options for our own behavior. In fact, the very things that we do to lower our anxiety usually just keep the old pattern going, blocking any possibility of intimacy. And the actual sources of the anxiety may be unclear or difficult for us to focus on and process.

When this kind of stalemate occurs, we need to work on the "I," and always in the direction of movement toward "more self." You may already have some idea of what this work entails. We move up on the selfhood scale (and the intimacy scale, for that matter) when we are able to:

- present a balanced picture of both our strengths and our vulnerabilities.
- make clear statements of our beliefs, values, and priorities, and then keep our behavior congruent with these.
- stay emotionally connected to significant others even when things get pretty intense.
- address difficult and painful issues and take a position on matters important to us.
- state our differences and allow others to do the same.

This is not *all* that "being a self" involves, but it's a good start. And it is the very stuff that intimacy is made of.

In the chapters that follow, we will see how moves toward intimacy always require us to focus on the self as the primary vehicle for change, while viewing the self in the broadest possible context. This is a difficult task in the best of circumstances. When anxiety is high, it is more difficult still.

4

Anxiety Revisited: Naming the Problem

"Anxiety is the pits!" I recently remarked to a close friend. I was having more than my fair share of it at the time. My friend, in her cheerful attempt to add perspective, reminded me that people don't die from anxiety—and that eventually it goes away. That was not a bad reminder. Anxiety can make you shake, lose sleep, feel dizzy or nauseous. It can convince you that you are losing your memory, if not your mind. But anxiety is rarely fatal. And eventually it will subside.

Of course, this is not the whole story. The things we do to *avoid* the experience of anxiety, and the particular patterned ways we *react* to it, may keep our relationships, and our selves, painfully stuck. What's reflexive and adaptive in the short run may carry the highest price tag over time. Even over generations.

The initial impact of anxiety on a relationship is always one of increased reactivity. Reactivity is an automatic, anxiety-driven response. When we are in reactive gear, we are driven by our feelings, without the ability to think about how we want to express them. In fact, we cannot think about the self or our relationships with much objectivity at all. We sincerely want things to be calmer and more intimate, but we keep reflexively doing what we always do, which only leads to more of the same.

Whatever our style of navigating key relationships under stress—pursuing, distancing, fighting, child-focus, overfunctioning, underfunctioning—we'll do it harder and with even greater gusto in an anxious emotional field. That's just normal. The important question is, What happens after that? Reactivity . . . and then what?

In some circumstances, we may be able to stand back a bit, tone down our reactivity to the other person, and do some problem solving. We can begin to identify our individual coping style, observe how it interacts with the style of others, and modify our part in stuck patterns that block intimacy. Sometimes, however, we cannot tone down our reactivity by an act of will. We need instead to address the source of anxiety that is revving us up. Frequently, our reactivity in one relationship is fueled by anxiety from an entirely different source. Let's take a look at how such a process can work.

Anxiety and the Pursuit Cycle

A couple of years back, my sister shared with me that she was having a terribly difficult time with her steady companion, David. Although Susan felt entirely committed to the relationship, David said he needed more time to work through his own issues in order to make a decision about living together. This was a difficult situation because Susan and David lived in two different cities, making for long and tiring weekend trips. However, this long-distance arrangement (and David's indecision) was nothing new and had been going on for quite some time.

What *was* new was my sister's sudden feeling of panic, resulting in her pressuring David for a decision he was not ready to make. Because my sister had been working for some time on her pattern of pursuing men who were distancers in romantic relationships, she was able to see her behavior like a red warning flag. She was unable, however, to tone down her reactivity and stop pursuing. By the time Susan called me, she was feeling terrible.

In thinking about my sister's situation, I was particularly struck by the *timing* of the problem. Susan's sense of desperation and her heightened reactivity to David's wish for more time and space followed a trip we took to Phoenix to visit our parents and to see our Uncle Si, who was dying from a fast-moving lung cancer. Si's diagnosis was a shock to us, for he was a vibrant, strapping man we had assumed would outlive everyone. Visiting with him was also a reminder of past losses, impending losses, and some recent health scares and downhill slides in our family tree. Of all of these stressors, the closest to home for Susan and me was an earlier diagnosis that our father had a rare, degenerative brain disease. Because my father surprised everyone by regaining considerable functioning, this devastating diagnosis was replaced with a more hopeful one.

During our phone conversation, I asked Susan if there might be a connection between her anxious focus on David, and all the emotions that were stirred up by our recent visit to Phoenix. This made intellectual sense to her, on the one hand, but on the other, it seemed a bit abstract since Susan was not experiencing a connection at a gut level. Indeed, any of us may have difficulty appreciating that key events in our first family—and how we respond to them—profoundly affect our current (or future) romantic relationships.

Soon thereafter, Susan came to Topeka for a long weekend and decided to consult with a family systems therapist during her visit. As a result, she began to more fully appreciate the link between recent health issues in our family and her anxious pursuit of David. Simply *thinking* about this connection helped Susan to de-intensify her focus on David and reflect more calmly and objectively on her current situation.

Susan was also challenged to think about the pursuer-distancer pattern she was stuck in. It was *as if* 100 percent of the anxiety and ambivalence about living together were David's. It was *as if* Susan were just 100 percent raring to go—no worries at all, she said, except how they would decorate the apartment. Such polarities (she stands for togetherness, he for distance) are common enough, but they distort the experience of self and other, and just keep us stuck.

Finally, Susan confronted the fact that she was putting so much energy into her relationship with David that she was neglecting her own work and failing to pay attention to her short- and long-term career goals. On the one hand, Susan's attention to this relationship made sense because ensuring its success was her highest priority. On the other hand, *focusing on a relationship at the expense of one's own goals and life plan overloads that relationship.* The best way Susan could work on her relationship with David was to work on her own self. This kind of self-focus is a good rule of thumb for all of us.

Having a Plan

Insight and understanding are necessary but insufficient pieces of solving a problem. The next challenge for Susan was translating what she had learned into action. What might Susan do differently upon her return home to lower her anxiety and achieve a calmer, more balanced relationship with David? By the time Susan left Topeka, she had formulated a plan. Whenever we are feeling very anxious, it can be enormously helpful to have a clear plan, a plan based not on reactivity and a reflexive need to "do something" (anything!), but rather on reflection and a solid understanding of our problem.

Breaking the Pursuit Cycle

This is what Susan did differently upon her return home. First, Susan shared with David that she had been thinking about their relationship during their time apart and had gained some insight into her own behavior. "I came to realize," she told David, "that the pressure I was feeling about our living together had less to do with you and our relationship, and more to do with my anxiety about some other things." She filled David in on what these other things were—family issues related to health and loss. David was understanding—and visibly relieved.

Susan also told David that perhaps she was letting him express the ambivalence for *both* of them, which probably wasn't fair. She reminded David that her own track record with relationships surely provided her with good reason to be anxious about commitment, but that she could avoid this pretty well by focusing on *his* problem and *his* wish to put off the decision.

This piece of dialogue was hardest for Susan, because when we are in a pursuer-distancer polarity, the pursuer is convinced that *all* she wants is more togetherness and the distancer is convinced that *all* he wants is more distance. Sometimes only after the pursuit cycle is broken can each party begin to experience the wish for both separateness and togetherness that we all struggle with.

Finally, Susan told David that she had been neglecting her own work projects and needed to put more time and attention into them. "Instead of driving up next weekend," Susan said, "I'm going to stay at home and get some work done." For the first time in a while, Susan became the spokesperson for more distance, *not in an angry, reactive manner but rather as a calm move for self.* Indeed, when Susan began to pay more attention to her work, she became quite anxious about how she had neglected it.

The changes Susan made were effective in breaking the pursuer-distancer pattern that was bringing her pain. If we are pursuers, such moves can be excruciatingly difficult to initiate and sustain in a calm, non-reactive fashion. Pursuing is often a reflexive reaction to anxiety. If it is *our* way, we will initially become *more* anxious when we keep it in check.

From where, then, do we get the motivation and the courage to maintain such a change? As one colleague of mine explains, we get it from the conviction that the old ways simply do not work.

Moving Back to the Source

Before Susan left Topeka, she considered another option aimed at helping her to calm things down with David. Whenever Susan found herself feeling anxious about the relationship and slipping back into the pursuit mode, she would contemplate *sitting down and writing a letter to our father instead, or calling home.* This may sound a bit farfetched at first, but it makes good sense. If Susan managed her anxiety about family issues by distancing, then she would keep her anxiety down in that arena but she would be more likely to get intense with David. If she could stay connected to the *actual source of her anxiety,* then she might become more anxious about our parent's failing health, for example, but the anxiety would be less likely to overload her relationship with David. Indeed, learning how to stay in touch with people on our own family tree, and working on key emotional issues at their source, lays the groundwork for more solid intimate relationships in the present or future.

Of course, staying connected to family members and working on these relationships is a challenge requiring considerable time and effort. Indeed, this work really has no end but by the limits of our own motivation. Had Susan been in therapy, she might have chosen to continue and deepen this work over time. But a small step can go a long way. For Susan, just keeping in touch with family helped to lower her reactivity to David's caution and occasional distance. And lowering her reactivity was the key element that allowed Susan to stay on course in modifying her reflexive pattern of pursuit.

A Postscript on Partners
Who Can't Make Up Their Minds

What if *your* partner can't make a commitment? What if he's not ready to think about marriage, not ready to give up another relationship, not sure that he is really in love? He (or she) may or may not be ready in two years—or twenty. Does Susan's story imply that we should hang around forever, working on our own issues and failing to address our partner's uncertainty? Does it mean that we should never take a position about our partner's distancing or lack of commitment? Certainly not! A partner's long-term ambivalence *is* an issue for us—that is, if we really want to settle down.

We will, however, be *least successful* in addressing the commitment issue—or any issue, for that matter—if we are coming from a reactive and intense place. Working to keep anxiety down is a priority, because anxiety drives reactivity, which drives polarities. (*All* he can do is distance. *All* she can do is pursue.) Of course, anxiety is not something we can eliminate from our lives. Our intimate relationships will always be overloaded with old emotional baggage from our first family as well as recent stresses that hit us from all quarters. But the more we pay attention to the multiple sources of anxiety that impinge on our lives, the more calmly and clearly we'll navigate the hot spots with our intimate other.

A Calm Bottom Line

Let's look at a woman who was able to take a clear position with her distant and ambivalent partner, a position that was relatively free from reactivity and expressions of anxious pursuit. Gwenna was a twenty-six-year-old real estate agent who sought my help about a particular relationship issue. For two and a half years she had been dating Greg, a city planner who had had disastrous first and second marriages and couldn't make up his mind about a third. Gwenna was aware that Greg backed off further under pressure, yet she didn't want to live forever with the status quo. How did she ultimately handle the situation?

As a first step, Gwenna talked with Greg about their relationship, calmly initiating the conversation in a low-keyed fashion. She shared her perspective on both the strengths and weaknesses of their relationship and what her hopes were for their future. She asked Greg to do the same. Unlike earlier conversations, this one was conducted without her pursuing him, pressuring him, or diagnosing his problems with women. At the same time, she asked Greg some clear questions, which exposed his own vagueness.

"How will you know when you *are* ready to make a commitment? What specifically would need to change or be different than it is today?"

"I don't know," was Greg's response. When questioned further, the best he could come up with was that he'd "just feel it."

"How much more time do you need to make a decision one way or another?"

"I'm not sure," Greg replied. "Maybe a couple of years, but I really can't answer a question like that. I can't predict or plan my feelings."

And so it went.

Gwenna really loved this man, but two years (and maybe longer) was longer than she could comfortably wait. So, after much thought, she told Greg that she would wait till fall (about ten months), but that she would move on if he couldn't commit himself to marriage by then. She was open about her own wish to marry and have a family with him, but she was equally clear that her first priority was a mutually committed relationship. If Greg was not at that point by fall, then she would end the relationship—painful though it would be.

During the waiting period, Gwenna was able to *not* pursue him and *not* get distant or otherwise reactive to his expressions of ambivalence and doubt. *In this way she gave Greg emotional space to struggle with his dilemma and the relationship had its best chance of succeeding.* Her bottom-line position ("a decision by fall") was not a threat or an attempt to rope Greg in, but rather a true definition of self and a clarification of the limits of what she could accept and still feel OK about in the relationship and her own self.

Gwenna would not have been able to proceed this way if the relationship was overloaded with baggage from her past and present that she was not paying attention to. During the waiting period, Gwenna put her emotional energy into working on her own issues, which included, among other things, her anger at her deceased father, who she felt had been unavailable to her, and her related pattern of choosing distant males with poor track records in relationships. Of course, hard work does not ensure that things turn out as we wish. While my sister and David now live happily together, Gwenna's story has a different ending.

When fall arrived, Greg told Gwenna he needed another six months to make up his mind. Gwenna deliberated a while and decided she could live with that. But when the six months were up, Greg was still uncertain and asked for more time. It was then that Gwenna took the painful but ultimately empowering step of ending their relationship.

Anxiety . . . From Where and When?

Anxiety. We all know it impacts on everything from our immune system to our closest relationships. How can we identify the significant sources of anxiety and emotional intensity in our lives?

Sometimes they are obvious. There may be a recent stressful event, a negative or even positive change we can pinpoint as a source of anxiety that is overloading a relationship. If *we* miss it, others may see it for us ("No wonder you've been fighting more with Jim—you moved to a new city just a year ago and that's a major adjustment!").

Sometimes we sort of know a particular event or change is stressful, but we don't fully appreciate just *how* stressful it really is. For example, we may downplay the emotional impact of significant transitions—a birth, a child leaving home, a graduation, a wedding, a job change, a promotion, a retirement, or an ill parent—because these are "just normal things" that happen in the course of the life cycle. Other people may even appear to breeze through. We fail to appreciate that "just normal things," when they involve change, will profoundly affect our closest ties.

In other cases we may simply *not* link anxiety from source A to stuckness in relationship B, or we may minimize or ignore the key events in our first family that raise intensity elsewhere. My sister, for example, was initially unaware that her reactive position with David was driven by the emotionality from her family visit, although one followed right on the heels of the other. Our narrow focus on one intimate relationship obscures the broader emotional field from our view.

A Look at the Emotional Field

Consider Heather, who found herself suddenly "swept away" by a married man named Ira and vulnerable to extreme highs and lows in response to Ira's alternating hot and cold attitude toward her. She felt so buffeted about by the intensity of her feelings that she called me to begin psychotherapy.

According to Heather's report, "nothing else was happening" in her life at the time her relationship with Ira heated up. That is, she believed that the beginning of their affair had occurred in a calm emotional field. When I inquired carefully, however, I learned that Heather's passionate attachment to Ira began shortly after the death of her maternal grandmother. Because this grandmother was a distant figure in Heather's life, this loss did not seem to Heather to be of particular emotional significance.

But such was not the case. Heather's widowed mother and grandmother had been extremely close, spending much of their time together. The grandmother's death raised uncomfortable issues for Heather concerning her mother's well-being and also evoked Heather's worry that she was next in line to fill up the empty space in her mother's life. It also stirred up strong feelings about the earlier loss of her own dad. As Heather was to learn, our distance from family members is by no means a protection from strong emotional reactions to their deaths.

The underground emotionality surrounding her grandmother's death created an anxious emotional field in which Heather's painful attachment to Ira took hold. Her reactivity to Ira's every move was sky-high. Yet from Heather's perspective, "nothing else was happening" when their steamy affair began.

Sometimes the source of anxiety or intensity that is fueling a current relationship problem is from an experience long past—incest, an early loss, or any number of "hot issues" in our first family which were never processed or resolved. The trauma, or the problem in the family that could not be talked about, might be from five years ago or fifty-five. The connection may be relatively easy to make ("I know that my problem with being intimate with Sam has something to do with my history of sexual abuse"). Or we may be unable to make a connection at all.

Consider, for example, Lois and Frances, two sisters in their late forties who barely speak to each other since their mother's death six years ago. Lois is still furious at Frances for not doing enough for their mother at the time of her greatest need, and Frances believes Lois made unilateral decisions about their mother's care without consulting her. The two sisters are locked in a mutually blaming stance, heading for a total cutoff that will likely continue in successive generations. Each considers "the problem" to be the fault of the other. Neither sister is aware that the intensity in their relationship (managed first by fighting and now by distance) has as its source the high level of anxiety surrounding their mother's terminal illness and death.

Staying angry and distant protects both Lois and Frances from the full experience of their grief, which they would meet head on if they truly reconciled and drew together. It also protects Lois from experiencing her anger *at her mother,* who left Frances more than half of the inheritance because Lois had a wealthier husband. Their stuck position blocks them from successfully mourning the loss of their mother, processing the issue of the inheritance, and affirming their important bond as sisters.

Six years after losing their mother, Lois and Frances have not yet moved out of their reactive way of relating to each other. Perhaps at some future time a crisis, or some other transforming life experience, will allow one of them to take the first bold move toward connectedness. If this occurs, it will surely constitute a courageous act of change.

Thinking About Anniversaries

Our closest relationships are like lightning rods that absorb tensions and anxieties from whatever source and from however long ago. *Anniversary dates will always kick up anxiety, whether we are aware of them or not.* For me, hitting my forties presents a challenge because my mother was diagnosed with her first cancer in her late forties—and her mother died at age forty-four. I trust the fifties will be easier, all other things being equal, which of course they never are. If a crisis hit your family when you were age six, you can be certain that you'll be operating in a more anxious emotional field when your child turns six and when you reach the age your mother was at that time.

This does not mean we will *feel* more anxious at an important anniversary date. When your daughter reaches age nine, the age you were when your parents divorced, you may not even remember that fact. Instead you may feel more critical of your husband, or perhaps feel more clingy and insecure. Or instead you may find that you and your daughter become quite distant—or that you fight with her daily about her school habits or choice of friends.

What we see most frequently at anniversary dates is the *outcome* of high anxiety, those predictable patterned ways in which people move under stress that rigidify and polarize our relationships. Some people *do* make the connection ("I notice I've wanted to leave Joe since I've been approaching the age of my mother's breakdown"). Most of us don't. Instead we just shift into a reactive gear and a particular relationship may take a downward spiraling turn. Or we just get reactive all over the place. Our boss criticizes our work and a cloud of depression settles over us all day. A boyfriend seeks more space and we feel panicky. We're just more vulnerable to automatic, intense reactions from whatever source.

Of course, none of this is exactly new. We all know there are multiple sources of stress that impact on a particular relationship at a particular time. And of course we are aware that anxieties and unresolved issues from our first family get us into trouble today. *Thinking* about key sources of anxiety, however, is a big challenge. *Working* on them is a bigger one still.

What Is the Problem?

Most of us confuse the *outcome* of high anxiety with "the problem." For example, I was viewed as "the problem" at the time of my mother's cancer diagnosis and I was sent to therapy. It would have been just as likely for anxiety to be managed by severe marital fighting or distance, in which case a "marital problem" might have been the diagnosis. In another family, Dad might have hit the bottle or Mother might have developed a severe depression with other family members getting organized around it in an unhelpful fashion.

When anxiety overloads a family beyond their resources to manage it, they will come to therapy naming the problem in one of three ways:

1. *Child-focus:* A child is seen as the problem and everything else may be viewed as OK.
2. *Marital fighting and/or distance:* "The marriage" is the problem.
3. *A symptomatic spouse:* One spouse is underfunctioning or has the symptom.

When *one* person or *one* relationship is labeled "the problem," other issues get obscured from view. For example, if my sister saw David's distancing (or her own pursuing) as "the real problem," she would have missed the point. On the one hand, it was helpful for her to observe and modify her own part in a pattern of distance and pursuit that was only bringing her pain. In that sense, the *pattern* was the problem. On the other hand, it was equally important that she widen her focus to include additional sources of anxiety that were fueling her reactivity.

Maintaining a broad perspective isn't easy. Naturally we want to focus where it hurts and we want to steer clear of other areas. For example, if we bring our child to therapy, we want the focus of treatment to be on the child. Our concern for our child is genuine enough. However, the *last thing* we want is to look at our own reactivity toward the child's father or stepmother, or how we are currently navigating our own relationship with our mother.

We want to look where we want to look. And the higher the anxiety, the more extreme our tunnel vision and the greater our vulnerability to be swallowed up by painful feelings. Yet, as the next chapter continues to illustrate, we cannot work on intimacy problems if we stay narrowly focused on one relationship or on any one definition of "the problem."

5

Distance and More Distance

Adrienne called me for an appointment with the goal of working on her marriage. She summarized the problem in these words: "Frank and I got along fine for the first few years. But after our second child was born, we began to fight a lot. And when we both had enough of that, we just stopped relating to each other and became like roommates sharing an apartment. I was devastated when I discovered he was having an affair, but I shouldn't have been surprised. I was looking at another man, too, even though I wasn't acting on it."

If not for the painful discovery of her husband's lover, Adrienne might not have come for help. "I knew the closeness had gone out of our relationship, both physically and emotionally," she explained, "but I wasn't that upset about it. Maybe I was denying the problem, but I figured it was just life. A lot of couples I know aren't intimate after they have kids. Every now and then the distance really bothered me, but at the same time I didn't take it that seriously. I suppose I got used to it."

When Adrienne first sought my help, she viewed distance as the problem in her marriage. Earlier, she had viewed marital fighting as the problem. Distancing and fighting, however, are not "the problem" between any two people. Both conflict and distance are normal ways of managing the anxiety that is freighting an important relationship.

Given sufficient time and the inevitable stresses that the life cycle brings, we can count on periods of reactive fighting and distance in even the most ideal partnerships. The fight-or-flight response is present in all species, our own included. The *degree* of trouble we get into in a particular relationship rests on two factors. The first is the amount of stress and anxiety that is impinging on a relationship from multiple sources, past and present. The second is the *amount of self* that we bring to that relationship. To the extent that we have not carved out a clear and whole "I" in our first family, we will always feel in some danger of being swallowed up by the "togetherness force" with others. Seeking distance (or fighting) is an almost instinctual reaction to the anxiety over this *fusion,* this togetherness which threatens loss of self.

The specific *way* we get into trouble has to do with our own particular style of managing anxiety and the dances we get stuck in with others. Adrienne's story will allow us to take an in-depth look at one common, if not universal, way of managing anxiety that can get us in trouble over the long haul in any close relationship: *emotional distance and cutoff.*

Distancing: The Problem or the Solution?

What is a distant relationship? Adrienne's description of her marriage to Frank provides a good example. At the time she discovered her husband's affair, they seldom fought, but at the same time they were not really close and they rarely shared their thoughts, feelings, and experiences. And rather than confront the distance in their relationship head-on, both of them were detouring their emotional energy toward a third party. Frank was having an affair, and although Adrienne was not sleeping with anyone, she had another man under her skin.

In one sense, Frank's affair—and Adrienne's affair of the mind—protected their marriage. Adrienne's erotic attachment to another man ensured that she would not fully experience her dissatisfaction with Frank, and thus the deeper problems in her marriage would not surface with real emotional force. When we look later at the complex business of triangles, we will see how third parties *do* serve to stabilize relationships and help keep the real issues safely underground. Of course, the solution is also the problem. Adrienne and Frank became so entrenched in an empty-shell relationship that it took a real crisis—Adrienne's discovery of the "other woman"—to get her to take a serious look at their marriage, and her life.

Most of us rely on some form of distancing as a primary way to manage intensity in key relationships, including those in our first family. For example, we may move to a different city or country as a way to avoid the difficult feelings evoked by closer contact with our parents or other family members. Or we may live in our folks' house but withdraw emotionally by keeping conversations superficial, by sharing little about our selves, or by avoiding certain subjects entirely. We may even have a sibling we don't speak to unless we happen to show up together at a family gathering.

Emotional distancing can be an essential first move to ensure our emotional well-being and even our survival. We all know from personal experience that a relationship can become so emotionally charged that the most productive action we can take is to seek space. And if we are in danger of violence or abuse, there is no higher priority than getting out of the situation to ensure that we will not be hurt.

Distancing is a useful way to manage intensity when it removes us from a situation of high reactivity and allows us to get calm enough to reflect, plan, and generate new options for our behavior. Often, however, we rely on distance and a cutoff to exit permanently (emotionally or physically) from a significant relationship, without really addressing the issues and problems. This may be the easiest and least painful way out in the short run—but whatever goes unresolved and unprocessed may cause trouble in our next relationship venture. As usual, it's a matter of short-term relief in exchange for a long-term cost.

In Adrienne's marriage the distance was extreme. At the same time, however, the triangles (Frank's affair and Adrienne's serious flirtation) stabilized the marriage so that neither partner was pushing for change—that is, not until the cat got out of the bag and there was no way to put it back in.

Back to the Emotional Field

All of us, without exception, have difficulty with intimacy, and over time, we will either move forward or drift backward in this dimension. Why did Adrienne move backward, and why did the distance in her marriage become so extreme?

According to Adrienne, marital problems "just happened" after the birth of Joe, their second son. But conflict in relationships does not "just happen," nor do people simply, without reason, drift into intractable fighting or distance. What, then, was the broader context for Adrienne and Frank's relationship difficulties? What was going on at around the time that Adrienne and Frank entered a period of constant fighting and bickering, and then one of unbridgeable distance, lack of communication, and infidelity? "Nothing much," according to Adrienne. On careful investigation, however, "nothing much" turned out to be a great deal, indeed.

Although Adrienne herself observed that marital tensions surfaced after the birth of Joe, their second son, she failed to associate the two events. Yet the connection was real enough. The birth of any child introduces extra stress into a marriage, and for this couple, the issue of second sons was a particularly loaded one. *What made it loaded was the history of "second sons" in the previous generation in each of their own families.*

In Adrienne's family, the second child, Greg, was born severely retarded and was placed in an institution when he was three. When I began seeing Adrienne in psychotherapy, she had not visited her younger brother for eleven years, because "he doesn't recognize anyone and there's no point." In Frank's family, the second and youngest son had been the "problem child," who was still considered something of a black sheep. Given these emotional issues surrounding second sons, it was no surprise that Joe's entrance into the family would evoke a fair share of underground anxiety and concern.

During Joe's first year of life, Adrienne's father was diagnosed with stomach cancer that was discovered at an advanced stage. Although Adrienne was terribly upset about her dad's diagnosis, she managed her feelings by distancing from him. She did not decrease the *amount* of contact she had with her father, but all her communication about his illness and her reactions to it were through her mother, who took the position that Adrienne's father needed to be protected from what was happening. When I first met with Adrienne, her father was at the terminal stage of his illness, but she had not yet found a way to even mention the cancer to him, to say good-bye, or to tell him how much she valued him as her father.

At the time that her marital problems intensified, Adrienne was also struggling with career issues. When Joe was born, Frank had managed his own anxiety by distancing into long hours of overtime work. On the surface, Adrienne fought with him about his unavailability, but she was also envious of his ability to lose himself in his projects. In contrast, she was experiencing increasing dissatisfaction with her own job as a lab technician but was unable to generate alternatives or to clarify what she wanted to do. By entering into a strong, erotic flirtation with a man at work, Adrienne put her own career issues on hold and helped to steady the marital boat—while she and Frank grew oceans apart.

It was an important first step for Adrienne to recognize the high stress she had been under since the birth of her second son, and to more clearly identify the key events that helped fuel the growing distance in her marriage. These were:

- the birth of a new baby, Joe, which evoked deep (although unconscious) feelings in Adrienne about her own retarded brother and his place in the family.
- the diagnosis of her father's terminal illness.

Adrienne's own career concerns and her difficulty formulating personal goals.

It was also reassuring for Adrienne to recognize that when anxiety and stress get high enough, or last long enough, marital distancing and/or fighting is one common way that it gets expressed.

From Insight to Action

As Adrienne looked carefully and objectively at how she negotiated other important relationships under stress, she began to observe that distancing was a long-standing pattern for her and other members of her family. It was, in fact, her familiar and preferred way of moving under stress, especially with men. In her first family, her relationship with two important males—her dad and her retarded brother—had always been distant, with her mother in the middle, conveying information between parties. Through therapy, Adrienne began to recognize that there was some connection between her distant position from the men in her first family and the dramatic distance that now characterized her marriage.

Wouldn't it be nice if "insight" automatically led to change? Typically it does not. Understanding the roots of a problem is not the same as knowing how to solve it.

As Adrienne learned more about herself in psychotherapy, she tried to move back into her marriage in a new way, hoping to achieve a deeper level of closeness. Some of what she did differently was ultimately productive. For example, she told Frank that psychotherapy was helping her to become aware of her *own* contribution to the distance in their marriage, which she was working to change. She also took a clear position that his extramarital affair was not acceptable to her and that he would have to end it in order for her to stay in the marriage. This he did.

But much of Adrienne's efforts to "push closeness" only interfered with its attainment. She became preoccupied with intimacy as a primary goal, keeping it in the forefront of her discussions with Frank and insisting that he join with her in the pursuit of it. The more she pursued Frank for greater closeness, and the more she focused on his lack of warmth, interest, and attentiveness, the more distant Frank became. And the more he distanced, the more Adrienne pursued.

What happened when Adrienne was able to break the pursuit-distance cycle? She accomplished this by de-intensifying her critical focus on Frank and by giving him more space, without returning to her earlier position of cold withdrawal. In response, Frank did make some tentative moves toward her. At this point, however, Adrienne responded negatively—she just wanted to be left alone. "To be really honest," she reflected in psychotherapy, "maybe it's too late. Or maybe I really don't want to be particularly close with him. But I don't want to lose the marriage."

Adrienne gradually recognized her own allergy to intimacy, which helped her to realize that she needed to make changes in her original family relationships before she could move differently in her marriage. This gave Adrienne the courage to go "back home" again. If she chose to remain cutoff from the males in her first family and failed to process emotional issues in that arena, then her marriage would remain overloaded. And Adrienne would continue to respond to the overload by distancing or with conflict.

"Dad, I'm Going to Miss You"

How did Adrienne move against the distance in her own family? First, she made a significant effort to connect with her dad directly about his illness rather than hearing all the details via her mom. The typical pattern was that Adrienne always began her visits with her dad by asking, "How are you?"—to which he responded with a superficial reply ("About the same") or with a somewhat loaded joke ("The doctors tell me I'm so healthy I could drop dead any minute"). Adrienne would then change the subject and they would chat about the weather or the grandchildren.

Adrienne made a big advance when she was able to cut through her father's distance (which was his attempt to offer Adrienne the protection *he* thought *she* needed) and ask him directly, "Dad, what are the doctors telling you about your cancer? I'd really like to hear the facts from you." When he gave his usual superficial and uninformative response, she let him know directly that although his cancer—and her awareness that she might lose him soon—was painful for her, she would feel much better if she knew the facts and was kept informed. When he said, "Mother will keep you informed," Adrienne responded, "She does, Dad, but I'd also like to hear it from you." This brief conversation was a big step for Adrienne in dealing more directly with her dad's impending death. It was also the first time that the word "cancer" had been used by any family member in her father's presence. He reacted awkwardly at first and then later with relief and greater openness.

Of course, there were times when Adrienne's dad did not feel like talking about his illness, and Adrienne was sensitive to his moods. It is of questionable virtue to push someone into discussing something because *we* think it is good to do so. But often we confuse sensitivity with an anxious "protectiveness" in which the lines of communication shut down in a family because everyone operates on the assumption that the *other* person doesn't want to hear it or can't handle it.

Initially, Adrienne was convinced that her father chose not to discuss his own dying ("He can't deal with it") and that bringing it up was intrusive. This notion was reinforced by her mother, who insisted that Adrienne's father "could never deal with reality." *Yet Adrienne herself was not asking her father questions that made clear her wish to keep the lines of communication open.* Adrienne made a courageous change in her own relationship with her dad when she began to calmly and clearly ask questions.

What sorts of questions? Adrienne's questions conveyed her interest in the facts of his illness as the doctors saw it ("Did you get the results of the test back?" "What is your doctor telling you about your prognosis and the course of the cancer?"). Her questions conveyed her interest in her dad's own perspective ("Do you agree with the doctors or see it differently?" "What's your own sense about this cancer and your prognosis?") And her questions conveyed her interest in her dad's thoughts and feelings about death.

When, through her questions and the sharing of her own reactions, Adrienne convinced her father of *her* genuine wish to know, he turned out to value the opportunity to talk about his terminal condition. A week before he died, Adrienne's father shared his "philosophy of death" with her and they did some crying together. Later that week Adrienne told me, "It was a good kind of crying—not a depressed crying, but just an emotional crying."

As Adrienne put her emotional energy into connecting with her family around her father's impending death, she experienced great sadness but also felt as if a load had lifted from her marriage. She became less preoccupied with "lack of intimacy" as a root difficulty in her marriage, and paradoxically, she became better able to achieve it. As her marriage became freer from the emotional overload of an important mourning process, Adrienne also became freer to share with Frank what she was going through as her dad was dying. She was able to focus more on how *she* was managing her own issues, and less on whether Frank was responding to her self-disclosures in just the "right way." As a result, she and Frank shared more instances of genuine closeness.

"My Brother Means Nothing to Me"

The most distant relationship in Adrienne's life was with her brother. She treated it as a "non-relationship" and did her best to render Greg invisible in her mind. It is not possible, however, to have a "non-relationship" with a parent or sibling. Distance and cutoff only cause intensity to go underground and resurface elsewhere.

For a long time in psychotherapy, Adrienne could not *think* about her brother, Greg, much less contemplate a visit to the institution where he resided. Each time I asked a simple factual question about Greg, or inquired about how his retardation and institutionalization affected the family, Adrienne gave the same predictable response: "I never knew him—he's too retarded to relate to—he means nothing to me."

Adrienne had not seen Greg for over a decade, and prior to that her contact with him had been minimal. His status as an "invisible" family member was more than apparent. Adrienne's older son, who was five, did not even know that his mother had a brother. Frank had never met Greg or seen a photograph of him as an adult. Adrienne herself might not have recognized Greg if she had run into him on the street.

Adrienne talked about her lifelong distance from Greg as if it reflected nothing more than disinterest ("I simply can't think of any reason why I'd go to the trouble to see him"). She was totally unaware of the underground feelings that threatened to surface if she made any move to reconnect. "This may sound callous," she would report blandly, "but I just don't consider him a member of the family."

We commonly confuse distance or cutoff with a defect of the heart. We hear this confusion in everyday talk, and even in the pronouncements of mental health experts. Labels like "unloving" or "uncaring" may automatically be applied to a mother who relinquishes or takes flight from her child, to a father who abandons the family and never looks back, to a brother who cuts off communication with his sister after she enters a psychiatric hospital or becomes ill.

It is important to understand that distance and cutoff between family members have nothing to do with an absence of feeling, or a lack of love or concern. Distance and cutoff are simply ways of managing anxiety. Rather than reflecting a *lack* of feeling, they reflect an *intensity* of feeling. The feeling may surround hot issues that have evolved over many generations and that cannot be processed or even mentioned easily.

Adrienne learned the true meaning of intensity only *after* she telephoned the institution where her brother lived and set up a date for the long trip to a neighboring state to see him. The week before the visit, she was unable to sleep well, had terrifying and violent nightmares, and experienced her first full-blown panic attack on the bus to work one day.

For reasons she could not articulate, she felt unable to tell her mom about the visit, so kept it a secret.

These dramatic reactions to Adrienne's planned visit forced her to recognize that seeing her brother was no small emotional matter. Still, it was only *after* she visited Greg that she could begin to identify and process the underground feelings that the distance and cutoff had held in check.

Fallout from Change

After so much anticipatory anxiety, Adrienne found the actual visit to Greg reassuring. Their meeting stayed on a calm note, and although Adrienne was convinced that her status as a sister went unappreciated, Greg seemed pleased by her presence. Having the chance to actually see Greg, to be with him, to observe the setting he was in, and to meet a few staff members who had daily contact with him made Greg into a "real person" for her, and allowed her to replace fantasy with a more realistic perspective on her brother. What made the deepest impression on Adrienne, though, was that one young staff member at the institution was obviously fond of Greg, a feeling he apparently reciprocated. "It never occurred to me that anyone could actually become *attached* to him—or vice versa!" Adrienne exclaimed during her next therapy session. "I mean this guy seemed to have a real affection for Greg, like they had a *real relationship.*"

Because Adrienne initially found the visit reassuring, she was unprepared for its emotional aftermath. Several weeks after she shared the news of her visit to Greg with her mom, Adrienne came to therapy nearly hysterical. Her mother, Elaine, was acutely depressed and had shared suicidal fantasies with her, although she had no plan to act on them. The following week, I saw Adrienne and her mother together.

Over the next several sessions with Adrienne and Elaine, a crucial family theme erupted—a theme that had seethed like an underground volcano since Greg's birth. This "hot issue" was Greg's retardation and, more specifically, the unspoken question in the family of "Who was to blame?" What emerged through Elaine's outpouring of tears and despair was her most profound sense of guilt and self-recrimination for the condition of her son.

Adrienne's cutoff from her brother had helped protect her mother from the conscious recognition of these feelings, and protected the family from having to deal with a subject that everyone feared was too hot to handle. At an unconscious level, Adrienne had always appreciated this fact. Children usually do.

During our time together, Adrienne's mother was able to share with her daughter the questions about her son's retardation that had haunted her for decades. Had she caused it? Was it a gene from her side of the family? Was it the bottle of wine she had drunk during that first month when she didn't know she was pregnant? Elaine also shared her profound guilt about the decision to institutionalize Greg. She told Adrienne, in a voice filled more with despair than blame, "When you kept talking on and on about how much that man liked Greg—and how they seemed to really be good for each other—I thought you were telling me that I was a monster for putting him away!"

In a way, all this was new to Adrienne. But in a way it was not, for she had always sensed the unnamed tension surrounding the subject of Greg. As Adrienne and her mother were able to share their thoughts and reactions on this difficult subject, her mother's depression rapidly lifted. At the same time, however, a second "hot issue" emerged, as Elaine got in touch with her previously repressed rage at her deceased husband. Elaine had always felt that her husband's family blamed her for the decision to institutionalize Greg, and she believed that her husband had not come to her defense. She and her husband had not talked about this directly, but it provided the backdrop for their own growing marital distance. Indeed, after *their* second child, Greg, Elaine and her husband had drifted into a growing distance, *a pattern that Adrienne could now recognize herself repeating.*

Both Adrienne and Elaine found it awkward and difficult to talk openly about these painful issues, but it was ultimately rewarding. As a result of getting things out on the table, mother and daughter shared a genuinely closer relationship and both were freer to stay in more emotional contact with Greg. Elaine's self-disclosure helped Adrienne to recognize that *she too felt guilty:* guilty because she had never wanted Greg to come along in the first place; guilty because she had wanted him gone from the moment he arrived; guilty because, in the omnipotent unconscious mind of the child, these "bad feelings" had *caused* her brother to be extruded from the family; and finally, guilty because her life was so easy and privileged compared to the hardship that Greg's handicap imposed on him.

When Adrienne could articulate these guilty feelings, think about them, talk about them with family members, and recognize that they were both *natural* and *shared,* her unconscious no longer needed to "do penance" for her sins. Much to Adrienne's surprise, she found herself thinking more creatively about her work situation, as her own guilt about having a retarded brother was no longer a restraining force.

Adrienne's guilt, however, did not derive entirely from early irrational sources. Adrienne also felt guilty because she had rendered her brother invisible and treated him as if he did not exist. *Because women are encouraged to feel guilty about*

*everything—and to take responsibility for all human problems—
we often have difficulty sorting out when guilt is there for a good
reason.* By "good reason" I refer to guilt that lets us know we
are not taking a responsible position in a relationship: *a
position that is congruent with our own values and beliefs as we
have struggled to formulate them, separate from pressures of family
and culture.*

Only *after* visiting her brother and breaking the old distancing pattern did Adrienne become aware of her strong
feelings of guilt for having stayed away. This awareness led to
changed behavior, as it should. Adrienne slowly began to
stay in reasonable contact with her brother, and she brought
her children and husband to meet him as well. Whether Greg
recognized her as family or fully appreciated her visits was
not entirely clear at the time Adrienne terminated her work
with me. Adrienne had nonetheless decided to stay connected—for her own sake.

What About Adrienne's Marriage?

Adrienne came into therapy with only one goal and only one
area of concern: She wanted to save her marriage. She had
no wish to talk about her father's impending death, and the
subject of her retarded brother was even more off-limits. "I
can't stand talking about this family stuff!" she would frequently say to me. "What does it have to do with anything?"

Adrienne's feelings were more than understandable.
Our desire not to focus where it hurts makes sense and
should always be respected. This is where Adrienne and I
began, and we might not have needed to look further. *In most
cases, however, couples cannot achieve greater intimacy by staying
narrowly focused on their relationship.* Because our current

relationship problems are fueled by other unresolved issues and affected by how we understand and navigate family relationships, it just doesn't help to stay locked into a narrow perspective.

As Adrienne was able to identify a long-standing pattern of distancing in her family (a pattern that had gone on for at least several generations) and then was able to connect more directly with her family members, her behavior with Frank gradually shifted. Rather than swinging back and forth between distance, on the one hand, and "pushing" for intimacy, on the other, Adrienne found a new middle ground. She moved from self-defeating attempts to be closer (like blaming Frank for being a distant person and pushing him to reveal himself) to constructive attempts (letting Frank know that she wanted to spend a weekend together in the city; sharing more of herself with him, without focusing on whether she got the "right" response). By dealing directly with issues in her own family of origin, rather than avoiding them, Adrienne gained the ability to think more objectively and calmly about her marital difficulties.

There was another reason why Adrienne could not achieve her goal of "closeness" by staying narrowly fixed on her marriage. Paradoxically, couples become less able to achieve intimacy as they stay focused on it and give it their primary attention. *Real closeness occurs most reliably not when it is pursued or demanded in a relationship, but when both individuals work consistently on their own selves.* By "working on the self," I do not mean that we should maintain a single-minded focus on self-actualization, self-enhancement, or career advancement. These are male-defined notions of selfhood that we would do well to challenge. Working on the self includes clarifying beliefs, values, and life goals, staying responsibly connected to persons on one's own family tree, defining the

"I" in key relationships, and addressing important emotional issues as they arise.

Surely, it was important for Adrienne to take the distance in her marriage seriously. For some time before discovering her husband's affair, she had not taken it seriously enough. And yet, it was equally important for her to let go of her overriding preoccupation with intimacy as a primary goal, in order to be better able to achieve it.

As Adrienne paid attention to her important family relationships she became more self-focused and less reactive to Frank's every move. Lowering our reactivity is always a challenge and a prerequisite for working on relationship issues in a productive way. Not surprisingly, the challenge is particularly difficult when that other person is pushing our buttons by not thinking, feeling, and reacting as we do—or as we think they should.

6

Dealing with Differences

"My brother's views on divorce drive me crazy!"

"I simply can't accept the fact that my sister doesn't visit Dad at the hospital."

"It infuriates me that my best friend refuses to join AA when she needs it so desperately!"

"Why doesn't he talk *about things when he's upset!"*

It's hard to feel intimate with someone we disagree with. Surely relationships would be calmer and simpler if everyone thought, felt, and reacted exactly as we do. Believing that one view of reality (usually our own) is the correct one, that different ways of thinking or being in the world mean that one person is "right" and the other is "wrong," is just human nature. We commonly confuse *closeness* with *sameness* and view intimacy as the merging of two separate "I's" into one worldview.

Some differences are bound to make us feel angry, isolated, and anxious at times—and for this reason it may be hard to keep in mind that *differences are the only way we learn.* If our world—or even our intimate relationships—were comprised only of people identical to ourselves, our personal growth would come to an abrupt halt.

But perhaps more to the point is the fact that people *are* different. *All of us see the world through a different filter, creating as many views of reality as there are people in it.* We view the world through the unique filter of our age, race, gender, ethnic background, religion, sibling position, and social class, for starters. And our particular view of a "correct" reality will be further refined by our family history, a history which has evolved particular myths, party lines, and traditions over many generations, along with particular requirements for sameness and for change. This is an easy point to "get" intellectually but not emotionally. Until we can truly appreciate and respect this concept of *a different filter,* we are bound to lose perspective. It will require just a little bit of stress to get us overfocused on what the other party is doing wrong—or not doing right—and underfocused on the self.

This is not to deny our strong human need to connect with people like ourselves. Certainly we feel a special closeness to others who share our deeply held beliefs and values, who enjoy similar interests and activities, and who do things our way. But in any close relationship differences will inevitably emerge—differences in values, beliefs, priorities, and habits, *as well as differences in how we manage anxiety and navigate relationships under stress.*

When anxiety lasts long enough, these differences may calcify into exaggerated positions in a relationship, as they did in my own family during my mother's illness. And if we react strongly to differences (distancing or focusing on the other in an intense way), things may go from bad to worse.

The examples I am about to share with you illustrate the challenge we face in accepting differences and becoming less reactive to that other person who is pushing our buttons or not doing things our way. We will see that this can be a relatively manageable challenge in some circumstances and feel virtually impossible in others.

Dealing with Differences

Suzanne was an anthropologist who had spent several years studying child-rearing patterns in Southeast Asia. She spoke three foreign languages fluently, and by virtue of both her training and personal bent, she was deeply interested in people of other cultures.

Learning to be a calm, nonjudgmental, and objective observer of differences was Suzanne's stock-in-trade. But like the rest of us, this did not generalize to her closest relationships. When Suzanne first came to my office for a consultation, she was furious at her husband, John, for being "tied to his parents' apron strings." John accompanied her to the session, begrudgingly, and only much later returned on his own initiative.

I learned that John, the firstborn and best educated of three sons, was the only sibling to have moved away from the New York area where his Italian grandparents had first settled. Six months ago, his mother had suffered a serious stroke, and John was struggling with guilt feelings about living so far from the family home, leaving his dad and two younger brothers to carry the major burden of day-to-day care. Suzanne felt increasingly unsympathetic to her husband's struggle, which included endless emotional phone calls home. "John has never really separated from his parents," Suzanne explained during our initial meeting, with no attempt to disguise the frustration she was feeling. "My husband is much more tied to *them* than he is to *me!*"

Suzanne had initially requested my help for "marital problems," but it quickly became evident that she viewed John—along with his "sticky, demanding family"—as the problem. Predictably, John was convinced that Suzanne was the problem. She was, by his report, cold and critical, without empathy or appreciation for his dilemma.

A Matter of Ethnicity

Ethnicity is just one of many filters through which we see the world, but since Suzanne was an anthropologist, it seemed like a logical place to help her adopt a more reflective attitude about the differences that concerned her. Suzanne came from an Anglo-Saxon, Protestant background, John from an Italian one. Could Suzanne begin to appreciate these two different "cultures" with the same objectivity, neutrality, and calm with which she contrasted child-rearing practices in America and China? Of course not. But perhaps she could move a bit in this direction. This was the challenge, and a difficult one at that, particularly because Suzanne was operating under the sway of such strong feelings.

What Is a "Family"?

Suzanne knew something about the differing traditions from which she and John came, but she hadn't really given it much thought. When she became curious enough to do some reading on the subject, she explored what was known about how these two ethnic groups think about family and how they define their responsibility to the older generations. The research made her feel right at home.

Italian families place the strongest emphasis on *togetherness.* One does not really think of the individual (the "I") apart from the family, nor of the nuclear family apart from the extended family. The marriage of a child, for example, does not signify the "launching" of that child into the *outside* world, but rather the bringing of a new person *into* the family. With such high value placed on *taking care of one's own,* no one should have to go *outside* the family resources to solve problems or ask for help.

For white Protestants of British origin, the definition of "family" contrasts sharply. For Suzanne's ethnic group, family is a *collection of individuals,* with a few distinguished ancestors that one is not supposed to boast about. A high premium is placed on children leaving home at the appropriate age—launched into the world as separate, self-reliant, and competent individuals.

No wonder Suzanne and John had differing beliefs on such key issues as family loyalty and closeness, and the caretaking of aging parents! As did their families. John's family wanted him home. They were proud of his successes but felt betrayed and puzzled by his move halfway across the country, away from his roots. Suzanne's parents, in contrast, valued the separateness of individual family members. Grown children were expected to be competent and responsible during family crises—but "responsible" did not mean "togetherness," which only made Suzanne's family uncomfortable, particularly at times of stress.

A Warning About Generalizations

Thinking about her marriage in terms of ethnic differences allowed Suzanne to gain a more respectful appreciation of the *different filters* through which we see the world. Generalizations are of course potentially problematic because they can be used to stereotype people rather than to help us recognize the unique screen through which we filter our experience. When we generalize about any group ("The Irish are this way," "Firstborns are that way," "Women are this way") we *exaggerate* similarities within the group and *minimize* similarities between groups. Obviously there is great diversity in any group and countless exceptions to every rule.

When generalizations are made about subordinate group members, we need to be especially wary. Throughout the recorded history of "Mankind," generalizations about women (made in the name of God, nature, and science) have served the interests of the dominant group, defining "separate but equal" spheres which keep women in place and obscure the necessity for social change. As women, over generations, have fit themselves to these prescriptions of what is right and appropriate for our sex, the costs have been incalculable.

Generalizations do not tell us anything about "right" or "wrong," "better" or "worse," "natural" or "God-given." *They are useful only when they foster a greater respect and appreciation for our different constructions of reality that evolve out of different contexts.* In Suzanne's case, for example, her willingness to turn a scholarly eye on the subject of ethnicity helped her to stop *diagnosing* her husband's guilty struggle with conflicting loyalties and begin to see it as a *difference* that was a natural evolution of family patterns and traditions. As she became less reactive to his behaviors and less focused on them, she took the first steps toward changing a stuck marital battle and moved the relationship toward a calmer and more respectful togetherness.

Opposites Attract—and Then What?

Suzanne and John illustrate that old adage "Opposites attract." *Differences* may draw us like a magnet to the other person; however, these *same* differences may repel us later on. What initially attracts us and what later becomes "the problem" are usually one and the same—like the qualities that were most and least valued in my women's group.

John came from a tightly knit family which operated in a "one for all and all for one" fashion. As he increasingly struggled to establish an identity of his own, he became allergic to the high degree of closeness, togetherness, and emotionality in his family. In reaction to this, John was drawn to women who modeled a position of emotional detachment and distance. He fell in love with Suzanne, whose family prized emotional separateness and placed a high premium on the calm self-reliance of individual family members.

Suzanne, for her part, was allergic to the distance and superficiality in her own family. She felt especially drawn to John's large and expressive extended family. But what were her complaints five years into their marriage? Suzanne felt closed in and suffocated by John's "demanding" family ("It's like a big sticky cocoon") and she was mad at John for not "cutting the apron strings." From John's perspective, the "cool and clean" emotional attitude that had first attracted him was now his primary source of dissatisfaction.

Getting Self-Focused

The more Suzanne could think in terms of "cultural differences" between herself and John, the more she could lighten up. And the more Suzanne lightened up, the more effectively John struggled with his own problem. Suzanne didn't really need to become an expert on ethnicity to improve her relationship. Ethnic differences, like birth order, are just one of countless factors that influence our definition of self, our life course, and how we negotiate relationships. For Suzanne, however, her "research" helped her become less negatively focused on John's problem. Her newfound objectivity was a crucial first step toward change.

As Suzanne became less reactive to her husband's struggle, she was able to pay more attention to her own unfinished business with her first family. Suzanne bristled over John's long phone calls home, in part because of her distance from her own family. Slowly, Suzanne began to establish more direct emotional contact with her parents and sister, and in turn she became less focused on what John was or was not doing with his parents and relatives. *When we are not paying enough attention to how we are connecting with our own family, we will be overreactive to our in-laws—or to how our spouse is conducting his family business.*

Although Suzanne learned to stay out of John's family affairs, she did speak up about issues that affected her directly. For example, she and John were planning an eight-day visit to the East Coast; John's family was insisting that he and Suzanne stay with them the entire time. Suzanne, for her part, felt "claustrophobic" about the arrangement and wanted to stay with friends and just visit John's family during the day. Her husband's initial position was that his family

would never understand or accept such an arrangement—
and that he would not even consider it.

In the old pattern, Suzanne would hover around John
during his calls, criticizing his parents' possessiveness and
unreasonable demands, and instructing her husband as to
how he should stand up to them. In the new pattern, Suzanne stayed out of her husband's negotiations with his parents, while speaking clearly to the issues that directly concerned her. She let John know, for example, that it was
important for her to have time alone with him, and she
explained how stressful she found their visits when they
spent all their time with family. John did end up telling his
parents that he and Suzanne would be staying three of the
eight evenings in a hotel together, because they wanted some
time alone. Suzanne also took responsibility to ensure her
own time away from John's family when she felt she needed
it. If John had insisted on staying all eight nights with his
family, Suzanne would have decided she could live with it, or
she would have made alternative arrangements.

It was a real challenge for John to begin to establish
some limits and boundaries with his parents when the "togetherness force" seemed overwhelming. Likewise, Suzanne
was challenged to move *toward* her family when the "separateness force" went into full swing. It was this work, however, which ultimately allowed them to stop fighting and find
their own comfortable balance between the forces of separateness and togetherness in their lives together.

The Moral of the Story

We may not identify with the specifics of Suzanne's
story. Gender roles being what they are, it is far more com-

mon that *he* distances and *she* seeks more togetherness—and that daughters, not sons, will struggle harder around issues of caretaking and family responsibility.

Nevertheless, Suzanne's struggle is universal. All of us come from a "different culture," with family roles and rules that have evolved over many generations. Whether the issues are the big ones (How are aging parents cared for? How is money managed? How are children disciplined?), the medium ones (Is it OK to complain, boast, or shine?), or the small ones (Do the onions get chopped or sliced?), we are all deeply affected by family patterns and traditions that may seem like Truth itself, rather than one perspective among many.

In particular, we may fail to appreciate differences in the patterned ways that individuals move in relationships under stress. If our style of managing a stressful event is to share feelings and seek greater togetherness, we may rail against that other person whose preferred mode of handling the same stress is to be more private and self-reliant. If we tend to shift into an overresponsible, "fix-it" mode when anxiety hits, we may get all ruffled about that other person who reacts to stress with underresponsibility or a bit of spaciness. And the more intensely we do *our* thing, the more they do *theirs.* Distancers distance more when they are pursued. Underfunctioners underfunction more around overfunctioners. And vice versa. And the more we get focused on the other person's behavior rather than our own, the more stuck we become.

The higher the level of anxiety in a relationship and the longer it continues, the more likely we are to become polarized around differences and to get locked into a rigid and entrenched position over time. We tend to manage anxiety by dividing into two camps, quickly losing our ability to see both sides (or better yet, *more* than two sides) of an issue.

A good illustration of this is the story of one couple who came to therapy on the verge of divorce. Their only child, a six-year-old daughter, had been physically disabled in a car accident two years earlier. During the same year, the father's father was diagnosed with Alzheimer's. Clearly, the level of anxiety in this family had been chronically high, and the child, Deborah, was now having emotional problems at school.

The parents—seeking help for the first time, at the initiation of the school counselor—were hardly able to talk together. "I can't stand being around my wife anymore!" the husband explained. "It's all doom and gloom—always going over how depressed she is about the accident, always talking about Deborah's problems, always acting like someone's died when nobody has died." From the wife's perspective: "My husband can't deal with his feelings, he won't talk about what's happened, he just wants to be away as much as possible. I can't stand being so alone with it."

This couple had become rigidly polarized in dealing with their daughter's disability. Both were out of touch with an important part of their own experience that was being carried by the other in an exaggerated form. The mother was drowning in her grief. The father was distancing from his feelings and insisting that they get on with their lives. In listening to their angry criticisms of each other, one might easily lose sight of the fact that *both* have to grieve and *both* have to get on with their lives—although not in the same ways or on the same timetable.

Reactivity: Toning It Down

Our own *reactivity* to differences is what leads us to exaggerated and stuck positions in relationships—positions that become so rigid and polarized that we lose our ability to relate to *both* the competence and incompetence in the other party —and to *both* the competence and incompetence in the self. Instead we become *overfocused* on the incompetence of the other and *underfocused* on the incompetence of the self. We are unable to see more than one side of an issue, to generate new options, and to observe and change our *own* part in a relationship pattern that is keeping us stuck.

We all get reactive at times, and we know it when it hits. That other person only has to step off the plane, enter the room, come home ten minutes late, or mention a particular subject, and we feel that clutching in the gut, that quick rise of anger, that sudden depressed feeling, or that heavy grip on the heart. Suzanne experienced an intense and automatic emotional response whenever she heard her husband pick up the telephone to call his family in New York. And the couple whose daughter was disabled in a car accident experienced it almost every time they were in the same room together and tried to talk about their child. Our reactivity may take the form of a migraine headache or an attack of diarrhea on the first or last day of every visit home. The more we get stuck in a reactive mode over time, the more our differences become exaggerated and polarized.

Legally Divorced—Emotionally Married

Consider June and Tom, who were like many divorced couples, legally but not emotionally separated. The differences between them were quickly apparent to even the casual observer. June managed anxiety by *overfunctioning,* which is typical for her sibling position as the oldest of four daughters. That is, when stress hit, she moved in quickly in an overresponsible fashion to take charge and fix the situation. The higher the anxiety, the more she functioned harder and harder, and the more she focused on others who did not fulfill their responsibilities or accomplish things. People who were fond of June admired her competence, maturity, and reliability. Those who didn't like her called her bossy, strict, overly assertive, and demanding. This portrait is typical of an older sister of sisters.

Unlike June, Tom *underfunctioned* under stress. He tended to become fuzzy and irresponsible, inviting others to criticize or take over for him. For example, he would tell June that he'd return the kids to her house by 6:00 P.M. Sunday evening, but he would show up at 6:40 instead. Rarely did he make it to the phone to let her know he'd be late, although he knew that lateness pushed June's buttons more than anything else. People who liked Tom admired his warm, laid-back, charming, and relaxed style. Those who weren't his fans thought he should grow up and become more reliable and thoughtful toward others. Tom, in many ways, was a typical youngest child.

June and Tom's respective life-styles also reflected their differences. June was an ambitious and successful real estate agent who was not apologetic about the fact that she enjoyed the finer things in life. Status and material comforts were important to her, and she worked hard to provide the best for herself and her children. Tom, in contrast, worked for low pay with retarded children, and he prided himself on his antimaterialistic values. His company of choice was a group of local artists, all of whom lived modestly.

When I first saw Tom and June in consultation, they were angrily focused on each other, as they had been for much of their marriage. They could sit in the same room together only because of their shared concern about their two children, a son and a daughter, who were both showing signs of emotional difficulties. During our first few sessions together, each blamed the other for "causing" the children's problems. June was convinced that Tom's irresponsibility and immaturity were a terrible influence, especially on the younger child, their son. Tom felt similarly about June's values and life-style ("Can you imagine buying a seventeen-year-old girl a new sports car? What is she trying to prove to that kid!").

The differences between June and Tom had once drawn them together. Tom, who had grown up in an unpredictable family, saw in June the stability and reliability he had yearned for. June, once a quiet, overresponsible child, saw Tom as someone who would teach her to loosen up and have fun. But as it happens, the differences that attracted them to each other became very quickly the focus of angry attention.

Now, eighteen years after marrying and six years after divorcing, their reactive anger *was the glue that kept June and Tom from really separating or divorcing in the emotional sense.* As long as they kept this up, they were as married as ever. Their reactivity to each other kept them close (albeit in a negative way), and neither was ready to let go.

Who was the villain and who the victim? June's friends sided with her, and Tom's friends sided with him. In fact, both Tom and June were competent enough parents and neither of their life-styles was inherently bad for themselves or for their kids. They were just different. Likewise, over-functioning and underfunctioning are normal, patterned ways of managing anxiety. When we get locked into extreme or polarized positions, however, we begin to operate at a cost to both self and other.

So with two kids headed for serious trouble, what was the problem and whose problem was it? The problem was *not* the individual traits, qualities, or values of either parent. Both Tom and June had their strengths and weaknesses.

Rather the problem was their *reactivity* to each other, which was unrelenting and intense.

For example, when Tom brought the kids home an hour late, June might say nothing, but the tension in the room was so thick that her daughter said she could feel it. Five minutes later she would be on the phone with her best friend, talking about how irresponsible and immature Tom was, and how worried she was about his influence on the children. June had all but lost her ability to focus on and relate to Tom's competence as a father.

Tom, of course, did his full share to keep the intensity going. Not only did he know exactly how to push his ex-wife's buttons and keep her involved (like not phoning when he'd be late), but he was also highly reactive to June. For example, when his kids went camping with him and his buddies, wearing the sixty-dollar hiking boots that June had bought for them, Tom all but had a fit. Several times during the camping trip, he took potshots at the "rich kids' boots," which of course was really criticism of the children's mother.

What about the kids? They in turn were reactive to their parents' reactivity. The younger one in particular was becoming increasingly anxious and angry as he struggled with the question of "whose camp" he was in. Unable to navigate a separate relationship with each parent, free from the intensity between them, he was acting up in school and getting into every sort of trouble.

Tom and June quit their work with me after several sessions. Months later, June called to let me know that she had placed her two children in individual psychotherapy and that she hoped this would give them a chance to work on their problems, which she believed her husband had caused. Tom was vehemently against this therapy and refused to drive the kids to their sessions or support it in any way.

According to June, the new therapist joined her in viewing the children as the appropriate focus for treatment and Tom as the irresponsible parent who was not acting in their interests. The negative intensity between Tom and June had escalated to the highest point in their relationship. I do not know whether things are better or worse at the present time.

This is a story about a *child-focused triangle* and later we will be taking a careful look at how such triangles operate. The story also illustrates how different people (including different experts) will *name the problem* in different ways. At this point, however, I am sharing Tom and June's situation to illustrate a few key points.

First, differences per se are rarely "the problem" in relationships; the problem is instead our reactivity to differences. In divorce, for example, kids can do just fine even when the parents have dramatically different values, life-styles, and ways of managing anxiety. Children do poorly, however, when reactivity or expressed emotional intensity is high between the parents, and even more so if they are the focus of it. And of course, the parents stay stuck as well.

Second, reactivity exaggerates and calcifies differences. For example, June's overfocus on her husband's incompetence (and her underfocus on her own issues) only provoked his irresponsible behavior further, and helped polarize their relationship. Similarly, Tom's angry focus on his ex-wife's materialism (and his need to prove himself the "opposite") made it far less likely that the two of them could be in touch with whatever values, beliefs, and desires they did hold in common. Naturally, the kids felt pressured to choose whether they would be "like Dad" or "like Mom" (an impossible loyalty struggle), rather than being able to identify with whatever aspects of both parents felt comfortable to them.

Toning down our reactivity is perhaps the most crucial and difficult step toward removing barriers to intimacy or toward solving any human problem. This is why I sent Suzanne to the library to learn more about ethnicity—so that she could start *thinking* about differences in her marriage rather than just reacting to them. It is also why I challenged her to get better connected with her own family of origin— so that distance and cutoff in this area would not leave her more vulnerable to intense reactions in her marriage or in any other primary relationship. As we have seen with Susan, and Adrienne as well, *change occurs only as we begin thinking about and working on the self—rather than staying focused on and reactive to the other.*

What exactly does it mean to become less reactive and less focused on your ex-husband's irresponsibility, your husband's depression, your boss's criticalness, your brother's distance, your father's drinking, your mother's complaining? By accepting and appreciating differences, are we simply accommodating to a relationship? Does it mean that "anything goes"? Does it mean that we stew inside and say nothing? *Of course not!*

Toning down our reactivity and getting unfocused from the other does *not* mean distance, cutoff, silence, or accommodation. It does *not* mean ignoring things that trouble us, because we are scared of making the situation worse. In fact, toning down our reactivity means putting *more* energy into reconnecting and defining where we stand on important relationship issues, but in a new way that is focused on the self, not on the other. Let's see how this works.

7

Defining a Bottom Line

"I used to get really reactive to my father's drinking," Kristen explained in group therapy, "but I've finally gotten out of that position." Kristen was sharing her story with Alice, another group member who was still trying to "cure" her husband's alcoholism.

"I learned the hard way," Kristen continued, "that I just can't change him. I mean I tried for about ten years. I gave him calm and logical advice. I had screaming fits. I begged and pleaded. I told him that he had a disease that was ruining the whole family. Twice my mom and I signed him up for a treatment program and dragged him down there. Nothing worked. It took me about a decade to come to terms with the fact that I can't stop my dad from drinking and that he's not going to change."

Alice was listening with rapt attention. She knew all too well that her own practice of emptying the liquor bottles down the drain wasn't working, and she was eager for advice. "So how do you handle your father's drinking now?" she asked.

"I just ignore it," Kristen said flatly. "I was home last weekend and I knew right away that Dad had been drinking. I arrived after lunch and he was already slurring his speech and looking terrible. On Sunday he could hardly carry on a conversation and he was pretty much out of it the whole time I was there. When he was down in the basement, my mother told me that he's drinking more and more—and he won't even go to the doctor for a checkup. Dad still denies that he has a serious problem. But I don't get into it with him. I've really come to terms with the fact that I can't help him."

"You mean that you ignore your father's drinking?" asked Alice. "You don't pay attention to it?"

"Yes," explained Kristen. "It took me a long time to learn that there is nothing else I can do. He drinks, and that's his choice. And if you're still trying to make your husband stop drinking, you won't get anywhere, either!"

Kristen's story is a common one that is by no means specific to alcoholism. It raises the broader problem of how we respond in relationships when a person close to us is a chronic underfunctioner, or behaves in ways we cannot easily accept or tolerate. What works for us and what doesn't?

When we are able to recognize and truly accept what does *not* work we are almost halfway along. Kristen shared with the group what she learned that did not work with her dad. What did not work was her being reactive to his drinking and staying anxiously focused on it. What did not work was her giving him advice about his problem or trying to solve it for him. What did not work was her trying to fix or rescue him in any way—or even thinking that this was possible. What did not work was her lying, excusing, or covering up his drinking to any other person. What did not work was criticism, accusation, or blame. As Kristen herself explained, it took her a decade to truly accept that these old behaviors did not work.

And indeed, they do not. Whether the issue is the other person's drinking, depression, irresponsibility, schizophrenia, or whatever—any or all of the aforementioned behaviors only reduce the likelihood that the other person will take responsibility to solve the problem. It may take some of us more than a decade—perhaps a whole lifetime—to truly own up to the fact that these behaviors just don't work. In fact, they operate at the expense of the underfunctioning party and compromise any possibility of closeness based on mutual regard.

Recognizing that the old ways don't work gives us an opportunity to stop, think, gather information, orient to the facts, and generate new options for our own behavior. But to do this in an anxious emotional field is an unusual if not remarkable achievement. When Kristen tried to change the old pattern, what "solution" did she adopt? By her own report, she now ignored her father's behavior entirely—a form of emotional distancing. As we know, distancing from an issue or a person is still a reactive position, driven by anxiety. It simply keeps the intensity underground in one place, leaving us more vulnerable and reactive elsewhere.

Staying silent, acting as if "nothing was happening" when her father was drunk, taking no position on an important issue that bothered her and still made her clutch inside —these are reactive rather than responsible positions in an important relationship.

Kristen now talked *about* her dad with her mom, but she did not talk *to* him, which only further entrenched the long-standing distance between them. Kristen was participating in a common family triangle in which mother and daughter consolidate their closeness through their disappointment and frustration with Dad, rather than each continuing to deal directly with him on their own relationship issues. Father, as well, participates fully in maintaining his outside, underfunctioning position in this triangle.

Kristen's relationship with her father, like Adrienne's relationship with Frank (Chapter 5), reflects two typical patterned ways of managing anxiety. Surely we can recognize these from our own experience: The first is an *overtly* reactive position, where much life energy (anger energy and/or worry energy) is focused on the other, in unsuccessful attempts to change or blame that person; the second is a *covertly* reactive one, where we avoid the experience of intensity by distancing from an individual or a particular issue. When these become ongoing rather than temporary ways of managing anxiety, we are bound to stay stalled.

Where, then, is the middle ground between overfunctioning and overresponsibility on the one hand, and distance and disengagement on the other?

Taking a Position

After long, hard work on Kristen's part, she arrived at a point where she could effectively *define a bottom line* in relationship to her dad and his drinking. What specifically did this entail?

First, Kristen stopped pretending that she was blind to her father's alcoholism, and she took a clear position that she would not stay in his home or talk to him on the phone if he was drinking. She was able to do this in a relatively calm, nonblaming way, *clarifying that she was acting for herself rather than for or against her dad.* Taking this position was difficult for Kristen on a number of counts, down to such details as having to arrange an alternate sleeping plan if she arrived with her kids at her parents' home after a four-hour drive and found her father drunk. With help from group therapy and an Adult Children of Alcoholics group, Kristen was able to stay on track—or more accurately, to get back on track following derailments.

For example, when her dad slurred his words on the phone and called it "a bad cold," Kristen said calmly, "Dad, you say you haven't been drinking, but I'm not able to carry on a conversation with you now. I'm hanging up the phone. Good-bye." When her dad was sober, Kristen worked hard to avoid the old guilt-inducing statements about *him* ("Why do you do this to us!") or about some *other* party ("Do you realize how much you upset Mother last weekend?"). Instead Kristen tried to stick with *"I" statements*—nonblaming statements about the self.

On one weekend visit, for example, Kristen canceled her plans to stay at her parents' home. Instead, she took herself and her children to a nearby motel after dinner because her father was obviously under the influence of alcohol. In a low-keyed way, Kristen made clear to her own kids why she had decided not to stay at her parents' home when her dad had been drinking. Later that week she communicated the following to her father:

"When you've been drinking, Dad, I'm going to do my best to stick to my plan to leave. It's not that I don't care about you. It's that I *do* care about you. I know that I can't do a thing to help you, but it's too painful for me to see that you've been drinking and especially to be reminded that I may not have you around for a very long time."

When her father became defensive, accusing her of exaggerating and making mountains out of molehills, Kristen heard him out and said, "Dad, I don't agree. I obviously see the problem as far more serious than you do—and you certainly know my beliefs about the need for treatment. In any case, I just feel too tense inside to be around you when I even *suspect* you've been drinking. So even if I *do* overreact at times, I'm still going to pick up and go, like I did last Saturday night."

Getting Put to the Test

In a chronically anxious emotional field such as this one, it is an extremely difficult challenge to think rather than react, especially when the "tests" and countermoves start rolling in. Late one night, Kristen's father called her from a phone booth about twenty minutes from her home. He had been in town that day on business and obviously was in no shape to drive home. Kristen immediately phoned her mother, who became hysterical and instructed Kristen to get her father right away, before he killed himself or someone else. But Kristen (who had been in this situation before) had already told her dad that she wasn't going to bail him out anymore when he drank, because it was too hard on her and not an acceptable way to have a relationship with him.

At this point, Kristen became so anxious that she could not think clearly, if at all. She knew that the old pattern of rescuing her dad did not work. At the same time, she wanted to respond appropriately to a situation of imminent danger. Kristen made another call, this time to the leader of her group of Adult Children of Alcoholics, which enabled her to calm down and make a plan. The outcome was that she called the police and explained the situation. She then called her mother to tell her that she had called the police. The police picked up her dad. And Kristen began steeling herself for the volcanic reaction from her folks that would now come her way.

"How Can You Do This to Dad??!!"

And so it goes. Countermoves and "Change back!" reactions are par for the course when we change our part in an old pattern, but knowing this fact may not make the situation any easier to deal with. Both of Kristen's parents acted enraged at her, if not ready to disown her. They attacked her on the phone in such a vitriolic manner that Kristen could barely refrain from hanging up. How dare she humiliate the family this way? Was she aware of the harm she had done to her father's driving record and to his professional reputation? Did she care about the expensive fine that she had imposed on him? What kind of daughter calls the police on her own father?

Kristen felt such a strong rise of anger on the phone that she knew she should wait to respond. She wanted to scream that *she* had not done this to her father, *he* had brought it on himself, and that his taking responsibility for the consequences of his actions was long overdue. But she resisted saying all this, because she knew from experience that it would only fuel the fire.

Instead, Kristen listened for as long as she could tolerate it. Then she told her parents that she needed to get off the phone, but would think about what they had said and then get back to them. "Don't bother!" were her father's last angry words. He was obviously quite sober.

Meeting intensity with more intensity—meeting reactivity with more reactivity—only escalates things further. Instead, Kristen wrote her parents a chatty, informative letter that began by sharing some news about her daughter's recent performance on the soccer field.

Then she addressed the hot issue in a *brief paragraph,* avoiding lengthy explanations and justifications that would only have added to the intensity. Kristen was direct and factual. She did not back down from her bottom line.

First, Kristen apologized for whatever grief, fines, and humiliation that she had caused her dad by calling the police, explaining that certainly it wasn't her intention to hurt him or cause trouble for the family: "I simply didn't see any other alternative," she wrote, "and I still don't. I wasn't going to come get you myself, because I've learned that I just can't do that and still have a relationship with you that feels acceptable to me. And I sure wasn't going to do nothing when I was feeling so scared that you might drive and be in danger. So I did the only thing I could think of, which was to call the police. Frankly, I'd do it again, because I wouldn't know what else to do." When Kristen's older brother got in on the act (*"How could you do such a thing to Dad!"*), she provided him with the same brief explanation.

Mother's Reaction

To Kristen's surprise, the family member who reacted most strongly to her changed behavior was her mother. Yet her mother's reaction was normal and predictable. For one thing, *all* family members (including ourselves) react with anxiety when a family member challenges an old pattern by moving differently. Understandably, Kristen's mother felt especially threatened *because her daughter's new behavior brought her face-to-face with her own position (or lack of position) vis-à-vis her husband's drinking.* It challenged her mother's deeply held belief that she was doing all she could, that nothing else was possible.

Over the long years of her marriage, Kristen's mother had increasingly put more and more energy into focusing on her husband's alcoholism and less and less energy into figuring out how she might live her own life as well as possible. She overfunctioned for her husband (bailing him out and pulling up slack for him) and she underfunctioned for herself (neglecting to clarify her own life goals and failing to set clear limits about what was and was not acceptable to her in regard to her husband's drinking behavior and what she would and would not do). Learning that alcoholism was a disease, she then used this belief to take no position regarding her husband's *management* of his disease. *She had no bottom line,* meaning that she engaged in endless cycles of fighting, complaining, and blaming, but she was unable to say, "These are the things that I cannot and will not tolerate in this relationship." Because Kristen's mother was truly convinced that she could not live *without* her marriage, she could not navigate clearly *within* it.

Kristen's mother did occasionally threaten divorce, but her ultimatums were reactive positions at times of high intensity ("Damn it! If you do this one more time, I'm leaving!"). Often they were expressions of desperation and last-ditch attempts to get her husband to shape up. *In contrast, a bottom-line position evolves from a focus on the self, from a deeply felt awareness (which one cannot fake, pretend, or borrow) of one's own needs and the limits of one's tolerance.* One clarifies a bottom line not primarily to change or control the other person (although the wish may certainly be there), but rather to preserve the dignity, integrity, and well-being of the self. There is no "right" bottom line for all individuals, but if we have *no* bottom line, a relationship (be it with a parent, child, co-worker, friend, lover, or spouse) can only become increasingly chaotic and impaired. This is so, whether we are convinced that the other person's behavior has been caused by illness, poor environment, bad genes, slothfulness, or evil spirits.

For almost four decades, Kristen's mother had participated in a dance with her husband that had high costs for all involved, and she had convinced herself that she had "tried everything." Kristen's new ability to de-intensify her anxious focus on her father's alcoholism, while clarifying a bottom line relative to his drinking behaviors and their relationship, struck at the heart of her mother's core beliefs, assumptions, and behavior. It challenged her mother's very reality of *how things are and how they must be.* It stirred her mother's deepest feelings about her *own* growing up.

Kristen's maternal grandparents had virtually sacrificed their lives for a son who was diagnosed as chronically mentally ill, exhausting themselves to the bone by tolerating all sorts of outrageous and irresponsible behaviors without setting clear limits and boundaries. They, too, saw no options ("We can't put our own son out on the street, can we?") and they blamed him (or his bad genes) for trapping them in an unhappy life. Professional help and community support were unavailable and the advice they did receive ("Kick him out if it's too hard for you") was not useful to them.

Kristen's mother repeated the family pattern—this time with a spouse—and accepted the family "reality" ("One cannot have a clear bottom line with a sick family member"). By replicating this pattern, Kristen's mother was able to deny the repressed rage she felt at the situation in her first family, which had been entirely organized and focused around her sick brother. By *doing the same,* Kristen's mother was proving to herself that nothing different could have been done, that there was no other way. And needless to say, it is a very difficult challenge for any of us to be able to set limits, rules, and boundaries in a solid fashion if our own parents were not able to do this with each other, with us, and with other family members.

The more we know about the broader multigenerational picture, the more we can begin to appreciate the enormity of the change Kristen was making. One does not challenge the legacy of generations without stirring up profound emotionality. It was predictable for Kristen's mother to become anxious about her daughter's new behavior and to express her anxiety by redirecting her anger and blame toward Kristen. It was Kristen's job to manage her mother's reactions without cutting her off or getting pulled back into the old pattern. Dealing with countermoves is what real change is all about.

If only change could take place in one hit-and-run maneuver—but it just doesn't work that way. It's a process that requires us to hang in as best we can. Following Kristen's call to the police, everyone's anxiety was up—and it was understandable that Kristen had difficulty staying in touch with family members who were angrily attacking her or giving her the cold shoulder. If Kristen was serious about real, substantive change, however, she would need to be creative in finding some way to stay in reasonable contact with her father and mother, retreating into distance only temporarily, when necessary.

If Kristen *had* cut off, a new, more functional relationship pattern would not have been established. And if her father's countermove was particularly dramatic (such as injuring himself in a car accident), Kristen's anxiety and guilt about her new position might have been unmanageable if she had failed to find some way to stay responsibly connected. Although the *actual* risk of serious injury or tragedy is far greater with the old pattern, this point is still an important one.

Most important of all, the ability to stay responsibly connected to family members, and to define a solid self in this arena, helps us to bring a more solid self to other intimate relationships. When family relationships have been especially painful and when there are cutoffs in the previous generations, maintaining connectedness is not easy. *But distance or cutoff from family members is always a trade-off.* The plus is that we avoid the strong uncomfortable feelings that contact with certain family members inevitably evokes. The costs are less tangible but no less dear. Family connectedness, even when these relationships are anxious and difficult, is a necessary prerequisite to conducting one's own intimate relationships free from serious symptoms over time and free from excessive anxiety and reactivity. The more we manage intensity by cutting off from members of our own kinship group (extended family included), the more we bring that intensity into other relationships, especially into those with children, if we have them. In some situations it can take years to figure out how to reconnect with a particular family member, but if we can slowly move in this direction rather than in the direction of more cutoff, there are benefits to the self and the generations to come.

Kristen's story had the kind of ending we all like to hear about. Her mother eventually sought help for her "codependency." Her Dad *did* get a handle on his drinking problem, and all the family members began to conduct their relationships more functionally. Not infrequently, this happens. And not infrequently, it doesn't. What is most relevant about this story is *not* that Kristen's changes eventually evoked positive changes on her parents' part. Rather, Kristen defined a responsible position in her family for her self —one that would put *her* on firmer footing for all her relationship ventures and one that would maximize other family members' chances of making use of their own competence.

Don't Just Do Something—Stand There!

The most useful thing you can do in response to Kristen's story is *only to think about it*. People commonly try to make changes they are not ready for or attempt to address a hot issue before they have competently addressed smaller problems. After you have read this book in its entirety, you will be better able to assess what, where, when, and if you wish to change. Surely we do not begin at the most difficult place.

Kristen's story illustrates the most difficult kind of change. Keep in mind, though, that between the "before" and "after" of her story, Kristen had the advantage of participating in both group therapy and in a group of Adult Children of Alcoholics. Clarifying a new position with her dad was not something she just decided to jump into one day. For all of us, such changes require careful preparation, planning, and practice, and in some cases, professional help.

What you can do, though, is to use Kristen's story as a springboard to thinking about your own pattern of responding to an underfunctioning person or to a significant other whose behavior is not acceptable to you. We will continue to learn more about the process of defining a self in relationships, and the implications of having or not having a bottom line. For now, keep in mind that patience is a priority; we can't learn to swim by jumping off the high dive.

Kristen's story does give us much to think about *that is not specific to having an alcoholic family member*. The changes Kristen made illustrate her struggle to *define a self* within the intense emotional field of family relationships. This struggle is relevant, indeed central, to all of our lives. And since we cannot hold the clock still, we are always navigating relationships in the direction of greater or lesser degrees of self.

We all do better in life when we can stay reasonably connected to important others; when we can listen to them without trying to change, convince, or fix; and when we can make calm statements about how we see things, based on thinking, rather than reacting. We all do better when we can process an important issue (in Kristen's case, her dad's drinking) and take a clear position rather than relying on silence or blame. We all do better when we have a clear bottom line ("I am not able or willing to live with these behaviors") rather than communicating through our own behavior that "anything goes." We all do better when we can deal directly with our most difficult family members rather than talking about them with other relatives. And finally, we all do better when we can de-intensify our anxious focus on the other's problem and put our primary energy into clarifying our own beliefs, convictions, values, and priorities, while formulating plans and life goals that are congruent with these.

Kristen's story illustrates some key aspects of defining a self. But there is more. Defining a whole and authentic self also means sharing *both* our overfunctioning and underfunctioning sides with significant others rather than participating in polarized relationships where we stay focused on the other person's problems but do not share our own. Every person, *without exception*, has strengths and competencies as well as weaknesses and vulnerabilities, but most of us have difficulty identifying and expressing both sides. This is especially the case when an overfunctioning-underfunctioning polarity gets set in motion and each person's behavior only provokes and maintains the behavior of the other.

It was as difficult for Kristen to consider sharing her underfunctioning side with her father ("Dad, I'm having a problem and I'd like your thoughts about it") as it was for her dad to exercise his competence to stop drinking. An overfunctioning style is very difficult to modify and the costs of overfunctioning are often hidden. For our selves, however, and for those close to us, it is a challenge worth thinking about.

8

Understanding Overfunctioning

Everyone knows that chronic *under*functioners need to change. If we underfunction—as Kristen's father did—we receive the diagnostic labels, get sent to therapy, and get placed in treatment centers or psychiatric hospitals. Our families may identify us as "the sick one," "the spoiled one," "the irresponsible one," "the troublemaker," "the black sheep." People may distance from us or become overfocused on us, often in unhelpful ways. We ourselves may be convinced that we are an emotional basket case, while others in our family seem to have no loose ends.

In contrast, if we *over*function, we may truly believe that God is on our side. Surely, we have done everything possible to be helpful and our greatest source of distress is the other person—who is unable or unwilling to shape up. Unfortunately, those around us may reinforce this attitude, this way of seeing only part of the picture. Or they may do the opposite and blame us for "causing" the problem through our own behavior—a similarly narrow and distorted view.

All of us have relationships and circumstances in which we overfunction, and this is not necessarily problematic, particularly if we can observe it and make a shift. For example, our daughter calls in tears because she was put on probation at work. Instead of asking her questions—or perhaps sharing something from our own experience—we try to lift her spirits or tell her three things to do. Later that day we reflect on the conversation and recognize that our advice was unsolicited and that we really weren't listening very well. So we call her back the next day to simply see how she's doing. We ask a few questions about the job situation and tell her we're sorry she's having such a hard time.

When we get *stuck* in an overfunctioning position, however, we may find change exceedingly difficult. This rigidity exists because overfunctioning is not just a bad habit, a misguided attitude, an overzealous wish to be helpful, or a behavior pattern caused by living with a chronically underfunctioning individual, such as an alcoholic spouse; overfunctioning, like underfunctioning, is a patterned way of managing anxiety that grows out of our experience in our first family and has deep roots in prior generations. This reactive response operates almost instinctually, without conscious awareness or intent. And it can keep us—and our relationships—incredibly stuck.

Those who come by overfunctioning most naturally are often (although by no means always) firstborns or only children. The tendency will be exaggerated if a firstborn has same-sex siblings (the older sister of a sister, the older brother of brothers). And it will be particularly intense if one parent was physically or emotionally unable to competently do his or her job and we stepped in as an overresponsible child—a fixer, a mediator, or the like. Because overfunctioners "look good" (like my sister "sailing through" at the time of my mother's cancer diagnosis), their needs and problems are often overlooked, even by themselves. That is until they get good and sick—or find some other way to collapse. It may take nothing less than a serious emotional or physical illness for a chronic overfunctioner to slow down and force attention to her own needs. And when overfunctioners *do* collapse under the strain of overfunctioning, they can do it in a big way.

Defining Our Terms

As we have seen, *overfunctioning* can be defined as *an individual's characteristic style of managing anxiety and navigating relationships under stress.* If you are a good overfunctioner, you will identify the following characteristics in yourself.

OVERFUNCTIONERS

- know what's best not only for themselves but for others as well.
- move in quickly to advise, fix, rescue, and take over when stress hits.
- have difficulty staying out of and allowing others to struggle with their own problems.
- avoid worrying about their own personal goals and problems by focusing on others.
- have difficulty sharing their own vulnerable, underfunctioning side, especially with those people who they believe have problems.
- may be labeled as people who are "always reliable" or "always together."

Overfunctioning, however, is not simply a description of an individual's defensive style. More to the point, overfunctioning (along with underfunctioning) refers to *a reciprocal (or circular) relationship pattern*. Given sufficient anxiety, the pattern will become polarized and "stuck," as illustrated by the examples of my sister and me. Viewed from this perspective, overfunctioning (like underfunctioning) is an attribute of a *relationship system* that cannot be understood apart from the whole. Let's take a closer look at this way of thinking.

De-Selfing and Pseudo-Self

When Dr. Murray Bowen, founder of Bowen family systems theory, first described the reciprocal pattern of overfunctioning and underfunctioning, he was referring to a common marital process in which one partner gives up self (de-selfing) and the other gains in pseudo-self. The person who sacrifices self is the *underfunctioner*. The person who is bolstered in self is the *overfunctioner*. Just how does this exchange work?

When couples pair up and stay paired up, they are usually at the same level of "self" or independence. That is, the amount of "true self" or "solid self" that they have carved out in their first family—and now bring to their relationship—is about the same. Or, we might say that they are at the same level of emotional maturity. For example, when Jo-Anne (our anonymous letter writer who canceled her subscription to *Ms.* magazine) first married Hank (as we will now call him) their "levels of self" might be depicted by a horizontal line (see figure A on page 106).

If we look at this couple several years down the road, however, their levels of self may *look* more like figure B (see page 106).

Over time, Jo-Anne has assumed the adaptive and un-

Figure A

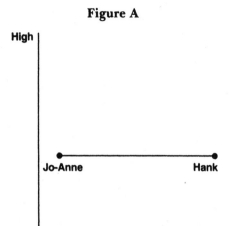

Figure B

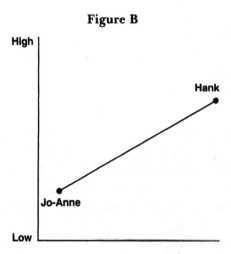

derfunctioning role, knuckling under to marital pressures and going along with someone else's program. She may be depressed and symptomatic, without personal and life goals. Hank, in contrast, may have no psychiatric or physical symptoms and may be up for a promotion at work. To all the world, he *appears* to have "more self" than his spouse and to be functioning well. Over time, the polarity may become firmly entrenched. Hank's reactivity to his wife's underfunctioning may take the form of angry distance and/or overfocus—but in either case, he will begin to share less of his *own* problems and vulnerability with her (if he ever did to begin with) and she will share less of her strength and competence with him.

The difference in their levels of functioning, however, is more apparent than real. In systems language, Hank has gained in pseudo-self in proportion to his wife's de-selfed position. She has "given up" self and he has "borrowed self." It's just like a seesaw. If, by some stroke of magic or plain hard work, Jo-Anne were to change in the direction of greater selfhood, we would predictably see this:

Figure C

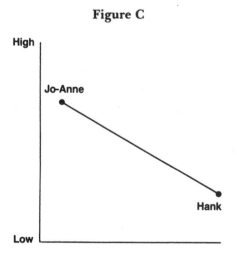

As Jo-Anne began to look better, Hank might get depressed and begin to look worse. Psychotherapists see this happen routinely, and predictably. We have observed it at the societal level as well, as when men first complained of feeling impotent or castrated in response to changes in women brought about by feminism. It is not simply that the strengthening of women is *confused* with the weakening of men. More to the point, the pseudo-self of men is actually challenged as woman stop giving up self.

If Jo-Anne were able to maintain a genuinely higher level of "solid self" (as opposed to overfunctioning at Hank's expense), the seesaw swing depicted in figure C would not stay static. Hank might ultimately meet the challenge of moving to a higher level of self in response to the real changes that his wife has made. Or several years down the road Hank and Jo-Anne may no longer be together.

Why Change?

From where, then, does the overfunctioner find the will to change? As Kristen's story illustrates, change can be a profoundly difficult and anxiety-arousing business. As frequently as not, the motivation is just not there or it runs out after the initial push. And understandably so. Where will we get the courage, to say nothing of the motivation, to begin to modify our overfunctioning ways? Why change if we are sitting at the top of the emotional seesaw, if we can avoid the full impact of our own unfinished business by focusing on the other, if we can derive that secret feeling of self-righteousness from diagnosing others and being "right," or if we are the "insider" that the family talks *to* ("Let me tell you what your brother did now!") rather than *about?*

It's a real dilemma. The will *not* to change is often particularly powerful in chronic overfunctioners. First, we tend *not* to see that we have a problem: We have only tried to be helpful to that other person, and if we have distanced or cut off, it is only after being convinced that we have tried all possibilities. Like Kristen and her mother, we cannot see how we are contributing to a painfully stuck relationship pattern because we cannot imagine (and may not really want to imagine) another way of relating. We may even be convinced that the other party cannot survive without our help ("My sister wouldn't eat if I didn't buy her groceries").

Second, we do not know *how* to modify our overfunctioning position. We may have no clear instructions, no well-marked road map, and no trained coach to guide us over the rough spots. In all probability, we may lack a realistic assessment of just how tough the going can get—if we really get going.

Finally, it is *emotionally painful* to modify a chronic overfunctioning pattern. As we will see, it may evoke strong feelings of depression, anxiety, and anger as our own vulnerabilities and needs come rushing to the surface—and who needs that! It's understandably hard to tolerate short-term pain, even for the promise of a more whole and grounded self later on.

Yet some of us do find the will to change, as Kristen's story illustrates. Such change requires us to move against our wish to fix things and our even stronger wish for distance once we find we can't fix things. But perhaps the most difficult aspect of modifying an overfunctioning pattern is to *share our vulnerability* with the underfunctioning person and to *relate to that person's competence*. Let's return to the last part of Kristen's story to see how this can be done—and to appreciate the strong emotionality it evokes.

Back to Kristen

In a later, second incident, Kristen again called the police to collect her father. In response, Kristen's father called her "terribly selfish"—at which point she lost control. In her next group-therapy session, Kristen described the experience: "At that moment, I exploded. *He* was calling *me* selfish! *He* was telling me how *I* hurt the family! I just let the bastard have it. I just couldn't take it anymore, and I didn't care if I was blowing it."

"Blowing it" is a normal part of the difficult process of change. We do not alter our part in a stuck relationship pattern without returning again and again to our old ways. The group empathized with Kristen's feelings and her surge of reactivity. Some thought it was good for her to have let her anger out full force. Most importantly, Kristen was able to get back on course again.

About a month later (and almost a year from her first call to the police), Kristen performed a bold and courageous act. She wrote her father a letter that included the following message.

> Dad, I've been giving some thought to your opinion that I've become selfish, and I've come to the conclusion that you have a point there. I *am* becoming more selfish. To be honest, I'm even *working* on becoming more selfish. I think that I've spent much of my life looking over my shoulder worrying about your drinking, or Mom's problems, and I've put very little energy into getting clear about who I am and where I'm going in my life. Focusing so much on *your* problems may have given me a place to hide, because I didn't have to look too hard at myself and my own problems. Now that I'm thinking about *me*, I realize I've been unhappy with my job situation for a long time and not doing anything about it. At the same time, I'm feeling hopeful because at least I'm starting to think about it.

In a later conversation with her dad, Kristen described a specific problem affecting her at work and also shared her ongoing indecision about career directions. She asked him if he had any thoughts or reactions to her dilemma and also expressed interest in learning whether he had ever struggled with similar issues. How had *he* decided on his particular line of work? Had he ever thought about a career change? What work issues did others in his family struggle with? Kristen let her father know that whatever he could share of his own considerable experience around work issues might help her to struggle more productively with her own decisions. Later that week she talked with her mother about work and career struggles on her mother's side of the family.

Soon thereafter, Kristen became profoundly depressed. Although she said her depression hit her "out of the blue," it was anything but surprising. By sharing her *own* underfunctioning side with her father, Kristen was challenging the roles and rules that constituted her family's "reality." She was changing the rules governing their dance by relating to *his* competence, by considering his perspective of value, by being more of a *self* in their relationship, and by no longer pretending that she had it all together. For example, one of the family's "realities" was that her father, as a "sick" alcoholic, should not be burdened by other family members' problems and surely could have no valuable advice to offer. Another unspoken rule was that fathers and daughters should not have real relationships.

By inviting her father to act like a father, Kristen also unleashed a torrent of buried emotions and unmet dependency needs within herself, needs and longings that she had kept safely blocked from awareness by chronically overfunctioning and overfocusing on the problems of others. Her father's positive response to her self-disclosure paradoxically unleashed her buried rage and disappointment about what she had *not* been able to get from him and her family throughout her lifetime. Her first, gut response was that whatever he could give her now was not enough—and too late.

Kristen could not understand why her new behavior, and her dad's positive response to it, left her feeling more miserable than ever. Her reaction, however, was predictable and par for the course. And it is because change is often *this* difficult that many of us choose to continue with our old ways.

On the other hand, the payoffs are high if we can do this work and stay on course (or more accurately, get back on course) over time. Sharing vulnerability and relating to the other person's competence are essential to restoring balance in a relationship with an underfunctioning individual. If we cannot do this, it is far less likely that the other person will put energy into their own recovery and they will have to work twice as hard to even be in touch with their own competence.

Even more to the point, this work allows us to move toward a more balanced and authentic self. It is our best insurance policy against continuing polarized relationships with new people in our lives and passing the pattern down the generations.

Finally, if we are able to modify a chronic overfunctioning pattern, we will begin to be in touch with the real costs to self of the old way. It is frustrating, exhausting, angering, and draining (both financially and emotionally) to overfunction—to be rescuing, bailing out, pulling up slack, or paying more attention to the problems of others than to one's own. And distancing from that other family member who just isn't doing well doesn't really leave us feeling very solid, responsible, or grounded in the long run, despite our attempts to convince ourselves otherwise.

So far, we have been looking at a *chronic* overfunctioning-underfunctioning pattern. By chronic, I mean that the pattern is fixed and long-standing, with roots that may go back for generations. Resistance to change is sky-high, both from within and without, and professional guidance is often necessary to help us lower reactivity, observe our part in the dance, and stay on course over time. Often the strong feelings stirred by moving differently are so uncomfortable we will tell ourselves we don't want to change, it's not worth it, or it's not possible.

Let's turn now to the story of Anita, who provides a typical example of *mild* overfunctioning that swung into full force at a particularly stressful time in the family life cycle. Anita was able to make changes relatively easily because the "stuckness" that brought her to therapy was only of several months' duration. When a relationship gets stuck in response to an acute reaction to recent stress, change is more manageable.

"I'm Terribly Concerned About Mother!"

Anita was a twenty-nine-year-old administrative nurse who came to see me several months after her seventy-eight-year-old grandmother had a serious fall. Anita was obviously tense and under considerable strain when she entered my office.

When we first talked on the phone, Anita said she was seeking help because of headaches and anxiety spells. But during our first session, she focused almost exclusively on her mother, Helen, who was deeply absorbed in caring for *her* mother, Anita's ailing grandmother.

Anita shared that she had initially felt sympathetic toward her mother's plight, but over time her sympathy had turned to frustration and then to outright anger. "My mother cares for Grandma at the expense of everything else in her life," Anita explained. "She's wearing herself to the bone, she's neglecting Dad, and most important, she's neglecting herself."

When we complain that our mothers (or whoever) won't listen to reason, it usually means that they won't see things our way or do what we want them to do. As with Suzanne and John (Chapter 6), one key issue here was reactivity to differences. Anita was clearly having a hard time accepting the fact that her mother's way of managing a difficult situation differed from her own. Our reactivity to differences will always be higher at particularly stressful points in the life cycle (for example, at a wedding or funeral) because anxiety is the driving force behind reactivity.

For most of Anita's adulthood, she and her mother had shared a close relationship and could talk together openly and comfortably. Their relationship was not too polarized, in that each could share problems and relate to the competence of the other in solving her own difficulties. But when Anita's grandmother's health began deteriorating after her fall, Anita became focused on how her mother was handling this difficult situation. It was during this particularly stressful point that Anita's tendency to overfunction went into full swing and another mother-daughter relationship became stuck.

The Way It Was

In the months after her grandmother's fall, the interaction between Anita and her mother had become increasingly strained. Helen would complain to Anita about her continual exhaustion and about her unrelieved responsibility for her mother. Anita would then suggest ways that Helen could lessen her load; for example, by asking other family members to pitch in or by hiring a nurse to stay with Grandma several hours a day. Helen, in response, would either ignore this advice or tell Anita why her advice would not work. Anita would continue to argue her point, while Helen would continue not to listen.

What did Anita do then? Sometimes she repeated the advice, although her mother was not making use of it. After a while, Anita would distance from her mother ("I just don't want to hear her complaining if she doesn't want to do anything about it"), or she would interpret and diagnose Helen's behavior ("Mother, I think you secretly enjoy being a martyr and doing this super-responsible trip. You keep asking me for advice only to reject it, and that makes me feel angry and helpless"). When they managed to get off the subject of Grandma, their conversation tended to be superficial.

Although Helen was overextending herself for her mother, she was actually underfunctioning in terms of problem solving around the caretaking issue. And the more Anita took on Helen's problem as her own or focused intensely on the issue, the more Helen continued to underfunction for her self. Of course, Helen's behavior invited Anita's overfunctioning, just as Anita's overfunctioning invited her mother's underfunctioning. That's how a reciprocal or circular dance works.

"How much of your worry energy—or emotional energy—is directed toward your mother at this time?" I asked Anita the third time we met. I asked her to be as specific as possible; I wanted a percentage figure.

"About seventy-five percent," she answered quickly. My estimate would have been even higher.

"If that problem were to be magically resolved, if there were absolutely no cause for concern about your mother, where would that seventy-five percent worry energy be going? What else would you be paying attention to?"

"I don't know," Anita said simply. "I've never thought about it."

And indeed, she hadn't.

How Overfunctioning Helps

One of the nice things about any kind of *other-focus* is that we will not experience the full impact of our own issues. Obviously, lots of emotions were stirred up inside Anita in response to her grandmother's downhill slide and the specter of her impending death. How did Anita want to relate to Grandma at this time? How much contact did she want to initiate? What, if any, unfinished business did Anita have with Grandma that she might want to address before it was too late? If Grandma died tomorrow, would Anita feel at peace with this relationship, or would she wish that she had said or asked one thing or another? These are just a few of the questions Anita was able to *not* think about—or not think *too hard* about—because she was thinking about Helen, worrying about Helen, and talking about Helen to her therapist, family, and friends.

Another piece of psychological business that was stirred up for Anita at this time involved the question of a daughter's responsibility to an aging dependent parent. Helen's total and selfless devotion to Grandma made Anita anxious, because she experienced her mother's behavior as an expectation that *Anita would one day do the same*. The notion that Anita would one day devote *her* life to her aging mother or father scared and angered her, although her parents had never voiced any such expectations. Nor had Anita consciously articulated her concerns—even to herself. Instead, Anita made an automatic, reflexive move away from her own anxiety to a worried and critical focus on her mother. That's how people work. And this is how we begin to change it.

New Steps

The first thing Anita was able to do differently was to stop giving advice. Learning how *not* to be helpful is an especially difficult challenge for those of us who move in quickly to fix the problems of other family members or to rescue those in distress. Of course, there is nothing wrong with Anita giving advice to Helen *if* Helen finds it useful and *if* Anita recognizes that her advice may not fit her mother ("Well, this is what I would do in your shoes, but that may not be right for you. What are your thoughts?").

In the old pattern, Anita was giving advice from an overfunctioning or overresponsible position. She was truly convinced she had the answers to her mother's problem, and she became angry when her mother ignored her advice. For this reason Anita would do well to stop giving advice, at least until she can shift to a more respectful position regarding her mother's need to find her own solutions.

When we overfunction for family members, we can be sure they will underfunction for themselves and act less competently to solve their own problems. Furthermore, Anita already knows that her mother resists her advice. Doing more of the same can only keep Anita more stuck.

When Anita was ready to break the old pattern, she stopped trying to change her mother and began to change her own responses. When Helen called and complained about feeling drained by Grandma's illness, Anita asked questions and listened empathetically. She did not advise her mother in any way. Anita's attitude conveyed respect for the fact that her mother was the best expert on herself and that she was struggling with a truly wrenching dilemma.

It Doesn't Mean Silence!

What do overfunctioners do when they get angry, frustrated, and exhausted? As we have seen, they typically move into a position of reactive distance. I speak here not just of physical distance ("I just won't call or write him anymore") but also of emotional distance around the issue of concern. Kristen, for example, initially confused distance with substantive change on her part when she went from trying to fix her father's drinking behavior to acting as if it were not happening.

Clarifying our position around an important issue is always a key part of defining the self. Anita learned to do this *by saying something about her own self rather than trying to be the expert on her mother.* After a telephone conversation in which Helen again presented herself as exhausted and stressed-out, Anita responded: "You know, Mother, your ability to take care of Grandma truly amazes me. If it were me, I simply couldn't do it. I would have to find some way to get help and get time for myself, no matter what it took."

When her mother responded by giving a dozen reasons why help was not possible, Anita did not argue the point. She just said again, "You know, Mother, I just couldn't do it. I'm not saying I have the answers for you. I'm just saying that I could not be doing so much for anyone, no matter how much I loved them. I don't think I'd even be physically capable of it. But I recognize that you and I are different."

Anita stayed on track, although she often had to bite her tongue to avoid going back to the old pattern of advice-giving and arguing. Over lunch several weeks later, Helen told Anita that caring for Grandma was taking a toll on her own health. At this point, Anita turned to her mother and said warmly, "Mom, I've always admired how good you are at taking care of everyone. Your ability to keep giving to others never ceases to amaze me. You've taken care of three children. And you've taken care of Dad. And when Uncle Harry was in trouble, you were the first to be there to take care of him. And now you're taking care of Grandma.

"But there's only one problem. Who is taking care of you, Mom? This is what I worry about sometimes. Who's taking care of Helen?"

Helen became teary, and Anita suddenly realized that she had never seen her mother cry. Helen told Anita that no one really took much care of her and that furthermore she probably wouldn't allow it. She talked some about her own childhood and how her father's early death had left her feeling that it wasn't safe to depend on anyone. When they parted that afternoon, Anita knew her mother better.

What allowed this conversation to happen was Anita's ability to share her genuine concern for her mother without going back to her overfunctioning pattern (which was similar to her mother's pattern) of advising, rescuing, or fixing. Anita was sharing from the self, without implying what Helen should think, feel, or do, and without telling her specifically how she should solve her problem. Not long thereafter, her mother did begin to use her competence to make a change in her situation. The solution wasn't one Anita would have chosen, but it offered Helen some relief.

The change on Anita's part was not just a strategic shift into "I" language. It came from a deeper place, from a growing recognition that we cannot know for sure what is best for another person—what they can and cannot tolerate, what they need to do, when, and why. Surely it is difficult enough to know this for one's own self.

The Hardest Part

In Anita's case, the challenge of sharing her own anxieties and issues with her hitherto focused-on mother was a manageable challenge, because she and Helen had had an open and flexible relationship before the crisis created by her grandma's ill health. And so, sitting together on a park bench one fall afternoon, Anita began to tell Helen what had been stirred up inside her in response to the recent events. Mother and daughter were able to talk about their reactions to Grandma's deteriorating health, and cried some together. This sharing of emotions contrasts with emotional reactivity, which is an anxiety-driven response. Anita also asked her mother *directly* if she, Helen, would expect the same kind of caretaking from her children in her old age that Helen was now giving to Grandma. Anita's anxiety was much alleviated as she and her mother talked openly about the subject; Anita no longer had to float around in her own fantasies and fears.

Easy conversations? No. But Anita had an easier job than many of us would, because the stuck relationship pattern that brought her into therapy was an acute reaction to the anxious emotional field created by Grandma's ill health. Prior to this crisis, she and her mother had had a mature and flexible relationship where each preserved a high degree of separate self. This meant that they could listen to the other's problems—*and stay in their own skin*—without rushing in to fix things and without getting too nervous about differences. They could give advice or feedback, when appropriate, but each could also relate to the competence of the other to find solutions to her own problems. They could state their own opinion on any issue, while leaving room for the view of the other. This makes the process of change about as easy as it gets. Which actually, from Anita's perspective, was not particularly easy at all.

At times of high stress, all of us can get stuck in an other-focused position. The process may be a temporary and circumscribed reaction, as in Anita's case, or it may evolve into an extreme, overfunctioning-underfunctioning polarity, as in Kristen's family. Or we may be somewhere along this continuum of acute to chronic, somewhere between "mild stuckness" and a carved-in-stone polarity.

In my first family, my sister, Susan, and I participated in an overfunctioning-underfunctioning polarity that was linked to an issue of survival. No wonder that today, some thirty years later, it doesn't take too much anxiety to get us back into doing our old thing. We've both come a long way in working on our part of the pattern, but I presume it will always be a challenge. Had the level of family anxiety been even higher and lasted longer, and had our family possessed fewer emotional resources to manage this anxiety, the challenge for us today would be greater still.

Of course, I have a few conspicuous areas of overfunctioning, just as Susan has significant pockets of underfunctioning. Although every person has a predominant operating style, we will manage anxiety in different ways according to context and circumstance, according to the particular relationship and the specific issue at hand. For example, a woman may be an overfunctioner at work and an underfunctioner in her marriage. Or she may be a chronic distancer with her father and a chronic pursuer with men in her love life. Far from being a "contradiction," my sister's experience with David (Chapter 4) illustrates that a woman's distance from her father (or more specifically, the unaddressed issues and emotionality that are managed by distance) may be what raises anxiety (managed by pursuit) in other intimate relationships.

Anxiety continues to be a key concept in understanding how stuck our relationships will get, how resistant we (and others) will be to change, and how much change can actually be tolerated. We have seen how anxiety locks us into polarized positions in relationships, blocking productive communication and problem solving, and making intimacy impossible to achieve. Anxiety hits us from all directions, moving vertically down the generations and horizontally as we pass through life-cycle events and just plain hard times. As our next example will illustrate, a particular *subject* may itself carry so much anxiety that it is difficult to discuss in an open and respectful way. If a topic feels too hot to handle, we may opt for silence at the expense of authentic connectedness—or we may feel we have to make a choice between having a relationship and being a self.

9

Very Hot Issues: A Process View of Change

What's a daughter to do about a mother?
When she's the apple of her mother's eye?
Does she make her mother squirm
By exposing the worm?
Or does she help her mother deny?

> "The Daughter's Song"

Where did I go wrong?
Am I the one to blame?
What was it that I did to her
To bring about this shame?
How did it happen?
How could it possibly be?
That she . . . she . . . she's
So different
From me?

> "The Mother's Song"
> Lyrics by Jo-Ann Krestan

Three weeks before her older sister's wedding, Kimberly flew from Kansas City to Dallas and told her parents that she was a lesbian. Mary, her lover of three years, was with her during this self-disclosure. Kimberly's father responded as if he had been struck across the face. He said nothing and left the room. Kimberly's mother wept and then fired accusing questions: "Why are you telling us this?" "How can you sit here and tell me that you are a homosexual?" "Are you getting help for yourself?"

Kimberly's attempts to defend herself fell on deaf ears. After about ten minutes or more of the same, she told her mother that she and Mary were not prepared to listen to insults and that they would stay overnight with a friend. Kimberly left the friend's telephone number on the kitchen table, with a note telling her parents to call if and when they were ready to discuss the subject in a civil fashion. Kimberly heard nothing. She returned to Kansas City and decided she would not recognize her parents' existence if they would not recognize her partner and respect her life choice. She also decided not to attend her sister's wedding, "partly for financial reasons," as she put it. She had already spent enough money on her recent visit home.

About six weeks later, Kimberly's position softened. She decided to give her parents "one more chance." She gathered together some literature on gay and lesbian issues and sent it off to Dallas, with a letter inviting reconciliation. She expressed a wish that her parents would read the material so they could confront their homophobic attitudes and adopt a more informed view.

Kimberly's parents opened the package and resealed and returned it without a word. They did, however, send her a birthday card the following month, signed, "Love, Mom and Dad," but without their usual note and gift. It was at this point that Kimberly declared herself an orphan, with no further use for her parents.

For several years prior to "D-Day," as Kimberly later called it, she had been wanting to share her lesbian identity with her parents, especially her mother. Although a previous therapist had encouraged her *not* to tell ("Your parents don't tell you about their sex life. Why do you feel this compulsion to tell them about yours?"), Kimberly nonetheless found herself moving in the direction of coming out. She was aware that keeping such a big secret from her family ensured that her relationships with both parents could only remain distant and superficial, colored by silence and lies. Her invisibility as a part of a couple also affected her relationship with Mary as well.

Kimberly's secret from her family was hardly a circumscribed one involving only "sexual preference," meaning with whom she was sleeping or to whom she was attracted. Her lesbian identity also included her primary emotional commitments, her choice of a woman-centered life-style, and the everyday details of living, both large and small: from whom she vacationed with and how she spent her free time, to her recent role as an active organizer in the lesbian community. The long-term effects of staying closeted not only precluded the possibility of authentic emotional contact with family members but slowly eroded Kimberly's sense of dignity and self-regard, as well. It also diminished her energies and joy (as holding secrets always does) in small, imperceptible, but cumulative ways and negatively affected her relationship with Mary.

Kimberly's decision to come out was an act of courage. Choosing not to come out, however, does not signify an absence of the same. As I said earlier, no one can predict the consequences of change—not for ourselves and surely not for others. We do not know how much change is tolerable for an individual at a particular time, nor how much anxiety she or he can sit with. We cannot really know another person's story. For several years Kimberly had *resisted* pressures from her friends to come out to her family. *Her resistance was also an act of courage,* because Kimberly could recognize that she was not emotionally ready or prepared to make this announcement.

Coming Out: A Woman's Issue

Let's look more carefully at Kimberly's situation, because *coming out is an issue for all women.* We all have emotionally charged issues in our family that are difficult to address. We all may find ourselves confronting a choice between authenticity and harmony in a particular relationship. We all have to deal with powerful countermoves and "Change back!" reactions—both from within and without—if we define the "I" apart from the roles and rules of family and culture. And we all, by virtue of being female, have learned to please and protect relationships by silencing, sacrificing, and betraying the self.

Kimberly's experience will allow us to consolidate some of the lessons we have already learned about defining the "I." Her story teaches us what we can prepare for when we bring up *any emotionally loaded issue* and try to process it with our significant others. It reminds us of the *dilemma of differences* which always threaten as they inform—and which implicitly question the assumptions of the similar. We can count on the subject of lesbianism to be an especially loaded difference for families in our homophobic society.

Keep in mind that emotionally loaded issues come in every shape and form. Some issues, such as incest, are obviously intense. Other issues may not *seem* that hot from an outsider's perspective ("Mom, I've decided to leave the church") but may feel totally untouchable to a particular individual in a particular family. For Adrienne, the facts and feelings surrounding the decision to institutionalize Greg made it an emotionally explosive issue. For Jo-Anne, our anonymous letter writer in Chapter 2, a statement to her husband that she planned to continue her subscription to *Ms.* magazine might be akin to "coming out" and feel no less dangerous. Sometimes a straightforward, factual question ("Dad, how did Uncle Bill actually die?") may take years to lead up to.

Why would we even bother to *think* about tackling a hot issue that no one wants to talk about? Why would we *share something* or *ask something* that makes us feel like we are dropping an emotional bomb on our family? Often, we won't. Sometimes, however, our failure to share something —or ask something—greatly impairs our experience of self, our sense of esteem and worth, and our ability to be intimate with significant others. Once again, intensity from a key family relationship does not go away when we manage it through distance and cutoff. It only goes underground.

How do we open up a difficult subject in a way that is ultimately healing, laying the groundwork for greater closeness? How do we avoid a confrontation that only evokes more reactivity and cutoff? These are the questions that Kimberly did *not* think about before she flew home to make her announcements.

"D-Day" Revisited

Kimberly came for therapy nine months after D-Day. The birthday card from her parents was their last communication and Kimberly was still furious at their response. She sought my help because she had heard I was an "anger expert"—and she was angry. At the same time, she was not motivated to reconnect with her family. She just wanted to "work through her anger," whatever that meant—preferably without ever having to *do* anything differently with the people involved.

Kimberly told me that she had disclosed her lesbianism to her parents in hopes of having "real relationships" with them, rather than distant and dishonest ones. But instead of a shifting toward greater intimacy, their relationships had moved from distance to more distance, and now into a period of cold war. What process had occurred—or failed to occur?

It *Is* a Process!

Although Kimberly knew better intellectually, she thought of coming out as something she would go home and "do" ("Well, I've done it!") *rather than as the first small step in a long-term process.* She confused her parents' *initial* response with what might come later from her efforts. Kimberly did not have a process view of change. In fact, she did not even have an objective view of her *own* process. There were many years between Kimberly's *first* acknowledgment of her own different and "bad" feelings and her ultimate positive acceptance of her emotional and sexual orientation to women.

As we have seen, the predictable response to substantive change is increased anxiety followed by countermoves ("Change back, or else . . ."). If we are serious about the work, we need to *anticipate* countermoves and *plan to manage our own reactivity in the face of them.* Countermoves ("You don't mean that!" "How can you be so selfish!") do not mean that our efforts toward change are misguided or have failed. It simply means that the process of change is proceeding along normal lines. It is our job to hold our ground in the face of countermoves, without becoming defensive, without trying to convince others to think or feel differently, and without cutting off.

Counting on Countermoves

Margie, a twenty-six-year-old woman I saw in therapy, said she felt like she was "coming out" when she began to share some of her troubles with her mother. Margie's label in her first family was "Little Miss Sunshine." For as far back as she could remember, she was the "Always-Happy-Child" who would give her mother nothing to worry about, unlike her father who was addicted to gambling and repeatedly involved in unwise business ventures. *It was clear that her mother was highly reactive to the slightest sign of distress in her daughter and was unable to relate to Margie's competence to manage the sadness and depression that life's circumstances inevitably evoke.*

Margie's earliest memory was of returning from kindergarten feeling tearful and rejected because her classmates had made fun of her. She wanted to be alone in her room, but her mother came in and "grilled her" about her feelings, trying desperately to lift Margie's spirits. When Margie became even more upset, her mother burst into tears herself.

As it turned out, her mother's brother had committed suicide in his twenties and two other family members had received the diagnosis of manic-depressive illness. An underground issue in this family was her mother's fear that she might have passed on the "depression gene" or "suicide gene" to her daughter. It was Margie's job in the family to *not* show depression so as *not* to worry her mother.

When Margie began therapy she was in a polarized arrangement in which her live-in lover was the depressed one. Margie *overfocused* on him and *overfunctioned* for him. She worked in therapy for more than two years to understand the legacy and meaning of "depression" in her own family before she was ready to experiment and slowly share with her mother a bit of her more vulnerable side.

At first, for as long as a year or more, Margie's mother disqualified or minimized Margie's self-disclosures, sometimes changing the topic when Margie shared a small piece of her underfunctioning side. Only gradually did the lines of communication open up around the hot issues of depression and suicide. Even now, four years later, at times of high anxiety Margie's mother will revert to her old pattern ("Just get more sleep and you won't feel sad, honey!") and Margie can gently tease her about it. To an outsider, Margie made "small changes" ("What's the big deal about telling your mother that you had a lousy week?"). For Margie, though, because she was a severe overfunctioner, the change was monumental. This first step helped her to modify her overfunctioning position with her lover and ultimately enlarged her capacity for genuine closeness.

Margie could not have initiated or sustained this change without keeping the long-term process in mind. Nor could she have navigated the change if she had insisted on moving in with a big bang (for example, a heavy confrontation or "deep discussion" with her mother) rather than moving in *slowly* and in *low-key* fashion, counting on countermoves that were as sure as the sunrise.

Resistance from Within

In Kimberly's case, she opted for cutoff, *in part because she really did not want to process the issue of her lesbianism.* Her resistance was quite normal and was manifested by her decision to "orphan herself" after receiving the birthday card signed, "Love, Mom and Dad." Considering the context, this card was a small but significant move *toward connectedness* by her parents—to which Kimberly responded with anger and more distance. *That was Kimberly's countermove to change.*

Processing a loaded issue is not easy. Not only must we define our own position clearly over time, which in Kimberly's case would include some sharing of both the joys and the hardships of being gay, but we must also listen to the *other* person's reaction *without getting too anxious about differences* and without rushing in to change or fix things. It means keeping our own reactivity in check.

When Kimberly finally *did* begin to process the issue with her mother, she found it hard to sit still through her mother's expressions of disappointment and pain. On the one hand, her mother's reactions were entirely predictable, given the negative attitudes toward homosexuality that her mother had absorbed. And in our mother-focused culture, it was no surprise that Kimberly's mother was waking up in the middle of the night obsessed with worry that she had "caused" her daughter's "illness."

But there was more than this. Kimberly's mother also grieved the loss of the unfolding of the generations, as she knew it, as well as the loss of her illusions about her daughter and her images of Kimberly's life. This sudden and forced recognition of profound difference felt to her at first like the severing of her own ties into the future, like the "end of the line," as she put it. That she could identify and express these feelings was ultimately useful. Had she responded only with false liberalism and glib acceptance ("It makes no difference to us that you're gay, honey. We just love you for who you are"), mother and daughter would have lost the opportunity to process the issue before them and to ultimately arrive at a deeper and more authentic dialogue.

Kimberly and her mother could talk together only after Kimberly was able to calmly invite her mother to share her reactions ("Mom, what is the hardest thing for you about my being gay?") and to hear her out over time without becoming critical or defensive. This happened at first through letters, which gave both parties a little more time and space to cool off and think about their own reactions. Only later did Kimberly's mother express an interest in looking through the material that Kimberly had sent her before.

Laying the Groundwork

When Kimberly first revealed her lesbianism, things got off to a particularly difficult start because she opened up the subject in the context of an extremely distant relationship with both her parents. In fact, before D-Day, she almost never discussed personal matters with them. Whether it was good news (organizing a poetry reading at a local university) or bad news (being in a car accident that left her unharmed but badly shaken), Kimberly did not share important information with her family. Distance was the name of the game.

Earlier, I mentioned that you cannot learn to swim by jumping off the high dive. This is particularly true when it comes to emotionally loaded issues. Before bringing up *a big one,* we need to practice bringing up the small ones. And then the medium ones. It may take us several years before we can even picture ourselves in the same room with that other person, talking about the weather.

At Glacial Speed

The more intense the issue and the greater the degree of cutoff, *the more slowly one moves.* For example, many years ago I began working with a woman named Rayna who came to see me because she was unable to enjoy sex with her steady boyfriend. She related the problem to a history of incest which began when she was eleven. More specifically, she had participated in sex play—twice leading to intercourse—with a brother who was seven years her senior.

For the first couple of years in therapy, Rayna worked on processing this incident and putting it in a broader family context. The incest had been one of a number of things that had happened in this family following a traumatic period of multiple losses and an unexplained disappearance in the extended family. Rayna also began reading about incest and attending lectures on it, and she joined a group of incest survivors. During the third year of our work together, Rayna was able to make some initial contact with this brother, starting with sending a Christmas card and later birthday cards to his children. A year later, she stopped briefly at her brother's home for lunch during a cross-country trip and spent two hours with him. A splitting headache preceded the visit, however, and severe back spasms followed it—perhaps signals from Rayna's unconscious that she was attempting too much too soon.

To make a long story short, it was many years before Rayna had established enough contact with her brother to open up and process the issue of incest. Rayna first wrote him a note saying that she had been thinking of many painful events that had happened in their family when she was young, including some between the two of them, and she wanted to talk with him about this at some point. Later, she sat down with him and brought up the subject directly. How did he understand that such a thing could happen in their family? Why did he think it had occurred? How did he make sense of it? Did he still think about it? How had it affected him?

Rayna had prepared herself for the worst-case scenario ("He could deny it and tell me I'm crazy") and had thought about how she would handle this if it occurred—which it didn't. Finally, she clearly let her brother know that she still struggled with this part of her past. She shared that she had been in therapy for years, trying to work through what had happened, and she told him that the incest continued to diminish her self-esteem and influence her relationships with men.

Later on, Rayna and her brother were able to talk about their family and the broader, troubled context in which the incest occurred. At the same time, Rayna did not back down from the matter of individual responsibility. When her brother said, "Well, you didn't stop me," Rayna told him how she saw it. "Look," she said, "I've struggled with terrible guilt about this and I've blamed myself for many years. But I did not initiate sex—and I was eleven and you were eighteen. To me, that is an important difference. I no longer accept the verdict of guilty, although I still struggle with the feelings." In a later letter she elaborated:

> I know that what happened between us did not occur in a vacuum. I've given lots of thought to the things that were happening in our family when the incest began. I've also given lots of thought to what men learn in our society, and how they are taught to dominate women and see women as existing *for* them, sexually and otherwise. I know this is all part of the picture. But I want to be very clear with you that I believe you were responsible for your own actions. If I deny this, or try to deny the anger that I still feel toward you, it will be all the harder for me to work on having a relationship with you. And as painful as it is to try to work this through, it would ultimately be more painful for me to pretend that I don't have a brother.

If the incest had been perpetrated by Rayna's father, the anxiety would have been greater still and Rayna would have moved even more slowly, allowing more time to process the trauma in therapy and understand its occurrence within the larger family context. *Moving at glacial speed* in the face of very high anxiety is the optimal way to proceed. Rather than signifying a lack of strength or perseverance, moving slowly—or sometimes not moving at all—may be necessary to preserving and protecting the well-being and integrity of the self.

Back to the Source

Is it really necessary or even helpful to process a traumatic event or a loaded issue at the source? Why can't we work it all through in a safe and supportive environment such as that provided by therapy or a women's group? These are places to begin—and many of us will end there too. The gains can be considerable. *I believe, however, that in the long run we will do better if we can move slowly toward some carefully planned contact and eventually unearth the issue with the other person who was directly involved.* The next generations, our children and grandchildren, will also reap the gains.

Processing an issue at the source is important with deceased family members as well. My friend Dorothy lost her father when she was eight, and he was remembered in the family as a superhero. She pictured him on the big screen, full color, with all the imperfections air-brushed out. The actual men in her life were inevitably disappointing because they couldn't fill her father's proverbial big shoes. Two years ago, Dorothy began connecting with her aunt and uncles on her father's side, and she has worked to get a more balanced, objective view of her dad's strengths and weaknesses. The many stories she has gathered, as well as the facts she has learned about his history, have challenged her to think about her father as a real person rather than a cardboard figure defined by family myths and Dorothy's own unconscious wishes and projections. Her contact with her dad's family has been difficult to sustain because it evokes her father's memory for everyone. But being in touch allows Dorothy to stay emotionally connected to her dad and to continue the grieving process in an ultimately productive way.

To the extent that it is possible for us to move slowly *toward,* rather than away from, the emotional issues in our family, we move toward a more solid self and a more objective perspective on others. When painful things have happened and intensity has been managed by distance and cutoff, the "slowly" is especially important because we need first to establish some viable connectedness with family members before trying to bring up a difficult subject.

What Rayna did is not possible for everyone. Even with professional help this may never become a realistic or desirable project for some of us. Ultimately, we each must judge this for our self and trust that we are the best judge of what we can handle. And as always, it's best not to do anything until *after* we have worked to get our own reactivity down.

Down with Reactivity—Up with Thinking

Making disclosures about the self (as Kimberly and Margie did) is not as "hot" as confronting another family member on an intense and taboo subject such as incest. From Kimberly's perspective, however, sharing her lesbianism was loaded enough. Yet prior to her self-disclosure, she put no effort into establishing more connectedness with her folks. Kimberly had talked at length with her friends about coming out, but when the spirit moved her she acted impulsively, without considering her various options (such as timing) or planning how she would handle the strong reactions that her self-disclosure would evoke.

Considering Questions

Part of my job was to help Kimberly *think about* her dilemma rather than *react to it*. Therapists often use *questioning* not only to gather information and to generate and refine hypotheses about the meanings of behavior, but also to foster ability to examine a problem in context, to help lower reactivity, and ultimately to generate new options for behavior. Here is a brief sample of questions that were useful for Kimberly:

When did Kimberly start calling herself a lesbian and what did the word mean to her, then and now? What meanings did she think the word "lesbian" had for each member of her family? How long did it take her to accept her own lesbian identity, and how long would it take family members—more or less? Who in the family did she anticipate would have the strongest negative reaction to the news? Who might accept her lesbian identity most quickly? Most slowly?

Had anyone in her nuclear and extended families ever revealed "a secret," and if so, how had it been received? Was any person on her family tree ever excluded or "denied membership" because of differences? Had Kimberly's family ever been excluded by the community? Were there any cut-offs on her family tree, and if so, what were the circumstances in which these occurred?

How did Kimberly decide to come out at the particular time that she did? Did she think the reaction might have been different if she had approached her parents a year earlier? A year later? Had Mary not been with her at the time, would her parents have listened more or less? How did she anticipate that coming out would alter her relationship with family members, both in the short run and in the long run? How had coming out influenced her relationship with Mary? What factors had influenced Kimberly's willingness, or lack of willingness, to remain invisible as a couple?

This sampling illustrates the kind of questions that ultimately elicit thinking rather than reactivity. Although it's not easy, we can learn to generate questions for ourselves and for others. *Questions enlarge our capacity for reflection and for seeing a problem in its broader context.* This allows us to move back more calmly into an anxiety-filled setting and to continue to process an issue with a more centered focus on the self.

A Matter of Timing

As Kimberly adopted a more reflective attitude, she made a connection between her sister's upcoming marriage and her own intensely felt need to hop on the plane with her lover and let the truth be known. Kimberly opened up an emotionally laden issue in the intense emotional field surrounding her sister's wedding, thus ensuring increased reactivity—her own included.

What specifically was the connection between the upcoming wedding and Kimberly's anxious need for self-revelation? "Competition, I guess," was Kimberly's honest response. "Maybe I was having trouble with the fact that the wedding was all anyone was talking about." Kimberly now appeared to be down on herself, and she spoke as if she were making a fairly heavy confession: "It was 'the wedding this, the wedding that'—everything was the wedding, the wedding, the wedding."

Kimberly's feelings were entirely normal. Feeling jealous and competitive, especially toward those we are close to, is simply a fact of emotional life. Kimberly's feelings were not the problem. The problem was her inability to recognize her feelings (and the associated anxiety), leading to her reactive decision to hop on the plane with Mary. She approached her parents with a heightened need to receive the affirmation that was being showered on her sister, which left her overfocused on getting a particular response from her parents and underfocused on the self.

When we define a new position in a relationship, we need to focus on what we want to say about the self and for the self. We need to be much less focused on the other person's reaction or countermove or on gaining a positive response. This is a goal we achieve *only more or less,* but Kimberly had not laid the groundwork necessary to achieve it more.

Using Feelings as a Guide

Kimberly found it painful to get in touch with her "sibling rivalry" and, perhaps more to the point, her anger toward a world that affirms, honors, and celebrates heterosexual marriage yet fails to recognize or legitimize lesbian bonding. It was only natural that her sister's wedding, which was done up in grand style, would elicit such feelings. But Kimberly's decision to *not* attend the wedding (which she rationalized on financial grounds) only consolidated her outside position in the family and solved nothing in the long run. Later on, Kimberly was able to write both her parents and her sister to apologize for not being with the family on this important occasion. To her sister, she explained that her own pain about having a closeted and uncelebrated partnership might have clouded her thinking. Her apology was much appreciated. At the risk of stating the obvious, I might add that learning to say "I'm sorry" goes a long way toward lowering intensity and shifting a pattern in *any* relationship.

The "negative feelings" that Kimberly at first wished to disavow, later became her guide and incentive for establishing an important marker in her life. She and Mary created their own formal ritual to affirm and celebrate their bond to each other in the presence of their community and before loving witnesses. Her parents and sister, although invited, chose not to attend.

No family member is yet at the level of acceptance where Kimberly would wish them to be. Both her mother and father tell her that they will never accept her sexuality and life-style as "normal." But there are no cutoffs and the lines of communication are reasonably open. Kimberly and

Mary are invited as a couple to family gatherings, and Kimberly's relatives know that Mary is her lifelong partner and not her best friend. Some families might take a decade to reach even this point. In others, this moderate degree of acceptance might not be achievable in a lifetime.

Coming Out or Staying In?

How do you react to Kimberly's story? Some of us will see her choice to come out as an act of great dignity and courage. Others may view it as an immature and selfish act that unnecessarily burdened her family. What do you think?

You don't have to be lesbian to appreciate that the costs of coming out can be very high. On the other hand, the cost of "staying in" may be no less dear, simply less obvious. No sudden and dramatic act of rejection or persecution occurs. One is not suddenly fired from a job, betrayed by a trusted friend, disowned by one's family, or taken to court over custody of one's child. And yet the costs, although harder to identify and easier to deny, may be no less insidious. Failing to come out—although it may be a necessary choice—may feed back a sense of dishonesty, deceit, and self-doubt that erodes one's self-esteem and encourages self-hate. Failing to come out affects the very fabric of relationships and the quality of our day-to-day life. Neither intimacy nor self can flourish in an atmosphere of secrecy and silence.

The question of coming out is not specific only to lesbianism, although those of us who are gay are uniquely vulnerable to discrimination and isolation. Rather, the theme of coming out runs continually through all our lives. Each of us must struggle, both consciously and unconsciously, with our wish to be true to our selves, both privately and publicly, and our wish to receive love, approval, validation, belongingness —or an inheritance, for that matter. It is a struggle we never entirely resolve but one we can work on—in our own way and at our own pace—in a variety of contexts and throughout our lives.

Moving on to Triangles

When we think about intimacy (or the lack of it), we tend to think in terms of *dyads;* that is, two-party interactions. There *are* no key relationships, however, where two people relate to each other uninfluenced and unencumbered by other relationship issues involving a third party. A "pure" person-to-person relationship is only an ideal.

It's an important ideal, at that. If, for example, Kimberly's mother is trying to talk openly with her daughter about lesbianism, one might hope that unresolved issues from her marriage, or from her relationship with her own mother, won't exert a powerful unconscious influence on the process. One might also hope that Kimberly and her mother can work to resolve their own issues relatively free from the influence of others who jump on the bandwagon (Kimberly's sister starts lecturing their mother on how she could handle Kimberly; Mary angrily tells Kimberly that if she's not totally accepted by Kimberly's parents, she won't step foot in their house again). Finally, one might hope that relationship issues would remain in the relationship where they belong rather than being detoured via a third party (if Kimberly's mother fears her mother or husband blame her for Kimberly's lesbianism, she will discuss the issue directly with these parties rather than getting more reactive to Kimberly).

One might *hope* for all of the above, but it's not how we operate. As we will see, the *triangle,* not the dyad, is the basic unit of human emotional functioning, especially under stress.

10

Tackling Triangles

What do you think of when you hear the word "triangle"? For most of us, the "eternal triangle," or extramarital affair, comes right to mind. Affairs are certainly one common form that triangles take in both heterosexual and lesbian couples. Adrienne and Frank's marriage (Chapter 5), for example, was a typical example of how triangles—in this case, his affair, and her affair of the mind—detour marital issues via third parties. An affair may calm the person who is experiencing the most anxiety or discontent and stabilize the marriage until the secret comes out.

After the secret is revealed, relationship issues may still be obscured because so much emotional focus is on the breach of trust that it is difficult for each partner to examine her or his part in the marital distance that predated the affair. The one *having* the affair—in this case, the man— may have difficulty taking appropriate responsibility ("She was so overinvolved with the kids and so sexually rejecting that I found someone who made me feel attractive"). The "done-in" partner may stay so riveted on the betrayal that she never reaches the point where she can get self-focused and work on her own issues. Or she may detour a large percentage of her rage toward the "other woman," which is not where the more serious betrayal occurred.

Because triangles are a natural response to anxiety, affairs often begin at stressful times or important anniversary dates. *He* begins an affair shortly after his dad's stroke or right as his wife approaches her thirty-second birthday, the age when his mother left the family. *She* begins an affair when her firstborn son reaches eleven, which was the age that her older brother was diagnosed with a brain tumor. When we don't find a way to work on anniversaries with our conscious mind, the unconscious will do it for us. Of course, affairs are only one kind of triangle. As we will see, human systems have endless possibilities for triangles and we are always in them.

A Look at an In-Law Triangle

"When I married Rob," Julie explained to me, "we should have moved at least halfway around the world from his mother, Shirley." Julie went on to describe Shirley as the world's most impossible mother-in-law, an intrusive and demanding woman who went from bad to worse after "losing" her only son to marriage. Shirley insisted that Rob and Julie spend every Christmas and Thanksgiving at her home. On weekends, she invariably needed Rob's help with gardening and household chores. Both Julie and Rob described his mother as a woman who simply would not take "No" for an answer.

Within a year after Julie and Rob's wedding, all the negative intensity came to rest between Julie and her mother-in-law. The two women could hardly stand each other, although each got along fine with Rob, who made exhaustive and ineffective efforts to help the two women in his life see each other's point of view. Julie criticized Shirley constantly to Rob ("Your mother is the most demanding, manipulative person I've ever met!")—and to anyone else who would listen. Shirley refrained from openly criticizing her daughter-in-law to Rob, but her negative feelings were obvious.

This is a typical "in-law triangle." The relationship between Rob and his mother—*where the real issues are*—can stay calm, because the intensity has been detoured via Julie and his mother. In fact, Rob doesn't even *recognize* his anger at his mother, because he is so busy coming to her defense in response to his wife's criticism. The triangle allows Rob and his mother to avoid having to navigate a comfortable balance of separateness and connectedness in their own relationship.

In addition, *marital issues are obscured,* as Julie fails to address her own concern about Rob's loyalty to her and *his* problem with setting limits and boundaries around their marriage. She blames his mother ("That woman acts like she's going to have a coronary if she's excluded from anything!") rather than confronting Rob firmly and consistently ("Rob, the repairs have gone unfinished for two weeks and I'd really like you to work on that job before you do your mother's garden"). This way Julie avoids the challenge of taking a clear position with her husband about her own wishes and expectations. Thus, she avoids testing out how Rob would ultimately navigate his loyalty struggle between his mother and wife—and what *she* would do then.

Also fueling the triangle is Julie's distance from her own family of origin, whom she had hoped to "escape" through

marriage and with whom she maintains only dutiful and superficial contact. Because Julie is not attending to issues in
her own family of origin (we *all* have them with family
members—living or dead), she more easily becomes overfocused and overreactive to Rob's mother.

The triangle composed of Julie, Rob, and her mother-
in-law looks like this. Two sides of the triangle remain relatively free of conflict while the negative intensity resides
between Julie and Shirley (Diagram A).

Diagram A

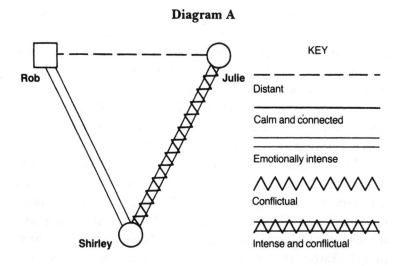

Enter, a Child!

Once little Emma came along, other triangles were set
in motion. In response to the anxieties of new fatherhood,
Rob withdrew further into work. To compensate for the lack
of marital intimacy and for her outside position with her
husband and mother-in-law, Julie moved toward forming an
"especially close" relationship with her daughter. The trian-

gle between mother, father, and daughter looked like diagram B:

Diagram B

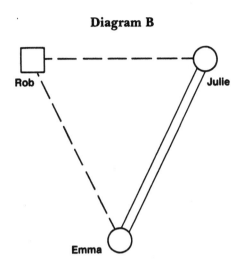

Emma was also an active participant in this triangle. She grew up sensing that her mother needed to be the "number-one parent" and that her dad was made uncomfortable by her emotional presence. Like many daughters, she had a radarlike sensitivity to the distance in her parents' marriage and to her mother's unhappiness. In time, she volunteered to be her mother's ally and "best friend," perhaps as an attempt to fill up her mother's empty bucket and to deflect attention from marital complaints. Even as a toddler, Emma began to put more energy into being "for mother" than into being for her self.

Sex-role pressures also played a major role in the drama of this all-too-familiar triangle. True to stereotype, Julie lacked personal goals and a life plan of her own, which led her to turn to Emma as a "career" rather than a relationship.

Rob became increasingly distant and work-oriented, reinforcing his odd-man-out position in the family.

Over time, each side of the triangle reinforced and
maintained the other two sides. The more distant and emotionally isolated Rob became in the family, the more the
emotional intensity and intimacy resided between mother
and child. And the more Julie and Emma tightened their
emotional bond, the more entrenched became Rob's distant
position.

A Third Triangle

In time, a third triangle developed, involving Julie,
Shirley, and Emma. Shirley began to openly criticize Julie's
mothering, even in front of Emma ("You just can't let her go
out dressed like that in this cold weather!") and to undermine her authority ("Emma, let's not tell Mommy that I took
you for this hot fudge sundae, because she just wouldn't
understand"). When anxiety was up, Julie and Shirley would
have tense exchanges in front of Emma about her care, and
later Julie would blame her husband for not defending her.
Rob did everything possible to maintain his distant position
in the triangle. It afforded him much relief to be outside the
intensity and to be protected from navigating the real emotional issues with his wife, his mother, and his daughter.

If you're feeling a bit lost in these triangles, that's understandable. It's difficult to "think triangles," and even
more so when we are in them. Although triangles are difficult to observe, we *all* participate in multiple interlocking
triangles, one or two of which are particularly central in our
emotional life. Our position in one triangle may be a transient reaction to stress. In another triangle, our position may
be rigid, fixed, and highly resistant to change. Triangles

solve a problem by lowering anxiety when it can no longer be contained between two persons. But triangles also create a problem by covering up the real relationship issues between any two of the parties and by operating at someone's expense.

Doing Something Different

What if Julie were able to shift her position in one of these stuck triangles? For example, what if she found a way to relate to her mother-in-law calmly and cordially and even stopped criticizing her to Rob? What if Julie also ceased fighting with her mother-in-law about Emma's care and found a way to lower her reactivity in this arena? For example, she might joke with her mother-in-law when Shirley criticized her parenting, instead of fighting with her about it: "Do you really think I'm raising Emma to be a stringbean? [*Laughing*] Well, we Hendersons [*her family name*] have so many pumpkins on our family tree, we could sure use a few stringbeans!" If Julie were feeling particularly courageous about trying out new moves, she might further shift her position in the triangle by asking Shirley to share her expertise, experience, and advice. That is, she could try to relate to Shirley's *competence,* which she has entirely lost sight of.

If Julie could maintain this new position over time, family relationships would shift. Tension and conflict would begin to surface between Rob and his mother. The issues in her own marriage with Rob would also become more clearly identifiable. The triangle might begin to look like diagram C (see page 150).

This would be a transitional stage on the way to more functional relationships. When intensity is up, mother-son

Diagram C

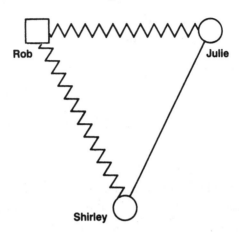

Rob   Julie

Shirley

and marital struggles would erupt, offering an opportunity for issues to be identified and addressed where they really are. In addition, Emma would benefit enormously from no longer being the focus of negative intensity between her mother and grandmother. She would have a much easier time growing up.

Of course, to initiate such a change, Julie would need to become more self-focused. She would have to put her primary energy into working on her *own* family rather than on reacting to Rob's. She would also need the courage to sit with the anxiety that is inevitably evoked when we change our part in a key triangle—and the real issues between parties begin to emerge. As we will see in the next chapter, changing our part in a stuck triangle is anything but easy.

Why is it Julie's job to change the triangle? It's not. Nor did Julie *make* the triangle happen. Each person in a triangle is responsible for their own behavior and any one person can change his or her own steps. The triangles that we get *most* stuck in are at least several generations in the making and their major ingredient is chronic anxiety. No one person "does it" to the other two.

As usual, the person who is concerned or in the most pain is often the one who finds the will to change. Rob could also change the triangle, but he is unlikely to do so because he is more comfortable with the status quo. The triangle protects him from facing the real emotional issues in his relationships with his mother, his wife, and his daughter.

So, What Is a Triangle?

Do you recall how anxiety can affect a relationship system? People divide into two camps, one or both parties get over-focused on the other (and underfocused on the self) in a blaming or worried way, and they ultimately wind up in extreme and polarized positions.

There is, however, an additional part to the story. *Two-person systems are inherently unstable. Anxiety and conflict will not stay contained between two parties for more than a short time.* A third party will quickly be triangled in (or will triangle him- or herself in). This process operates automatically, like a law of physics, without conscious awareness or intent.

The third party in a triangle may be in one person's camp at the expense of a relationship to the other (you don't see your Uncle Joe since your mother stopped speaking to him; you are cut off from your dad since he divorced your mother). The third party may be in a mediating, peace-making, or fix-it position (your parents fight and you move in to advise the parent with whom you have the most influence). Or the original two parties may get focused on a third individual, in a worrying or blaming way (as marital distance increases or an important anniversary date approaches, you and your husband become increasingly anxious about a child; you and your dad talk frequently about your mother's depression, convinced that you both know what's best for her).

Triangles take countless forms, but we can count on the fact that when tensions rise between two parties, a third will be triangled in, lowering anxiety in the original pair. The third party may be *inside* the family (a child, stepmother, grandparent, or in-law)—or *outside* the family (an affair or best friend). Even a therapist can be a third leg in a triangle if he or she joins the client's camp at the expense of a spouse or other family member. Such triangulation can also occur if a therapist is fostering a "special" close relationship that detours intensity from real relationships rather than increasing the client's motivation to solve emotional issues at their source.

A Word About Gossip

Gossip is a universal form of triangling with which we are all familiar. The higher the underground anxiety between two parties, the more the conversation will focus on a third. For example, when you meet your mother for lunch, a big chunk of the conversation may be about your dad, or the problems of your younger brother. There may be little real sharing of self by either you or your mom that doesn't involve a worried (or blaming) focus on someone else.

You can just about measure the level of anxiety in a work system or family system by the amount of gossip. By "gossip," I mean talk *about* another person, with a focus on that person's incompetence or "pathology." We consolidate our relationship with one party at the expense of a third—or we attempt to dilute our anxiety by getting others in our camp. Gossip has nothing to do with intentions. Our conscious intentions may be only the best.

A friend of mine returned from a Christmas dinner with her extended family where the underground anxiety had been quite high. This Christmas was the first without her maternal grandparents, who had both died during the past year. "It was a zoo!" my friend exclaimed upon her return home. "My aunt was cornering me to tell me how my mother is not taking care of her appearance; my mother was angry at her brother and didn't want me to sit next to him; my father cornered me to tell me in hushed tones about my mother's crying spells . . . and so it went!" No one talked about the missing grandparents and how sad the family was that they were not there.

Does talking about a third party *always* indicate a triangle? Of course not. For example, we may have a problem with a friend or co-worker and approach a third party for support or to obtain a more objective perspective. This kind of discussion may allow us to calm down and consider new options for dealing with the original party. Often, however, we have the best intentions for talking *about* a particular individual ("I just want my daughter to know the truth about her father!") when actually we are inviting someone into our camp and operating at the other party's expense. This is particularly true if the person we are talking to (e.g., our daughter) needs to have a relationship with the person we are talking *about* (e.g., her father).

If dyads are inherently unstable, triangles are inherently stable, just as a tricycle is more stable (although less functional) than a two-wheeler. Triangles can last for years, for decades, and over generations. They are not "wrong," "bad," or "sick," but rather are natural ways to manage anxiety in human systems. They serve the adaptive function of stabilizing relationships and lowering anxiety when it can no longer be contained between two parties. Triangles are simply the basic unit of human emotional functioning. As with any relationship pattern, the question is how flexible or fixed is the process?

Child-Focused Triangles

Children are ready-made for triangles; they absorb and detour anxiety from any source. Let's look briefly at a typical child-focused triangle that was a relatively *transient* reaction to anxiety and stress.

"For Willy's Sake"

Bill, a thirty-seven-year-old high school principal, became anxious when his wife, Sue, was accepted into a doctoral program in counseling psychology. Like many men, he was unable to articulate his fears directly, even to himself. Instead, he worried about the well-being of their two-year-old son, and confronted his wife on the child's behalf: "Willy needs you at home! I won't have him raised by a stranger!"

As Bill and Sue argued about "Willy's needs," their son became more anxious and began to react loudly to his mother's departures. A vicious cycle ensued as Bill intensified both his concern about his son and his criticism of his wife ("You see how sensitive he is to your absence!"). Willy, in turn, became even more ill-behaved and clingy.

It took only a few months of nonproductive fighting and blaming for both Bill and Sue to become self-focused and to address the issues between them. Sue, a black woman, was the first person in her family to enter a doctoral program; she had more than her fair share of anxiety, which she avoided by fighting with Bill. Bill got in touch with how threatened he felt about Sue's graduate studies, and with his discomfort at his own father's criticism of Sue's decision.

With a little help, Bill was able to articulate his fears to Sue and to talk directly with his dad about his disapproving attitude. Sue got in touch with her own discomfort about her pioneering position in her family, including her anxiety and guilt about having opportunities that were not available to previous generations of women, or men, in her family. She was able to talk with her mother, sister, and grandmother about her fear of both success and failure, and so learned more about their reactions to her decision to pursue a doctorate.

As Bill and Sue began to work on their *own* issues, little Willy stopped acting out. No longer the focus of parental anxiety, he was also less afraid that something bad would happen between his parents if his mother went back to school. Within a few months, the entire family had calmed down enough to weather Sue's transition to graduate student with a minimum of stress. Although this couple was unusually quick to get unstuck from a child-focused process, their situation illustrates that it can be done.

A Societal Triangle

This child-focused triangle is also evident at the *societal level*. Think back to the initial male response to the women's movement. Men did *not* typically say, "I'm scared and threatened by the changes women are making." Or, "I don't *want* to share housework and child care, and so I feel resentful when my wife asks me to do so." At the early stages of feminism, we did not often hear men speak about the self, or in "I" language, or with their own voice.

Instead, the media focused relentlessly on "the needs of children," which pulled everyone's heartstrings. In the '70s we all were treated to the picture of the small child staring glassy-eyed at the institutional walls of the day care center—while his mother ran off to fulfill her potential. The image itself was enough to frighten and induce guilt in any would-be feminist, and then *Kramer vs. Kramer* became a big hit. This "Change back!" reaction was a countermove to women's efforts to define the self, and not surprisingly, it took the form of blaming women and focusing on children.

Of course children have needs. But so do mothers and fathers. This focus on "the needs of children" did not reflect an *actual* investment in supporting the many children and families who needed help. Rather, it was a typical societal triangle, similar to the one between Bill, Sue, and Willy. Focusing on "the needs of children" ("Mama stay home!") protected us from identifying the locus of the problem's existence—*between* grown men and women. How *easy* it was to express worry that children would be damaged by misguided women in flight from their maternal responsibilities. How *difficult* it was (and still is!) for men and women to *work together* in order to change policy, work institutions, and family roles so that we can be a nurturant and cooperative society *truly* attentive to the needs of children and families!

Whenever adults are not actively working to identify and solve their own problems, then the focus on children may be especially intense or children may volunteer to deflect, detour, and act out adult issues in most imaginative ways. Indeed, children tend to inherit *whatever* psychological business we choose not to attend to.

A good friend tells the story of becoming extremely reactive after a teacher's conference in which she was told that her second-grader might be an "underachiever." She began to monitor her daughter closely, looking for any evidence of a problem; her daughter, in turn, became more anxious. Several weeks later, as my friend found herself lecturing this seven-year-old child on "goal setting," she suddenly realized that she herself had been feeling particularly stuck regarding her *own* professional directions. She had recently arrived at an important anniversary date, the age when her own mother—a bright and colorful woman—took a downhill turn and became increasingly unable to use her own competence. With this greater degree of self-focus, my friend was able to apologize matter-of-factly to her daughter for being on her back and explain that the issue was really her own. As she put her energies into working on it, her daughter's anxiety lessened.

Rampant Reactivity:
From Child-Focus to Self-Focus

Child-focused triangles can be extraordinarily intense, depending on the level of anxiety fueling them. Consider this firsthand report.

Several years ago, my family went out to dinner and then to a Saturday night baseball game in Kansas City. At the restaurant, I found myself concerned about my son Matthew's sluggishness and apparent fatigue. Later I noticed that he got up to go to the restroom four times during the game: he looked sick to me. Shortly before the ninth inning, I suddenly "knew" in my bones that Matthew (then age ten) had juvenile diabetes. The idea hit me not as just a possibility or a concern, but as a dreadful and unbearable truth.

My husband, Steve, often minimizes his concern in proportion to my exaggerated position, but not that night. By the time we got home that evening, Steve was well into the marital fusion and he was scared too. He called the pediatrician early Sunday and described the symptoms (fatigue and constant urination) that we had observed in Matthew the night before. The pediatrician suggested we wake Matthew immediately and meet him at the hospital emergency room. In retrospect, I imagine that the doctor's own sense of urgency (he might simply have told us to watch Matthew that day and get back to him) was partly a response to our contagious anxiety.

Steve woke Matthew and explained the terrible situation with as much calm as he could muster. With a heavy heart, I watched them head off to the hospital. I stayed home with our younger son, Ben, so unable to contain my own anxiety that I called my friend Emily to stay with me during the waiting period. I have faced far more potentially serious crises than juvenile diabetes in my lifetime, but I have never experienced anything worse than that Sunday morning. Until I received the report that Matt's blood test was normal, I could hardly stay within my own skin.

Obviously, my emotional reaction far exceeded even the reality of juvenile diabetes, had this unlikely diagnosis been confirmed. Later, I felt terrible about what I had dumped on Matthew, who was understandably shaken by being the focus of such extreme intensity.

Back to Self-Focus

The emotional process in my family on that particular weekend was as intense and dysfunctional as one could find in any family on this planet. If anxiety gets high enough, none of us is immune from going off the deep end with however we manage anxiety—be it overfunctioning, under-functioning, distancing, fighting, or child-focus. Significantly, however, I did not stay *stuck* in reactive gear; that's what makes the difference. I hope I would not have stayed too long in the reactive gear even if the diagnosis had been different.

Once I was able to call on the *thinking* part of my brain (which took time and help from my friends), it was evident I had my work cut out for me. I needed to get a clearer perspective on my own health anxieties—anxieties that have roots in issues and events that have come down over many generations. I thought I had "dealt with all that," because I had had several weighty conversations with family members about my mother's first cancer and my grandmother's early death from tuberculosis. Of course, it's a *process,* and working through the emotionally loaded issues on our family tree may take several lifetimes. Working on them *consciously*—even a little bit—offers many advantages over letting the unconscious do it for us.

And so I was on the phone again with my mother and sister, asking questions about the legacy of health issues and "worry" on our family tree. I felt somewhat chagrined by my failure to connect my worry about Matthew to my own mis-diagnosis with diabetes years earlier. And only two weeks before the ball game, a routine physical had revealed sugar in my urine. I had seen an endocrinologist, who diagnosed my condition as glucose intolerance.

Another obvious factor (which I had not thought about) was that my mother's diagnoses of cancer and diabetes had occurred the same year and were thus mixed up in my mind, just as I was prone (as are we all) to mixing myself up with my mother—and with my children. And when I took out my genogram (family tree) to study a bit more, I also realized why diabetes was a loaded issue for me and why "survival" anxieties had surfaced during this particular month. The details of my family history are only important here in that they enabled me to put my emotional energy back into my own issues. We all have important emotional issues—and if we don't process them *up* the generations, we are more than likely to pass them on *down*.

A Familiar Lesson

Kids aside, we are always in triangles of one sort or another because we always have "stuff" from our first family (as well as elsewhere) that we are not paying attention to and that may overload other relationships. Throughout this book, we have examined how we detour anxiety and emotionality from one relationship to another. Seeing the process in our own lives, however, is no easy matter, and working on it is even harder.

Working on triangles means more than identifying and addressing issues with our first family that fuel anxiety elsewhere. It also means observing and modifying our current role in key family triangles. Sometimes a triangle will last only a day, a week, or several months, as the examples in this chapter illustrate. But any relationship pattern can become chronically stuck if we don't become calm enough to examine our part in it.

Let's look now at an entrenched family triangle where anxiety was chronically high and where an underfunctioning-overfunctioning polarity had been in high gear for as long as anyone could remember. We'll also think a bit more about our own position in triangles, which should help us further understand the fine points of the overfunctioning-underfunctioning dance.

11

Bold New Moves: The Story of Linda

Linda, a twenty-eight-year-old financial planner, came to see me with the goal of working on her "poor judgment with men." One week after her first appointment, however, a family crisis placed another matter at the top of the agenda. Her younger sister, Claire, was acting depressed and, according to her mother, was leaving her apartment a mess and eating poorly. Both parents responded with intense anxiety, scooping Claire up and taking her back to stay with them in their small nearby apartment. There they cooked for her, did her laundry, and set her up with a therapist whom Claire refused to see after three appointments.

Linda herself was anxious about her sister, who fourteen months earlier had been hinting that she was considering suicide. At the same time, however, Linda was angry with her parents, especially her mother, whom she blamed for her sister's problems. "My mother has never let Claire grow up, *that's* the problem!"

During anxious times such as this one, Linda dispensed copious advice to her mother about how to manage Claire, which her mother ignored. Linda, in frustration and anger, would then seek distance from her entire family. "The best thing I can do for my own mental health," she stated flatly during our early work together, "is to stay as far away from that crazy group of people as possible!"

So, What's Wrong Here?

Linda began therapy with the notion that telling other family members what they were doing wrong (or not doing right) was the hallmark of assertiveness and selfhood. As we have seen, however, this belief is hardly true. *True selfhood and assertiveness are self-focused, not other-focused.*

Linda also thought that her mother made Claire sick. *Mothers cannot make their children sick.* Mothers are only part of a much larger picture and they do not have power over the whole.

In addition, Linda saw herself as having the answers to their family problems, and she blamed her mother for failing to follow her good advice. Linda did not recognize how her own behavior contributed to the problem she was trying to fix.

Finally, Linda thought that the best thing for her own mental health was to distance as much as possible. But that didn't work either. It lowered her anxiety, but only temporarily. Linda began eating excessively, and often awakened early in the morning anxiously preoccupied with the fear that her sister might kill herself.

Tracking the Triangle

What was Linda's position in this common family triangle? When anxiety was low, her relationship with her mother

seemed calm and close, although their "closeness" rested
heavily on their mutual focus on Claire. Claire, a chronic
focus of concern, had the more distant relationship to both
her mother and her sister. (See Diagram D.)

Diagram D

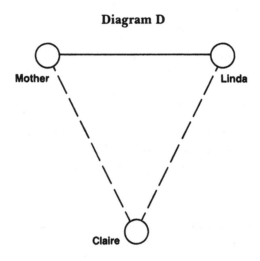

Claire's outside position in the triangle could get quite
pronounced as her mother and Linda consolidated their
relationship at her expense. For example, her mother would
tell Linda "secrets" that were not for Claire's ears, because
Claire would get "too upset" or "tell the wrong person."
Linda participated in the secret-keeping business at a cost to
both Claire and their relationship as sisters. Claire also did
her part to maintain her role as the fragile one, or the one
who couldn't be counted on.

When anxiety was up, the "inside" positions in the triangle became far less comfortable. Calm gossip turned into
angry tension between Linda and her mother, as Linda
would tell her mother what to do about Claire and her

mother would discount her advice. During one visit home, for example, Linda watched her mother wash and fold two baskets of Claire's laundry, while Claire sat on the living room couch thumbing through magazines. Linda phoned her mother the next day and let her have it. "Claire will never grow up if you keep treating her like a baby! She has arms! She has legs! She's twenty-three years old! She can carry a laundry basket!" Linda's mother, for her part, felt misunderstood and believed that Linda failed to appreciate the gravity of Claire's situation. During the particularly stressful period after Linda began therapy, the triangle looked like this:

Diagram E

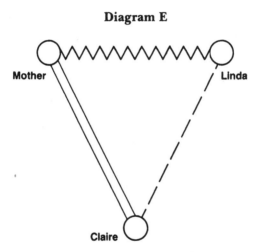

When Linda and her mother talked (or argued) about Claire's problems, both were concerned about her. Surely they did not intend to have a relationship at her expense. As we have seen, however, the patterned ways in which we move under anxiety are rarely helpful. It is simply not helpful to an

underfunctioning individual to overfocus on her (or him)—
or to talk *about* her at the expense of talking *to* her. And
efforts to mediate, make peace, or fix another family relationship are just about doomed to failure. We cannot be
therapists in our own family.

So what *does* help? And how does one begin to move out
of such a triangle in order to create a new dance?

Out of the Middle

Linda's first challenge was to try to *stay out* of the relationship issues between her mother and her sister, and to work
toward having a separate, person-to-person relationship
with each of them. At the beginning of therapy, Linda could
not move in this direction, because *like any good overfunctioner, she was convinced that her mother and sister needed her
help and that she had the answers for them.* For a long time,
Linda clung tenaciously to this view despite her mother and
sister's failure to solve their problems and despite seeing her
advice only temporarily heeded at best.

What exactly would staying out look like to Linda—or
to any of us, for that matter? Staying out does *not* mean that
Linda crosses her arms in front of her chest and announces
firmly to her mother and sister, "Please keep me out of this
triangle! You don't take my advice anyway, and it's not helpful for me to be involved!" Such a position would still reflect
a reactive, "I-really-know-what's-best-for-you" stance. And
it's a blaming and distancing position as well.

Let's look at what staying out actually requires. We will
also learn more about the fine points of overfunctioning,
because learning how *not* to function for other people is a

big chunk of the task at hand. When we *take responsibility for* another person, in contrast to *taking a responsible position in* that relationship, we are operating at that person's expense. Because this notion challenges the worldview of the over-functioning individual, many of us just don't "get it."

As we look at the specific changes that Linda made in her family, try to think about your own relationships. Keep in mind that the specific players and the specific symptoms (for example, Claire's depression) are less important than understanding the patterned ways in which we operate under stress. This triangle could have been with Linda, her mother, and her father; it could have been with Linda, her mother, and her grandmother; or it could have been with Linda and her two best friends. Instead of depression, Claire could have had any other emotional or physical problem. The principles of stuckness and change remain the same.

Getting off Claire

When Linda was ready to work on this core triangle, she began by trying to keep the conversation with her mother focused *less* on Claire and *more* on the two of them. Because core triangles are pretty intense (your mother is off the plane only five minutes before she says, "Let me tell you what your father has done now!"), shifting the focus can be quite a challenge.

Linda handled it pretty well. She stayed nonreactive when her mother talked about Claire, and she did not participate in diagnostic conversations or offer advice. She shifted the conversation toward *sharing more about herself* ("I've been having a real dilemma at work this week") and *learning more about her mother's family* ("Mom, wasn't Aunt Carole on some kind of medication for depression? Did she ever talk with you about the problem?").

Moving out of the triangle did not mean that Linda flatly refused to talk about Claire, which of course is a distancing position. Linda just didn't get into it in the old way. She still gave her mother occasional feedback when appropriate, but *not in an intense, advice-giving, or instructive way.* Here's an example of her changed behavior, which illustrates this crucial distinction.

One afternoon when Linda and her mother were shopping, her mother's focus on Claire was particularly intense. The situation at home had become unbearable, she said, with Claire just hanging around the house making impossible and manipulative demands. Linda heard her out and then said lightly, "Well, Mom, you're just so competent at doing for others and doling out all that good stuff—it makes sense to me that other people would be more than eager to take all they could get."

In this brief statement, Linda shifted significantly from the old pattern. She gave feedback (that is, by clarifying her own thoughts on an issue) in a light manner, without becoming instructive and without asking her mother to follow her advice. The perspective that she shared did not blame or take sides, but was, rather, a calm reflection on the dance as she saw it (their mother was good at giving, Claire was good at taking). When her mother ignored her comment, Linda did not take it further, recognizing that her mother's anxiety was too high to allow her to absorb even light feedback. Her mother and Claire would either solve their problems together, or they would not.

Getting Put to the Test

Moving out of a triangle is a process that will test us over and over. When we start to move out, others in the triangle will intensify their efforts to invite us back in, which is just human nature and the normal resistance to change. Linda's efforts to shift her position in the triangle with her mother and sister encountered this kind of "Change back!" reaction.

Claire was preparing to leave for a three-day trip to Cape Cod, where she planned to stay with some friends who were renting a summer cottage. At this time, however, she was acting mopey and depressed, and she had commented twice to her parents that life didn't seem worth living. Her mother did not think Claire was fit to go on the trip and tried to convince her to stay home. When this failed, she phoned her daughter's friends to express her concern. She asked them to provide a "low-stress" visit for Claire, to watch her for signs of depression, and to call if they noticed anything that looked "serious." Claire's mother did not tell her about the call, and she asked her daughter's friends to keep the call confidential. On the last day of Claire's visit, however, one of them spilled the beans.

Claire was furious with her mother about the incident, and unconsolable. Mother felt Claire was "overreacting"— blowing things entirely out of proportion. Claire, still living at her parents' home, began refusing meals with them, choosing to eat at a nearby McDonald's instead. At this point, her mother called Linda and implored her to "talk some sense" into her sister. This call provided Linda with an opportunity to practice *not* returning to her old pattern.

Linda rose to the challenge. She told her mother that she really didn't have the slightest idea how to be helpful to the two of them, and she expressed confidence that both parties could work out their difficulties over time. When her mother pressed her, she did not return to her old overfunctioning position, but rather responded empathetically to the struggle facing her mother and sister, indicating that she knew it was not easy. She said, "Mom, it sounds like you and Claire are really at a standoff. I love you both and I'm sorry that this is such a tough time. I know it looks impossible right now, but maybe later on things will look different."

At the same time, Linda did not back down from sharing her perspective when asked. Again, the ability to share our thoughts, values, and beliefs is part of *defining a self. Such sharing is not overfunctioning—if we can do it calmly, with respect for differences (others need not see things our way), and with an understanding that our way may not work for or fit others.*

And so—when asked—Linda let her mother know that she also would have been upset if she had been Claire, because she would have wanted her mother to deal with her directly rather than secretly call her friends. When her mother said, "You mean *you* wouldn't have made the call if you were scared to death about your daughter?!" Linda replied thoughtfully, "Well, if I had made the call, I would have told Claire about it. That's just my way."

When her mother angrily accused her of not understanding that Claire was impossible to talk to directly, Linda didn't argue. Instead, she said lightly, "Well, I'm just sharing my own thoughts about managing a difficult situation. I'm not saying I have the right answers." When her mother added, "And your sister is just trying to make me feel guilty by eating her meals in McDonald's every night!" Linda laughed and said, "I guess I wouldn't be doing things *her* way either. Nothing in the world would get me to eat a Big Mac if your home cooking was on the table!" At this point, her mother laughed too, and the tension eased a bit.

And Again, and Again!

Of course, this was not the last test Linda had to deal with. As we have seen, substantive change is a process that is never quite finished. The following week, the relationship between Claire and her mother escalated to a fever pitch. When Linda dropped by one afternoon to pick up a package, her mother cornered her in the bathroom. As Linda described it, "Mother looked so tense and puffed up that I thought she was about to pop." Mother put her face right up to Linda's and spoke in an angry whisper. "Do you know what your sister is doing now! She has stopped speaking to me! Can you believe that she is behaving this way! What do you think of *that! You* would never do anything like that, would you!?"

At first Linda clutched inside. She felt momentarily panicky, the way Kristen (Chapter 7) did when her dad called her to insist that she drive him home. But then she was able to think. "You know, Mother," Linda reflected, "you're probably right. I don't think I'd handle the situation the way Claire is because that's not my way. I think it would just be too painful for me to be feeling that distant from a family member. But as I've shared with you, I wouldn't have handled the situation your way either." Linda smiled and then added warmly, "I guess it makes sense that I'd handle the situation in my *own* way, since I'm different from both of you."

Her mother looked exasperated and said that she needed to start dinner. When she called Linda later that week, she did not mention Claire. When Linda visited several weeks later, it was obvious that her mother and Claire were sharing the easiest communication Linda had seen in a long time. "I feel kind of humbled by the whole experience," Linda told me later that week in psychotherapy. "They really are doing better without my help." It was Linda's first real experience of staying *calm* and *connected*—yet *outside* the old triangle.

These dialogues were dramatic turning points for Linda, and they came after much hard work in therapy. Yet Linda needs to appreciate that the work she is doing will always be "in progress." Whenever anxiety is high in her family, everyone, including Linda, will tend to reinstate the old pattern. Such is the nature of triangles and human systems. What is important is not that Linda always stay calm and "get it right," which is simply not humanly possible, but that she slowly move forward, and not backward, over time.

Connecting with Claire

As Linda stopped having the answers for other family members, she became more in touch with her *own* worry about her sister, as well as her own distance. Claire had talked suicide long before Linda had started therapy, but Linda had not really asked Claire direct questions or shared her own fears.

Linda was occasionally anxiously preoccupied with the subject, and like a true big sister, she had prescribed everything from exercise and medication to psychoanalysis. But the lines of communication were not really open. When I asked Linda how serious her sister had ever been about suicide (Had Claire ever made a plan?), Linda was not sure. Nor did she know what Claire's *own* perspective was on her depression, what efforts she had made to solve it, and what she had found helpful or not.

And so, Linda made a courageous act of change when she asked her sister *direct questions about suicide* and *shared her own reactions*. She put the issue squarely on the table: "Claire, I may be overreacting, but are you actually thinking about suicide?" When Claire's answer still left Linda feeling vague about the facts ("Well, Tuesday night I was sort of thinking about it, but I think I'm doing better now"), Linda asked questions that demanded more specificity. For example: "Where are you now on a one-to-ten scale, if *one* means that suicide is just a fleeting thought and *ten* means that you have a specific plan you're about to carry out?" "If tomorrow night you had a plan, would you let someone in the family know?"

Given the profound degree of anxiety surrounding a subject such as suicide, questioning may quickly take on a blaming, diagnostic, or overfunctioning tone. Linda was better able to avoid this because she was working in therapy to manage her own anxiety and to maintain a high degree of self-focus. Over time, she had reached a deeper and more genuine recognition that she could not change or fix her sister, or even know what was best for her. Certainly, no family member could keep Claire alive or solve her problems. What Linda *could* do for her sister was to care about her and to keep in touch.

Learning to ask clear questions—to go for the facts—is a skill, as well as a courageous act. If we are concerned that a significant other is in trouble, be it from an eating disorder, AIDS, suicide, drugs, or low grades, for that matter, it is not helpful to avoid asking direct questions. We all have reasons *not* to ask ("I can't do anything anyway," "If I mention drugs, he'll just deny it," "If I say anything, it may just put ideas in her head"). Over the long haul, however, we all tend to do better when we have open lines of communication with our significant others.

Sharing a Reaction

Opening up the lines of communication requires more than becoming a skilled questioner. It also requires sharing our reactions and giving feedback. "I" language is a priority here. Often we think we are *sharing about self*, when actually we are trying to be an expert on the other.

Linda shared her reactions with Claire when she told Claire how shaken she was at the thought of losing her: "Claire, the thought that you might ever try to kill yourself terrifies me. I love you and you're the only sister I have. I can't imagine how I would handle it if you were gone." When Linda finished speaking, she burst into tears. It was the first time in Claire's adult life that she had seen her big sister cry.

These words may seem so *obvious,* or even trite, that you might wonder why they constitute a courageous act of change. Yet the higher the anxiety, the more difficulty an overfunctioner (or distancer) has simply sharing pain, fear, and concern without anger or blame and without having answers or advice for the other person. It's hard to find the right words to say the simplest things: "I don't know how I'd handle it, to lose you in this way. I love you, and I want you to be around for as long as possible. I can't bear the thought that I could lose you now. I know that I can't do a thing to help you solve this problem, but I want you to know how much I care about you."

Setting Limits—Taking a Position

Of course, stepping out of overfunctioning does *not* mean that we fail to set limits and take a position on emotional issues. As we saw with Kristen and her dad, relationships can only become more chaotic and impaired when we cannot clarify limits or do not state clearly what we will and will not do.

What position did Linda ultimately take around the suicide issue? First, she clarified that she would not keep the issue of suicide a secret from any family member. Nor would she aid and abet her sister's self-destructive behavior in any other way. Again, regardless of the nature of the problem, our challenge is to define a clear and responsible position in the relationship, *for self* and not as an attempt to function for the other party. A look at a conversation between these two sisters illustrates how to "take a responsible position for self" and how difficult doing so can be. Such interactions are tough on both parties.

At one point, Linda asked Claire to let her know if she ever felt suicidal, and she expressed her wish for a closer relationship. Linda said she'd like for them both to feel free to call each other when they felt down. Claire immediately challenged this move toward more connectedness.

"Why should I tell you if I'm suicidal?" demanded Claire. "You can't do anything to help me when I'm depressed."

"I know that," Linda answered. "I don't even have the answers to my own problems, let alone yours. But even if I could only give you a hug and tell you I care, I would still like to know."

"Well, you'll have to promise me that you won't tell Mom and Dad. They would just overreact or put me in a hospital or something."

"I can't make you that promise," Linda replied. "I would never keep it a secret if I thought your life was in danger. For one thing, my *own* anxiety would be out of control if I held that kind of secret. I just couldn't do it. Yes, I'd call Mom and Dad. No, I wouldn't keep it a secret from anyone in the family."

"If Mom and Dad were away, would *you* ever put me in the hospital?" Claire asked accusingly.

"Claire, if I thought you might kill yourself . . . I'd call the police, the fireman, the hospital, or whoever I could think of. If you told me you were in immediate danger, I wouldn't know what else to do. I know you'd be furious with me, but I'd just have to live with that. I *couldn't* live with the feeling that I had aided your killing yourself. I just couldn't live with that."

"But you can't stop me anyway if I really want to."

"I know that, Claire. Of course I can't stop you. But as I said, I wouldn't sit around and be part of it happening. I'd be on the phone to everyone who loves you."

"Well then, forget it!" was Claire's quick and angry reply. "I'm not telling you *anything*." Claire left the room then.

Linda sat by herself for about five minutes. Then, before leaving, she told her sister: "Claire, I'm really hoping you'll reconsider what you said about not telling me anything, because I care about you. As your sister, I feel terribly sad to think we could end up not being able to talk about things that are important to us. I've been thinking about Mom and Aunt Sue [*a sister from whom their mother is cut off*] and I think how much I *don't* want us to end up like that."

This conversation illustrates the key aspects of "defining a self" that we have touched on in earlier chapters. Let's summarize:

First, Linda is maintaining a nonreactive position. Emotional, yes. Linda cried when she told Claire she was scared of losing her, and that she felt terrible about the prospect that they might end up as distant as their mother and Aunt Sue. But Linda was *thinking,* and she was maintaining her new position rather than reacting to anxiety in her usual patterned ways.

Second, Linda defined a clear bottom-line position ("No, I won't keep suicide a secret. Yes, I'd call the police or hospital, if necessary") and stood behind it, even in the face of intense emotional pulls to do otherwise. Linda resisted the temptation to back down from her position, and then perhaps to blame her sister for "manipulating" or "blackmailing" her.

Finally, Linda stayed entirely self-focused and stuck with "I" language—nonblaming statements about the self. She put her energy into taking a responsible position in the relationship—and not into taking responsibility *for* her sister, or acting as if she could solve her sister's problem. She did not lapse back into overfunctioning. At no time did Linda suggest that she was a better expert on Claire than Claire was on her self. This was part of a new pattern for Linda where she stayed in her own skin and worked to *relate to her sister's competence*—something we easily forget how to do when we are relating to a chronically underfunctioning individual.

Sharing Underfunctioning

What else did Linda need to do to create a different dance with Claire? Linda slowly shared some of her *own* problems with Claire, as well as with her parents. She started slowly, with small pieces of information, because of the extreme difficulty of modifying overfunctioning. Sharing one's vulnerability with family members and seeing the underfunctioners as having something to offer are not easy shifts.

Thus, Linda did *not* begin by telling her sister about her poor track record in choosing men, which had led her to therapy because she despaired of ever having a decent relationship. Instead, when Claire became depressed and called her one evening, Linda told her she wasn't really able to listen or be helpful right then. "Everything has gone wrong today," Linda complained to her sister. "In fact, I was just about to call you. I messed up a meeting at work, I burned my dinner, and I'm just feeling totally stressed-out." For Linda, this sharing was yet another courageous act of change. It pushed against the polarities in her family, where there was *too much focus* on the incompetence of one member and *not enough focus* on the incompetence of others. Later, when she was ready, she shared with Claire some of her problems with men and openly acknowledged that this was *her* significant area of underfunctioning. She also asked her sister for advice and help in areas where Claire had a history of expertise.

Linda and Men

When Linda first came to see me, her primary concern was her long-standing problem with men. Her relationships tended to intensify quickly, and equally quickly she would lose her ability to be objective about the man she was dating. She described herself as "a leaf blown about by the wind" when it came to romantic involvement—a stark contrast to her usual sense of mastery and control on the job.

Many firstborn, overfunctioning daughters share Linda's experience. And although the connection may seem elusive, the work she did on her own family was particularly helpful. Linda worked to modify her overfunctioning position and to share a more whole and balanced self with her sister and parents, which included *both* her competence and vulnerability. She also worked in therapy to obtain a more objective and balanced view of both the strengths and weaknesses of other family members. *In turn, she began to look more objectively at the men she was dating.* Things still heated up fast, but Linda could then step back to consider the strengths and weaknesses of a prospective mate.

Over time, Linda put much effort into observing and changing her part in some old patterns, polarities, and triangles in her family. In addition to the shifts she made with Claire and her mother, she also connected more with her father, who was an extreme distancer and something of an invisible phantom on the family scene. As Linda learned more about her dad's own family and history and shared more of herself with him, she was also on firmer footing with her male partners. The more we can stay connected and define a clear and whole self in the intense field of family relationships, the more grounded we are in other relationships.

At the time Linda terminated psychotherapy, she was not dating anyone in particular nor did she feel a great need to be. She was, however, doing a fine job of avoiding relationships that would ultimately waste her energy or bring her pain.

A Postscript: The Dilemma of Overfocus

When another person underfunctions—be it a misbehaved child, a depressed husband, a symptomatic sibling—significant others may become focused on that person. Over time, the focus on the other may increase, whether through blaming, worrying, fixing, bailing out, protecting, pulling up slack, covering up, or simply paying too much attention with too much intensity. To the same extent, the focus on self decreases, with less energy going toward identifying and working on one's own relationship issues and clarifying one's own goals and life plan. When this happens, the underfunctioner will only tend to underfunction more and longer.

We cannot simply *decide* to deintensify our reactivity and focus on another person's problems. It's not something we can just "do," nor is it something we can pretend. If we try to fake it, our efforts will be short-lived at best, or we may flip from overfocus to reactive distance—the other side of the same coin. We can deintensify our focus on the other only *after* we find the courage to work on other relationships and issues that we do not want to pay attention to. Each of us has enough to work on for at least several lifetimes. If we move forward with these challenges for self, we can avoid becoming overfocused on and reactive to that other party.

So, Who's Responsible for Claire's Depression?

When something goes wrong in a family, we naturally look for someone to blame. Or perhaps we point the finger at two or three people. But Claire's depression, like any serious problem, was probably several hundred years in the making; it may have been affected by issues, patterns, and events that were passed down over many generations. Whatever our particular theory (and there are countless biological and psychological theories that will continue to change and be enlarged over time), we are best to be humble. There is far more that we *don't* know about human behavior than we *do* know. Our most esteemed experts would have, at best, only a partial and incomplete explanation of Claire's depression.

So, who is responsible for curing Claire's depression or solving her problem? There is only one person who can do this job, although others will try, and that is Claire. It is *her* job to use her competence to become the best expert on her self and to figure out how she will work on her problem. Others may make it easier or harder for her to work toward recovery, but the challenge is hers.

But what of all the good work Linda did? Didn't this help Claire? Linda got out of the middle of the relationship between Claire and their mother. She modified her overfunctioning. She opened up communication. She set limits with Claire and defined a position around the suicide issue while letting Claire know she cared about her. She shared her underfunctioning side. She worked to deintensify her focus on Claire and to put more energy into her own issues, such as her distance from her father. She stayed in touch. These are extremely helpful actions that we as family members can take when someone we care about is underfunctioning. However, that's all they are. Only helpful. They do not solve the other person's problem, nor is doing so our job.

To what end, then, did Linda change? The work she did will give her the best chance of keeping her own anxiety down, having solid family relationships, and proceeding with her own life as well as possible. Linda's changed behavior will also make it easier, rather than harder, for Claire to use her competence to work on her own problem. But there is nothing that Linda or her parents can do to either cause or cure Claire's depression. Claire will either find a way to work on her problem when she is ready—or she will not.

12

Our Mother/ Her Mother/Our Self

Before all else, we are daughters. Our relationship with our mother is one of the most influential in our lives and it is never simple. Even when we have been separated from our mother at birth—or later by death or circumstance—a deep and inexplicable bond connects daughter to mother, mother to daughter.

As adult daughters, this bond may be one of profound ambivalence. We may still be blaming our mother, trying to change or fix her, or we may still be keeping our emotional distance. We may be absolutely convinced that our mother is "impossible," that we have tried everything to improve things and that nothing works.

So, what is the problem?

The problem is that these are cardinal signs of being stuck in this key relationship. They are signs we have not negotiated our ultimate separateness from our mother, nor have we come to terms with her separateness from us. If we are still blaming our mother, we cannot truly accept our self. If we are still fighting or distancing, we are *reacting* to the intensity in this relationship rather than working on it. And if we fail to carve out a clear and authentic self in this arena, we won't have a clear and separate self to bring to other important relationships. As we have seen, whatever goes unresolved and unaddressed in our first family will go underground—and then pop up somewhere else, leaving us in a more shaky, vulnerable position with others.

By working on the task of reconnecting with our mother, we can bring to this relationship a greater degree of self and can learn to appreciate the "separate self" of this woman we call mother. We hear much about how a *mother* impedes her daughter's separateness and independence. We hear less about the *daughter's* own difficulty in experiencing her mother as a separate and different "other," with a personal history of her own.

In the pages that follow, we examine the changes that one woman, Cathy, was able to make in her relationship with her mother. Her story, like others I have shared, will illustrate the process of moving toward a more mature intimacy in which we can define the self and respect the emotional separateness of the other. While we have already examined this process in depth, Cathy's struggle will allow us to summarize and appreciate anew the complexity of change and help us to think further about our own relationships.

Cathy and Her Mom

"My mother is really impossible!" concluded Cathy after a recent evening in her parent's home. "She's totally defensive and she won't listen to anything I say!"

"What was it you were wanting her to hear?" I inquired. Cathy had been in psychotherapy only briefly, and I knew relatively little about her family.

"First of all, there are a whole bunch of things I've been angry about for a long time, and I wanted to clear the air. I figured it would be good to get things out in the open, instead of just sitting on my feelings."

Cathy paused to catch her breath and then continued, with obvious exasperation in her voice, "My mother simply cannot deal with my anger! Each time I'd raise a legitimate complaint, she would say, 'Yes, but . . .' and then she'd end up criticizing *me*. I tried to get through to her—but as always, it's impossible."

"What were you trying to get across to her?" Cathy still hadn't answered my earlier question.

"First of all, my younger brother, Dennis, is doing poorly in school, and my mother constantly grills him about whether he's trying drugs and why he's out till midnight with his friends. That's one thing I was trying to give her feedback about. Then, there's the way she treats my dad, making all sorts of decisions for him. And finally, she's always intruding into my life, especially since my divorce. She worries constantly about my son, Jason, and she is always telling me to pray to Jesus. She needs to be totally in control of everything and everybody, and the whole family is suffering."

"Anything else?" I asked, as if that wasn't enough.

"Well, those were my main agenda items for this visit. But of course there's more. A lifetime more."

Cathy's complaints sounded familiar. I had heard them countless times before—in countless forms—from countless women in psychotherapy. And Cathy, like Linda and like so many of us, was doing the very things with her mom that only served to preserve the status quo. She blamed her mother for unilaterally "causing" family problems. She assumed that she (Cathy) was the expert on how her mother should handle her relationships (such as with Cathy's dad and brother). And she alternated between silence and distance, on the one hand, and fighting and blaming, on the other. As we have seen, these behaviors keep us stuck by ensuring that problems will not be addressed in a productive way, that old patterns will not be changed, and that intimacy will not occur.

Mother-Blame/Mother-Guilt

Cathy, like the rest of us, approached her mother, Anne, with only the best intentions. Her intention was not to blame Anne and certainly not to hurt her. According to Cathy, she confronted her mother because she wanted to lay the groundwork for a better relationship and because she wanted to help Anne deal with other family problems.

"How do you understand the fact that your mother couldn't hear a word you said?" I knew the question was premature, because Cathy's reactivity to her mom was still so intense I could not expect her to reflect on this problematic relationship and, in particular, her part in maintaining it.

"Because she's so defensive. She just feels accused and tries to protect herself."

Without knowing Cathy's mother, I could safely assume Cathy was on target here. Anne felt accused and tried to protect herself; she became defensive. So, what else is new? Or, to put it differently, why shouldn't she?

Our mothers have let us all down because they have lived with impossible and crippling expectations about their role. It is natural for a mother to react to her daughter's criticisms with anxiety and guilt. In fact, guilt is woven into the very fabric of womanhood. As one family therapist puts it, "Show me a woman who doesn't feel guilt, and I'll show you a man." Feelings of guilt run deepest and are most ingrained in mothers, who are the first to be blamed and the first to blame themselves. For example, recall Adrienne's mother, Elaine (Chapter 5), who felt responsible both for having a retarded son and for not keeping him at home. Or Kimberly's mother (Chapter 9), who stayed awake at night thinking she had "caused" her daughter's lesbianism—or that others would see it that way.

Mother-guilt is not simply the personal problem of individual women. Rather, it stems naturally from a society which assigns mothers the primary responsibility for all family problems, excuses men from real fathering, and provides remarkably little support for the actual needs of children and families. A mother is encouraged to believe she *is* her child's environment, and that if only she is a "good enough" mother, her children will flourish. It is only natural that Cathy's mother was sensitive to blame, and defensive in response to being accused of not being a good enough mother. Only a remarkably flexible and secure mother would react otherwise.

Let's look more closely at how Cathy navigated her relationship with Anne, with an eye toward consolidating some of the lessons we have learned about changing our own part in the relationship dances that block intimacy and keep us stuck. Underlying most mother-daughter distance and conflict is anxiety about navigating separateness and independence in this key relationship—and the usual confusion about what "separateness" and "independence" really mean. Cathy thought confronting her mother was a courageous expression of her "real" and independent self. In fact, her behavior made it more difficult to achieve this goal.

A Matter of Differences

Cathy's relationship with Anne had always been strained, but it had gone from bad to worse following Cathy's divorce two years earlier. "Mother always made my business her business," explained Cathy, "but since I've been living alone with my son, Jason, she really tries to run my life."

According to Cathy, Anne expressed a never-ending concern about Jason's well-being and about Cathy's lack of religious values. "My mother worries that Jason has been traumatized by the divorce," Cathy said, "and she doesn't like the way I'm raising him. Religion is the biggest issue between us. Saturday I had Mother over for lunch and I had to sit through her religion lecture for the tenth time—and in front of Jason!"

Anne's "religion lecture" took a variety of forms, but it basically boiled down to the following: First, Anne believed that Cathy should take Jason to church on Sundays. Second, Anne wanted Cathy to give religion a more central place in her own life. Whenever Cathy expressed sadness or anger over the divorce, Anne instructed her to pray. Cathy had no patience with her mother's advice or criticism (although Cathy had plenty of advice and criticism for Anne), and she did not like her parenting to be criticized in front of her son.

Cathy felt chronically tense in her mother's presence. She believed she had tried everything she could to change their antagonistic relationship; when nothing changed, she diagnosed the situation as hopeless. In reality, however, Cathy had explored no option other than moving from silence and distance to fighting and blaming, and back again. And both she and her mother acted as if they were the best expert on the other.

The Old Dance

Although Cathy periodically confronted Anne about her mismanagement of *other* family relationships, Cathy more typically said nothing at all when *she* was the target of her mother's criticism and unsolicited advice. She excused her failure to speak out. "My mother won't listen; it only makes things worse. My mother just can't hear the truth!" Sometimes Cathy refused to see Anne: "Mother upset me so much after the divorce that I avoided her for several months. If I could have afforded the plane ticket, I would have gone to China."

By distancing and failing to speak out on her own behalf, Cathy kept her relationship with her mother calm. As a way of managing anxiety, distancing *does* work in the short run, and that's why we do it. However, in Cathy's attempts to preserve a pseudoharmonious "we," Cathy was sacrificing the "I." *The degree to which we can be clear with our first family about who we are, what we believe, and where we stand on important issues will strongly influence the level of "independence" or emotional maturity that we bring to other relationships.* If Cathy continues to avoid taking a stand on emotionally important issues, she will remain "stuck together" with her mom, and she will be on less solid ground in other relationships as well.

According to Cathy, she did occasionally "take a firm stand" and "share her true feelings." But just what did she mean by this? Typically, it meant that Cathy moved from silently seething in her mother's presence to letting it all hang out. Like a pendulum that has swung too far in one direction, she occasionally went to the other extreme with

Anne. When this happened, Cathy would come to therapy describing an interaction that sounded like a confrontation between Godzilla and *Tyrannosaurus rex*. "My mother went off on her religion kick again, and I told her that she just used religion as a crutch—a simple solution to all of life's problems. Things escalated and she ended up storming out of the house in her usual dramatic fashion."

Fighting and blaming, like silence and distance, protected both mother and daughter from successfully navigating their separateness from each other. Again, "separateness" does not mean emotional distance, which is simply one means of managing anxiety or emotional intensity. *Rather, separateness refers to the preservation of the "I" within the "we" —the ability to acknowledge and respect differences and to achieve authenticity within the context of connectedness.* How well we do this within our own kinship group largely determines our capacity for intimacy elsewhere, and influences how well we will manage other relationships throughout our lives.

Defining a Self

One of the first steps in achieving independence or in "defining a self" is to move beyond silence and fighting, to begin making clear statements about our own beliefs and our position on important issues. For example, Cathy might choose a time when things were relatively calm to say to Anne, "Mom, I would really prefer that you don't discuss how I'm bringing up Jason in front of him. If you'd like to talk about my not taking him to church, let's find a time when just the two of us can discuss it."

Cathy can learn to address the real issues at hand rather than marching off to battle without knowing what the war is really about. In the old pattern, Cathy argued endlessly with her mother about whether Jason needed to go to church, and about the role of religion in their family life. Such fights were bound to go nowhere, and they kept Cathy stuck for two reasons: First, Cathy was trying to change her mother's mind, which was not possible. Second, she was behaving as if there were only one truth (about religion, child-rearing, or anything else), which both she and Anne should agree on.

The fact is that Cathy and Anne are two separate people who understandably have two different views of the world. Failure to appreciate this blocks real intimacy, which requires a profound respect for differences. We have seen how vulnerable we all are to confusing closeness with sameness and behaving as if we should share a common brain or heart with the other person.

This is especially true between mothers and daughters. With our beliefs about "women's place" shifting so dramatically over the past two decades, it is no surprise that mothers, in particular, may react strongly to their daughters' declaration of themselves as *different* from the generations of women who have come before. A mother may unconsciously experience such difference as disloyal or as a betrayal—a negative comment on her own life, or perhaps simply a reminder of options and choices that were unavailable to her. And of course, a daughter's "declaration of independence" can be especially hard for a mother who may feel she has nothing—not even a self—to return to after her children are grown. When women are taught that mothering is a "career" rather than a relationship, "retirement" becomes an understandable crisis. And because many daughters *do* handle their struggles with independence by distancing, blaming, or cutting off, then a mother's feeling of loss is understandably great. Mental health professionals may also contribute to the problem by instructing mothers "to separate" from their daughters, as if "to separate" means only giving something up, rather than working slowly toward a new and potentially richer kind of connectedness.

In sum, Cathy's job is to address the real issue in her relationship with Anne—the fact that she is a separate person with thoughts, beliefs, priorities, and values that differ from her mother's. To do this, Cathy must stop trying to change, criticize, or convince her mother; she must instead begin to share more about her own self, while respecting her mother's right to think, feel, and react differently.

For example, Cathy might say to Anne, "Mom, I know that religion has an important place in your life, but it's not where I'm at right now." If her mother begins to argue the point or criticize, Cathy can avoid getting drawn back into the old fight, because she knows from experience that intellectual arguments go nowhere and only keep her stuck. Instead, she might listen respectfully to everything Anne says and then merely reply, "Mom, I know how helpful your faith has been to you. But it's not my way." If Anne becomes hysterical and tells Cathy she is bringing disgrace to the family and causing her mother to have a coronary, Cathy can say, "I'm sorry if I'm hurting you, Mom, because that's not my intention." When her mother brings up religion for the 120th time, Cathy can joke with her or lightly reply, "I understand your feelings, but I see things differently."

Sound simple? Such conversations require a lion's share of courage, because they bring the separateness between mother and daughter into bold relief and, as a result, evoke tremendous anxiety. If Cathy stays on track, her mother will react strongly to her daughter's changed behavior by upping the ante in some way, perhaps by criticizing and blaming Cathy, or by threatening to sever their relationship.

It is important to keep in mind that countermoves or "Change back!" reactions occur whenever we move toward a higher level of assertiveness, separateness, and maturity in a key relationship. When we are the one initiating a change, we easily forget that countermoves express anxiety, not lack of love, and they are always predictable. The challenge for Cathy is to hold on to a process view of change, and to sit still through her mother's countermoves without returning more than temporarily to the old pattern of distancing or fighting. She can learn to sound like a broken record, if necessary, in the face of countless "tests." We have seen how change in a stuck relationship often feels like an uphill battle. It can require stamina and motivation, as well as a good sense of humor, to keep moving against the enormous and inevitable resistance from both within and without.

Moving Toward the Hot Issues

How did Cathy actually do in this difficult task of "defining a self" with her mother? In some areas, quite well. For example, she was extremely clear and consistent with Anne about *not* discussing her parenting in front of Jason, and when her mother continued to "drop comments" in front of him, Cathy didn't take the bait. Instead, she'd joke with her mother or otherwise deflect her criticisms—and then bring up the subject later when Jason was not within hearing distance. Cathy did not get intense or reactive to her mother's "tests" and countermoves, and she was clear in her own mind that *she* would not participate in arguments about Jason in his presence—even when "invited" to do so.

Whenever the religion issue came up, however, Cathy had a far more difficult time. As she put it, "Every time my mother brings Jesus into the conversation or tells me to pray, I just clutch and lose it." Over time, Cathy gained more control over her behavior, but not over her strong emotional response. "When my mother gets going about religion, I get knots in my stomach and I just feel like screaming at her," explained Cathy. "The best I can do is to drop the issue and change the subject."

In one sense, Cathy is correct. The worst time to try to discuss a hot issue in a stuck relationship is when we are feeling angry or tense. Emotional intensity only makes people more likely to *react* to each other in an escalating fashion rather than to think objectively and clearly about their dilemma. If Cathy is clutching inside and feels like screaming, it's not a bad idea for her to drop the issue, change the subject, take a walk, or escape to the bathroom to seek temporary distance. Over the long haul, however, Cathy will do best if she can begin to move *toward* the subject of religion, to get a broader perspective on her mother's attitude and on her own strong emotional response to the subject. How can Cathy move toward opening up such a difficult subject?

The Broader Picture

Every family has its hot issues, which come down the pike, unprocessed in one generation and played out in the next. In Cathy's family, religion was one hot issue, especially between mother and daughter. You can recognize a hot issue in your family if a subject is focused on incessantly and intensely, or if it cannot be talked about at all. You can be sure it's a hot issue if you clutch inside when the subject comes up.

How could Cathy gain a calmer and more objective perspective on this hot issue in her family? First, she had to widen the focus a bit. To this end, I asked Cathy a number of questions to help her think about what religion meant to her family in previous generations. What was the place of religion in her mother's own family as she was growing up? Did her mother have differences of opinion with her own mother; if so, were they openly expressed? If such differences existed, how were they handled? How would her grandmother have reacted if Anne had become a self-declared atheist, like Cathy? How did Cathy's mother arrive at her religious and spiritual beliefs, and in what way did they evolve over time? At what age did her mother become religious, and what significantly influenced her religiosity? Who else in the previous generations had "left" religion? Who had been most involved in it? What else was going on when important changes in such involvements occurred?

It was understandably difficult for Cathy to approach her mother calmly, factually, and warmly about this particular subject. By definition, the hot issues in a family can't easily be discussed objectively and productively, and of course, the more we avoid discussion, the hotter they become. When Cathy was finally able to get the subject out on the table, in a genuinely curious and uncritical way, the deep emotionality surrounding the subject of religion in her family took on a new meaning for her.

A Piece of History

What ultimately emerged in Cathy's talks with her mother was the story of a traumatic, early loss in her mother's own family. When Anne was five years old, her three-year-old brother, Jeff, died after ingesting a toxic substance in the family home. In addition to profound feelings of loss, Cathy's grandmother must have struggled with a deep sense of guilt and despair regarding her own fantasied or real contribution to Jeff's death. She was the only person home with her son when the tragic event occurred.

Anne didn't know all the facts surrounding her brother's poisoning, because this loss became the hot issue in her own family—a taboo subject that was never discussed. From what Anne was able to share with Cathy, it seemed that her mother's own religious attitudes had intensified after Jeff's death, as she struggled to survive the loss. On those rare occasions when Jeff's name was mentioned, it was only in the most *positive* of religious terms: "God takes only the best for himself." "It was God's will." "Jeff is happy with God." "God wanted Jeff with him." Both parents clung desperately to this one framing of the tragedy, in a manner that discouraged other questions and reactions from emerging openly among family members.

Cathy had long known that her mother had lost a brother in childhood. But this fact had not been *real* to Cathy, nor had she thought about its actual impact on her mother's life. Now Cathy learned that Anne had never seen her way clear to question her *own* mother's religious beliefs —in fact, after the tragedy, Anne "protected" her mother by suppressing differences of opinion on many issues. Anne believed that religion was her mother's lifeline, that it quite literally kept her mother alive. To question her mother's assumptions, or even to believe differently herself, was not an option for Anne. And now her own daughter, Cathy, was disavowing *all* religion, which only reactivated the old buried feelings surrounding a tragic death that had never been processed and emotionally put to rest.

This new information allowed Cathy to make connections between two generations of mothers and daughters. Anne's "solution" to the difficult challenge of selfhood with her own mother was to inhibit and deny expressions of difference, not only in religious matters, but also concerning any number of important issues. Cathy's "solution" was the opposite—which was really the same. Cathy was trying to define a separate self by being as *unlike* her mother as possible. If Anne said "apples," Cathy was sure to say "bananas." *Having to be different from our mother expresses our real self no more than having to be the same.*

The Pluses for Cathy

How did it affect Cathy to learn more about this crucial event in her mother's own family? For one thing, Cathy was able to feel somewhat more empathic and less reactive when the subject of religion reared its controversial head. In fact, reflecting on the impact of Jeff's death allowed Cathy to put many of her mother's "obnoxious behaviors" in a broader perspective. For example, Cathy felt extremely bugged by her mother's anxiety about her brother and especially about Jason's well-being after his parents' divorce. Cathy was now able to see how her mother's anxiety in these relationships was fueled by the intense, unresolved mourning process in her own family. Surely the issue of the survival and well-being of sons was an understandably loaded one for Anne.

As Cathy began to detoxify the hot issue of religion by getting it out on the table and broadening her perspective, she was also able to think through her own beliefs on this subject more clearly. Cathy's position on religion ("I'd drop dead before I'd bring Jason into a church") was a reactive one, and no more a statement of independent values than was her mother's desperate clinging to religious clichés. As Cathy began to view the legacy of religious values in her family through a wide-angle lens, thus gaining a better sense of her mother's own history, she was able to better formulate her *own* views on religion without mindlessly rebelling against the beliefs of two generations of women before her.

Perhaps most important of all, Cathy's conversations with her mother allowed her to experience Anne as a "real person," a separate and different "other" who had a personal history of her own. *Gathering information about our parents' lives, whether they are living or dead, is an important part of gaining a clear self, rooted in a factual history of our family's development.* And as Cathy discovered, information about each previous generation alters and enlarges the very meaning of behavior. For example, as Cathy learned more about her maternal grandparents' traumatic immigration from Poland, including the massive losses and severed ties that each experienced at the time, she viewed their "extreme" personalities in a new light. Her earlier glib and critical response ("Those folks became religious fanatics after the kid died") was replaced by a respectful appreciation of her grandparents' multiple losses and their strength and courage in finding a way to continue their lives after losing their son.

A Postscript: So You Think You Know Your Family?

Like many of us, Cathy began therapy convinced that she knew her family. This meant that she had stories to tell about family members and a psychiatric diagnosis for just about everyone on her family tree. But the stories we tell about our family frequently reflect the polarities that characterize systems under stress ("My mother the Saint," "Uncle Joe the Sinner") and have little to do with the complexity of real people and actual history. When anxiety has been high, we know who the good guys are, we know who the bad guys are, and we know whose camp we are in.

If we can move toward gathering a more factual history of our family, and enlarge the context over several generations, we will gain a more objective perspective on family members. We can begin to see our parents, as well as other relatives, as *real people in context* who have both strengths and vulnerabilities—as all human beings do. And if we can learn to be more objective in our own family, other relationships will be a piece of cake.

The best way to begin this process is to work on your own genogram, or family diagram. Instructions on doing a genogram can be found in the appendix at the back of this book. On the face of it, this may seem like a simple and straightforward task, as a genogram is nothing more than a pictorial representation of family facts. The facts included on a genogram are dates of births, deaths, marriages, separations, divorces, and major illnesses, as well as the highest level of education and occupation for each family member.

If you approach the task seriously, you will find that your genogram is a springboard to thoughts about many of the ideas presented in this book—or you may simply notice things of interest. You may find, for example, that you have considerable information about one side of your family and almost none about the other. You may become clearer about the hot issues and cutoffs on your family tree as you are confronted with the facts that you *don't* have and that you are uncomfortable asking about. ("How and when did Aunt Jess die?" "What is the exact date of my adoption?") You may begin to notice certain patterned ways that anxiety is managed on a particular side of the family; for example, on your father's side there may be considerable distance, including a good number of divorces, cutoffs, and people who don't speak to each other. You may observe there are few people on your family tree that you have a real relationship with— and that those relationships you *do* have are pretty intense.

The genogram is also your source of important anniversary dates and provides a context for understanding why relationships intensified or fell apart at a particular time. The ages of those who suffered losses, deaths, divorces, or downhill slides in the previous generations will give clues as to what years (as well as what issues) were particularly anxious ones in your past, and what ages may be particularly loaded ones for you in the future. You may notice certain patterns and core triangles repeating over generations or you may make observations about sibling position, as when Adrienne (Chapter 5) identified an issue around second-born sons in her family. The more facts you gather, the more questions you will generate.

Over time, working on a genogram helps us to pay primary attention to the self in our most important and influential context—our first family. It helps us to view relationship problems from a much broader perspective, over generations, rather than focusing narrowly on a few family members who may be idealized or blamed. As we are able to think more objectively about our family legacy and connect with more people on our family tree, we become clearer about the self and better able to take a position in our family, as Cathy did with Anne. It is not that we can ever gather a complete family history or be entirely objective about our own family. Obviously we can't. But we can work on it.

13

Reviewing Self-Focus: The Foundations of Intimacy

Compared to the Good Old Days (or the Bad Old Days, depending on how you look at it), prescriptions for intimacy are improving. We are now encouraged, at least in principle, to bring to our relationships nothing less than a strong, assertive, separate, independent, and authentic self. Yet these agreeable adjectives have become cultural clichés, their meanings trivialized or obscured. Popular notions of "selfhood" do not easily translate into clear guidelines for genuine intimacy and solid connectedness with others. In the name of either *protecting* or *asserting* the self, we may fail to take a position on something that matters or we may cut off from significant others, operate at their expense, or behave as if we have the truth of the universe.

I hope that this book has helped you appreciate the challenge of intimacy and all that it requires. Working toward intimacy is nothing short of a lifelong task. The goal is to be in relationships where the separate "I-ness" of both parties can be appreciated and enhanced, and where neither competence nor vulnerability is lost sight of in the self or the other. Intimacy requires a clear self, relentless self-focus, open communication, and a profound respect for differences. It requires the capacity to stay emotionally connected to significant others during anxious times, while taking a clear position for self, based on one's values, beliefs, and principles.

Laying the groundwork for intimacy is such a difficult challenge because what we do "naturally" will naturally take us in the wrong direction. As we have seen, our normal and reflexive ways of managing anxiety inevitably lead us to participate in patterns, polarities, and triangles that keep us painfully stuck. The higher and more chronic the anxiety, the more entrenched the pattern—and the more courage and motivation we must summon to sustain even a small change.

How You Can Best Use This Book

Go slowly and thoughtfully, for starters. The book's lessons are far too complex to translate into a list of how-to skills, although careful attention to each woman's story will provide you with more than enough ideas about what you might work on for the next decade. My first book, *The Dance of Anger*, lays out clear and specific guidelines for changing stuck relationship patterns. If you are interested in learning more about triangles, reactivity, styles of managing anxiety (pursuing, distancing, overfunctioning, underfunctioning, and child-focus), and countermoves, I suggest that you read *The Dance of Anger* as well. Each book will help you appreciate and consolidate the lessons of the other. You may also decide to start a *"Dance"* group with other women, using these books as a springboard for discussion and for work on important relationships.

You will make the best use of this book if you are willing to struggle with *theory* rather than to focus narrowly on *tech-*

nique. When a relationship is going badly, or not going at all, we obviously want "techniques"—that is, we want to know what we can *do* to make things different. We may want a six-step program to fix things, a list of Do's and Don'ts, and (if we're honest) new maneuvers to change or shape up the other person. Even the best how-to advice, however, will at best yield short-lived results unless we struggle to understand the underlying theory or principles—in this case, a theory about how anxiety is managed and how relationship systems operate under stress.

The fact is, there are no techniques to "make intimacy happen," although countless self-help books offer this promise. Intimacy can happen only after we work toward a more solid self, based on a clear understanding of our part in the relationship patterns that keep us stuck.

The principles in this book may sound clear and simple when they are illustrated through the lives of other women. But when you try to apply what you have learned to your own relationships, you will see how quickly complexities and ambiguities arise. In this final chapter, I will help you to review and consolidate some important concepts that provide a foundation for thinking about intimacy. The more solid your understanding, the more clearly you will make your own decisions about how, when, if, and with whom you want to experiment with change. Let's look first at *feelings and reactivity,* and then at the complex principle of *self-focus.*

Thinking About Feelings

When I started writing this book, I asked eight people to define "an intimate relationship." The majority responded with a variation of the same theme: "A relationship in which you can express your true feelings." The word "feelings" was unanimously emphasized, their free and spontaneous expression highlighted. I would agree: A truly intimate relationship is one in which we can be who we are, which means being open about our selves. Obviously the sharing of feelings is an integral part of intimacy.

And yet if you go back through this book, you will notice little focus on "getting out feelings" and none on "letting it all hang out." Rather, I have emphasized observing, thinking, planning, and learning to stay calm in the midst of intensity. Does this mean that feelings are wrong or bad, or that their full and spontaneous expression will always impede rather than facilitate the process of intimacy and change?

Certainly not. In flexible relationships, the emotional tone we use to take a position becomes relatively unimportant—a matter of personal style. With my husband, children, and certain friends, for example, I occasionally engage in impassioned arguments about "who's right," and if things don't get too stuck, I enjoy these exchanges. At certain times, however, and in other relationships, I will proceed with as much thoughtfulness and calm as I can muster.

It is always important for us to be *aware* of feelings. Our feelings exist for good reason and so deserve our attention and respect. Even uncomfortable feelings that we might prefer to avoid, such as anger and depression, may serve to preserve the dignity and integrity of the self. They signal a problem, remind us that business cannot continue as usual, and ultimately speak to the necessity for change. But as I explained in *The Dance of Anger, venting* feelings does not necessarily *solve* the problem causing us pain.

Venting our feelings may clear (or muddy) the air, and may leave us feeling better (or worse). When we live in close quarters with someone, strong emotional exchanges are just a predictable part of the picture and it's nice to know that our relationships can survive or even be enhanced by them. But venting feelings, *in and of itself,* will not change the relationship dances that block real intimacy and get us into trouble. In stuck relationships, venting feelings may only rigidify old patterns, ensuring that change will not occur.

In some instances, a passionate display of intensity is a turning point, even in a stuck relationship, because it indicates to ourselves and others that we "really mean it." It is part of a process in which we move toward clarifying the limits of what is acceptable and what is not. But just as frequently the opposite is true: reactivity serves to "let off steam," following which things will continue as usual. Reactivity and intensity often breed more of the same. When it becomes chronic, reactivity blocks *self-focus,* which is the only foundation on which an intimate relationship can be built.

Emotions are not bad or wrong, and women certainly are not "too emotional," as we have often been told. The ability to recognize and express feelings is a strength, not a weakness. It does not help anyone, however, to be buffeted about by feelings or to drown in them. It *does* help to be able to think about our feelings. By "thinking," I do *not* mean intellectualizing or distancing from emotional issues, which men tend to do especially well. I simply mean that we can reflect on our feelings and make conscious decisions about how, when, and with whom we want to express them.

Even as we strive for objectivity, it is not easy to distinguish between true emotionality and anxiety-driven reactivity.

When Adrienne (Chapter 5) cried with her dad about his impending death, they were sharing an emotional experience. But when she avoided dealing with his cancer—and instead fought with or distanced from her husband—that was reactivity. When Linda told her sister, Claire, how terrified she was of losing her, and later shared how scared she was that they would end up as distant as their mother and their aunt Sue, she was in touch with her real feelings. But when she angrily lectured her sister or mother about what they should do differently, that was reactivity. Reactivity is an anxiety-driven response that blocks a truly intimate exchange—one that encourages the open sharing of thoughts and feelings, as well as problem solving around difficult issues.

Because anxiety will always be hitting us from all quarters, reactivity is simply a fact of emotional life. As we have seen, the question is reactivity . . . and then what? To move toward a more gratifying togetherness and authentic emotional exchange, we may first need to deintensify the situation to lower the anxiety. When an important relationship is stuck, we become powerful and courageous agents of change by making a new move in a low-key way, by taking a new position with humor and a bit of teasing, by making our point in a paragraph or two rather than in a long treatise. Trying out new steps slowly and calmly is also what allows us to keep in check our own anxiety and guilt about change, so that we can stay on course and stay *self-focused* when the powerful countermoves start rolling in.

Understanding Self-Focus

When couples enter therapy for "intimacy problems," they are invariably other-focused; that is, they see the other person as the problem and they believe the solution is for that person to change. I use the term "couple" here in the broadest sense, to mean any and all ongoing relationships between two persons.

What happens if a couple remains other-focused over time? *She* continues to insist that the only way the relationship will improve is for him to become more responsible. *He* says that instead she must become less critical and more sensitive to his needs. *What happens is that no change will occur.* I have yet to see a relationship improve unless at least one individual can give up his or her negative or worried focus on the other and put that same energy back into his or her own life.

Every courageous act of change that I've described in this book, like those in our own lives, requires a move toward greater selfhood or self-focus. Whether the other party is our lover, spouse, child, sibling, parent, friend, or boss, self-focus requires us to give up our nonproductive efforts to change or fix the other party (which is not possible) and to put as much energy into working on the self. Only then can we move out of stuck patterns and create a new dance.

We need to understand, however, that self-focus does *not* mean self-blame. It does *not* mean that we view our selves as the "cause" of our problems, or that we view our struggles as being isolated from the broader context of family and culture. It certainly does not mean that we remain silent in the face of discrimination, unfairness, and injustice.

To clarify the point, let's momentarily consider the changes brought about by the second wave of feminism. None of these changes could have occurred had we denied and disqualified our anger at men or maintained a narrow focus on the question "What's wrong with me?" At the same time, however, feminists could not have become effective agents of change if we had gotten stuck in reactive gear and focused our primary energies on trying to transform men or make them into nicer and fairer people. The women's movement changed and challenged all our lives because feminists recognized that if we did not clarify our own needs, define the terms of our own lives, and take action on our own behalf, *no one else would do it for us.* Thus, feminists began busily writing women back into language and history, establishing countless programs and services central to women's lives, starting new scholarly journals and women's studies programs in universities, to name just a few actions. Only in response to our changing our own selves, and to our taking individual and collective action on our own behalf, would men be called on to change.

Moving toward self-focus does not mean narrowing our perspective. To the contrary, it means viewing our intimacy problems in the broadest possible context of family and culture. This broader perspective helps us think more calmly and objectively about our situation and how we might change our own part in it. Our part in it is the only thing we can change.

Self-Focus and Humility

Self-focus requires more than an appreciation of the fact that we cannot change the other person and that doing so is not our job. It also requires a transformation of consciousness, a different worldview from what comes naturally. I refer here to the challenge of truly appreciating how little we can know about human behavior and how impossible it is to be an expert on the other person. As I emphasized at the start of this book, we cannot know how and when another person is ready to work on something and how she or he (and others) will tolerate the consequences of change. These things are difficult enough to know for our own selves. Yet in the name of love and good intentions, we readily assume an "I-know-what's-best-for-you" attitude. This attitude precludes the possibility of intimacy and makes it much harder for other persons to assume responsibility for solving their own problems and managing their own pain.

Self-Focus and Being a Self

At the same time, we have seen that taking the focus off the other does not mean silence, distance, cutoff, or a policy of "anything goes." Rather, it means that *as we become less of an expert on the other, we become more of an expert on the self.* As we work toward greater self-focus, we become *better* able to give feedback, to share our perspective, to state clearly our values and beliefs and then stand firmly behind them. As Adrienne and Linda's stories have illustrated, we can do this as part of defining a self, and not because we have the answers for the other person. The following story shows another example of a woman working toward greater self-focus.

Regina's husband, Richard, became severely depressed after losing his job and his father in the same year. He spent more and more time in bed, isolating himself from others and failing to put much effort into seeking new employment. For several months, Regina, a natural overfunctioner, organized herself around his problem. She did double-duty housework and childcare, because Richard said he couldn't handle it. She circled help-wanted ads in the newspaper and brought Richard leads about job openings. She turned down social engagements he wished to avoid. Increasingly, she accommodated to her husband's problem or tried to solve it. Richard's depression persisted and worsened.

After several months, Regina was feeling exhausted and out of sorts. She told Richard that she wasn't taking good care of herself and that she needed to make doing so a priority. She joined an exercise class, began going out with friends, and accepted social invitations even though Richard stayed home. She also stopped covering up or functioning for him. For example, when the phone rang and he said, "Tell Al I'm out. I'm too depressed to talk," she handed him the phone and said warmly, "Tell him yourself." When Richard insisted that she keep his depression a secret, she clarified a position she could comfortably live with. "Look, I won't tell your mom or Al, because I figure that's your job. But I *have* talked with my parents and Sue about it, because I can't have a relationship with them and keep such a big secret." Increasingly, Regina struggled to clarify a responsible position for herself and she stopped organizing her behavior around Richard's symptoms and his demands.

When Richard continued to remain in hibernation, Regina walked into the bedroom one Saturday and said, "Richard, if this continues for one more week, *I'm* going to be so depressed myself that I'm going to crawl into that bed with you. Then this family will really be in a fix. So what are we going to do about it?"

These were *not just words* on Regina's part. She really meant it. She had no answers for him, although she had a few suggestions if he were interested. What she *did* know was that she could not continue with the status quo for much longer, for her own sake—and out of her concern for him and the family as well. At this point she was no longer willing to keep his depression a secret from any friends or family.

Regina ended up taking a bottom-line position that Richard had to do something because she could no longer live with the situation. Richard was briefly hospitalized and then began psychotherapy. Regina was able to give him lots of space to struggle with his depression because she empathized with his pain *without focusing on it*. She put her primary energy into her own problems, which she shared with him. And when he initially "couldn't listen," she addressed this with him over time ("Rich, I hear you saying that because your problems are so much more serious than mine, my feelings don't really count. The situation at work with Joe is real distressing to me and I need to be able to talk with you about it—if not now, then sometime soon").

This shift from other-focus to self-focus is particularly hard for overfunctioners who truly believe that the other person will die without our help. We may not pay attention to the fact that they may be dying with our help.

Does a shift toward self-focus bring intimacy into a troubled relationship? Not in the short run. When you set new limits and boundaries, the other may not respond positively. This is true whether you are telling your husband that you will no longer pack his lunch or informing your bulimic daughter that if she vomits in the morning, she has to clean up after herself, even if it makes her late for school. A move toward "more self" in a relationship is usually followed by anxiety (our own and the other person's) and countermoves ("How can you be so selfish?"). If we can hold to a new position, however, without distance or blame, intimacy may come later—or at least the relationship has the very best chance. *But you can't initiate a courageous act of change because the other person will love you for it.* The other person may not love you for it, at least not in the short run and possibly never.

Self-Focus and Emotional Separateness

As we become more self-focused, we define a responsible position in a relationship, based on our own values, beliefs, and principles rather than in reaction to how the other person chooses to define the relationship. As we have seen, this self-focus requires lowered reactivity and a high degree of emotional "separateness" from the other.

Consider Janine, a woman who married out of her own religion and converted to Catholicism. In response, her mother and an older brother would not attend the wedding and refused to acknowledge her as a family member. They did not respond to Janine's attempts to explain her decision to convert, nor to her pleas for greater flexibility and tolerance on their part. Their resolve to cut her off was so firm that neither acknowledged the arrival of a new granddaughter.

Janine was ultimately able to accept her mother and brother's decision, although she did not like it. As she gathered more information about her family history, she recognized that for several generations people in her family had cut off from each other around differences. There were two warring factions in her extended family, which included relatives who had not spoken to each other for many years. It was Janine's job to consider whether she wished to continue this pattern of managing anxiety and pass it down through the generations.

Janine ultimately decided that the position *she* would take in the family was one of connectedness rather than cutoff. Although her mother and brother had proclaimed her "dead," she sent each of them cards with brief notes on holidays, birthdays, and other life-cycle events. *In these communications, she did not attempt to change their minds or move them toward reconciliation.* She made clear to both her mother and brother that she understood the pain her conversion to Catholicism had brought them, and that she accepted the fact that they did not want to have a relationship with her. But she also explained that it was not possible for *her* to pretend she did not have a mother or brother. She simply found it too painful to deny the existence of people who were so important to her.

When Janine first decided that she would stay connected, she wrote her mother and brother a short note in which she mentioned her awareness of the many people in the family who did not speak to each other. She said that while she respected this as a necessary choice for some, she personally would feel devastated if she stopped speaking to a family member. Although Janine was clear about her own resolve to maintain some contact, she kept subsequent communications short and low-key, recognizing that to do otherwise would be to disregard the position of distance that her mother and brother had chosen to take. She also refrained from either criticizing or explaining them to other family members, thus avoiding triangles.

Four years later, Janine's mother called her. Earlier that week she had received a fiftieth birthday card that Janine had sent. She explained to Janine that she had been sitting in church that Sunday and suddenly realized that God did not want her to reject her daughter. "It is not God's will that I should lose a good daughter," she said with deep emotion. Then she pulled herself together and added matter-of-factly, "Life is too short for this. I want to see my grandchild." Janine's brother continued to avoid her at this time.

Would this reconciliation between Janine and her mother have taken place if Janine had responded to her mother's anger and cutoff with more anger and cutoff? We do not know. What was important was *Janine's* decision to take a position of responsible connectedness rather than cutoff, *whether or not her mother or brother ever spoke to her again.* Janine defined a position that allowed her to feel like a more solid and responsible individual in her own family. She initiated new steps in a family dance that had been ongoing for generations. This example, like many others we have seen, illustrates the "separateness" that self-focus requires. It is a separateness that ultimately allows for a more solid connectedness with others.

Thinking About Our First Family

Slowly moving toward *more connectedness* rather than *more distance* with members of our own kinship group is one of the best insurance policies for bringing a more solid self to other relationships. When we have few connections with extended family, and one or more cutoffs with a nuclear family member (a sibling or parent), our other relationships may resemble a pressure cooker, particularly if we start a family of our own. The degree to which we are distant and cut off from our first family is directly related to the amount of intensity and reactivity we bring to other relationships.

Of course the goal is not just to move toward connectedness—meaning *any* kind of connectedness. Rather, the challenge is to move toward a connectedness that preserves the dignity of the self and the other, allowing for the creation of real intimacy. Each example in this book illustrates a move in such a direction, and each woman's story is worth a careful rereading if you think it may apply to you.

Before you are inspired to plan your own courageous act of change, I suggest that you *first* do your own genogram (family diagram) and study it. This task may itself require courageous new behaviors, because you won't be able to get the necessary information without reconnecting with people on your own family tree (see appendix). As I mentioned at the conclusion of the previous chapter, paying attention to your genogram will help you stay self-focused, and you'll get a broader view of who is family, apart from the few people you interact with. Our current problems with intimacy are not "caused" by the bad things that one or two family members have done to us. They are part of a much larger, multigenerational picture of events, patterns, and triangles that have come down through many generations.

Your genogram can also help you evaluate the level of chronic anxiety in your family. How intense are the triangles? How pervasive is conflict and distance? Are there cutoffs among family members? How extreme are the overfunctioning-underfunctioning polarities?

To what extent have important issues in the family been processed and talked about? How open are the lines of communication? How much tolerance does your family have for differences? How easily do family members polarize around hot issues such as sex, religion, divorce, illness, responsibility to aging parents, and Uncle John's drinking? Extreme positions over the generations reflect chronically high anxiety, indicating that the process of change will require very slow and small moves on your part.

A Matter of Timing

Plodding slowly forward is probably a good idea for us all. If I keep repeating this point, it is because the examples in this book are bound to invite an overly ambitious attitude. I have described changes certain women have made over a period of years, sometimes with the help of therapy, and have condensed these changes into a chapter or even into a page or two. *This makes change look too easy, no matter what I say to the contrary.* Do remember that courageous acts of change include, and even require, small and manageable new moves, along with inevitable frustrations and derailments. How small (and how frustrating) depends on how hot the issue, how chronic the anxiety, and how entrenched the patterns. Trying to do too much will only give us a great excuse to end up doing nothing at all. Let's look at two brief illustrations of seemingly small moves, which required large amounts of courage.

A woman named Marsha worked in therapy for several years before she felt ready to ask her father the names and birthdates of her grandparents. Her father had been adopted at age four, after losing his mother in a flu epidemic. There were countless unanswered and unspoken questions. What happened to Marsha's grandfather after her grandmother died? Why didn't he—or some other family member—raise her father? What did her father know about his birth parents and their families? Marsha's father never spoke of his past and had become overinvolved in his wife's family. He also was vulnerable to severe depression—which Marsha was unconsciously attuned to—and the unspoken family rule was to never question Dad about his past or talk with him about anything emotionally important. On Marsha's genogram, her father's side was entirely bare in terms of biological kin.

Marsha herself was depressed and had sought therapy for this reason. She had no intimate relationships and not much sense of self. Her father was extremely intense and child-focused, reflecting the extreme degree of cutoff from his own family. *Asking her dad the names and birthdates of his birth parents was a courageous act of change that was all Marsha felt ready to do for quite some time.* It was, for Marsha, a significant first move toward selfhood and connectedness. She did it with her heart pounding in her chest, but she did it.

A year later (perhaps in response to changes that Marsha was making) her father began the equally courageous task of initiating a small move to track down his own roots. He had long stifled curiosity about his past out of loyalty to his adoptive parents and his profound inner trepidations about what he might discover. This prohibition under which he operated was an important factor in his depression and colored all his relationships. Although to this day he has chosen to learn "just a little bit," this little bit may make a significant difference in his life.

When patterns are entrenched and reactivity is high, it can be useful and sometimes necessary to enlist professional help. A friend of mine named Eleanor was in an extremely rigid triangle in which her parents were legally but not emotionally divorced and the intensity between them was so high that probably nothing short of her funeral would have gotten them in the same room together. Her part in the triangle was to be in her father's camp at the expense of a relationship with her mother, who had had multiple affairs during her marriage which she had lied about. Eleanor saw her father as the "done-in" spouse, and to wave his banner, she unconsciously sacrificed her relationship with her mother. This core triangle and Eleanor's inability to work on having a person-to-person relationship with each parent, *free from the intensity between them,* affected all of Eleanor's relationships. Eleanor's position in the triangle also made it *less likely* that her parents would tackle their unfinished marital business and really separate. Triangles, once they get "fixed," operate at everyone's expense.

Family systems therapists do not coach their clients to jump in and do something different. Eleanor met once a month with her therapist, working hard to become more objective about the emotional process in her own family. It took a long time before she could stop blaming her mother and view this core triangle in the context of other interlocking triangles and key family events that had occurred over several generations. Only *after* she had achieved this calmer, broader, and more objective perspective was she ready to think about slowly shifting her part in this core triangle.

Eleanor's first courageous act of change with her father was a low-key allusion to the fact that she had a mother. "I was mowing over at Mom's this morning and I think I got a bit too much sun," Eleanor said, moving on to talk about the unseasonably hot weather. If you are not impressed, that's because you don't know Eleanor and the family context.

A Postscript on Self-Focus: Having a Life Plan

In the dances we get stuck in, we can only change and control ourselves. Each person in a relationship, however, does not have equal power to make new moves. Children who are supported by their parents do not have the same power to create a new dance as do the adults. A woman who is one husband away from poverty does not have the same power as her spouse.

If we are truly convinced that we cannot live without our husband's support, our mother's inheritance, our current job, or the room in our parents' basement, our own bottom-line position may be "togetherness at any cost." We may not articulate this bottom line or even be conscious of it, but in such circumstances we may find it impossible to initiate and sustain courageous acts of change. Kimberly, for example, might not have felt free to share her lesbianism with her parents if they were paying her apartment rent and if she saw no other options for generating income.

Think of Jo-Anne, our anonymous letter-writer in Chapter 2 who, according to her own report, canceled her subscription to *Ms.* to save her marriage. She may engage in endless cycles of nonproductive fighting, complaining, and blaming. She may invite thousands of *Ms.* readers to join her camp, siding with her against her husband. But in the end, she *protects* rather than *protests* the status quo. Only *after* Jo-Anne is confident that she can ensure her safety, her survival, and some reasonable standard of living can she go to her husband and say, "I will not cancel my subscription to *Ms.* magazine." Only then can she maintain this position with dignity and firmness.

Paradoxically, we cannot navigate clearly within a relationship unless we can live without it. For women, this presents an obvious dilemma. Only a small minority of us have been encouraged to put our primary energy into *formulating a life plan that neither requires nor excludes marriage.* We may have generations of training to *not* think this way. Countless internal obstacles and external realities still block our path when it comes to planning for our own economic future and formulating long-range work and career goals. Yet such planning—which requires both personal and social change —not only ensures the well-being of the self but also puts us on more solid ground for negotiating relationships with intimate others.

My point here is not to undervalue the role of homemaker or of any unsalaried or underpaid worker. Women have been divided from each other by the media's invitation for "Moms" and "Career Women" to pit themselves against each other. The issue is not, nor has it ever been, whether homemaking is more or less valuable, challenging, or fulfilling than running a corporation, for who among us could begin to make such a judgment? The real issue is that the role of homemaker places many women in a position of profound economic vulnerability, particularly given the current divorce rate, the lack of high-level training and re-entry programs for displaced homemakers, the low or uncollectible child-care payments, and negligible alimony. These facts are reflected in the alarming statistics on the poverty of single mothers.

You may already be one of these statistics. Or you may unconsciously be so afraid of becoming a statistic that you are not yet ready to risk making a courageous act of change with someone you depend on.

Having a life plan means more than working to ensure economic security as best you can. It also means working toward clarifying your values, beliefs, and priorities, and then applying them to your daily actions. It means thinking about what talents and abilities you want to develop over the next two—or twenty—years. Obviously, a life plan is not static or written in stone, but is instead open to constant revision over time.

Finally, having a life plan does *not* mean adopting masculine values and pursuing career goals single-mindedly. Some of us may be striving to lighten our work commitments so we can spend more time with our friends and family, or in other pursuits such as spiritual development or the peace movement. What is significant about a life plan is that it can help us live our own lives (not someone else's) as well as possible. How we do this, and how we conduct our relationships with our own family of origin, is the most valuable legacy we can leave the next generation.

When we do *not* focus our primary energy on working on our own life plan, our intimate relationships suffer—just as they suffer when we cut off from our own kinship group to start a family of our own. Without a life plan, our intimate relationships carry too much weight. We begin to look to others to provide us with meaning or happiness, which is not their job. We want a partner who will provide self-esteem, which cannot be bestowed by another. We set up a situation in which we are bound to get overinvolved and overfocuse on the other person's ups and downs because we are underfocused on the self.

Intimate relationships cannot substitute for a life plan. But to have any meaning or viability at all, a life plan must include intimate relationships.

How essential are intimate relationships, really? In my own life, there are times when I am either so anxious or so eager about personal projects that the most treasured people in my life feel like distractions; my highest priority is to be left alone to do what I want to do. At other times—such as when a real crisis hits my family—nothing is more important than the love of my family and my friends and the support of my community; so necessary is this love, and my connectedness to others, that nothing else seems to matter.

Obviously, we will have varying and changing needs for distance and connectedness throughout the life cycle, and even during the course of a week or a day. It is as normal to seek distance occasionally as it is to seek togetherness; there is no "right" amount of intimacy for all couples or for all relationships. But without a viable connectedness in our kinship group and community, we just won't do very well when the going gets tough. Since everyone's life includes some hardship and some tragedy, we can count on the going getting tough.

Throughout history, women have stood for connectedness by working to maintain ties to past and future generations. Unfortunately, we have often done this at the expense of the self, sacrificing personal and career goals central both to our self-esteem and to our economic security. Not surprisingly, men have had a complementary problem; they have tended to focus on moving up and measuring up, at the expense of responsible connectedness to past and future generations. The success, if not the survival, of our intimate relationships rests on our being able to get this in balance. So, too, does the success and survival of our world.

Epilogue

Just as the female legacy does not promote thinking in terms of a life plan, it is also not part of our legacy to view ourselves as powerful agents of change. Women often feel powerless to initiate change, whether in their personal lives or in the public sphere. Like our fairy tale heroines, we may believe that we have to lie helpless in the teeth of the wolf, or asleep in a glass coffin, until we can be rescued by a handsome prince. We have been told that our sex is passive-dependent —that it is men who take charge and make change happen in the real world.

Such feelings are understandable, because in reality, women have been deprived of power. Men chart the stars, create language and culture as we know it, record history as they see it, build and destroy the world around us, and continue to run every major institution that generates power, policy, and wealth. Men define the very "reality" that—until the current feminist movement—I, for one, accepted as a given. And although women throughout history have exercised a certain power as mothers, we have not created the conditions in which we mother, nor have we constructed the predominant myths and theories about "good mothering." Even today, there is no female equivalent of America's best-known child-rearing experts, Dr. Spock and Dr. Brazelton.

(This is not because women do not know as much about taking care of babies as men do.)

Because of our condition of inequality, it is easy to feel powerless and to view women as ineffective agents of change. But, as we are learning, nothing could be further from the truth. Over the past two decades, women and minorities have been excavating the rich treasure of their history. If you studied women's history today, you would be surprised and exhilarated by the lives of our foremothers—and stunned by how these women's pioneering accomplishments have been overlooked in our culture's great texts. A detailed genogram of your own family over three or four generations will likely help you discover the women on your own family tree who were bold and courageous pioneers of change. Knowing the strength of our own legacy is empowering.

This book has focused on individual change and intimacy, surely a personal subject. Yet it is my hope that we will work toward becoming more courageous and effective agents of social change as well. It is the larger context of our lives—which we call the "social," "political," "societal," or "cultural" context—that gives shape and form to our most intimate interactions and to our very definition of family.

Although the connections are not always obvious, personal change is inseparable from social and political change. Intimate relationships cannot flourish under conditions of inequality and unfairness. Indeed, all our intimate relationships will look entirely different to us in a future where women are truly valued and equally represented alongside men in every aspect of public life. Just *how* such relationships will look, and just *when* such a future will be, we can only begin to imagine—but we must continue to work for those relationships and that future.

— *Appendix: Creating a Genogram* —

A genogram, or family diagram, is a pictorial representation of the facts of a family system for at least three generations. It is a springboard to help you think about your family and a useful format for drawing a family tree.

The genogram is a widely used tool in psychotherapy and family assessment. Some therapists use it simply to keep track of the cast of characters and dates in a particular family. For others, the genogram serves as a rich source of hypotheses regarding complex family emotional patterns. The genogram shows the strengths and vulnerabilities of a particular individual, or a particularly troubled family relationship, in a much larger context to give new meanings to problems and behavior.

Although the genogram is widely used by therapists of varying orientations (as well as by family physicians, historians, biographers, and the like), it is most frequently associated with Bowen family systems theory. Additional sources of information about the genogram can be found at the end of this appendix.

Genogram Symbols

Because there is diversity in how genograms are drawn, other therapists may use symbols somewhat different from those shown here.

Female

Give name, age, birthdate (*b.*), highest level of education, occupation, significant health problems, and date of diagnosis (*dx*).

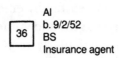

Sue
b. 8/18/53
MA
Social work
migraines dx 2/79

Male

Give name, age, birthdate, highest level of education, occupation, significant health problems, and date of diagnosis.

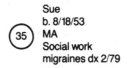

Al
b. 9/2/52
BS
Insurance agent

Index Person

You are the index person in your own genogram. Darken the outline of your gender symbol.

Death

Give age, date of death (*d.*), and cause.

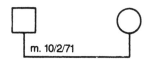

b. 2/12/10
d. 3/21/80
Heart attack

b. 2/9/70
d. 5/12/75
Leukemia

Marriage

Give date of marriage (*m.*).
(Husband—left; wife—right)

m. 10/2/71

Separation and Divorce

Separation (*s.*)—one diagonal line with date
Divorce (*d.*)—double diagonal line with date

m.10/2/71   s. 3/78   d. 12/1/80

Living Together or Significant Liaison

Draw a dotted line.

Multiple Marriages

(Mary was twice divorced before marrying Joe. Joe was widowed.)

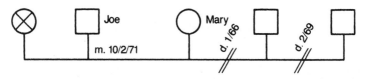

Children

List in birth order beginning with oldest child on the left.

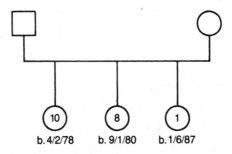

Twins

Indicate whether identical or fraternal (*I.* or *F.*).

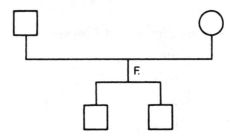

Adoption

Give birthdate, adoption date (*a.*), and any information about biological parents. (Do two genograms if information about birth family doesn't fit.)

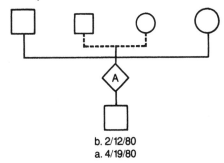

b. 2/12/80
a. 4/19/80

Foster Placement

Draw a dotted line from biological parents. Give date of foster placement (*F.P.*).

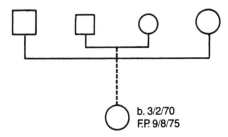

b. 3/2/70
F.P. 9/8/75

Pregnancy   *Miscarriage*   or   *Abortion*

3 mo.   9/1/72   9/1/72
              3 mo.   3 mo.

Stillbirth or Intrauterine Death

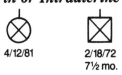

4/12/81   2/18/72
                 7½ mo.

STRAUSS FAMILY GENOGRAM*

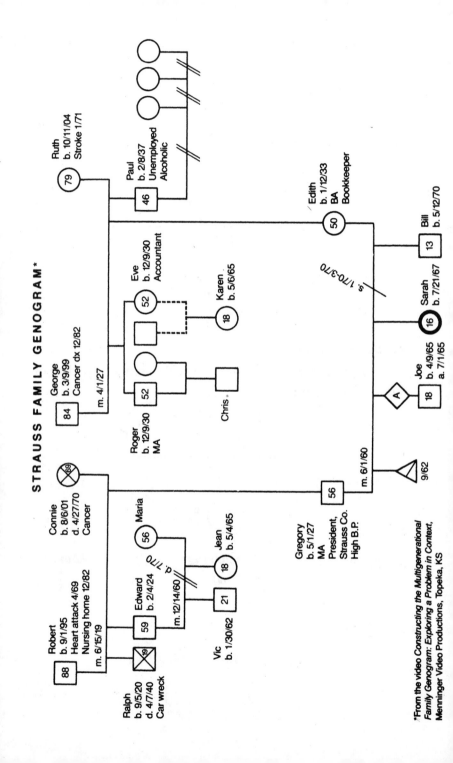

*From the video Constructing the Multigenerational Family Genogram: Exploring a Problem in Context, Menninger Video Productions, Topeka, KS

The Strauss Family Genogram

Sarah is the index person. She is the second child and first-born daughter in her sibling group. She has an older, adopted brother, Joe, whose entrance into the family followed a miscarriage. Sarah has a younger brother, Bill.

Sarah's father, Gregory, is the youngest of three sons. Gregory's older brother, Ralph, the first-born son, died in a car accident at the age of nineteen.

Sarah's mother, Edith, is a middle sibling. Her two older siblings, Roger and Eve, are twins. Eve had a child, Karen, with a man whom she chose not to marry. Edith's younger brother, Paul, has been married and divorced three times and has no children from his prior marriages. He is an alcoholic.

The genogram helps us to see that Sarah's father, Gregory, is at an important anniversary time. His youngest child, Bill, has turned 13, the age that Gregory was when Ralph was killed. Joe (who is in Ralph's sibling position) will soon be 19, the age when Ralph died. In addition, Sarah's three living grandparents are in very poor health. From this information alone one can speculate that this might be a stressful time in the life cycle of Sarah's family.

The genogram also suggests that Sarah's brother Bill was born into a particularly anxious emotional field. Just before Bill's birth his parents separated and reconciled and his paternal grandmother died of cancer. During the first year of Bill's life, his uncle Edward divorced and his maternal grandmother had a stroke. These events surrounding Bill's entrance into the family may have predisposed his early relationship with one or both parents to be emotionally intense. As a youngest child, Bill shares a common sibling position with his underfunctioning uncle Paul. How might this influence the relationship between Bill and his mother?

This genogram is only partially completed for purposes of illustration. Keep in mind that the usual amount of information included on a genogram are age, birthdate (and adoption date), highest level of education, occupation, significant health problems (including date of diagnosis), and date and cause of death for every circle and square on your family diagram and for as far back as you can search.

You may want to put other significant information on your genogram such as immigrations, retirements, and drug and alcohol problems, constructing your own shorthand or symbols to save space (for example, *ALC* or Ⓐ for alcoholic). To keep your genogram from becoming too cluttered, use a large piece of oaktag or oversized paper and keep track of important information elsewhere (job changes, re-locations, ethnic and religious backgrounds, psychiatric hospitalizations, etc).

Bibliographical Information on Genograms*

Genograms in Family Assessment by Monica McGoldrick and Randy Gerson (New York: Norton, 1985). This informative book provides a detailed description of constructing a genogram along with an introduction to its underlying interpre-

---

* References on the theory and therapy of Dr. Murray Bowen, who pioneered the use of the genogram, can be found in the notes. While most sources are directed toward therapists, they are valuable reading for non-professionals as well.

tation and application. The authors use genograms of famous people such as Sigmund Freud, Margaret Mead, Virginia Woolf, and Jane Fonda to illustrate their points.

Constructing the Multigenerational Family Genogram: Exploring a Problem in Context. Available for rental or sale through Menninger Video Productions, Box 829, Topeka, KS 66601, 1–800–345–6036. This video illustrates the construction and use of the multigenerational family genogram. A detailed case vignette highlights the important areas of information a genogram can provide.

Notes

Chapter 1   The Pursuit of Intimacy: Is It Women's Work?

PAGE

5   On the impact of marriage on women's mental health see E. Carmen, N. F. Russo, and J. B. Miller, "Inequality and Women's Mental Health," in the *American Journal of Psychiatry* 138/10 (1981): 1319–1330, which also appears in P. Reiker and E. Carmen, eds., *The Gender Gap in Psychotherapy* (New York: Coward McCann, 1983). Also see Jessie Bernard, *The Future of Marriage,* 2nd edition, (New Haven: Yale University Press, 1982) and M. Walters, B. Carter, P. Papp, and O. Silverstein, *The Invisible Web: Gender Patterns in Family Relationships* (New York: Guilford Press, 1988).

5–7   See Jean Baker Miller, *Toward a New Psychology of Women* (Boston: Beacon Press, 1986), for an appreciation of the complex links between women's relationship orientation and women's subordinate group status. Miller's pioneering work has inspired new psychoanalytic perspectives on women's investment in connectedness and relatedness. See *The Stone Center Working Papers* on women (The Stone Center, Wellesley College, Wellesley, MA 02181). Also see Carol Gilligan, *In a Different Voice* (Cambridge: Harvard University Press, 1982).

Chapter 2   The Challenge of Change

PAGE

10   The story of the New England farmer (and related insights
          about the quest for personal growth) is from Robert J.
          McAllister, *Living the Vows* (San Francisco: Harper & Row,
          1986), pp. 127–143.

11   On the subject of change (and resistance to change in
          families) see Peggy Papp, *The Process of Change* (New York:
          Guilford Press, 1983).

Chapter 3   Selfhood: At What Cost?

22   "Letter to the Editor," *Ms.* magazine, September 1980.

23–25   More about women's compromised and de-selfed position
          in marriage and with men can be found in H. G. Lerner,
          The Dance of Anger (New York: Harper & Row, 1985),
          chapter 2. Also see H. G. Lerner, *Women in Therapy,*
          (Northvale, NJ: Jason Aronson, 1988; paperback edition
          from Harper & Row, 1989), chapters 11 and 13.
                  See also Paula Kaplan, *The Myth of Women's Maso-
          chism,* (New York: E. P. Dutton, 1984).

31–33   Traditional psychoanalytic concepts of self and theories
          regarding dependency and autonomy in women continue
          to be re-examined and revised by feminist theorists such as
          Jean Baker Miller and the work of the Stone Center, *op. cit.*
          See also Lerner, *op. cit,* 1988, Gilligan, *op. cit.*, 1982, Luise
          Eichenbaum and Susie Orbach, *What Do Women Want*
          (New York: Coward McCann, 1983), and Nancy Cho-
          dorow, *The Reproduction of Mothering* (Berkeley: University
          of California Press, 1978).
                  The concept of self and the complex interplay be-
          tween separateness and connectedness have been most

fully elaborated in psychoanalytic theory and Bowen family systems theory. For a comprehensive review of Bowen theory see Michael Kerr, "Family Systems Theory and Therapy," in Alan Gurman and David Knistern, eds., *Handbook of Family Therapy* (New York: Brunner/Mazel, 1981), pp. 226–64 and Michael Kerr, "Chronic Anxiety and Defining a Self," *The Atlantic Monthly* 262/3 (September 1988): 35–58. Also see Michael Kerr and Murray Bowen, *Family Evaluation* (New York: Norton, 1988).

Bowen family systems theory differs from other systemic approaches in its attempts to root theory in evolutionary biology rather than general systems theory. Because the writings of Bowen and his colleagues are singularly male-centered in language and worldview, it may be difficult to appreciate the value of Bowen's ideas for the psychotherapy of women. For a feminist critique of Bowen theory see Deborah A. Luepnitz, *The Family Interpreted: Feminist Theory in Clinical Practice* (New York: Basic Books, Inc., 1988), chapter 3, pp. 36–47. For the clinical application of Bowen's ideas by a feminist therapist see Lerner, *op. cit.*, 1988, chapters 12 and 13 and H. G. Lerner, "The Challenge of Change" in Carol Tavris, ed., *Everywoman's Emotional Well-being* (New York: Doubleday & Company, 1986), chapter 18.

34   Overfunctioning-underfunctioning reciprocity, fighting, distancing, and child-focus have been described at length in the family systems literature as ways of managing anxiety and navigating relationships under stress. See Murray Bowen, *Family Therapy in Clinical Practice* (New York: Jason Aronson, 1978), Kerr, *op. cit.*, 1981, and Kerr and Bowen, *op. cit.*, 1988.

Chapter 4   Anxiety Revisited: Naming the Problem

37   The pattern of pursuit and distance has been widely described in the family therapy literature. See Phillip Guerin

and Katherine Buckley Guerin, "Theoretical Aspects and Clinical Relevance of the Multigenerational Model of Family Therapy," in Philip Guerin, ed., *Family Therapy* (New York: Gardner Press, 1976), pp. 91–110.

On breaking the pursuit cycle see the example of Sandra and Larry, chapter 3, in Lerner, *op. cit.*, 1985.

46   Most therapeutic approaches strive for the reduction of anxiety and the awareness of its sources. On the impact of anxiety moving down and across generations see Betty Carter and Monica McGoldrick, "Overview: The Changing Family Life Cycle," in Betty Carter and Monica McGoldrick, eds., *The Changing Family Life Cycle: A Framework for Family Therapy,* 2nd edition, (New York: Gardner Press, 1988), pp. 8–9. Also see Betty Carter, "The Transgenerational Scripts and Nuclear Family Stress: Theory and Clinical Implications," in R. R. Sager, ed., *Georgetown Family Symposium* 3 (Washington, D.C.: Georgetown University, 1975–76).

Chapter 5   Distance and More Distance

54   I am grateful to the well-developed theoretical insights of Murray Bowen regarding distance and cutoff from nuclear and extended family.

Chapter 6   Dealing with Differences

73–75 My interest in ethnicity in the therapeutic process was sparked by a workshop conducted by family therapist Monica McGoldrick, whose teachings are reflected in this clinical example. Also see Monica McGoldrick, J. K.

PAGE

Pearce, and J. Giordano, *Ethnicity and Family Therapy* (New York: Guilford Press, 1982) and Monica McGoldrick and N. Garcia Preto, "Ethnic Intermarriage: Implications for Therapy," *Family Process* 23/3 (1984): 347–364.

80   Reactivity should not be confused with effectively voiced anger that serves to challenge the status quo and preserve the dignity and integrity of the self. On the importance of female anger and protest see Teresa Bernardez-Bonesatti, "Women and Anger: Conflicts with Aggression in Contemporary Women," in the *Journal of the American Medical Women's Association* 33 (1978): 215–19. For a comprehensive overview on anger see Carol Tavris, *Anger: The Misunderstood Emotion* (New York: Simon & Schuster, 1982).

81–85 Marla Beth Isaacs, Braulio Montalvo, and David Abelsohn have written a useful book for therapists (and others involved in the divorce process) to help divorcing parents move out of intense, child-focused triangles toward more functional parenting. See *The Difficult Divorce* (New York: Basic Books, Inc., 1986).

Chapter 8 Understanding Overfunctioning

102   I am grateful to Katherine Glenn Kent for helping me to appreciate the fine points of the overfunctioning-underfunctioning reciprocity in my clinical work. More on this subject can be found in Bowen, *op. cit.*, 1978, Kerr, *op. cit.*, 1981, and Kerr and Bowen, *op. cit.*, 1988.

108–12 On modifying an overfunctioning-underfunctioning pattern see the example of Lois and her brother in Lerner, *op. cit.*, 1985, chapter 4.

Family therapist Marianne Ault-Riché has co-produced an educational videotape describing her attempts to modify her overfunctioning position in her family of origin. See *Love and Work: One Woman's Study of Her Family of Origin,* (Menninger Video Productions, The Menninger Foundation, Box 829, Topeka, KS 66601).

113   Part of this case example was previously published by H. G. Lerner, "Get Yourself Unstuck from Mom," in *Working Mother,* December 1986, pp. 64–72.

Chapter 9   Very Hot Issues: A Process View of Change

123   Lyrics by Jo-Ann Krestan from the musical *Elizabeth Rex or The Well-Bred Mother Goes to Camp.* Produced by the Broadway-Times Theatre Co. New York City, December 1983. Used by permission.

On a daughter's disclosure of lesbianism to her mother see Jo-Ann Krestan, "Lesbian Daughters and Lesbian Mothers: The Crisis of Disclosure from a Family Systems Perspective," in Lois Braverman, ed., *Women, Feminism, and Family Therapy* (New York: The Haworth Press, 1988).

125   On the costs of secrecy for the lesbian couple see Jo-Ann Krestan and Claudia Bepko, "The Problem of Fusion in the Lesbian Relationship," *Family Process* 19 (1980): 277–289.

137–38 I am indebted to Sallyann Roth and Bianca Cody Murphy for these and other questions and for their lucid work on systemic questioning with lesbian clients. See Sallyann Roth and Bianca Cody, "Therapeutic Work with Lesbian Clients: A Systemic Therapy View," in M. Ault-Riché, ed., *Women and Family Therapy* (Rockville, MD: Aspen Systems Corporation, 1986), pp. 78–89.

Chapter 10   Tackling Triangles

143   Triangles are a key concept in most family systems approaches. I am grateful to the teachings of Katherine
Glenn Kent on triangles in family and work systems.

For a comprehensive review of triangles within marriage and the family see Philip Guerin, L. Fay, S. Burden,
and J. Gilbert Kautto, *The Evaluation and Treatment of
Marital Conflict* (New York: Basic Books, 1987). Also see
Kerr, *op. cit.,* 1981 and Kerr and Bowen, *op. cit.,* 1988.

Chapter 11   Bold New Moves: The Story of Linda

162   For a detailed description of moving out of a child-
focused triangle, see Lerner, *op. cit.,* 1985, chapter 8. Also
see Maggie Scarf, *Intimate Partners* (New York: Random
House, 1987).

Chapter 12   Our Mother/Her Mother/Our Self

184   Part of this case example appeared in Lerner, "Get Unstuck from Mom," *op. cit.,* 1986.

For more on the subject of navigating separateness and
connectedness in the mother-daughter relationship see
Lerner, *op. cit.,* 1985, chapter 4. Also see Lerner, *op. cit.,*
1988.

186   Mother-blaming and a narrow mother-focused view of
family problems still characterize both psychoanalytic and
family systems theory and therapy. See Nancy Chodorow
and S. Contratto's "The Fantasy of the Perfect Mother,"
in B. Thorne and M. Yalom, eds., *Rethinking the Family:*

Some Feminist Questions (New York: Longman, 1982), pp. 54–75. Also see Lerner, *op. cit.*, 1988, pp. 255–285 and Evan Imber Black, "Women, Families, and Larger Systems," in Ault-Riché, ed., *op. cit.*, 1986, pp 25–33.

See also Adrienne Rich, *Of Woman Born* (New York: W. W. Norton, 1976), Lois Braverman, "Beyond the Myth of Motherhood," in Monica McGoldrick, C. M. Anderson, and F. Walsh, eds., *Women in Families* (New York: W. W. Norton, 1989), chapter 12, Luepnitz, *op. cit.*, 1988, and Walters, Carter, Papp, and Silverstein, *op. cit.*, 1988.

187   Thanks to Rachel Hare-Mustin, a pioneer in feminist family therapy, for her quote on women's guilt.

187   Psychoanalytic theory has tended to "pathologize" the mother-daughter dyad, focusing narrowly on the darker side of separation struggles in this relationship. For new psychoanalytic contributions that challenge traditional views see J. V. Jordon and J. L. Surrey, "The Self-in-Relation: Empathy and the Mother-Daughter Relationship," in T. Bernay and D. W. Cantor, eds., *The Psychology of Today's Woman* (Hillsdale, NJ: The Analytic Press, 1986), pp. 81–104. Also see J. L. Herman and H. B. Lewis, "Anger in the Mother-Daughter Relationship," in Bernay and Cantor, eds., *op. cit.*, 1986, pp. 139–168.

Chapter 13 Reviewing Self-Focus: The Foundations of Intimacy

209   Communicating from a self-focused position requires the ability to take an "I" position on important issues. Thomas Gordon, founder of Parent Effectiveness Training has done pioneering work on "I" messages. His book *Parent Effectiveness Training* (New York: New American Library, 1975) is a useful model of self-focused communication for all relationships. See also Lerner, *op. cit.*, 1985, chapter 5.

216–17 Bowen theory and therapy are especially useful in gaining a broader, more objective perspective on the emotional process (including cutoffs and triangles) in one's own family and working to gradually modify one's own part in the patterns that block growth.

The adoption experience is an example of a particularly intense cutoff where the adoptee's inquiry and search for birth parents may consciously or unconsciously be experienced as a disloyalty, threat, or betrayal. See Betty Jean Lifton, *Lost and Found: The Adoption Experience* (New York: Harper & Row, 1988) and *Twice Born: Memoirs of an Adopted Daughter* (New York: Penguin Books, 1977). As a rule, any significant cutoff from a key family member binds intense underground anxiety and emotionality that may hit one like a ton of bricks during (and not until) the process of re-connecting.

218 While the importance of a life plan for women may seem more than obvious, I am grateful to Betty Carter and Katherine Glenn Kent for their insightful thoughts on the subject.

A life plan is crucial for women, not only because of our special vulnerability to poverty, but also because economic dependence on a man impedes or precludes the process of defining the self and taking a bottom-line position in that relationship. See Lerner, *op. cit.*, 1988, pp. 243–246 and Walters, Carter, Papp, and Silverstein, *op. cit.*, 1988.

Epilogue

223 Any attempt to understand, diagnose, or treat human problems apart from the socio-political context (including the profound impact of gender-determined family and work roles) is necessarily problematic. For a provocative commentary on current psychiatric diagnosis see Matthew P. Dumont, "A Diagnostic Parable (First Edition–Unre-

vised)," in *Readings: A Journal of Reviews and Commentary in Mental Health* 2/4 (December 1987): 9–12.

223–24   Feminist psychoanalytic thinkers have long challenged and revised traditional phallocentric views on female psychology, and they continue to do so. Only recently are family systems thinkers re-examining theory and practice from a feminist perspective. See McGoldrick, Anderson, and Walsh, eds., *op. cit.*, 1989, chapter 1, for a brief history of feminist contributions to the family therapy field. Also see Judith Myers Avis, "Deepening Awareness: A Private Study Guide to Feminism and Family Therapy," in Braverman, *op. cit.*, 1987, pp. 15–46 and Walters, Carter, Papp, and Silverstein, *op. cit.*, 1988.

To raise one's consciousness and to keep current on ideas and issues central to women's lives I recommend subscribing to *New Directions for Women* (published since 1972), 108 West Palisade Avenue, Englewood, NJ 07631.

Index

The Dance of Deception

A Guide to Authenticity and
Truth-Telling in Women's Relationships

In memory of AUDRE LORDE,
who taught us that women have gained nothing
from silence.

Contents

Acknowledgments

The *Dance of Deception* completes a trilogy. Unlike its predecessors, this book does not fall into the category of "self-help" or "how-to." I have set out to be thought-provoking rather than prescriptive, although where I believe there is a right or better way to go about things, I spell it out.

I discovered early on in writing this book that I didn't want to limit my terrain. My greatest delight was in choosing a subject as vast, multilayered, shifting, and subjective as human experience itself. So the reader should not expect an orderly, comprehensive text, or an airtight argument to think or behave in a particular way. Instead, I hope the reader will feel jolted, shaken up a bit, pushed to think about a rich variety of subjects, and rewarded for the journey.

A book that deals with so large a subject owes a multitude of acknowledgments. I regret that I cannot begin to name all the people who have contributed over many years to my work. Freshest in my memory are the many friends who gave generously of their time and talents while this work was in progress:

Acknowledgments

My dear friend Jeffrey Ann Goudie cheered me on (and cheered me up) from start to finish. In addition to timely hand holding, she made excellent suggestions throughout the manuscript. Her husband, Thomas Fox Averill, also read the entire draft and offered vital criticism. It is a blessing to have two such splendid friends, both writers themselves, who took time away from their own valuable projects to lend assistance and support.

This book owes its existence to my manager, Jo-Lynne Worley, who pulled me out of my proposed early retirement (I didn't really mean it, anyway) and convinced me that the best was yet to come. Her steady and loving friendship, her abiding belief in my work, and her quiet, remarkable competence in managing everything, allowed me to begin and complete this book. She has extended, enriched, and organized my life in countless ways.

My close friends in the Topeka community critiqued all or parts of this manuscript, talked and thought with me about my subject, or in some way encouraged and helped me along. My love and thanks to Emily Kofron whose work and presence in the world inspires me. Special thanks also to Ellen Safier, Nancy Maxwell, Marianne Ault-Riché, and Judith Koontz. From out of town, Harris E. Weberman and Sherry Levy-Reiner commented on earlier drafts. Countless women I interviewed informally gave me uncompromisingly honest responses to tough questions about deception and truth-telling in their intimate lives.

This is my third book to pass through the (ever-wiser) hands of Janet Goldstein, my terrific editor at Harper-Collins. She has the gift of knowing immediately when something is "off" and the rare talent for making small suggestions that make a big difference. I also appreciate the fastidious copyediting by Ann Adelman and the careful work of others on the staff of HarperCollins who have done a fine job with the production, promotion, and publicity of all my books. It's a privilege these days to find a publisher one wants to stay wedded to. I also want to thank Karen Wald, Lisa Liebman, Stephanie von Hirschberg, and the staff at *New Woman* magazine, where I have the good fortune to write a monthly advice column.

I am blessed with an extraordinary and ever-widening network of feminist friends and colleagues. My heartfelt thanks to Holly Near and Jeanne Marecek for critiquing each chapter with great care, to Patricia Klein Frithiof for encouraging my work and bringing it to Sweden, to Sonia Johnson and Jade Deforest for their love and generous sharing of ideas and themselves, and to Mollie Katzen for responding so enthusiastically to the final draft.

The Menninger Clinic has provided me with a solid home base from which to work. Peter Novotny has affirmed and supported my projects from my earliest years at Menninger and others have joined in along the way, lending the administrative support that made it possible for me to combine writing and clinical work. I'm especially indebted to Mary Ann Clifft whose careful and meticulous editing is unsurpassed. The entire manuscript has had the benefit of her keen eye. Thanks also to the Menninger library staff and to Eleanor Bell for providing editorial help with the chapter notes.

I am deeply grateful to Carolyn Conger, who is, in the fullest sense of the word, a teacher. Her ability to awaken insight, to empower others to connect with their own wisdom and worth, is remarkable. She taught me about truth from a new angle.

My husband Steve Lerner has been, along with everything else, a precious friend and colleague for almost a quarter of a century. From him, and with him, I've learned much about the subject of this book. I'm grateful for his love, encouragement, and his unwavering belief in my work. He has enhanced my life in more ways than I can articulate.

Intellectual Debts

Writers commonly explain that books are the products of many people's ideas and that the intellectual debt an author owes to others cannot be adequately acknowledged. Never before have I felt this to be so true. Because my subject is at the heart of both feminist theory and the practice of psychotherapy, all of my professional training and my education as a feminist have contributed to this work. It is difficult, if not impossible, to sort out the "ownership" or origin of ideas and probably spurious to try. Although I've done my best to acknowledge my intellectual debts in the Chapter Notes, I apologize in advance for the inevitable omissions.

I want to mention certain people up front, particularly where I have drawn directly or heavily from their work: Sisella Bok has written two important books on ethical implications of secrecy and lying; Pauline Bart loaned me her title for Chapter 5; I'm also deeply indebted to the important work of Carolyn Heilbrun (Chapters 5 and 6), Peggy McIntosh (Chapter 6), Evan Imber-Black and Peggy Papp (Chapter 10), Peggy Vaughan (Chapter 11), Rosabeth Moss Kanter and Elizabeth Kamarck Minnich (Chapter 13), and Audre Lorde, Sonia Johnson, and Jean Tait (Chapter 12).

I especially need to thank Adrienne Rich for her classic texts, *Of Woman Born* and *Lies, Secrets, and Silence*, which are pivotal to my subject. I love the way Rich tells the truth and writes about truth-telling—incisively, urgently, uncompromisingly, and passionately. My gratitude for her brilliant work (which includes thirteen books of poetry) is part of my larger debt to the intellectual revolution wrought by feminism. Without the presence in my life of a feminist community, I would be groping around in the dark or writing comfortably and tamely in a voice that was not my own.

I have learned much from my immensely gifted friend Marianne Ault-Riché who generously included me as an equal partner in two vital projects that she originated—our early communication workshops in Topeka ("Talking Straight" and "Fighting Fair") and the "Women in Context" conference series at Menninger. I also want to thank Elizabeth Kamarck Minnich for her enlightening, inclusive, and hopeful vision of democracy, and her husband, Si Kahn, for keeping this vision alive through his organizing and music.

In writing this book I also drew heavily on my experience as a clinical psychologist and psychotherapist. Throughout my professional training I have had many fine teachers of psychoanalytic and family systems theory. I'm particularly indebted to Katherine Glenn Kent for teaching me to "think systems" over our many years of friendship, and for helping me to apply Bowen family systems theory to my life and work. Her influence is reflected in this book, as is the pioneering work of Murray Bowen. I'm also indebted to an excellent paper on deception by Stephanie Ferrera. Of course, my adoption of other people's ideas doesn't mean they like what I did with them. No one I thank shares all my opinions or necessarily agrees with my conclusions. As always, the ultimate responsibility for this book is mine alone.

Many feminist psychoanalytic thinkers have enriched my life, beginning with my friend Teresa Bernardez, who was the first in the mental health field to focus on the subject of women's anger. Jean Baker Miller's classic text, *Toward a New Psychology of Women*, carefully links the subordination of women to dilemmas regarding authenticity and truth. I thank her for this important work and for all that has followed from her visionary efforts.

For assorted assistance and comeradeship thanks to Susan Kraus, Joanie Shoemaker, Georgia Kolias, Jo-Ann Krestan, Claudia Bepko, Elaine Prostak Berland, Jennifer Nell Hofer, Betty Hoppes, Patricia Spiegelberg Hyland, Nancy Jehl, Doris Jane Chediak, my women's group, and my wise and witty long-distance pal, Carol Tavris. My love to my parents, Rose and Archie Goldhor, my sister (and co-author in juvenile publishing) Susan Goldhor, and my dear sons, Matt and Ben Lerner. Finally, thanks to my readers who continue to overwhelm me with messages of affection, gratitude, and thoughtful challenge.

The Dance of
DECEPTION

Except for the friends and family who have given permission to appear in this book, names and identifying characteristics of individuals mentioned have been changed in order to protect their privacy.

1

Tony and the Martians

When I was twelve, I told a lie that grew to epic proportions. I told my friend Marla, who lived across the street from me in Brooklyn, that I had been contacted by a man named Tony who came from another planet. Since first grade, Marla and I had been on-again, off-again best friends.

I told Marla that Tony told me to find a date. Since no one had asked me out yet (and I believed that no one ever would), Marla had to fix me up with a blind date because Tony said that something bad might happen to me otherwise. Marla, who could accomplish almost anything she set her mind to, went about this project with her usual vigor and enthusiasm. The blind date came and went. Tony did not.

A few minor characters from the same planet were added to the drama, as the personality and presence of Tony grew and became part of my deepening friendship with Marla. Tony emerged as a good-hearted, playful fellow who told me funny things that I could tell only Marla—and that she could tell no one. At a time when my other girlfriends were dropping one best friend for another, my special status with

Marla was secure. Tony stabilized our friendship and strengthened our sense of camaraderie and commitment. And I was in charge—an active director and orchestrator of the threesome: Tony and Marla and me.

I don't remember how often Tony visited or how long he stayed around, but I think it was at least a year before I let him drift out of our lives. Years later, when Marla and I were both graduate students in Berkeley, California, I tearfully told her I had made Tony up. Until then, we had both walled off the Tony business, not bothering to reflect on it or even to remember. Marla protected me and our friendship by choosing not to subject this interplanetary drama to close scrutiny. After all, anything is possible. When we finally talked about it, Marla was lighthearted and forgiving, as I hoped she would be with our long history of friendship binding us together.

In the early 1970s I entered psychoanalysis during my post-doctoral training program in clinical psychology and confessed my "Tony story." I half-jokingly voiced my concern that my analyst would downgrade my diagnosis to something either very bad or very sick. My uneasiness was hardly surprising. Although lying is commonplace in both personal and public—especially political—life, the label of "liar" is a profound condemnation in our culture, bringing to mind pathology and sin. I know parents who punish their children more severely for lying to them than for any other behavior. I have heard otherwise calm parents scream at their children, "Don't you *ever* lie to me again!" So heavy are the negative associations of intention and character that it is difficult to think lovingly, or even objectively, about the role that lying plays in the lives of children and adults.

My analyst (coincidentally also named Tony) was, as always, empathic and nonjudgmental. In psychoanalysis—as in the rest of life—insight and self-understanding do not flourish in an atmosphere of self-depreciation or blame. He and I explored Tony in the context of my distant relationship with my father and my related desperation about getting the "blind date" that I first used Tony for with Marla.

Many years later, after the birth of my second son in 1979, I faced a personal crisis, a health scare, that pushed me to learn more about my mother's diagnosis of advanced endometrial cancer when I was twelve. While talking to my parents at this time, I recognized that I had brought Tony into the picture when my mother, then forty-eight, had been given one year to live. Although I was unaware on a conscious level of her diagnosis and prognosis, I am certain that my unconscious knew everything.

As I reconstructed that year, multiple lies emerged, beginning with my mother's harrowing experience with a medical system that did not provide her with facts. After a long period of misdiagnosed vaginal bleeding, my mother hemorrhaged and was hospitalized for an emergency D&C. This procedure led to the unexpected diagnosis of a hitherto unknown invasive cancer. Her physician (who may himself have been reacting to the long period of misdiagnosis and neglect) told my father the facts—but swore him to secrecy. After the initial procedure, my mother was packing her bags to return home when she was told that an additional stay in the hospital was necessary for a second surgery to "stretch her uterus." With this improbable, mystifying explanation, her doctor performed a complete hysterectomy without her knowledge or permission. She awoke from the surgery, confused and disoriented, and suffering from inexplicable, intense pain.

My mother did not confront her doctor until immediately before her discharge from the hospital, when he referred her for radiation treatment. She demanded to know her diagnosis. He did not answer, but instead took her hand and told her to enjoy life and to try to have enjoyable sex in the year to come. He didn't mention cancer and she didn't push it. A part of her, too, must not have wanted to hear the word spoken out loud. With a referral for prolonged radiation treatment, however, my mother knew the name of her problem even though the medical establishment did not voice it.

In the year that followed, the word "cancer" was never spoken in my family. My mother's health was not even discussed. Inexplicably, she did not die, as predicted, and so we have had the opportunity to talk as adults about that traumatic year after her diagnosis. Our conversations have allowed me to appreciate more deeply how helplessly out of control I must have felt when I brought Tony down from another planet.

My mother, the emotional center of the family, seemed to be dying. Susan, my only sibling, had started college at Barnard and would soon be looking for an apartment in the city. She was getting launched, leaving me for her own grown-up life. My mother had quietly made plans for her brother and sister-in-law, then living in a different part of Brooklyn, to take me in after her death because she did not think that my father could care for me by himself. I was on the edge of losing everyone. Into this precarious world, threatening to pull apart at the seams, I brought Tony.

During the year after my mother's diagnosis, my most important relationships had a lie at their center. In my family, the lie was perpetuated through silence. There was a survival issue in my family that no one was talking about. Only once did I give voice to reality, to truth, in an incident that I myself do not remember. My mother tells me that some time after she had finished her radiation treatment and had recovered her energy and spirits, she came down with a bad cold and took to bed—a singularly rare occurrence for her. I stormed into the bedroom and screamed at her for lying down. "Get up!" I commanded with the full force of early adolescent rage. "You'd better not die—do you hear me?—or I'll never forgive you!" My mother recalls this outburst— over as suddenly as it began—as our family's only direct expression of feeling, our only articulation of danger.

Apart from this isolated outburst, I blanketed myself in denial, screening out my mother's illness and my questions about how I would be cared for if she died. Reading back through my diary—my one place to tell the truth—I do not find a word during that year about my mother being sick or about my being afraid. I numbed my consciousness, both language and feeling. But because the unconscious seeks truth, I acted out all over the place—in trouble at school and a mess at home.

With Marla, my best friend, the lie was told in words, not in silence. I constructed, elaborated, and kept alive a narrative, immersing myself so fully in the drama that I did not experience myself as standing outside it. Only much later did I piece together enough context to make sense of my behavior, to think more objectively of its meaning.

Perhaps I wanted to be caught. One evening I found myself in my sister Susan's bedroom, spontaneously telling her that I had become friends with a man from another planet. If Susan had taken this revelation seriously, a confrontation about Tony might have pushed us all toward addressing the deeper issue. But for better or worse, Susan merely listened to my story, perhaps never giving it a second thought.

Thinking about Context

If my behavior with Marla was viewed out of context, an observer might say, "She lied because that's how she is. She is a liar, out for herself, that sort of child." Or a psychological interpretation might be based on a particular notion about human behavior: "Because she is insecure, she needs to manipulate and control—that's why she lies."

In the absence of context, we tend to view particular behaviors as fixed "traits" or as "personality characteristics" that exist within us, rather than as part of a dance happening between and among us. My creation of Tony, for example, could be viewed as evidence of my manipulative, controlling, and deceptive intentions—words that fit with our culture's general description of how women have wielded power. Of course, these *were* my intentions—to manipulate, control, and deceive, just as my intentions were to love, to connect, strengthen, protect, and survive.

Context allows us to put lying—or any other behavior—into perspective. By broadening our view, we are challenged to take a more complex reality into account, to ask questions (rather than provide answers) about where lies begin.

Did the lie begin, in my case, with a frightened adolescent girl who desperately wanted to avoid any further threat of loss by holding on to her best friend by whatever magic possible?

Did it begin with my parents, unable to address, even with each other, a terrifying illness, then handed down as a death sentence? Or did it begin with *their* parents, Russian Jewish immigrants who could not begin to speak about the massive losses and separations they had endured?

Did the lie begin under the hand of patriarchy, with the male-dominated medical system withholding facts from my mother, mystifying and falsifying her experience, denying her deepest instincts, protecting her from essential knowledge "for her own sake," creating for her a situation of unutterable loneliness? Did truth-telling become less possible still when the doctor told my father to keep my mother's condition a secret, for which she did not easily forgive him? And what of my mother's unspoken plan to transfer me to a relative's home upon her death? Was patriarchy (its consequences then hidden, unspoken, denied) at the heart of a mother's felt knowledge or belief that it might be unwise to leave an adolescent daughter alone with an emotionally isolated father?

I was in my thirties before I connected Tony to my mother's diagnosis of cancer, a connection which cast a new perspective on my behavior of twenty years earlier—as did the facts about my mother's hospital experience then, and the culturally enforced silence surrounding any diagnosis of cancer at that time. Deception is larger than the particular individual responsible for it, larger even than a family. We can never know for sure where a lie begins, with whom it originates, or the many factors that sustain it. We can, however, move toward an increasingly accurate and complex understanding of ourselves as we widen our view of a lie, secret, or silence— or any deceptive behavior, for that matter.

This story about Tony illustrates the importance of context, and how empathy and understanding increase with the bigger picture of family, culture, and the addition of more facts. Further, this story illustrates that our most dramatic and colorful lies—the ones we can decide either to keep secret or to confess—are not necessarily at the center of our emotional life and not where we need to focus our primary attention. My lie to Marla was symptomatic of the paralyzing silence in my family surrounding my mother's illness. My family's silence was symptomatic of a culture which placed cancer, as well as other painful subjects, in the realm of the unspeakable. It is the unspoken, all that we cannot name and productively address, that gets us into trouble; lying is merely one expression of that trouble.

In truth, I did not experience myself as a "liar." Or, more accurately, I knew I was lying to Marla about Tony but I told myself I was *pretending*. We were, perhaps, all pretending— the doctors who withheld information from my mother (for her own sake), my parents who withheld information from us children (for our sake), and the children, myself included, who didn't persist in asking questions (for the family's sake). We were a family like any other, with strengths and vulnerabilities, doing our best to stay afloat in the face of massive anxiety about my mother's—and our own—survival.

2

~

Deception and Truth-Telling

Whether our motives are unconscious or intentional, pristine or nefarious, deception is a part of everyday existence. It wears countless faces in daily life and takes on an endless array of forms and functions. Our language itself speaks to the multiplicity of ways that we depart from truth-telling and engage in deceit:

> We say, she fibbed, fabricated, exaggerated, minimized, withheld.
> We say, she told a white lie, a partial truth, a falsehood, a tall tale.
> We say, she embroidered her story, she pulled the wool over our eyes.
> We say, she keeps secrets (and also, she can't keep a secret).
> We say, she covered up, covered over, concealed, misled, misinformed, twisted, distorted, falsified, misrepresented the facts.
> We say, she is false, elusive, evasive, wily, indirect, tricky,

treacherous, manipulative, untrustworthy, unfaithful, sneaky, scheming, calculating, conniving, corrupt.

We say, she is deceitful, deceptive, duplicitous, dishonest.

We say, she is a hypocrite, a cheat, a charlatan, a callous liar, a fraud.

We say, she presented a clever ruse, a bogus deal, an artifice, a pretense, a fiction, a sham, a hoax.

We say, she is phony, artificial, affected.

We say, she is pretending, charading, posturing, faking, holding back, being an imposter, putting up a good front, hiding behind a facade.

We say, she did not own up, come clean, or level with me.

We say, she gaslighted me, messed with my mind, mystified my reality, betrayed and double-crossed me.

We say, she is two-faced; she speaks out of both sides of her mouth.

We say, she speaks falsely.

We say, she cannot face reality; she cannot face the truth; she engages in self-deception.

We say, how brave she was to reveal nothing, how clever to throw them off track.

We say, she acted with discretion.

We say, she lied out of necessity; she lied for the greater good.

We say, she lied with honor.

Our language provides us with incredibly rich possibilities for describing our departures from truth-telling. Different words and phrases evoke varied images of deception, connoting a range of implications about intention and motivation, and the seriousness of harm done. We may have learned to associate some of these words more with women, some more with men. In either case, we have more words to describe the nuances of how we deceive each other than to describe how we love.

Deception is not a "woman's problem" or even a uniquely human phenomenon, for that matter. From viruses to large mammals—from disease-causing microbes to baboons and chimps—deception is continually at play: an African beetle kills a few ants and attaches their carcasses to its body in order to enter an ant colony to feast undetected; a chimp misdirects her group away from a food source, covers up her own movements so that the location of the food can't be traced, and returns later to dine by herself. Many baboons and chimps, when threatened, make themselves appear larger. Deception has played a major role in the evolution of human life. It is interesting to think about the fact that deception and "con games" are a way of life in all species and throughout nature. Organisms that do not improve their ability to deceive—and to detect deception—are less apt to survive.

Do only humans engage in calculated deception? Not according to the finest animal trainers, who attribute a capacity for moral understanding to a number of species other than our own. Trainers, notes Vicki Hearne, distinguish horses who are trustworthy ("Relax, there isn't a tricky bone in that horse's body") from those who are "sneaky" ("Don't worry, he'll come around okay, he's no real criminal, just a juvenile delinquent") and even "irredeemably dishonest." Although such anthropomorphic, morally loaded language is criticized as naive, even heretical, the scientifically minded critics are hopelessly behind the trainers when it comes to engagement in the real world of animal-human encounters.

The subject of deception pertains to every member of our species, but this book speaks directly to women, and undoubtedly to some women more than others. I invite men to read it, too, of course, not just to learn about the women in their lives but also to find themselves in these pages. Much of what follows is "generically human"; where it isn't, it's useful for the reader to define both commonalities and differences. We can all benefit from examing how we hide the real and show the false. Unexamined deception is now threatening our survival far more than enhancing it.

How, specifically, do we engage in deception?

We lie outright, as I did to Marla, with the intention of convincing the other person of what we know is not true, of what we do not even believe ourselves. As our language illustrates, words and phrases which connote deliberate deception tend to condemn, reflecting our feelings about being on the receiving end of deception. When we are the active players, however, we are more likely to experience ourselves as lying to prevent harm, not create it.

We also depart from truth-telling through silence, as my family did, by failing to speak out. We do not ask an essential question or make a comment to clarify the facts. We withhold information from others that would make a difference in their lives. We do not even say, "There are some things I am not telling you."

In contrast to how we react to stated lies, we are slower to pass negative judgment on what is *withheld*. After all, no one can tell "the whole truth" all the time. (A friend commented recently, "Can you imagine what an impossible world it would be if we could all read each other's minds!") Deception through silence or withholding may be excused, even praised: "My daughter is lucky I never told her about her father"; "The doctor was kind enough to spare her the truth about her illness"; "How incredible that she is always cheery for her children when she is feeling so wretched."

When we are silent or withholding about the self, we may call it "privacy," a word suggesting that our failure to disclose is neutral or harmless. We would all agree that we don't have to tell anyone everything, although the more intimate the relationship the greater both the possibility and the longing to tell—and the bigger the emotional consequences of not telling. Privacy differs from deception. But when we say, "This is nobody's business but my own," we may obscure the full meaning and consequences of secrets and silence, of a life in hiding in which we do not allow ourselves to be known.

Then there are lies, secrets, and silences that begin with the self. We are not clear about what we think, feel, and believe. Our priorities and life goals are not really our own; our behavior is not congruent with our stated values and beliefs. On important matters, we give in, go along, buckle under. We may not feel genuine or real. We are not "centered," "grounded," or in touch with ourselves. As a result, we are not fully present in our most important relationships.

Because of the enormous human capacity for self-deception, we may fail to recognize when we are lying—or when we are not living authentically and truly. In any case, we can be no more honest with others than we are with the self.

Pretending and Truth-Telling

In thinking about women's lives, I have come to pay particular attention to the words "pretending" and "truth-telling," words that touch on all of our actions and relationships as well as who we are and what we might become.

"Pretending" is a word that may help us to suspend our moral judgments about what is good or bad, better or worse, so that we can think more objectively about a difficult subject. It also fits more appropriately into the fabric of women's lives. Our failure to live authentically and to speak truly may have little to do with evil or exploitative intentions. Quite the contrary, pretending more frequently reflects a wish, however misguided, to protect others and to ensure the viability of the self as well as our relationships. Pretending reflects deep prohibitions, real and imagined, against a more direct and forthright assertion of self. Pretending stems naturally from the false and constricted definitions of self that women often absorb without question. "Pretending" is so closely associated with "femininity" that it is, quite simply, what the culture teaches women to do.

In some instances, however, we will rightfully be wary of the word "pretending" precisely because (like "privacy") its neutral and benign connotations would have us trivialize and gloss over what does need our attention, if not our moral judgment. It is not useful to sanitize the fact that under patriarchy, women are continually lied to, and that in the struggle for love, sanity, and survival, we continue to tell lies. Sometimes, only a harsh word like "lying" will do.

Truth-telling, the heart of my subject, is a central challenge in women's lives. The term "truth-telling" seems more encompassing, more courageous, and more richly textured in meaning than the word "honesty." When I say "truth-telling" out loud, I think of bold and pioneering acts, as well as enlivened conversation on the headiest of subjects. For example, "What is truth?" "Who defines what is true and what is real for each of us?" "Do women really have a 'true self' to uncover, find, or, alternatively, to invent?" "Whose truth counts?" Under patriarchy, women are well schooled in pretending and deception. We also have developed an extraordinary capacity to tell the truth, or at least to whisper it.

Reflections on this subject remind me of the tendency to organize our world into dichotomous categories: good and evil, masculine and feminine, yin and yang, gay and straight, and now, pretending and truth-telling. People, of course, are far more complex and multifaceted than the polarities or "opposites" we create.

Truth-telling is, on the one hand, closely linked to whatever is most essential in our lives. It is the foundation of authenticity, self-regard, intimacy, integrity, and joy. We know that closeness requires honesty, that lying erodes trust, that the cruelest lies are often "told" in silence.

Yet this perspective is only part of the overall view. In the name of "truth," we may hurt friends and family members, escalate anxiety nonproductively, disregard the different reality of the other person, and generally move the situation from bad to worse. I have watched my clients—and myself—make every variety of error about who to tell, what to tell, when to tell, how much to tell, and how to tell. And, of course, there are situations in which it may be wiser to be strategic than spontaneous. In my early years at the Menninger Clinic, for example, I was the sole identified feminist; I thus made it my job to openly confront every injustice and to raise the consciousness of my colleagues. In my efforts to convince others of "the truth," I quickly became encapsulated in a role that made it impossible for them to hear what I had to say.

In the real world, the seemingly contradictory activities of pretending and truth-telling are not always "opposite" or discrete. Pretending, for example, may be an indirect move toward the truth, rather than a misdirected flight from it. In pretending love or courage, we may discover that it really does exist—or that we can enhance our capacity for it. Sometimes pretending is a form of experimentation or imitation that widens our experience and sense of possibility; it reflects a wish to find ourselves in order to *be* ourselves. Similarly, at a particular time, pretending may be necessary for survival, or we may feel that it is absolutely essential.

My goal, then, is not to create another false polarity, or to try to push the reader along an unexamined, linear path from pretending to truth-telling. Nor will I provide "answers," "how-to" instructions, or reassurance, although my values and beliefs about a "right" course of action will surely come through. What follows are my reflections on aspects of deception and truth-telling that are vital to our lives. My primary focus is on relationships, including one's relationship to the self. My hope is that you will join me in examining how all of us engage in deception and approach truth-telling—a subject that is at the heart of who we are in the world and what kind of world this is.

3

To Do the Right Thing

In 1970, Dr. Robert Wolk and Arthur Henley published a book called *The Right to Lie*, the first "how-to" guide on using deceit in everyday life. The authors provide numerous examples of "constructive" and "worthwhile" lies that purportedly strengthen intimate relationships.

There is the case of Evelyn G., for example, who with her husband consults a doctor after trying unsuccessfully for a year to become pregnant. Following fertility tests, the doctor telephones Evelyn and asks her to visit him privately. He then informs her that her husband is sterile, but asks her to consider whether her husband should be told. The authors continue:

> Evelyn is deeply disappointed. She has an impulse to tell her husband, "See, I'm not to blame! It's all your fault!" But she knows that this will strike at the heart of his self-esteem. The doctor agrees, adding that such an accusation might possibly even make Paul G. impotent.
>
> To preserve her sex life and her husband's sensibilities, Evelyn decides to tell a lie. She takes full blame for her

inability to conceive. It is a "loving" lie, that protects the marriage. As Evelyn had expected, her husband is sympathetic and tells her not to feel badly, that he will be just as happy to adopt a baby. That is **his** loving lie and concludes an even exchange of deceits that strengthens the relationship.

According to the authors, the "constructive lies" that Evelyn and Paul exchange are born of necessity and kindness, and serve to reinforce the loving bond between them. Happily, the specifics of their story is dated, as is my mother's hospital experience around the time of her first cancer. If nothing else, a physician who joins with one spouse to falsify medical facts to the other might fear a malpractice suit. People still justify lying, however, if they believe it serves a protective end or a greater good. What has changed are cultural norms, and we have changed with them. As creatures of culture and context, our beliefs about "constructive lies" shift with the political climate of the day.

I have thought hard about the impact of culture and context, particularly as I watched the televised congressional hearings in 1991 that turned into a painful and outrageous attack on Anita Hill, as she tried to tell the truth about Supreme Court Justice nominee Clarence Thomas. In the midst of the moral outrage I felt on her behalf, I recalled an experience I had in 1962, more than a quarter of a century ago.

I was spending my junior year of college in Delhi, India, in a program sponsored by the University of Wisconsin, where I was an undergraduate. Midway through the year, I moved from Miranda House, a college dorm in Old Delhi, to a room in a nearby hotel. At this same hotel lived a distinguished American, perhaps forty years my senior, who had retired from a high government position. He was, in his own words, "a very important man." Indeed, he was the most important man I had ever encountered close up.

For months he pursued me aggressively and inappropriately for sex. Later that year, when I came down with malaria, he made advances toward a close woman friend who was caring for me at the time, and was also an American student in the program. After my recovery, I was relieved to find that he continued to pursue her rather than me.

I always found this man's advances unwelcome and discomfiting. Yet never for a moment did I question the "right" of so prominent a man—a veritable force in history, as I saw it—to persist in his efforts to get what he wanted. I was always more attuned and vigilantly protective of his feelings than of my own. My friend and I discussed his advances only with each other. We said nothing to the leader of our program in Delhi.

The following year, back in Madison, Wisconsin, my friend and I sat with this same program leader in the cafeteria of the Student Union. He was visiting briefly from Delhi and was about to return there. Suddenly departing from small talk, he told us that a student was currently reporting sexual advances from this same man. He quickly added that this honorable gentleman would never do such a thing. The student could only be mistaken.

"Right?" he said in our direction. It may well have been meant as a question, but I heard it as a declaration or challenge. My friend and I nodded affirmatively and nothing more was said on the subject. It wasn't until 1991, as I watched, in astonishment, the enemies of Anita Hill, that I thought with sorrow and disbelief about my nod and subsequent silence. Why did I leave that brave student, halfway across the world, in a position of isolation and vulnerability?

What was her name? What price did she pay for speaking the truth? Why had I not spoken out? I felt ashamed of myself—particularly because I had felt not the slightest hint of shame at the time.

I'm sure that I lied for many of the usual reasons people lie: to make myself most comfortable at the moment, to escape disapproval and censure, to avoid complexity and complication, to keep at bay my own emotions, which were linked to my earlier experience. My friend and I feared, perhaps rightfully so, that our disclosure might also be discounted or held against us. Our program head was a compassionate and intelligent man, but the cultural climate of the day enforced denial.

More to the point, I thought at the time that I was doing *the right thing.* I believed that it was my responsibility to protect the reputation of this very important man. I figured that the woman, whoever she was, could handle the situation. But the public image (and personal feelings) of an older man of high status was another matter. Like Evelyn G., who lied to protect her husband from injury and impotence, I believed that my lie was "constructive," even honorable.

How could I have thought this way? Or, given that I did think this way, why is my current perspective so radically different? A generous friend explains, "Well, you're obviously much braver now." I share her view that courage, like good taste, is acquired with age. But I was courageous during my college years, and was not one to submit to injunctions that violated my conscience. No, my individual bravery was not the issue here. Rather, the bravery of other women transformed cultural norms.

The first to speak out about abuses of power must be particularly brave or thick-skinned. When I was in college, terms such as "sexual harassment," "date rape," "sexual abuse," and

even "sexism" had not yet been invented. The word "patriarchy" wasn't in my vocabulary. We called these things "life,"
and I never considered the necessity, or even the possibility,
of women creating and codifying language. Without the
vocabulary, however, I was unable to name, much less protest,
what was happening inside and around me. Also, as more
women told the truth, my beliefs about what constitutes
"honorable lying" changed, and I began to reexamine the
question of who needs protection from whom. Watching
Anita Hill reminded me of how much—and how little—has
changed in the world since my undergraduate days.

If even one heroic male senator had stood up in eloquent
outrage at the abusive treatment of Anita Hill, the "ordinary
folks" watching television might have been better able to
open their eyes to the abuses of our patriarchal fathers. Yet
when it comes to interpreting the motivations of others, we
can never know the whole story. In protecting the president's
nominee, these politicians might also have convinced themselves that they were engaging in an honorable lie or a noble
silence. They might have believed that protecting "a very
important man"—and the collective rule of men—served a
greater good. Perhaps they believed that they were acting on
behalf of higher principles, such as "loyalty" or "solidarity."

Does the epidemic of lying, duplicity, and concealment
on the part of "honorable men"—the leaders of our country—make it easier for us to rationalize our own private
departures from the truth? Most of us do see our lies in a
benevolent light. So how can we decide in our daily lives
whether deception in its countless manifestations is right, or
harmless, or justified, or necessary, or good for somebody?
How accurately do we observe ourselves and take note of the
times we are less than honest or forthright, even over the
course of a single day?

What's Your HQ?

I recently came across a quiz in a women's magazine that invited readers to assess their "HQ" (Honesty Quotient) by ranking themselves on a scale of 1 to 10 for truthfulness. Obviously, this rating scale—like others of its kind—could not begin to do justice to human experience or the complexity of even a day in the life of a real human being. Real life is complicated, messy, contextual, unquantifiable, full of paradoxes and contradictions. In a single conversation, I may be truthful, untruthful, and sort of truthful, without even noticing the discrepancies.

Consider the scene that followed a talk I had with my younger son, Ben, about the importance of being honest. As we leave the shopping mall, we pass a video arcade and he demands to play a game. I tell Ben that I have no change, and I pull him along with me toward the exit. I probably do have the change, but we're both in a terrible mood and it seems easier to put it this way than to risk a fight. When we get home, the phone rings and I overhear Ben's impatient response: "Why do you keep bothering me? I don't want you to come over!" I'm mad at Ben for this display of tactlessness, and I whisper to him: "Why don't you just tell him you're busy and can't have friends over today?"

On my better days, I behave more solidly. I tell Ben why I'm not giving him money for a video game and I deal directly with his reaction. I approach the subject of his telephone etiquette without coaching him to fib to a friend. This may seem like a small distinction, but perhaps not. True enough, no single trivial lie undermines my integrity or my relationship with my son. But fibbing, including "polite" or social lies, can become part of the daily fabric of living—a way of avoiding conflict and complication that becomes so

habitual we fail to notice even the fact of it and its imperceptible erosion of our integrity and our relationships.

In the abstract, people almost unanimously applaud honesty,
which, as popular wisdom has it, is "the best policy." If we
actually could measure a person's "HQ," we would each
aspire to a high score and would strive to surround ourselves
with others who rate high on our ten-point scale. Honesty,
like authenticity, is one of our culture's most deeply held values. It is always a slur to say, "She is a dishonest woman," or,
"This man does not tell the truth." It is always a compliment
to speak of someone's honesty and commitment to the truth.

But what happens when we move away from abstract values and focus instead on specific incidents in the lives of real
human beings? Then we have Evelyn and Paul exchanging
their "loving lies" on the infertility problem; we have me
back in my college days nodding my head in the wrong
direction to protect "a very important man." Or, more
recently, fourteen white, male senators protecting the president's Supreme Court nominee.

Within my own profession, psychologists hold widely
divergent views on whether lies harm or benefit their recipi-
ents. Some years ago, this news item appeared in the *San
Francisco Chronicle:*

> A pale, slight 11-year-old boy, injured but alive, was pulled
> yesterday from the wreckage of a small plane that crashed
> Sunday in the mountains of Yosemite National Park. The
> boy had survived days of raging blizzards and nights of sub-
> zero temperatures at the 11,000-foot-high crash site, swad-
> dled in a down sleeping bag in the rear seat of the snow-
> buried wreckage. . . . "How is my mom and dad?" asked the
> dazed fifth-grader. "Are they all right?" Rescuers did not tell

the boy that his stepfather and his mother were dead, still strapped into their seats in the airplane's shattered cockpit, only inches from where he lay.

Dr. Paul Ekman, a professor of psychology and noted expert on lying, selected this news item to illustrate "an altruistic lie, benefiting the target, not providing any gains to the rescuers." He stated that few would deny this fact. But when my husband (also a psychologist and family therapist) and I discuss the same news clipping, we imagine that this lie made the rescuers feel more comfortable and perhaps occurred at the expense of the child. Had we been at the scene, we would not have volunteered the facts. But we try to imagine what the rescuers did tell the boy, who undoubtedly feared (or knew) the worst and asked directly for information about his family.

For days after reading that news item, I found myself thinking about the assault on this boy's reality and on his future capacity to trust that adults would tell him the truth. While knowing more details might shift my perspective, I question the same lie that my fellow psychologist applauds.

It has been fascinating for me to listen to women voice their moral judgment on a range of examples of deception and truth-telling. Sometimes there is a predictably shared response, as when a colleague tells how her parents invented a web of lies and trickery to hide a Jewish family in their home from the Nazis. Her story is unarguably one of courageous and honorable deception in the service of a higher ideal.

But more commonly, and more interestingly, we differ in our responses to the myriad ways that people deliberately distort or conceal the truth—and to how they reveal it, for that matter. What one woman considers a necessary revelation, another considers an inappropriate disclosure. While one person claims, "He deserves to have the facts," another insists that "he should be protected from the truth." What one woman calls a "healthy venting of true feelings," another labels a "hostile, inappropriate outburst."

In regard to tolerating or even inviting deceit, we also differ. In her book, *Lying,* the philosopher Sissela Bok claims that everyone, even deceivers, wants to avoid being deceived. Yet some of us consistently demand the truth, while others ask to be "spared." Consider some examples of the second option.

The wife of a university professor says to me, "If my husband is sleeping with other women, I don't ever want to know it."

A mother in a family therapy session looks her daughter directly in the eye and says, "If you're on drugs, don't tell me about it. I can't handle it."

A woman who has been sexually abused by two maternal uncles attends a movie with her mother that includes the theme of incest. As they leave the theater, her mother says, "If anything like that ever happened in our family, I wouldn't want to know about it."

A therapy client tells me she is worried that her brother might be suicidal but then adds, "I really don't want to know. There's nothing I can do anyway."

No one *wants* to be tricked, manipulated, or duped. But we may feel, at a particular moment, that we can't handle a more direct confrontation with what we already suspect or know. We are unlikely to seek "more truth" if we feel unable to manage it, or if we are not confident that potentially painful information is ultimately empowering and could lead to productive problem solving, more informed decision making, and a more solid self in relationships. We vary widely in the degree to which we are in touch with our competence to manage painful facts, and our readiness and willingness to move toward them.

We differ, too, in our capacity to detect deception and, more generally, in our ability to observe and name reality. We all repress, deny, project, distort, tune out, and get sleepy. Our knowledge and interpretation of "the truth" is, at best, partial, subjective, and incomplete. But we do have varying capacities for empathy, intuition, reflection, autonomy, objectivity, integrity, maturity, clarity, and courage—all of which enhance our ability to detect deception and incongruity in ourselves and in others.

We also differ from each other in our subjective experience of lying. One friend tells me, "When I don't tell the truth, I feel it in my body. So I don't get off the phone, for example, by making excuses, like someone's at the door or I'm late for an appointment. Telling a big lie, like faking sexual pleasure, would make me physically sick." She adds, "My body keeps me honest, even if my head wants to get away with things."

This friend describes herself as being committed to the principle of veracity at "a cellular level." She seeks an honest way to express herself, no matter how inconsequential the issue or insignificant the interaction. In contrast, another woman tells me that she comfortably engages in every variety of "social" and "face-saving" lie. She reports feeling fine about this behavior "as long as no one is hurt."

Our cultural emphasis on how women differ from men (consider the phrase "the opposite sex") obscures not only human commonalities but also the range of differences *within* our own gender grouping. Of course, women differ from each other. We differ not only in matters of conscience and moral judgment but also in our philosophy about truth-telling, and in our beliefs about what is productive and growth-enhancing in relationships. We differ in our ability to accurately perceive and process information and to detect deception in ourselves and others. And our ideas about lying and truth-telling are colored from birth onward by our race, class, culture, and unique personal history. All of our life experiences combine to shape our philosophy of what is and is not the truth—and when and how we should tell it.

How often do we articulate our differing philosophy on the many rich and complex dimensions of deception and truth-telling, of speaking and holding back? Since the beginning of recorded time, philosophers and scholars from varied disciplines have debated the nature of truth, as well as the moral, ethical, legal, psychological, and evolutionary aspects of deception and the forces that drive it. But despite the profundity, centrality, and immediacy of this subject in everyday private and public life, we may avoid discussing with others our own personal beliefs about it. Perhaps we should initiate and sustain more such conversations. Clarifying our commonalities and differences helps us examine how we are choosing to live in the world and how we are making decisions about doing "the right thing."

Hiding a Life

An attorney named Lena who was flying from Miami to Boston was engaged in friendly conversation with an older woman next to her. They talked about their respective jobs, then the woman showed Lena a photo of her family, which included a new grandson she was visiting for the first time. Midway into their flight, she asked Lena, "Are you married?" "No," Lena responded matter-of-factly, "but I've been living with a woman for five years and we think of ourselves as married." The woman stared at her blankly, so Lena explained further, "I'm a lesbian. My partner, Maria, is a woman." Her flight companion fell silent and kept her eyes riveted to a magazine for the remainder of the flight.

Lena had left a distant, unsatisfactory marriage that had lasted for nine years. When she came out as a lesbian three years later, she decided that she would never again "live a lie." From that time forward, she has been open about her lesbianism, resisting all temptations to pass as a heterosexual. Some of Lena's friends believe she makes herself unnecessarily vulnerable, but this is what Lena chooses, explaining: "If I'm quiet about Maria in any situation where I would have mentioned my husband or son, I'm acting as if my life and loving is shameful and wrong." Lena will have no part in this, no part in hiding or in pretending through silence to be what she is not.

Lena's family "love her anyway," as they collectively put it, which is among the milder of the homophobic responses she has encountered over the years. There have been more dramatic consequences of her dedication to being truthful: Lena's car has been vandalized by high school students, she has been sexually harassed in her neighborhood, and she almost lost custody of her son, who is now eleven. But the ignorance and hatred she has faced have only strengthened her resolve to be more open. Even to avoid the pain of prejudice, Lena says she would no sooner hide her life than would a black civil rights leader pretend to be white. This deeply held value of living without deception or concealment does not allow Lena to hide the honest affections of her good heart.

Lena believes that silence about her sexual orientation constitutes a lie. "It is lying," Lena argues, "because heterosexuals deny not just our right to love openly but the very fact of our existence." Sure, Lena could have said to her flight companion, "No, I'm not married." But that factually correct statement would have been, from Lena's perspective, intended to mislead. "Silence is a lie," Lena insists, "if you are deliberately going along with another person's false belief. In this case, the false belief happens to erase and degrade the lives of ten percent of the population."

Moreover, Lena reminds me, passing for what one is not never involves a solitary lie. As many have observed, it is easy to tell a lie, but it is almost impossible to tell only one. The first lie may need to be protected by others as well. Concealing something important takes attention and emotional energy that could otherwise serve more creative ends. When we must "watch ourselves," even when we do so automatically and seemingly effortlessly, the process dissipates our energy and erodes our integrity. "It also creates a disturbance in the air," Lena tells me. "Before I was out, I'd bring Maria to office parties and I knew everyone was saying behind my back, 'Are they? Aren't they?' Now they know. And they know that I know they know. It's less crazy-making."

As we discuss the airplane conversation, Lena talks about how trivialities add up. One doesn't say, "Oh, my partner is in the same field as your husband!" One doesn't pull out a photo of one's own to show. One doesn't mention, even if asked, that the purpose of one's flight is to attend a concert to benefit gay and lesbian rights. One doesn't step off the plane and freely embrace one's lover. One doesn't hold hands by the baggage claim. Any of these ways of holding back, of not speaking, of not acting, may seem trivial. But the life this adds up to, Lena says, is a life half-lived.

Is She Honest or Crazy?

I asked a group of Lena's friends—all gay, all out of the closet, and all committed to fighting homophobia—about their reaction to the airplane incident. A vast diversity of opinion was expressed among friends bound by common values and politics.

HELENE: If we were all like Lena, it would be our strongest weapon against homophobia. Lena is unflinchingly honest and brave, and I love her for it. And I'm grateful. It's like what Adrienne Rich says—that when a woman tells the truth, she is creating the possibility for more truth around her. Imagine our collective power if ten percent of the population was, every moment, visible and out!

CLARA: I think you're romanticizing Lena's behavior. I don't tell strangers on airplanes that I'm a lesbian. It's none of their business. Personally, I think that she does so partly for shock value. There is some need for privacy and discretion.

ROGER: What Lena calls "honesty" is a failure to protect herself. It's downright crazy. I worry about her a lot. She could get herself killed by some asshole. It would be more honorable if she would choose her battles.

ROSA: I don't approve of Lena's behavior, because it doesn't accomplish anything positive. It's not useful. I'm pretty open about being gay, but I let people get to know me before I tell them. If people have a relationship with you first, it makes a dent in their stereotypes. If they like you, they may open up their hearts or at least confront their own prejudice. But if you just announce that you're gay right up front, it pushes people away. They never give you a chance. They don't even see you as a real person. It's not strategic.

HELENE: Strategic? Life is not a chess game. There comes a time when you have to stop thinking about strategy and what works and who will think what. You have to say, "I won't take this anymore!" You have to be yourself, *now.* That's where Lena is coming from. She's beyond hiding. She's beyond waiting for some hypothetically "just" world to arrive in which we can all be free. She's *creating* that world, by living it now.

MIKE: I think that we shouldn't try to judge Lena's behavior. It's not our place. What she does is right for her—there could be no other way for Lena. But it certainly wouldn't be right for me. I think that the worst thing we do to each other is to make these judgments. We have to respect and validate our differences. It has to be okay for each of us to be in a different place about what we can share and what we can handle.

HELENE: I disagree. If we don't make judgments, we are morally bankrupt. There *are* matters of right and wrong in this world, good and bad. It's wrong to hide. It's bad to be in the closet. We don't have to blame or condemn each other, we can be loving and supportive. But we still need to push each other to stop the hiding and secrecy which is so destructive to ourselves and to the world.

Honesty—the matter of who, what, when, where, how, and why we tell—is a complex business. Even among a small group of generally like-minded friends, important differences emerge. Clara questions the virtue of Lena's motives, while Helene has nothing but respect for Lena's refusal to hide. Roger believes that protecting oneself should take precedence over revealing oneself, particularly considering the real risks involved. Rosa places the highest value on strategy and believes that patience and timing is the best way to change hearts and minds. Helene believes in confronting injustice directly, forcefully, and immediately. Mike emphasizes the importance of respecting differences. In contrast, Helene impatiently views "respect for difference" as a way of condoning inaction, fence-sitting, or a lack of courage and conviction.

But perhaps Lena's friends would concur in placing her at the high end of the "HQ" scale. (That is, if they agree to define honesty as "being oneself.") Then again, they might not rate her openness so highly. True, Lena is boldly and courageously "herself" in refusing to hide her affections and her woman-centered life. But Lena also tends to distance herself from friends and family, and she leaves much unsaid. She has trouble sharing her feelings of vulnerability with those close to her, and she rarely acknowledges her own need for help and support. She describes herself as a "do-it-your-selfer" rather than one who believes in the healing power of confiding in others. Even Lena's best friend, Helene, does not view Lena as one of the more "open" people in their social group.

Fortunately, we don't have to be rated (or to rate others) on a scale that measures our "HQ" because even close friends or colleagues won't necessarily view a specific incident of revelation or concealment in the same light. We might not even agree on the meaning of such terms as "truth" or "authenticity." At times I have felt like throwing up my hands in the face of seemingly endless unravelings.

Yet I don't really believe, or, more to the point, I don't live as if decisions about truth-telling and deception are hopelessly subjective, infinitely complex, and ultimately unquantifiable. Instead, I decide with confidence that some people and some sources of information are more trustworthy than others. I choose with conviction friends whom I think are open, authentic, and real. I make assessments about which contexts—public or private—provide individuals with more (or less) opportunity to discover, invent, and share their own truths. I observe the power of context to shape and limit the stories we tell. But I also observe the power of individuals to transcend and shape context, to create new stories, and to find new meanings in even the most oppressive circumstances. My work as a clinical psychologist and psychotherapist is guided by these convictions.

And sometimes—such as when watching Anita Hill and Clarence Thomas on television—the question of what is right, what is true, and what is real, appears simple and obvious after all.

4

In the Name of Privacy

My friend hates her large, soft breasts. She is so self-conscious about them that she never relaxes with her husband when they are naked together. He loves her body and seems not to sense her feelings of shame or the constraint she feels with him because of it. My friend tells me, "In bed, even if we are just hugging, I make sure that my breasts don't flop around or slide into my armpits. When we're making love, I press my arms against my sides to give them shape. I've been doing this for so long I don't think about it, but yes, I know it interferes with my experience of being physical with him."

Her husband knows nothing of her feelings. "There's no point in telling him all this," my friend explains, "because I'd become even more tense, more self-conscious, and less spontaneous in bed." She goes on to express another fear, that she acknowledges as less rational. "If I tell him, he might notice how floppy and squishy my breasts really are. I'm afraid he'd get turned off if I draw his attention to them."

I comment to my friend that she and I are different—that I couldn't keep such a big secret from my husband. My friend bristles at my choice of the word "secret," because she thinks that I think secrets are a bad thing in a marriage. "No," she corrects me. "I don't keep secrets from my husband. We are speaking here of privacy. I am a more private person than you are." I agree that she is the more private person, but I still think she is keeping a secret from her husband.

Our conversation pushes me to clarify the difference between privacy and secrecy in my own mind. The distinction between the two categories seems apparent in common language. A private path is not a secret path. The upcoming surprise party I am planning for a friend is a private party but a secret from the guest of honor. With those we love, or seek to love, keeping secrets is different from requiring privacy. But what my friend calls a matter of privacy, I consider a matter of secrecy. How do I distinguish between these overlapping and intertwining concepts in my private (not secret) life?

Is It Private . . . or Secret?

Privacy is a human right. My right to privacy includes my right to control access to a certain amount of emotional and physical space that I take—correctly or not—to be "mine." Privacy protects me from intrusion and ensures my separateness as a human being among others. I do not want my mail opened, my journal read, my phone tapped, my behavior monitored, my property searched, my medical records or sexual history published in the local newspaper. I close the door to my home, my office, the bathroom, and the voting booth. I require periods of time each day when I am not spoken to, looked at, or focused on.

I do not seek privacy in order to fool others or engage in acts of deception. Rather, I seek privacy primarily to protect my dignity and ultimate separateness as a human being. Thus, I publically defend my "right to privacy." In contrast, I don't recall ever using the phrase, my "right to secrecy," although surely I have the right to keep some secrets, my own and others. Secrets may, as lies always do, demand justification. In contrast, it is the violation of privacy, not the guarding of it, that demands justification.

My right to privacy also includes my right to protect my body, and any decisions regarding it, from unwanted control and intrusion by others. The possibility that the government could force me to carry a fetus to term, for example, is as terrifying to me as the possibility that the government could order a fetus ripped from my womb. I feel entitled to make personal choices about reproducing, loving, and dying—without state intervention. If I do not control my own body, I do not control my own life, and I am in no position to seek or define my own truths.

There is also a certain amount of physical space *around* my body that I take to be private, or "mine." If I'm standing with someone who violates this space, I step back. Once, when an elegantly dressed woman positioned herself shoulder to shoulder with me in an otherwise empty, spacious elevator, I was startled. I reflexively moved away and recalled an elderly woman from my graduate school days in New York. This woman, who appeared to be psychotic, ritualistically walked the streets of Broadway near Columbia University with a closed umbrella in hand. When someone stepped inside what seemed to be a near-physical boundary surrounding her person, she umbrellaed them out of her territory, shouting, "You're invading my life space!" I affectionately remembered this woman, and for a moment on the elevator I identified with her, although I did not protect my "life space" so colorfully.

Protecting one's personal space occurs both within and between species. One species will flee from another at a particular "flight distance," for example, six feet for a wall lizard. Within species, each animal has a "social distance," a minimal distance that the animal routinely preserves between itself and others of its kind. "Having space" is a critical aspect of privacy and self-preservation.

Alida Brill, who has written a splendid book on privacy, reminds us that privacy is an accorded right, granted to individuals only when others let them have it. No matter how fiercely we tell others, "Keep out!", they may choose not to respect our wishes or even our legal rights. The ability to protect privacy rests firmly on privilege. Brill speculates that the reason that citizens of the former Soviet Union have such a translation problem with the word "privacy" has as much to do with spatial limitations as it does with political ideology. She reminds us that the homeless, engaged in their morning ablutions in public places, rely totally on the kindness of strangers to avert their eyes, in order to maintain the thinnest slice of private life.

Our society's vulnerable groups—the poor, children and the elderly, lesbians and gays, people of color, girls and women, the sick and disabled—are both most in need of privacy and most vulnerable to having their privacy invaded. Disempowered groups can't count on having privacy unless those in power—that is, those not of "their kind"—will grant it to them. For example, the most crucial decisions about what should and should not be private in the lives of women is ultimately decided in legal and political arenas that include few if any women as decision makers.

Because I consider privacy my right, I am neither secretive nor guarded about requesting or defending it. I openly define my privacy needs to others. I say, "Please knock before coming in," or, "Don't read my mail," or, "Move over, I want more space." Or simply, "That's private." In the ultimate of paradoxes, I go public about my abortion (a private matter) to help protect this most basic right of privacy in women's lives. In contrast, I guard not only my secrets but also the fact that I am keeping them.

In her book *Secrets*, Sissela Bok explores the ethics of concealment and revelation and refines the distinctions between privacy and secrecy. Secrecy always involves the intention to hide or conceal information from another person, just as lying always involves the intention to convince another of what we ourselves do not believe to be true. Keeping a secret over time can require energy and intense, active attention. Secrets may be guarded through silence, or they may require constant vigilance and a complex web of new deceits to protect the old. Secrets forge boundaries, create bonds, isolate, connect, and estrange. Secrets produce coalitions, triangles, insiders and outsiders. Keeping a secret can make us feel powerful, superior, special, and loyal—or anxious, burdened, guilty, and ashamed. Secrets can serve the most loving or malevolent of intentions. We may keep secrets about matters that are trivial or lethal, but there is no one who has not guarded secrets—their own and others—or who has not been affected by the secrets of others.

Privacy and secrecy have overlapping functions in our lives. We rely on both to control the flow of separateness and connectedness in relationships, and to provide us with a layer of protection against intrusion, reaction, and encroachment. In personal relationships, both privacy and secrecy reflect the need to create a boundary around the self by exercising some control over what we conceal and reveal to others. Both give us breathing space.

Privacy and secrecy have so many layers of nuance and meaning in private and public life that no single definition could adequately define either concept or distinguish between them in all instances. Both terms are invoked to defend concealment. As I see it, however, privacy shifts into secrecy when an act of deliberate concealment or hiding has a significant impact on a relationship process. Secrecy, as I define it here, is deliberate concealment *that makes a difference.*

Thus, when my friend chooses not to reveal feelings about her breasts to an inquiring neighbor—or to her husband—she is being private and secretive, respectively. With her husband, the person with whom she seeks to have her most intimate emotional and physical relationship, the concealment or revelation of emotionally sensitive information makes a difference.

What difference does it make that she fails to tell him the truth—that she hates her breasts, that she postures herself in bed with him to firm them up, that she can't relax in the process, that she thinks somehow she is fooling him, that he would "see something," or love her less if she let go and allowed her breasts to fall into their natural shape? In telling him, she would initially feel more vulnerable and less in control. Her husband might respond as she most fears. But even if he leapt from the bed, shrieking, "My God! Get those

floppy, squishy breasts out of here!", where might the process of openness and truth-telling take them over the course
of months, or years, or a lifetime—compared to, say, a decision on her part to reveal nothing?

Secrecy protects my friend from being open to the full
range of her husband's reactions and responses to her real
self. Indeed, this is the purpose of secrecy. But secrecy ultimately compounds the painful feelings it is meant to deflect.
At the very least, it blocks possibility. If my friend can't bring
her feelings out in the open, there is no potential for healing
and resolution, for self-acceptance and a deeper intimacy.
She will ultimately lose sight of what is possible for her in
bed, and rightfully attainable. With secrecy, my friend has no
chance to receive her husband's comfort, wisdom, and understanding, to relax into his body knowing she is accepted and
desired for herself, to laugh and joke with him about her
floppy breasts. Until she shares her secret, she can't begin to
understand and assimilate its meanings, look it in the eye, cut
it down to size, neutralize it, and drain it of its destructive
power.

Keeping secrets involves self-deception because we allow
ourselves only to be aware of the positive or protective functions that our secrecy serves. We usually keep secrets with the
conscious intention to preserve—not fracture—what is precious to us. We keep a particular secret "for a reason," and it
may be a good one at that. But we won't know the emotional
costs of keeping a secret until *after* we tell it. The impact of
secrecy, or any form of deception, is usually obscured until
after a process of truth-telling is well under way.

In my friend's case, concealing her feelings about her
body was significant because the content had great emotional
meaning to her. But secrets can have reverberating consequences through relationship systems even when the infor-

mation concealed is so trivial that any outside observer might well ask, "Why would anyone go to such trouble to keep *that* a secret?"

Insiders and Outsiders

Vicki came to see me shortly after marrying her second husband, Sam, a kind and attentive man whom she met by placing an ad in the personal section of a Kansas City paper. A year earlier Vicki had extricated herself from an unhappy marriage of almost two decades. She described her first husband, Jim, as a mocking, belittling, and arrogant man, who devalued her without pause. Vicki was ultimately able to leave him, but not to stand up to him, either before or after the divorce.

Vicki had custody of their two daughters, Betty, eighteen, and Joey, sixteen. She described Joey as "her best friend" in the family, while Betty was viewed as immature and problematic. During our first meeting, Vicki joked about the unorthodox way she met Sam. To illustrate her first husband's critical attitude and arrogance, she added, "That's the kind of information Jim would love to get his hands on. If he knew that I met my husband through the personal ads, he'd never hide his criticalness and contempt."

He would not, however, find out. While Joey knew the true story, Betty hadn't been told. "I swore Joey to secrecy," Vicki explained, "and made her promise that she wouldn't share this information with her sister or Jim. I can't tell Betty because she can't be trusted to keep things confidential from her dad."

"What will you tell Betty," I inquired, "if she asks how you and Sam met?"

"She won't ask," replied Vicki. "She doesn't ask about things."

"And if she did?" I pushed.

"I don't know." Vicki stated flatly. "I'd think of something."

Some secrets are dramatic. Many families hide information of critical emotional importance to their members' identity and sense of reality: Father is alcoholic, Mother relinquished a child before marriage, Little Susie is adopted, Grandmother is dying, Uncle Charlie jumped rather than fell to his death from the third-floor window, six-year-old Paula is being abused. The telling and not telling of secrets as large as these may profoundly affect every aspect of family life for generations to come.

In light of the critical truths that families hide, Vicki's secret about meeting her second husband through the personal ads seems hardly noteworthy. In the broader scheme of things, it is a rather minor piece of information that Vicki chooses to selectively withhold and disclose to her daughters and ex-husband. Yet the consequences of concealing even the most "ordinary" information in families can be far-reaching, because the selective sharing and guarding of information is the stuff of which "insiders" and "outsiders" are made in social groups. Sometimes the *relationship process* which evolves with secrecy may be far more important than the content of the information withheld.

Such was the case in Vicki's family: Joey's role as mother's "best friend" was a compelling one for any girl. Although she was the younger of two sisters, she was entrusted not only with the secret about the personal ad but also with other small details of her mother's life that she was asked to keep confidential from her sister, Betty, and her father, Jim. While no single secret carried particular meaning, the process of secrecy took its toll.

At the time I began working with Vicki, and then with Sam and the children, the emotional cost to Betty was immediately apparent. Betty was the "outsider" in the family—the one who didn't know the facts. She was learning not to ask, to look the other way, to discount her own sense of curiosity and reality. Betty also had to struggle increasingly hard to show her competence, when the family treated her as incompetent by failing to include her.

Not surprisingly, Betty sensed Joey's special position with their mother and blamed her sister for her own hurt feelings. Joey, by agreeing to withhold information from her sister, widened the emotional chasm between them.

Joey's connection to her father was deeply affected as well. The accumulating "Don't tell your dad" messages invited Joey to plant herself firmly in her mother's camp at the expense of her relationship with her father. Joey felt she had to be "for her mother," rather than free to be herself in all relationships.

Vicki's growth was also compromised. By placing her younger daughter, Joey, in the middle of issues with her ex-spouse ("Don't tell your father *anything* he could use against me"), she bypassed the challenge of dealing directly with Jim. Her reactivity and helpless behavior in the face of Jim's criticism had not changed following the divorce. Thus, she continued to give him too much power, and she made him too important in the emotional life of her new family. Vicki behaved as if she could find no way to stand up to Jim, to be real with him, to use her wonderful wit and humor to respond directly to whatever arrogant comment he might make about the personal ad or anything else. She was also teaching her daughters that one must hide from a difficult person rather than be oneself—and then manage the response one gets. Until Vicki learned to hold her own with Jim, which she ultimately did, she remained emotionally hooked on him.

Sam's entrance into the family was also contaminated by the personal ad secret, which involved him. At first, Sam was unable to articulate his feelings, beyond sensing that there was "something wrong" with the requirement that he selectively conceal how he met his wife. It wasn't that he felt compelled to share this information or even that it was on his mind. But Sam knew in his bones that the requirement of secrecy kept Jim lurking in the shadows of the new marriage and skewed his new connections with his two stepdaughters, Joey (whom he could tell) and Betty (whom he was instructed not to tell). Although it was a small thing, Sam's complicity with the secret left him feeling that he was starting a new family in a less than straight and legitimate way. To his credit, Sam eventually told Vicki exactly what he felt. He expressed his wish, and later his intention, to be out of the secret-keeping business.

This family had no intention to hurt, divide, or exclude its members. Yet when I first saw them in therapy, each individual was disempowered, each relationship compromised. The keeping of secrets brought some family members closer, but at the expense of other individuals and other family relationships. When we operate at the expense of others, we compromise ourselves, as well.

Is It Privacy or Patriarchy?

I have defined secrecy, as distinguished from privacy, as intentional concealment that makes a difference in a relationship process. When I evaluate whether I am "being private" or "keeping a secret" from, say, my husband, this is the criterion I apply. Yet, when we examine the complexity of real life, this neat distinction between privacy and secrecy collapses. Privacy, too, may involve concealment that makes a difference. In fact, we may invoke the concept of privacy to justify concealment and to pretend that it makes no difference.

Even when we consider a "pure" example of privacy, concealment may still make a difference. In our shame-based culture, women (like my friend with the squishy breasts) do not simply exercise the right to privacy out of free choice and on behalf of the self. When we say to each other or to ourselves, "This is private; It is my business," we express a basic and essential human right. But in so doing, we may also preserve lies that oppress us, rather than lay claim to our individual freedom. In the name of privacy, we withhold from each other our honest experience. We fail to know each other and be known. We fail, individually and collectively, to scrutinize the "personal" or private in ways that would challenge us to seek new truths and revise old ones.

Under patriarchy—which is all we have known—privacy (a legitimized form of silence) is, for women, both necessary and dangerous. Privacy is necessary not only because it is a human need, but because speaking out—and *being* out—can place some of us emotionally and physically at risk. Privacy is dangerous, however, because the failure to share what is most private or personal isolates us, shames us, and keeps us trapped in narrow, false myths about female experience. Feminism taught us that when we share what is most shameful and private, we learn that it is most universal and shared. The commonality of female experience allows us to challenge old lies and create the space for truth.

*   *   *

Let's look again at my conversation with my friend who hates her breasts. In this exchange, she disclosed feelings to me that she had never before revealed to anyone. She had often complained about her body, but in a funny, bantering way that masked her sorrow and shame. Now she showed real feeling, specificity, and depth.

A particular incident had inspired this shift toward greater truth-telling. Earlier that evening, she attended a lecture I was giving in the city where she lived. My subject was "The Advice-Giving Industry for Women: Is it Hazardous to Your Health?" During this lecture I facetiously credited self-help books with providing us with such wonderful tips as "How to keep your arms tightly at your sides when you're making love, so that your breasts don't disappear or fall into your armpits." At these words, ripples of laughter arose from the audience. Within seconds, women all through the room were laughing unrestrainedly and breaking into applause.

My friend told me later that this comment alone was worth the price of admission. Really, it was not the quip that she valued. Rather, it was the experience of sitting among hundreds of women of all ages, shapes, and sizes, and being part of the shared response that swept through the room. In those moments of contagious laughter, each woman knew she was not alone in "positioning" her breasts—or worrying about them—when she lay down with a lover.

My friend's joy and relief was in having the private made public, the shameful made silly, the personal made political. She was not alone, and certainly not the first to struggle in a particular way with particular feelings. The lessening of shame that always accompanies this recognition of shared experience led her that evening to speak more openly and truthfully. She hadn't yet told her husband and perhaps she will never choose to. But talking openly with me was possibly a move in that direction.

The next step might bring my friend—and all women—to widen the context. Why are so many of us dissatisfied with our breasts? Recognizing a shared experience helps us stop pathologizing ourselves. Instead of maintaining a narrow and singular focus on the question, "What's wrong with me?", we can begin to ask other questions, like "Who says?", "What group of people has created this reality for us?", "How does it serve them?", "What would be different if we stopped believing it?"

Questions such as these begin to create a new context in which each woman can begin to discover what is true about herself and say it out loud. The process is circular and unending. As one woman speaks the truth—from her private or secret self—she widens the space for more truth around her.

5

A Funny Thing Happened on the Way to the Orifice

In the summer of 1970 I sat in a circle of about twenty women in Berkeley, California. We were in the process of trying to form consciousness-raising groups. One of the women asked who among us had never faked an orgasm. I don't know if she was conducting research or merely being curious.

Only a few women raised their hands. At the time, the business of faking orgasms did not strike me as particularly noteworthy. It was simply a matter of women learning what the culture taught about getting and keeping a man—bolstering the male ego, reflecting men at twice their natural size, listening wide-eyed to *his* ideas, no matter how boring.

I was raised to pretend with men. Pretending was as natural as breathing and as ordinary as good manners. In my growing-up years in Brooklyn, I took the task seriously. When a sixth-grade teacher advised us girls that it was endearing to misspell big words in notes to boys, I consulted my dictionary, to be certain of my misspellings.

My teacher's advice, as silly as it sounds today, simply reflected the predominant prefeminist teachings of the day, which urged women to be smart enough to catch a man but never to outsmart him. Women were encouraged to feign weakness, helplessness, and dependency if they were not fortunate enough to possess these traits naturally. To quote one expert in female popularity, Arlene Dahl, whose book *Always Ask a Man* found its way into my personal library:

> The successful female never lets her competence compete with her femininity. Never upstage a man. Don't top his jokes even if you have to bite your tongue to keep from doing it. Never launch loudly into your own opinions on the subject. . . . Instead draw out his ideas to which you can gracefully add your footnotes from time to time. If you smoke, don't carry matches. In a restaurant let your mate or date do the ordering. You may know more about vintage wine than the wine steward but if you are smart you'll let your man do the choosing and be ecstatic over his selection even if it tastes like shampoo.

Faking orgasms, as I viewed the matter in 1970, was hardly separable from, and no more alarming than, biting our tongues or drinking wine that tastes like shampoo (one can glimpse here the excruciating activity behind female "passivity"). These behaviors, I believed, were merely the prescribed etiquette for middle-class white women like myself, to be shed like a false skin after a good relationship was under way.

I failed to appreciate the enormous unconscious power of the paradoxical rule behind these cultural teachings—the rule that women should strengthen men, and our bond with them, by relinquishing our own strength, and that to do otherwise, or simply to be ourselves, was unfeminine, unlovable, castrating, destructive, and, yes, even life-threatening to men.

I did not comprehend the degree to which we women internalized and played out this rule unconsciously in other important relationships, not just with men whom we believed needed proof of their manhood or those who had economic power over us (such as husbands and bosses) but also with our sisters, our mothers, our best friends, our female lovers.

I did not think much about the terrible cost to our lives—and to men's lives, too—when we behaved not as authentic women but as "female impersonators," to use Carolyn Heilbrun's phrase.

And not until some months after the question of faking orgasms was first raised did it again draw my attention, this time as I was beginning to practice psychotherapy.

So, What Do Little Girls Have?

One of my clients, a twenty-two-year-old graduate student named Krista, had something important to tell me that she could not bring herself to say out loud. For years, she had harbored a profound and corrosive feeling of shame about a secret she had carried. As a new therapist, I wanted to help Krista by respecting her own sense of timing about when she was ready to share. Our work together, however, was a time-limited venture, and I ended up pushing her to get it out on the table. I did not know what to expect.

The secret that Krista ultimately revealed was that she could not achieve orgasm during intercourse unless she stimulated her clitoris at the same time. I confess that I had expected a more colorful revelation.

What struck me as interesting, however, about this simple physical need of hers was Krista's feeling of shame. For years she had kept silent about it, had in fact told no one before me—not her women's group, not her male partners, not her closest female friends. Why? I asked her.

For starters, Krista believed that she was the only woman in San Francisco, in the United States, or even on the planet who had to stimulate her clitoris during intercourse to have an orgasm. Here was a woman who faked orgasm with her longstanding partner, because she wasn't going to do *that* while engaged in the romantic act of making love. It would destroy the emotional climate, Krista explained, and furthermore, she feared she might ultimately lose him to a "real woman" who didn't have this regrettable complication.

Second, Krista felt ashamed to say the word "clitoris" out loud because, until the moment she said the word to me (and I said it back to her), she had never heard it spoken. She was not certain how to pronounce it. No one had ever told her she had one. Krista had unconsciously interpreted this peculiar silence to mean that this very real part of her body, which embodied her sexuality, was forbidden, unspeakable, and confusing, perhaps even grotesque.

During the 1970s, the articulation of such feelings was believed by psychoanalysts to reflect "penis envy." But when my supervisor suggested to me that Krista wanted a penis, that she wanted to be a man, I silently disagreed. I thought that Krista wanted permission to be a woman. She wanted most to be herself.

Around this time I began to understand that the wide-spread female practice of faking orgasms (or pretending greater enthusiasm about intercourse than is felt) is an act with deeper meaning: It reflects cultural pressures for women to be more concerned with the pleasure that we arouse in others than with the pleasure we might feel within ourselves. Faking orgasm is an important example of pretending and self-betrayal in women's lives that bolsters our sexual partners and protects them at the expense of the self. It reflects the myths we have internalized about what men need from women and have a right to expect from us.

Krista's pattern of "faking it" was also linked to her inability to view her clitoris as a valid aspect of her sexuality. Her silence and inauthenticity was not simply evidence of a personal neurosis, but rather reflected the false labeling of female genitals as well as the predominant beliefs of the day. In psychoanaltyic circles, for example, many of my colleagues still considered the clitoris to be a vestigial organ in adult sexuality; women who preferred clitoral to vaginal stimulation were labeled "masculine" or "phallic" (as were those of us who aspired to be mathematicians or engineers), and were diagnosed as manifesting penis envy or sexual immaturity. Although Masters and Johnson's research challenged these views in the sixties (Why didn't they just *ask* us?), Freud's traditional views had great staying power. Krista's sense that her clitoris was not a central or even legitimate aspect of her sexuality was paralleled by expert opinion which held the same.

Psychoanalytic theory has since been appropriately revised, but not much has changed. What's between our legs is still *misnamed* or *not named* by the dominant group culture, and women are still complicitous with this lie. Perhaps, this is where serious pretending begins.

Raising Vulva Consciousness

I was at the local YWCA when I overheard the following conversation:

"That's his penis, isn't it, Mommy?" squealed a preschool girl pointing to a naked baby boy in the locker room. The mother, more amused than embarrassed by her daughter's unabashed curiosity, answered affirmatively.

"And what's *that?*" the girl asked, pointing now to the crotch of a naked little girl standing nearby.

"That's her *vagina*," the mother answered with that false brightness adults reserve for addressing the very young and the very old.

I cleared my throat—but then bit my tongue. The year was 1990, and I wanted to lean over to this mother and say, "Hey, I think I know something that you don't know." Or maybe, "Vagina! You must be kidding! Do you have X-ray vision, lady?" But apart from pestering my good friends, I try to restrain myself in public places from correcting other people's language. Now, more than two decades after working with Krista in psychotherapy, I know that the misuse of the word "vagina" for everything "down there" is still remarkably persistent.

Most of us were raised on some variation of "boys have a penis and girls have a vagina." To quote again from my personal library: "A girl has two ovaries, a uterus, and a vagina which are her sex organs. A boy's sex organs are a penis and testicles. One of the first changes (at puberty) will be *the growth of hair around the vaginal opening of the girl*." Such partial and inaccurate labeling of female genitalia might inspire any pubescent girl to sit on the bathroom floor with a mirror and conclude that she is a freak. Maya Angelou shares just such a traumatic experience in her first autobiographical account of her life, *I Know Why the Caged Bird Sings*.

The widespread practice of mislabeling female genitalia is almost as astounding in its implications as is the silence that surrounds this fact. True, Americans do not excise the clitoris and ablate the labia, as is practiced in other cultures on countless girls and women of color. Instead, we do the job linguistically—a psychic genital mutilation, if you will. Obviously the two crimes are not equivalent. But language can be as sharp and as swift as the surgeon's knife. What is not named does not exist.

How could Krista—or any woman—feel "permission" to be a sexual being when she has been taught from childhood that she has a vagina (which is internal and difficult to examine) but not that she has a vulva which includes the clitoris and labia? What does it mean for a little girl to discover her clitoris as the prime source of sexual stimulation and gratification, but to have no label for or validation of this reality? ("Only boys have something on the 'outside'"). What new meaning might Freud's concept of "penis envy" take on, if we consider the fact that in his lifetime the words "clitoris," "vulva," and "labia" were not included in the dictionary and, in this country, the only word in Webster's dictionary for female genitalia was "vagina"? Who decides what words are included in the dictionary and who decides what is real?

To this very day, my colleagues continue to say "vagina" when they mean "vulva." And so do the scores of mostly white middle-class parents I have informally interviewed over the years since working with Krista. Most people still misuse the word "vagina" to refer to "what girls have," and many educated parents report that they have never heard the word "vulva," including a large number who think the term refers to a Swedish automobile. When my friend, Nancy, was diagnosed with vestibular adonitis—an uncommon disease of the unspeakable parts—she called the National Institutes of Health and presented the facts to the woman in charge of directing her call. "Vulva?" the woman replied querulously. "Vulva? . . . Is that heart and lungs?"

Those who are knowledgeable about the correct words give the most imaginative reasons for not using them: "Telling my daughter about her clitoris is like telling her to go masturbate"; "I can't tell her about something that tiny [her clitoris] and I'm not even sure how to pronounce it"; "Vulva is a medical term, and I don't want to burden her with words that her friends don't know"; "She'll spread the news to her classmates and how will we deal with that?"; "'Vulva' and 'clitoris' are technical terms" (this one from parents who taught their small daughter about ovaries and Fallopian tubes); and (from a particularly forthright father), "I don't want my daughter to become a sex maniac or to grow up thinking that men can be replaced with a vibrator."

It is not simply that privileged men, the creators and codi-fiers of language, have named women in accordance with their own unconscious wishes, fears, and fantasies. It is also that we are not yet able to muster the clarity and courage to say "vulva" when that is what we mean and to say "vagina" when that is what we mean. This is not just a matter of lin-guistic precision, but rather of the deepest levels of truth-telling. If we cannot tell our daughters what they have, we are inviting each new generation of women to pretend—to blur language, sensation, and thought.

Of course, the subject of vulvas is one of countless exam-ples of how female experience is distorted, denied, and falsi-fied. This particular example brings us back to the little girl in the locker room who asked her mother, "And what's *that?*"

How would you answer her?

Renaming Krista's Problem

I don't recall providing Krista with any brilliant insights in my work with her so long ago. I do remember encouraging her to come out of the closet with her secret, and she did. When she returned to therapy after her initial self-disclosure, she told me that she had initiated a frank discussion about sex in her women's group and had learned that about half the women needed clitoral stimulation to achieve orgasm during intercourse. I interpreted this fact to mean that each of these women stimulated her clitoris during lovemaking—or otherwise had her needs met—but I was wrong. Krista went on to explain that these women, like herself, faked orgasm. "What a relief," Krista told me, "to find out that a whole bunch of us have the same problem."

"And what is the problem, as you see it?" I inquired.

"That we can't come in the normal way," Krista answered matter-of-factly.

"And who says what's normal?" I pushed further. I recall this particular exchange because, at the time, I was struck by how even "scientific communications" on female psychology went in circles. Once something was defined as "unfeminine" or "gender inappropiate," the old rules could not easily be challenged. When women differed from the theories, the exceptions only proved rather than probed the rule, and it was the women—not the theories—who were brought into question. Women were still trying to fit themselves to the predominant theories of the day, rather than the other way around.

Perhaps because I was new at the business of psychotherapy, I felt that I was not particularly helpful to Krista. No doubt she inspired my thinking more than I inspired hers. But her women's group took a great leap forward on the orgasm issue when they later began asking, "Who says?"

It was the women's group that helped Krista to rename her problem—a problem that stemmed not from some shameful personal anomaly, but rather from the narrow and false definitions of female sexuality that Krista had accepted without question. Soon Krista could articulate her dilemma without pathologizing herself: Should she be honest with her boyfriend, lay claim to her own legitimate sexual desires, and risk his distancing from her? Or should she continue faking orgasms and protect the status quo? Krista chose to do the latter.

That was 1970. For Krista and for me, the women's movement was just beginning.

Innocent Pretending?

Although sexual lying is considered by many to be an unethical act (as in having an ongoing affair and denying it), "pretending" is not so disparaged. There is a certain lightness or frivolity associated with words such as "pretending," "faking," and "feigning"—words that may evoke images of discretion, ladylike behavior, or even good manners. Women still tell me that they view sexual faking as an inconsequential act, just something women do, and not a bad idea at that. Not so long ago, when my mother was my age, certain gynecological texts advised physicians to instruct their patients to fake orgasm, noting that such "innocent deception" and "innocent simulation" would help women in their wish to please their husbands. Many women still have no concept that their bodies and their sexuality exist for themselves—no concept that their lives can be lived for themselves.

Why do the words "lying" and "pretending" ring so differently in our ears? We think of lying as a self-serving, self-promoting, or self-protective activity. In contrast, pretending may be done in the service of enhancing another person at the expense of the self. Sexual pretending, for example, has changed cultural forms over the years, requiring women to conform to whatever men wanted to hear at that particular period of history.

Thus, the "modern woman" may feign multiple orgasms whereas the Victorian lady denied sexual pleasure by "lying still"—bending to cultural pressure so strong that she might seem, even to herself, as devoid of instinctual life as the sleeping Snow White. Likewise women throughout history have denied erotic and sensuous ties to other women, or have been granted a kind of limited heterosexual freedom—only to be warned not to exercise it. In high school and college, I had my desires acknowledged, but was told not to act on them lest I "spoil" myself for marriage by decreasing my value, worth, and marketability in the eyes of men who prized virginity. Of course, there have always been courageous women who have resisted these societal strictures, refused to be complicitous, disbelieved what men have told them or said about them, insisting instead on uncovering and living their own truths, sexual and otherwise.

Why do we minimize or soften an act of self-betrayal, even placing it within the category of feminine virtue? Why do we fail to take seriously the act of faking orgasm or exaggerating—or denying—sexual desire? Why do we accept rather than refute the ubiquitous practice of misnaming our most intimate places, symbolically erasing and mystifying our sexuality? Throughout history and around the world, women have not simply "pretended" as an act of feminine goodwill, but instead have been forced to tell sexual lies to men as a matter of self-preservation. "Lustful" nuns and "difficult" wives have been subjected to clitoridectomies; unfaithful women, those who chose to live outside male control (especially those who chose to love other women), have been subjected to ridicule, censure, and violence. For married women who would prefer to be left alone in bed, sexual lying is a matter of economic and emotional necessity, since intercourse is still considered a husband's right and a woman's obligation. And for many, pretending has become a way of life, even when nothing obvious is at stake.

We may not be aware that we are pretending out of fear, or that we are pretending at all. When we learn that our bodies are not for ourselves, we stop tuning in to the signals that our bodies give us about our particular sexual desires and rhythms—as well as our lack of interest. Instead, we feel exhausted at bedtime, or question what is wrong with us for "not wanting it." We may "try to get into it," or think of someone or something else while we're "doing it." Pretending becomes habitual, reflexive, and unexamined.

Of course, it is overly simplistic to define lying as "for the self" and pretending as "for the other." Sorting out the two is difficult until after both the lying and the pretending have stopped. Only then can we determine who exactly is being protected and from what. When we are anxious or threatened, we try to get comfortable, which is where lying and pretending may begin.

So Krista did not fake orgasm just "for him," but also as a strategy to keep him. She wanted to protect his feelings, but she also wanted to protect herself from dealing with those feelings. And Krista may have been inhibited by any number of anxieties about sexuality and intimacy that prevented her from being more truthful in bed. Nor was her pretending necessarily "good for him," because her boyfriend might have felt more than slightly shaken that he had been deceived and more than slightly angry that he had been denied the opportunity to develop a more authentic intimacy.

It has long been the woman's job, whether in the bedroom or boardroom, to magnify men, making them seem larger than life by reflecting and mirroring them back to themselves. As early as 1929, in *A Room of One's Own*, Virginia Woolf wrote about this connection between the enforced inferiority of women and their role of enlarging men in all aspects of private and public life:

> For if she begins to tell the truth, the figure in the looking-glass shrinks; his fitness for life is diminished. How is he to go on giving judgments, civilizing natives, making laws, writing books, dressing up and speechifying at banquets, unless he can see himself at breakfast and at dinner at least twice the size he really is?

Krista once said that she played the part of the perfect lover so that her boyfriend would feel like the perfect lover. But Krista's pretending was surely an attempt, however misguided, to protect her own self-esteem, along with his. In a culture that failed to name or validate real or diverse female experience, Krista was trying to conform to how "a real woman" feels and behaves. She was trying to act "like a woman," to be "like other women," because she had learned that her own truths were inadequate, unnatural, not good enough—or else because she did not yet know what her own truths were.

Consciousness Raising: Naming Our Own Truths

I was a graduate student in New York City when the Women's Liberation movement got rolling in the late sixties. Around the country, women like Krista were joining together in consciousness-raising groups to tell their stories, to say, "This is what it is really like for me." Whether the "it" was orgasm, marriage, housework, friendship, fat, or shaving our legs, women began to tell the truth about their experience.

My first reaction to the Women's Liberation movement was one of disinterest. What did it have to do with me? Partially blinded by my arrogance at having "made it" in a man's world, I saw nothing to complain about, and if I wasn't complaining, I didn't see why anyone else should be. After all, *I* had never been discriminated against as a woman. If other women were tired of feeling like glorified scullery maids, why didn't they get out of the kitchen?

Only slowly did I begin to feel uncomfortable and dishonest in the face of my condescension to feminist protests. It was especially difficult for me to confront the fact that I, too, like Krista, had lied about my pleasures and my pain out of my fears of losing approval and privilege, to say nothing of relationships. The truth—or even the fact of patriarchy—did not suddenly reveal itself to me in a single flash of lightning that brightened a previously darkened terrain. Rather, consciousness raising occurred slowly, imperceptibly, as women around me created new realities that allowed me to stand back and see the old one.

It was consciousness raising, not psychotherapy or expert advice, that led countless women to tell the truth about their lives and to create passionate new visions of self, of female community, and of a fair world. This happened because consciousness-raising groups provided a new context in which women gave priority to their own stories and exchanges over the communications of men. Also, consciousness-raising groups had no leaders. There was no therapist, no expert, no facilitator who might fit the new territory to his or her own map, or who was empowered to "know best" or speak the truth for others in the group. Consciousness-raising groups were not therapy groups. The purpose of these groups was not to privatize, individualize, and pathologize "women's problems," but rather to understand these through the lens of gender and the socially constructed fabric of our lives.

This collective sharing of private experience allowed women to articulate and challenge the doctrines of patriarchy which had been so pervasive as to be accepted as "laws of nature." Many women broke the silence about male violence in their lives and, for the first time, were heard. The psychiatrist Judith Lewis Herman writes, "In the protected environment of the consulting room, women had dared to speak of rape, but the learned men of science had not believed them. In the protected environment of consciousness-raising groups, women spoke of rape and other women believed them."

The outpouring of anger, creativity, intellectual passion, erotic energy, and political action that this early stage of modern feminism inspired was simply incalculable. Armed with the credo that "The personal is political," women arose from a collective slumber and began to change ourselves and the world. All this could not have happened had individual women brought their secrets, their self-disclosures, their confessions, to their psychoanalysts or to their husbands or best friends. Nor could it have happened if women had met together to analyze their problems and pain through the narrow explanatory lens of "bad mothers," "toxic parents," and "dysfunctional family systems" (a term reminiscent of broken stereo components). The refusal of women to pathologize and privatize our lives turned truth-telling into a revolutionary act.

Until women collectively articulated authentic experience, feelings of shame, guilt, and inadequacy flourished ("What's wrong with me?"). These feelings, which blocked healthy anger and protest, are inevitable when women are divided and isolated from each other, when we do not have a safe place to discover our commonalities, to explore our differences and diversity, and to understand the particular social-historical context in which these arise.

Of course, some women are more private than others. It is not the way of all women to disclose their selves in a group, or to discuss the intimate details of their lives. Nor do I wish to glorify these early consciousness-raising days when many white, heterosexual, middle-class, mostly young feminists assumed they comprised and could define the category of "women." But despite the problems, a profound transformation occurred when previously isolated women created groups and offered one another the most personal accounts of our lives. Women who felt like monsters for not fitting the available female scripts moved beyond individual guilt to protest popular myths about female experience.

Was There Therapy (or Truth-Telling)
Before Feminism?

Feminist scholar Carolyn Heilbrun regrets the passing of consciousness-raising groups and notes that either women will exchange and create new stories in groups, or we will live our lives isolated in the houses and the stories of men. She also wonders how much any individual woman before feminism was helped by therapy or expert advice. I wonder, too. Before feminism, depressed housewives in therapy learned to compromise and adapt. Women who passionately quested for ambition and achievement along with, or in place of, marriage and motherhood, were viewed as envying or imitating men. Women who loved women were similarly pathologized, as were heterosexual women who expressed anger and unhappiness about "being a woman," as being a woman was defined. Mothers were blamed for everything, including their own unhappiness.

Before the recent wave of feminism, many women were so guilty about their unspeakable feelings that they could not voice them, not even to themselves. When I joined the staff of the Menninger Clinic in the early seventies, it was common for an exhausted, unhappy, and isolated mother of small children to begin therapy with the following goal: "Make me a better wife and mother to my husband and children." She had no other story to put forth, no other vision for herself that felt acceptable and rightfully obtainable. Faking motherhood went deeper than faking orgasms; her feelings were a secret she kept even from herself.

But the unconscious, seeking truth, would voice a protest. The woman would develop symptoms which frequently took the form of an unconscious wildcat strike against her "sacred calling": "I am too depressed/fatigued/

confused/sick to run the household and care for my children." The woman herself experienced inordinate guilt and proclaimed her inadequacies with a vengeance in order to protect herself from her unspeakable rage. It was the rage of one who had so accommodated to someone else's program that she had betrayed, if not lost, her own self.

In my prefeminist days, I took as truth the predominant theories of the day regarding how the "good mother" (or "good-enough mother") feels and conducts herself. I didn't challenge the "scientific literature" on motherhood, written by experts who were neither women nor mothers—nor probably even home enough, for that matter, to know much about fathering. Actually, I did register that there was something wrong in much of what I was being taught about female psychology; but before I was part of a supportive network of feminist scholars, I felt too vulnerable and alone to articulate my feelings.

The intentions of mental health professionals, myself included, have always been to expand, not limit, self-knowledge. The goal of psychotherapy or psychoanalysis is to help women clarify their own choices and discover their own truths in a "neutral" and "value-free" emotional climate. But this is not possible, not then, nor ever. Despite good intentions, no therapist is free from the historical particularities of family and culture, of time and place. Therapists could not begin to move beyond the conventional, man-made narratives of a woman's life until women, collectively, did it first. Of course, any interpretation of experience privileges one story, or particular framing of reality, above others, and edges out other meanings and alternative explanations.

Women are wise to maintain a healthy skepticism toward

all experts who would presume to tell us what is true, and to prescribe how we should think, feel, and conduct ourselves. "Expert opinion" often reflects the privileged and dominant voices in our culture who have access to meaning-making and the media to disperse it. As the poet Audre Lorde says, "The master's tools will never dismantle the master's house." Perhaps the most trustworthy experts on women are those who put forth their theories as partial and tentative speculations and those who share the particulars of their own experience, recognizing that their most deeply held "truths" may or may not be useful to an individual woman as she seeks to uncover her own.

Today, women as a group are less obedient. We no longer accept patronizing or guilt-inducing pronouncements about the "good mother," the "true vaginal orgasm," or the "appropriate place" and "true nature" of women. Nor do we accept the suspect status of those of us who are not mothers or choose not to pair up with men. To all of this, we are saying, "Enough!" It is not that we are more courageous than the women who came before us. Women have always been brave. Rather, we are no longer among the first, or the few, to speak out and share authentic experience. Feminism has created the space for more truth-telling and for the restoring and re-storying of our lives.

6

~

We Are the Stories We Tell

Is there a "true story" of female experience? If so, then surely it cannot be told by experts who have never been women, nor can any one of us speak for all. Each woman is ultimately the best expert on her own self. But to begin to know our own truths, we need to examine our own stories and those of other women. Telling a "true story" about personal experience is not just a matter of being oneself, or even of finding oneself. It is also, as we will see, a matter of *choosing* oneself.

Re-Storying Female Ambition

My friend Sue overheard a telephone call I made to my dad. I was telling him about a recent speaking engagement and he asked, as he always does, how many people came to hear me. "Oh," I responded enthusiastically, "the hall was packed! There must have been close to a thousand women there." My father was pleased.

Actually, I was exaggerating by a couple of hundred women, and Sue called me on it. Boasting is bad enough, she said, without distorting the facts. By her own report, Sue neither lies nor tolerates lying from others. She is firmly in the camp of those philosophers, theologians, and ethicists who argue that lying is never justified, and that it invariably erodes the soul, annihilates human dignity, and exacts a toll, however imperceptible, on relationships. Sue believes that any lie, no matter how seemingly small, fools with the reality of another human being and impedes trust.

The following day, however, Sue behaved in a way that struck me as dishonest. In a crowded coffee shop as we waited in a long, slow-moving line, we chatted at length with two women, both probably in their fifties, from a rural part of western Kansas. When a table for four became available, they asked us to join them and we accepted, glad to continue our conversation. They spoke poignantly about worsening farm problems and then asked what each of us did for work. "I work with children in a hospital," Sue responded. Both women assumed she was a nurse, and referred to her as such in the conversation that followed. Sue, a pediatric surgeon at a New York City hospital, did not correct this misperception.

For as long as I have known Sue, she has denied or minimized her accomplishments and status. Several months earlier, for example, she decided not to tell her mother and sister about an important promotion because "they were both in such difficult places in their lives." Whenever people seem intimidated by Sue's profession as a surgeon, she explains that she is actually a glorified seamstress, and that surgical expertise requires no more complex skill than the precise handwork that women have created for generations. This has been a repetitive theme or pattern in Sue's life. While I

veered from truth-telling by exaggerating my accomplishments to my father, Sue *minimized* hers to the world.

As we talked about the coffee shop incident, Sue
explained why she had described her work in words that concealed her status and then failed to clarify the facts as the
conversation progressed. In her experience, people are often
intimidated to learn she is a doctor; that information creates
distance between her and the people she meets. Sue thought
this barrier might be especially likely to surface with these
two rural Kansas women. Also, these women were having
wrenching financial struggles; given popular stereotypes
about "rich doctors," Sue felt it would be in poor taste to
mention her profession.

While Sue condemned my exaggerating about the workshop attendance, she saw her behavior as "pure." She was
simply trying to make these two women feel comfortable,
and she hadn't actually *said* she was a nurse. More to the
point, Sue viewed downplaying individual accomplishment
as a virtue, but exaggerating as a vice. Thus, I had told a lie,
while she had acted with honor. Such was not my worldview.

Our differing ethnic backgrounds were probably at play
here. Sue's Anglo-Saxon Protestant family thinks it sinful to
boast, even about distinguished ancestors. By contrast, my
Jewish family considers it sinful for children not to give their
parents something to boast about. Sue and her sister were
discouraged from "standing out" or "showing off," while my
sister and I were encouraged to dazzle and shine. In my family, hitting the winning home run was far more important
than being the good team player Sue was expected to be. In a
number of ways, our experiences in our respective families
led us to respond differently to common dilemmas women
face about work.

Claiming Achievement

The small departures from truth-telling that Sue and I encountered in each other may seem insignificant in comparison to faked orgasms, or other more serious deceptions we have all known. But the tension between Sue and me about what constitutes an honest self-presentation in the arena of work and success was neither trivial nor coincidental.

Like love, work is at the center of all human existence. But women seldom tell the truth, even to ourselves, about the meaning of work in our lives. And patriarchal definitions of what it means to be a woman—to have womanly desires and hopes and ambitions—have, until recently, made truth-telling virtually impossible. Before modern feminism, stories of female ambition were silenced or erased; even now, they are told with apology ("Yes, it's a great honor to be a Nobel Prize laureate, but really, what I love best is staying home and being a mother to Kevin and Annie"). In this larger historical context, my critical reaction to Sue took hold and gathered meaning.

Following the prescriptions of culture, Sue failed to lay claim to honest achievement—failed to give the world a narrative of her life that might expand for all women our sense of risk, adventure, curiosity, and possibility. I think our lunch companions would have appreciated knowing that Sue was a surgeon, and I found it unnecessary and insulting to "protect" such sturdy rural women (or anybody, for that matter) from the facts. I would resent such protection myself, I told Sue. Isn't it our responsibility to speak accurately about the diverse realities of our lives? Shouldn't we refuse complicity with the disastrous, feminine prescription to protect and bolster others by denying our ambition and hiding our ability?

Yet, like Sue, I have often felt pulled to act out some variation of this prescribed female script.

Here's one example. About a year ago, I sat down to write a brief speech in response to being named Woman of the Year by the local chapter of the National Women's Business Association. I was particularly touched by the recognition I was about to receive for my contributions to my own community. In addition, the day of the award ceremony would be proclaimed by both the mayor of Topeka and the governor of Kansas as "Dr. Harriet Goldhor Lerner Day." In response to these honors, I wanted to say something significant, especially to the audience that included people I loved. I decided that I would share my personal reflections on my journey to successful authorhood. I would tell an honest story.

But once seated before my computer, I found myself writing a talk that attributed my success to good luck. I meant it and, in part, it was true. Success does require a large measure of timing and luck, and is hardly a result of talent and perseverance alone. Indeed, I could think of countless women, past and present, whose extraordinary work had not been recognized or even valued, let alone published, promoted, and prized.

But I chose not to tell that story. What stopped me short was Carolyn Heilbrun's book, *Writing a Woman's Life*, which documents how patriarchial culture defines and limits women's lives by determining what stories about women will be told. Helibrun explains that well into the twentieth century, women were unable to claim achievement or admit ambition in the telling or recording of their own lives. Those who were able to achieve and recognize their accomplishments often attributed their success either to luck or to the efforts or generosity of others. This description was not of an outdated phenomenon, but rather one that I observed daily in my consulting room—and in the acceptance speech I wrote and almost presented in my own community.

On reflection, I recognized that I had as much bad luck as good luck in the publishing world. While writing my first book, *The Dance of Anger*, I was fired, rehired, and fired again by my first publisher. Enormous determination, perseverance, and will kept me going, as the book was then rejected by almost every major publishing house in the country. When it miraculously saw the light of day, I did not release it passively into the world like a bottle left to drift aimlessly out to sea. Instead, I promoted it energetically and aggressively, enlisting my large network of friends and colleagues to do the same.

This summary of events was part of the story I ultimately told—a story about luck (both very good and very bad), but mainly about determination and perseverance against great odds. And while I spoke frankly about the unanticipated cost of fame and glory, I stated emphatically that I have found these stresses far preferable to the stresses of having my work undervalued and rejected.

I thought I had made a bold move toward truth-telling when I shifted from publicly attributing my success to "luck," a historically rooted form of female apology and self-disparagement, to telling the true tale of my individual determination and spirit. The "luck story," I had concluded, was a dishonest narrative. It not only reflected historical forces that make women deny ambition, but indicates the forces that keep us feeling illegitimate when we do receive public acclaim. Women, like other marginalized groups, internalize countless messages: we do not belong in important places; we do not really count; we do not really shape history and culture. And so, when we do achieve recognition, we tend to attribute our success to luck, or if not that, then to something, anything, other than our competent and entitled selves.

A decade or so earlier, I could not have told my story as truthfully, without fear of censure and ridicule, without fear of invidious interpretations ("penis envy" was the label once applied glibly in psychoanalytic circles to women for whom ambition and achievement were central), without fear that my very femininity would be suspect. Now, none of this concerned me, not because I had matured with age (although that too), but because feminism had widened the range of stories women could construct and share about our lives. I credit feminism, more than any other force in my life, with allowing me to move toward the truth, toward greater congruence between my private life and public image.

I wanted Sue, too, to be honest about her brilliant career, especially with her family and friends. To me, this had nothing to do with boasting, or arrogance, or insensitivity to the feelings of others. It simply had to do with telling our stories, and particularly with telling the stories that could not be told earlier. It was a matter of telling the truth. Throughout time, accounts of women's lives—those we have told as well as those told for and about us—have suppressed and distorted the truth about female experience, have made it conform to the narrow scripts society has written for us. I did not want Sue to follow this tradition.

Sue saw it differently. Rather than attributing honesty and virtue to my revised acceptance speech, she doubted the veracity of my story. On the one hand, she shared my concern about false and constricting scripts of women's lives and she agreed that women should feel entitled to ambition, recognition, and honor. On the other hand, Sue felt that the last thing women needed was another narrative that spoke to false notions of individual superstars. This was not an authentic way, she felt, to restore and re-story women's lives.

Feeling Like a Fraud: McIntosh's Double Vision

As I tried to unravel the tension that developed between Sue and me, the work of Peggy McIntosh was pivotal to my understanding. Peggy McIntosh, an associate director of the Wellesley College Center for Research on Women, has written two critically acclaimed papers weaving together the apparently opposed points of view that Sue and I each voiced. In her examination of feeling like a fraud, McIntosh argues both that we shouldn't let the world make us feel like frauds—and we must keep alive in ourselves the wise sense of fraudulence that may overtake us in public places. From her perspective, Sue and I both held positions of integrity, though both should be present in each person.

The first part of the dual consciousness that McIntosh promotes is perhaps the easier to grasp. Women and other disempowered groups must resist feeling fraudulent when these feelings reflect internalized value systems that tell us we don't belong in spheres of power or authority in public life. And so, we can move against our feelings of fraudulence and learn to stand behind the podium or pulpit and "deliver the goods." This perspective was what made me think Harriet Goldhor Lerner Day in Kansas was a terrific idea, and why I refused to apologize for that honor.

But McIntosh also articulates a second perspective, which she hopes we can preserve along with the first. She wants us to keep alive our valid sense of fraudulence because it can help us to spot and critique the fraudulence in the roles we are asked to play. When we feel fraudulent, or even tentative, apologetic, silenced, and self-doubting, it may reflect our honest refusal to internalize the idea that having power, prestige, or public exposure proves merit and authority. Feeling like a fraud in such circumstances may express our awareness that the dominant culture's form of leadership and authority—and the concomitant images—*do* require fraudulent behavior. From this perspective, we may not hate being behind the podium so much as we hate the podium itself, because we wish instead to create alternative, more collaborative, less rigidly hierarchical ways of exchanging ideas.

McIntosh writes:

> We feel fraudulent, I think, partly because we know that usually those who happen to get the high titles and the acclaim and the imagery going with them are not "the best and the brightest," and we don't want to pretend to be so either. When we entertain nagging thoughts about whether we belong or deserve to be at the podium, or in the boardroom, or tenured, or giving an interview to a newspaper, or earning a good salary for what we like to do, we may be deeply wise in feeling anxious and illegitimate and fraudulent in these circumstances. Those men who feel the same way in such settings may be deeply wise as well, for the public forms and institutions tend to demand that one appear to be an authority figure, an expert, "the best." The public forms and institutions insisting on these images do require fraudulent behavior of us, and they will turn us into frauds if we accept the roles as written. The roles are dishonest and people who are still in touch with their humanity and with their frailty will properly feel fraudulent in them.

And so, McIntosh advocates the dual vision of recognizing that it is bad for us to feel like frauds insofar as that feeling *perpetuates* hierarchies, and yet it is good for us to feel like frauds insofar as that feeling may help us to *undermine* hierarchies. When necessary, we can help each other to overcome feeling fraudulent while acknowledging that such a feeling is normal because we're taught it, and not by accident. Our recognition of the feeling of fraudulence can be a guide to developing ways of behaving which feel more authentic to us.

In Sue's case, she knew that being a surgeon was not inherently more valuable than being a highly skilled carpenter, artist, teacher, or conversationalist. And so she felt properly fraudulent when her work was glorified. She knew her ranking in hierarchical structures lent her power and prestige beyond genuine differences in merit, intelligence, and personal excellence. As McIntosh puts it, "People who feel in public like imposters are perhaps more to be trusted than those who have never experienced feelings of fraudulence." She notes that *the ability to feel fraudulent rests on our capacity to be in touch with our own authenticity.* By knowing what is "real" in ourselves, we can recognize when the self is being violated by institutions or roles that ask us to put aside an integral part of ourselves or to pretend to be what we are not.

Both McIntosh's work and Sue's criticism of my acceptance speech raised questions: How do people make it to the top? Who decides whose work is worthy of attention and economic reward and whose is not? Do those who "make it" get there because they are really the hardest workers, the most persevering, the most deserving, and the very best? If I had spoken more honestly, would I have put less emphasis on individual merit and more on privilege—and yes, luck, including the luck of time and place, birth and circumstance?

Did the world really need another narrative that spoke to false notions of individual merit of the "rugged individual"?

Sue wished that I had used Harriet Goldhor Lerner Day to dethrone myself where others had set me up, to challenge the equation of status and merit, and to underscore the importance of creating new definitions of "success" and a less rigidly stratified world. I might have done this, Sue added, not apologetically or self-disparagingly, not out of prescribed feminine modesty or guilt, but rather from a realistic and balanced regard for myself and others.

And what of Sue choosing to "pass" as a nurse? From her perspective, this choice was not an apologetic self-portrayal, as I had interpreted it. There were good reasons why Sue was troubled by the image that accompanied her status as a doctor and the power that accrued to it. Yes, she wanted praise for work well done, and the power to influence decisions in her field that mattered. But she did not want to be glorified, magnified, even deified—which her status seemed to pull for. She did not want to be falsely set apart from or above other human beings.

I had reacted negatively to how she protested one kind of charade with another by misrepresenting herself at the coffee shop. Pretending to be what one is not, or failing to clarify who one is, did not strike me as a good "solution." I wanted Sue to be clear about her professional status, while being the kind of doctor and person she really wanted to be in her public and personal life. But I now understand Sue's behavior in a different, or rather, an additional light. It is not simply that she has succumbed to the pressures exerted by family and culture, which lead women to feel like "imposters" in positions of authority and power. She is also reacting against the divisiveness of hierarchical roles.

The tension between Sue and me developed around the

subject of how we *portray* our success to others. Women often feel phony simply for being successful, without articulating why, as Sue did. We may feel fraudulent in response to any variety of recognition, attention, success, or praise. Beyond crediting luck, or the generous efforts of others, we may feel that we have deceived, tricked, or fooled others, that we are undeserving, and that we are in danger of being "found out."

These feelings are not exclusive to women, but are remarkably common among us, inspiring a growing number of thinkers and writers to pay attention to how women apologize for success on the one hand, or ensure the lack of it, on the other. Feminist therapists, myself included, have viewed this "fear of success syndrome" or "imposter syndrome" as pathological or problematical, something to help women get past, through, or over as we analyze the forces of family and culture that stand in the way. It has been difficult to keep voices like McIntosh's at the center of our attention—voices that identify some roles and rules of success themselves as dishonest and fraudulent.

Choosing Our Stories

These days, I think of Peggy McIntosh's work when I sit through a formal public introduction of myself: "An internationally acclaimed expert on the psychology of women" . . . "One of the most important relationship experts of our times" . . . and so forth. In response to this glorified image, I think, "Who is this person?" and "How intimidating that sounds!" And even, "Is this true?"

This reaction is not a self-depreciative response, for I

believe that I am probably as worthy of such laudatory introductions as other psychology experts who are similarly described. But I am also aware that no one in my field is worthy of such an inflated description. Far more remains unknown than known in the area of human emotional functioning, and all psychotherapists have a partial, subjective, and incomplete perspective. Such an introduction is not "me" (or anyone else for that matter), nor, paradoxically, does such an intimidating list of my achievements begin to speak to my actual talents as a thinker, therapist, or human being. Yet I am also hesitant to disclaim an elevated status that historically has been denied to all women, and I want my ideas to count as much as those of other "renowned experts" in my field.

So, what is true? In some settings, I accept and even help shape the glorified introduction, just as I gave a speech in my community attributing my success to determination and talent over luck. In other settings, I tell a different story—one that recognizes the falsity of elevating my talents and achievements above those of "ordinary women." It is not that I am chameleonlike in my self-presentation. Rather, there are multiple ways we can name or frame what is true and real, and countless ways we can story and re-story our experience. As I share my stories, and listen to the stories of others, I do not only ask myself, "Is this authentic and true?" I also consider who is served or disempowered by a particular story or construction of reality.

Of course, there are many stories that I will never begin to imagine because my context does not evoke or allow for them, or because one dominant story I tell about myself suppresses and marginalizes other truths.

Angela and Jan

Two young women, Angela and Jan, worked as administrative assistants in a nonprofit service organization housed in a renovated brownstone in Philadelphia. Although they rarely socialized outside of their work, they developed a close friendship that later expanded to include several women on the secretarial staff. Despite low pay and little opportunity for learning or advancement, both Angela and Jan felt satisfied with their positions. The atmosphere was warm and relaxed, they enjoyed each other's company, and they liked the organization.

After working alongside Angela for five years, Jan applied for a position in another public service organization that offered better pay and more challenge. She had applied "just for fun," and expressed reservations when she was offered the position. The new job was across town, in a sterile, fluorescent-lit office where Jan would have little chance to interact with anyone other than her boss.

Angela discouraged Jan from making the change, arguing that money and opportunity were a poor substitute for the warm, collaborative atmosphere of their current setting. "Maybe it's because I'm not one of those ambitious women," Angela said over lunch, "but a friendship like ours and a place like this is hard to come by. I guess I put people first. And money just isn't that important to me." After considering Angela's view and weighing the pros and cons, Jan decided to stay put.

Less than a year later, Angela's brother-in-law offered her a position in a private firm that paid well and provided opportunities for training, travel, and advancement. Angela had not been looking for a new job, but when this one fell in her lap, she decided not to turn it down. Jan felt angry and betrayed by Angela's decision; Angela felt torn and guilty, but explained to Jan that she owed it to herself to make the change.

By Angela's last week of work with Jan, their friendship had reached the breaking point, culminating in a fight in which Jan called Angela a "two-faced liar." For a long time to come, Angela would remember Jan's angry words: "You said that you weren't one of those ambitious women—that people came first! Well, given the opportunity, you sure *became* one of those ambitious women very fast, didn't you? Funny, isn't it!"

Jan's assumptions were both right and wrong. She was right that given the opportunity, Angela did become "one of those ambitious women." But she was wrong in concluding that Angela had lied to her. At the moment when Angela had said, "I don't care about money," or, "People are the most important thing to me about a job," or, "I'm not ambitious," she had told the truth. Only *after* Angela had the promise of real opportunity, more money, and greater power did she begin to value them. In her new job, Angela turned out to be very ambitious indeed. As she put it to Jan many months later, "Maybe I just couldn't let myself know how much I wanted something until I really had it."

Perhaps none of us can say with certainty what we do not want, until we have the opportunity to turn it down. Angela's explanation, however, implies that she had always been ambitious and that she had defensively denied that aspect of herself in her first work setting. This may or may not be true. A more parsimonious explanation is that dead-end jobs evoke dead-end dreams, while new opportunities evoke new desires and, ultimately, new stories about our "true self."

We do not create our stories—or ourselves—in a vacuum; we are always shaped by and shaping our context.

Many of the stories we assume to be "true" or "fixed" about ourselves change dramatically when the context changes, and particularly as we gain (or lose) economic and social power. Even more to the point, there is no such thing as a "true story" (or a "true self") that unfolds separate from the influence of family and culture—free from the particular social, political, and economic factors of the time. From the moment we are first wrapped in a pink or blue blanket, we learn what stories we can tell and whether there is an ear to hear them.

7

~

Our Family Legacies

My friend Liz Hoffmeister movingly describes her first experience with death in these evocative words:

> Not yet three years old, I stood at our mother's funeral, a brother on either side, our arms touching. Grown-ups flowed around us, mouthing words. The most clearly remembered are: "Poor little things, they don't know what has happened." We stood there, impassive, their words disallowing us any show of grief. Our faint pressure on each other's arms and our short life with our mother held us up, eyes dry, while they made many empty sounds that day.
>
> At not quite three, to know your mother is in a box that is to be buried; to hear the grown-ups free to cry; to hear them say that you don't know what has happened is a form of still, cold terror. And not quite so simply that you have lost your mother, and not quite so simply that their words will not let you cry, but that at not quite three you can already wonder what kind of world you find yourself in.

The first world we find ourselves in is a family that is not of our choosing. It is our most influential context. In the best of circumstances, children would feel free to speak their own truths, to give voice to their deepest sorrow, and to know that they would be heard and understood by other family members. But, as Liz's words remind us, and as Bea's story will illustrate, this is not the world in which we find ourselves.

"Who Is This Unhappy Girl?"
The Story of Bea

Bea came to therapy after ending a five-year relationship with a man she found boring from the start. She was depressed and pessimistic about future relationships. When I asked her how supportive her parents were to her at this difficult time, she said that she told them nothing. "My father and I talk about the weather," Bea explained, "and my mother can't deal with me when I'm depressed. She can't even begin to hear it."

As far back as Bea could remember, her mother, Ruth, had disqualified Bea's sad feelings. Bea, who had an older brother, was "the happy girl" in the family—a role that was rigidly enforced. Whenever Bea got down in the dumps, her mother would approach her with false brightness and say, "Who is this unhappy girl? This is not my Bea! My Bea has a pretty smile on her face! Let's make this sad little girl go away so that my *real* Bea can come back!" Ruth also went to absurd lengths to protect Bea from anything she thought might disturb her. When Bea was five, her mother refused to take her to a birthday party because she'd heard that a girl with severe cerebral palsy would also be among the party guests.

During Bea's adult life, her mother continued to respond

anxiously to any hint of her daughter's unhappiness. Whenever Bea shared a problem, Ruth would reflexively rush in to fix it, or she would offer unsolicited advice or glib admonitions to "look on the bright side" and "keep a positive attitude." In response to her mother's allergic reaction to depression, Bea had long ago stopped sharing real feelings with her.

The ideal family encourages the optimal growth of all its members and provides a safe space where individuals can more or less be themselves. At their best moments, families promote a sense of unity and belonging (the "we"), while respecting the separateness and difference of individual members (the "I"). Parents make and enforce rules that guide a child's behavior, but they do not regulate the child's emotional and intellectual life. Individual family members can feel free to share their honest thoughts and feelings on emotionally loaded subjects, without telling others what to think and feel, and without getting too nervous about differences. No family member has to deny or silence an important aspect of the self in order to belong and be heard.

That's the ideal, but not the reality for most families, including Bea's. As she was growing up, her parents anxiously avoided a wide range of subjects. Bea sensed what topics were not "safe" and automatically avoided these "high-twitch" areas. Like many children, she silenced herself, disavowed her perceptions, and flattened her curiosity about issues that might threaten family harmony or disrupt family relationships. She also concealed important aspects of herself—such as her sadness and vulnerability. As Bea put it, "I just couldn't be real; I couldn't be myself. No one was honest in my family. It was all pretend."

Yet honesty was valued, if not rigidly prized, by Bea's parents. They punished the children not only for lying and cheating, but also for exaggerating and telling tall tales. "My parents were fanatics about honesty," Bea explained. "They wouldn't even let us believe in Santa Claus. My dad was the type who would make us walk a mile in the snow to return an extra dime the store clerk gave us by mistake. And we had to keep our word no matter what. If you said you would do something, it was considered a major crime to change your mind."

So intense were the sanctions against "dishonesty" that Bea was initially taken aback when she viewed the interior of other families. "When I was in fifth grade, I learned that my best friend's mom made long-distance personal calls from her work phone. She also brought office supplies home for the kids, like paper, pens, and Scotch tape. My friend was encouraged to lie about her age to get cheaper movie tickets or bus fares. Her parents accepted the fact that children don't always tell the truth. At first I was shocked because these behaviors would not have been tolerated in my family. But the paradox was, their family *felt* more honest than mine, more relaxed and spontaneous. In my friend's family, they were direct with each other. They actually talked about what was happening in their lives."

In Bea's family, "honesty" meant sticking to the facts, keeping one's word, and playing by the rules. It did not, however, include the honest sharing of feelings and personal experience. "My mother wasn't honest about her life," Bea explained. "When I asked her about herself, she would only tell me what she thought I should hear or what she thought was good for me." There was a striking incongruity between Ruth's upbeat messages, her behavior, and the almost palpable thickness of her unhappiness, which Bea felt "in the air."

Beyond Intentions

We grow up assuming that our parents will not intentionally lie to us, or deliberately conceal information about things that matter. We take on faith the information they give us. We ask, "Where were you born?" or, "How much did our house cost?" or, "Why has Uncle John stopped visiting us?" We expect straight answers, or, if not that, to be told that some things are private and will not be shared or discussed with us. If we are not told the truth, we cannot trust the universe—including our internal universe of thoughts, feelings, and perceptions.

Like all human beings, however, our parents can be no more honest and direct with us than they are with themselves. The discrepancy Bea sensed between her mother's words and her mother's true feelings probably reflected Ruth's own confusion rather than her deceptive intentions or dishonorable character. It isn't easy for mothers to share their personal feelings when they cannot name them and have been taught so many fictions about female experience.

Also, our parents are guided by the ethic of what is "good for us" rather than what is true. Ruth may have withheld or distorted information with the intention of protecting her daughter—that is, "for her own good." To prepare a daughter for a "happy marriage" and to teach her to be a "good mother," mothers pass down all sorts of myths from one generation of women to the next.

Family therapist Betty Carter notes that mothers routinely tell their daughters what they think is helpful rather than conveying their true doubts, fears, struggles, and uncertainties. This, she notes, reflects a mother's effort to fulfill her impossible responsibility of raising perfect children. Carter writes that "Trying desperately to be 'good mothers' and to guide their daughters, mothers withhold their *deepest personal experience* and try to convey to their daughters how *it should have been* and *how they want it to be for their daughters—instead of how it really is or was for them.*" Although the daughter may be angry at her mother for lying, she may also attempt to fulfill her own maternal responsibility by passing down the same myths in turn to her own daughter.

Within the family, women rarely describe their reality to each other with candor. This failure constitutes a tremendous loss, for it is through our stories, which create an authentic connection to other women, that we begin to uncover our deepest truths. It is not enough to exchange stories in a consciousness-raising group, at a women's conference, or with our five closest friends. Our sense of what is real and true suffers when we are unable to do this in our own families. The difficulty of pushing against silence and secrecy in a family depends on the amount of anxiety surrounding a particular subject and the emotional climate of family relationships.

The Family Emotional Climate

When Bea says about her family, "I just couldn't be real; I couldn't be myself," she is referring to the anxious emotional climate in which she was raised. Family members do not intentionally create an anxious climate for themselves or for each other. Nor do they notice it. Like a fish in water, we don't pay attention to the "givens" of our surroundings.

The level of underground anxiety or emotional intensity in a family is a function of multiple factors. It reflects the real stresses that impinge on the family as it moves through the life cycle, and the parents' economic and social resources to deal with these stresses. It also reflects societal stresses and social inequalities that affect the family. It reflects the parents' level of maturity and emotional functioning, which includes their connections to their own families of origin and the unresolved emotional issues they bring from this source. In the history of a family, anxiety accumulates over many years. Painful events that have not been processed in past generations will remain embedded in a family, and will be reenacted with each new generation.

The level of underground anxiety or emotional intensity in a family determines how much freedom individuals have to discover, clarify, and express their own truths—and how accurately they will see themselves and others. Anxiety drives people toward polarities, toward fusion or cut-off, toward glorifying or hating a difference, toward disclosing too much or too little, toward avoiding a subject entirely or focusing on it incessantly. Anxious families deny differences, sweeping them under the rug in a "group think" mentality that compromises individual autonomy, or they exaggerate differences and magnify them out of proportion.

Anxiety drives projections and distortions. People take things too personally and read too much into the other person's responses—or they do the opposite and entirely miss the nuances and subtleties of both the words and the nonverbal communications. Chronically anxious families are characterized by rigid, authoritarian rules—or the family operates like a glob of protoplasm, without clear parental leadership and generational boundaries. Anxious families deny the realities of change and try to hold the clock still—

or family functioning is so fluid and chaotic that there is no consistent, predictable structure to be counted on. Anxiety pushes us to one extreme or the other.

Anxiety drives triangles. As anxiety mounts, people talk about other family members ("I'm just so worried about the way your brother is behaving!") rather than directly *to* them. As tensions escalate, family members take sides, lose objectivity, overfocus on each other in a worried or blaming way, or join one person's camp at the expense of another. Anxiety heightens reactivity, which makes us quick to tell each other off and to try to shape each other up ("I'm so sick of playing games with my mother that I blew up and let her know how she manipulates everyone!"). Family members equate these intense, anxiety-driven confrontations with being honest, then blame the other person for not changing (". . . and then my mother got so defensive! She just can't accept the truth"). In reality, openness and truth-telling don't begin until at least one person calms down, steps out of the soup, and begins to really think rather than to merely react.

Bea's family had all the hallmarks of a chronically anxious system. Family roles were rigid and polarized; the labels applied to individual family members denied both the complexity of human experience and the inevitability of change. Bea was "always happy"; her older brother, Rob, was "the irresponsible one"; Aunt Mary was "selfish and untrustworthy." Information that challenged family myths and labels was disqualified, as if family coherence required that these remain as sure as sunrise and as fixed as the stars.

Whenever "always happy" Bea showed sadness, her mother would push anxiously for the return of the "real Bea." When "irresponsible Rob" acted responsibly, the family held its collective breath, just *knowing* that he would screw up shortly. When Bea violated an unspoken family rule against visiting her "selfish" Aunt Mary—and Aunt Mary responded warmly and generously in return—the rest of the family intensified their criticism, telling Bea that Aunt Mary was only out to "use her." All families have their myths, party lines, and labels, but when these are rigidly fixed, they exert a profound constraint on "realness." Like a pedestal or a prison, fixed labels that are either positive or negative leave one with little space in which to move around.

In Bea's family, the importance of "togetherness" also mandated that significant differences stay beneath the surface. This anxiety-driven fusion (the loss of the separate "I's" within the "We") was particularly intense between mother and daughter, so that if Ruth said "apples," Bea, as a child, felt unable to say "oranges." Later, as she entered adolescence, Bea did the opposite (which is really the same) and felt compelled to say "oranges" every time her mother said "apples." The enforced "togetherness" between them was so great that Bea felt compelled to push the differences. She suffered from what the poet Lynn Sukenick has called "matraphobia"—the fear of being one's mother. When we must be as unlike our mothers as possible, we rule out the opportunity to discover and invent our real selves, just as we do when we feel compelled to be exactly the same as her.

Even in calmer, more flexible families, differences challenge mothers and daughters. With the role of women changing so fast, it is not surprising that a mother may experience her daughter's expression of difference as disloyalty or betrayal, as discontinuity or loss, and as a judgment on the mother's own life and choices. Such tensions are understandable as a mother watches her daughter struggle to find new and different explanations for what it means to be an adult woman compared to what was prescribed over countless generations.

When it came to expressing her real feelings, Bea did no better with her dad, with whom she also could not articulate honest differences. The entrenched distance in their relationship, however, made things appear calmer and less intense. Like many daughters, Bea had learned to expect nothing from her father and everything from her mother. Although she complained that she couldn't be her "true self" with either parent, Bea focused her negative attention on Ruth.

Our Mothers' Daughters

The relationship with the same-sex parent is, of course, particularly pivotal for the development of authenticity and self-regard. As her mother's apprentice, a daughter watches to see what it means to be a wife, a mother, and an adult woman. A daughter is sensitively attuned to the quality of her mother's life and to how her mother conducts her key relationships, including those with her own family of origin. When a daughter senses her mother's unhappiness or sees through her lies and silence, she may volunteer to fill up her mother's empty bucket, fix her depression, live out her thwarted dreams, or wave her mother's banner at the expense of having a relationship with Dad. It is not simply that parents assign their children to a particular role, like "the happy one" or "Mom's best friend." A child may volunteer for such an impossible job in the family without even being asked.

During a summer on Cape Cod, my psychiatrist friend Teresa Bernardez and I taught a seminar on the subject of mothers and daughters. One participant, a social worker, shared the following story: When she was a little girl, she would ride in the back of her parents' car, as children do. On family trips, she invented an "imaginary twin" to sit with her—or, more accurately, an exact duplicate of herself. Even as a small child, she was able to articulate her reasons for inventing this fictitious double. "This way," she told herself, "I can grow up, travel to faraway places, and live a life of fun and adventure. And my twin can stay home and *be for mother*."

Her story fascinated me because it illustrates how the child consciously and deliberately did what many daughters do with little or no awareness or intention. Women frequently leave a part of themselves at home. That is, we may sacrifice important aspects of the self in an unconscious effort to *be for* our mothers. A daughter senses her mother's hopes, fears, dreams, compromises, losses, and unfulfilled longings. The greater the suffering in the previous generations of women, the more a daughter may find herself unable to carve out a different life plan for herself—one that includes a large measure of joy, ambition, and zest. Or the daughter may feel compelled to succeed for her mother's sake, to express her mother's unacknowledged ambitions, or to prove that the compromises and hardships of previous generations have not been in vain.

For obvious reasons, the father often appears to be the less intense or less anxious parent. Fathers have been exonerated from parenting in any real sense, while mothers, in contrast, are taught that they *are* the child's environment, and that they are singularly responsible for what their children become.

The myth that motherhood is a "career" rather than a

responsibility and a relationship is a particularly disastrous
one. Bea complained frequently in therapy, "My mother
needed me to have a happy smile so she could show the
world what a good mother she was." Well, why not? In our
ambitious, competitive, production-oriented society, a
mother may naturally want to create a good product—to
show herself, the world, and her own mother that she is a
"good mother," that she has done her job well.

One Father's Emotional Legacy

Of course, our fathers, too, for an endless variety of unconscious reasons, will need us to be (or not to be) a particular
way for their own sakes. Our parents' perceptions and
expectations of us are always colored by their unfinished
business with their own families of origin and with each
other—and by all the emotional issues, past and present,
that affect them.

Bea's dad, Frank, for example, went off the deep end
whenever Rob and Bea departed from telling the truth, following rules, or keeping their word. All children break rules,
test limits, and engage in deception, but Frank had no flexibility to lighten up about even minor transgressions or a simple change of mind. "Once I promised to take a boy in the
neighborhood to the circus and then backed down because it
turned out to be the day of a big school event," Bea said.
"My father reacted as if I had committed a criminal act."

Frank described his own dad, Bea's grandfather, as a "no-
good lying drunk" who could not be counted on. His father's
colorful behavior increased in proportion to his alcohol consumption, making him a frequent focus of town gossip in
their small Oklahoma community. Frank's mother felt help-

less to deal directly with her husband or to leave him. By the time Frank was eight, he had assumed the role of his mother's confidant and emotional ally against his dad.

As the firstborn and only son, Frank set about to restore his family's good name through his own exemplary behavior. He was so overcontrolled that the danger of becoming undercontrolled may always have lurked in the shadows of his unconscious. His own "bad" and mutinous impulses must have terrified him, as they suggested he was like his dad and so might betray his mom.

Frank's experience of his parents was so polarized that he could not acknowledge any competence in his "no-good father" or any shortcomings in his "perfect mother," whom he described as a saint. Even after his parents' death, Frank remained "for Mom" and "against Dad," never gaining a broader, more richly textured understanding and integration of family patterns and his part in them. As a man, Frank always knew who the good and bad guys were—and whose side he was on.

This emotional legacy deeply colored his expectations, perceptions, and reactions to his children, particularly to Rob, also a firstborn and only son. Frank's unconscious fear that his son would be like his own father (combined, perhaps, with his wish that Rob would act out the unacceptable impulses that Frank denied in himself) contributed to a particularly anxious emotional climate for father and son.

As Bea learned more about her dad's family, she was able to understand why being "honest" and "rule-abiding," particularly in the eyes of the community, was not just a virtue or a deeply held value to Frank. It was, instead, a rigid, anxiety-driven focus of concern.

* * *

When anxiety is high enough, or lasts long enough, parents can lose the capacity to separate their emotional issues from ours. A woman told the following story at a National Women's Studies Association meeting: When she was a teenager, her mother, a Holocaust survivor, constantly pressured her to eat more and put on weight. Why? Because "in the camps" her mother explained, "those people who had a few extra pounds could survive a few extra days."

How crazy such thinking sounded to an American-born daughter! Yet this mother was doing what parents usually do, even when they have not been traumatized. Parents do not view their children objectively, as separate "real" selves. Rather, our parents see us through the distorting filter of their own history and life circumstances. Indeed, it was to this mother's credit that she could connect her current behavior with a past trauma, thus giving her daughter some context in which to understand her anxious concern about weight. In response to her daughter's challenge, she could have yelled back, "Because this is what we do in this family!" or, "Because you must eat more to stay alive!" When parents get intensely focused on some aspect of a child's behavior, they typically have no clue about what force from their own past is driving them.

Families are not fair, and we do not choose the family we are born into. Our parents, being human, cannot create the perfect climate, like a garden greenhouse, to foster the blossoming of our true, authentic selves. Too much has happened long before we even enter the scene. When viewed over several generations, no family is free from the emotional ripples or, more accurately, the tidal waves that result from anxious events—immigrations, cut-offs, poverty, and untimely losses—that affect a family's functioning over generations.

Nor do we have one "true self" that might unfold in

some ideal "free" environment, unfettered by roles, rules, traditions, and myths of family, culture, and context. The self does not "unfold," but instead is continually reinvented and re-storied through our interactions with others. Depending on a multiplicity of factors, including time, place, and historical circumstance, we have more (or less) space to be open and flexible in this process.

As adults, we can choose how honestly and authentically we navigate relationships with our first family. Moves toward greater truth-telling require us to define ourselves more clearly, to see others more objectively, to talk straight about issues that matter, and to acknowledge in oneself and others the full, shifting range of competencies and vulnerabilities that make us human. This is where honesty, truth-telling, and "realness" begin. Not with the revelation or the uncovering of dramatic deceptions and secrets, but rather with the dailiness of what we call "being oneself."

Adults have the capacity to reshape the emotional climate of family relationships and to be inventive about truth-telling. Children also influence other family members and make their own choices about concealment and disclosure. A child's capacity for thinking and problem solving, however, is limited, and is coupled with a condition of total economic and emotional dependence. Children are the least empowered family members; as such they can afford to take few risks, whether real or imagined, with adults on whom their very survival depends.

Our Mothers' Stories

When I first saw Bea in therapy, she never disclosed anything of emotional significance to her family members. When her mother asked, "How are you?", Bea replied, "Fine." Only much later could Bea venture to say, "Well, I'm not so fine. I just broke off with this guy and I'm feeling terrible." Such a disclosure might not impress us as a bold act of truth-telling, but it was for Bea, who ultimately learned to appreciate her mother's predictable response ("Oh, you're not really sad, honey") as nothing more than *information* about Ruth's way of managing anxiety. Instead of retreating back into silence and blame, Bea found creative ways to continue the conversation.

Sometimes Bea teased Ruth about her avoidant behavior ("Hey, Mom, are you allergic to sadness? Or do you think that I'm not tough enough to handle feeling miserable?"). She also challenged her in a light, caring way ("So, Mom, when did you start working for the American Red Cross? How did you get this job of rushing in to rescue me by changing the subject every time I'm down?"). As Bea felt calmer and more centered in her mother's presence, she began to ask questions that expanded the context surrounding her mother's behavior.

Bea told Ruth that she would be able to get a better grip on her own ups and downs if she could learn something about how other women in the extended family had managed depression and grief. She asked about Aunt Rhonda, Aunt Mary, Grandma Belle, and Great-Grandma Trina. How depressed had the most depressed family member ever gotten? How did other family members respond? In what generation did this allergy to depression start? What was Ruth's "philosophy" on dealing with depression, and how did it differ from Grandma Belle's beliefs? What was the saddest thing that had ever happened in the family over the past two hundred years?

* * *

As Bea became a more skilled questioner, her mother became more disclosing. When I first met Bea, she was too angry and intense to broach an emotionally loaded subject with Ruth. Intensity breeds more intensity, only adding to the anxious emotional climate that blocked truth-telling to begin with. Moves toward truth-telling may require us to maintain a calm, emotional presence in an anxious emotional field. Paradoxically, this translates into being "less real" in order to help create an emotional climate in which people can be "more real." That is, if "being real" is defined as doing what comes naturally, which in Bea's case meant angrily avoiding or confronting Ruth. This kind of "realness" or "truth-telling" invariably shuts the lines of communication down even further.

What a huge challenge it is to arrive at a place where our wish to understand the other person is as great as our wish to be understood! Only when Bea had reached that point could her mother begin to share her stories and to reveal her secrets. Bea, who knew only of Ruth's two sisters, learned that her mother had had a twin brother who drowned at the age of three in a lake on family property. Ruth's mother, Grandma Belle, felt overwhelmingly guilty for not having supervised her son more closely. She subsequently drowned in her own grief, never surfacing long enough to breathe fully again. When Grandma Belle died at age sixty-three, all her son's clothes, toys, and possessions were just as they had been on the day he died. Ruth said, "Time stopped for my mother on that day."

In response to their loss, Bea's grandparents were rigidly polarized. Grandmother could do nothing but grieve while Grandfather could do anything but grieve. They blamed each other for their respective coping styles, and a chilly distance settled like fog into the cracks and corners of their household. Marital problems intensified further because Grandma Belle felt certain that her husband's family blamed her for the drowning, although no one spoke directly to the subject of responsibility and blame. Grandma Belle told Ruth she was devastated by her husband's failure to support her, although she could not speak out on her own behalf either, nor even forgive herself. The family drew apart, with no professional or community resources available to help them support each other in their grief so that they could move ahead with the business of living.

No wonder Ruth was at a loss to respond to her daughter's unhappiness, or to know what to do with her own. Ruth grew up with two adults who pushed the extremes in managing depression and vulnerability. Her father's philosophy was to press forward and "get on with things," as he put it. Her mother, for her part, could get on with nothing. Somewhere along the line, Ruth chose her dad's way for herself and for her own daughter as well. Whenever she noticed Bea showing the normal tears and vulnerabilities of childhood, she also saw, at those very moments, her own mother never coming out of grief. It probably didn't help matters that Bea bore a striking physical resemblance to Grandma Belle, for whom she was named.

Ruth never grieved for her lost twin, worried as she was about her mother's relentless sorrow and the climate of bitterness between her parents. Ruth's underreaction was in direct proportion to her mother's overreaction. "I never cried for my dead brother," Ruth said, "and I haven't cried at a funeral since." At a particularly honest moment, Ruth told Bea, "Maybe I can't stand seeing you upset because if I ever let myself cry, I'm afraid I'd never stop." Later, Ruth did cry in conversation with her daughter, and she did stop.

Bea was ultimately able to tell Ruth why her "protectiveness" was problematic. She let her mother know specifically what she found helpful when she was depressed. Ruth was able to tell Bea how "clutchy" she felt when Bea was feeling down, and she also said frankly that worrying was the only way she knew to be close to her daughter. Their conversation continues, I hope, to this day.

8

~

Honesty versus Truth

Not long ago, I had the privilege to introduce the performing artist Holly Near at a Menninger women's conference. I felt unusually anxious about my role in this event because Holly is one of my favorite singers, as well as a political heroine and role model in my life. I had sat in the audience at many of her concerts, and here she was, from Carnegie Hall to the Ramada Inn in Topeka, Kansas. I was as nervous as I was thrilled to walk on stage and introduce her.

But at the height of my anxiety, a friend pulled me aside and criticized my behavior earlier that day: I had failed to make an appropriate introduction and had left her feeling invisible and unimportant. She was correct about my behavior, but not about my motives. I apologized and explained that it had been my "spaciness" at work rather than any lack of love and regard for her. I just hadn't paid attention.

The next day my friend apologized to me for her bad timing. She knew how anxious I was before this big event and she also knew, firsthand, the terrors of public speaking. After confronting me, she later regretted having acted on her feelings of the moment and wished she had waited a day to reproach me. I appreciated her apology and told her so. I want my friends to be honest and spontaneous with me, but I also want them to consider my feelings. I want to hear their criticisms, but not at moments when I feel the most vulnerable or overloaded.

Most people can probably name countless examples in their own lives when their timing, or someone else's, has been off. Or when a bit of tact might not only have spared someone pain, but might also have maximized the chances that two people would really listen to each other, rather than anxiously *react*. When I was younger, I believed that timing and tact were the opposites of honesty. Now I believe instead that timing and tact are what make truth-telling possible in the most difficult circumstances and in regard to the toughest subjects.

Nor do I feel compelled to tell "the whole truth" to people who aren't important to me. For example, I've turned down repeated lunch invitations from one woman I find obnoxious. When she asked me directly whether I was avoiding her for personal reasons, I said, "I'm so busy these days that I hardly see my close friends." This was true enough, but it begged the question. Had she been important to me, I would have struggled to figure out just what I found "obnoxious" about her, and I would have sought a way to talk with her about it.

Honesty in the Moment

Some of us equate "honesty" and "being ourselves" with the uncensored expression of thoughts and feelings. It is indeed wonderful to have a relationship so relaxed and intimate that we can share anything and everything without first thinking about it. Yet honesty, as so defined, may also block deeper levels of truth-telling. Consider Clark Moustakas's story about his struggle to distinguish between honesty and truth.

Moustakas, a psychotherapist who led encounter groups, was once advised by his colleagues that in order to be effective and to live a full life himself, he should learn to ferret out and evoke expressions of anger and conflict within the group experience. In so doing, he would find his own angry expressions, serving as a model for others. Although this advice suggested an alien path, not in keeping with "being himself" or with how he wanted to live, Moustakas did not want to close himself off from what might be learned by following his colleagues' advice. Still, he was not convinced that spontaneous angry encounters were necessary for authentic living and growing.

Nonetheless, for about six months, Moustakas pushed himself to experiment with the "anger formula" he had been told was essential to the group process. He found that while it took only minutes to express his anger, it took hours to deal with its consequences. The group meetings were lively but troubling. He observed the upheaval and havoc he was causing in the lives of others, particularly since his own communications as group leader carried great weight.

Eventually, Moustakas experienced stomach pains, headaches, and other physical symptoms that he interpreted as a sign the confrontational style of leadership was alienating him from his own values. He began to ask himself questions: What was the real value of honesty? What was happening to him in these emotional encounters? Then he began to consider deeper questions: Who am I? What do I seek in my life with others? What are my values, ideals, desires?

When others had categorized his previously nonconfrontive leadership style as a weakness or a lack, Moustakas had responded with a willingness to experiment. In the process, however, his body signaled its own truths. Ultimately, Moustakas concluded that he had abandoned a vital pattern of being: "I came to see that my body tensions and headaches were a protest against the denial of my own self. Thus while I was being 'honest' in the moment when I angrily confronted other people, my honesty was often a lie in the sense that it denied something essential in me, something rooted in the values and ways of my life."

Like Moustakas, or anyone else, I hold values, beliefs, and goals that may transcend the impulse to "be myself" or to "be honest," without invitation, at any particular moment. I do not, for example, wish to hurt another human being unnecessarily. I value kindness and compassion. Sometimes the very urgency or intensity of my emotions is the red flag that signals me to stop and think, to separate out fleeting reactions from my more enduring and significant feelings.

I also do not want to be "honest" at my own expense. In certain situations, my efforts to be open and frank have led downward in a spiraling process that made me the focus of negative attention or concern. There have been countless instances in my personal and professional life when being strategic rather than spontaneous was the best approach toward deepening levels of knowing and truth-telling.

With honesty, as with all good things, we can have too much. If a casual acquaintance spills out her deepest feelings and darkest secrets at an office party, we may question her maturity rather than admire her openness. As we grow up, we learn to restrain our uncensored selves, and to make thoughtful and informed choices about how and when to tell what to whom.

Is It Our Anxious, or Real, Selves?

During the writing of my previous books on the subjects of anger and intimacy, I struggled with a conceptual tangle regarding momentary honesty and enduring truth-telling. Sometimes I felt as if I were wearing two different hats, or taking my readers in two directions at once.

On the one hand, my goal was to legitimize the open, direct, and forthright expression of female anger and protest. As subordinate group members, women operate under profound injunctions against voicing any thoughts or feelings that might threaten others or disrupt relationship harmony.

On the other hand, my clinical practice was filled with women who were venting their "real feelings" in a manner that *protected* rather than *protested* the status quo. Getting angry was getting nowhere or even making things worse. My clients' efforts to "tell the truth" or to "be honest" often froze relationships rather than moved them forward.

In my efforts to guide my readers, I sometimes felt like the English professor who wrote on a student's composition, "Be yourself!" and then added, "If this is yourself, be someone else."

Some efforts to be truthful reflect a simple failure to protect ourselves. Sally, a teacher of learning-disabled children, consulted with me after receiving a performance evaluation that failed to do justice to the high quality of her work. Her senior supervisor, a distant man who didn't relate well to the students, criticized Sally as being "too emotional" and "over-involved with individual children at the expense of group discipline." In Sally's opinion, her supervisor had little knowledge of her actual work. She was incensed by his criticism, which labeled as a "weakness" what Sally believed to be the very essence of her strength with the children.

At the first opportunity, Sally confronted her supervisor. She began on a reasonably calm note, but when he became defensive and argumentative, Sally responded with interpretations: "I think that *you* have trouble relating to people and that you have a problem with my style. The children really connect with me, and I believe there's an issue of competition in our relationship that you've never dealt with." The next day, a colleague reported her supervisor's reaction: "Sally's immature response to her evaluation only confirms its accuracy."

The situation deteriorated even more as Sally focused tenaciously on convincing her supervisor of the truth, and he, in response, dug in his heels. Sally then turned to her co-workers, criticizing her supervisor and pressing the other teachers to side with her against him. Perhaps they, too, had complaints about him; however, the zealousness with which Sally attacked him led them to respond in his defense. The more Sally voiced her anger, the more the other women denied their own.

It was evident that Sally was contributing to her own isolation and distress. Her attempt to convince other people of her side of things elicited their disapproval and defensiveness rather than their sympathy. This only increased Sally's sense of bitterness and injustice, and a vicious cycle ensued. Yet when Sally first came to see me, she didn't question her own behavior. She believed unequivocally in saying *what* she felt *when* she felt it, particularly when she felt that truth was on her side. She didn't distinguish between honesty in work situations and honesty in intimate relationships where closeness is the goal.

If, indeed, Sally's first priority was to confront her boss with the full force of her emotionality, irrespective of his response, then her behavior was congruent with her values. From this perspective, she was, indeed, "doing the right thing." But as Sally felt increasingly unhappy at work, she began to reconsider what she wanted to accomplish. Did she simply want to express her feelings to her supervisor? If so, was it necessary or useful to try to process the underground issue of competition, or anything else, between them? Or did she want instead to maximize her chances of being heard and reevaluated, or evaluated more positively the next time around?

When Sally decided that she wanted to champion her own cause more effectively, she shifted gears, interacted more thoughtfully, and proceeded with greater awareness of what she wanted to accomplish and how her behavior affected those around her. She ultimately stood firmly and assertively behind her position, but without becoming defensive or attacking. Her earlier honesty not only reflected a failure to protect and regard herself; it also made it more difficult for her supervisor to be objective or to appreciate the truth of her position.

Truth-telling obviously requires us to "be ourselves." But it may also require us to exercise restraint, as we consider matters of timing and tact, and what we hope to accomplish in a relationship. Also, it takes time and effort to clarify for ourselves—no less for others—what we really think and feel, and where we stand on important issues. At the very moment we lay claim to being "most honest," we may be anxiously reacting to the other person rather than expressing our deepest feelings. Whatever we experience with the greatest emotional intensity may be what we may mistakenly assume to be "most real."

Thinking versus Emoting

Consider, for example, a nineteen-year-old woman, Peg, who has invited her mother, Anna, to join her in therapy sessions with me so that they can "resolve their relationship." Their interactions are colorful and intense; each blames the other for her unhappiness and confronts her with "the truth" as she sees it. A psychiatric resident, who observes several sessions from behind a one-way mirror, tells me he is impressed that "real feelings" are being expressed.

From my perspective, however, there is little exchange of real feelings between this mother and daughter, although I don't doubt the presence of real pain. The contagious reactivity between them is so high that they behave like two nervous systems hooked together. Almost any topic triggers immediate intensity from the other, so that within moments they are rigidly polarized in opposing camps. Neither can identify and address the core issues, hear the other objectively, or take a position without blaming or telling the other what to do.

Anna and Peg are unquestionably honest with each other. Their freedom to give full vent to their emotions may well be a testimony to the durability of their mother-daughter bond. Surely, their fighting keeps them connected. But they are not in a process of truth-telling, of knowing and being known, of refining and deepening their disclosures to one another. To help them move in this direction, I remain a calm presence in this anxious emotional field and begin to ask questions that facilitate thinking rather than emoting.

Multiple sources of anxiety fuel reactivity in any family relationship. As I question Anna, I learn that her younger sister recently died and that Anna's husband has been unsupportive at this difficult time. Also, her daughter Peg, at nineteen, is now the same age that Anna was when her own father abandoned the family. At this time, Anna sacrificed her plans to study art and design, returning home instead to care for her devastated mother. Caretaking became Anna's full-time job until she married and got pregnant with Peg. She never resumed her career plans.

Now Peg is planning to head west to study violin at a conservatory of music. Without consciously knowing Anna's history of loss and self-sacrifice at her age, Peg nonetheless senses her mother's underlying grief. And Peg is nothing short of masterful at pushing her mother's buttons and sustaining a lively, angry engagement that protects her mother from becoming depressed. As therapy progresses, Peg discovers that she prefers dealing with a "bitchy" mother rather than a sad mother. She fears she could lose herself in waves of compassion for her mother's life, and lose sight of her own wishes for independence, making her struggle to pursue her career goals even harder.

This is not to deny the importance, or the necessity, for giving full voice to our immediate and uncensored reactions. We may—in a particular moment of truth—swear, scream, moan, curse the darkness, or otherwise show another person the full force of our rage or pain. I value the raw, unbridled emotional exchanges I have shared with my husband, which are part of knowing each other so deeply and trusting that we can survive almost anything. But I am glad that these are only moments, that they are few and far between, and that we can step back from them to reflect and talk about what they mean. I also value my capacity to withhold or conceal my emotions, and to use both intuition and thinking to make choices about whom to tell what.

No single moment of honesty, self-disclosure, revelation, or emotionality can determine how truth-telling will proceed over time. Truth-telling is a *process*—and one that cannot be sustained in a chronically anxious or distant emotional field. Remember how Bea managed to reconnect with her mother, Ruth, before asking her about the legacy of depression in their family? Rather than confronting her mother in a blaming way, Bea kept the emotional intensity down by teasing her about being allergic to depression. And as Bea learned to interpret her mother's avoidant behaviors as expressions of anxiety, rather than as personal rejection, she was able to "lighten up" around Ruth. She worked slowly over time to create the conditions of safety that ultimately allowed Ruth to reveal the secret of her twin brother's death, and the family's reaction to that loss.

Most family relationships are emotionally intense, although when the intensity is managed by distancing, it gives an appearance of calm. Anna and Peg—like Bea and Ruth—moved forward in the process of truth-telling only after they were able to reflect on the broader context in which their intensity developed. Only then could they listen respectfully (rather than reactively) to each other. And as Peg slowly became genuinely interested in her mother's history, she began to understand that this was her history as well, and thus "about her." As a true exchange of stories took place, they both developed a more accurate and objective picture of themselves and each other.

Truth-telling in families is a slow, bumpy process without end. Each question and each disclosure evokes new questions, new feelings, and new disclosures. The revelation of personal feelings, or previously concealed information, can mark the beginning of future disclosures and uncoverings, or the opposite. Depending on how we define honesty, it may impede or facilitate truth-telling.

My dictionary equates honesty with moral excellence: honesty implies truthfulness, integrity, sincerity, fairness, and an absence of deception or fraud. As so defined, honesty is unarguably—and always—essential to the process of truth-telling. But when people reveal personal examples of "honesty," they typically focus on incidents when they have reacted, sometimes after a long silence. "I finally got up the courage to tell my mother that she's ruining my sister's life," one woman says. Another explains, "I told my boss that he's totally insecure and threatened by competent women." Yet another reveals, "I called my mother on her birthday and said, 'Sit down, Mom, I'm a dyke.'" When one tracks the specific interactional sequences following disclosures like these (who said what, when, and then what), they often result in the relationship shifting from bad to worse. The solution to the problem is not to become less honest, but rather to become better truth-tellers.

Truth-Telling as a Process

During my college year in India, I conducted research on the attitudes of a young group of Harijan ("Untouchable") women toward the caste system. Although the caste system had been legally abolished, its rigid hierarchical structure still pervaded some aspects of Hindu society. Harijan women remained in the lowest position in the social stratum, in essence outside the system. My questions of these women concerned their attitudes toward untouchability and the caste system, and whether they internalized the deep-rooted prejudices against them. I wanted to know how they viewed their lack of status and opportunity. How did they feel about being assigned by birth to the "low and dirty" work of cleaning latrines and sweeping dirt with inadequate brooms? What of value or comfort did they find in their assigned, unalterable roles? What changes did they hope for and how might these come about?

Although these questions were deeply personal, I hoped not to be lied to, or shunned, or viewed with suspicion. To this end, I did not parachute down to their village from the sky, pencil and pad in hand, and begin my soul-searching inquiry. First, I studied the language and culture. I worked with the women daily, cared for their children, and participated with them in major life cycle events such as births, weddings, and funerals. Before asking the more difficult questions that my research required, I talked with each woman about everyday concerns.

Then I formulated my questions with care, so as to minimize any anxiety, shame, or discomfort they might evoke. I also listened with care, suspending all judgment. Still, my research did not always proceed smoothly. My Hindi wasn't good enough to work without a translator. My presence did not always inspire trust. The interviews were not conducted "my way," either. A woman might fail to show up for an interview scheduled at noon, but then arrive in the early evening with five extended family members. Although the process was sometimes frustrating, I learned a great deal. I attributed problems and misunderstandings to cultural differences and my status as an outsider.

In a culture closer to home, such as our own families, however, we are so emotionally hooked into the system that we can easily lose, or never develop, such a process-oriented view of gathering and sharing information. Instead, we may descend on our family with our own agenda, and without having laid any groundwork for truth-telling. We may know next to nothing about our parents' history and culture. We may have maintained only superficial contact, if that, over the years. We may have exerted only minimal effort to attend or even acknowledge important family events. We may have little objective perspective on family patterns and our part in them. We may approach a family secret or "hot issue" in a clumsy or confrontational way.

Then, when we meet with resistance, we may bolt rather than be able to implement a long-term plan for whatever it is we hope to accomplish. As a result, we may be too quick to blame and diagnose the other person ("My father just won't talk about the past") rather than to consider how we, ourselves, might become more skilled and patient in gathering information.

Of course, we will always be more reactive and "twitchy" when we are within a system rather than outside it. That's why therapists and consultants can be invaluable to families, businesses, and other organizations, particularly if they can avoid being drawn into the anxious emotional field they are there to observe. But even in the midst of the problems, even when we're in the soup, we can learn skills for climbing out and getting clearer about the real isues and how best to address difficult truths.

Anthropologists know how much is to be learned before carrrying out research projects like the one I undertook as a college student in India. As a family systems therapist, I know how much is to be learned about opening up conversations within families and other systems where lies, secrets, and silence have prevailed. Whether the "hot issue" is incest, religion, a father's drinking, marital dissatisfaction, or a daughter's responsibility for an aging parent, one theme emerges clearly in my work with families. Doing what comes naturally may just as naturally land us in trouble. In the name of either "honesty" or "truth," we are likely to drive anxiety higher rather than promote the conditions of safety that encourage truth-telling. Much of what we call "telling the truth" involves an unproductive effort to change, convince, or convert another person, rather than an attempt to clarify our own selves.

To discover new truths or reaffirm old ones, we must be willing to experiment with different ways of being in relationships and to persevere in the face of resistance. Issues that cannot be talked about frankly (and relationships in which real talk occurs rarely, if at all) have often been encapsulated in anxiety from generation to generation. It is no surprise that substantive change occurs slowly, with inevitable frustrations and derailments. Our challenge is to approach "high-twitch" subjects in ways that are likely to sustain connection rather than cut-off, and to maximize the opportunity for deepening conversation over time, rather than "hit-and-run" disclosures, revelations, and confrontations.

"Why bother?" That was my response to a friend many years ago who challenged me to open up an emotion-laden issue in my own family—slowly, responsibly, and with care, and with a plan to manage the inevitable resistance evoked by change. Interestingly, it was no bother to me to try steadily yet clumsily to be in conversation with women halfway around the world. Today, my response would be, instead, "Why *not* bother?" There is, perhaps, no more direct route to discovering our own truths than to unearth the stories in our immediate and extended family. The stories of our family members are *our* stories, these stories "are us," and it is in the exchanging and refining of personal experiences that we can come to know our own truths.

9

~

Just Pretending

L et's pretend!"
      And why not? Pretending can be a creative, even magical act. A child says to her best friend, "Let's pretend we're astronauts." A teacher says to her dance students, "Pretend that you're an animal of your choosing and *be* that animal." Pretending stretches our imagination, enhances empathy, expands our sense of possibility, and provides a vehicle for self-expression and self-discovery.

When pretending involves deception—as it often does— it can still be a playful form of inventiveness and "make-believe." One of my most cherished childhood memories is of riding the train from Brooklyn to Manhattan with my sister, Susan, who was taking me to the fanciest stores on Fifth Avenue. Our parents could only afford to give us subway tokens, but we planned to masquerade as millionaires. Our first stop was Tiffany's: "Do you think we should buy Mother this diamond necklace for her birthday?" I inquired loudly of Susan, pointing to the most expensive item in view and hoping to capture the attention of the well-heeled shoppers nearby. "Oh, don't be silly!" Susan replied in her most grown-up, haughty voice. "Mother has several *exactly* like it, you know." In this way, we spent a happy, memorable afternoon.

But pretending can also be a most serious venture: "I pretended to be sleeping whenever my father came into my room and touched me"; "He escaped the Nazis by pretending he was a crazy man"; "My brother and I tried to pretend that things were normal in our family." When reality is limiting, harsh, or dangerous, pretending is an act of coping, self-preservation, and survival.

Between what is playful and what is desperate, we could name countless forms and functions of pretending in everyday life. Whether the intention is to dazzle or distract, confuse or camouflage, masquerade or malinger, impress or impersonate, pretending is an ever present adaptational strategy throughout all of nature. A particular act of pretending may elicit censure ("Why must she always pretend to have it all together?") or admiration ("I was amazed that she was able to give such an uplifting performance when her heart was breaking"). In either case, the human capacity to hide the real and display the false is truly extraordinary, allowing us to regulate relationships through highly complex choices about how we present ourselves to others.

But how do we distinguish pretending from other forms of deception, such as lying. Interestingly, people do routinely distinguish between the two, at least where their own behavior is concerned. When, for example, I ask friends to provide me with specific examples of lies they have told recently, there is an initial, palpable silence. Not so when I ask the same friends for examples of pretending: "I pretended to be out when my friend called"; "I acted like I was interested in the conversation"; "I pretended that nothing was wrong when I had lunch with my folks"; "When she was telling me about the authors who influenced her work, I kept nodding my head as if I had heard of them."

Not one person asked me to define my terms. People assumed that they knew when they were pretending, and to what end. Unlike other forms of deception, acts of pretending were described without defensiveness or apology, and with conscious recognition of their adaptive value. A young woman called Beth whom I met briefly in Denver described an incident of pretending that highlights how we typically distinguish between pretending and lying.

Beth, an experienced woodswoman, had recently led a group of Girl Scouts on a weekend wilderness trip. A severe and unexpected thunderstorm washed out the main trails and created hazardous conditions. Beth lost her way, and went from feeling nervous to fearing for the survival of the group. Teetering on the edge of panic, Beth "talked herself down," as she put it, and forced herself to act as if she was feeling calm and confident. On top of this deception, she added another: "I pretended to myself that I was an actor, that the group was being filmed for a television show, and that the film crew was just out of sight." In this way, she managed to get a grip on her anxiety and to keep a clear head.

In Beth's situation, pretending had clear adaptational advantages over authenticity. Beth's primary task was to ensure the safety of the group, not share her true feelings. "Fear can be contagious," she explained, "and I didn't want mine spilling over into the group." Feigning courage and calm also helped her muster these qualities in herself. "When I let myself feel fear, I become more fearful," Beth explained. "When I act brave, I'm better able to *be* brave."

There's a postscript to this story. In the Scout meeting that followed this dramatic adventure, Beth encouraged the girls to talk about the experience. Early in the discussion, one girl said to Beth, "You were telling us not to worry, but you looked scared to me." Several other girls nodded in assent. They, too, had picked up on Beth's anxiety but had also pretended not to notice it.

Beth calmly explained that she had, indeed, felt scared, particularly because she was responsible for their safety. To veer from truth-telling at this juncture would have required Beth to lie. The group's primary task now was emotional rather than functional: the job at hand involved processing the frightening experience they had been through together. Beth felt that anything short of the facts would disqualify the girls' perceptions, invalidate their sense of reality, and impair their trust in authority. She intuitively decided how much to share—for example, she didn't describe the morbid images of dead Girl Scouts that flashed through her mind when she was most afraid. But she knew that honesty was essential to helping the group process their experience and move on.

A Definition of Terms

What *are* the distinguishing features of pretending?

First, pretending conveys the possibility—and sometimes even the wish—to fool not only others but also oneself. When Beth, for example, pretended to be calm and courageous, she wanted most of all to convince herself.

Second, this word describes feigning or faking, but not stating a lie. As my younger son Ben put it, "I can pretend that I'm not angry with my friend. But if he says, 'Are you angry at me?' and I say, 'No,' then I'm lying." His example reminded me of my friend Sue, who didn't feel dishonest passing as a nurse because she didn't explicitly lie about her status.

The third and most salient feature of pretending builds on the first two. Like sexual pretending, pretending in general (at least from the pretender's perspective) implies a *mild* act of feigning or faking that neither rattles the conscience nor demands careful examination. We don't typically associate the word with a shattering personal betrayal, a flagrant lie, or an unforgivable breach of trust. Rather, it calls to mind the suggestion that this particular form of insincerity or false appearance is personally okay or culturally sanctioned.

According to one dictionary, pretending is "mild in force" and implies "no evil." The two dictionaries in my library don't even include the words "lie" or "deceive" among the synonyms provided. Pretending is a "soft" verb. As such, it is the form of deception we are least likely to scrutinize. The very word "pretending," like the word "privacy," invites us *not* to pay attention.

And yet, as I listen to women reveal how they pretend in their own personal lives, I hear stories of grave, ongoing deceptions. Of necessity, these must be shored up by lying and self-betrayal: "I pretended that I was in love with him, because I was desperate to get married"; "I pretended to want sex"; "I pretended to enjoy motherhood"; "I pretended to be happy in my marriage." Patriarchy schools women to pretend as a virtual way of life, and then trivializes its eroding effects on ourselves and our partners.

Women's ways of pretending demand our most careful attention. We must take pretending seriously, precisely because we are taught not to. Pretending, by definition, is inconsequential. But this itself is a lie, or at best only a partial truth. If women stopped pretending tomorrow, the world as we know it would also stop. So, too, is the case with "privacy." What is private is by definition nobody's business but our own. But when women collectively came forth and made the private public—then all that we took to be "true" under patriarchy was challenged and reviewed.

Contrary to what the dictionary tells us, pretending is potentially the most serious form of deception because it can involve *living* a lie, rather than telling one. And we are least likely to catch ourselves in the act. When we tell an outright lie, we feel jolted. But pretending is imperceptibly woven into the fabric of daily life and so leads to the construction of a false self. We may not feel any jolts along the way, because we are, after all, "just pretending." In time, we don't notice ourselves doing it at all.

Pretending, patriarchal style, deadens our passion, calcifies our choices, and blocks us from knowing and acting on our own truths. But there are also other types of pretending that can help rather than harm us.

There is pretending that enlightens and enlivens, that leads us to invent and discover new truths, that helps us not only to find but also to choose ourselves. This kind of pretending is illustrated by Beth's comment, "When I act brave, I'm better able to *be* brave." Bold and courageous acts of pretending can help clarify and expand what is real and true about ourselves, just as momentary honesty can impede truth-telling.

Beth's story about feigning courage with her Girl Scouts reminds me of my own efforts at pretense during a time of crisis. Shortly after President George Bush declared war in the Gulf, I was scheduled to present a workshop in Texas. I didn't want to go. I felt despair about living under a government more concerned with profits and power than with human lives, in particular, with lives of color. For the first time in my adult life, I felt that my work made absolutely no difference in the world. My professional focus on individuals and families seemed wildly unimportant.

As I packed for the workshop, I cried about the war and felt hopeless about the world's future. I decided, however, to pretend to feel hope, because I believe that maintaining hope is a moral imperative. As long as we can *feel* hope, there is hope. Also, for me, acting hopeful was perhaps the quickest route to being hopeful.

At the workshop I talked about warring families and warring nations. I focused on the extraordinary challenge of moving from blaming people toward understanding escalating patterns of conflict and our own part in them. I told the participants that my firsthand experience with individuals and families who have successfully met this challenge in the most difficult of circumstances encouraged me to maintain hope. As I stood at the podium and made these comments, I actually felt hopeful. I was no longer pretending, although that had been my starting point.

If I had truly lost all capacity to feel hope at the time of the Gulf war, pretending would have been of no value to me. I have never been able to shake myself free from pain or pessimism with false reassurances that deny a deeper reality. Glib affirmations to "think positively" and "look on the bright side" can alienate us from our bodies and our unconscious, by serving to conceal emotional complexity rather than uncover what is hidden or lost. Sometimes, however, we only learn what is true, or real, or possible, or "still there" by experimenting with pretending and by restraining our so-called true selves.

The Courage to Pretend

An attorney friend of mine, Molly, called me for advice on a family matter. She had just returned from her brother's wedding in Des Moines, where things hadn't gone well. Molly told me that their mother, Ethel, had been narcissistic and self-centered, trying to control the whole show and coldly distancing when things didn't go her way. Ethel disapproved of the non-traditional wedding ceremony, and she sat through it with a look of undisguised exasperation. There were no raised voices during the four-day family gathering, but an unremitting tension had settled between mother and daughter.

Molly's mother, whom I had met briefly on several occasions, was a competent, energetic, "take-charge" person. Although Molly valued her mother's style, she didn't respond well to its more extreme manifestations, which predictably surfaced at anxious times such as family events. I asked Molly whether Ethel would have behaved differently if Molly's father, Sam, had survived his unexpected heart attack fifteen months earlier. As far as Molly knew, he hadn't been mentioned during the ceremony or in any family conversation. Molly's response to my question was, "Thank God he didn't live to see it!" Sam had been a rabbi. The bride had been raised Catholic. The wedding took place in a Unitarian Fellowhip, and the woman marrying them was, as Molly put it, "weird." No wonder, I joked with Molly, that everyone seemed a bit tense.

When Molly returned home to Lawrence, Kansas, her anger at her mother mounted rather than dissipated. She sat down at the computer and wrote her mother a four-page, single-spaced letter. In it she shared her observations of the recent family dynamics, with particular emphasis on Ethel's self-centered behavior and Molly's reactions to it. True to her legalistic background, she documented each point in careful detail. In an attempt to be fair, she also noted the contributions of herself and other family members to the problems. She concluded by saying: "I know we have all contributed to the dysfunction of our family, as well as to the denial of this dysfunction."

Although Molly felt driven to write the letter ("Someone has to tell the truth in this family"), she found herself hesitant to mail it, and called me instead to get a different perspective on the situation. I asked her whether she was aiming for momentary honesty or enduring truth-telling. That is, did she want to share her reactions with her mother, as Sally first did with her supervisor, irrespective of the response she might evoke? If so, then mail the letter. Or did she want to take the hard road and begin to lay the groundwork for greater truth-telling to develop? Molly indicated the second choice.

Molly wanted my reaction to her letter, and she asked specifically what I'd do in her shoes. I told her that I wouldn't mail it. The letter was long and extremely intense. And the content was blaming, even though honesty, not blaming, was Molly's good intention. Since Molly had frequently complained to me in the past that her mother couldn't handle even minor criticism, she didn't need me to predict that Ethel would get defensive reading the letter.

What then, was the "right" way for Molly to proceed? There are undoubtedly many right ways. Molly, however, wanted to know what kind of letter I would write, based on the family systems perspective that guides my work as a therapist. I told her I'd write a shorter, chattier letter to Ethel. I'd keep it low-keyed, because I'd be aiming to reduce anxiety and reactivity, not raise it further. I'd address the family tension in a paragraph or two, rather than in a treatise. And

I'd stick to sharing my own truth rather than criticizing my mother.

"So, after commenting on the weather and the wheat fields, you'd say *what* in this paragraph or two?" Molly insisted. I told her that I would say something like the following:

"Mom, I felt some tension between us when I was home for the wedding. I'd be interested in hearing your thoughts, because I've been trying to sort my feelings out since I returned. I was pretty tense around the time of the wedding and I realize that this was the first time our family has been all together since Dad's death. I think the wedding was a vivid reminder to me that Dad isn't around anymore. I also find myself wondering how Dad would have reacted to the wedding, if he had lived to see it."

Molly said that the "low-keyed part" made sense to her, but that the rest didn't fit because she hadn't thought about her dad during the wedding or since. According to Molly, Sam had been a distant and critical father, whose death left her largely unaffected. As she mulled over our conversation the next day, however, she decided "to pretend," to try it out or "try it on," as she explained, to see what might be learned from such an experiment. She began the letter, but when she started to write the part about her dad, she burst into tears.

Molly's reluctant attempt at pretending ended up evoking real feelings. As she wrote the letter, her grief about her father surfaced, along with genuine curiosity about her mother's experience. What had it been like for Ethel to be at the wedding without Sam? How was she affected by knowing how upset Sam would have been about their son's departure from the family's religious and cultural tradition?

Molly mailed the new letter, and Ethel wrote back the same day that she received it. Molly described her mother's response as a long litany emphasizing how glad she was that Sam died before the wedding because the very thought of how he would have suffered caused Ethel more grief than anyone could imagine. Molly was initially taken aback by her mother's response, since Ethel's "poor me" attitude never failed to push her buttons. As we talked about the letter, however, Molly was able to step back a bit and regain a process-oriented view.

From my perspective, I viewed Ethel's response more positively, as evidence of her willingness to engage with her daughter around emotional subjects. Even if Ethel had failed to respond to Molly's communication, I would not have felt particularly discouraged. Rather, I would have viewed Ethel's distancing as information about her way of managing anxiety, and I would have encouraged Molly to think about where to go from there.

Molly responded to her mother with a note that asked a few empathic rather than critical questions. For example, she expressed interest in how her paternal grandparents had responded to Ethel and Sam's wedding years earlier. Although Molly's grandparents had been orthodox Jews, her parents had been married in a reformed synagogue, thus departing significantly from the traditions of the previous generation. Molly worded her questions respectfully, rather than in her usual legalistic manner. She learned that her paternal grandmother had been too upset to attend the wedding, and that Ethel had never felt accepted by her mother-in-law. This revelation eventually led to her mother disclosing other family stories and secrets that had never been told, nor asked about.

Over time, Molly began to address the question of how differences were managed in their family. She shared with Ethel her observation that many of their family members seemed to have a hard time with differences, and that the problem appeared to be generations in the making. "As I get older," Molly wrote, "I'm realizing that loving my family doesn't mean we all have to be the same." In a subsequent phone call to her mother, Molly mentioned that she felt as if both Sam and Ethel reacted critically whenever she did something differently than Ethel would. And so, her relationship with her mother began to move forward, although with some moves backward. Most importantly, however, Molly began to see more movement forward than backward over time.

We can approach truth-telling as a lifelong process, or as hit-and-run confrontation. We can be focused on our own part in the process, or on "getting" a certain response. Obviously, we will all yo-yo back and forth between reflection and reactivity, but it is useful to think about where we ultimately want to stand.

Truth-telling, as we have seen, is a thing of accumulation. Truths are not "told" but rather enlarged on and refined over time. Like a long-distance run, truth-telling takes endurance, the capacity to push forward in the face of enormous resistance. At the same time, truth-telling requires restraint. It asks us to sit still when we feel fired up to act. Finally, it requires us to develop the wisdom and intuition to know when to do what.

Realistically speaking, we're not wired to take the high road. With Molly, I could easily adopt a thoughtful, process-oriented view of change, because it's not my family and it does fall within my area of professional expertise. Like an anthropologist studying a society to which she does not belong, I can hear Molly—as I heard the Harijan women in

India—with interest and curiosity. If I view Molly as an emissary from a complex culture, I can more easily see that over many generations, her family has developed a set of values, beliefs, and rules that govern each member's behavior around the difficult issues that can't easily be talked about. I can also appreciate the slow pace often required by truth-telling and the necessity at some points to move at glacial speed.

Yet, in my own family, I can lose objectivity as fast as anyone else does in theirs and it takes me effort to regain it. Humans lean toward dichotomous, polarized thinking under stress. As we divide into opposing camps, multiple and complex truths are easily lost, with each party overfocused on what the other is doing wrong and underfocused on our own options for moving differently. Whether we are talking about individuals or governments, it is a remarkable achievement to move against our automatic, patterned responses, which block the possibility of open conversation and the experience of a more nuanced and complex view of what we name reality. Changing how we habitually behave in a relationship may require an initial willingness to pretend, to act, to silence our automatic responses, to do something different even when it initially feels nothing like "being oneself." One can discover in pretending that one has allowed for the emergence or invention of something "more real."

Playing Dumb

"Do you know how to act dumb?" I once teased Lenore, a client of mine. In the jargon of family systems theory, Lenore was an entrenched overfunctioner, who always knew what was best, not only for herself but for others as well. She was quick to advise, rescue, take over, and fix. She had little capacity to stay in her own skin and allow others to struggle with their problems and manage their pain. If someone itched, she scratched. Her partner, Beverly, underfunctioned with as much gusto as Lenore overfunctioned. Throughout their ten-year relationship, each unwittingly reinforced the other's behavior.

During this particular therapy session, I was challenging Lenore to do something different, something "unnatural" at that. "Playing dumb" is hardly a therapeutic prescription for women, but I was wondering whether Lenore could attempt a courageous act of change that would disrupt the relationship pattern for which she sought help.

Could she, for example, experiment with saying, "I don't know," when Beverly asked for help in finding her car keys? Could she let Beverly leave the house with their four-month-old daughter without going through her usual checklist: "Do you have the diapers? Did you pack the formula? Did you remember to bring another sleeper?" When Beverly did leave the diapers behind, or otherwise acted less than competently, could Lenore underreact rather than overreact, allowing Beverly an opportunity to sit with the emotional and practical consequences of her underresponsibility? And if Lenore couldn't do this for a week, would she be willing to try it for, say, two days?

The next time I saw Lenore, she gave the following report on her experiment: "When I saw that Beverly was going to leave the house without Anna's pacifier, I literally had to go to the basement to keep myself from reminding her. Anna can't go for long without it. Thirty minutes later, Beverly came back home to get it. I sat there working on a report and forced myself not to say a word. She ended up being late to meet a client, which was a disaster. When she started to complain about it that evening, I stayed calm and told her I was sorry she'd had a hard day. Again, I had to stop myself from getting preachy. I was amazed at how hard it was for me to stay emotionally separate from her—to just stay out. Anyway, yesterday when Beverly took Anna to the pediatrician, she forgot to pack the diapers. But this time she came back for them before she'd even pulled out of the driveway."

My goal as a therapist was not to provide Lenore with a technique to help shape up her partner. Rather, I wondered what Lenore might learn about herself by modifying her own part in an overfunctioning-underfunctioning polarity that had gone on as long as their relationship had. While Lenore's small experiment with Beverly was hardly significant in itself, it drew meaning in the context of the work that Lenore was doing in therapy.

Many painful events had happened in Lenore's first family, and anxiety had been chronically high. Her parents did not approach problems calmly and factually, or with an eye to a solution, but rather with intense emotional reactivity and symptomatic behavior. Lenore, who had no living siblings, unwittingly supported her parents' incompetence by providing them with limitless care, both functionally and emotionally. When she first entered psychotherapy, she had no experience in being emotionally present in the face of neediness or pain without trying to find answers and solutions. She had sporadically distanced from, or set limits with, her parents, but only *after* she was angry for having done or given too much. Then the intensity in her voice only fueled their anxiety and neediness.

Finally, Lenore had never considered sharing her own problems or vulnerability with either of her parents, nor did she view any other family member as having anything to offer her. But she saw no connection between her inability to reveal her vulnerability and her parents' inability to assume competence.

Only slowly did Lenore understand and modify her automatic and "natural" ways of responding to her parents. In acting any way other than how she always had, Lenore felt that there was initially a strong element of "pretend" or experimentation, as when she let Beverly leave home without all the baby's supplies. What initially felt like "pretending," however, ultimately led her to discover new insights about family patterns and her part in them.

More Pretending

A psychotherapy client says to me: "My friend is dragging me to this meeting about adoptees searching for their birth parents. I pretended to be interested because she needs my support, but I've never been curious about my biological mother or father." In this apathetic spirit, my client attends the meeting and all emotional hell breaks loose for her. So it is that we sometimes learn more about what is "really real" by placing ourselves in a new context. Or, like Molly and Lenore, we *create* a new context by changing our own behavior in an old one.

Consider Jen, who is frantic about the fact that her live-in boyfriend keeps hedging on setting a marriage date. Jen had a disastrous first marriage, but believes now that she's met the "perfect man." The more she pressures him to make a commitment, the more he distances, and vice versa. By the time she seeks my help, the pattern that has been set in motion has a life of its own. All she can do is express dependency and neediness. All he can do is experience a cool distance and a need for space. She's anxiously pursuing and he's putting on his track shoes. Jen is so focused on marriage that almost no energy is going into her work, her friendships, and her life plan.

I advise Jen to consider a bold act of pretending. Can she set aside a period of time—say eight weeks—to stop focusing on her boyfriend and begin to put her energy back into her own life? Can she be the one to seek more separateness, for example, by going out with her own friends a few evenings a week? Can she initiate a conversation in which she expresses her own doubts about marriage? (We all have them.) Can she stay warmly connected to her boyfriend (rather than swinging into a cold, reactive distance), without pursuing him or mentioning marriage?

For a "natural" pursuer, this challenge is difficult. And because such advice smacks of the old "hard-to-get" tactics that women have been taught to play, it may sound phony or manipulative. But there's nothing authentic or true in continuing a pattern where she only pursues and he only distances. Polarized relationships (she stands for togetherness, he for separateness) distort the experience of self and other, and keep us stuck in a narrow view of truth and possibility. Sometimes interrupting the pursuit-distance cycle allows each partner to acknowledge the more difficult and complex—but internally more whole—experience of both wanting and fearing intimacy.

Let's take one final example: A friend of mine, Michelle, was intensely critical of her mother-in-law, Sylvia. Dedicated to expressing her true feelings, she constantly criticized Sylvia to her husband, who invariably came to his mother's defense. This was a typical "in-law triangle," with the negative intensity settling between the wife and her mother-in-law. The two women sparred with each other while the man stayed outside the ring.

From Michelle's perspective, she was dealing candidly with an impossible situation. She told her husband regularly how much she hated his mother. In response to Sylvia's unsolicited advice and critical scrutiny, Michelle became openly sarcastic and coldly withdrawn. Michelle described her own behavior as honest and forthright, but she was unwittingly running interference for the other two. Wherever a wife and mother-in-law are slugging it out, there is a mother and son who aren't addressing the emotional issues between them.

I challenged Michelle to pretend, to experiment with behaviors that at first struck her as unnatural and even phony. I suggested that she lighten up, stop criticizing Sylvia to her husband, and try to relate instead to Sylvia's good qualities, which Michelle had totally lost sight of. I encouraged her to create a less intense emotional climate between herself and her mother-in-law, and to approach her with humor and interest rather than distance and blame. I also suggested that she deal more directly with her own parents to avoid overfocusing on her husband's family.

My point was not to persuade Michelle to do something different for its own sake ("Let's throw red paint on your mother-in-law and see what happens"). Rather, I was challenging her to become an expert on how triangles operate and to change her part in this one.

What began as pretense, as "experimenting," led in time to a more richly textured view of family realities. A year later, Michelle was underreacting to Sylvia while her husband had begun to overreact to his mother. Conflicts were surfacing in Michelle's marriage, as well as between her husband and his mother. These real relationship issues had been totally obscured by the old triangle, which had sidetracked the negative intensity into the relationship between Michelle and Sylvia.

Pretending can facilitate truth-telling (or truth-knowing) when it makes a dent in unproductive, habitual ways of responding to others. As an old Spanish proverb reminds us: Habits at first are silken threads, then they become cables. We can't see what's "true" or possible in a relationship or in a human being until *after* we change our behavior. Sylvia, for example, softened her critical attitude (which reflected, in part, her misguided wish to feel helpful and included) when Michelle moved toward her, inviting and valuing her perspective rather than bristling at her unsolicited advice.

Goethe once wrote (before inclusive language): "If you treat man as he appears to be, you make him worse than he is. But if you treat man as if he already were what he potentially could be, you make him what he should be." We can never know the totality or the potential of other human beings (or what they "should be," for that matter), but who they are with us always has something to do with how we are with them.

W. Brugh Joy has paraphrased Goethe's quotation as follows: "If I treat myself as I think I appear to be, I make myself less than I am. But if I treat myself as if I already were what I potentially could be, I make myself what I should be." Both quotations are intriguing meditations on the power of imagining and pretending—and the relationship between the two.

10

〜

Family Secrets:
A Disturbance in the Field

During many of my growing-up years in Brooklyn, I kept a lock-and-key diary that I hid in a dresser drawer beneath my sweaters. After each entry, I put the diary back at a particular angle so I could tell if it had been tampered with. I lived in terror that my parents would read it or that my best friend's brother would make good on his threat to find it. Whoever violated my privacy would also discover my most carefully guarded secrets. Ironically, it was my younger son who recently found these same diaries in an attic box and gleefully thumbed through them. Fortunately, enough years had passed that I reacted mostly with amusement when he unabashedly reported his adventure.

Every family has secrets dividing those who "know" from those who "don't know." Secrets between parents and children often reflect healthy boundaries, allowing each generation to have its separate sphere. Other secrets that adults keep from children, and vice versa, are deeply problematic.

Children conceal information from their parents and engage in deception for many reasons. A child may choose to keep a secret to avoid punishment or disapproval, to protect a parent from worry, to carve out a private space, to consolidate relationships with siblings and peers, or to foster autonomy and separateness. Hiding information or feelings from parents can help children feel powerful and independent, and can stave off unwanted attention and intrusion. Children, however, do not always "choose" the secrets they keep or the ways in which they get trapped in someone else's story. Some secrets, such as incest, reflect both the adult's abuse of power and the child's utter terror, confusion, and helplessness.

Parents routinely keep some secrets from their children. Adults need to maintain privacy and naturally want to shield their children and themselves from unnecessary and painful disclosures. Parents make daily decisions about what information to impart to their children and how and when to do so.

But parents differ dramatically in the degree to which they view children as needing protection from "the truth." Bea's mother Ruth, for example, tried to buffer her daughter completely from the inevitable sadness and grief that life brings. By the time Bea was an adult, there was little real communication or exchange of feelings between them. Other parents may do the opposite. They may tell children too much, thus failing to shield them appropriately from adult problems, or they may pressure their children to open up to them. Either extreme reflects an anxious family's efforts to adapt; both extremes are problematic.

How do we distinguish a "family secret" from the countless things that parents choose not to tell their children, and vice versa? The term "family secret" usually refers to the concealment of events and facts (rather than thoughts and feelings) relevant to the person who does not have the information. The term is reserved for subjects that are emotionally loaded in our culture. Family secrets commonly involve matters of alcoholism, drug addiction, imprisonment, suicide, physical and mental diagnoses, untimely losses, migration status, parentage, infertility, adoption, sexual orientation, affairs, employment and financial status, divorce, incest, and violence. If a mother hides what she paid for the new lawn furniture, this act of concealment is unlikely to find its way into the literature on "family secrets," although her failure to disclose the information may have a profound meaning in her family.

The extent to which a piece of information is concealed or mystified is a barometer of family anxiety. In turn, the extent of anxiety reflects the personal meanings that parents bring to a particular subject from their own families and the degree to which a subject is stigmatized within the broader culture.

When I was in the sixth grade, my friend Arlene kept her parents' divorce a secret from every one of her classmates at her mother's request. Her mother not only felt responsible for the failure of her marriage, but she also did not want Arlene to suffer from being the only one in her class from a "broken home." This secrecy would be unusual in the nineties because divorce is now ubiquitous and far less stigmatized in most communities.

Stigma and secrecy are mutually reinforcing and entwined. The more a subject is stigmatized and misunderstood, the more likely it is that stigmatized individuals will resort to secrecy. Yet the keeping of secrets further exaggerates shame and increases our sense of being stigmatized.

But individual acts of insight or courage alone cannot

bring an end to this vicious cycle. Rather, change occurs only when individuals join each other to collectively form a social and political force to be reckoned with. The civil rights movement, the adoption reform movement, and the women's movement all illustrate how a social movement can alter the previously stigmatized meanings that the dominant culture assigns to certain groups. As new meanings develop and become established, more people come forth to reveal their secrets. As a result, individuals begin to feel a positive sense of identity and pride where stigma and secrecy once prevailed. Information among family members (for example, that Mother really is an alcoholic) can then flow more freely, which strengthens relational resources within the family and between the family and the community.

Of course, a secret can be made of any content, and it need not be shaped by stigma and shame. As Vicki's story illustrated, even a secret as neutral and trivial as meeting one's spouse through a personal ad can have a dramatic effect on family relationships, separating "insiders" from "outsiders" and creating hidden alliances and triangles that operate at great cost. Secrets influence relationships, even those secrets that are kept by a single family member who tells no one. The negative power of secrecy derives both from the emotional importance of what is not spoken (the content) and the convoluted alliances, triangles, and distance that secrets can create (the process).

In her book *Secrets in Families and Family Therapy*, Evan Imber-Black offers a dramatic example of the rapid triangular shifts that can occur when secret-keeping has become the relational modus vivendi for a family: Although a mother agreed with her adult son to keep his drug abuse a secret from his father, she revealed it within hours. In turn, the father agreed to keep his knowledge of the information secret from the son and from Imber-Black, their therapist. But then the father came to the next family therapy session alone and disclosed the secret, insisting that the therapist not tell his wife he had done so. In a joint family session, Imber-Black focused on how information flowed in the family, and how their wish to protect each other from harm was connected to the mutually felt experience of constant betrayal.

As the following story about Linda illustrates, the hidden alliances created by secrecy are not always fluid. Rather, triangles can become rigidly fixed—over years, decades, and generations. Secrecy is typically maintained in the name of "protection," and implicit calls to family loyalty hold secrets in place. It is difficult, however, to sort out who is protecting whom and from what—particularly considering the serious consequences of secrecy on individual and family life.

"Your Father Can't Handle Difficult Things"

When Linda came to see me in therapy, she was twenty-two years old and had recently become pregnant with her first child. She was the oldest of four daughters from a Kansas farm family and she was enrolled in a master's program in public health administration. Since her freshman year of college, she had been unable to speak comfortably in front of groups and she sometimes felt panicky even raising her hand in class. She described herself as being afraid that she would blurt out something "stupid or inappropriate."

Despite earlier attempts at therapy, Linda's problem stayed with her. Now an even more distressing symptom led her to seek help once again. Since learning that she was pregnant, she worried constantly about developing a health problem that would require diagnostic X-rays that would damage the fetus. Linda could not understand why she was haunted by this anxious preoccupation since she had no history of medical problems nor, apart from her fear of speaking in public, any remarkable history of worrying.

During Linda's second therapy session, while I was putting together a family genogram (a detailed family tree), Linda revealed a family secret that she initially viewed as being irrelevant to her symptoms. At age ten, Linda had attended the funeral of a neighboring farmer. After the service, the man's daughter told her that Linda had had an older brother who had died from "a heart problem or something" when he was a month old, on Christmas Day. Linda at first thought that the girl was lying, but she later asked her mother, who confirmed this fact and then refused to discuss it further.

During that brief and tense conversation, Linda's mother asked her not to mention the subject to any other family members. There was no reason, she said, for Linda's younger sisters to know or for their father to be reminded of this loss because "your father can't handle difficult things." It was best, she explained, that he remain unaware that Linda even knew. Linda's deep sense of family loyalty led her to put the news behind her rather than dwell on it. I was the first person she had ever told.

Linda's knowledge of her brother's death allowed her to make sense of otherwise inexplicable and mysterious aspects of her past. Her mother, for example, was "inside a dark cloud" during the holiday season, the anniversary of the loss. Linda's father, for his part, expressed profound disappoint-

ment that he did not have a son to help him farm. All their
daughters were affected by his obvious sorrow and dissatisfaction, but only Linda knew the rest of the story.

One reason that such family secrets wield so much negative power is that a parent can hide crucial facts, but cannot
hide the intensity of feelings surrounding these facts. In my
family, for example, my mother's cancer diagnosis could be
concealed, but the survival anxiety was in the air. When children sense a disturbance in the field, but do not feel free to
ask questions, they flounder in unconscious fantasies that
cannot be put to rest. As the family therapist Peggy Papp
notes: "When children sense information is being withheld,
they become confused and anxious, lose their sense of trust,
and often end up blaming themselves. In searching for a way
to explain the inexplicable, they create private beliefs, myths,
and fantasies. These often get acted out through symptomatic behavior and become a metaphor for the concealment in the system. The tensions and conflicts produced by
secrets remain irresolvable as long as the information necessary for their resolution remains inaccessible."

In Linda's case, she knew the secret. But the forbidden
subject was still off limits, so Linda didn't ask questions
about all the things she did *not* know: What exactly had her
brother died from? What caused the problem? Why couldn't
it be fixed? Where was her brother buried? What was his
name? Why was his death so terrible that no one was allowed
to talk about it? If Linda suddenly died, would the family
never again speak her name? Does death mean that one is
erased forever from family history and memory? And how
did the loss of the firstborn child affect Linda's entrance into
the family?

When a subject is taboo for ongoing discussion, children
stifle their feelings, as well as their natural curiosity to make

sense of their world. Sensing her mother's anxiety, Linda repressed her questions and put all thoughts of her brother out of consciousness. At the time of her first pregnancy, however, that underground emotionality surfaced as symptoms and perhaps as metaphor. X-rays not only harm (as expressed in Linda's worry about the survival and well-being of her own firstborn) but they also expose what is hidden from sight. Similarly, Linda's longstanding fear of publicly blurting out something stupid or inappropriate might also have reflected the burden of secret-keeping and her unconscious wish to talk openly about the truth.

Once Linda was able to examine the forbidden subject in the broad light of day, she felt lighter, less burdened, and more calm. She then told her husband about the secret she had discussed in therapy. He was glad to have information that helped explain her seemingly inexplicable fear that some unknown danger threatened their firstborn. Feeling supported and eager to control her anxiety, Linda gathered the courage to open up the secret in her family.

Linda spoke first to her mother, Fern. She picked a calm time and told her mother how fearful she felt about being pregnant. She asked Fern to help her get a grip on her anxiety by providing a bit of information about her brother's death. Linda began by asking a few factual questions ("What was his name? Did you have a normal pregnancy? Who first noticed there was a problem?"), rather than inquiring about difficult feelings or expecting to cover a broad territory all at once. Linda also told her mother that it was only when she became pregnant herself that she understood how devastating it would be to lose a child. She had anticipated a cold response from Fern. Instead, they cried together.

In a later conversation, Linda let her mother know that she planned to talk about the loss with other family members, including her dad, John. At this point, Fern's anxiety skyrocketed and she angrily accused Linda of being selfish, disloyal, and disrespectful. But Linda was able to maintain a firm stance without distancing or becoming defensive. She told her mother, "You know, Mom, I suppose I *am* being selfish, because I need to do this for myself. I'm sorry that I'm hurting you because that's not my intention."

Linda explained to Fern that keeping the secret was too big a burden for her because it kept her distant from the other family members. She also told her mother that she loved her family and wanted to be able to talk with them about important things. Linda didn't try to change or convince her mother—only to be as clear as possible about where she stood and what she needed to do for herself. Getting *out* of the secret-keeping business in families is as important a skill as keeping a confidence when appropriate.

In excavating a family secret, one revelation leads to another. Linda began to learn about other losses in the previous generation that had never been grieved or openly talked about. She learned from her father that her brother had died of a viral illness rather than some kind of heart problem. Her parents had felt particularly devastated because of their own failure to call a doctor in time. As a result, they had never bothered to clarify false rumors about the cause of their infant son's death.

As Linda replaced fantasy with fact she was able to separate out her own pregnancy from her mother's painful experience. Her fear of speaking out in groups diminished and her preoccupation with X-rays all but disappeared. Linda's parents, however, initially became *more* anxious as the fragile equilibrium in their distant marriage was disturbed by their daughter's challenge to secrecy and silence.

For Fern and John, having to face their grief about their son's death once again was not the only difficult aspect of the change initiated by Linda. Linda's move toward her dad also defied a long-established, multigenerational legacy of father-daughter distance. In her effort to share her own fears with him, and to ask him about the losses in his life, Linda challenged the myth that fathers must be protected (or more accurately, excluded) from family emotional life. When Linda told Fern, "I can't keep such a big secret from Dad," she was refusing to collude with John's outsider status. In so doing, she made waves that rippled throughout the entire system and ultimately affected all their family relationships.

Insiders and Outsiders

With family secrets, there are countless ways that the boundaries are drawn and redrawn between insiders and outsiders. In Linda's family, for example, John thought that he and his wife were keeping a secret from the children. But, in fact, from the time Linda was ten years old, his wife and daughter had kept a secret from him.

Secrets have different "locations" in family life. A mother may have a secret, such as her addiction to Valium, that she tells no one. Or she may tell her adolescent daughter and swear her to secrecy. All the family members may know about her addiction but may behave with each other as if no one knows. Or the children may be warned not to mention their mother's secret to anyone outside the immediate family. Another kind of secret might involve a child and one parent and an outside agent, as when a child's problem is discussed by one parent and a teacher or therapist, but the other parent is not told.

In her book *Deborah, Golda, and Me*, Letty Cottin Pogrebin observes that most of her family's secrets were guarded by women, who revealed information bit by bit like time-release pain capsules. She speculates that shame was a major factor that might account for this guardedness, perhaps because women are socialized to be more conscious of appearances than men and to rely more on "how it would look" or "what people might think" in the absence of more concrete measures of worth. Pogrebin also wonders whether keeping certain behaviors under wraps allowed the women to look presentable yet do what they wanted to do anyway.

In recalling the secrets in her own family, including who was in cahoots with whom, Pogrebin also draws a connection between secrecy and power: "While men control the history of nations and civilizations, women use family history as their negotiable instruments. And if knowledge is power, clandestine knowledge is power squared; it can be withheld, exchanged and leveraged. For women, who traditionally were excluded from prestige-building occupations or the exercise of worldly influence, guarding secrets may have been the only power they know."

I agree with Pogrebin's premise. While women and men may not consciously intend to exclude each other, there is surely a connection between women's outside position in the public sphere and men's outside position in the private sphere of family emotional life.

When Fern told her ten-year-old daughter, "Don't tell Dad," her stated intention was to protect her husband from unnecessary upset. But when Linda, twenty-two years old and pregnant, did tell her dad, it became clear that her mother had most needed to protect herself from grief and rage stemming both from the loss of her son and her husband's emotional withdrawal from her. Perhaps she also wanted to protect her emotionally central position with her children. Fern taught all her daughters that their father couldn't be expected to deal with difficult things and that he mustn't be bothered. Whatever her intentions, she reinforced rather than challenged John's outside position in the family.

Yet family secrets, more often than not, are profoundly disempowering, even for the secret-keepers. Secrets erode connection, block authentic engagement and trust, and strip the family of spontaneity and vitality. Secrets not only rob individuals of relational resources within their families, but they also rob the family itself of external supports. Keeping a secret from the outside world ("Don't tell anyone Dad lost his job") lowers family self-esteem and may lock the family into an atmosphere of shame, silence, and social isolation.

Secrets support pathological family processes, bonding insiders together with false bonds and estranging outsiders. Secret-keepers may become physically but not emotionally present, "missing in action," as a friend puts it. As outsiders remain blocked from knowing what is true, they may become increasingly unable to recall the past, gather facts in the present, and anticipate and plan for the future. And what begins as one family secret often spreads to ever-widening circles of lying, silence, suppression, and denial.

The negative effects of secrecy on children may stay underground for years, even decades, until the child reaches a key anniversary age or a particular stage in the family life cycle. Linda, for example, moved forward with her life, despite her fear of speaking publicly, until she conceived her first child. At this time, her anxiety became almost incapacitating.

Some children react to secrecy on the spot, as I did in response to the silence surrounding my mother's first cancer diagnosis. A child or adolescent's symptomatic or acting out behavior may be a random, anxious response to secrecy. Or it may speak metaphorically to what is being concealed and may serve to blow the whistle on the family.

Secrets and Symptoms

Many years back, a wealthy, socially prominent couple from Kansas City requested my professional help. They were concerned about their adolescent daughter, Catherine, whose downhill slide both embarrassed and alarmed them. Catherine had refused individual psychotherapy but agreed to see me with her parents.

At the start of our first meeting, Catherine's father bluntly stated his view of the problem, while his wife nodded in assent. Catherine was "looking like riffraff, behaving like riffraff, and hanging out with riffraff." Her recent appearance, something between punk and porn, humiliated her parents, who were both highly visible in the business community and especially concerned with image and status. Also, Catherine had begun staying out all night and engaging in promiscuous adventures, which she flaunted rather than concealed from them. Her father responded by lecturing Catherine on matters of morality, while her mother expressed panic about her daughter's safety and the risk of AIDS. Catherine, for her part, dug in her heels, insisting that she would do as she pleased with her life.

My initial attempts to help the parents work as a team to formulate clear rules and discipline were not helpful. Suspecting the concealment of crucial information, I asked that

Catherine's older brother be invited to join the sessions. In a meeting that included only the two children, a family secret did indeed emerge. Catherine's brother let it be known that their mother was going to elaborate lengths to avoid acknowledging that her husband was having an affair with his business partner. He explained, "The two lovebirds are screwing all over the country and everyone knows it but Mom."

Catherine had also suspected her father's affair from its inception a year earlier, having overheard bits and pieces of flirtatious telephone conversations. It was not her conscious plan to "blow the whistle" on her family through her own less-than-respectable behavior, but she did just that. And while Catherine was contemptuous of her father's hypocrisy and deception, she was angrier still at her mother's unwillingness to face reality and stand up for herself.

At sixteen, Catherine understandably had little perspective on the profound economic, emotional, and social vulnerability of women in marriage. As she looked into her mother's eyes and worried about her own future, she saw only a woman who was "phony," "cowardly," and "superficial," and who would not defend or define herself. Catherine was furious that her mother seemed unwilling either to protest the affair or even to react to it. As a result, she ended up doing the job for both of them.

Symptoms can serve both to *protest* and to *protect* the status quo in family life. Catherine's problematic behavior brought her family into treatment, making it impossible for business to continue as usual. She did, indeed, blow the whistle on her family's deceptive image of propriety. At the same time, she protected her parents from confronting her father's secret affair, and the profound marital distance surrounding it. Like a lightning rod, Catherine attracted to herself all the negative attention. She provided both of her parents with an ongoing focus of concern, so that by the time the family entered therapy, Catherine was all her parents talked about—and perhaps their only "safe" topic of conversation.

Shortly after the secret came out in the open and the spotlight focused on her parents, Catherine began to settle down. At her own initiative, she had an HIV test, which proved negative, and she announced in a therapy session that she was "taking a vacation from sex" to catch up with her schoolwork. Catherine's mother was no longer able to stick her head in the sand, although she initially felt totally at a loss about how to respond to her husband's affair. When the facts were out on the table, she first reported feeling dead inside and unable to react. However, as she waited for the results of *her* HIV test, rage and fear swept through her like a tornado.

My own attention was now focused on helping the parents address the affair and turn their primary concern toward their own marital problems, which had been obscured by their concentration on Catherine. I dismissed Catherine and her brother from the therapy sessions, encouraging them to get on with their own lives, as their parents needed to deal with adult problems that were private. Only much later did I work briefly with Catherine and her parents to help restore communication and establish mutual regard.

While I have focused on the negative effects of secrecy in families, the subject is far too complex to allow for glib generalizations or sweeping conclusions ("All secrets in families are bad and should be immediately revealed"). The challenge for parents is not to rush in to "tell all," or for therapists to ferret out all that is hidden. As we have seen, revelations and confrontations may do more harm than good when family members bounce into each other's lives, often in a context of distance or tension, and try to do too much too fast. Telling a secret may not be productive if it occurs in an anxious emotional field, before at least one adult is motivated and thoughtful enough to get a grip on their own intensity.

There is little agreement on what constitutes a "family secret" or on definitions of what is "normal" or "functional" secret-keeping in families. Some family therapists believe that all secrets are toxic. Others pay attention to the strategic and adaptational value of secrets, which functions differently depending on their location in a particular family, ethnic group, generation, community, class, and culture. From my perspective, the challenge of revealing secrets is one of process and direction, of creating an emotional climate in which sensitive information can be shared and the conversation can continue long after the secret is revealed.

It is one thing, for example, to tell a preschool-age child that she is adopted. It is another to create a calm emotional climate where the child can feel safe to ask questions and share a range of honest emotions, including grief over her loss of significant people, separation from her birth mother, and the possibility she may never meet her birth parents. As children mature, they raise new questions, or the same question changes in meaning over time. The question "Who is my mother?" means one thing to a kindergarten child, and another to an adolescent girl wanting genealogical information to help clarify her identity and make sense of her world.

Whatever the subject, at least one family member will pay a price when an important matter can't be noticed, talked about, or even remembered. In the shadow of secrecy, children are especially vulnerable to acting out or developing symptoms. They are the most dependent family members and, as such, are fiercely loyal to unspoken family rules and traditions. No matter how outrageously children and adolescents behave, they *"know"* at a deep, automatic level what not to ask about. When they sense undercurrents of hostility, fear, or distance in the family, they are most likely to create self-blaming fantasies to fill in the missing pieces or to explain the tension. Children also put on blinders that obscure more than the original secret from view.

No Thinking Permitted Here

Peggy Papp worked as a family therapist with Billy, an eleven-year-old boy with a "learning deficit" in history who was unable to remember dates or places. His symptom was a puzzling one, for he did well in all his other school subjects. In therapy Papp discovered that Billy had been kept from learning his own history, which was filled with mystery and chaos. Billy's mother wanted to protect him from any knowledge of his father's alcoholism and job losses. Billy, for his part, wanted to protect his mother by not asking her upsetting questions, like why the family kept moving from one place to another and why he and his mother suddenly left his father.

For Billy, the past was dangerous territory that could not be explored or even thought about. When Papp was able to help Billy integrate the facts of his past with his current life, he was able to recall historical dates and places, and his "learning block" disappeared. The taboos that had prohibited Billy from gaining knowledge of his family history had generalized to a prohibition of learning the history of the world around him. In a similar light, Papp reports the work of another therapist who treated a girl with a "selective math disability," related to the fact that she had never been told about her adoption. Once she was permitted in therapy to add up the facts of her own life and to compute the arithmetic related to her birth (she was fifteen months old when her adoptive parents married), her "math disability" disappeared.

Any large family secret, or mystification of what is real, can ultimately lead to a more generalized prohibition against knowing, seeing, talking, feeling, and asking. This occurs even when the broader culture *prescribes* secrecy and mystification in family life, as with the ubiquitous practice of mislabeling female genitals ("Boys have a penis, and girls have a hole where the baby comes out"). False and mystifying communications create broader taboos against a child's clear articulation of inner experience and outer reality.

One woman I saw in psychotherapy was unable to think clearly about geography, directions, and maps—a confusion related to the prohibition against "figuring out" her genitals. In therapy, it emerged that her inability to comprehend the geography of her genitals, or her world, was a promise to "not look." Looking meant that she would see something (her vulva, especially her clitoris) that wasn't supposed to be there. "What I had that felt good didn't have a name," she explained. "It wasn't supposed to exist. Only boys had something on the outside. So I couldn't have my clitoris and still be a girl." As she put it, "Everyone knows that men have a penis, and everyone can say the word—even at parties. But the only word that people will say to describe what women have is 'vagina.'"

Is the clitoris a societywide family secret? The idea sounds silly enough to demand that we consider it. The fact that a secret is normalized or culturally sanctioned does not make it less of an assault on female reality. It only makes it harder to look squarely at its implications. When women publicly examine "the trivial" or "unimportant" (like the cultural prescription to keep our age a secret, to joke or even lie about it), we may begin to move toward the center of what keeps us sleepy and disempowered.

Family secrets appear to be private business, derived from the deepest interior of family life; but patriarchal injunctions promote silence and denial even about life-and-death matters, such as the horror and extent of male violence in women's lives. The cultural context determines not only which secrets can be told, but also which secrets can be remembered and which secrets can be heard. Today, for example, my colleagues and I see a startlingly large number of women who have been victims of incest or sexually abused. Why were we not hearing all these stories fifteen years ago? Did our cultural climate then deny our clients their capacity to remember? Were women remembering yet not telling their therapists? Or were they telling their therapists and not being heard? However one understands it, something in the cultural emotional climate has shifted to allow for the honest memory and frank disclosure of even the most horrific of family secrets.

Significantly, discussions about violence and sexual abuse are taking place *among* women, as stories move more freely between the therapist's office and the public sphere. As women make the transition from the private to the public, they can begin to understand their personal experience within a wider context of gender and power. As more women remember, the ability to do so is renewed within us all, which makes remembering more likely for any one of us. The presence of powerful social and political movements—the civil rights movement, the feminist movement, the human rights movement, to name a few—ensures that once we remember and speak, we will not forget and fall silent. Nor will our stories be erased from history and the future.

11

An Affair Is a Big Secret

Jane had been living with her lover, Andrew, for five years when she found herself attracted to Bill, a man she worked with closely in a small veterinary clinic. Their flirtation, playful at first, intensified over time. For several months, they did not act on, or mention, the obvious sexual energy between them. But Bill was on Jane's mind and under her skin. At home, she talked to him in her head and thought about him while making love with Andrew. The nature of their work and the setup of the office kept Jane and Bill in close physical proximity, even had she wished otherwise.

Jane never questioned her primary commitment to Andrew. Not for a moment did she consider leaving him for Bill. She was, however, surprised by the strength of this attraction, and particularly by its emotional hold on her. She was confused about its meaning, not knowing, as she later put it, whether her feelings were "real" or whether she was getting into "some crazy, addictive, crushlike thing." As Jane felt increasingly anxious and driven by the attraction, she concluded that getting to know Bill better, rather than forcing distance, was the only route to gaining greater clarity about her feelings.

In keeping with a mutual agreement to tell each other about sexual temptations, Jane had, until now, been open with Andrew whenever she had felt attracted to someone else. This time was different. Jane feared that he would be inconsolable if he knew how compelling the attraction to Bill was, and she predicted that the emotional atmosphere at home would become so highly charged that she would be pressured to cut off from him entirely. She imagined Andrew anxiously grilling her every day after work, even insisting that she leave the job she loved. Jane wanted the time and space to move toward Bill and to sort out her feelings, time and space that would not be available if she brought the situation out into the open.

Jane also suspected that ending her relationship with Bill at this point would ensure that she'd stay stuck on him, if only in fantasy. She believed their ongoing contact would "normalize things" and "add more reality to the relationship," ultimately helping her to find her way out of the emotional woods. Also, Andrew wasn't asking questions about Jane's relationships at work, suggesting that perhaps he didn't really want to know about any possible rivals.

When Jane slept with Bill for the first time, vowing it would never happen again, she began to feel overwhelmingly anxious at home. In a panicky moment, she revealed everything to Helene, a long-time best friend who was also like a sister to Andrew. Sharing her secret helped alleviate Jane's anxiety only temporarily, because Helene became increasingly uncomfortable in her role as confidante. "I can't keep hearing about this," she finally told Jane during a late-night phone call. "I feel like it's putting a big wedge between me and Andrew, and I'm worried about the whole thing." Jane became terrified that Helene would violate her confidence.

Then Jane became anxiously preoccupied with the idea that she might have contracted the AIDS virus from Bill and passed it on to Andrew. She began having difficulty sleeping through the night and often awoke in the early morning with fear radiating through her bones. Jane had slept with Bill a total of three times and had practiced safe sex each time. Nonetheless, her anxiety and guilt increased, focusing on the chilling thought that she had brought the deadly virus home.

In response to her escalating anxiety, Jane stopped sleeping with Bill and made a concerted effort to renew her closeness to Andrew. When Bill became romantically involved with another woman, Jane felt wounded but ultimately relieved. In the months that followed, Bill became increasingly committed to his new lover and Jane's attachment to him lessened. She still revealed nothing of the affair to Andrew, though, because she was afraid to do so so soon after its occurrence. "Later . . . " she promised herself. And at other times, "What's the point of bringing it up? It's over."

Several months later, about a year after her relationship with Bill first heated up, Jane finally told Andrew about the affair. Helene had been pushing her to get the truth out into the open, because the secret was at Andrew's expense in their close threesome. Jane did not reveal the details easily, or in one sitting, but she did begin the process of laying the facts out on the table. Andrew felt enraged and devastasted, but their relationship survived and deepened over time as they ultimately learned to request more from each other in the way of intimacy and self-disclosure.

* * *

An affair is a big secret because increasingly, and in ever-widening circles, it causes the persons involved to operate in a "pretend" way in their primary relationship. The longer Jane continued her emotional and sexual involvement with Bill, the more censored and less centered she felt with Andrew, so that eventually she was physically but not emotionally present in her primary relationship. She often *appeared* to be attentive, because her efforts to be solicitous to her partner increased in direct proportion to her growing anxiety and guilt about the betrayal. But her solicitousness was more deliberate than spontaneous, more tacked on than deeply felt.

In his book *Private Lies,* the family therapist Frank Pittman notes that it is the secrecy more than the sexiness in an affair that creates distance and disorientation in a marriage or primary partnership. The secrecy also helps make the lover a more emotionally compelling partner than the spouse. Typically, the lover knows all about the spouse, while the spouse knows nothing—for certain. The sharing of facts and feelings can be relatively free and uncensored with the lover, while the opposite is true with the spouse. No matter what the potential for intimacy in a marriage, it is impossible to feel close to a person one is hiding from, confusing, throwing off track, deceiving.

Thus, the very way the three players are positioned in this triangle keeps the spouse in an outside and increasingly distant position. Pittman's advice to men who have fallen in love with the "other woman" is: "Bear in mind that a man feels closest to whichever woman shares his secrets. And he feels uncomfortable around anyone to whom he's lying. If you've been deceiving your wife while sharing your innermost thoughts and feelings with your affair partner, of course you will feel in love with her and out of love with your wife.

This is why having an affair—although it is not a loving thing to do—does not necessarily mean you don't love your wife. See what happens when you tell your wife the truth and start lying to the other woman." Pittman concludes that the issue is less whom one lies with, than whom one lies *to*.

The Unconscious Seeks Truth

What made it impossible for Jane to continue her double life? Some of us continue in one or more affairs over several years, even decades, never coming clean with our partners. Infidelity may be congruent with our family and cultural legacy, or sanctioned by our social group and close friends. Or, we *believe* one way and *behave* another, without allowing ourselves to acknowledge the incongruity between our beliefs and actions. We compartmentalize our experience, keeping contradictory beliefs and behaviors separate, so that they don't rub up against each other and cause us trouble. And, of course, all of us have a refined ability to rationalize, to fool not only others but also ourselves.

Jane, however, was not wired this way. She was committed to monogamy and, even more strongly, to honesty. When she found herself first having an emotional affair with Bill, and later a sexual relationship, she did not engage in multiple self-deceptions to comfort herself. She did not tell herself, "If Andrew doesn't know, it won't affect him," or, "My attraction to Bill livens things up in bed with Andrew, so it's not such a bad thing." Jane knew she owed Andrew the truth. She believed everyone has a right to live life based on facts rather than deception.

At the same time, Jane felt in her guts that she needed to allow her relationship with Bill to develop, unimpeded by

Andrew's emotionality. "I needed to do what I needed to do," she later explained, "so I just couldn't tell." Still, being deceptive—even toward an end Jane viewed as necessary or irresistible—violated the dictates of her conscience. The contradiction between her values and her behavior eventually took an emotional toll.

Jane did not exactly think her way out of this moral dilemma—that is, her decision to back off from Bill was not made from the neck up. One might say that Jane's unconscious, speaking through her body, ultimately pushed her to set limits with Bill and later to tell Andrew about him. When our behavior violates our core values and beliefs, our unconscious and our body seek truth. If we ignore a signal—in Jane's case, anxiety—we may receive a bigger one, and then a more urgent one still, until we are forced to pay attention.

As Jane failed to put limits on the intensity with Bill, or to talk to Andrew about him, she experienced increasingly higher levels of anxiety. When she could no longer contain her anxiety, she established a potentially unstable triangle by confiding in a friend who was also best friends with Andrew. She subconsciously chose a confidante who would kick her anxiety higher; she now worried constantly about how long Helene would keep the secret at Andrew's expense.

Jane persisted in trying to ride out the anxiety without letting go of Bill, or telling Andrew, but it didn't work. Her sleep was disrupted by an anxious, obsessive preoccupation about bringing death home in the form of AIDS. At this point, Jane stopped having sex with Bill and moved toward Andrew. If Jane had continued her relationship with Bill, she might have gotten herself "caught," as so frequently happens when anxiety about betrayal mounts. Or she might have developed a more severe emotional or physical symptom. A friend quotes her old country doctor as saying, "If we do something wrong and pretend to ourselves that we don't know what we are doing, we will get very sick—physically, or in our head, or both."

Of course, we all know people who do not seem to feel guilty enough in response to lying and deceiving others. Some of these people occupy top governmental positions—or share our beds. At one time or another, we ourselves may fall into this category. Sometimes, however, guilt is there, unfelt and unacknowledged until triggered by time or circumstance:

A business executive once sought my help for severe depression after the death of his fifteen-year-old son. He had been having an affair with his assistant over a period of several years, and experienced no apparent guilt or remorse for lying endlessly to his wife. But one evening while he was enjoying a clandestine romantic dinner with his lover, his son was struck and killed by a truck while jogging.

On learning of his son's death, this man felt such intense anxiety that he ended the affair the next day. Then he told his wife everything en route to the funeral. He did not examine his motivation for telling, nor did he consider the matter of his timing. His "honesty" was a reflexive attempt to lower an unmanageable degree of emotionality that threatened to overwhelm him.

When I saw him during his period of crisis, his mourning for his son was complicated by his fantasy that his behavior had contributed to his son's death. He had arranged for his assistant to be transferred, and the thought of ever having another affair was beyond his imagination. A year later, however, he had formed a new sexual relationship which he kept secret from his wife. His initial self-disclosure had been motivated by an acute state of panic, not by anxiety that signals a violation of well-integrated values and beliefs. Most importantly, he and his wife had not looked honestly at their own relationship following the disclosure of the first affair. Instead, they had reacted to their traumatic loss by moving even farther apart into a position of entrenched distance.

Finding Out . . . Then What?

Why a secret comes out into the open is less important than what happens after it is discovered or revealed. The discovery of an affair can wreak havoc on a marriage, or it can strengthen it, depending on the commitment of both partners to honesty and to each other.

Andrew initially felt devastated by Jane's involvement with Bill. He and Jane alternated between explosive interchanges, marathon late-night talks, and passionate lovemaking. These heightened levels of both positive and negative intensity surprised them both by enlivening their relationship at a time of crisis. Yet emotional intensity, either positive or negative, is often an anxiety-driven response, more likely to impede than foster clear thinking about the relationship. Despite being a necessary first step in processing the pain of sexual betrayal, it is no more than that.

How does a couple process infidelity and rebuild trust? For starters, Jane and Andrew recognized how very distant their relationship had become prior to the affair. They both had become lazy about paying attention to each other. Andrew, for example, was not registering important information about his partner, including obvious signals during the time of the affair that something was different or "not right." When we aren't receiving and processing information from the other person, we become dishonest with ourselves.

We are all responsible, in part, for how our relationships go; we may collude with or even invite dishonesty. But Andrew neither caused Jane's affair nor could he have prevented it. Most importantly, Andrew and Jane used the revelation of the affair as a springboard to deeper levels of truth-telling and self-disclosure. The affair served as a vivid reminder that sexual temptations are a reality of life, especially, but not exclusively, when a primary relationship is distant. Denying that one's partner, or oneself, is vulnerable to powerful outside attractions is a form of sleepwalking. Jane and Andrew both decided they would keep the subject of sexual and romantic attractions in their consciousness and conversation, while trying not to overfocus anxiously on each other. They recognized that trusting each other—when "trusting" meant taking each other for granted and not paying attention—was not useful.

The dishonesty and secrecy of Jane's affair made it intolerable to Andrew, and he wanted to know the facts, no matter how painful. How could they establish an emotional climate in which honesty about sexuality was increasingly possible? Toward this end, they renewed their promise to each other to openly share any outside attraction before acting on it. This would include revealing strong emotional and romantic attractions, not just genital ones. The one listening would try to respond with honest feelings, without punishing the other for honesty by becoming overly reactive or controlling. Both would feel free to ask each other about outside attractions, and to remind each other that honesty, not monogamy, was their most important shared value.

In her book *The Monogamy Myth*, Peggy Vaughan underlines the fact that we cannot assume monogamy without discussing it, nor can we assure it by extracting promises or issuing threats. Only honesty can create the groundwork for monogamy. Attractions kept secret from a partner are far more likely to intensify and be acted on.

In keeping with their goal of increasing intimacy, Andrew eventually asked Jane for more detailed information about her sexual and emotional experiences with Bill. Although it was painful to hear the details, Andrew knew he would do better with the facts than with fantasies and fears. As Andrew gradually asked the questions that he was ready to hear answers to, Jane refined and expanded on the truths she shared. In turn, Andrew told more about his own sexual history and fantasies. He had a few transgressions of his own to share.

Andrew talked to a few good friends and supportive family members about Jane's affair, enlisting their much-needed empathy and support without inviting them to come to Jane's defense or to side against her. He learned as much as possible about how others manage the crisis of infidelity, whichever side of it they are on, and about the more general issue of sexual attractions outside committed relationships. Jane did the same. How did her sisters experience and deal with sexual temptations outside their marriages? What beliefs and values did others have about telling or asking their partners about their sexual feelings and fantasies? What did her good friends expect from themselves and their partners in the way of sexual truth-telling? Where did people draw the line between privacy and secrecy?

As Jane and Andrew engaged other people in deeper levels of conversation, both were surprised by the remarkably diverse beliefs about sexual honesty they encountered. These differing perspectives helped each of them to refine and clarify their values on the subject. Being open with others was a crucial part of the process of being more open with each other.

* * *

Individuals hold very different views about what constitutes honest and appropriate self-disclosure between sexual partners. We each have our own "philosophy" on the subject, even if we don't articulate it to ourselves or our partner. What one woman deems essential information about her spouse or lover another woman may consider irrelevant, inappropriate, or invasive.

Consider, for example, two very different perspectives voiced by Jane's sisters, women who otherwise shared similar values and worldviews. On matters of honesty and fidelity, Bess is concerned only about what her husband does. Mary Anne, in contrast, cares primarily about whether her husband is *emotionally* present in bed.

In Bess's words: "My only rule is that George keeps his hands off other women. It's like that old saying, 'It doesn't matter where his appetite comes from as long as he dines at home.' I don't want to know who he's thinking about when we're having sex and I would never ask him. Fantasies are private and I can't see anything useful in sharing them. George can think about the Pope if he wants to, as long as he's in *my* bed and no one else's."

In Mary Anne's words: "I would feel most betrayed if Sid had an affair of the heart—even one he didn't act on. Last year Sid was infatuated with a woman at work and for months he was thinking of her every time we made love. It was incredibly painful for me *not* to have this information and to learn about it much later. It was also dishonest of Sid to keep this secret from me. Now we have an agreement to talk when this happens. We don't share every passing fantasy about another person or grill each other after sex. But when a fantasy gets so heavy or persistent that one of us isn't really *present* with the other in bed, we tell. When we're open about it, we get through the problem and become close again."

Mary Anne demands more in the way of intimacy from her husband than Bess does. This difference between them is not a matter of "right" or "wrong," "better" or "worse," because there is no correct amount of closeness or distance for all couples, or even for a particular couple over time. It is useful, however, to be clear about our own beliefs and expectations about sexual honesty and to act accordingly. We are never guaranteed that the other person will tell us the truth, but if we want *really* to know, we need *really* to ask, over time and from the heart.

The Monogamy Paradox

Jane and Andrew responded to the crisis of betrayal by deepening their connection to each other. A more typical response, however, is to try to control a partner or swear him or her to monogamy. Naturally, we may *want* our partner to swear fidelity, but none of us can make an absolute promise about what we will or won't do over the course of a lifetime. To do so is again a form of pretending. When people marry, they take an oath in front of God and everyone to forsake all others; yet statistics suggest a very high incidence of both divorce and extramarital sex. There are well over a dozen species of mammals (including wolves and gibbons) more monogamous than our own. We tend to desire both the security of a lifetime partner and the excitement and liveliness of sexual and emotional variation.

Societal untruths about monogamy (like that one that it

is the only normal and normative way to live for everbody)
invite us to be less than honest with ourselves and our partners. Another cultural myth inviting dishonesty is that the
"real reason" behind an affair is a faulty spouse or bad marriage. True enough, marital distance and discontent is often
managed by overinvolvement with a third party, be it a lover,
child, therapist, or whomever. But affairs, like other triangles, are often a reflexive response to anxiety from any hidden source.

Jane, for example, began sleeping with Bill as she
approached the age of her dad when he died in a work-
related accident. People commonly begin affairs on the heels
of an important loss or, as in Jane's case, at the anniversary of
an earlier one. Lying about an affair may signal that a more
anxious emotional issue is unacknowledged or unaddressed.

The myth that we are a perfectly monogamous species,
and that affairs are terrible aberrations that never happen
among good people in loving relationships, encourages self-
deception and denial ("My partner is never attracted to other
women"), isolation and shame ("I wouldn't want anyone to
know that my husband betrayed me"), and exaggerated feelings of personal responsibility and failure ("What was wrong
with me that he needed to go outside the relationship?"). As a
result, many people are hesitant to talk openly and frankly
about the reality of affairs, both before and after they happen.

While Jane and Andrew responded to the crisis of betrayal
by working toward deeper levels of honesty, not all couples
respond similarly. The following sequence of events is more
typical:

Rosa called for a brief consultation after learning of her
husband's infidelity. She told me that several months earlier

she had become suspicious about a "funny distance" in her marriage. At the time, she grasped her husband by the shoulders, looked him in the eye, and said firmly, "John, I have a very strong feeling that you are having an affair. If you are, I want you to know that I'm leaving you. I really need to know the truth about this."

John said, "Nothing is going on," so when Rosa later discovered a different truth, she was outraged. "It's unbelievable," she told her friends, "that John lied in the face of such a direct confrontation." Rosa did not ask John questions about this relationship but insisted that he end it, which he did. Then she asked him to swear, over and over, that he would never again be unfaithful. John renewed his vow to Rosa and she reiterated her bottom line: "If I ever find out that you're screwing someone, we're finished, no questions asked!" To me, she said, "I can't get over feeling devastated. I wonder, and I wonder, how I'll trust him again."

Of course Rosa wondered. Threats and promises do nothing to guarantee fidelity or bolster trust. Nor can we ensure that a partner will remain monogamous forever. What we can do, though, is work toward establishing increasingly greater levels of honesty and open communication in a relationship, which is the only foundation on which trust can be built. Rosa did the opposite. The rigidity and finality of her ultimatum ("If I ever find out . . . we're finished!") only served to invite deception, shut down the lines of communication, and make future affairs more likely.

Paradoxically, monogamy becomes more attainable when we honestly recognize that we can't guarantee it. Then we can talk openly about the fact that strong attractions, and affairs, occur in the best of marriages. Future temptations may well arise for both Rosa and John, depending on opportunity and circumstance. Rather than saying, "If it happens again, I can't take it," Rosa might say—as Jane did—"Of course, temptations will be there again . . . perhaps for me as well. I want us to be able to talk about it. And I want to do my part in making such conversation possible."

Rosa could not sanction extramarital affairs because she required monogamy to feel comfortable in her marriage. When I first saw her in therapy, however, she could find no middle ground between accepting infidelity or immediately bolting. Through our work, Rosa took a new position with John. She asked him to talk openly about attractions before they were acted on, and to tell her the facts directly if he did have sex with another woman. She told him, "Of course, it would be devastating to hear the truth from you. But I would stay in the marriage long enough to struggle with the issue and to try to get some clarity about it, so we could make a thoughtful decision about where we would go from there. If I discovered you were having an affair and lying to me about it, our marriage would be in far greater jeopardy."

As Peggy Vaughan emphasizes, there is a huge difference between issuing threats about what we would do if our partner is not faithful, and asking for a commitment to honesty—not only about present and future sexual attractions but also about all emotional issues affecting our relationship. Trust evolves only from a true knowledge of our partner and ourselves and a mutual commitment to increasing levels of sharing and self-disclosure. Monogamy can neither be demanded nor taken on faith.

Not all "honest sharing" is motivated by the wish for greater intimacy and deeper levels of self-disclosure with a partner. A friend of mine was married to a man who, early in their marriage, described his lusty fantasies for other women in vivid detail. His wife initially felt jealous, then alienated and put off. When she told him so, he did some soul-searching and recognized that these provocative communications reflected his insecurities and created distance.

Several years later, he approached his wife about his intensifying feelings of sexual attraction to his business partner. He was, as he put it, becoming intoxicated. He was scared to open up this conversation with his wife, but felt it was a matter of conscience to do so. His self-disclosure was fueled by his commitment to keep his marriage primary and to detoxify and defuse the power that attractions have when kept secret. He also wanted to create the conditions in which he would be least likely to act on his desire. Telling his wife ensured that she would continue to ask questions and express her pain. It ensured that he would consider her, even during those moments when he might prefer not to.

His wife, to her credit, recognized that her husband's honesty reflected his wish to protect their marriage and keep himself in line. Thus, she did her best not to distance herself from him, or try to control him, or otherwise punish him for his truth-telling. While her gut reaction to his disclosure was a fight-or-flight one, she managed to move toward him with love, while sharing her own feelings of threat and hurt.

To Tell or Not to Tell

The cost of confessing a sexual betrayal is obvious and immediately felt. In telling, we deal with our partner's pain and rage, with our own conscience or lack of it, with a lengthy process of reviewing and rebuilding intimacy. If the affair is ongoing, we can no longer have our cake and eat it too; either we end the affair, or deal with the consequences of refusing to do so, or else resume lying again.

In telling—in extending the possibilities of truth between two people—we also open the door for greater integrity, complexity, depth, and closeness in a relationship. Concealing an affair, even when it is long past, brief, and unsuspected, creates a subtle distance, disorientation, and emotional flatness in a relationship. Apart from issues of morality and conscience, concealing or confessing an affair has a great deal to do with the amount of distance we want or will tolerate in a primary relationship. And when we say, "I can't tell, because it will cause him too much pain," what we really mean is, "I don't want to deal with his pain and anger"—which is a different matter.

Whether we tell, or are told, also depends on the spoken or unspoken "contract" that evolves between spouses or intimate partners. We may communicate, as Rosa did, that we had better not find out about an affair because we couldn't take it. We may say this explicitly or we may convey it through our failure to ask questions that will allow us to know our spouse better as a sexual human being.

There is nothing wrong with communicating to our partner that we do not want the entire truth at a particular time about sexual fidelity, or any other issue. Being honest about our vulnerability, and our wish to be spared the whole story, may be a self-loving and self-protective act. Whatever the subject, we can be direct with others about what information we want and are ready to handle. Obviously we do not share information that may evoke violence or precipitate abuse.

But we should be clear with ourselves that extended silence ultimately invites secrecy (which requires lying and deception to maintain it), not only about affairs but about other emotionally painful issues that affect a relationship. It is simplest, of course, to ask our partner to conceal from us what brings pain, to spare us from the truth. But if we go along with such a contract, we narrow the possibilities of truth-telling and connection between two people.

12

The Body Seeks Truth

Some folks have bodies that won't let them lie. Or perhaps, more correctly, some folks *are* bodies that won't lie. A friend reminds me that we are our bodies. We don't just reside in them, like borrowed or rented space.

This friend is an honest body. He had a one-night stand and then confessed it to his wife the following evening, not from choice but from necessity. He cried rather than slept after it happened. He went through the motions at work the next day, feeling exhausted and nauseated. "I felt like I had the mental flu," he told me, when I asked him about the timing of his disclosure. "So I just collapsed into bed and waited for my wife to ask, 'What's wrong?'"

He didn't reflect on the timing of a revelation determined only by the extent of his own distress. His timing, in fact, was lousy, because his mother-in-law was visiting from Philadelphia and was inescapably drawn into private business. But reflecting on his actions, or even waiting to reveal them, wasn't an option. He couldn't have bluffed his way through his symptoms without engaging in further deception.

His wife, also a friend of mine, was distraught. I could empathize well enough with her shock, anger, and pain. But I also found myself thinking, "I'd vote for this man for president. I, for one, would sleep better at night if we had a president with an honest body. A president who *was* an honest body."

I don't know what combination of personal integrity and biological wiring brings on a mental flu, or why, for that matter, my friend's guts didn't kick up in protest *before* the act. I do know that his body (feeling nauseated and exhausted), not just his head, kicked him into truth-telling, just as his body (feeling aroused) contributed to his transgression.

In different contexts, this same friend can be a "natural liar." Once, I enlisted his help in an elaborate plot designed to throw my husband off track when a family surprise was being planned for him. My friend schemed, concealed, connived, and kept secrets with the rest of us. Despite my worry that his voice would crack, his face would turn red, or his body would otherwise leak the truth—he lied like a trooper.

But not when he had slipped into another woman's bed.

Most of us can count on our bodies, like the dreams of our unconscious, to at least *try* to keep us honest. If we engage in deceptions that violate our values, we may not immediately get a dose of mental flu, or even a jolt. But like Jane, who was sexually involved with her partner at work, we may get a little signal that changes into a bigger one over time if we fail to pay attention. Similarly, our bodies may react to the deceptions of others, as when a child becomes anxious, depressed, or otherwise symptomatic in response to a family secret.

Clark Moustakas's description of his experience with encounter groups illustrates how our bodies can grab us by the collars when our behavior is incongruent with our true values and beliefs. Moustakas, you may recall, was encouraged by his colleagues to try a more aggressive style of leadership. But when he experimented with pounding away at the defenses of others, his body gave him a pounding of its own. Ultimately, he couldn't ignore the physical signals which revealed that, at least for him, something was wrong with this confrontational style of leadership.

Our bodies react to our own deceit, even to a single incident of lying, particularly if we feel conflicted and guilty about it. These clues provide important nonverbal information to others in relationships. The last time I told an outright lie, I reflexively turned my face away while speaking, knowing that my expression might "give me away." Similarly, I rely on my reading of other people's bodies to detect deception, as we all do: I register what is popularly called "body language." I note obvious incongruities (my client says she's not angry but looks angry). I pick up subtle ones (my husband says he is paying attention, but I sense he's distracted). When a person's words tell me one thing ("I'm feeling close to you") and my automatic "knowing" intuits something different (I sense distance, a "not-thereness"), I put more trust in what my body registers than in the words I hear.

It's not surprising that our bodies register the lies and incongruities of others. Nor is it surprising that we respond with detectable physiological changes when we are dishonest and we know it. What is more remarkable is how the deceptions that we are denying or, indeed, living, sound a wake-up call to which the body responds. Turning points in my own life have occurred when my body has acted up to prod me away from a false path. A couple of instances stand out vividly.

The Body Protests

Early in my career I formed part of a multidisciplinary team in a psychiatric hospital. I was unhappy and believed I shouldn't be there. I had been told, however, that my skills as a psychologist were needed on this particular team and that I did not have the option of leaving. So I convinced myself that I must stay and that staying was the responsible thing to do. I redoubled my efforts to be heard, but I felt ineffective in that particular context.

During staff meetings, I became increasingly tense but decided this was life. After all, no one has a perfect job. I differed theoretically and personally from the psychiatrist in charge, but I reminded myself that differences present a challenge as well as being a fact of existence. Then I began to nod off during staff meetings. My struggle to stay attentive and involved became so intense that I was constantly battling sleepiness. Paradoxically, sleepiness was itself a "wake-up call," and I finally got the message. In the midst of this turmoil, I had a health scare, which proved to be a false alarm but provided me with the final incentive to find a way out. I became inventive and created a new career option where I had believed none existed.

At an earlier turning point in my life, my body gave me a more dramatic signal that I was about to make an important wrong turn. I was a graduate student in clinical psychology, living in an apartment on New York's Upper West Side. Eager for love and marriage, I became seriously involved with a fellow graduate student who met the checklist of qualifications I was looking for. He was bright, funny, ambitious, kind, fair—an all-around wonderful person. We shared similar interests, from playing the guitar to our love for psychology. But I didn't love him passionately or even romantically. And at the time I couldn't get clear about how much this mattered.

He was a terrific buddy and I felt comfortable in bed with him. I don't know whether my lack of passion was a matter of chemistry or one of circumstance. He and I had shared a "previous life" together on East 9th Street in Brooklyn. During my early teens, he had been pals with my friend Marla's older brother and we all had hung out together at Marla's house. Now, I couldn't separate out the old stuff from the man and woman we had become. But I thought I should because I didn't see anyone better out there.

I have never been an indecisive person, particularly not in matters of the heart. For the first time in my life, I understood how excruciating it is to feel suspended in a state of ambivalence and confusion. Should I break up with this man or marry him? I wanted to avoid doing either for the wrong reasons. I had met a number of attractive men at Columbia University who stirred more passionate and romantic feelings. But after dating them briefly or knowing them more intimately, none was, as I put it back then, "a really good catch."

I did everything I could think of to clarify the matter. I talked to countless people and solicited their advice and perspectives. I weighed the pros and cons. I tried to envision the future and to imagine worst-case scenarios. I also tried to be silent and meditative, to listen to the wisdom of my own soul. But I kept swinging first one way, then the other.

Eventually, there came a point where I could no longer tolerate the situation. After carefully considering everything I could think of, I decided to make marriage my goal. I resolved to stop looking around and to make a full emotional commitment. And I believed, by all objective criteria, I was doing the right thing. All logic, all rational thought, urged me to hold on to this man and "work on it." That night, I fell asleep feeling relieved.

But when I awoke the next morning, I was so depressed I could hardly rise from the bed. I had never felt so depressed, nor depressed in that particular way. It was paralyzing, but it didn't last through the day; it lasted just long enough for me to get the message.

My body was warning me about my self-deception and pretending. It was proving false what I was trying at the time to convince myself was true: "Passion eventually goes out of relationships, anyway"; "All relationships require compromise"; "My chances of finding someone better are slim"; "There is no perfect marriage." But I was deceiving myself. Without a crystal ball, I could never know which choice would ultimately prove "best" for me. But the absence of romance, or passion, or chemistry, or whatever, was too big a compromise to make.

Lying in bed that morning, heavy and immobilized, I knew I would never marry my friend. Yet for whatever reasons, I didn't have the strength, integrity, or will to end it then and there, or even to speak frankly with him. Instead, I behaved ambivalently, indeed, obnoxiously enough to bring about the inevitable. Shortly thereafter, he met and married a terrific woman who loved him without reservation.

The body, guided by the unconscious, can be a primary

source of personal truth and self-knowledge. We rely on this source of wisdom because the capacity for self-deception is extraordinarily well developed in our species. Women, in particular, are socialized as a class to pretend, to settle, and to call our compromises "life." Our bodies are harder to fool.

Interpreting Gut Feelings

"The body seeks truth," I tell a friend.

"The body misleads," she responds.

We know we're both correct, so we begin to refine our ideas further. We conclude that the body, seeking truth, sends a signal. But decoding it, interpreting its meaning, and knowing how to proceed from there is another matter entirely.

My friend, also a psychologist and psychotherapist, challenges me on the interpretation of my experience. We talk first about the example of my unhappy work situation and how it lulled me into sleepiness. She tells me about her experience, several years earlier, of becoming sleepy whenever a particular client talked about sexual abuse. Later, my friend uncovered repressed memories of sexual abuse in her own life that were similar to her client's: that is, for both women the abuse occurred while they were being bathed by their fathers. Sleepiness—like recurrent headaches, or other symptoms—is a signal to examine unconscious conflict, my friend says, not to leave the field.

The same friend challenges my interpretation about the immobilizing depression I felt after deciding I would compromise and marry without passion. "Who knows?" she asks. "Maybe it meant that you had conflicts about intimacy. Maybe you had an unconscious fear of commitment. Maybe your depression was a signal that you needed therapy to explore what was blocking you from a richer, more passionate response."

I'm not one to bolt from either love or work. I tell her simply, "I knew." That is, I knew in both instances what I needed to do.

Our conversation turns to a colleague, Sybil, who lives in California. Sybil, who is thirty-two years old, has metastasized breast cancer. My friend says that Sybil lives a compromised life, always withholding her honest responses, desires, and evaluations. She wonders if Sybil has chosen illness or death as a way out of an unbearable family situation that she can neither tolerate nor leave. My friend says, "I work frequently with breast cancer patients. They cannot begin to heal themselves until they uncover the meaning of the disease in their lives."

I have a powerful negative response to my friend's interpretation of Sybil's illness. It's not that I doubt a connection between our emotional and physical well-being. When we live unauthentic lives, our bodies may indeed give us a signal, in the form of illness or physical distress, that something is wrong. When our relationships or selves are severely compromised, our immune systems may also be compromised. Surely our bodies can only be strengthened when we live examined lives that include a large share of love, wisdom, truth, courage, and risk.

But I'm also convinced that Sybil, whom I met only briefly, did not cause her cancer. I don't believe that acquiring a life-threatening disease means that one hasn't lived authentically or truly enough. Following one's true path is undoubtedly a good and healthful idea, but it is no guarantee against getting cancer or preventing its return. I remind my friend that countless numbers of dishonest, fraudulent folks will continue to ripen to a mean-spirited old age while alarmingly large numbers of joyful, loving women will continue to die prematurely of breast cancer. From my perspective, it is profit madness—the poisoning of our soil, water, food, and sky—not personality deficit that is leading to a startling increase of cancer among the young people we know. It is our environment, not our psyches, I tell her, that demands a cleanup.

Despite our differences, my friend and I agree on one main point. The body may signal us, but it will not tell us how to interpret the signal. There is no instruction manual, no map. We both tentatively conclude that the body does not mislead. Rather, to be more accurate, *we misread.* We overanalyze, on the one hand, or on the other, we fail to pay attention at all.

Being in touch with our bodies, or more accurately, being our bodies, is how we know what is true. From moment to moment, we read our bodies so automatically that, like a cat, we don't think about it. We know, through our bodies, when we feel like sitting, or standing up, or leaving a restaurant. We know, through our bodies, whether we want to lie in someone's arms or just go to sleep. We know, through our bodies, whether a particular interaction leaves us feeling energized, uplifted, and inspired, or the opposite.

Our most direct route to self-awareness, to personal truth, is through the gut. We say, "I'm bored," or, "I want to be left alone." We say, "I love her," or, "I just don't trust her." We say, "I'm terrified." All this comes to us through the body.

Yet we do misread and lose touch with what we are feeling, especially when it threatens to overwhelm us or make waves in our lives. We may misname our most basic emotions. "No, I'm not angry," we say, as we transform an unacceptable emotion into tears and hurt. Or perhaps we do it the other way around. But even when we call it straight ("Yes, I'm furious"), emotions are only starting points. We still must think about feelings, decode them, and decide on the next step. The quest for truth has at its center the struggle to identify the body's deepest truths and to distinguish these from automatic conditioned responses that begin in the body and then mislead.

Take Anger, for Example

Anger is in the body, a signal worth attention and respect. Perhaps we are doing more or giving more than we can comfortably do or give. We may be failing to clarify what we expect from or will tolerate in a relationship. Or our behavior is incongruent with our stated beliefs: that is, we say we can't live with something, but then we continue to put up with it. Anger exists for a reason; it can inspire us to define our own truths and to take a new and courageous action on our own behalf.

But the opposite occurs as well, and just as frequently. Anger creates tunnel vision that leads to a narrow, rigid view of what is true and whose truth counts. Anger, like any strong emotion, tells us that something is not right, but it doesn't tell us *what* the real issues are, or even *with whom* the real issues are, or how best to proceed. When we feel angry and intense, we may be convinced that there is only one truth, our own, and our job is to convince the other person to see things our way.

Anger can sharpen our passion and clarity, but it can also

blur it. When we angrily confront another person, convinced
that truth is on our side, we often move the situation from
bad to worse. When anxiety is high, people divide into
opposing camps and lose the capacity to see both—or better
yet, four or five—sides of an issue. The capacity for empathy
and for creative problem solving that considers the needs of
all is diminished. The emotional climate may become
increasingly intense, ensuring that people will have to struggle harder to uncover and share their own truths, to hear
each other, or simply to stay in the same room.

Venting anger rarely solves the problem from which our
anger springs, nor does it necessarily clear a wider path for
truth-telling. When it comes to anger, or any form of emotional intensity, we will have difficulty distinguishing anxiety-driven emotionality from true feeling, and deciding what
to do next.

Decoding anger, or even feeling it to begin with, requires a
sense of entitlement and possibility. The challenge is not
only to "get in touch with our bodies," but also to create a
context that makes this awareness possible and that validates
our response. For most of us, private experience has no name
when there is no ear to hear it, no cultural legitimacy for
what we feel in the gut.

One girl in my high school in Brooklyn often made a fuss
about apparently trivial things that didn't seem to matter.
Judy just couldn't leave well enough alone. "Why is God
male?" "Why does she give up her name and go by Mrs.
John Smith?" "Why should she hide her age, calling herself a
girl?" We thought Judy was overreacting, always making
something out of nothing. I don't think Judy was seeking
political analysis back then; just validation for her own gut

reactions. Looking back, I imagine that she felt sexism in her bones the same way an African-American man felt racism when he was called "colored boy," or told to sit in the back of the bus. But there was no word "sexism" back then, and the rest of us were in a coma. To be awake in a world of sleep-walkers is possible but never easy. So, like a child, or like a woman, Judy was seen but not heard.

Now, three decades later, my body can detect sexism like radar. I register it somewhere in my chest, before I have words to explain what is wrong or to justify my irritation. Today, the feminist analysis that begins in my gut is cheered and read by other women. I am privileged to be part of an extraordinary movement of women, raising questions like Judy's, rethinking and re-viewing everything, taking nothing as a "given." Some women still say, "Me? I'm not angry," or, "How trivial," but most of us say differently. I wonder what happened to Judy, who had no one to affirm or support her, or even to listen.

Anxiety and Fear

Anxiety—like anger—requires interpretation. Like other messages from the body, the true meaning of anxiety may be obscured. Yes, we're anxious. But what is the danger? Is it past or present, real or imagined? Should we stop to consider it or try to ignore it? Are we feeling anxious because we are boldly charting new territory, or because we are about to do something stupid? Who is being served or protected by our fear?

Anxiety drives other emotions. When anxiety is high, we are most likely to fly into a rage or fall mindlessly in love. Or we may feel just plain scared. Anxiety, like anger, may propel us into action, but just as often it operates like a stop sign or a flashing red light that says, "Danger! Do not enter here!"

I've learned through experience (the name we give to our mistakes) to recognize and pay heed to a particular type of anxiety or tension as if it were a stop sign. My body is warning me to come to a halt because I'm off track. Perhaps I should not mail a letter or make a phone call, or rush into a particular conversation. Anxiety makes me think twice.

When I'm anxious, I become intense. I may feel an urgent need to confront a friend with "the truth," or, more specifically, to tell her what she is doing wrong. But when I feel this way, I've learned to wait, to see whether the need endures over the course of a day or two. Usually, the intensity dissipates because it's been driven by my own stress. Waiting also allows for a clearer intuitive response about how to put things and whether to even bother.

I've learned that I'm obnoxious when I offer unsolicited "truths" to friends at the time I feel most driven to confront them. I also distinguish between different sorts of emotional intensity. There's a difference, in my body, between an anxious, uncentered sort of intensity, and the passion—the fire in the soul—that lends energy and zest to friendship and work.

Sometimes I feel anxious and I decide to ignore it. If anxiety were *only* a warning sign, I might never show up for my mammogram, get behind the podium, or speak out when my heart is pounding. There are many occasions when I feel anxious or frightened and I just decide that I won't let it hinder me from doing what I need to do.

During a year when I was terrified to fly, or more accurately, terrified to crash, I crisscrossed the country on countless airplanes. Waves of anxiety washed over me as I imagined my plane, engulfed in flames, plummeting to the ground. These fearful imaginings began days before every departure, but I flew so much that my fear eventually went away. Another therapist with the same story says: "When people tell you they don't fly because they are afraid of flying, you need not believe them. They don't fly because they don't buy airline tickets."

We need to respect our anxiety and pay attention to what our bodies are trying to tell us through it. But we don't have to succumb to fear. Fear is women's worst enemy. And it is not by accident that we are taught to fear. Fear serves to paralyze women, holds us in place, saps our energy and attention from important work, and limits our creativity and imagination. Fear keeps us close to home. It silences us. And if we wait until we are unafraid, or fixed, or analyzed, we may have waited too long.

In Audre Lorde's book *The Cancer Journals*, she speaks eloquently on this point. "I realize that if I wait until I am no longer afraid to act, write, speak, be, I'll be sending messages on a Ouija board, cryptic complaints from the other side. When I dare to be powerful, to use my strength in the service of my vision, then it becomes less important whether or not I am afraid." She warns us not to allow our fear to fossilize into silence because imposed silence in any area of women's lives is a tool for separation and powerlessness.

Audre Lorde makes no claim to have banished fear entirely. In describing her response to the crisis of breast cancer, she tells us that fear remains an uninvited companion, but one that she refuses to surrender to, or to dissipate her energies fighting. Breast cancer heightened Lorde's clarity about the necessity for women to break our silences, to scrutinize and speak our truths. She exhorts us to work and speak when we are afraid, just as we work and speak when we are tired. "For we have been socialized to respect fear more than our own needs for language and definition, and while we wait in silence for that final luxury of fearlessness, the weight of that silence will choke us."

Our silence, Lorde reminds us, does not protect us. Women can be silent our whole lives for safety and we will still die. Our invisibility on matters both personal and political may help us to feel less vulnerable, but not, in the long run, less frightened. "We can sit in our corners mute forever while our sisters and our selves are wasted, while our children are distorted and destroyed, while our earth is poisoned, we can sit in our safe corners mute as bottles, and we still will be no less afraid."

The body's first response to anxiety is not courage. Rather, when we are anxious, we seek comfort, which means doing what is reflexive and familiar. "Doing what comes naturally" can lull us into a psychic slumber, a life on automatic pilot where our commitment is to security and safety rather than truth and honor.

Dr. Sonia Johnson is a nationally prominent speaker, feminist author, and excommunicated Mormon who once ran for president of the United States. In her passionate quest to discover her own truths, she has never been stopped by the immensity of her fear. To the contrary, she has interpreted her experience of greatest terror as proof that she was mucking about in the deepest strata of patriarchal taboos. In working to strip herself of layer after layer of indoctrination, she became most distrustful of what initially felt deceptively natural, comfortable, safe, and right. Early in her feminist life, she learned that the first emotions she identified in herself at any given moment were not her genuine feelings. And in her quest to discriminate between her conditioning and her true feelings, she has over and over stepped into alien, lonely, and uncharted territory, no matter how great her terror.

I respect Sonia's courage for jumping off the high dive and creating a radically new vision of female reality. Her unraveling of all that patriarchy has taught as "true" and "real" has taken her on a couragous personal quest, which she generously shares in her books. In the process of inventing and discovering what is most authentic and alive within herself, she has discarded both relationships and sex, at least as the rest of us define these. Today, Sonia could no sooner return to her old beliefs than she could fit herself into the outgrown clothes of her youth.

Sonia's glorious leaps out of her patriarchally conditioned mind make almost everyone nervous. Even some of my more radical feminist friends have concluded that she has gone off the deep end. Sonia might happily agree, since she observed early on that truth is reversed in patriarchy, and thus to go out of our minds is to become most truly sane. Visiting her in the mountains of New Mexico, I found her to be anything but crazy. Rather, I felt admiration and love in response to her uncompromising commitment to free herself from patriarchial injunctions.

Yet I have no less respect for women who move slowly and cautiously on their own path toward greater truth-telling and self-discovery. Perhaps that's because I'm one of the slower ones. I believe that the direction of our lives is more important than the speed at which we travel them. Laying the groundwork for truth-telling can be a slow process for those of us who try to preserve both our connections and our integrity. Our bodies may not only protest deception but also warn us about the hazards of precipitous honesty.

Respecting Resistance

Maria sought my help at a time when she was struggling with a profound dilemma in truth-telling. She hadn't told her parents that she was living with an African-American man in a love relationship that spanned almost two years. Her partner, Cyrill, lost patience. At first, he encouraged Maria to tell her parents. Then he pushed her to do so. Now he was delivering an ultimatum: "Tell them the truth or I'm history." It was at this crisis point that Maria came to see me.

When Cyrill criticized Maria for keeping his existence and their relationship a secret from her family, Maria concurred and said nothing in her own defense. She told me that she hated herself for being a coward, yet she couldn't bring herself to tell her parents the truth because she feared their rejection. Cyrill argued that if Maria's parents rejected her, they weren't worth worrying about and that acceptance had no meaning when it was founded on deception.

Maria's silence violated her own values. Yet she felt paralyzed to act. A month earlier she had gone back home with the intention of telling her parents about Cyrill. She became so nauseated that she couldn't proceed with her plan. More than once, her body acted in protest—not of deception but of honest self-disclosure. Once she developed back spasms while having an imaginary conversation with her mother in which she told her about her love for Cyrill and their plans to eventually marry.

Maria thought that she should plow through her resistance. She compared herself unfavorably to Cyrill, who was not in hiding, even though his parents were vehemently opposed to their son dating or marrying outside his race and culture. Yet Maria felt frozen in place. Then, as we constructed a genogram of Maria's family and examined how dif-

ferences were managed over the generations, her gut resistance began to make sense.

Families have differently patterned ways of managing
anxiety and emotional intensity. Over four generations,
Maria's family had developed a predominant way of navigating relationships under stress: emotional cut-off. Many family members did not stay connected in the face of differences.
Instead, when people got mad, they might not speak to each
other for, say, a couple of hundred years.

The stated "reasons" behind cut-offs ran the gamut from
the sacred to the absurd. Maria's Irish grandparents, for
example, never allowed her mother back into their home
after she married out of the Catholic faith and converted to
her husband's religion. Her father's siblings stopped speaking
when they could not agree about the settlement of their
deceased mother's limited estate. Maria's maternal uncles
severed their ties following a feud about the sale of Amway
products. A number of first cousins had never met because
their parents weren't on speaking terms. Also, forgiveness
was not culturally valued in their family. If someone did
something bad to you, you weren't supposed to forget it.
One prominent family therapist, herself Irish, jokingly call
this the "Irish grudge syndrome."

Cyrill's family, like most, also had a difficult time managing differences. But while family members flared up in
anger, there were no emotional cut-offs. In the end, blood
proved thicker than water. Family was family, no matter
how much you disapproved of, or gossiped about, your
crazy relatives. As far as Cyrill knew, no family member had
ever been extruded from the family because of a conflict or
difference.

Both Maria and Cyrill faced a racist society. And both
would have to deal with friends' and co-workers' reactions to

their relationship. But they did not face the same family. How might Maria approach the challenge of truth-telling, considering the family legacy of cut-off? This was her challenge. As I saw it, her body was warning her to slow down and proceed with care.

And so she did. At glacial speed, Maria finally started to move. She began laying the foundation for truth-telling by first increasing the amount of contact she had with each of her parents. Before telling them about Cyrill, she initiated any number of conversations with family members about how differences were handled in the family. She inquired about relatives who had been excluded or "denied membership" because they believed or behaved differently. She told her parents how painful it would be for her if a family member didn't recognize her existence.

Most importantly, Maria entered into all these conversations with a loving heart and from an emotional space that was free from judgment or blame. Although she hoped for acceptance, she became increasingly less focused on needing her folks to change or respond in a particular way. When she did finally tell her parents about Cyrill, about two months after our initial meeting, she felt good because she was navigating her part of the process in a solid way. She didn't receive the acceptance she had hoped for, but neither was she cast out by her family.

In my work with Maria, I didn't want her to succumb to anxiety. I did, however, wish for her to respect it. The body, which is closely linked to the unconscious, has a particular wisdom about matters of timing. If we are absorbing too much anxiety, we may need to slow down or make a different plan.

The Body Stores Truth

The body not only seeks truth (again, to be distinguished from momentary honesty) but also, for want of a better word, it *stores* truth. When we're ready, our body may provide us with clues about painful truths that our conscious mind has repressed. Many of us receive the precious gift of memory through the body first.

Consider the matter of early sexual abuse and how we begin to remember: One close friend experienced "a tornado" moving up through her chest—an intense experience that took her by surprise as she casually thumbed through a book on incest. This physical reaction was her first awareness of a sexual trauma that occurred on a train when she was four. Another friend, in the course of psychoanalysis, began to experience a "suffocating feeling" in her throat, accompanied by difficulty swallowing. Along with her dreams (another primary source of truth and wisdom), her body was beginning to give her knowledge of a childhood experience of being orally sodomized by an uncle.

The body does not "forget." It is not uncommon for people to begin to uncover traumatic memories during movement, breathing exercises, deep massage, or various kinds of therapeutic body work. The profoundly wise body/unconscious "knows" what truths we can handle when and in what doses. The return of memory—along with the emotions surrounding early trauma—marks the beginning of transformation and healing. As we begin to recall an incident of sexual abuse, for example, our past and present lives make better sense and we view our world and ourselves with a new clarity. The gift of memory usually does not come to us first by "thinking things through," although thinking is essential in figuring out how to process new information and what to do next.

Of course, our mind/body/unconscious are not truly separate entities. Granted, we may *experience* the distinction, as in the examples I have described where the rational mind says, "Go!" and the body says, "No!" We may even describe different "ways of knowing" as if we were a composite of different selves that inhabited separate spheres.

For example, I ask an acquaintance about how she uncovers her deepest truths and she tells me about her intuitive self, her intellectual self, her spiritual self, and her body wisdom. She refers also to her "inner wise woman" and to "the child within," as well as to her "masculine" and "feminine" sides. These distinctions may be useful to her but they are not real. The categories we create reflect our limited understanding of the infinite and mysterious complexity of how we ourselves "know" and think/feel/intuit our own truths.

Love and Connection

Regretfully (or happily), there are no "how-to" guidelines for deciphering the body's signals. Obviously, we can "read" our bodies more accurately during a calm, meditative moment than during an anxious, frenetic time. And we will be in tune with our bodies only if we truly love and honor them. We can't be in good communication with the enemy.

Alienation from our bodies leads us to ignore signals as basic as those regarding hunger and touch. Few of us, for example, eat when we are hungry, stop when we are no longer hungry, or even recognize what our bodies are signaling to us. Instead, countless women are trapped in cycles of dieting and self-contempt that may last a lifetime. Our sexuality is similarly encumbered with emotional baggage. Many of us have difficulty staying "in the moment" and feeling whatever we are (or are not) feeling. Instead, we may prod our bodies to feel aroused or to achieve orgasm. Our attention may shift to how we look, what our partner is thinking, whether we are taking too long to get excited, to come, or whatever.

Over the past year or so, I have experimented with the challenge of listening to and regarding my body and refusing to push myself to do what I do not feel in the moment. I have not so much "succeeded" in these experiments as I have arrived at a deep appreciation for the layer upon layer of female conditioning that removes women from a truly loving, respectful connection with our bodies/selves and thus from a deeper knowledge of our power and personal truths.

As women, we are taught to hate our bodies and to disconnect from them. On my desk, for example, sits a full-page ad from two full-service hospitals. It features a glamorous young blonde in pink lingerie holding a single rose. *Life Looks Better When You Do*, reads the caption of the advertisement inviting women to begin the "natural" process of "Becoming" through plastic surgery. The "You're Becoming" program offers breast proportioning, nose improvement, face, brow, or neck lift, eyelid surgery, chin reshaping, ear modification, suction lipectomy for the reduction of localized body fat, and other corrective procedures to help women gain the "beauty, confidence and health" (yes, health) we wish to project to others.

There's no particular reason to single out the plastic surgery industry—or the cosmetic industry, the diet industry, the fashion industry, the pornography industry—as *the* problem. What we learn about "being a woman," being "like other women," and "satisfying male demand" involves massive deception, concealment, and self-betrayal that ultimately breeds shame, alienation, and disconnection from our bodies/selves, and even from our place in the life cycle. How extraordinary, for example, that we are told to withhold, to joke about, or even to lie about our age. How remarkable that any one of us would actually agree to mystify and conceal the number of years we have been alive, thus perpetuating the notion that there is something shameful or lesser in growing older, which is, after all, everyone's goal.

It is not only possible but natural for each of us to love our bodies, to find ourselves beautiful—no matter how different, disabled, old, or battle-scarred we may be. I love Audre Lorde's description of her decision to avoid prosthesis after her mastectomy, to go proudly into the world as a beautiful, one-breasted black warrior, to find the strength that came from her own perception of her body, and the courage to challenge what we learn is "normal," meaning the "right" color, shape, size, or number of breasts. I'm further inspired by a vision she shared more than a decade ago of an army of one-breasted women descending upon Congress and demanding that the use of carcinogenic, fat-stored hormones in beef feed be outlawed.

It is not any one thing we do: wearing clothes and shoes that constrict movement or comfort; covering our gray hair, wrinkles, and smells; kissing or embracing without connection or desire; eating when we aren't hungry. None of these things on any particular day is "a big deal." But the larger picture, the infinite ways we are taught that we do not belong to ourselves, may amount to a total erosion of connection with and love for our bodies and what they stand for.

We are all products of a culture, but we are also shapers of culture. Here is the oldest and deepest feminist challenge: to create the contexts in which we can define more authentically our own desires and aesthetics, and to be more connected to our bodies and how we wish to use them.

13

Will the Real Me Please Stand?

Pat Parker, a poet of humor and passion, once told a friend that she was waiting for the revolution that would allow her to take all her parts with her wherever she went—"not have to say to one of them, 'No, you stay home tonight, you won't be welcome, because I'm going to an all-white party where I can be gay but not black. Or I'm going to a black poetry reading and half the poets are anti-homosexual.'"

Parker, who died in 1989, did not spend her life sitting back waiting for such a revolution. Like countless women, she was creating it. "If I'm advertised as a black poet, I'll read dyke poems," she once said. Most of us are not so bold, but all of us can probably identify with Parker's words about leaving parts of ourselves at home.

It's not that women are openly exhorted to hide or silence important aspects of the self. Quite the contrary. Experts everywhere encourage us to express our "true selves," despite whatever anger or disapproval this might evoke from others. Such advice, which I myself have sometimes advocated, is both accurate and absurd.

It is accurate because living more authentically and truly is unarguably a good idea. The dictate "Be yourself!" is an agreeable cultural cliché—and as a friend of mine quips, no one else is as qualified for the job. Surely, there are times when we must gather the courage to clarify and stand behind our beliefs and values, even when doing so leaves us feeling separate and alone. And, undoubtedly, we all might benefit from accommodating less to others and becoming more attentive to our own inner voice.

But the advice to be one's true self, and to value one's true self apart from context and how others respond to us, is as absurd as it is advisable. For starters, we are relational beings who need approval and appreciation from significant people in our lives. Our wish to be valued, and to belong, is not excessive dependency but a basic, enduring human need.

Also, we don't have one "true self" that we can decide to reveal on the one hand or hide on the other. Rather, the particulars of our situations define, limit, and expand what we assume to be "real" and "true" about ourselves. Nor is there ever a point in human life when the self is "finished" or "set." Situations are always redefining who we are. It's not just a matter of what we present to others but also what we *become* within different contexts.

Take the workplace, for example. The story of Angela and Jan in Chapter 6 reminds us that people don't just bring their true selves to the job. Jobs also "create" people. You may recall that Angela behaved "like a woman" (affiliative, "people-oriented," and devoid of ambition) in a low-opportunity work setting. But she behaved more "like a man" when she was offered economic opportunity and status.

Similarly, men in dead-end jobs begin to resemble the

female stereotype. The sociologist Rosabeth Moss Kanter has pointed out that men in jobs with little or no opportunity for advancement "limit their aspirations, seek satisfaction in activities outside work, dream of escape, interrupt their careers, emphasize leisure and consumption, and create sociable peer groups in which interpersonal relationships take precedence over other aspects of work." In her book *Men and Women of the Corporation* Kanter demonstrates how the differing fate of men and women in the workplace is largely a matter of the structure of work systems themselves, rather than a function of psychological, biological, or socialization differences between the sexes. Many gender differences that we take to be "true" or "fixed" disappear, or even reverse themselves, when the context changes.

We can never unravel the tightly interwoven fabric of situation and self, because "self" does not exist in isolation. For example, the "feminine" traits, qualities, and behaviors identified as the "special" strengths and weaknesses of our sex are identical to those that characterize subordinate, oppressed, or disempowered groups. What, then, are we observing or measuring when we define a trait or behavior as "masculine" or "feminine"? Only after we begin to change our situations, or someone else changes them for us, can we appreciate how remarkably contextual is our "true self"—male or female.

A Seminar on the River

In a moment of either ignorance or courage, I accepted an invitation to join a group of colleagues conducting a seminar for business executives on the subject of how to understand human behavior. I had participated in these executive seminars before, as both a lecturer and a small group leader, so the work was not new to me. This particular seminar, however, would not be held at the familiar conference center on Menninger grounds. With the cooperation of Colorado's Outward Bound program, the week-long executive seminar would take us down the Yampa and Green rivers in Utah and Colorado. A core Menninger staff group had been conducting river seminars for some time and several had become veteran whitewater rafters. But this was a first for me.

On land or on water, women executives are a numerically scarce commodity. This posed a dilemma for our seminar staff, who had to determine the composition of the small discussion groups that would meet twice a day as a key part of the experience. As only a small fraction of our participant group was female, we had limited options for group assignments. We could sprinkle one or two women in each group; we could create two mixed-gender groups and twice as many men's groups; or we could put all the women together in one small group. I argued for the third alternative, and—as the only woman on the professional staff of this trip—volunteered to lead that group.

The first option (sprinkling a woman or two in each group) was objectionable to me because I was concerned about the negative impact of tokenism, a word used to refer to the intentional placement of a minority person in a visible position of power in a group or organization, so as to convey the appearance of inclusiveness when there is no real commitment to this goal. Tokenism, however, also refers to the *fact of numerical scarcity*, irrespective of how it came about or why it is maintained. The negative effects of tokenism need not reflect the questionable intentions of the leadership, but rather the skewed proportions of the group. In a skewed group where there is a large preponderance of one type of member over another, the "rare" individuals are tokens.

The handful of women participating in the river seminar were tokens in their work setting. Like them, I was a token in the Menninger staff group. By placing the women participants together in the small group, I argued, we could provide them with one context in which they would not continue to suffer that predictable fate within the group.

What is such a fate? Rosabeth Moss Kanter's careful research on tokenism is in keeping with my own observations of the behavior of the numerically scarce. Kanter reports that tokens often feel they have to "do better" while maintaining a low profile and playing down their successes. The fear of visibility often displayed by the numerically scarce is yet another way to understand the "fear of success syndrome" that has been observed in women and other marginalized groups. Numerically scarce individuals usually end up conforming to stereotypes—or bending over backward to fight stereotypes. In either case, the amount of "watchful effort" required often precludes the option of relaxing and being oneself.

Tokens typically show excessive loyalty to the dominant group culture and do not generate alliances with other tokens that might influence the group. The numerically scarce are unable to establish effective support systems among themselves and will meet resistance from their own kind when they attempt to do so. ("I just don't feel the need to meet together as women"; "What will people think if they see black people sitting together at lunch once a week?")

In the end, Kanter notes, tokens *underline* rather than *undermine* the dominant group culture. For example, exaggerated macho conversation is more likely to be displayed and tolerated in a skewed group than in one where women are either entirely absent or well represented. The flip side of such behavior is that those in the dominant group end up carefully "watching" what they say in front of tokens. Both macho talk and "gentlemanly" behavior highlight masculinity and isolate the women.

Tokens themselves unwittingly protect, rather than protest, the status quo. When women, for example, are included in token numbers in group life—medical school, say, or the military—they are viewed not as individuals but as representatives of their kind. The pressures to be "as tough as the boys" and to avoid doing anything "out of line" make it difficult to support or identify with other women. Also, the gratification of being viewed as "special" and the distinction of occupying a position previously denied to members of one's own group further increase the pressure to conform.

Kanter reports that as ratios shift (just over 2 to 1), tokens become a minority and have the possibility to behave differently: "Minority members can find potential allies in one another, can form coalitions, and can affect the culture of the group." Balanced groups (at a ratio of about 3 to 2 or better) put the least negative constraints on group members and offer the greatest possibility for people to behave naturally and be viewed objectively. As groups become balanced, people can begin to relate to one another as individuals rather than as "types" or representatives of a particular kind. Kanter's work suggests that tokens are unaware of the negative constraints of tokenism until after the relative numbers shift and they are no longer tokens.

A factor as apparently simple as relative numbers, then, profoundly shapes our experiences in group and organizational life, determining how much of our "true selves" we can experience and express. But mitigating the impact of tokenism was not my only reason for wanting to create same-sex discussion groups on the river trip. I knew that women's groups help women define themselves with imagination and without constraint, and I was experienced both as a facilitator and as a member of such groups. Men, too, would be "more themselves" in a men's group, rather than in a group that included one woman. The seminar leader agreed to the same-sex group composition and I was satisfied. I forgot that tokens identify with the majority culture and thus I assumed, mistakenly, that the female participants would share my enthusiasm.

Just Like a Woman?

I was entirely unprepared for the resistance I encountered when my small group met for the first time. The women, feeling like lower-caste citizens excluded from the real action, demanded to know why this act of segregation had occurred. Although the men were satisfied to be together, the women felt ghettoized. Their negative comments about our group's composition implicitly set the men up and put the women (i.e., themselves and me) down.

When I reported on my small group experience during an evening staff meeting, my colleagues voiced no surprise. Surely women tend to prefer the company of men. Haven't women always been complicitous with sexist attitudes, viewing their own activities as inferior to what men do? From this perspective, the women were simply behaving "like women." What else is new?

But did my group's negativity reflect their gender or their position as tokens? Was I observing something "natural" and enduring about women, or was I observing the outcome of an unnatural (i.e., numerically skewed) context? Contrast the river seminar experience with an activity such as a feminist conference, where women, rather than being tokens, are the creators of the group culture and the leaders who sustain it. What happens when tokens become dominants?

Here's one example: My friend and colleague Marianne Ault-Riché and I co-directed a national women's conference at Menninger from 1983 to 1990. Because the format included small discussion groups, Marianne and I struggled over the years with the dilemma of group composition. How should we distribute the handful of tokens (in this case, men) who participated in the conference?

Because we were familiar with Kanter's work on tokenism, we were committed to putting no less than three men together in a discussion group. Our first conference included two mixed-gender groups and twice that many all-female groups. Complaints were voiced by the women in the mixed groups, who were disappointed and angry that they were not assigned to women's groups. In the next two conferences, we put all the men together in one small group led by two male adjunct faculty members. Now the women were satisfied but the men complained bitterly. Even though the conference brochure stated clearly that participants would be placed in same-sex discussion groups, the men felt cheated, marginalized, and removed from the center of learning and the heart of the emotional experience. As would be expected from their position of numerical scarcity, their behavior was like that of the women in the river seminar.

From my perspective, the women in the river seminar were not behaving "like women." Rather, they were behaving like *people in a particular context*, one in which they were numerically scarce, one in which their "own kind" held no power (the executive seminars were created and led by men), and one in which their group leader was the newest staff member as well as the least skilled and most anxious about navigating the rapids and the wilderness. The members of my small group did transcend their initial disappointment. But we can never fully transcend the impact of tokenism. Tokens themselves may not complain, and may even feel honored to be included among the dominants. But we cannot begin to know what tokens do "naturally" in groups until the relative numbers shift and they are tokens no more.

Tokenism is just one of the countless variables that affect how "naturally" we behave in group life and what we take to be true or real about ourselves and others. But it is hardly a new or startling idea that we are continually influenced by context and circumstance—by power or the lack of it. Why elaborate on the obvious?

Most of us fail to appreciate how profoundly we influence each other and how larger systems influence us. Instead, we learn to think in terms of individual characteristics, as if individuals are separable from the relationship systems in which they operate. Obviously, we do have aspects of the self that are relatively stable and enduring, predictable, and even rigidly patterned. And some aspects of the self are not negotiable under relationship pressures. We do not, however, have one "true self" that we can choose to either hide or authentically share with others. Rather, we have multiple potentials and possibilities that different situations will evoke or suppress, make more or less likely, and assign more or less positive or negative values to.

What Counts?

When I was on the river, I learned how it felt to be the least competent and most frightened person in a work group. I enlisted for this trip without any prior camping or whitewater experience, and I was entirely unprepared for the grit and skill required for wilderness living and whitewater rafting. I was particularly unprepared for how slowly I learned outdoor skills in comparison to the seminar participants, who were both more experienced and far quicker to learn.

I had difficulty mastering everything from tying the gear securely into the raft to understanding what commands I should shout ("Right!" "Left!" "Stop!" "Backpaddle!") to guide my raft safely down the rapids when it was my turn to captain. As the week progressed and the wilderness became my "real world," I imagined what it would be like to live out my life in this setting. How would my experience of myself and my self-worth change in this context? Back home, my particular skills were socially and economically valued, while skills requiring physical ability were typically assigned a lesser worth. In the wilderness, these values were reversed: my individual talents were irrelevant to adaptation and survival and, in fact, seemed just plain unimportant.

As I struggled to start a fire, or tie a knot, or control my anxiety, I thought about how closely our definition of "what counts" is linked to time and place. My feelings of inadequacy reminded me of how difficult it can be to value ourselves when our own special talents and abilities are not "what really counts." Of course, one could argue that I was failing to consider context in viewing myself as hopelessly incompetent in the great outdoors. A friend who runs wilderness trips for women reassures me that, in the right setting, I could learn both confidence and skills on the water. I'm not convinced, but I suspect I would do better than I think I might, and worse than she imagines. In any case, I know it wouldn't come easily.

My river experience, like my conversation with Sue about my award ceremony, pushed my thinking about what counts and about who *decides* what counts. In the wilderness, doing things well is far more important than talking or writing well. But in our everyday lives, who determines "the truth" about the relative importance of our talents, interests, and skills? Who decides whose work and experience is worthy of attention and economic reward—and whose is not?

All of us internalize the dominant group's values, transmitted through family and culture, about who and what count. We may, to take just one example, question our intelligence without asking who has defined "intelligence," who benefits from this definition, and what other definitions are possible. A particular view of "the truth"—created by a specific group of people—is presented as representative of the whole, or as relevant to all humankind.

In my mother's generation, for example, I watched countless women discount their remarkable intelligence (or question their "IQ") because they never asked, "Who says?" Who says that a man is brilliant when he solves mathematical problems but fails to notice that someone in the room is crying? Who says that the ability to grasp the nuances of a social interaction is a lesser measure of "intelligence" than the ability to grasp the principles of engineering? Who says that the complex skills women traditionally excel in reflect "intuition" rather than intelligence?

Intelligence comprises more factors than we can ever begin to quantify; it includes such complex skills as the capacity for friendship, for empathy, for being perceptive, caring, alert, and emotionally present in the world. But the construction of standardized intelligence tests, like the construction of much of our reality, tells a different story—one that reflects racial, class, and gender biases. There are no universal, ultimate, or fixed "truths" about what constitutes intelligence. Nor can individual intelligence ever be captured by so arid a concept as IQ.

How then do we expand the possibilities of knowing what is "true" about our selves and our world? Only by recognizing how partial, subjective, and contextual our "knowing" is can we even hope to begin to enlarge it. Only as we understand that a very small group of privileged human beings have defined what is true and real for us all can we begin to pay attention to the many diverse voices (our own, included) that we have been taught to ignore. Only by viewing human behavior in context, by placing ourselves in new contexts, and by trying out new behaviors in the old contexts, can we begin to move toward a more complex truth about ourselves and others.

Who Defines Truth . . . and for Whom?

Feminist consciousness raising began with white, middle-class women awakening to the fact that privileged, white, Euro-American males defined the nature of things, including the nature of women and human nature itself. Yet amazingly (or perhaps not surprisingly), modern feminism repeated and mirrored old errors. In creating new truths about "women," the voices of dominant women silenced a diversity of female stories, as men had silenced theirs.

One needn't be a feminist scholar to observe that women differ from one another by virtue of age, race, class, physical ability, ethnicity, sexual orientation, and other factors that combine to form a filter or vantage point from which we define what is real or true. Less obvious are the ways that dominant voices submerge others, and purport to define what is true or real for all. Nor is it necessary to harbor discriminatory intentions to erase another's authentic voice, or to elevate oneself at another's expense. The process may be automatic and covert, a matter of who is included, in what proportions, and who is paying attention. Errors of exclusion and tokenism run deep, as my own experience illustrates.

When Marianne Ault-Riché and I organized the first feminist women's conference at the Menninger Clinic, our goal was to create a safe space in which to critique theory and share personal experience. We knew that the freedom to speak honestly and openly required a conference setting that offered a radical departure from patriarchal structures. Our first conference was called "Women in Context." Subsequent conferences focused on such themes as "Women and Self-Esteem" and "Mothers and Daughters." Marianne and I were proud of creating and co-directing a successful feminist conference series in our workplace.

Our self-congratulatory stance, however, was tempered over time. Minority women began to challenge the white, middle-class, heterosexual "culture" of the conference. Initially, I felt defensive and said things to myself like "But we *are* a white institution," and "I don't really know women of color who could lecture on this subject," and "Won't the quality of the conference suffer if we try to invite speakers of every race, class, and creed?"

These are the same arguments that privileged men use to exclude women, but the parallel didn't register. Similarly, Marianne and I were attuned to the dilemma faced by token males in the women's conference, but we didn't recognize the dilemma of the token females. As I recall complaining to Marianne, we surely couldn't be expected to create a space for *everyone's* story. Wasn't it sufficient that we had added African Americans and lesbians to our conference staff? How could we begin to make room for the multiplicity of female voices: Native American, Hispanic (Latina, Chicana, Puerto Rican, Cuban), Mexican-American, Asian, old, poor, disabled . . . The list was endless. I could imagine only problems rather than benefits from such rich diversity.

In fact, there is nothing wrong with any group of people getting together with their own kind to teach and articulate their own truths. Nothing wrong, that is, as long as they make no pretense of representing anyone other than themselves. As the philosopher Elizabeth Kamarck Minnich points out, both clear thinking and truth-telling itself demand that we name our sample or reference group. This is what Marianne and I had failed to do. Ours was not, in fact, a conference "on women," but rather an exclusive gathering organized by, about, and for women who were just like us.

When we attend a conference on "African-American Mothers and Daughters," we understand that the subject matter is partial and particular. There is no pretense of putting forth truths for all womankind. The very presence of the prefix or marker "African-American" acknowledges the existence of others whose experience may be different but no less central. As Marianne said in her introductory comments at our final conference, "We should have called our first conference, 'White, Middle-Class, Heterosexual Women in Context.'"

The point is not to divide the human family into endless categories and minute subdivisions. Rather, as Minnich illustrates in her book *Transforming Knowlege,* truth-telling (indeed, democracy itself) falters when we pretend that one group represents the variety of humankind by claiming generality, let alone universality. Admittedly, she notes, it sounds funny when dominants "prefix" themselves ("I met the most charming white male heterosexual banker last night") because dominants (whether dominant by virtue of gender, class, color, culture, numerical frequency, or all of the above) take themselves and their experience to be what is whole, real, inclusive, true, and important.

Thus the brochure on my desk promotes an upcoming panel on "Black Women Writers at Work." If the panel consisted of white males, it would be called "Writers at Work." As Minnich observes, the number of prefixes, or "markers," increases as we move down the traditional hierarchy. One can study "Women's History" or "Black Women's History" or "Black, Third-World Women's History."

But what of the white Euro-American heterosexual privileged male? His history is simply "history." His writing is simply "literature." He alone is not prefixed. He then, Minnich notes, becomes the generic human, the defining center, the one whose partial and particular truths are generalized to the whole. Meanwhile, as feminist scholars point out, the prefixed groups become "alternative," "nontraditional," "special interest," and implicitly "lesser than." Although these groups together compose the majority of humankind, as women now compose the majority of students on American college campuses, it is assumed that they can be covered by a course here and there, or the addition of a few works written by women or minorities in an otherwise unexamined curriculum ("Just add women and stir").

Marianne and I unwittingly replicated this error. We falsely believed that sprinkling a few minority voices throughout the conference *as we had designed it* would make everyone happy. When we finally co-directed an inclusive conference, giving real space to those women's voices long silenced and oppressed, I felt anxious and threatened. We did not all sit in a circle, hold hands, and sing "We Are the World." Significant differences emerged, including criticisms of our leadership. Some questioned whether a conference held in a white institution under the leadership of two white women was fully inclusive. Others questioned the politics of white women "giving space" in *their* conference to black women and others. In keeping with the research on tokenism, these important challenges did not emerge (and probably wouldn't have been heard) until there were significant numbers of minority women among us.

I learned more about myself in that conference, albeit through my errors, than I had in any other. And I gained a deeper appreciation of the fact that truth-telling is not simply a matter of individual insight or courage. It is, first and foremost, a matter of context. For context determines not only what truths we will feel safe to voice, but also what truths we can discover and know about ourselves.

Truth-telling demands far more than "honesty" and good intentions, as these are conventionally defined. It also requires us to relinquish our habitual, patterned modes of reaction and thought, so that we can move toward an expanded vision of reality that is multilayered, complex, inclusive, and accurate. The process requires us to be in conversation with other women similar to and radically different from ourselves. And it requires that the *context* of this conversation be a safe space where everyone can be herself, where no woman feels she must leave behind a part of herself (the African-American part, the lesbian part, the Jewish part).

A Category Called Woman?

Can we even begin to speak of "a common female experience"? Are there truths "about women" that include us all?
Perhaps it's too early to make universal pronouncements.
When family therapist Rachel Hare-Mustin complained as a
child to her mother, "Everyone hates me!" her mother
replied, "Everyone hasn't met you yet." Like Rachel, we
haven't heard yet from all women, or even from representatives from all categories of women.

Of course, we all generalize. We do need to talk about
"us," as my own use (and misuse) of the collective and unpre-
fixed "we" illustrates. Talking about "us" helps create unity,
solidarity, belongingness, and group identity. The recognition of common female experience moves us beyond shame
and guilt, beyond pathologizing widely shared problems that
are evoked by subordination. When *we* generalize about us
("Black is beautiful") we create more accurate, affirming, and
empowering messages than when *they* generalize about us.
This is particularly so if "they" are the dominant group. In
the history of dominant and subordinate groups, the "truths"
that dominants create about subordinates invariably serve to
justify and maintain the status quo.

Generalizations about any group (women, Irish,
Methodists, firstborns, schoolteachers) are useful when they
help us appreciate the particular sets of filters through which
different categories of people tend to see the world. At the
same time, we cannot be too cautious about the generalizations we speak and hear. Who is doing the generalizing?
From what sample? Who is served or disempowered in the
process? Who is prefixed and who isn't?

Generalizations are particularly hazardous if they purport to tell us what is right or wrong, good or bad, normal or

unnatural, for individuals who may or may not fit the generalizations constructed about their particular kind. Generalizations are stories that we become if we believe them. "Beware of the stories you tell," one psychologist warns, "for you will surely be lived by them."

We need also to pay attention to how generalizations can erase the experience of other human beings. I once spotted a famous runner on an airplane and asked him for an autograph for my younger son. He responded warmly and wrote: "To Ben, Run for Jesus." My family is Jewish, and I was startled both by this man's assumptions and by my own inability to speak up at the time. Later, I regretted that I hadn't gathered the courage to tell him we were Jewish and to ask him for another autograph.

Dominant, un-prefixed groups tend to think like the runner. I've done it myself, albeit in more subtle forms. Shortly after this experience, I gave a lecture on the West Coast that I called "Mothers and Daughters: The Crucial Connection." When I took questions from the audience, an African-American woman raised her hand and pointed out that what I had said was not accurate to her experience, and certainly not for black women in general. I told her quite frankly that I had little experience with black mothers and daughters. She said, "Well, if you're talking about white mothers and daughters, why don't you say so?"

I felt defensive and initially put off by this public criticism. Later I thought how courageous she was to make this point in front of a predominantly white audience. I also recalled my airplane experience and recognized that she was correct. How many times a day, I wondered, do groups like lesbians and disabled women face precisely this experience? How often do I construct generalizations about women that render an entire group nonexistent? How could I be complicitous with dominant thinking when, as a woman, I know exactly what it's like to be educated by dominants who make generalizations that don't describe me, on the one hand, or that fail to recognize my existence, on the other?

What part can we play in creating a world with space for more women to tell and know a more honest story? Those of us who have enough privilege to, say, put together an un-prefixed program (for example, "Motherhood in the Nineties") can use our privilege responsibly. If we are a panel of dominants, we can prefix ourselves ("Our panel will speak to you from the perspective of white, middle-class, married mothers—one perspective of many"). Better yet, we can also put together programs—or create spaces—that are inclusive and diverse. This is a difficult challenge because we tend to feel most comfortable huddled together with folks "just like us."

To the extent that we can make room for a rich weave of women's stories and voices, we will be better able to identify those universal threads that do unite us as women. Such unity will not be based on the silence, suppression, and shedding of difference, but rather on the recognition and celebration of difference. The truths that we then construct about the "I" and the "we" will be more complex, encompassing, richer, and accurate, as will be our lives.

Epilogue

When the Lion Learns to Write

There is a fabled tale about a little boy who questioned how Tarzan could have defeated all the jungle animals, including the mighty lion. The child's mother replied, "My son, you'll get a different story when the lion learns to write." Contained in her response are two valuable lessons in truth-telling. First, there is always more than one version of the truth. Second, the one with the pen (Freudian symbolism intended) is at the defining center and can tell a story that is (mis)taken to be inclusive, real, and whole.

At the center of a woman's life is the quest to discover, speak, and live her own truths, to cease living a life dictated and defined by others—that is, a life lived in another person's story. I hope I have inspired readers to reflect on the many faces of deception in our lives, and to consider the lies, secrets, and silences—our own and others—that affect us. I hope too, that the reader has learned something about the slow, bumpy process of truth-telling. Like peacemaking, truth-telling does not just "happen," or burst forth in our midst. Rather, it must be worked toward, plotted, and planned.

The struggle toward truth-telling is at the center of our deepest longing for intimacy with others. The poet Adrienne Rich speaks to this point in her notes on women, honor, and lying. It is not, she writes, that we have to tell everything, or to tell all at once, or even to know beforehand all that we need to tell. But an honorable relationship, she reminds us, is one in which we are trying, all the time, to extend the possibilities of truth between us, of life between us. She acknowledges that it is painful and exhausting for a woman to begin to uncover her own truths in a culture that validates only male experience, but that the politics worth having, the relationships worth having, demand that we go this hard route.

For women to go the hard route is to fly in the face of all that has been prescribed for us regarding possibility and place, to say nothing of good manners. It also requires us to protest the exclusion of women from public life. When we collude with the objectification, diminishment, and invisibility of women, we compromise all manner of clarity, truth, and honor.

As a dominant group, men have created for themselves many dehumanizing forces that block them from acting and reacting from an authentic center. There are, however, many categories of pretending in which men will not participate. Men will not pretend, for example, that words like "she" or "chairwoman" could ever truly include them. Men will not pretend that the works of womankind represent humankind. Men will not fail to notice when they are excluded from a particular subject, event, discourse, or governing body. In fact, most men have the opposite problem; they assume that to speak of women *is* to exclude them. (I'm often asked by men, "Why do you write books for women? Why do you exclude men?")

Truth-telling cannot co-exist with inequality. Our vision of truth is profoundly eclipsed by the loss of diverse voices and visions that give complexity, texture, and depth to what we name reality. Thus, it is not sufficient for us to stop lying to each other, to stop concealing the facts. It is also necessary for us to *include* each other and to create space for those voices, including parts of the self, that have long been silenced.

This is part of what it means to be an honest woman, at this particular time, in this particular place: We can take, or leave, what others insist is true for us and for our own good. We can pay passionate attention to our own experience, to the stories of other women, and to the voices of those men we have learned "don't count." We can understand the inseparability of the personal and the political, because deception and duplicity thrive when certain groups and individuals have the power to elevate their own truths by diminishing, silencing, even eradicating, others.

Women make up over half the world's population, yet as a group we wield virtually no economic or political power and have no social authority. We have been taught to pretend that our special role as wives to men and mothers to children somehow accounts for this fact, or makes it tolerable or even natural. When women are fully represented and valued in every aspect of language, politics, and culture, the world will have different visions of what's true and what matters.

There is never a resting place in the struggle for personal and political integrity. When anxiety is high, and resources appear scarce, some individuals and groups will always operate at the expense of others. But we can long for and work toward that unrealized world where the dignity and integrity of all women, all human beings, all life, are honored and respected. More to the point, we can live *today* according to the values that we wish would govern the world in the hypothetical future we are working for. To honor diversity, complexity, inclusiveness, and connection in our lives now is to widen the path for truth-telling for everyone.

~

Notes

1 Tony and the Martians

1   Thanks to Marla Beth Isaacs for our friendship that has lasted since the first grade.

2 Deception and Truth-Telling

9–11   Drawing from the theoretical perspective of Murray Bowen, Stephanie Ferrera has written an excellent paper that discusses human deception in the context of deception in nature. See "Deception in Nature and the Family" in *Midwest Symposium on Family Systems Theory and Therapy*, May 1991 (Center for Family Consultation, 820 Davis Street, Suite 221, Evanston, IL 60201).

11   The examples of deception in nature are reported from the *St. Louis Post-Dispatch*, Section D, March 12, 1991, p. 1. Among those authorities quoted on a biocultural approach to deception are the theologian Loyal Rue, the molecular biologist Ursula Goodenough, and the anthropologist Robert Sussman. Readers interested in deception in nature, see Robert Trivers, *Social Evolution* (Menlo Park, Calif.: The Benjamin/Cummings Publishing Company, 1985); and R. W. Mitchell and Nicholas S. Thompson, eds., *Deception:*

Perspectives on Human and Nonhuman Deceit (Albany: State University of New York Press, 1986).

11 Trainers, notes Vicki Hearne . . . : From Vicki Hearne, *Adam's Task* (New York: Vintage Books, 1987), pp. 8–9. Hearne, an English professor, poet, and professional animal trainer, has written a remarkable book on animal–human encounters which begins with a discussion of the anthropomorphic, morally loaded language of trainers and the conflicting world of intellectual and academic discourse.

3 To Do the Right Thing

17–18 Robert Wolk and Arthur Henley, *The Right to Lie* (New York: Peter H. Wyden, 1970), pp. 172–73.

21 If even one heroic male senator . . . : See Peter Breggin's article on the Hill/Thomas hearings: "Abuses of Privilege," *Tikkun* 7, no. 1 (1992): 17–22; June Jordan, "Can I Get a Witness?" *Progressive*, December 1991, pp. 12–13. See also Toni Morrison, ed., *Race-ing Justice, En-Gendering Power: Essays on Anita Hill, Clarence Thomas and the Construction of Social Reality* (New York: Pantheon, 1992).

21 Does the epidemic of lying . . . : Readers interested in ethical/philosophical considerations regarding lying, see Sissela Bok, *Lying: Moral Choice in Public and Private Life* (New York: Vintage Press, 1978).

24 Paul Ekman, *Telling Lies: Clues to Deceit in the Marketplace, Politics, and Marriage* (New York: Norton, 1985), p. 63. Story from the *San Francisco Chronicle*, January 9, 1982, p. 1.

25 Bok, *Lying*, p. 23.

27–30 The psychiatrist Nanette Gartrell and many others in my field have sharpened my consciousness regarding homophobia. On the freedom to openly love whom we choose, I am indebted to the passionate work of Minnie Bruce Pratt, Barbara Smith, Audre Lorde, Adrienne Rich, Suzanne Pharr, Holly Near, and June Jordan.

4 In the Name of Privacy

The philosopher Sissela Bok defines secrecy as intentional concealment, and privacy as "the condition of being protected from unwanted access by others—either physical access, personal information or attention." I am particularly grateful for her careful definitions, distinctions, and elaborations of the language of concealment. See *Secrets: On the Ethics of Concealment and Revelation* (New York: Vintage Press, 1989), pp. 10–11.

The distinction between privacy and secrecy is addressed in the family therapy literature. Mark Karpel distinguishes between privacy and secrecy by determining the relevance of the information to the person who doesn't know it. See "Family Secrets: I. Conceptual and Ethical Issues in the Relational Context. II. Ethical and practical Considerations in Therapeutic Management," *Family Process* 19 (1980): 295–306.

Regarding distinctions between privacy and secrecy, see also Evan Imber-Black, ed., *Secrets in Families and Family Therapy* (New York: Norton, 1993).

36   If I do not control my own body . . . : On "truth" and the abortion controversy, see Harriet Goldhor Lerner, "Whose Truth Counts?" in *New Woman*, October 1991, p. 34.

37   On "flight distance" and "social distance," see Edward O. Wilson, *Sociobiology* (Cambridge, Mass.: Harvard University Press, 1980), Chapter 12; also, Bok, *Secrets*, p. 11.

37–38   See Alida Brill, *Nobody's Business: The Paradoxes of Privacy* (New York: Addison-Wesley, 1990). In her prologue, Brill writes, "Privacy is granted to you by others, by their decency, by their understanding, by their compassionate behavior, by the laws of the land. It exists only when others let you have it—privacy is an accorded right." Brill pays careful attention to the privacy issues for disempowered groups and addresses the paradoxes of privacy regarding reproduction, sexual choice, and ways of dying.

41–44   For more on family secrets, see Chapter 10 notes.

44–45   Along with gender, differences in race, class, and culture shape beliefs about what must be kept private or secret. See Chapter 10 notes.

45   Many feminists have explored the connections between women's silence/privacy and patriarchy. See Robin Morgan, "The Politics of Silence," in *The Word of a Woman: Feminist Dispatches 1968–1991* (New York: Norton, 1992), and Tillie Olsen's *Silences* (New York: Delacorte Press, 1978). I am particularly indebted to Adrienne Rich's work, *On Lies, Secrets, and Silence: Selected Prose 1966–1978* (New York: Norton, 1979), which includes her essay, "Women and Honor: Some Notes on Lying," 1975, pp. 185–94. I am similarly indebted to all the work of poet and writer Audre Lorde, including her books, *The Cancer Journals* (San Francisco: Spinsters/Aunt Lute Books, 1980) and *Sister Outsider* (Freedom, Calif.: Crossing Press, 1984).

The linguist Deborah Tannen's popular work on male–female communication also addresses the meanings of silence. See *You Just Don't Understand: Women and Men in Conversation* (New York: William Morrow, 1990); also, D. Tannen and M. Saville-Troike, eds., *Perspectives on Silence* (Norwood, N.J.: Ablex Publishing Corporation, 1990).

Joan Laird has written an account of the many forms of silence in women's lives. See Joan Laird, "Women's Secrets—Women's Silences," in Imber-Black, ed., *Secrets in Families and Family Therapy.*

47   As one woman speaks . . . : Adrienne Rich wrote in 1975, "When a woman tells the truth she is creating the possibility for more truth around her" (*On Lies, Secrets, and Silence,* p. 191).

5 A Funny Thing Happened on the Way to the Orifice

Special thanks to Pauline Bart for the chapter title. See Pauline Bart and Diana Scully, "A Funny Thing Happened on the Way to the Orifice: Women in Gynecology Textbooks," *American Journal of Sociology* 78, no. 4 (1973): 1045–50.

48–50   On pretending and protecting men, see Harriet Goldhor Lerner, *Women in Therapy* (New York: Harper & Row, 1989), Chapter 11, pp. 158–69.

49   Arlene Dahl, *Always Ask a Man* (Englewood Cliffs, N.J.: Prentice-Hall, 1965), p. 8.
       On female strength going underground in adolescence, see Carol Gilligan, Nona Lyons, and Trudy Hanmer, eds., *Making Connections: The Relational Worlds of Adolescent Girls at Emma Willard School* (Cambridge, Mass.: Harvard University Press, 1990). Also, C. Gilligan, A. G. Rogers, and D. L. Tolman, eds., *Women, Girls and Psychotherapy: Reframing Resistance* (New York: The Haworth Press, Inc., 1991); also, Carol Gilligan, *In a Different Voice* (Cambridge, Mass.: Harvard University Press, 1984).

50   Carolyn Heilbrun writes, "It is perhaps only in old age, certainly past fifty, that women can stop being female impersonators, can grasp the opportunity to reverse their most cherished principles of 'femininity.'" From *Writing a Woman's Life* (New York: Ballantine Books, 1988), p. 126.

53–56   On the false and incomplete labeling of female genitalia, see Harriet Goldhor Lerner, "Parental Mislabeling of Female Genitals" in *Women in Therapy*, pp. 23–37. "Raising Vulva Consciousness" appeared as "And What Do Little Girls Have?" in *New Woman*, February 1991, pp. 110–11. (First published in *New Directions for Women*, May/June 1990, p. 10.)
       Alice Walker's novel *Possessing the Secret of Joy* (New York: Harcourt Brace Jovanovich, 1992) deals with the catastrophic procedure of genital mutilation. The dedication reads: "With Tenderness and Respect to the Blameless Vulva." Audre Lorde also reminds us that female circumcision is a crime against black women; see Lorde, *Sister Outsider*, p. 120.
       On genital mutilation, see Robin Morgan and Gloria Steinem, "The International Crime of Genital Mutilation," in Steinem's *Outrageous Acts and Everyday Rebellions* (New York: New American Library, 1983), pp. 292–300. Also in Gloria Steinem's *Revolution from Within: A Book of Self-Esteem* (Boston: Little, Brown, 1992), pp. 356–57.

53   Quote from K. Taylor, *Almost Twelve*, (Wheaton, Ill.: Tyndale House, 1972), italics mine.
            The historian Thomas Laqueur has written a well-researched book about the making and unmaking of sex over the centuries. See *Making Sex: Body and Gender from the Greeks to Freud* (Cambridge, Mass.: Harvard University Press, 1990).

57–58   On feigning orgasms, "lying still," and women's distorted relationship to their sexuality and powers of reproduction under patriarchy, see Rich, "Women and Honor: Some Notes on Lying"; also see Rich's classic text, *Of Woman Born* (New York: Norton, 1976) and her article, "Compulsory Heterosexuality and Lesbian Existence," in *Signs: Journal of Women in Culture and Society*, 5, no. 4 (1980): 631–60.
            See also Sonia Johnson, *Wildfire: Igniting the She/Volution* (Estancia, N. Mex.: Wildfire Books, 1990) and Sonia Johnson, *The Ship That Sailed into the Living Room: Sex and Intimacy Reconsidered* (Estancia, N. Mex.: Wildfire Books, 1991). Sonia Johnson's books and tapes can be ordered from Wildfire Books, Star Route 1, Box 55, Estancia, NM 87016; phone (505) 384-2500.

57   Gynecological texts . . . : See Scully and Bart, "A Funny Thing Happened on the Way to the Orifice."

59   Adrienne Rich, in *On Lies, Secrets, and Silence*, p. 189, mentions clitoridectomies for "lustful" nuns and "difficult" wives.

60   Virgina Woolf, *A Room of One's Own* (New York: Harcourt Brace Jovanovich, 1929), p. 37.

61–63   I am indebted to Carolyn Heilbrun's eloquent words on consciousness raising and the necessity for women to articulate authentic experience in groups to protest the available fictions about female experience. See Heilbrun, *Writing a Woman's Life*, chapter 1. See also Teresa De Lauretis, *Alice Doesn't: Feminism, Semiotics, Cinema* (Bloomington, Ind.: Indiana University Press, 1984), p. 186.
            I have been a member of a women's group since 1976. Women's groups are free, and anyone can start one. See Harriet Goldhor Lerner, "Getting a Women's Group Started," *New Woman*, March 1992, p. 30. Also see Gloria

Steinem's "Helping Ourselves to Revolution" in *Ms.* November/December 1992, pp. 24–29. Steinem, who offers practical advice for starting women's groups, notes, "If two white male alcoholics could start a network of free, leaderless, accessible meetings, so can we."

62   Judith Lewis Herman, *Trauma and Recovery* (New York: Basic Books, 1992), p. 29.

64   Carolyn Heilbrun in *Writing a Woman's Life*, p. 47, notes, "There will be narratives of female lives only when women no longer live their lives isolated in the houses and the stories of men."

64–65   On motherhood as institution and experience, see Adrienne Rich's essential book, *Of Woman Born*. See also the sociologist Jessie Bernard's classic texts, *The Future of Marriage* (New York: Bantam, 1973) and *The Future of Motherhood* (New York: Dial, 1974).
          On female depression as a protest against women's "sacred calling," see Rich, *Of Woman Born* and Lerner, *Women in Therapy*, pp. 202–03.

65   Therapists could not begin . . . : See Heilbrun, *Writing a Woman's Life*.

65   Of course, any interpretation of experience . . . : Postmodern views challenge the notion of an objective "truth" and view interpretation in therapy as privileging one meaning or story (usually that in line with the dominant culture) over others. See, for example, Rachel Hare-Mustin and Jeanne Marecek, eds., *Making a Difference: Psychology and the Construction of Gender* (New Haven, Conn.: Yale University Press, 1990), pp. 22–64.
          The psychotherapy literature reflects a growing emphasis on a "narrative perspective" regarding human problems. In the words of the psychologist George S. Howard, this perspective views identity as an issue of life-story construction; psychopathology as instances of life stories gone awry; and psychotherapy as exercises in story repair" ("Culture Tales: A Narrative Approach to Thinking, Cross-Cultural Psychology and Psychotherapy," *American Psychologist*, March 1991, p. 187). For a psychiatrist's description of his work helping

people create new, growth-enhancing stories, see James Gustafson, *Self-Delight in a Harsh World: The Main Stories of Individual, Marital and Family Psychotherapy* (New York: Norton, 1992).

66   "The master's tools. . . ": Lorde, *Sister Outsider,* p. 110.

Readers interested in feminist revisions of traditional views of women might begin with Jean Baker Miller's classic and accessible book, *Toward a New Psychology of Women* (Boston: Beacon Press, 1986).

Feminist thinkers continue to critique and transform psychoanalytic and family systems views of women. For a psychoanalytic perspective, see, for example, Judith Jordan, Alexandra Kaplan, Jean Baker Miller, Irene Stiver, and Janet Surrey, *Women's Growth in Connection: Writing from the Stone Center* (New York: Guilford Press, 1991). From a family systems perspective see, for example, Marianne Walters, Betty Carter, Peggy Papp, and Olga Silverstein (The Women's Project in Family Therapy), *The Invisible Web: Gender Patterns in Family Relationships* (New York: Guilford Press, 1988). See also Lerner, *Women in Therapy.*

Thanks to Rachel Hare-Mustin for her pioneering work in feminist family therapy.

6 We Are the Stories We Tell

I am deeply indebted to two critically important papers by Peggy McIntosh, "Feeling Like a Fraud, Part One," *Work in Progress,* The Stone Center Working Papers Series, No. 18 (1985); and "Feeling Like a Fraud, Part Two" *Work in Progress,* The Stone Center Working Papers Series, No. 37 (1989). These papers can be ordered directly from Peggy McIntosh, Wellesley College, Center for Research on Women, Wellesley, MA 02181.

67   Is there a "true story" of female experience?: Psychologist Carol Tavris has written a wise and engaging book examining popular myths about sex differences. See *The Mismeasure of Woman* (New York: Simon and Schuster, 1992). See also Hare-Mustin and Marecek, eds., *Making a Difference.*

69   Our differing ethnic backgrounds . . . : Ethnicity, like gender, is a key factor that shapes what one conceals and reveals about personal achievement. Thanks to family therapist Monica McGoldrick for her pioneering work on ethnicity and family therapy.

70–74   On the denial and erasure of ambition, adventure, and achievement from stories of women's lives, see Carolyn Heilbrun's acclaimed book, *Writing a Woman's Life*. Heilbrun illustrates how patriarchal culture has defined and limited what stories about women's lives could be scripted and told.

72–78   Feminist scholars from many disciplines have explored the forces that block women from success in the public sphere, or leave women feeling illegitimate, guilty, or self-doubting and out of place when they do rise in male-dominated hierarchies. In addition to the work of Peggy McIntosh and Carolyn Heilbrun, see the pioneering work of Jean Baker Miller, *Toward a New Psychology of Women*; see also Rosabeth Moss Kanter, *Men and Women of the Corporation* (New York: Basic Books, 1977).

        Also see, Harriet Goldhor Lerner, "Work and Success Inhibitions," in *Women in Therapy*, pp. 171–99; see also Irene Stiver, "Work Inhibitions in Women," *Work in Progress*, The Stone Center Working Papers Series, No. 3 (1982).

74   See McIntosh, "Feeling Like a Fraud, Part One," and "Feeling Like a Fraud, Part Two."

75   Quote from McIntosh, "Feeling Like a Fraud, Part One," p. 5.

77   The belief that "rugged individualism," "separateness," and independence define maturity or mental health has been challenged by new theories of female development that emphasize connection and context. Work by Jean Baker Miller, Carol Gilligan, Peggy McIntosh, and the writings from The Stone Center (See Jordan et. al., *Women's Growth in Connection*) reflect this new perspective. Psychotherapists and other interested readers can order working papers from The Stone Center, Wellesley College, Wellesley, MA 02181-8268; phone (617) 283-2838.

The capacity for connection and cooperation is no less essential for men. See Alfie Kohn, *No Contest: The Case against Competition* (Boston: Houghton Mifflin, 1987) and Mark Gerzon, *A Choice of Heroes: The Changing Faces of American Manhood* (Boston: Houghton Mifflin, 1992).

81   Dead-end jobs evoke dead-end dreams . . . : See the sociologist Rosabeth Moss Kanter's groundbreaking book about how jobs "create" people, *Men and Women of the Corporation.* See also Chapter 13 notes.

7 Our Family Legacies

83   From Liz (Elizabeth Sprague) Hoffmeister's self-published book, *The Crawdad Nest* (Topeka, Kans.: 1976).

87–88   Betty Carter quotation (author's italics) from *Mothers and Daughters* by Elizabeth (Betty) Carter, Peggy Papp, Olga Silverstein, and Marianne Walters, The Women's Project in Family Therapy Monograph Series, vol. 1, no. 1, (Washington, D.C., 1983), p. 16 (out of print).

88–92   Thanks to psychiatrist Jerry Lewis and other early researchers on family functioning. I am especially indebted to the work of Murray Bowen, the founder of Bowen family systems theory, who died October 9, 1990, at the age of seventy-seven. His theoretical contributions include his pioneering efforts to describe human emotional functioning from a multigenerational perspective, and his concepts of triangles, emotional reactivity, emotional cut-off, and differentiation of self. Bowen and his colleagues, especially Jack Bradt, also pioneered the use of the multigenerational family genogram. Despite important differences in our worldview, all three of my *Dance* books draw heavily from Bowen's work. For a review of Bowen theory see Michael Kerr, "Family Systems Theory and Therapy," in Alan Gurman and David Knistern, eds., *Handbook of Family Therapy* (New York: Brunner/Mazel, 1981), pp. 226–64.

Also, see Stephanie Ferrera's summary of anxious family functioning, "Deception in Nature and the Family," based on Bowen's theory, and Roberta Gilbert's book, *Extraordi-*

nary Relationships (Minneapolis, Minn: CHRONIMED Publishing, 1992). The address for CHRONIMED Publishing is P.O. Box 47945, Minneapolis, MN 55447-9727. Contact Georgetown Family Center for information on Bowen theory, therapy, or training at 4404 MacArthur Blvd. N.W., Suite 102, Washington, DC 20007; phone (202) 965-0730.

My greatest intellectual debt is to Katherine Glenn Kent whose generous sharing of ideas has greatly enhanced my understanding of the process of truth-telling in families. What I understand of Murray Bowen's theory comes from her teaching and our countless conversations over many years of friendship.

Family therapists and readers interested in the emotional challenges of family life, see the following important texts, which address gender issues. Betty Carter and Monica McGoldrick, eds., *The Changing Family Life Cycle: A Framework for Family Therapy*, 2nd ed. (Boston: Allyn & Bacon, 1988); Monica McGoldrick, Carol Anderson, and Froma Walsh, eds., *Women in Families: A Framework for Family Therapy* (New York: Norton, 1989); Walters, Carter, Papp, and Silverstein (The Women's Project in Family Therapy) *The Invisible Web*.

In addition to the above texts, Virginia Goldner, Rachel Hare-Mustin, and other scholars in family therapy have articulated how the fate of women in families is shaped largely (and invisibly) by gendered power arrangements. See, for example, Thelma Jean Goodrich, ed., *Women and Power: Perspectives for Family Therapy*, (New York: Norton, 1991.) Also see Evan Imber-Black, "Women, Families, and Larger Systems," in Ault-Riché, ed., *Women and Family Therapy* (Rockville, Md.: Aspen Systems Corporation, 1986), pp. 25–33.

91   The poet Lynn Sukenick coined the phrase "matraphobia," the fear of being one's mother. Also see Rich, *Of Woman Born*, p. 235.

92–93   Thanks to Betty Carter for her insights about a daughter as her mother's "apprentice" and for her inspiring teaching and work with families. For enriching my understanding of the mother-daughter relationship, and for locating this relationship in the broader context of culture, class, and gender, I also thank Olga Silverstein, Laura Silverstein, Monica McGoldrick, Evan Imber-Black, Marianne Walters, Lois Braverman, and many other family systems therapists I continue to learn from.

On relationships between African-American mothers and daughters see Patrica Bell–Scott et al. *Double Stitch: Black Women Write about Mothers and Daughters* (Boston: Beacon Press, 1992). For a scholarly feminist challenge to conventional theories about the mother-daughter relationship through an examination of media representations, popular culture, and image making, see Suzanna Danuta Walters, *Lives Together, Worlds Apart: Mothers and Daughters in Popular Culture* (Berkeley: University of California Press, 1992).

94 As early as 1970, Phillip Slater wrote about the hazards of motherhood as a "career" in a production-oriented society; see *The Pursuit of Loneliness: American Culture at the Breaking Point* (Boston: Beacon Press, 1970). I am also grateful for the pioneering feminist insights of psychoanalyst Robert Seidenberg, and for the early support of psychoanalyst Anthony Kowalski.

96 Because "in the camps". . . : From audiotape ("Feminist Jewish Women's Voices: Diversity and Community"), Eighth Annual National Women's Studies Convention, Fourth Plenary, National Women's Studies Association.

97–101 Our Mothers' Stories: For a detailed guide on opening up the lines of communication with family members, see Harriet Goldhor Lerner, *The Dance of Anger* (New York: Harper & Row, 1985) and *The Dance of Intimacy* (New York: Harper & Row, 1989).

99–101 Untimely loss poses the most difficult emotional challenge for families to cope with. Facts and feelings surrounding death frequently go underground. I am grateful to my friend Libby (Elizabeth) Rosen, nurse and child-birth educator, whose work in this area has inspired me. Also see Froma Walsh and Monica McGoldrick, eds., *Living Beyond Loss: Death in the Family* (New York: Norton, 1991); Freda Herz Brown, "The Impact of Death and Serious Illness on the Family Life Cycle," in Carter and McGoldrick, eds., *The*

Changing Family Life Cycle. Also see psychiatrist Sue Chance's plainspoken account of her emotional journey following her son's suicide, *Stronger than Death* (Norton, 1992).

8 Honesty versus Truth

102   Holly Near, a foremother of women's and political music is a rare performing artist who has never veered from speaking, singing, and living her own truths. Her music can be ordered from Redwood Cultural Work, 1222 Preservation Parkway, Oakland, CA 94612. See also her autobiography, *Fire in the Rain, Singer in the Storm* (New York: William Morrow, 1990).

105   Clark Moustakas, *Loneliness and Love* (Englewood Cliffs, N.J.: Prentice-Hall, 1972), p. 109.

106–12 The distinction between thinking and anxiety-driven reactivity is central to Bowen family systems theory and therapy.

112   Definition of "honesty" from *The American Heritage Dictionary* (Boston: Houghton Mifflin, 1985), p. 620.

9 Just Pretending

121   Pretending is a "soft" verb: *The American Heritage Dictionary,* p. 981; and *Random House Webster's College Dictionary* (New York: Random House, 1991), p. 1069.

129–32 The concepts of overfunctioning and underfunctioning are elaborated in Bowen family systems theory. For a helpful book on overfunctioning/overresponsibility, see Claudia Bepko and Jo-Ann Krestan, *Too Good for Her Own Good* (New York: HarperCollins, 1990).

132   On secrecy surrounding adoption, see Chapter 10 notes.

132–35 The pattern of pursuit and distance has been so widely described in the family literature that it is difficult to trace its origins. Philip Guerin and Katherine Guerin wrote about it as early as 1976. The concept of triangles is also central in the family therapy literature and has been carefully elaborated by Murray Bowen.

Part of the text on Jen and Michelle appeared in Harriet Goldhor Lerner, "My Mother-in-law Is Driving Me Crazy," *New Woman*, July 1992, p. 42, (mother-in-law triangle), and "He Won't Make a Commitment," *New Woman*, November 1992, p. 34 (pursuing and distancing). For more on these patterns, see Lerner, *The Dance of Anger*, chapter 8, and *The Dance of Intimacy*, chapter 10.

135   Quotation by Goethe and paraphrase by Joy in W. Brugh Joy, *Joy's Way*, (Los Angeles: Jeremy P. Tarcher, Inc., 1979), p. 63.

10 Family Secrets: A Disturbance in the Field

As the chapter notes indicate, I am especially grateful to family therapist Evan Imber-Black, for her book, *Secrets in Families and Family Therapy*, which pays careful attention to the wider context in which family secrets are embedded.

I know of two books for nonprofessional readers on the subject of family secrets: Harriet Webster, *Family Secrets*, (Reading, Mass.: Addison-Wesley Publishing Company, 1991); and Kittredge Cherry, *Hide and Speak: How to Free Ourselves From Our Secrets* (San Francisco: HarperCollins, 1991), a self-help guide about secrets.

136   Every family has secrets...: I am indebted to Peggy Papp for her work on secrecy between parents and children. See "The Worm in the Bud: Secrets Between Parents and Children" in Imber-Black, *Secrets in Families and Family Therapy*.

137   How do we distinguish...: On defining a "family secret," see Karpel, "Family Secrets," and Imber-Black, *Secrets in Families and Family Therapy*.

138   Evan Imber-Black, Marilyn Mason, Jo-Ann Krestan, Claudia Bepko, and other family therapists have addressed the connections between shame, stigma, and secrecy and the

broader societal context. See Imber-Black, *Secrets in Families and Family Therapy*.

On secrecy, stigma, and AIDS, see Gillian Walker, *In the Midst of Winter: Systemic Therapy with Families, Couples, and Individuals with AIDS Infection* (New York: Norton, 1991)—chapter 8 deals with issues of secrecy, confidentiality, and the duty to warn. Also see Lascelles Black, "AIDS and Secrets," in Imber-Black, *Secrets in Families and Family Therapy*.

140–45   Untimely and nonnormative loss commonly lead to secrecy and a shutdown of communication among family members regarding facts, feelings, and fantasies about who's to blame. See Chapter 7 notes.

142   Peggy Papp, in Imber-Black, *Secrets in Families and Family Therapy*.

145   On "locations" of family secrets: Janine Roberts, using some ideas of Evan Imber-Black, has expanded on Mark Karpel's original topology to include the location of secrets when therapists and larger systems are involved. See Janine Roberts, "On Trainees and Training: Safety, Secrets and Revelation," in Imber-Black, *Secrets in Families and Family Therapy*.

146   Letty Cottin Pogrebin, *Deborah, Golda, and Me* (New York: Crown Publishers, 1991), p. 13.

149   "Blow the whistle". . . : Peggy Papp describes a child or adolescent's symptomatic or acting-out behavior as an unconscious attempt to blow the whistle on a family secret. (In Imber-Black, *Secrets in Families and Family Therapy*.)

150–52   Family therapist Edwin Friedman takes the position that all family secrets have a profoundly negative effect on family life and should be revealed. Other family therapists (see Imber-Black, *Secrets in Families and Family Therapy*) emphasize that secrets have both pathological and adaptational value, and they stress the importance of assessing whether the opening of secrets will be healing or harmful. There are widely divergent views regarding the function, adaptational value, and therapeutic management of family secrets.

Therapists dealing with family secrets need to be informed about issues of race, culture, and class. Nancy Boyd-Franklyn, for example, illustrates how therapists working with African-American families must understand the history of slavery and racism and how it contributes to the process of secret-keeping within families. "Racism, Secret-Keeping, and African-American Families," in Imber-Black, *Secrets in Families and Family Therapy*.

Fiction writers such as Maxine Hong-Kingston and Amy Tan have dealt with the subject of secrets and silence between generations in Asian families. Writers from all marginalized groups invariably address the subject of shame, stigma, secrecy, and enforced silence as shaped by gender, generation, sexual orientation, and the specific history of culture, class, and race. See Cherrie Moraga and Gloria Anzaldua, eds., *This Bridge Called My Back: Writings by Radical Women of Color* (New York: Kitchen Table/Women of Color Press, 1983); Barbara Smith, ed., *Home Girls: A Black Feminist Anthology* (New York: Kitchen Table/Women of Color Press, 1983); Elly Bulkin, Minnie Bruce Pratt, and Barbara Smith, *Yours in Struggle: Three Feminist Perspectives on Anti-Semitism and Racism* (Ithaca, N.Y.: Firebrand Books, 1984); Claudia Tate, ed., *Black Women Writers at Work* (New York: The Continuum Publishing Corporation, 1983); and Pogrebin, *Deborah, Golda, and Me*.

151   A helpful guide for adoptive parents is Lois Ruskai Melina, *Making Sense of Adoption* (New York: Harper & Row, 1989). I also highly recommend Ann Hartman's important article, "Secrecy in Adoption," in Imber-Black, *Secrets in Families and Family Therapy*.

152–53 The case of Billy was reported by Peggy Papp in Imber-Black, *Secrets in Families and Family Therapy*. The example reported by Papp of the adopted child with a "selective math disability" is from Deborah Donovan and Denis McIntyre, *Healing the Hurt Child* (New York: Norton, 1990). Donovan and McIntyre note that family secrets lead a child to wear "cognitive blinders" that impede school performance.

153   On secrecy and addictions, see Jo-Ann Krestan and Claudia Bepko's "On Lies, Secrets, and Silence: The Multiple Levels

of Denial in Addictive Families," in Imber-Black, *Secrets in Families and Family Therapy*. Therapists see Krestan and Bepko, *The Responsibility Trap: A Blueprint for Treating the Alcoholic Family* (New York: Free Press, 1985).

153   One woman I saw in psychotherapy. . . : See Lerner, *Women in Therapy*, pp. 23–37.

154   When women publicly. . . : For more on women who comply with the cultural prescription to lie, joke, or keep secret about their age, see Harriet Goldhor Lerner, "Hiding Our Age," *New Woman*, October 1992, p. 37.

154–55 In the February 1992 *Lear's* report on incest by Heidi Vanderbilt, she notes that as recently as the early 1970s, experts in the psychiatric community estimated only one to five cases of incest per one million people.

In her book *Trauma and Recovery*, Judith Lewis Herman writes, "In the absence of strong political movements for human rights, the active process of bearing witness inevitably gives way to the active process of forgetting" (p. 9). See also her earlier book, *Father-Daughter Incest* (Cambridge, Mass.: Harvard University Press, 1981). I also want to thank Robin Morgan, Audre Lorde, June Jordon, Susan Brownmiller, and other theorists and activists who have offered a feminist analysis of the silence surrounding violence against women.

11 An Affair Is a Big Secret

159   Frank Pittman, *Private Lies: Infidelity and the Betrayal of Intimacy* (New York: Norton, 1989).

159–60 Pittman quotation from "Mending Broken Ties," *New Woman*, November 1990, p. 42.

164–65 I am indebted to Peggy Vaughan's excellent self-help book, *The Monogamy Myth* (New York: Newmarket Press, 1989).

On a radically different note, see Sonia Johnson's feminist challenge to monogamy. She rejects the notion of fidelity and sexual exclusivity: ". . . the red herring of numbers that focuses us on how many lovers we are taking naked to bed instead of what condition our souls are in and what is in our hearts as we lie with them." *The Ship That Sailed into the Living Room*, p. 112.

12 The Body Seeks Truth

176   Clark Moustakas, *Loneliness and Love*.

176   On techniques that detect deceit by reading body language, voice, and speech patterns, see Ekman, *Telling Lies*.

182   It is profit madness . . . : We must speak openly about the primary role of environmental contaminants in causing higher rates of breast cancer and other cancers in particular neighborhoods and communities. To do otherwise is to engage in the deadliest of deceptions. I am grateful for the work of Jay Gould, Benjamin Goldman, Terry Tempest Williams, Rita Arditti, Tatiana Schreiber, Judith Brady, and other individuals and groups documenting the connections between environmental contamination and cancer, and promoting activism and national debate.

     I am grateful to my dear friend and colleague Emily Kofron for our many conversations about psychological theories regarding cancer patients and for her activism to increase funding for breast cancer research. Kofron has written an important article on breast cancer in the *The Family Therapy Networker*, January/February 1993. Also see Susan Sontag, *Illness as Metaphor and AIDS and Its Metaphors* (New York: Anchor, 1990) and Harriet Goldhor Lerner, "Can We Cause Our Own Cancer?", *New Woman*, January 1992, p. 28.

183–84   On women's anger and the complex forces that prohibit its expression, see the pioneering work of Teresa Bernardez, "Women and Anger: Conflicts with Aggression in Contemporary Women," in the *Journal of the American Medical Women's Association* 33 (1978): 215–19. See also Bernardez, "Women and Anger—Cultural Prohibitions and the Feminine Ideal. *Work in Progress*, The Stone Center Working

Papers Series, No. 31 (1988), and Lerner, *The Dance of Anger*. For a comprehensive overview on the uses and abuses of anger in truth-telling see Carol Tavris, *Anger: The Misunderstood Emotion* (New York: Simon and Schuster, 1983).

186   "Experience is the name everyone gives to their mistakes." Oscar Wilde, *Lady Windemere's Fan*.

187   Airline ticket quotation from David Reynolds's book, *Even in Summer the Ice Doesn't Melt*, excerpted in *Yoga Journal*, May/June 1992, p. 55. Reynolds is the founder of Constructive Living, based on the Japanese Morita and Naikan psychotherapies, and has authored numerous books.

187–88 Audre Lorde's *The Cancer Journals*, pp. 22–23. Lorde, who describes herself as a "black lesbian feminist warrior, poet" has written the first passionate, compelling feminist text on breast cancer and on the transformation of women's fear and silence into language and action. I also recommend *Chemo-Poet and other Poems*, by Helene Davis (Cambridge, Mass.: Alice James Books, 1989).

Audre Lorde died on November 17, 1992, in her home on St. Croix, U.S. Virgin Islands, after a fourteen-year struggle with breast cancer. She was fifty-eight years old. Lorde published seventeen volumes of poetry, essays, and autobiography. Her numerous honors include becoming the poet laureate of New York State in 1991 and receiving honorary doctorates from Hunter, Oberlin, and Haverford colleges. In her writing and political activism, Lorde spoke courageously and eloquently against racism, homophobia, and all forms of prejudice and violence. Her work has touched the hearts of countless women and men, worldwide.

In honor of Audre Lorde's life, a scholarship for black women writers has been established in her name. Donations, made payable to the Astrea Foundation/Audre Lorde Memorial Fund, can be sent to the Astrea Foundation, 666 Broadway, Suite 520, New York, NY 10012.

189   Sonia might happily agree....: "Since truth is reversed in patriarchy, to go out of our minds is to become most truly

sane." From the foreword of Sonia Johnson's book *From Housewife to Heretic* (Albuquerque: Wildfire Books, 1981). Johnson chronicles her run for president of the United States, along with her other political and emotional journeys.

189   My heartfelt gratitude to Jade Deforest and Sonia Johnson for their love, their wisdom, their lives, and their generous sharing of everything.

191   I first heard the term the "Irish grudge syndrome" from family therapist Monica McGoldrick.

193   On denial, repression, dissociation, and the recovery of history, memory, and connection for victims of sexual and domestic violence, see Herman, *Trauma and Recovery*. Her book also explores the experience of other traumatized people such as combat veterans and the victims of political terror. Also see the self-help guide *The Courage to Heal*, by Ellen Bass and Laura Davis (New York: HarperCollins, 1992).

194   For persons interested in spirituality and the psychic/sacred arts, I recommend workshops or other opportunities to learn from the psychologist Carolyn Conger. To be placed on her mailing list, call (800) 833-0611.

There is a vast number of books on body/mind/spirit connections. For example, see Deepak Chopra, *Quantum Healing: Exploring the Frontiers of Mind/Body Medicine* (New York: Bantam Books, 1989), p. 33. See also Steinem, *Revolution from Within*, pp. 197–248.

194–95   On the subject of weight, dieting, and hunger, see Jane R. Hirschmann and Carol H. Munter's helpful book, *Overcoming Overeating* (New York: Fawcett Columbine, 1988). Regarding physical touch "in the moment," I am grateful to conversations with Jade Deforest and Sonia Johnson.

Psychologist Carol Tavris challenges popular myths about women's bodies, sexuality, and "diseases" in *The Mismeasure of Woman*.

195   See, for example, Naomi Wolf, *The Beauty Myth: How Images*

of Beauty Are Used Against Women (New York: William Morrow, 1991). See also Steinem, *Revolution from Within.*

196   Lorde, *The Cancer Journals*, pp. 16, 64. See also Marsha Saxton and Florence Howe, eds., *With Wings: An Anthology of Literature by and about Women with Disabilities* (New York: The Feminist Press, 1987). A self-help video, *Chronic Illness: The Constant Companion*, features psychologist Meredith Titus, who is also its co-writer and producer; it is available from Menninger Video Productions, (800) 345-6036.

13 Will the Real Me Please Stand?

198   Pat Parker quotations come from a conversation with the poet Judy Grahn. See Dorothy Allison, "Memorial: Pat Parker 1944–1989," *Out/Look, National Lesbian and Gay Quarterly*, Fall 1989.

199–205 I am indebted to Rosabeth Moss Kanter's critically important work on the impact of tokenism and numerical scarcity in organizational life, *Men and Women of the Corporation* (see especially pages 206–42). Kanter's research illustrates how power, relative opportunity, and tokenism (numerical scarcity) shape the behavior and attitudes of men and women in the workplace. She provides an in-depth view of why "individual" or psychological models of change cannot address the "woman question" and she makes a compelling argument for the necessity of organizational reform (that is, policies and programs to balance numbers, enhance opportunities, and provide equal access to power).

200   Rosabeth Moss Kanter quotation, *Men and Women of the Corporation*, p. 161.

202   Do women have a "fear of success" or, rather, a fear of visibility that is characteristic of persons in token roles? See Kanter, *Men and Women of the Corporation*, p. 221.

203   Rosabeth Moss Kanter quotation, *Men and Women of the Corporation*, p. 209.

208–09   Part of this appeared in Harriet Goldhor Lerner, "Should I Find Out My IQ?" in *New Woman*, July 1991, p. 38.

210   I am grateful to Marianne Ault-Riché for her vision, courage, and hard work in creating and sustaining the "Women in Context" conference series at the Menninger Clinic (December 1983–November 1990). We both extend our heartfelt thanks to the conference staff who have enriched the conferences over many years.

211–13   On the matter of prefixing I am deeply indebted to the work of the philosopher and educator Elizabeth Kamarck Minnich. She writes, "we can add the prefixes, or markers . . . on the grounds that accurate scholarship, truth-telling itself, demands that we name our sample. If a course covers only white people, and/or is taught from the analytic perspectives developed within an exclusively white tradition, it should be so labeled and the perspective claimed as such. . . . Courses titled 'Man and His World' can still be taught, but now as courses in which gender analysis is central, not weirdly absent. Still, courses on 'Woman and Her World' are at this moment in history much more important to teach." From "The Circle of the Elite to the World of the Whole" in Carol Pearson, Donna Shavlik, and Judith Touchton, eds., *Educating the Majority* (New York: Macmillan, 1989), pp. 277–93 (a vital book for those interested in higher education).
           Elizabeth Kamarck Minnich's essential text, *Transforming Knowledge* (Philadelphia: Temple University Press, 1990) uncovers the ways in which our unexamined habits of language and thought perpetuate old exclusions, devaluations, and hierarchies.
           In 1973, Adrienne Rich wrote a visionary feminist essay, "Toward a Woman-Centered University," reprinted in *On Lies, Secrets, and Silence*, pp. 125–55.

212   "Just add women and stir.": A quotation from Charlotte Bunch, which originated in conversation and is frequently quoted among those in Women's Studies.

214–16   To appreciate the hidden power of false generalizations to influence how and what we think, see Minnich, *Transforming Knowledge*.

215   "Beware of the stories you tell. . . ": A paraphrase of Shakespeare by George S. Howard, "Culture Tales: A Narrative Approach to Thinking, Cross-cultural Psychology, and Psychotherapy," *American Psychologist* 46, no. 3 (March 1991), pp. 187–97, quotation, p. 196.

          Carolyn Heilbrun notes, "Power consists to a large extent in deciding what stories will be told," *Writing a Woman's Life*, p. 44.

216   On wanting to huddle with folks "just like us," see Bernice Johnson Reagon, "Coalition Politics: Turning the Century," in Smith, *Home Girls*, pp. 356–68. Reagon reminds us that coalition work is difficult and if we prefer to feel safe and nurtured, we should return to a little village or barred room where we let in only people just like us. Reagon is an internationally acclaimed lecturer and scholar of African-American, community-based cultural life and history. She is also the founding member and leader of Sweet Honey in the Rock, an ensemble of African-American women whose sound is rooted in the African-American tradition of congregational choral style and its many extensions.

Epilogue: When the Lion Learns to Write

217   "My son, you'll get a different story. . . ": Quoted in Linda Webb-Watson, "The Sociology of Power," in Goodrich, *Women and Power*, p. 54.

218   See Rich, "Women and Honor: Some Notes on Lying" in *On Lies, Secrets, and Silence*.

218–19   Elizabeth Kamarch Minnich notes that the assumption that to talk about women is to exclude men, reverses the usual assumption that to talk about men is to include women.

219–20   Many feminist women of color have contributed to a more complex, diverse, and multilayered vision of human reality.

In addition to those writers already mentioned in my earlier chapter notes, I am grateful for the work of Joy Harjo, Maya Angelou, Angela Davis, bell hooks, Paula Giddings, Louise Erdrich, Sandra Cisneros, Toni Morrison, Toni Cade Bambara, Paula Gunn Allen, Luisah Teish, Michelle Cliff, Mary Crow Dog, Alexis De Veaux, Paule Marshall, and Mary Helen Washington. This is a very partial list. Thanks also to Barbara Smith, who is co-founder (with Audre Lorde) and current publisher of Kitchen Table/Women of Color Press.

The feminist community has challenged me to think more inclusively and accurately. I rely on feminist publications to prod and inform me, including *Ms.* magazine, *New Directions for Women, Sojourner, Women's Review of Books*, and *Belles Lettres*. I encourage others to support these and other vital feminist publications by subscribing.

I also rely on Redwood Cultural Work to tie music, culture, and politics together from a multicultural feminist perspective. For twenty years, Redwood has championed cultural rights and social justice, producing and presenting new music rooted in the folk traditions of the many cultures that exist today in the United States. To get their catalog or information about concerts, call (800) 888-SONG.

Index

39092 09437132 7